Preventing money laundering

A legal study on the effectiveness of supervision in the European Union

Published, sold and distributed by Eleven International Publishing
P.O. Box 85576
2508 CG The Hague
The Netherlands
Tel.: +31 70 33 070 33
Fax: +31 70 33 070 30
e-mail: sales@budh.nl
www.elevenpub.com

Sold and distributed in USA and Canada
International Specialized Book Services
920 NE 58th Avenue, Suite 300
Portland, OR 97213-3786, USA
Tel: 1-800-944-6190 (toll-free)
Fax: +1 503 280-8832
orders@isbs.com
www.isbs.com

Eleven International Publishing is an imprint of Boom uitgevers Den Haag.

Book cover design: Laurens van den Broek

Many thanks to the *Muntgebouw Utrecht* (<www.muntgebouw-utrecht.nl>) for allowing to take and to use a picture of the *Gulden Middenweg*. The Gulden Middenweg is a path within the building that is covered with coins of the former Dutch currency, the Dutch guilder. It brings together two important elements of this research: money and Utrecht.

Layout: Klaartje Hoeberechts, Utrecht University

ISBN: 978-94-6236-577-3
E-ISBN: 978-94-6274-336-6

Printed in The Netherlands

Preventing money laundering

A legal study on the effectiveness of supervision in the European Union

Voorkomen van witwassen

Een juridisch onderzoek naar de effectiviteit van het toezicht in de Europese Unie

(met een samenvatting in het Nederlands | with a summary in English)

Proefschrift

ter verkrijging van de graad van doctor aan de Universiteit Utrecht
op gezag van de rector magnificus, prof. dr. G.J. van der Zwaan,
ingevolge het besluit van het college voor promoties
in het openbaar te verdedigen
op vrijdag 5 juni 2015
des ochtends te 10.30 uur

door

Melissa van den Broek

geboren op 14 januari 1987
te Haarlem

Promotoren: Prof. dr. G.H. Addink
Prof. dr. B. Unger
Copromotor: Dr. A.P.W. Duijkersloot

Acknowledgements

'It always seems impossible until it is done'
~ Nelson Mandela, 1918-2013

Although the wise words of the late Nelson Mandela have absolutely nothing to do with writing a PhD thesis, these words definitely depict my life as a PhD researcher. Doing research required a lot of perseverance and hard work, but this is the moment where I can finally say with pride: it is done! The past four years can be characterised as a period of ups and downs. Moments of true inspiration and joy were followed by moments of despair, thinking I would never get it done. Luckily, I was accompanied by friends, family and colleagues along this journey. I would like to express my gratitude to the people who have been very helpful to me during the time I carried out this research.

First of all I would like to thank my supervisors Henk Addink and Brigitte Unger and my daily supervisor Ton Duijkersloot for their guidance during my PhD research. Henk, it was you who introduced me to the academic world back in 2008 when I became your assistant. Later you also provided me the opportunity to carry out a PhD research under your supervision. Thank you very much for your trust in me, for your encouraging support and our inspiring discussions. Brigitte, thank you for involving me in the ECOLEF project. During this project I have acquired many new skills, including how to pack a bag in the most efficient way for our numerous travels across Europe. I am genuinely happy that the project turned out to be a success. Ton, you became my daily supervisor in the second year of my PhD research. Thank you very much for the regular meetings we had, and especially for the moments where I could spontaneously knock on your door to tell you about my great new discoveries or to ask for your advice. Your laid-back personality and practical suggestions were really the things that I needed.

I would also like to thank the members of the assessment committee: Aletta Blomberg, Anna Gerbrandy, Valsamis Mitsilegas, Adrienne de Moor-van Vugt and Rob Widdershoven. Your valuable suggestions and comments, even the minor ones, allowed me to make the necessary improvements to my PhD research at its final stages. A special thanks to Rob Widdershoven for the fruitful discussions we had with regard to my thesis on a number of occasions.

This PhD research could not have been completed without the help of several experts in the field. I highly appreciate the cooperation I received from all the representatives of the different anti-money laundering supervisors, ministries, departments and professional associations. I would like to thank them for investing their time and effort in providing me the information, as well as their insights and experiences, which I needed to carry out this research successfully.

Many thanks to Peter Morris for editing my English, and to Titia Kloos and Klaartje Hoeberechts for making my manuscript camera-ready. Furthermore, I would like to thank Mariska Duindam at Eleven International Publishing for her assistance in the publication of this research.

Ruim zes jaar ben ik werkzaam geweest bij de afdeling die tegenwoordig de naam Staatsrecht, Bestuursrecht en Rechtstheorie draagt. Ik ben altijd met veel plezier naar mijn werk gegaan en heb met veel collega's een goede band opgebouwd. Dank voor jullie interesse gedurende het schrijfproces. Alyssa, jou wil ik daarnaast nog bedanken voor de nodige afleiding in de vorm van concerten, festivals en avondjes uit. Ook mijn collega-promovendi, in het bijzonder Paulien, Sandra, Daan, Margot, Herman Kasper, Anoeska, Jasper, Marloes, Eva, Hanneke, Willem, Mark, Elvis, Dayla, Joras en Ioana, wil ik bedanken voor alle inhoudelijke praatsessies, de samenwerking en de altijd gezellige PhDates zoals de PhDrinks, de PhDinners en de PhDances in de Derrick of in andere foute bars. Daan, bedankt voor de wekelijkse koffiemomentjes buiten de deur. Margot, jij bent het laatste jaar stiekem mijn grote voorbeeld geweest. Dank voor al je goede adviezen. Ook wil ik graag mijn kamergenoten van ASP 200, kamer 3.01, bedanken. Paulien en Sandra, ik had me geen betere 'roomies' kunnen wensen. Jullie waren er voor me toen ik het zwaar had, gedurende en buiten kantooruren. Elvis, I can only imagine how hard it must have been for you in our girls' office. It was a pleasure sharing thoughts and a workplace with you.

Inmiddels ben ik alweer een aantal maanden werkzaam bij de Autoriteit Financiële Markten. Bij de afdeling Kwaliteit Accountantscontrole en Verslaggeving zit ik helemaal op mijn plek. Dat heb ik met name te danken aan Maaike. Wij kenden elkaar al van de universiteit waar wij allebei onderzoek deden naar de preventie van witwassen. In maart 2012 mocht ik zelfs jouw paranimf zijn. Ik vind het ontzettend leuk dat ik nu weer jouw collega ben en ik hoop dat wij de komende jaren nog veel mooie projecten op ons mogen nemen.

Ik prijs me gelukkig met de lieve vrienden en vriendinnen die ik heb. Jullie hebben de afgelopen jaren – soms tot vervelens toe – moeten aanhoren hoe het met mij (lees: mijn onderzoek) ging. Toch bleven jullie altijd geïnteresseerd. Hopelijk geeft dit boek een idee waar ik me de afgelopen jaren mee bezig heb gehouden. In het bijzonder wil ik Cilia, Sandra, Cristel, Fardow, Monique, Frank, Pim, Teun, Xandra en Ellen noemen. Ook de beruchte 'Mirande chicks' mogen hier natuurlijk niet ontbreken: Eva, Froukelien, Laura en Sabine, bedankt voor jullie bijdrage!

Ik heb de twee beste paranimfen die ik me wensen kan. Paulien, het feit dat ik je naam nu al voor de derde keer in dit dankwoord noem laat duidelijk zien hoe belangrijk jij voor mij bent. Naast een toponderzoekster en betrokken collega, ben je vooral een ontzettend lieve vriendin. Ik denk met heel veel plezier terug aan de vele leuke dingen die wij samen ondernomen hebben (o.a. Cuba, Leuven, Londen, Straatsburg en Heidelberg) en ik vind het enorm fijn dat jij mijn paranimf wilt zijn. Laurens, hoewel je inmiddels ver boven mij uittorent, blijf je mijn kleine broertje. Je aarzelde om mijn paranimf te worden toen ik je vertelde dat je een rokkostuum aan zou moeten trekken tijdens de ceremonie, maar gelukkig zei je toch 'ja'. Dank je wel voor het mooie ontwerp van de cover. Ik vind het heel speciaal dat jij dit voor mij hebt willen doen.

Lieve mama, dit boek is voor jou. Je hebt het je misschien niet altijd gerealiseerd, maar jij bent de drijvende kracht achter dit proefschrift geweest. Ik weet dat ik altijd op jouw onvoorwaardelijke steun kan rekenen en ik ben je daar enorm dankbaar voor. We hebben het niet gemakkelijk gehad na papa's dood in 1995, maar dankzij jouw kracht en doorzettingsvermogen heb ik het tot hier mogen schoppen. Ik weet zeker dat papa trots op ons is.

Lieve Benjamin, jij kwam het laatste – en tevens belangrijkste – jaar van dit onderzoek in mijn leven. Ik heb je af en toe horendol gemaakt met mijn stemmingen waarin pure frustratie en euforie elkaar in rap tempo afwisselden. Gelukkig bleef jij op die momenten kalm en kookte je weer een heerlijke maaltijd. Zonder jou zou ik het laatste jaar grotendeels op kant-en-klaarmaaltijden hebben geleefd. Samen met jou, Joep en Leo ben ik gelukkig. Ik hou van jou.

Melissa
Utrecht, maart 2015

Acronyms and abbreviations

AAT	Association of Accounting Technicians (United Kingdom)
AML	Anti-money laundering
BFT	*Bureau Financieel Toezicht* (Financial Supervision Office, the Netherlands)
CCT	Conduct & Compliance Team (AAT, United Kingdom)
CDD	Customer due diligence
CTF	Combating terrorist financing
DNB	*De Nederlandsche Bank* (Dutch Central Bank, the Netherlands)
DNFBP	Designated non-financial businesses and professions
DTCA	*Belastingdienst* (Dutch Tax and Customs Administration, the Netherlands)
ECOLEF	Study on the Economic and Legal Effectiveness of Anti-Money Laundering and Combating Terrorist Financing Policy (JLS/2009/ISEC/CFP/AG/)
ECJ	Court of Justice of the European Union
ES	Spain
FATF	Financial Action Task Force
FCA	Financial Conduct Authority (United Kingdom)
FI	*Finansinspektionen* (Swedish Financial Supervisory Authority, Sweden)
FIU	Financial Intelligence Unit
FMI	*Fastighetsmäklarinspektionen* (Swedish Estate Agents Inspectorate, Sweden)
ICAEW	Institute of Chartered Accountants in England and Wales (United Kingdom)
LATSS	Local Authority Trading Standard Services (United Kingdom)
MIP	Members in Practice (AAT, United Kingdom)
MONEYVAL	Committee of Experts on the Evaluation of Anti-Money Laundering Measures and the Financing of Terrorism
NL	The Netherlands
OFT	Office of Fair Trading (United Kingdom)
PAC	Practice Assurance Committee (ICAEW, United Kingdom)
PAS	Practice Assurance Scheme (ICAEW, United Kingdom)
QAD	Quality Assurance Department (ICAEW, United Kingdom)
RCB	Regulation and Compliance Board (AAT, United Kingdom)
RN	*Revisorsnämnden* (Supervisory Board of Public Auditors, Sweden)
SE	Sweden

SEPBLAC	Servicio Ejecutivo de la Comisión de Prevención del Blanqueo de Capitales e Infracciones Monetarias (SEPBLAC, Spain)
STC	Sentencia Tribunal Constitucional (Spain)
STS	Sentencia Tribunal Supremo (Spain)
Third Directive	Directive 2005/60/EC of the European Parliament and of the Council on the prevention of the use of the financial system for the purpose of money laundering and terrorist financing (OJ L 309/15, 25 November 2005)
UK	United Kingdom

Table of Contents

PART II

1 Introduction

1.1 Introduction

Striking headlines like 'Spanish Princess Cristina de Bourbon charged with money laundering and fraud in major corruption investigation', 'Messi caught up in 1m money laundering mess', 'HSBC sets aside $700m for money-laundering fines', 'Vatican Priest charged with money laundering', 'Public Prosecution Office continues to catch lax gatekeepers', or 'Lawyer and book keeper convicted of laundering £1.8m', can be found regularly in newspapers and on websites these days.[1] They reflect the results of the ongoing fight against money laundering worldwide.

1.1.1 What money laundering is and why it should be combated

Money laundering is a generic term used to describe the process of concealing illegally obtained proceeds. It is criminalised all around the world and is considered a grave danger to society due to its strong interaction with organised drugs and white-collar crime.[2] It is a complex phenomenon with a wide variety of appearances. In the most simplified picture, the process of money laundering consists of three stages: the *placement* of criminal proceeds in a financial institution or the purchase of an asset; the *layering* of proceeds where the criminal attempts to conceal the origin of the proceeds, for example by creating a false paper trail; and lastly, the *integration* of the proceeds into the legitimate economic and financial system.[3] Various money laundering methods, also known as typologies, can

1 The Independent, *Spanish Princess Cristina de Bourbon charged with money laundering and fraud in major corruption investigation*, 25 June 2014, Marca, *Messi caught up in 1m money laundering mess*, 8 June 2014, available at: <www.marca.com/2014/06/08/en/football/barcelona/1402228989.html>, last visited on 1 August 2014, The Guardian, *HSBC sets aside $700m for money-laundering fines*, 30 July 2012; Het Financieele Dagblad, *Priester Vaticaan aangeklaagd wegens witwassen*, 21 January 2014, Trouw, *OM zet jacht op verzakende poortwachters door*, 8 October 2013; BBC News, *Lawyer and book keeper convicted of laundering £1.8m*, 29 January 2013.

2 Stessens, G. (2000), *Money Laundering: A New International Law Enforcement Model*, Cambridge University Press: Cambridge, at 6-14; Gilmore, W.C. (2011), *Dirty Money: the evolution of international measures to counter money laundering and the financing of terrorism*, Council of Europe Publishing, 4th edition, at 15-21.

3 See about these stages in more detail: Mitsilegas, V. (2003) *Counter-measures in the European Union: A New Paradigm of Security Governance versus Fundamental Legal Principles*, Kluwer Law International: The Hague-Boston-London, at 27-30; Gilmore (2011) at 34; Ferwerda, J. (2012), *The Multidisciplinary Economics of Money Laundering*, Tjalling C. Koopmans Dissertation Series, USE 007 (doctoral thesis Utrecht University), at 5-8.

be used to launder money.[4] Examples are the laundering of proceeds through trade in diamonds and the use of virtual currencies like *Bitcoin*.[5]

Money laundering has a strong international dimension.[6] This phenomenon has been a law enforcement priority since the early 1990s. The international nature of money laundering, combined with estimations on the scope and the distorting effects it may bring about, make money laundering a grave danger to national and international financial markets. There have been numerous attempts to measure the scope of the problem.[7] The International Monetary Fund (IMF), for example, estimated in 1998 that the total global money laundering accounted for 2 to 5 percent of global GDP.[8] Unger calculated that between 3 to 6 billion Euros are laundered within the Netherlands, and that 14-21 billion Euros flow into the Netherlands from the twenty countries in which most money is laundered.[9] Schneider roughly estimated that the worldwide turnover of organised crime in 2006 had a value of 790 billion US dollars, which also gives an indication of the extent of money laundering.[10] And the UNODC presented estimations in 2011 concluding that criminal proceeds amounted to 3.6 percent of global GDP, of which 2.7 percent is laundered.[11] Money laundering is said to bring about negative effects for society. The Financial Action Task Force (FATF), the IMF and other international organisations have often referred to the distortive nature of organised crime activities against financial markets, which may threaten the investment climate as investors lose confidence in their economic systems.[12] Widespread financial abuse is furthermore said to bring about an increase in crime

4 Gilmore (2011) at 34-47; Unger, B. (2007), *The Scale and Impacts of Money Laundering*, Edward Elgar Publishing Ltd: Cheltenham, at 89-108.

5 FATF (2014), *Money laundering and terrorist financing through trade in diamonds*, January 2014; FATF (2014a), *Virtual Currencies: Key Definitions and Potential AML/CFT Risks*, June 2014.

6 Stessens (2000) at 209-214; Amrani, H. (2012), *The Development of Anti-Money Laundering Regime: Challenging issues to sovereignty, jurisdiction, law enforcement, and their implications on the effectiveness in countering money laundering*, doctoral thesis Erasmus University Rotterdam, available at: <http://hdl.handle.net/1765/37747>, at 169-187.

7 See for example: Walker, J. (1999) 'How Big is Global Money Laundering', *Journal of Money Laundering Control*, vol. 3, issue 1, pp. 25-37; Argentiero, A., Bagella, M. and Busato, F. (2008), 'Money Laundering in a Two-Sector Model: Using Theory for Measurement', *European Journal of Law and Economics*, vol. 26, issue 3, pp. 341-359; Walker, J. and Unger, B. (2009), 'Measuring Global Money Laundering: "the Walker Gravity Model"', *Review of Law and Economics*, vol. 5, issue 2, pp. 821-853; Bagella, M., Busato, F. and Argentiero, A. (2013), 'Using dynamic macroeconomics for estimating money laundering: a simulation for the EU, Italy and the United States', in: Unger, B. and Van der Linde, D. (eds.), *Research Handbook on Money Laundering*, Edward Elgar Publishing Ltd: Cheltenham, pp. 207-223; Unger, B. and Ferwerda, J. (2014), 'Threat of money laundering', in: Unger, B., Ferwerda, J., Van den Broek, M. and Deleanu, I., *The Economic and Legal Effectiveness of the European Union's Anti-Money Laundering Policy*, Edward Elgar Publishing Ltd: Cheltenham, pp. 9-19. (This last book is hereafter referred to as: Unger et al. (2014).)

8 *Money Laundering: the Importance of International Countermeasures*, Statement made by Michel Camdessus, Managing Director of the International Monetary Fund at the Plenary Meeting of the Financial Action Task Force on Money Laundering, February 1998, available at: <www.imf.org/external/np/speeches/1998/021098.htm>, last visited on 30 July 2014. The background for these estimations can be found in: Quirk, P.J. (1996), 'Macroeconomic implications of money laundering', *IMF Working Paper*, no. 96/66.

9 Unger (2007) at 57-88 and 184.

10 Schneider, F. (2010), 'Turnover of organized crime and money laundering: some preliminary empirical findings', *Public Choice*, vol. 144, issue 3-4, pp. 473-486.

11 UNODC (2011), *Estimating Illicit Financial Flows Resulting From Drugs Trafficking and Other Transnational Organized Crimes: Research Report*, Vienna, October 2011, at 39.

12 Quirk (1996).

and corruption, it can lead to societal upheaval, and in extreme situations it can even undermine the democratic basis of government.[13] Unger made an inventory of all possible effects of money laundering. She makes a distinction between short-term and long-term effects.[14] The short-term effects of money laundering can be unfair competition or missing revenues for Governments.[15] An example of a long-term effect is the damaged reputation of the financial sector.[16]

The various claims of the dangers and seriousness of money laundering are also received with criticism.[17] The estimations should be used with great caution and the lack of (good) empirical evidence of the volume, nature and impact of money laundering makes some wonder about the true necessity of fighting it. In this respect, Alldridge considered that '[m]oney laundering has become one of the great moral panics of our day. A range of sources, including mass media, assert that it is bad, very interesting, and slightly daring, but do not so much deal with what it is, how it is done or why (otherwise than as a form of complicity in some previous offence) it is so damaging'.[18] And for Van Duyne et al. the lack of empirical evidence leads them to conclude that 'more attention has been devoted to fear factors of crime-money than to a detached balancing of various legal and social interests'.[19] Others believe that the most serious aspect of money laundering as such is not the crime itself, but the fact that it facilitates other crimes and allows criminals to access and enjoy the fruits of their illicit behaviour.[20] All in all, Ferwerda concluded that '[a]ll these effects of money laundering are therefore in need of empirical testing'.[21]

Despite these critical sounds, there has been an increasing consensus since the end of the 1980s that money laundering must be combated. The fight against money laundering features high on the international agenda and is, as the headlines of the newspapers above show, not an unnoticed one.

---

13 FATF, *How does money laundering affect business?*, available at: <www.fatf-gafi.org/pages/faq/moneylaundering/>, last visited 30 July 2014.

14 Unger (2007) at 109-181. Cf. Ferwerda, J. (2013), 'The Effects Of Money Laundering', in: Unger, B. and Van der Linde, D. (eds.), *Research Handbook on Money Laundering*, Edward Elgar Publishing Ltd: Cheltenham, pp. 35-46; Masciandaro, D. (2013), 'Money Laundering And Its Effects on Crime: A Macroeconomic Approach', in: Unger, B. and Van der Linde, D. (eds.), *Research Handbook on Money Laundering*, Edward Elgar Publishing Ltd: Cheltenham, pp. 47-56.

15 Unger (2007) at 111.

16 Ibid., at 145-146.

17 For example: Van Duyne, P.C. (1994), 'Money Laundering: Estimates in Fog', *Journal of Financial Crime*, vol. 2, issue 1, pp. 58-74; Reuter, P. (2013), 'Are Estimates of The Volume of Money Laundering Either Feasible Or Useful?', in: Unger, B. and Van der Linde, D. (eds.), *Research Handbook on Money Laundering*, Edward Elgar Publishing: Cheltenham, pp. 224-231.

18 Alldridge, P. (2008), 'Money Laundering and Globalization', *Journal of Law and Society*, vol. 35, issue 4, pp. 437-463 at 437.

19 Van Duyne, P. C., Groenhuijsen, M.C. and Schudelaro, A.A.P. (2005), 'Balancing Financial threats and legal interests in money-laundering policy', *Crime, Law and Social Change*, vol. 43, issue 1-2, pp. 117-147 at 141.

20 Mulig, E.V. and Smith, M. (2004), 'Understanding and Preventing Money Laundering', *Internal Auditing*, vol. 19, issue 5, pp. 22-25.

21 Ferwerda (2012) at 5 and 29-38.

1.1.2 Existing efforts against money laundering

Originally based on concerns with regard to organised drugs crime, the worldwide fight against money laundering has today become multifaceted.[22] Over the past twenty years, a 'twin-track approach' against money laundering has evolved.[23] On the one hand, this approach consists of a *preventive policy*, which aims at the prevention of money laundering through the setting of identification and reporting obligations for financial institutions, certain non-financial institutions and legal professionals like lawyers and civil-law notaries. Administrative law and disciplinary law play an important role in this policy, both in terms of the substantive obligations as well as enforcing compliance with these obligations.[24] On the other hand, the twin-track approach consists of a *repressive policy* of which the objective is to punish the money launderer through the use of criminal law and by the freezing, seizure and confiscation of assets. The anti-money laundering policy was connected to the anti-terrorist financing policy shortly after the 9/11 attacks and has been, and still is, a policy that is developing at high pace.[25]

The fight against money laundering takes place at the international, regional and national level. At the international level various United Nations Conventions have played an important role in the development of measures against money laundering.[26] However, the international standard-setting body is the Financial Action Task Force (FATF). This body was established at the 1989 Paris summit by seven nations with the most advanced economies in the world (the G-7).[27] Although the FATF has 'just' 36 members (in 2014), through the network of FATF Regional Style Bodies its Forty Recommendations on money laundering, the financing of terrorism & proliferation are adhered to by virtually

22 See: Gilmore (2011); Mitsilegas, V. and Gilmore, W.C. (2007), 'The EU legislative framework against money laundering and terrorist finance: A critical analysis in the light of evolving global standards', *International and Comparative Law Quarterly*, vol. 56, issue 1, pp. 119-140.

23 Stessens (2000) at 82 and 108-112. Cf. Mitsilegas (2003) at 31 who, referring to other studies, speaks about a 'two-fold goal'.

24 Enforcing compliance with the preventive obligations takes place through education, guidance and the creation of awareness on the other hand, but also by verifying compliance through supervision (inspections) and sanctioning. This means that even within the preventive policy repressive elements can be found. The difference with the repressive policy, however, is that criminal law plays a limited role and that the preventive policy is not primarily aimed at catching the money launderers themselves.

25 In October 2001 the issue of countering the financing of terrorism was specifically added to the FATF mandate, which connected the fight against money laundering to the fight against terrorist financing by formulating eight special recommendations. In 2008 the FATF mandate was again broadened to include combating the financing of the proliferation of weapons of mass destruction. See: <www.fatf-gafi.org>.

26 Most important are the UN Convention against Illicit Traffic in Narcotic Drugs and Psychotropic Substances 1988 (Vienna Convention); UN Terrorist Financing Convention 1999; UN Convention on Transnational Organised Crime 2000 (Palermo Convention); UN Convention against Corruption 2005 (Merida). See: Mitsilegas (2003) at 40-44; Gilmore (2011) at 53-84; Unger, B. and Van den Broek, M. (2014), 'Implementing international conventions and the Third EU Directive', in: Unger et al., *The Economic and Legal Effectiveness of the European Union's Anti-Money Laundering Policy*, Edward Elgar Publishing Ltd: Cheltenham, pp. 46-61 at 46-50.

27 Mitsilegas (2003) at 48-50; Gilmore (2011) at 91-94; Roberge, I. (2011), 'Financial Action Task Force', in: Hale, T. and Held, D. (eds.),*The Handbook of Transnational Governance: Institutions and Innovation*, Polity Press: Cambridge, pp. 45-50; Van den Broek, M. (2011), 'Gelijkwaardigheid in het antiwitwasbeleid: de FATF en de EU', *SEW: Tijdschrift voor Europees en Economisch Recht*, vol. 59, issue 10, pp. 422-428.

all countries around the world.[28] The international initiatives against money laundering have strongly influenced the efforts taken at the regional and national level to combat money laundering. At the regional – in this research the European – level we can find two important Council of Europe Conventions.[29] And the European Union's core framework in the fight against money laundering and terrorist financing consists of the Directive on the prevention of the use of the financial system for the purpose of money laundering and terrorist financing (hereafter 'Third Directive'[30]), the Council Decision concerning arrangements for cooperation between financial intelligence units of the EU Member States, as well as the Wire Transfer and the Cash Control Regulations.[31] One of the main purposes of the Third Directive was to provide a common EU basis for the implementation of the FATF Recommendations.[32] The process of the adoption of a new Directive is currently heading towards is final stages.[33] The third level concerns the national level, which for the most part is the result of the implementation of the international and European norms.

1.1.3 Current knowledge of these efforts

In the broad field of the study of money laundering by far the most attention has been devoted to the measuring of the amounts and effects of money laundering.[34] Compared to these economic and criminological studies, legal studies on money laundering are relatively scarce. Moreover, these legal studies often focus on the criminal law aspects of money laundering.[35] A topic that received a great deal of attention is the obligation for legal professionals to report suspicions of money laundering to the competent authorities

28 FATF (2012), *High-Level Principles and Objectives for FATF and FATF-style regional bodies*, October 2012. About MONEYVAL, see: Gilmore (2011) at 204-211.

29 CoE Convention on Laundering, Search, Seizure and Confiscation of the Proceeds from Crime 1990, ETS No. 141; CoE Convention on Laundering, Search, Seizure and Confiscation of the Proceeds from Crime 2005 (Warsaw), CETS No. 198. See: Gilmore (2011) at 175-194.

30 Directive 2005/60/EC of the European Parliament and of the Council of 26 October 2005 on the prevention of the use of the financial system for the purpose of money laundering and terrorist financing, [2005] OJ L 309/15 ('Third Directive'). The Directive is completed by Commission Directive 2006/70/EC laying down implementing measures for Directive 2005/60/EC of the European Parliament and of the Council as regards the definition of 'politically exposed person' and the technical criteria for simplified customer due diligence procedures and for exemption on grounds of a financial activity conducted on an occasional or very limited basis, [2006] OJ L 214/29.

31 Council Decision 2000/642/JHA of 17 October 2000 concerning arrangements for cooperation between financial intelligence units of the Member States in respect of exchanging information, [2000] OJ L 271/4; Regulation (EC) 1781/2006 on information on the payer accompanying transfers of funds, [2006] OJ L 345/1; Regulation (EC) 1889/2005 of the European Parliament and of the Council on controls of cash entering or leaving the Community, [2005] OJ L309/9.

32 Consideration 5 Third Directive.

33 More about this in § 1.8.

34 See Ferwerda (2012) at 11-24 for a literature overview on models to estimate the amount of money laundering.

35 For example: Stessens (2000); Alldridge, P. (2003) *Money laundering law: forfeiture, confiscation, civil recovery, criminal laundering and taxation of the proceeds of crime*, Oxford: Hart Publishing; Mitsilegas (2003); Ping, H. (2004), *The fight against money laundering: a comparative perspective*, doctoral thesis Erasmus University Rotterdam; Mitsilegas, V. (2009) 'The third wave of third pillar law: which direction for EU criminal justice?', *Queen Mary University of London, School of Law Legal Studies Research Paper* No. 33/2009; Amrani (2012); Vervaele, J. (2013), 'Economic crimes and money laundering: a new paradigm for the criminal justice system?', in: Unger, B. and Van der Linde, D. (eds.), *Research Handbook on Money Laundering*, Edward Elgar Publishing Ltd: Cheltenham, pp. 379-396.

in relation to the fundamental principle of legal professional privilege.[36] Some studies specifically focus on the preventive anti-money laundering policy (hereafter also the 'preventive AML policy'), but there one can observe that the focal point generally lies with the implementation of the international and European norms into the national policies or on the role of financial intelligence units.[37] Limited attention has been paid to the matter of supervision in the preventive policy so far.[38] This is lamentable, because this means that there is not much insight into the role of administrative and disciplinary law in the prevention of money laundering.

Moreover, as a result of the attention paid to the volume and effects of money laundering, research on the effectiveness of the measures that are need to prevent and combat money laundering has remained behind as well.[39] The FATF is undertaking serious attempts

36 For example: Yasin, N.M. (2004), 'Lawyers, legal privilege and money laundering: The UK and Malaysian experience', *Journal of Banking Regulation*, issue 5, pp. 364-386; Faraldo Cabana, P. (2007), 'Legal professionals and money laundering in Spain', *Journal of Money Laundering Control*, vol. 10, issue 3, pp. 318-336; Tilleman, A. (2007), 'Money laundering and the professional sector. Supervision of lawyers and civil-law notaries in the Netherlands – what about professional secrecy?', in: Van Duyne, P.C., Maljevic, A., Van Dijck, M., Von Lampe, K. and Harvey, J. (eds.), *Crime Business and Crime Money in Europe. The Dirty Linen of Illegal Enterprise*, Wolf Legal Publishers, pp. 43-68; Komárek, J. (2008), 'Legal Professional Privilege and the EU's fight against Money Laundering', *Civil Justice Quarterly*, vol. 27, issue 1, pp. 13-22; Stouten, M. and Tilleman, A. (2013), 'Reporting Duty for Lawyers versus Legal Privilege: Unresolved Tension', in: Unger, B. and Van der Linde, D. (eds.), *Research Handbook on Money Laundering*, Edward Elgar Publishing Ltd: Cheltenham, pp. 426-434. In 2007, the European Court of Justice came up with a judgment on this topic: Case C-305/05, *Ordre des barreaux francophones et germanophones and Others v Conseil des Ministres* [2007] ECR I-05305. More about this case: Luchtman, M.J.J.P and Hoeven, R. van der (2009), 'Case C-305/05, Ordre des barreaux francophone et germanaphones et al. v Conseil des Ministre, judgment of 26 June 2007, Grand Chamber; [2007] ECR I-5305', *Common Market Law Review*, vol. 46, issue 1, pp. 301-318.

37 British Institute of International and Comparative Law (2006), *Comparative Implementation of EU Directives (II): Money Laundering*, City Research Series, no. 10, City of London; Katz, E. (2007), 'Implementation of the Third Money Laundering Directive – an overview', *Law and Financial Markets Review*, vol. 1, issue 3, pp. 207-211; Costa, S. (2008), 'Implementing the new anti-money laundering directive in Europe: Legal and enforcement issues – The Italian Case', *Global Business and Economics Review*, vol.10, issue 3,pp. 284-308; Deloitte (2011), *Final Study on the Application of the Anti-Money Laundering Directive*, Service Contract ETD/2009/IM/F2/90; Thony, J.F. (1996), 'Processing Financial Information in Money Laundering Matters: The Financial Intelligence Units', *European Journal of Crime, Criminal Law and Criminal Justice*, issue 4, pp. 257-282; Stessens (2000), at 183-199; Van den Broek, M. and Addink, G.H. (2013), 'Prevention of money laundering and terrorist financing from a good governance perspective', in: Unger, B. and Van der Linde, D. (eds.), *Research Handbook on Money Laundering*, Edward Elgar Publishing Ltd: Cheltenham, pp. 368-378.

38 Rietrae, J. (2007), 'The 3rd EU anti-money laundering directive: main issues and intriguing details', in: Van Duyne, P.C., Maljevic, A., Van Dijck, M., Von Lampe, K. and Harvey, J. (eds.), *Crime Business and Crime Money in Europe. The Dirty Linen of Illegal Enterprise*, Wolf Legal Publishers, pp. 15-42; Stessens (2000), at 200-208; Faure, M., Nelen, H. and Philipsen, N. (2009), *Evaluatie tuchtrechtelijke handhaving: Wet ter voorkoming van witwassen en financiering van terrorisme en haar voorlopers*, Boom Juridische uitgevers: The Hague, Stouten, M. (2012), *De witwasmeldplicht: Omvang van handhaving van de Wwft meldplicht voor juridische en fiscale dienstverleners*, Boom Juridisch uitgevers: The Hague (doctoral thesis Utrecht University); Van den Broek, M. (2011a), 'The EU's preventive AML/CFT policy: asymmetrical harmonisation', *Journal of Money Laundering Control*, vol. 14, issue 2, pp. 170-182.

39 See Harvey, J. (2005), 'An evaluation of money laundering policies', *Journal of Money Laundering Control*, vol. 8, issue 4, pp. 339-345, who argues that this is difficult due to a lack of empirical evidence on the actual amounts of money laundered. Because the effectiveness of countermeasures are in her view to be measured as a reduction of the money laundering volume, not having proper data on the money laundering volume leads to not being able to measure the effectiveness of the countermeasures.

in this field, but always faces the problem that country evaluations are carried out over different periods of time and that research team compositions change, which may lead to different judgments concerning effectiveness. Comparisons between countries are therefore difficult to make. The ECOLEF study is one of the first studies in which EU Member States' policies have been compared within the same time frame and by a single team of researchers in relation to threats of money laundering, as well as their policy responses both in the repressive and preventive anti-money laundering and combating terrorist financing policy.[40]

1.2 Definition of the problem and research question

As a result of the limited attention that has been paid to supervision in the preventive anti-money laundering policy in research so far, an insight into the contours and contents, the similarities and differences between countries, let alone into the effectiveness thereof, is largely absent. An important finding from the ECOLEF study is the fact that while the substantive norms in the preventive AML policy, meaning the obligations in place for institutions and professionals subject to regulation such as customer due diligence and the reporting obligation, have to a large extent been harmonised within the European Union, this is not yet the case for norms concerning supervision and sanctioning.[41] The Third Directive provides some minimum conditions, but the design of supervision is largely left to the Member States' procedural autonomy. As a result, there exists a patchwork of supervisory regimes throughout the European Union.[42] In spite of the fact that for a long time the international and European standards paid little attention to the matter of supervision, the last two years have shown a shift in thinking and careful attempts to harmonise supervision and sanctioning have been made or are underway.[43] The aim of this research is to obtain an insight into differences in supervision under the preventive AML policy, to analyse these on a systematic basis and to compare the regimes to find which one is the most effective, and to create a learning effect for other countries in order to strengthen their systems. This leads to the following research question:

In which of the Member States of the European Union is supervision within the preventive anti-money laundering policy the most effective, and what can other Member States do to reach the same level of effectiveness?

40 Unger et al. (2014), *The Economic and Legal Effectiveness of the European Union's Anti-Money Laundering Policy*, Edward Elgar Publishing Ltd: Cheltenham. More about this study in § 1.7.

41 Van den Broek, M. (2014), 'Supervisory architectures in the preventive AML policy', in: Unger et al., *The Economic and Legal Effectiveness of the European Union's Anti-Money Laundering Policy*, Edward Elgar Publishing Ltd: Cheltenham, pp. 62-86.

42 Van den Broek (2011a).

43 Chapter IV, sections 2 and 4, Third Directive; 2012 FATF Recommendations 26-28 and 35. The Interpretative Notes to the 2012 FATF Recommendations provide detailed guidance on how to design a risk-based approach to supervision, which powers supervisors must have and on the adequacy of supervisors' resources.

In order to come to a synthesis that can lead to an answer to this research question, three supportive questions should be addressed:

- When is supervision effective, viewed principally from a legal perspective?
- How are EU Member States different in designing their supervisory regimes?
- What does anti-money laundering supervision look like at the national level?

The first supportive question allows for the development of the theoretical framework of this research (Chapter 2). Based on this theoretical framework the supervisory regimes of the EU Member States will be analysed and compared. The second supportive question requires a description of the different supervisory regimes within the European Union and serves as the foundation for the country selection in this research (Chapter 3). This aspect builds on work that I have done within the ECOLEF study, about which more is explained in § 1.7. The third supportive question aims for detailed analyses of AML supervision in the Member States selected (Chapters 4-7). The analyses closely follow the elements identified as part of the theoretical framework.

1.3 Scope of the research

Given that the research question is fairly broad, it is important to narrow down the scope of this research. This is done in three ways: country selection, the selection of supervisors, and the focus on money laundering. These delineations will now be explained.

The research question refers to 'the Member States of the European Union'. It is, however, challenging, if not impossible, to carry out an in-depth study on AML supervision in 28 EU Member States within a timeframe of four years. Therefore, the number of Member States included in this research has been narrowed down. I have chosen to include four EU Member States in this research. This choice is the direct result of the supervisory models that can be identified within the European Union.[44] Chapter 3 thoroughly discusses the models and explains in more detail the choice for Spain, the Netherlands, the United Kingdom and Sweden as 'representatives' of these models. Although it is the ambition of this research to draw conclusions on the effectiveness of AML supervision in the European Union, the choice for one country per supervisory model inevitably means that the findings should be handled with great care and should, at times, be put into perspective as well. It is nevertheless anticipated that the findings on the AML supervision in these four EU Member States can be generalised to the (more abstract) level of the supervisory models, and thus to allow one to say something about the effectiveness of AML supervision in the European Union.

A second delineation to the scope of this research concerns the focus on AML supervision on banks, accountants and real estate agents. This choice is made because of the fact that the preventive AML policy has a very wide coverage, ranging from large international financial conglomerates to next-door jewellery shops. Without such a delineation, the

44 See § 1.7 and Chapter 3.

choice for the four countries would result in a total of 39 AML supervisors.[45] Because the scope of the preventive AML policy can generally be distinguished into three categories of institutions and professionals and in order to include a representative part of this scope in this research, I have decided to include one sector or profession for each category. The first category is the group of *financial and credit institutions*. This group includes, inter alia, banks, insurance companies, money exchange offices, and investment companies. I chose banks to represent this category of institutions, because banks have a long experience with the preventive AML policy and these are present in all four Member States. The second category concerns *legal and fiscal service providers*. This group includes civil-law notaries, lawyers, tax advisors, accountants and other independent legal professionals. Accountants represent this category for two reasons. As explained, a great deal of research has already been done on notaries and lawyers' split between the reporting obligation and legal professional privilege, also in relation to supervision.[46] Accountants are faced with this split to a lesser extent. Moreover, the accountancy profession is interesting because in some Member States this profession is subject to forms of self-regulation. This may lead to the formal or informal involvement of professional associations in AML supervision. The third category concerns *non-financial businesses and non-legal professionals*. This is a default group and varies from real estate agents, trust and company service providers to dealers in (high-value) goods. The group of dealers is very diverse and can range from car dealers, jewellers, to dealers in precious stones and metals, but can also be as broad as to include any dealer in goods when accepting cash payments exceeding 15,000 Euros or more. Because of the comparatively high risk of money laundering in the real estate sector, I have selected this profession as representative of the third category.[47]

The choice for the AML supervision of banks, accountants and real estate agents in the four countries narrows down the total of AML supervisors to 21. This is still a very high number, most prominently caused by the accountancy sector in the UK where 11 professional associations have AML supervisory responsibility.[48] In order to have a fair balance between the four countries included in this research, I have decided to include two professional associations. I have specifically chosen for the Institute of Chartered Accountants in England and Wales (ICAEW) and the Association of Accounting Technicians (AAT), because they are different from each other in terms of their age, size and jurisdiction. ICAEW is one of the oldest and largest professional associations in the accountancy sector in the UK and members of this association are allowed to use the title 'chartered' accountant. AAT is a relatively small and young professional association.

45 Chapter 3. The county administrative boards in Sweden are for the purpose of this research counted as one AML supervisor.

46 Supra, n. 35.

47 Ferwerda (2012) at 80-81 lists a number of characteristics that make the real estate sector susceptible to money laundering. Cf. FATF (2007), *Money laundering and terrorist financing through the real estate sector*, Paris; OECD (2007), *Report on tax fraud and money laundering vulnerabilities involving the real estate sector*, Centre for Tax Policy and Administration.

48 HM Treasury (2013), *Anti-Money Laundering and Counter Terrorist Finance Supervision Report 2012-13*, par. 7, available at: <www.gov.uk/government/publications/anti-money-laundering-and-counter-terrorist-finance-supervision-reports/anti-money-laundering-and-counter-terrorist-finance-supervision-report-2012-13>, last visited on 8 May 2014. If one would include the number of professional associations for tax advisors as well, one would come to 17.

ICAEW's jurisdiction is limited to England and Wales; AAT operates throughout the entire UK territory. Together they reflect the variety that is present among the different professional associations carrying out AML supervision. This research analyses the AML supervision exercised by 12 supervisors in total.

Above I briefly mentioned that since 2001 efforts to combat money laundering have been connected to efforts to combat terrorist financing. Although money laundering and terrorist financing are closely related, terrorist financing has a distinct character and, therefore, '[a]cademically the two are distinct concepts'.[49] The primary motivation of terrorism and hence, terrorist financing, is often not financial gain, as is the case with money laundering. Rather, terrorists and terrorist financiers aim to seek the greatest publicity for their group, a cause, or an individual.[50] Furthermore, terrorist financing is not necessarily about making 'black money' white, in other words turning illicit money into licit money. Of course, funds that support terrorism can come from illegal activity, but it is often also generated by means of fundraising.[51] Finally, terrorist financing does not involve the high amounts of money that are generally believed to be involved with money laundering. De Goede demonstrated that the costs for the terrorists committing the 9/11 attacks in New York are estimated to be between 300,000 and 370,000 Euros.[52] This is peanuts compared to the billions that are estimated to be part of global money laundering flows. This research focuses on the prevention of money laundering, which is why reference is made to the preventive AML policy and why this research talks about AML supervision. This delineation does not mean, however, that the prevention of terrorist financing is completely left out of the scope of the research. The findings of this research may be applied *mutatis mutandis* or are equally relevant in the context of the prevention of terrorist financing.

1.4 Terminology

It is important to provide some information about the terminology and common definitions. In this research there are many references to preventive anti-money laundering policy. This policy is to be understood as a particular set of legal, regulatory and policy norms which aim at the prevention of money laundering activities. It can also be referred to as the preventive (anti-money laundering) regime. In this research both expressions are used interchangeably and have the same meaning. Moreover, 'anti-money laundering' and, to lesser extent, 'combating terrorist financing' are commonly used in this research.

49 Ferwerda (2012) at 10.

50 Matusitz, J. (2013), *Terrorism and Communication: A Critical Introduction*, Sage Publications Inc., at 4.

51 The International Bank for Reconstruction and Development, the World Bank and the International Monetary Fund (2006), *Reference Guide to Anti-Money Laundering and Combating the Financing of Terrorism, Second edition and Supplement on Special Recommendation IX,* at I-1 to I-10, available at: <http://siteresources.worldbank.org/EXTAML/Resources/396511-1146581427871/Reference_Guide_AMLCFT_2ndSupplement.pdf>, last visited on 30 July 2014; Eckart, S.E. (2008), 'The US regulatory approach to terrorist financing', in: Biersteker, T.J. and Eckart, S.E. (eds.), *Countering the financing of terrorism*, Routledge, pp. 218-219.

52 De Goede, M. (2007), *Terrorism Financing and Money Laundering*, Presentation held at the conference 'Tackling money laundering', Utrecht, available at: <http://www2.econ.uu.nl/users/unger/conference%20slides/de%20Goede%20AML%20and%20TF.pdf>, last visited on 1 August 2014.

In order to ease the reading of the text, anti-money laundering and combating terrorist financing are often referred to as AML and CTF. For other abbreviations used in this research, I refer to the list of abbreviations.

This research focuses on supervision and sanctioning within the preventive AML policy. Different meanings can be attached to the term supervision.[53] The term supervision is used in two ways in this research. In the broad context, it includes both the supervision as well as the sanctioning activities of the AML supervisors, i.e. all activities aimed at compliance with the norms in force by the obliged institutions and professionals. In the narrower context, when it is positioned next to sanctioning, it means the activity of obtaining information by the competent authorities with the aim of verifying the compliance of obliged institutions and professionals with the applicable norms in force. This includes the forming of an opinion about the information collected as well as trying to persuade non-compliant institutions and professionals to become compliant. Activities like education, training and advice can also be included under the term supervision. Sanctioning refers to the imposition of sanctions in the case of identified non-compliant behaviour. A synonym intermittently used for the word sanctioning in this research is enforcement. It should be borne in mind that this research strongly focuses on administrative and disciplinary law sanctioning, and that it does not in principle deal with criminal law or private law sanctioning.

Finally, the term 'AML supervisor' in this research means the authority that has been awarded the supervisory responsibility under the domestic anti-money laundering legislation for a specific group of institutions or professionals. This term is used interchangeably with 'AML supervisory authority'. When reference is made to the natural persons working at the AML supervisors, I generally refer to inspectors and in the case of professional associations to reviewers.

1.5 Methodology

Analysing the effectiveness of norms, a policy field or system is not typical to legal research. This does not mean that lawyers are never confronted with questions of an empirical nature.[54] In the context of supervision it is not easy to stipulate exactly what is required for it to be effective, as this depends on the approach one takes. This research takes a legal approach, with support from insights from other disciplines. This means that it is not the aim of this research to measure the effectiveness as such (are the goals actually attained?) or to measure the effects of supervision, but rather to develop a legal framework within which, if fulfilled, the effectiveness is presumed.

53 Cf. Michiels. F.C.M.A. (2013), 'Handhavingsrecht en handhavingsbeleid', in: Michiels, F.C.M.A. and Muller, E.R. (eds.), *Handhaving*, Kluwer: Deventer, pp. 21-31 at 23-24.

54 Leeuw, F.L. (2011), 'Can legal research benefit from evaluation studies?', *Utrecht Law Review*, vol. 7, issue 1, pp. 52-65; Schrama, W. (2011), 'How to carry out interdisciplinary legal research: Some experiences with an interdisciplinary research method', *Utrecht Law Review*, vol. 7, issue 1, pp. 147-162.

This research combines several research methods to answer the research question and supportive questions. This first concerns the common legal research methods of a literature study (books, doctoral theses, articles in journals, scientific reports) as well as an analysis of the applicable laws, regulations, policy documents and, where available, (sanctioning) decisions from the AML supervisors and case law. The availability of policy documents, decisions and case law differs widely between the countries and even between the AML supervisors. With this research method both primary and secondary sources of law are studied.[55] It is important to note here that the sources of the literature study are not limited to legal texts alone. Understanding that law cannot be seen separately from the context in which it operates, literature from other disciplines, such as economics and criminology, that deals with effective supervision is also studied to a certain extent. These sources are supportive in formulating an answer to the research question.[56]

The second principal method applied in this research is comparative legal research. The legal systems of four EU Member States are compared in order to gain insight into the legal and practical differences in supervision in the preventive anti-money laundering policy. Clearly, the differences between the legal systems are taken into account in the analysis wherever possible. Especially the common law tradition in the United Kingdom and the fact that British administrative law differs on various accounts from the continental administrative law systems in Sweden, the Netherlands and Spain is something that is taken into account throughout this research.[57] The comparison in this research is principally based on a juxtaposition method. This means that all country chapters are structured in a similar way and that the data for each country is presented in a similar pattern. By doing so, I aim to bring some simplicity to the complexity and wealth of the data presented. In the synthesis a functional comparative method is applied.

The two legal research methods are supported by data collected through interviews. The interviews have been used to discuss questions arising from information stemming from public sources as well as to complete the lacking information needed for this research, all with the final aim of getting a better insight into the (effectiveness of the) supervisory practice of the AML supervisors in the different countries. The common legal research methods would not allow to, or to a very limited extent, say something about the law in practice. Representatives from all but one AML supervisors included in this research,[58] as well as a number of other authorities involved in the preventive AML policy in the

55 Jacobstein, J.M. and Mersky, R.M. (1990), *Fundamentals of legal research*, Foundation Press: New York, at 2.

56 Cf. Taekema S. and Van Klink, B. (2009), 'Dwarsverbanden: Interdisciplinair onderzoek in de rechtswetenschap', *Nederlands Juristenblad*, issue 36, pp. 2559-2566, who distinguish five ways (with different levels of intensity) in which lawyers can include methods and insights from other disciplines into their research.

57 One example is the fact that British administrative law does not have a separate system of administrative courts: Wade, H.W.R. and Forsyth, C.F., *Administrative Law*, Oxford University Press: Oxford, 11th edition, at 8-9.

58 Despite various attempts over a time span of several months, I have not been able to conduct an interview with the Swedish Board of Public Auditors (*Revisorsnämnden*). This means that for this AML supervisor only public sources could be used.

countries concerned, have been willing to talk to me once or twice about their work.[59] In total, I conducted 32 interviews for this research of which nearly 50% took place within the ECOLEF study. Sometimes interviewees forwarded additional information after the interviews had taken place. In all cases, they have allowed me to use this, sometimes non-public, information and to refer to this information in my research.[60] I am not blind to the potential pitfalls that accompany the use of interviews as a research method. One can particularly think of the dependence on data provided by the AML supervisors during and after interviews, and the fact that the non-public information cannot be verified by outsiders. For some AML supervisors, however, it appeared to be the only way to obtain information about the exercise of AML supervision at all. I firmly believe that a useful, comparative research on the effectiveness of AML supervision without the use of interviews would not have been feasible. In order to minimise the potential pitfalls as much as possible, I used semi-structured interviews based on topic lists.[61] The topic lists provided the structure needed for the interviews and closely followed the elements from the theoretical framework. Topics were divided into institutional questions, organisational questions, questions regarding the exercise of supervision and sanctioning, cooperation with other stakeholders, and factual questions. For each interview the questions were adjusted and extended depending on the information already available for the authority concerned. The topic lists were, upon request, forwarded to interviewees beforehand. After each interview, I made an interview report and sent this to the interviewees. They were given the opportunity to respond to the interview reports and, through this, to give their approval to use the final interview reports in this research. Part of the agreement with the interviewees is that the final interview reports are not attached to this research and that the personal names of the interviewees are not released.[62] Another way through which I have tried to minimise the above-mentioned pitfalls is to use as much as possible public data in the first place, or alternatively to connect the data from interviews with the public data available. Where this appeared to be necessary, I explicitly state in the text or footnotes that the data presented stems solely from interviews or (non-public) information provided.

1.6 Relevance

Besides being an added value to the existing (academic) literature on money laundering, this research is also scientifically relevant for its innovative character. The innovation can be found in the use of the notion of effectiveness. This research presents a theoretical framework in which effectiveness is analysed principally from a legal perspective. Another

59 See Table of interviews. It contains a table that lists the dates, authorities, location of the interviews and whether the interviews formed part of the ECOLEF study or not. The set-up of the interviews conducted within the ECOLEF study was a little different from those specifically held for this PhD research. That is why all AML supervisors that were interviewed during the ECOLEF study were also interviewed at a later moment. This does not hold true for all other authorities involved in the preventive AML policy.

60 The non-public sources are not attached as annexes to this research. Only upon request and after written approval from the interviewees am I able to provide these data.

61 Van Thiel, S. (2010), *Bestuurskundig Onderzoek: Een methodologische inleiding*, Uitgeverij Coutinho: Bussum, § 8.4.

62 Only upon request and after written approval from the interviewees am I able to provide the final interview reports.

relatively novel element is the use of insights from other disciplines in the development of this theoretical legal framework. The multidisciplinary approach is also reflected in the research methods used in this research, which go beyond the use of the common legal research methods alone. Altogether, this research proves that it is not impossible for lawyers to work with the notion of effectiveness. This research is also innovative because of the use of (self-developed) supervisory models in the preventive AML policy as the basis for the country selection in this research.[63] To my knowledge, this research is the first research in which supervision in the preventive AML policy within the European Union has been analysed in such a comparative way. This makes the research more profound, as it allows for a switch between discussions on the national level and a more abstract level, and gives it more validity in terms of methodology. The selection of countries is accounted for.

1.7 ECOLEF

The ECOLEF study has already been mentioned a few times in this introduction. ECOLEF is an acronym for a study called *The Economic and Legal Effectiveness of Anti-Money Laundering and Combating Terrorist Financing Policy*.[64] I have been involved in this study as a legal researcher, carrying out research on the preventive AML policies of the EU Member States. Because the present research and the ECOLEF study have had a considerable overlap in work and time it is advantageous to explain how the two research projects are related. First, some more background information about the ECOLEF study is given.

The ECOLEF study is a study financed through an action grant by the European Commission. It formed part of the Prevention of and Fight Against Crime Programme operated by Directorate-General Home Affairs. The research was carried out by an interdisciplinary team of economic, legal and criminological researchers from Utrecht University and the University of Wollongong (Australia). The objective was to establish a framework for an encompassing cost-benefit analysis for evaluating anti-money laundering and combating terrorist financing policy, including countries' threat assessments. The study was conducted between 2009 and 2012 and performed in three phases. The first phase (December 2009-August 2010) consisted of setting up the project, the collection of contact data for the Member States, and the design of five surveys. The second phase of the project ran from September 2010 until June 2012 and consisted of the first analysis of all EU Member States' anti-money laundering and combating terrorist financing policies. During this period desk studies were performed, interviews were locally held with national authorities involved in the anti-money laundering and combating terrorist financing policy, and four regional workshops were organised for the country representatives. The final phase (July 2012-December 2012) consisted of an overall analysis of the Member

63 This part of the research was carried out within the framework of the ECOLEF study. See § 7.
64 Project reference: JLS/2009/ISEC/CFP/AG/.

States' policies, the organisation of a final conference and the writing of the final report. A book based on this report was published in March 2014.[65]

The ECOLEF study dealt with a wide variety of topics within the AML/CTF policy.[66] One of the findings was that although many international and European standards require various essential elements of money laundering and terrorist financing to be criminalised, a considerable divergence between the Member States has remained in existence.[67] Other findings in relation to financial intelligence units (FIUs) were that the budget of FIUs and the number of staff are significantly higher when FIUs have their own premises, that most FIUs have staff with a mixed background and that most FIUs have additional tasks and the number of additional duties increases once FIUs undergo organisational changes.[68] Regarding international cooperation, the study found a variety of judicial and FIU cooperation channels in the fight against money laundering and that international cooperation generally takes place between homologous institutions.[69] The study furthermore dealt with the collection of statistics and undertook a cost-benefit analysis.[70] In relation to the prevention of money laundering, three matters were studied in more detail: the harmonisation of substantive norms and effectiveness issues, the (timeliness of the) implementation of the Third Directive and international norms, and the matter of supervision at a more abstract level. All in all, the ECOLEF study demonstrated a diversified picture of the fight against money laundering and terrorist financing in the European Union.

The ECOLEF study and this research are related in that relevant data obtained during the ECOLEF study have been used in this research as well. Although the ECOLEF study was much wider in scope, it allowed some first interviews to be held with representatives of AML supervisors throughout the European Union and thus gave the opportunity to build a network for the purpose of this research. The ECOLEF study also provides an important methodological fundament of this research. The development of supervisory architectures for the then 27 EU Member States during the ECOLEF study is used as the starting point for this research. This research picks up the models from the ECOLEF study and builds

65 Unger et al. (2014), *The Economic and Legal Effectiveness of the European Union's Anti-Money Laundering Policy*, Edward Elgar Publishing Ltd: Cheltenham.

66 For the full details and an explanation of the conclusions of the ECOLEF study: Unger et al. (2014) at 221-241.

67 Ferwerda, J. (2014), 'Definitions of money laundering practice', in: Unger et al., *The Economic and Legal Effectiveness of the European Union's Anti-Money Laundering Policy*, Edward Elgar Publishing Ltd: Cheltenham, pp. 87-96.

68 Deleanu, I. (2014), 'FIUs in the European Union – facts and figures, functions and facilities', in: Unger et al., *The Economic and Legal Effectiveness of the European Union's Anti-Money Laundering Policy*, Edward Elgar Publishing Ltd: Cheltenham, pp. 97-124.

69 Deleanu, I. and Van den Broek, M. (2014), 'International cooperation', in: Unger et al., *The Economic and Legal Effectiveness of the European Union's Anti-Money Laundering Policy*, Edward Elgar Publishing Ltd: Cheltenham, pp. 147-161.

70 Ferwerda, J. (2014a), 'Collection of statistics', in: Unger et al., *The Economic and Legal Effectiveness of the European Union's Anti-Money Laundering Policy*, Edward Elgar Publishing Ltd: Cheltenham, pp. 162-186; Ferwerda, J. (2014b), 'Cost-benefit analysis', in: Unger et al., *The Economic and Legal Effectiveness of the European Union's Anti-Money Laundering Policy*, Edward Elgar Publishing Ltd, pp. 205-219.

further on these by carrying out more in-depth research on the effectiveness of AML supervision at the national level in the European Union.

1.8 Developments after March 2014

History never stands still and, as mentioned, especially the AML policy is developing at an incredibly high pace. Numerous developments of obvious importance have taken and continue to take place, which makes it very challenging to engage in long-term research in this policy field. Throughout the four years of this research, developments have taken place at all levels, even in the months, weeks and days leading up to the finalisation of this research. At the international level the clearest example is the adoption of the revised FATF Recommendations in February 2012. Not only were the standards considerably changed, leading to a new structure for the Recommendations, these were also expanded in terms of their content and scope.[71] In order to make the finalisation of this research possible, I chose to set a final date up until which all developments at the international, European and national levels have been incorporated. This research is up to date until the 31st of March 2014. Developments that have taken place after this period are not included in the country analyses, nor in the synthesis and conclusion. Some important developments are explained hereafter.

The first and foremost development that could not be included in this research concerns the adoption of a European directive that should replace the current Third Directive. Throughout this research the adoption of this directive was planned, delayed, planned, and delayed yet again. This shows the sensitivity of the matter and the high (political) interests surrounding the adoption of this instrument. At the moment of the finalisation of this research, the European Parliament had adopted a first reading of this Fourth Directive.[72] Because the directive has been in 'the near future' throughout most of the research, I pay some attention to the changes that the Fourth Directive is likely to bring about in relation to AML supervision in Chapter 2.[73] More against the background of this research, developments have taken place in relation to the creation of the European System of Financial Supervision (EIOPA, ESMA and EBA) in 2010 and to the Single Supervisory Mechanism (SSM) that grants the European Central Bank a supervisory role in relation to the financial stability of banks starting in November 2014.[74] With the changes in the EU-wide supervisory structure and the move towards a European

71 FATF (2012), *International standards on combating money laundering and the financing of terrorism & proliferation: The FATF Recommendations*, February 2012.

72 *European Parliament legislative resolution of 11 March 2014 on the proposal for a directive of the European Parliament and of the Council on the prevention of the use of the financial system for the purpose of money laundering and terrorist financing*, COM(2013)0045, 2013/0025(COD).

73 See § 2.3.3.

74 For the European System of Financial Supervision, see: Ottow, A. (2014), 'The New European Supervisory Architecture of the Financial Markets', in: Everson, M., Monda, C. and Vos, E. (eds.), *European Agencies in Between Institutions and Member States*, Kluwer: Alphen aan de Rijn, pp. 123-143. For SSM, see: Council Regulation 1024/2013 of 15 October 2013 conferring specific tasks on the European Central Bank concerning policies related to the prudential supervision of credit institutions, OJ L-287/63, 29 October 2013; Ferran, E. And Babis, V. (2013), 'The European Single Supervisory Mechanism', *University of Cambridge Faculty of Law Legal Study Research Papers* 10/2013.

banking union, principles that have played a fundamental role for a long time in banking supervision, such as the home state control (or home country) principle, are likely to fade and ultimately be abandoned. As is currently expected, AML supervision of banks will remain the responsibility of the national supervisors. Nevertheless, the developments described above may affect their supervisory responsibility and the way in which they give shape to and exercise their AML supervision, especially where this is embedded within their prudential supervision programmes.

Various important developments have taken place at the national level as well. In May 2014, the Spanish legislator finally adopted the long-awaited Royal Decree under the Spanish AML Act.[75] Because the adoption took place more than a month after the set date of this research, the lack of a Royal Decree is still described in the country analysis for Spain and is included in the synthesis and conclusion. In the Netherlands some legislative developments are worth mentioning as well. Whereas in January 2014 the EU Capital Requirements Regulation entered into force, the Dutch legislator implemented the EU Capital Requirements Directive into national legislation with the aim of strengthening capital requirements for banks and banking supervision in August 2014.[76] This has affected the Dutch AML Act as well: the amendments provide for tougher administrative fines and an extension of sanctioning powers for the DNB – with a direct reference to the Dutch Financial Supervision Act[77] – in relation to the most serious offences under the AML Act committed by banks.[78] It also affected the categorisation of offences under financial legislation, most importantly Sections 3:10 and 3:17 of the Financial Supervision Act (*Wet op het financieel toezicht*, Wft).[79] Moreover, in line with one of the findings in this research, the DNB published in June 2014 for the first time a good practices report that resulted from its thematic supervision.[80] In the United Kingdom a very important institutional development took place in April 2014: the Office of Fair Trading, the AML supervisor of real estate agents, was abolished on the 1st of April 2014. Its supervisory

75 *Real Decreto 304/2014, de 5 de mayo, por el que se aprueba el Reglamento de la Ley 10/2010, de 28 de abril, de prevención del blanqueo de capitales y de la financiación del terrorismo*, BOE no. 110, Sec. I, 6 de mayo 2014, 34775-34816.

76 *Wet van 25 juni 2014 tot wijziging van de Wet op het financieel toezicht en enige andere wetten ter implementatie van richtlijn 2013/36/EU van het Europees Parlement en de Raad van 26 juni 2013 betreffende toegang tot het bedrijf van kredietinstellingen en het prudentieel toezicht op kredietinstellingen en beleggingsondernemingen, tot wijziging van Richtlijn 2002/87/EG en tot intrekking van de Richtlijnen 2006/48/EG en 2006/49/EG (PbEU 2013, L 176) en ter implementatie van verordening (EU) nr. 575/2013 van het Europees Parlement en de Raad van 26 juni 2013 betreffende prudentiële vereisten voor kredietinstellingen en beleggingsondernemingen en tot wijziging van Verordening (EU) nr. 648/2012 (PbEU 2013, L 176) (Implementatiewet richtlijn en verordening kapitaalvereisten)*, Stb. 2014, 253; *Besluit van 15 juli 2014 tot wijziging van het Besluit prudentiële regels Wft, het Besluit bestuurlijke boetes financiële sector en enige andere besluiten op het terrein van de financiële markten ter implementatie van de richtlijn kapitaalvereisten en de verordening kapitaalvereisten (Implementatiebesluit richtlijn en verordening kapitaalvereisten)*, Stb. 2014, 303. Hereafter 'Implementation Act' and 'Implementation Decree'.

77 See § 5.6.3.3 as to why this is relevant.

78 Sections 28(5) and 28a AML Act, as amended. Chapter 5, however, demonstrates that not a single offence under the AML Act is categorised in the highest category (third category offences). The Implementation Act and Implementation Decree have not changed this.

79 Article II Implementation Decree. See § 5.6.3.1.

80 DNB (2014), *Good practices bestrijden corruptie*, 25 June 2014, available at: <www.toezicht.dnb.nl/binaries/50-230094.pdf>, last visited on 30 July 2014.

powers under the Money Laundering Regulations 2007 were transferred to HM Revenue and Customs (hereafter 'HMRC') on that date. Because of the set date, references are made to this transfer of supervisory responsibility in the country analysis and, where possible, the findings for the Office of Fair Trading are viewed in the light of the transfer to HMRC. Because HMRC had not taken up AML supervision during the period of this research, nothing more could be done in this respect. In Sweden, the legislator amended the AML Act on four occasions in the period from April to August 2014.[81] Amendments concerned, among other things, the expansion of the scope of the AML Act,[82] the references to the Swedish FIU as a result of the reorganisation of the Swedish National Police per January 2015, and the implementation of the prohibition on depositing money in a bank account if there are suspicions of money laundering. None of the amendments has directly affected the (powers of the) AML supervisors included in this research. Nevertheless, on the 1st of July 2014 the Swedish Ministry of Finance released a Memorandum (*Promemoria*) in which it proposes some more amendments to the AML Act. One of these proposals concerns the strengthening of the sanctioning powers of the county administrative boards, which is a welcome development as will become clear from this research.[83] In implementing the EU Capital Requirements Directive, the Swedish legislator has also been active in strengthening banking legislation and regulations.[84] Amendments have affected the powers of the Swedish Financial Supervisory Authority as described in this research. One of the most outstanding changes is the removal of the statutory cap of 50 million SEK for the imposition of administrative fees (fines) by the Authority.[85] The Authority also amended its regulations and general guidelines governing measures against money laundering and terrorist financing in June 2014.[86] Finally, a number of reports were published in the four countries after the 31st of March 2014 as well. One can think of the annual reports for the year 2013 of some AML supervisors and relevant stakeholders, like national FIUs, and reports issued by Governments. The Swedish Government, for example, published its national anti-money laundering strategy on the 19th of June 2014.[87]

81 *Lag om ändring i lagen (2009:62) om åtgärder mot penningtvätt och finansiering av terrorism,* SFS 2014:278 (adopted on 30 April 2014; entry into force on 1 July 2014) ; *Lag om ändring i lagen (2009:62) om åtgärder mot penningtvätt och finansiering av terrorism,* SFS 2014:314 (adopted on 15 May 2014; entry into force on 1 July 2014); *Lag om ändring i lagen (2009:62) om åtgärder mot penningtvätt och finansiering av terrorism,* SFS 2014:663 (adopted on 12 June 2014; entry into force on 1 January 2015); *Lag om ändring i lagen (2009:62) om åtgärder mot penningtvätt och finansiering av terrorism,* SFS 2014:795 (adopted on 19 June 2014; entry into force on 1 August 2014).

82 Act 2014:278 extended the scope to (managers of) alternative investment funds, to providers of payment service activities under the Swedish Payment Services Act (SFS 2013:561) without being a payment institution and to providers of certain professional activities with consumer credit including the supply or provision of credit to consumers (SFS 2014:275).

83 See Chapter 7; Finansdepartementet (2014), *Införande av visa internationella standarder i penningtvättslagen,* Promemoria June 2014, available at: <www.regeringen.se/sb/d/18204/a/243403>, last visited on 9 September 2014. The proposed amendments should enter into force in May 2015.

84 *Lag om ändring i lagen (2004:297) om bank- och finansieringsrörelse,* SFS 2014:982; *Lag om särskild tillsyn över kreditinstitut och värdepappersbolag,* SFS 2014:968.

85 Chapter 15, Sections 7-9 Lag om ändring i lagen (2004:297) om bank- och finansieringsrörelse, SFS 2014:982

86 *Föreskrifter om ändring i Finansinspektionens föreskrifter och allmänna råd (FFFS 2009:1) om åtgärder mot penningtvätt och finansiering av terrorism,* FFFS 2014:9.

87 *En nationell strategi för en effektiv regim för bekämpning av penningtvätt och af finansiering av terrorism,* SKR 2013/14:245.

It goes without saying that the findings of this research are valid until the 31st of March 2014. It should be borne in mind that the developments discussed above may affect or have affected the findings presented in this research.

1.9 Readers' guide

In order to present the aspects described above in an accessible way, this research is divided into three parts which all have a different structure. *Part I* contains the theoretical framework of effective supervision (Chapter 2) and explains the country selection by presenting the models of supervision in the preventive AML policy (Chapter 3). This is followed by *Part II* that consists of four country chapters (Chapters 4-7): Spain, the Netherlands, the United Kingdom and Sweden. This part is particularly relevant for those who are interested in the specific details of the AML supervision of banks, real estate agents and accountants in the four countries. Those who are interested in an actual comparison between the countries should immediately jump to *Part III*. This part is the most vital part of the research and contains the synthesis (Chapter 8) and conclusion (Chapter 9), where an answer to the research question is given.

Please note that translations from Dutch, Swedish and Spanish to English are my own and that all errors and omissions that may, in spite of my efforts to be as accurate as possible, still be found in this research remain mine.

PART I

2 Effective supervision

2.1 Introduction

What makes supervision effective? In order to answer the research question posed by this research, a theoretical framework is needed on the basis of which the countries' supervisory architectures can be analysed. This chapter presents the theoretical framework of effective supervision, in which effectiveness is assessed principally from a legal perspective.

Originally effectiveness was not a legal notion. This makes working with this notion a difficult task for lawyers, although it does not mean that lawyers have nothing to say about effectiveness at all.[1] Effectiveness is an ambiguous term in itself and can be applied in many different ways. In the context of supervision it is not easy to stipulate exactly what is required, as this depends on the approach one takes. The effectiveness of supervision, as explained, is approached here from a legal perspective. It is important to emphasise that it is not the aim of this research to measure effectiveness as such (are the supervisory goals actually attained?) or to measure the effects of supervision, but rather to develop a legal framework within which, if fulfilled, effectiveness is presumed.

This chapter starts with the theoretical embedding of effectiveness in law (§ 2.2). Based on the effectiveness principle some abstract directions for effective supervision can be identified. After that, requirements stemming from the Third Directive are analysed (§ 2.3). The Directive is an instrument of minimum harmonisation and the requirements for AML supervision and sanctioning are, therefore, minimum requirements.[2] Section 2.4 contains a literature study on the effectiveness of supervision. It demonstrates that a common core of requirements can be identified in literature, which can complement the abstract directions from the effectiveness principles and minimum requirements stemming from the Directive. Academic literature, (inter)national studies and other relevant sources are included in this literature study. Finally, this chapter presents in § 2.5 the criteria that are used for researching the effectiveness of the supervisory architectures in the Netherlands, Spain, the United Kingdom and Sweden.

1 Aelen, M. and van den Broek, M. (2014), 'De dubbele rol van het recht bij de effectiviteit van het financieel toezicht', *Tijdschrift voor Financieel Recht*, issue 1/2, pp. 12-22.

2 Article 5 Directive 2005/60/EC of the European Parliament and of the Council of 26 October 2005 on the prevention of the use of the financial system for the purpose of money laundering and terrorist financing (Third Directive).

2.2 Effectiveness as a legal principle

This section presents effectiveness as a legal principle within the notion of good governance (§ 2.2.1) and as a principle of European Union law (§ 2.2.2). Although this section presents effectiveness within these two concepts as two distinct principles, it should be borne in mind that in reality there is some overlap and interaction between the principles of effectiveness.[3] The principle of effectiveness is a highly developed principle in EU law and has, therefore, influenced the ideas underlying and meaning attached to the principle of effectiveness as a good governance principle. On the other hand, while, broadly speaking, the EU principle of effectiveness is primarily concerned with the effectuation of EU law into national law, the principle of effectiveness as a good governance principle has expanded the application of the effectiveness principle to the national level as well. This section ends with some concluding remarks (§ 2.2.3).

2.2.1 Good governance

Because supervision is the concluding piece of regulation and requires actions to be taken by or on behalf of the public administration, the concept of good governance provides a framework in which the requirements for effective supervision can be further developed. Good governance can be seen as a normative framework that provides the public administration with internal fundamental basics, which it must respect when making decisions or in the performance of other public tasks such as supervision.[4] Good governance aims to ensure that citizens' rights are respected and that the policy objectives of the public administration are attained at the same time. It is a 'framework concept on the basis of the rule of law and principles of procedural justice which draws together a range of rights, rules and principles guiding administrative procedures with the aim of ensuring procedural justice, public administrative adherence to the rule of law, and sound outcomes for administrative procedures'.[5] In literature, good governance is considered to be a legal concept.[6] The notion is given shape by a set of legal principles, or public values,

3 See in a broader context: Addink, G.H. (2011), 'De doorbraak van het beginselenrecht in het bestuursrecht: enkele opmerkingen over een conceptueel beginselenrecht', in: De Gier, T. et al. (eds.) (2011), *Goed verdedigbaar: vernieuwing van bestuursrecht en omgevingsrecht* (liber amoricum prof. mr. P.J.J. van Buuren), Kluwer: Deventer, pp. 3-16 at 11.

4 I say 'can be seen' on purpose, because there is much debate in the academic circle about what good governance is, resulting in an unsettled meaning and different uses of the notion of good governance. Some authors have a broader understanding of governance and are consequently of the opinion that all public organs, including political and judicial authorities, are subject to this notion. See for example: Leftwich, A. (1993), 'Governance democracy and development in the Third World', *Third World quarterly*, vol. 14, issue 3, pp. 605-624 and Addink, G.H. (2010), *Goed Bestuur*, Kluwer: Deventer, at 6. However, I apply a narrow definition of good governance which is limited to public administration. The terms good governance and good administration are in this research therefore equal to each other.

5 Hofmann, H.C.H. and Mihaescu, C. (2013), 'The Relation between the Charter's Fundamental Rights and the Unwritten General Principles of EU Law: Good Administration as the Test Case', *European Constitutional Law Review*, vol. 9, issue 1, pp. 73-101 at 84.

6 Curtin, D.M. and Dekker, I. (2005), 'Good Governance: The concept and its application by the European Union', in: Curtin, D.M. and Wessels, R.A., Good *Governance and the European Union: Reflections on concepts, institutions and substance*, Intersentia: Antwerp, pp. 3-20 at 4-8 consider good governance to be both a legal quality and a legal personal relationship. Cf. Esty, D.C. (2006), 'Good Governance at the Supranational Scale: Globalizing Administrative Law', *The Yale Law Journal*, vol. 115, issue 7, pp. 1490-1562

that regulate the institutional settings of and the processes within the public administration and manages the public-private relationship.[7] In order to obtain a good understanding of the notion of good governance, attention will first be paid to the origin and emergence of good governance. This is followed by a presentation of the good governance principles, and the principle effectiveness as a principle of good governance specifically.

2

2.2.1.1 Origin and emergence of good governance

Influenced by earlier failures of its reform programmes in third world countries, the term good governance was first coined by the World Bank in 1989.[8] Third world countries had to fulfil a number of requirements before the World Bank allowed them to make use of its lending policy. Good governance was considered to be the solution and its building blocks were an efficient public service, a reliable and independent judicial system, and an accountable administration. The notion of good governance was picked up soon thereafter by other international organisations like the International Monetary Fund, the World Trade Organisation and the UN High Commissioner for Human Rights.[9] At the European level, the European Commission's White Paper on European Governance from 2001 is considered to be the masterpiece on good governance in the European Union, although it is fiercely criticised at the same time.[10] The five principles that underpin the notion of good governance in the White Paper are openness, participation, accountability, effectiveness and coherence.[11] The European Ombudsman has been actively engaged in the development of good governance at the European Union level as well.[12] In the 2000s the increasing popularity of the notion culminated in the inclusion of the right to good administration in the Charter of Fundamental Rights of the European Union (hereafter

at 1523; Addink (2011) at 12-15; Addink, G.H. (2012), 'Het concept 'goed bestuur' in het bestuursrecht en de praktische consequenties daarvan', *Ars Aequi*, April 2012, pp. 266-275 at 269.

7 Legal scholars tend to talk about principles (e.g. Addink (2010)), while governance scholars rather seem to write about values (e.g. Van der Wal, Z. (2008), *Value solidity: Differences, similarities and conflicts between the organizational values of government and business*, Enschede: Print partners Ipskamp (doctoral thesis VU University)). In some studies the terms are used interchangeably. In this research principles and values have the same meaning.

8 World Bank (1989), *Sub-Saharan Africa: From Crisis to Sustainable Growth*, Washington DC, at 60-61; World Bank (1992), *Governance and Development*, Washington DC; World Bank (1994), *Good Governance and Fiscal Transparency*, Washington DC; World Bank (1997), *Corruption and Good Governance*, Washington DC.

9 Wouters, J. and Ryngaert, C. (2005) 'Good Governance: Lessons from international organizations', in: Curtin, D.M. and Wessels, R.A., Good *Governance and the European Union: Reflections on concepts, institutions and substance*, Intersentia: Antwerp, pp. 69-104 at 70-78; Chowdhury, N. and Skarstedt, C.E. (2005), *'The Principle of Good Governance'*, *CISDL Draft Legal Working Paper*, Oxford, at 4-5.

10 European Commission (2001), *White Paper on European Governance*, COM(2001) 428 final; Curtin and Dekker (2005) at 4. See for a large collection of critical publications: Joerges, C., Meny, Y. and Weiler, J.H.H. (eds.) (2001), 'Mountain or Molehill? A critical appraisal of the Commission's White paper on Governance', *Jean Monnet Working Paper*, No. 6/01.

11 European Commission (2001) at 10. See also: Lavrijssen, S.A.C.M. (2006), *Onafhankelijke mededingstoezichthouders, regulerende bevoegdheden en de waarborgen voor good governance*, Boom Juridische uitgevers: The Hague (doctoral thesis Utrecht University) at 57-92.

12 European Ombudsman (2005), *The European Code of Good Administrative Behaviour*, Brussels; Ponce, J., (2005), 'Good Administration and Administrative Procedures', *Indiana Journal of Global Legal Studies*, vol. 12, issue 2, pp. 551-588, at 565-576; Mendes, J. (2009), 'Good Administration in EU Law and the European Code of Good Administrative Behaviour', *EUI Working Papers Law* no. 2009/09.

the CFREU or 'the Charter) that formally entered into force with the Treaty of Lisbon in 2009.[13] Authors consider this both an innovation and a retrograde step at the same time. It is the first time that a European (or even international) charter of fundamental rights explicitly recognises the right to good administration, but the formulation of Article 41 CFREU is more limited in scope than the case law of the European Court of Justice on the right to good administration.[14] Currently, developments with regard to the creation of a European Law of Administrative Procedure are taking place, which should apply to all EU institutions, agencies and other institutions in relation to administration and administrative decisions. In January 2013, the European Parliament adopted a resolution prepared by the Committee of Legal Affairs of the European Parliament, requesting the European Commission to develop a proposal for a regulation on a European Law of Administrative Procedure and to include good governance aspects therein.[15] The Council of Europe also pays attention to the notion of good governance, most notably in relation to local governance.[16] And quite recently, the European Court of Human Rights has started to use the notion of good governance in cases related to the protection of property as enshrined in article 1 of the First Protocol to the Convention for the Protection of Human Rights and Fundamental Freedoms.[17]

Likewise, the attention to good governance is increasing at the national level. This increased attention can primarily be explained by the modernisation of administrative law. Traditionally, administrative law served citizens against arbitrariness on the side of the administration, but administrative law is more and more focused on its instrumental function(s).[18] Member States have adopted and implemented various kinds of legally binding and non-binding documents which give content to the notion of good governance. In 2005 the Swedish Agency for Public Management compared principles of good administration in various EU Member States and concluded that a common core

13 Article 41 CFREU. Wakefield, J. (2007), *The right to good administration*, Kluwer: Deventer; Addink, G.H. (2008), 'Goed Bestuur: een norm voor het bestuur of het recht van een burger?', in: Addink, G.H., Jurgens, G., Langbroek Ph. M. and Widdershoven, R.J.G.M., *Grensverleggend Bestuursrecht*, Kluwer: Deventer, pp. 3-25; Hofmann and Mihaescu (2013).

14 Hofmann and Mihaescu (2013) at 83-86.

15 European Parliament resolution of 15 January 2013 with recommendations to the Commission on a Law of Administrative Procedure of the European Union, Strasbourg, 2012/2024(INI). See: Craig, P. (2013), 'A General Law on Administrative Procedure, Legislative Competence and Judicial Competence', *European Public Law*, vol. 19, issue 3, pp. 503-524; Addink, G.H. (2014), 'Europees bestuursrecht in ontwikkeling: op weg naar een Europese Awb', *Nederlands Tijdschrift voor Bestuursrecht* 2014-24. In the summer of 2014 ReNEUAL, a research network on EU administrative law, published Model Rules that are designed as a draft proposal for binding legislation: ReNEUAL Model Rules on EU Administrative Procedure, available at: <www.reneual.eu/>, last visited on 10 September 2014.

16 Conference of European ministers responsible for local and regional government, *Good local and regional governance – the European Challenge*, MCL-15(2007)5 final; Additional Protocol to the European Charter of Local Self-Government on the right to participate in the affairs of a local authority, CETS No. 207; Addink, G.H. (2009), *Local and Regional level participation in Europe: A comparative exploratory study on the application of the participation principle at local and regional level within the framework of the Council of Europe*, Utrecht University.

17 For example: ECtHR, 15 September 2009, *Moskal v Poland*, app. no. 10373/05; ECtHR, 20 October 2011, *Rysovskyy v Ukraine*, app. no. 29979/04; ECtHR, 16 May 2013, *Maksymenko and Gerasymenko v Ukraine*, app. no. 49317/2007, *EHRC*, 2013/153 annotated by Henk Addink; ECtHR, 26 November 2013, *Bogdel v Lithuania*, app. no. 41248/06.

18 Van Wijk/Konijnenbelt & Van Male (2014), *Hoofdstukken van het bestuursrecht*, Kluwer: Deventer, at 46-47.

of principles can be identified, but that Member States' legislation shows a great variety in the way in which the principles are implemented.[19] In the Netherlands, the National Ombudsman and the Court of Audit play an important role in developing the notion of good governance.[20] Moreover, the Ministry of Interior Affairs and Kingdom Relations drafted its own Good Governance Code for the public sector.[21] The Spanish Government also adopted a Good Governance Code in 2005, which applies to Members of Government and senior officers of the General State Administration.[22] And, finally, in the United Kingdom the Independent Commission on Good Governance in Public Services adopted a Good Governance Standard for Public Services.[23]

2.2.1.2 The principles of good governance

Good governance is an umbrella term. One cannot in general say what constitutes good governance, because it strongly varies according to the context in which it is used.[24] The notion is given content through the principles of good governance. These principles are sometimes linked to the notions of the rule of law or democracy, but often have their own meaning and content.[25] The principles of good governance are not a single set of principles. In literature, the variety that can be identified at the international, European and national level, as well as between different organisations and countries, has been typified as a 'cacophony of values'.[26] Various governance and legal studies have dealt with

19 Statskontoret (2005), *Principles of Good Administration in the Member States of the European Union*, 2005:4.

20 Algemene Rekenkamer (2008), *Goed Bestuur in uitvoering: de praktijk van onderwijsinstellingen, woningcorporaties, zorgorganisaties en samenwerkingsverbanden*, The Hague (in English: *Good Governance in practice: The practice at education institutions, housing associations, care organisations and alliances*); Algemene Rekenkamer (2005), *Essentials of Good Governance*, The Hague; Nationale Ombudsman (2005), *De maakbare overheid: jaarverslag 2005*, Den Haag; Nationale Ombudsman (2014), *Behoorlijkheidswijzer*, available at: <www.nationaleombudsman.nl/sites/default/files/behoorlijkheidswijzer_nl_februari_2014.pdf>, last visited on 19 March 2014.

21 Ministerie van Binnenlandse Zaken en Koninkrijksrelaties (2009), *Nederlandse Code voor Goed Openbaar Bestuur: beginselen van deugdelijk overheidsbestuur*, The Hague.

22 *Orden APU/516/2005, de 3 de marzo, por la que se dispone la publicación del Acuerdo del Consejo de Ministros de 18 de febrero de 2005, por el se aprueba el Código de Buen Gobierno de los miembros del Gobierno y de los altos cargos de la Administración General del Estado, Boletín Oficial del Estado (BOE), no. 56, sec. I, 7953-7955*. An English translation of the Code is available at: <www.oecd.org/dataoecd/17/35/35521364.pdf>, last visited on 19 March 2014. The Code was complemented by *Ley 5/2006, de 10 de abril, de regulación de los conflictos de intereses de los miembros de Gobierno y de los Altos Cargos de la Administración General del Estado, BOE, no. 86, Sec. I, 13954-13961* (in English: *Act on conflicts of interest of members of the government and senior officials of the administration*) *and Real Decreto 432/2009, de 14 de abril 2009, por el que se aprueba el Reglamento, por el que se desarrolla la Ley 5/2006, de 10 de abril, de regulación de los conflictos de intereses de los miembros de Gobierno y de los altos cargos de la Administración General del Estado, BOE, no. 91, Sec. I, 34657-34713.*

23 Independent Commission on Good Governance in Public Services (2004), *The Good Governance Standard for Public Services*: OPM: London.

24 Curtin and Dekker (2005) at 5; Botchway, F.N. (2001), 'Good Governance: The Old, The New, The Principle and The Elements', *Florida Journal of International Law*, vol. 13, pp. 159-210, at 180 et seq.

25 Addink, G.A., Anthony, G., Buyse, A. and Flinterman, C. (2010), *Source Book on Human Rights and Good Governance*, SIM Special no. 34, at 14. Addink considers good governance as a concept standing at equal footing with Rechtsstaat and democracy: Addink. G.H. (2015), *Good Governance: Concept and Context*, OUP: Oxford (forthcoming), Ch. 5 and 6.

26 Huberts, L.W.J.C. and Van Hout, E.J.Th. (2011), 'Goed bestuur: kiezen of delen?', *Bestuurskunde*, vol. 20, issue 2, pp. 53-62, at 57. Cf. Wouters and Ryngaert (2005).

the identification and categorisation of principles of good governance. As a result there exists a wide variety of lists of principles or values.[27] Hereafter, the principles of good governance are explained following Addink's categorisation: accountability, transparency, participation, properness, human rights and, lastly, the principle of effectiveness.

Accountability, transparency, participation, proper administration and human rights

Accountability as a principle of good governance requires that the public administration gives an account of the activities that it has performed, and the results and the resources that it has used.[28] The forums to which account must be given differ. This can be, for example, the Government, Parliament, another hierarchical authority, or the wider public.[29] A common way to give account is the publication of annual plans and reports.

Transparency is strongly related to the concept of democracy and has many appearances and meanings.[30] As a good governance principle, it refers to the question of how the public administration applies its powers in the performance of its public tasks. Citizens or third parties need information in order to understand what the administration is doing and what they can expect from it. By being transparent the public administration can create more legitimacy, trust, and strengthen its own position vis-à-vis society.[31] Transparency can be given by providing access to documents and by the active provision of information.[32] The principles of accountability and transparency are strongly related: for accountability a level of transparency is needed: '[t]ransparency may be considered part of accountability or a prerequisite to it: how can the public hold public authorities accountable if the public

27 Van der Wal (2008) identified thirty public values and brought these back to thirteen most important principles for public authorities; Beck Jørgensen, T. and Bozeman, B. (2007), 'Public values: an inventory', *Administration & Society*, vol. 39, issue 3, pp. 354-381 compiled a list of eight core principles; Kernaghan, K. (2003), 'Integrating Values into Public Service: The Values Statement as Centerpiece', *Public Administration Review*, vol. 63, issue 6, pp. 711-719 identifies four categories; Van Montfort, C. (2008), *Besturen van het onbekende: Goed bestuur bij publiek-private arrangementen*, Uitgeverij Lemma: The Hague at 29 applies four clusters; Addink (2010) identifies six principles.

28 Accountability is thus understood as a mechanism. Cf. Bovens, M. (2010), 'Two Concepts of Accountability: Accountability as a Virtue and Accountability as a Mechanism', *West European Politics*, vol. 33, issue 5, pp. 946-967.

29 Bar Cendón, A. (2000), 'Accountability and Public Administration: Concepts, Dimensions, Developments', in: Kelly, M. (ed.), *Openness and Transparency in Governance: Challenges and Opportunities*, Maastricht: EIPA, pp. 22-61 at 27.

30 Buijze, A. (2013), *The Principle of Transparency in EU law*, Boxpress: 's-Hertogenbosch (doctoral thesis Utrecht University); Scholtes, E. (2012), *Transparantie, icoon van een dolende overheid*, Boom Lemma (doctoral thesis Tilburg University) at 50-55; Dyrberg, P. (2002), 'Accountability and Legitimacy: What is the Contribution of Transparency?', in: Arnull, A. and Wincott, D. (eds), *Accountability and Legitimacy in the European Union*, Oxford University Press, pp. 81-96 at 81-84.

31 Scholtes (2012) at 107.

32 See e.g. Curtin, D. (2009), *Executive Power of the European Union: Law, Practices, and the Living Constitution*, Oxford University Press, pp. 204-246; Adamski, D. (2014), 'Access to Documents, Accountability and the Rule of Law – Do Private Watchdogs Matter?', *European Law Journal*, vol. 20, issue 4 pp. 520-524; Heliskoski, J. and Leino, P. (2006), 'Darkness at the break of noon: The case law on Regulation 1049/2001 on access to documents', *Common Market Law Review*, vol. 43, issue 3, pp. 735-781; Grønbech-Jensen, C. (1998) 'The Scandinavian Tradition of Open Government and the European Union: Problems of Compatibility?', *Journal of European Public Policy*, vol. 5, issue 1, pp. 185-199; Héritier, A. (2003), 'Composite democracy in Europe: the role of transparency and access to information', *Journal of European Public Policy*, vol. 10, issue 5, pp. 814-833; Addink et al. (2010) at 57 et seq.

is not allowed to know what goes on within the public authorities, or if what goes on is obscure?'[33]

Participation as a principle of good governance ensures that citizens are able to exert influence on the public administration at various stages in decision-making procedures. The principles of proper administration have been developed in various European jurisdictions 'as tools to cope with [...] unavoidable legal uncertainties' arising from unclear legislation and the discretionary use of powers by the administration.[34] The principles of proper administration give a (minimum) standard to decision-making activities by the public administration. Examples are the principle of due care, the principle of proportionality, the principle of legality (*Gesetzmäßigkeit*), the principle of motivation, the principle of legal certainty, the principle of equality (*egalité, Gleichheitsgrundsatz*), and the prohibition of misuse (excess and abuse) of power (*détournement de pouvoir*). Finally, the principle of human rights in a good governance context requires that the public administration fully respects fundamental rights. It has been stated that '[b]oth groups of norms for the government (...) can only be realized by each other: human rights needs good governance and good governance needs human rights'.[35]

The principle of effectiveness

Turning to the principle of effectiveness, it can be observed that effectiveness is gaining importance in legal theory as a principle of good governance.[36] Given the interest of lawyers in knowing whether legislation and regulations actually work in practice, and under the influence of social and economic sciences, it is understood that policies must be effective and timely. They must deliver what is needed based on clear objectives.[37] Effectiveness requires that legislation and regulations set goals and that those goals are accomplished as effectively as possible. From a legal perspective, it requires that there are no legal hindrances, or factual hindrances that may bear legal consequences, which make the application of the law and regulations (by the public administration) more burdensome, as a result of which legislative or regulatory goals cannot be achieved.[38] Effectiveness is sometimes framed by lawyers into notions such as proportionality and subsidiarity.[39] This is logical, because these are notions that lawyers are acquainted with. At the same time, however, it also gives a too narrow picture of effectiveness. This is demonstrated at the end of this chapter, when the theoretical framework for effective supervision is finalised.

Different from the other principles of good governance, the principle of effectiveness entails a strong instrumental character. For this reason, the principle of effectiveness sometimes clashes with the other principles of good governance that usually have a protective

33 Dyrberg (2002) at 83.
34 Addink et al. (2010) at 31.
35 Ibid., at 112. Cf. OHCHR (2007), *Good Governance Practices for the Protection of Human Rights*, New York-Geneva.
36 Addink (2010) at 30 et seq.; Aelen and Van den Broek (2014).
37 European Commission (2001) at 10; cf. Addink et al. (2010) at 80.
38 Stouten (2012) at 22.
39 European Commission (2001) at 10; Buijze, A. (2009), 'Effectiviteit in het bestuursrecht', *Nederlands Tijdschrift voor Bestuursrecht* 2009-31.

(safeguard) dimension in the first place. I will now briefly discuss the relationship between the principle of effectiveness and other principles of good governance.

2.2.1.3 Relationship between effectiveness and the other principles of good governance

What is the relationship between the principles of good governance? Do the principles reinforce each other, are they incompatible with each other, or are they even immensurable?[40] The close relationship between accountability and transparency could already be observed. But what happens when the principles conflict with each other; do all principles carry equal weight or should one principle be preferred over other principles?

On the whole the public administration, in the exercise of public tasks, should be democratic, legitimate, incorruptible (*integer*) and performance-oriented.[41] Connecting these requirements to the principles as just presented above, one could argue that participation is closely related to the democracy aspect, whereas accountability, transparency and properness belong to the aspect of legitimacy. Respect for human rights can be seen as part of the integrity of the administration and effectiveness as part of the performance-oriented administration.[42] The four overall requirements that the public administration must adhere to do not always coincide and even conflict at times.[43] This also holds true for the principles. Especially effectiveness may clash with the other principles: governance studies mostly demonstrate a strong tension between effectiveness, on the one hand, and the democracy-related principles of good governance, on the other.[44] A number of so-called coping strategies have been developed in order to overcome conflicts between the principles (values).[45]

> Two examples of cases where effectiveness clashes with other principles are the following. Suppose, for example, that a public administrative authority wishes to take a decision that affects a large number of citizens. The principle of participation requires that these citizens need to be given a possibility to become involved in the decision-making process. Participation at the same time slows down the decision-making process and conflicts with the principle of effectiveness, because the goals of the public administrative authority may not be attained in time. In such situations, it may be necessary to weigh the importance of the different principles in light of the circumstances of the case, or even to set aside one or more principles. Effectiveness may also conflict with the protection of fundamental rights as a good governance principle: while it would be highly effective to

40 De Graaf, G., Huberts, L. and Smulders, R. (2013), *Publieke waarden: De beginselen van goed bestuur in de dagelijkse praktijk van ziekenhuis en gemeente*, onderzoek in opdracht van het Ministerie van Binnenlandse Zaken en Koninkrijksrelaties, at 15, who refer to a number of studies, in particular to the work of Spicer, M. (2010). *In defense of politics in public administration: A value pluralist perspective*, The University of Alabama Press.

41 Bovens, M.A.P., 't Hart, P. and Van Twist, M.W.J. (2012), *Openbaar bestuur: beleid, organisatie en politiek*, Deventer: Kluwer, at 24-35.

42 This is just one possible categorisation of the principles of good governance along the lines of these four requirements. One could also argue that transparency should be part of the 'democratic public administration'.

43 Cf. Lavrijssen (2006) at 76.

44 See for an overview of various studies: De Graaf et al. (2013) at 31-33.

45 See for an overview of the literature on this point: De Graaf et al. (2013) at 34-35.

> have lawyers reporting to the competent authorities when they suspect that their client is involved in money laundering, this would at the same time infringe citizens' fundamental right to speak openly with their lawyer, and the right to a fair trial.[46]

At the same time the different principles can reinforce each other. This is particularly the case when good governance is seen as a tool for creating (more) legitimacy. Transparency, for example, is said to further participation, because transparency mechanisms increase possibilities for civil society to obtain information and participate in the authorities' decision-making procedures.[47] Regarding the exercise of supervision by a public authority, it seems that accountability and transparency are closely related to effectiveness. In this context it has been stated that transparency as to the functioning of supervision, and accountability about the effectiveness thereof, are essential components of good democratic governance, and altogether contribute to the legitimacy of supervision by the State.[48] Also in legal requirements concerning accountability, one can sometimes find references to effectiveness as well.[49] In the Netherlands, for example, Section 20 Government Accounts Act *(Comptabiliteitswet)* requires Ministers to ensure the effectiveness and efficiency of their policies and to account for that via periodic evaluation reports.

The relationship between the principles, in particular the relationship between effectiveness and the other principles of good governance, is twofold. Later in this chapter this will become clear, when accountability and transparency are incorporated into the notion of effective supervision.

2.2.2 The EU principle of effectiveness

The principle of effectiveness is not exclusively a principle of good governance and it is used in other contexts as well. Because the principle of effectiveness is extensively referred to in European law, this section focuses on the particular obligations stemming from the European principle of effectiveness.

2.2.2.1 Background of the principle of effectiveness in European Union law

The principle of effectiveness is most extensively elaborated within European Union law. It is connected to the principle of loyal cooperation as enshrined in Article 4, third paragraph, of the Treaty on European Union (TEU), which obliges Member States to take appropriate measures in order to ensure the full effect of the obligations arising out of the Treaties or resulting from the acts of the institutions of the Union, as well as to refrain from taking any measure that could jeopardise the attainment of the Union's objectives.[50]

46 See in this context: Van den Broek and Addink (2013) at 374-375.
47 Dyrberg (2002) at 82.
48 Welp, P. (2012) 'Effectiviteit van toezicht: tijd voor *responsive evaluation*', *Tijdschrift voor Toezicht*, issue 2, pp. 7-22 at 12.
49 Aelen and Van den Broek (2014) at 14-16.
50 Jans, J.H., De Lange, R., Prechal, S. and Widdershoven, R.J.G.M. (2007), *Europeanisation of public law*, Europa Law Publishing: Groningen, p. 199 et seq.; Hatje, A. (2001), *Loyalität als Rechtsprinzip in der Europäischen Union*, Nomos: Baden-Baden; Kapteyn, P.J.G., VerLoren van Themaat, P. (2008), *The law of the European Union and the European Communities*, Kluwer: Deventer, at 147-156.

The principle of loyal cooperation must be respected by all levels of the national administration and is considered to be the basic principle for enforcement in a European law context.[51] The principle of effectiveness is also strongly connected to the principle of national procedural autonomy.[52] This principle entails that unless European law provides otherwise, national law and national authorities must ensure that the European norms are applied and complied with, where necessary after implementation in national law.[53] Hence, European norms must be implemented, brought into effect at the national level and enforced where necessary.[54] The choice for national procedures and institutions is in principle entirely left to the Member States' discretion. This is where the principle of effectiveness comes to the fore: as a means to mediate between the national interest of achieving maximum autonomy and the European interest in achieving the maximum application of the European norms.[55] In sum, the principle of effectiveness primarily sees to the effectuation of EU law in national law.[56]

> The European influence on national procedural autonomy via the principle of effectiveness has to do with the fact that historically the European Union does not have its own agents to enforce its norms, but must rely on national authorities.[57] While Member States are in principle responsible for the enforcement of European norms, in policy fields like customs, fisheries, fraud, as well as financial, energy and environmental law there is a clear trend of the 'Europeanisation' of enforcement.[58] In those policies, the EU has assigned the European Commission as the main supervisor, created networks or even European regulatory authorities.[59] In more general terms Delistopoulos states that

51 Blomberg, A. (2008), 'European Influence on National Environmental Law Enforcement: Towards an Integrated Approach', *Review of European Administrative Law*, vol. 1, issue 2, pp. 39-81 at 43.

52 Blomberg (2008) at 43; Van Gerven, W. (2000), 'Of rights, remedies and procedures', *Common Market Law Review*, vol. 37, issue 3, pp. 501-536 at 502; Verhoeven, M. (2011), *The Costanzo Obligation: The obligations of national administrative authorities in the case of incompatibility between national law and European law*, Intersentia: Antwerp, pp. 96-102 (doctoral thesis Utrecht University).

53 Jans et al. (2007), at 18.

54 See more about national procedural autonomy, points of discussion and difficulties: Gerbrandy, A. (2009), *Convergentie in het mededingingsrecht*, Boom Juridische uitgevers: The Hague, at 24-25, Accetto, M. and Zleptnig, S. (2005), 'The Principle of Effectiveness: Rethinking Its Role in Community Law', *European Public Law*, vol. 11, issue 3, pp. 375-403 at 395-397; Verhoeven (2011) at 49-52. Cf. Delicostopoulos, J.S. (2003), 'Towards European Procedural Primacy in National Legal Systems', *European Law Journal*, vol. 9, issue 5, pp. 599-613.

55 Accetto and Zleptnig (2005), at 403. Cf. Tridimas, T. (2006), *The General Principles of EU Law*, Oxford EC Law Library, 2nd edition at 424 who argues that the scope of the principle of national procedural autonomy is difficult to pin down and that its minimum content can best be defined negatively. He states that the Court always takes as a starting point the principle of effectiveness.

56 Ottow, A.T. (2006), *Telecommunicatietoezicht. De invloed van het Europese en Nederlandse bestuurs(proces) recht*, Boom Juridische uitgevers: The Hague (doctoral thesis University of Amsterdam), at 66; Aelen en Van den Broek (2014) at 13.

57 Jans et al. (2007) at 200; Accetto and Zleptnig (2005) at 381; Snyder, F. (1993), 'The Effectiveness of European Community Law: Institutions, Processes, Tools and Techniques', *Modern Law Review*, vol. 56, issue 1, pp. 19-54 at 22.

58 De Moor-van Vugt, A.J.C. (2011), 'Netwerken en de europeanisering van het toezicht', *SEW: Tijdschrift voor Europees en Economisch Recht*, issue 3, pp. 94-102.

59 Adriaanse, P.C. et al. (2008), *Implementatie van EU-handhavingsvoorschriften*, WODC: Den Haag; Ottow, A. (2011), 'Europeanisering van het markttoezicht', *SEW: Tijdschrift voor Europees en Economisch Recht*, issue 1, pp. 3-17; De Moor-van Vugt (2011); De Moor-van Vugt (2001), *Toezicht achter matglas: Over de betekenis van transparantie voor toezicht op de naleving van regelgeving*, Boom Juridische uitgevers: The Hague, at 11-12.

European legal order has moved 'from national procedural autonomy to a combination of national procedural competence and European procedural primacy'.[60] Still, the success of European legislation mostly depends on the Member States' willingness to design adequate enforcement systems as EU law is mainly enforced indirectly.[61] From a European point of view it is thus necessary to establish some minimum requirements on enforcement to minimise the European enforcement deficit.[62] One of these minimum requirements is effectiveness.

The effectiveness principle itself is a jurisprudential principle, not enshrined in any Treaty provision and developed most prominently by the European Court of Justice in its case law.[63] Despite its character, it is considered to be one of the most important instrumental requirements that need to ensure a full implementation and application of European Union law.[64] The broad effectiveness principle can be divided into two *species*, namely the principle of effectiveness in procedural law ('Rewe effectiveness'), and the principle of effective judicial protection. The principle of effective judicial protection is enshrined in Article 19, first paragraph, TEU and entails that Member States are responsible for providing sufficient remedies to ensure effective legal protection in the fields covered by Union law.[65] It is codified in Article 47 CFREU as well.[66] In academic circles there is much talk about the relationship between the two effectiveness species. Some consider that both belong to an overarching principle of effectiveness, whereas others separate the effectiveness principle and the principle of effective judicial protection from each other.[67] The Court itself has also not clearly indicated what the relationship between the two is. In one case it applies the principle of effectiveness, while in other cases it turns to the principle of effective judicial protection. The *DEB* case exemplifies this uncertainty. In this case the ECJ translated of its own volition a preliminary question about the principle of effectiveness into a question about effective judicial protection.[68] In the *Pontin* case, the Court had positioned the principles of effectiveness and equivalence within the framework

60 Delicostopoulos (2003) at 609 et seq.

61 Adriaanse, P.C. et al. (2008a), 'Implementation of EU Enforcement Provisions: Between European Control and National Practice', *Review of European Administrative Law*, vol. 1, issue 2, pp. 83-97 at 86.

62 Jans et al. (2007) at 199-200.

63 Tridimas (2006) deals extensively with the case law of the ECJ on the principle of effectiveness.

64 Although, as could be seen above, it is related to and operates in conjunction with other principles. See: Accetto and Zleptnig (2005) at. 385-388. Cf. Jans et al. (2007), at 206; Blomberg (2008).

65 E.g. Case 222/84 *Johnston* [1986] ECR 1651, Case 222/86 *Heylens* [1987] ECR 4097, Case C-424/99 *Commission v Austria* [2001] ECR I-9285, Case C-50/00 P *Unión de Pequeños Agricultores v Council* [2002] ECR I-6677, and Case C-432/05, *Unibet* [2007] ECR I-2271.

66 Cf. Tridimas (2006) at 455-456; Pernice, I. (2013), 'The Right to Effective Judicial Protection and Remedies in the EU', in: Court of Justice of the European Union, *The Court of Justice and Construction of Europe: Analyses and Perspectives on Sixty-Years of Case Law*, Asser Press: The Hague, pp. 381-397.

67 For example: Tridimas (2006) at 418-476 includes both the 'Rewe effectiveness' and effective judicial protection under a wider principle of effectiveness; Ottow (2006) at 66 et seq. states that effectiveness is further elaborated in the principle of effective judicial protection and also embeds this in her theoretical framework on effective supervision; Accetto and Zleptnig (2005) at 388 also consider effective judicial protection as a feature of the overarching principle of effectiveness. See differently: Gerbrandy (2009) at 22 et seq., who derives the principle of effective judicial protection from the notion of *Rechtsstaat* (the rule of law). She discusses the possible relationship between the principle of effectiveness and the principle of effective judicial protection, but considers them as two separate principles.

68 Case C-279/09, *DEB [*2010] ECR I-13849, paragraphs 28-29.

of the principle of effective judicial protection.[69] And in *Alassini*, the Court used both the tests with respect to the principle of effectiveness and the one with respect to effective judicial protection, as each principle has a different focus.[70]

Prechal and Widdershoven have analysed the ECJ's case law and point at notable similarities and differences between the two species. They identify the relationship as 'a poorly articulated and uneasy' one.[71] Because of differences in the characteristics, focus and underlying rationales, they conclude that a separate application of principles of effectiveness and effective judicial protection is most desirable. Following this line of reasoning, I consider the principle of effectiveness and effective judicial protection as two separate principles. In my opinion, the principle of effectiveness refers primarily to the implementation, application and/or enforcement of European Union law. It has a strong instrumental, procedural and top-down focus whereby the protection of citizens' rights only comes into play incidentally – if at all. On the contrary, the principle of effective judicial protection aims to protect the individual in the first place, has a bottom-up focus, and is strongly related to the fundamental right to a fair trial. Here the judge plays a central role in the enforcement of the law. Taking into account that this research deals with the effectiveness of supervision from a more instrumental perspective, no further attention will be paid to aspects of legal protection in this research.[72]

On the basis of the principle of effectiveness in procedural law, the Court has also developed more specific effectiveness criteria in relation to (adequate) enforcement.[73] The next subsection presents the principle of effectiveness in procedural law, and specifically in relation to enforcement. In particular the requirements stemming from the principle of effective enforcement are important for the theoretical framework of this research.

2.2.2.2 The principle of effectiveness as a requirement for adequate enforcement

The general instrumental requirements for adequate enforcement that stem more directly from the case law of the ECJ with respect to enforcement are effectiveness, equivalence, dissuasiveness and proportionality.[74] Besides these instrumental requirements, European law also requires that the enforcement systems of the Member States observe fundamental

69 Case C-63/08, *Pontin* [2009] ECR I-10467.

70 Joined Cases C-317/08 - C-320/08, *Alassini* [2010] ECR I-02213.

71 Prechal, S. and Widdershoven, R. (2011), 'Effectiveness or Effective Judicial Protection: A Poorly Articulated Relationship, in: Baumé, T., Oude Elferink, E., Phoa, P. and Thiaville, D. (eds.), *Today's Multilayered Legal Order: Current Issues and Perspectives*, Paris Legal Publishers: Zutphen, pp. 283-296 at 296.

72 See for interesting literature: Van Gerven (2000); Tridimas (2006) at 443-456; Arnull, A. (2011), 'The Principle of Effective Judicial Protection in EU Law: an Unruly Horse?', *European Law Review*, vol. 36, pp. 51-70; Dougan, M. (2011), 'The Vicissitudes of Life at the Coalface: Remedies and Procedures for Enforcing Union Law before the National Courts', in: Craig, P. and de Búrca, G., *Evolution of EU Law*, 2nd edition, Oxford: Oxford University Press, pp. 693-746.

73 Enforcement in relation to the European effectiveness principle refers to the imposition and execution of sanctions.

74 Cf. Case 33/76, *Rewe*, [1976]; ECR I-1989; Case C-45/76 *Comet BV v Produktschap voor Siergewassen* [1976] ECR 2043; Case C-68/88, *Commission v Greece* [1989] ECR 2965 (Greek Maize); Case C-354/99, *Commission v Ireland* [2001] ECR-07657. See: Jans et al. (2007) at 206-213.

rights, general principles of law and Treaty freedoms.[75] These are the so-called protective (safeguard) requirements for adequate enforcement. The principle of effectiveness as a requirement for adequate enforcement is a refinement of the principle of effectiveness in procedural law, also called 'Rewe effectiveness'.

Rewe effectiveness

The landmark cases for this principle are the *Rewe* and *Comet* judgments.[76] In *Rewe*, the ECJ decided that it is in principle up to the national legislatures to determine which procedures apply and how these are organised in the national legal order, but at the same time held that for the application of European norms the minimum requirements of effectiveness and equivalence have to be respected.[77] Briefly, effectiveness means that the national norms must 'not render virtually impossible or excessively difficult' the exercise of rights conferred by the European legal order.[78] Equivalence (non-discrimination) requires that norms governing a dispute with a European law dimension must not be less favourable than those governing similar domestic disputes.[79] Equivalence and effectiveness are complementary and are considered to be the 'outer-limits' of national procedural autonomy.[80] Later case law has taught us that in case of a conflict between the principles of effectiveness and equivalence, the first takes precedence and sets aside the principle of equivalence.[81] Furthermore, if the national procedural norms do not fulfil the requirements of effectiveness and equivalence, the Court held in *Barra* and *Deville*, although not explicitly, that these national norms must be rendered inapplicable.[82] In examining whether national procedural norms or national procedures comply with the principle of effectiveness, the ECJ has developed two types of tests in its case law: the direct test and the 'procedural rule of reason' test.[83]

> In the direct test the ECJ concludes whether a national norm renders the exercise of (European) rights virtually impossible or excessively difficult and which consequence should follow therefrom.[84] In the second test, effectiveness is balanced with other national principles that may serve as a justification in concrete cases for impeding the

75 Jans et al. (2007), at 213-220; Adriaanse et al. (2008) at 33.

76 Case 33/76, *Rewe*, [1986]; ECR I-1989; Case C-45/76 *Comet BV v Produktschap voor Siergewassen* [1976] ECR 2043.

77 Case 33/76, *Rewe*, [1986]; ECR I-1989. See: Tridimas (2006) at 423-425.

78 Cf. Case 61/79, *Denkavit* [1980] ECR I-1205 in which the Court speaks about 'impossible in practice to exercise the rights conferred by the Community legal order'. See for more details about the development of the effectiveness principle in the case law of the ECJ: Craig, P. and De Búrca, G. (2008), *EU law: Text, Cases and Materials*, Oxford University Press: Oxford, 4th edition, pp. 313-325.

79 E.g. Joined Cases 66/79, 127/79 and 128/79 *Salumi* [1980] ECR 1237; Case C-260/96, *Ministerio delle Finanze v Spac* [1998] ECR I-4997; Case C-295-298/2004, *Manfredi* [2006] ECR I-6619; Craig and De Búrca (2008) at 325-328.

80 Tridimas (2006) at 423; Prechal and Widdershoven (2011) at 295.

81 Case 199/82, *San Giorgio* [1983] ECR I-3595.

82 The Court stated that Community law 'precludes' such national procedural norms: Case 309/85, *Barra* [1988] ECR I-355; Case 240/87, *Deville* [1988] ECR I-3513. This was repeated in Case C-228/96 *Aprile* [1998], ECR I-07141.

83 Tridimas (2006) at 424; Ottow (2006), at 68 et seq.

84 Widdershoven calls this the '*rechttoe-rechtaan toepassing*'. See: Joined Cases C-317/08 - C-320/08, *Alassini* [2010] ECR I-02213, *AB 2010/157*, annotated by R.J.G.M. Widdershoven.

effective application of European norms.[85] The ECJ still uses both tests and it is not clear when it uses which test.[86]

The Rewe effectiveness is aimed at the effectuation of EU law in national law and primarily addresses national legislatures. I will now turn to a refinement of the principle of effectiveness as applied in typical enforcement (sanctioning) cases. This is of more relevance in the context of effective supervision.

The principle of effectiveness in an enforcement context

In enforcement cases adjudicated by the ECJ the principle of effectiveness is not only linked to equivalence, but is itself further divided into three separate requirements, namely effectiveness, proportionality and dissuasiveness. In its case law the Court has decided that sanctions for breaches of a Directive or the implementing norms must satisfy these conditions.[87] While in *Von Colson and Kamann* the ECJ decided that Member States are free to decide on their sanctions but that these must be effective and have a deterrent effect, the 'effectiveness, proportionality and dissuasiveness' formula was first explicitly mentioned in the so-called *Greek Maize* case.[88] In later case law, particularly the *Spanish Strawberries* case, the ECJ stated that Member States are also under an obligation to intervene when private groups interfere violently with the intra-Community movement of goods, hence Member States should also enforce when a negatively formulated Treaty provision is not complied with.[89] This principle of effectiveness is primarily aimed at national legislatures, but applies in a derived fashion to national supervisory authorities too. After all, it is the supervisory authorities that decide which instrument(s) they use and the question whether these comply with the requirements of effectiveness, proportionality and dissuasiveness partly results from this choice.[90]

Greek Maize was about the failure of Greek authorities to take any action against identified fraud by a Greek company that had claimed to export Greek maize to Belgium, which was in fact Yugoslavian maize. The Commission started an infringement procedure against Greece and argued that it had acted in breach of the principle of loyal cooperation by not taking any criminal or disciplinary action against the perpetrators of the fraud. The Court held that 'where Community legislation does not specifically provide any penalty for an infringement or refers for that purpose to national laws, regulations and administrative provisions, Article 10 of the Treaty [now: article 4(3) TEU] requires Member States to take all measures necessary to guarantee the application and effectiveness of Community law'. It continued by stating that '[f]or that purpose whilst the choice of penalties remains within their discretion, they must ensure in particular that infringements of Community law are penalised under conditions, both

85 Ottow (2006) at 70; Accetto and Zleptnig (2005) at 399-400. Joined Cases C-430-431/93 *Van Schijndel and Van Veen* [1995] ECR I-4705; Case C-312/93 *Peterbroeck* [1995] ECR I-4599 are the first cases in which this test was used.

86 Joined Cases C-317/08 - C-320/08, *Alassini* [2010] ECR I-02213, *AB 2010/157*, annotated by R.J.G.M. Widdershoven.

87 Case 68/88, *Commission v Greece (Greek Maize)* [1989] ECR 2965.

88 Case 14/83, *Von Colson and Kamann* [1984] ECR 1891; Case 68/88, *Commission v Greece (Greek Maize)* [1989] ECR 2965.

89 Case C-265/95, *Commission v France (Spanish Strawberries)*, [1997] ECR I-6959; Adriaanse et al. (2008a) at 34.

90 Aelen and Van den Broek (2014) at 14.

> procedural and substantive, which are analogous to those applicable to infringements of national law of a similar nature and importance and which, in any event make the penalty effective, proportionate and dissuasive'.

Although the Greek Maize formula has been used on various occasions in other judgments by the ECJ, it remained for a long time uncertain what was really meant with the requirements of effectiveness, dissuasiveness and proportionality.[91] Only in casuistic terms has it become clear how the Court interprets these requirements. The Court has held, for example, that symbolic compensation for damages was insufficient, as well as a national limitation on the amount of compensation for damages.[92] In the *Berlusconi* case, Advocate General Kokott attempted to give more substance to the formula. Kokott explained effectiveness in the sense that there may be no legal impediments in the procedure, thereby referring to the Rewe effectiveness, while she positioned the requirements of dissuasiveness and proportionality to the available sanction as such:

> '88. Rules laying down penalties are effective where they are framed in such a way that they do not make it practically impossible or excessively difficult to impose the penalty provided for (and, therefore, to attain the objectives pursued by Community law). (...)
> 89. A penalty is dissuasive where it prevents an individual from infringing the objectives pursued and rules laid down by Community law. What is decisive in this regard is not only the nature and level of the penalty but also the likelihood of its being imposed. Anyone who commits an infringement must fear that the penalty will in fact be imposed on him. (...)
> 90. A penalty is proportionate where it is appropriate (that is to say, in particular, effective and dissuasive) for attaining the legitimate objectives pursued by it, and also necessary. Where there is a choice between several (equally) appropriate penalties, recourse must be had to the least onerous. Moreover, the effects of the penalty on the person concerned must be proportionate to the aims pursued.'[93]

Scholars have attempted to shed more light on the meaning of and the relationship between the requirements as well. In Harding's view, the effectiveness of a sanction depends on the evaluation of its proportionality and dissuasiveness, for which questions such as the method of enforcement, the type and level of the sanction, the general and individual levels of dissuasiveness and evidence of its dissuasive effect occupy a central role. At the same time, effectiveness should be positioned in a comparative way as it 'presupposes a comparative enquiry into possible divergence in national enforcement' and that 'comparisons may [...] throw a very different light on matters'.[94] Hence, the effectiveness of an enforcement regime in a particular Member State would be compared on several accounts, such as the resources and expertise at the disposal of the supervisors, the (prosecution) policy in place, the procedural and evidential rules and the application of sanctions in practice. Faure has pointed out that the notion of dissuasiveness strongly resembles the notion of

91 Examples of cases are Case C-7/90, *Vandevenne* [1991] ECR I-4371; Case C-29/95, *Pastoors* [1997] ECR I-285.

92 Case 14/83, *Von Colson and Kamann* [1984] ECR 1891; Case C-271/91/, *Marshal II* [1993] ECR I-4367.

93 Joined Cases C-387/02, C-391/02, and C-403/02, *Berlusconi and Others* [2005], Opinion of AG Kokott, delivered on 14 October 2004, ECR I-3565.

94 Harding, C. (1997), 'Member State Enforcement of European community Measures: The Chimera of 'Effective Enforcement'', *Maastricht Journal for European and Comparative Law*, vol. 4, issue 5, pp. 5-24 at 15-21.

deterrence, which is an important concept in law & economics literature in relation to criminal law.[95] An effectiveness test should, in his view, entail an examination on whether the policy and legal instruments chosen are suitable in order to attain the goals set by the legislator, while the proportionality of a penalty 'most likely refers to a relationship between the type of penalty on the one hand and the type of infringement on the other hand'.[96] Blomberg is of the opinion that for the question whether a sanction is effective, dissuasive and proportionate, the specific circumstances of the case must be considered, 'in particular the nature of the violation in conjunction with the interests at stake on the one hand and the nature and impact of the imposed sanction on the other (...), determine the effectiveness and dissuasiveness of an enforcement action'.[97] It is doubtful whether the principle of effectiveness in an enforcement context can be further specified. It will possibly remain dependant on the Court's interpretation on a casuistic basis.

2.2.3 Concluding remarks

This section's aim was to demonstrate how effectiveness operates as a legal principle in different contexts. Within the legal notion of good governance, the principle of effectiveness requires that goals are set and that those goals are accomplished as effectively as possible. It requires that there are no legal hindrances, or factual hindrances that may bear legal consequences, that make the application of the law and regulations by the public administration more burdensome, as a result of which legislative or regulatory goals cannot be achieved. The foregoing showed the interplay with the other principles of good governance, most importantly with accountability and transparency. Sometimes effectiveness conflicts with other principles. However, within the framework of supervision, accountability, transparency and effectiveness are said to reinforce one another. The principle of effectiveness is most extensively elaborated within European Union law and here it closely relates to the notions of loyal cooperation and national procedural autonomy. The principle of effectiveness in relation to procedural law is concerned with the implementation, application and enforcement of EU law at the national level. It teaches us that the national norms must not render virtually impossible or excessively difficult the exercise of rights conferred by the European legal order. More specifically in relation to enforcement, the principle of effectiveness is linked to proportionality and dissuasiveness. The exact content of these principles remains undetermined and must be decided on a case-by-case basis, although scholars have attempted to distil some more concrete requirements from it.

Together, effectiveness as a principle of good governance and as an EU principle provide some first contours for effective supervision. They nevertheless remain too abstract in themselves for application in a theoretical framework. Therefore, I will now turn to

95 Faure, M.G. (2010), 'Effective, Proportional and Dissuasive Penalties in the Implementation of the Environmental Crime and Ship source Pollution Directives: Questions and Challenges', *European Energy and Environmental Law Review*, vol. 19, issue 6, pp. 256-278.

96 Ibid., at 264.

97 Blomberg (2008) at 46.

secondary EU law in order to see whether this provides more specific requirements for effective supervision.

2.3 Minimum requirements for supervision in the Third Directive

Departing from the more abstract visions on effectiveness in relation to supervision, it is now time to turn to the policy field at hand. In the developments in the area of the prevention of money laundering and terrorist financing, European directives have paid more and more attention to the matter of supervision and sanctioning. Whereas the first two Directives from 1991 and 2011 only imposed very broad obligations and left the supervision under the preventive anti-money laundering policy to the procedural autonomy of Member States, the Third Directive sets some requirements in order to ensure effective and adequate supervision.[98] This Directive, which is an instrument of minimum harmonisation, has two sections that are specifically on matters of supervision and sanctioning.[99] These are discussed in § 2.3.1 and 2.3.2, and form part of the theoretical framework. In § 2.3.3, I turn to the proposal for a Fourth Directive, which should replace the Third Directive in the near future. The proposal (as amended by the European Parliament) shows an increased focus on the matters of supervision and sanctioning. Because the new Directive has not been adopted during the period in which this research was carried out, the new provisions are only included as a source of inspiration for the theoretical framework of effective supervision.

2.3.1 Supervision

The Third Directive obliges Member States to require that all supervisors 'effectively monitor compliance'. Supervisors must be able to take the necessary measures to ensure compliance with regard to the obligations derived from the Directive, and have adequate powers.[100] This should at least include the power to compel the production of any information that is relevant to monitoring compliance and performance checks, as well as the availability of adequate resources to carry out the supervisory functions. The Directive does not say what adequate resources are, thus leaving this to the Member States' discretion.

Taking into account the wide range of institutions and professionals that fall under the scope of the preventive AML policy, the Third Directive indicates that supervisors for specific groups of institutions and professions need to be able to have additional instruments. The Directive states that currency exchange offices, trust and company service providers, as well as money transmission or remittance offices, shall be licensed or registered, and casinos must be licensed, in order to operate the business legally.[101] To

98 Van den Broek (2011a) at 176-178.

99 Chapter V, Sections 2 and 4 Third Directive. Article 5 Third Directive lays down explicitly that Member States have the power to impose stricter measures. See also: Buisman, S. (2011), 'The Influence of the European Legislator on the National Criminal Law of Member States: It Is All in the Combination Chosen', *Utrecht Law Review*, vol. 7, issue 3, pp. 137-155 at 140.

100 Article 37(1) and (2) Third Directive

101 Article 36 Third Directive.

that effect, the persons who effectively direct or will direct the business or the beneficial owners of these entities must be fit and proper persons. A second additional instrument is that the supervisors of credit and financial institutions and casinos must be provided with enhanced supervisory powers, notably the possibility to perform on-site inspections.[102] For the AML supervisors of auditors, external accountants, tax advisors, notaries, lawyers and other independent legal professionals, trust and company service providers, dealers in (high-value) goods and real estate agents, the Directive allows the exercise of supervision on a risk-sensitive basis. The supervision of auditors, external accountants, tax advisors, notaries, lawyers and other independent legal professionals may be carried out by self-regulatory bodies (professional associations), provided that they have adequate powers and resources.[103]

2.3.2 Sanctioning

Member States should ensure that all 'natural and legal persons covered' can be held liable for not complying with preventive AML obligations. Supervisors should be able to impose sanctions in case of an infringement of the obligations that are effective, proportionate and dissuasive.[104] The Directive does not further explain how these general criteria should be fulfilled: the type of sanctions, as well as their amount or duration, is left to the discretion of the Member States. However, for financial and credit institutions, the Third Directive states that Member States must at least ensure that administrative measures can be taken against or administrative sanctions can be imposed on these institutions for non-compliance with the preventive AML obligations.[105] No similar provision can be found for the supervisors of the other obliged institutions or professionals. The Directive furthermore obliges Member States to ensure that legal persons can be held liable when breaches of the preventive obligations are committed by any person with a leading position within the legal person, either individually or as part of the legal person, for the benefit of that legal person. One can think of Board members, directors or compliance officers. The leading position of a natural person is to be determined by the power of representation of the legal person, the authority to take decisions on behalf of the legal person or the authority to exercise control within the legal person.[106] Again, the type of liability – administrative, civil or criminal – is left to the Member States' discretion. In any case, legal persons must be held liable where the lack of supervision or control by a person with a leading position has made possible the commission of infringements for the benefit of a legal person by any person under his authority.[107]

102 Article 37(3) Third Directive.
103 Article 37(4) and (5) Third Directive.
104 Article 39(1) Third Directive. This is the so-called *Greek Maize* formula, discussed in § 2.2.2.2.
105 Article 39(2) Third Directive.
106 Article 39(3) Third Directive.
107 Article 39(4) Third Directive.

2.3.3 Proposal for a Fourth Directive

On the 5th of February 2013 the European Commission published a proposal for a new Directive on the prevention of the use of the financial system for the purpose of money laundering and terrorist financing.[108] The proposal showed the intention to make changes in a wide range of aspects, including – inter alia – the risk-based approach, the inclusion of tax crimes as predicate offences to money laundering, the definitions and obligations concerning politically exposed persons and ultimate beneficial ownership, public registers, simplified due diligence, record-keeping, internal policies and procedures. The revision of the Third Directive was broadly steered by changes to the FATF Recommendations in February 2012, as well as various reports and assessments conducted by or on behalf of the European Commission.[109] The proposal was discussed thoroughly at the European Parliament, which adopted the first reading on the 11th of March 2014. The EP made 150 amendments to the original proposal.[110] Due to negotiations with the Council of Ministers and the need for a second reading of the draft after the European Parliament elections have taken place, it is expected that the Directive will be adopted in early 2015. With regard to supervision the proposal contains the following changes and additions:[111]

- Money transmission or remittance offices are no longer required to be registered or licensed in order to operate their business legally. New is that gambling service providers must be authorised;[112]
- Member States must ensure that AML supervisors of DNFBPs[113] take the necessary measures to prevent criminals or their associates from holding or being the beneficial owners of a significant or controlling interest, or holding management functions in those obliged institutions;[114]
- Article 45(2) states that Member States shall ensure that competent authorities have adequate powers, including the power to compel the production of any information relevant to monitoring compliance and to perform checks. It now also refers to adequate 'financial, human and technical' resources and states that supervisory staff must maintain high professional standards, including standards of confidentiality and data protection, with a high level of integrity and appropriate skills;
- In the case of credit and financial institutions and providers of gambling services, competent authorities must have enhanced supervisory powers, notably the possibility to conduct on-site inspections. Moreover, '[c]ompetent authorities in charge of supervising credit and financial institutions shall monitor the adequacy of the legal advice they

108 European Commission (2013), *Proposal for a Directive of the European Parliament and of the Council on the prevention of the use of the financial system for the purpose of money laundering and terrorist financing*, COM(2013) 45 final (hereafter 'proposal').

109 Ibid., at 3.

110 *European Parliament legislative resolution of 11 March 2014 on the proposal for a directive of the European Parliament and of the Council on the prevention of the use of the financial system for the purpose of money laundering and terrorist financing*, COM(2013)0045, 2013/0025(COD). The legislative resolution is also available at: <www.europarl.europa.eu/sides/getDoc.do?type=TA&language=EN&reference=P7-TA-2014-0191>, last visited on 24 March 2014.

111 It is important to bear in mind that the text of the proposal as amended by the EP (first reading) can still be amended and will not enter into force after the Council of Ministers and EP have approved the text and amendments thereto.

112 Article 44(1) proposal. Cf. Article 36(1) Third Directive. See also § 2.3.1.

113 Designated non-financial businesses and professions.

114 Article 44(3) proposal. DNFBPs are designated non-financial professions and businesses.

receive with a view to reducing legal and regulatory arbitrage in the case of aggressive tax planning and avoidance';[115]
- Member States shall require that obliged institutions with branches or subsidiaries in other Member States respect the national provisions of that other Member State pertaining to this Directive, and shall ensure that the relevant competent authorities of the host and home state cooperate in order to ensure effective supervision of the requirements of the Directive;[116]
- Whereas the Third Directive allowed the risk-based approach to supervision for AML supervisors of legal and fiscal service providers and other non-financial and credit institutions, Article 45(6) demonstrates that this becomes the standard for all AML supervisors;[117]
- The assessment of the risk profiles of the obliged institutions and professionals must be reviewed periodically as well as after the occurrence of major events or developments in the management and operations of the obliged institutions. Likewise, Member States must ensure that supervisors take into account the degree of discretion or flexibility that underlies the preventive obligations of obliged institutions, appropriately reviewing the risk assessments, as well as the adequacy and implementation of the policies, internal controls and procedures;[118]
- Article 45(9) extends the possibility for supervision by self-regulatory bodies to real estate agents;
- The European regulators (EBA, EIOPA and ESMA) shall issue guidelines addressed to the national AML supervisors on factors to be applied when conducting supervision on a risk-sensitive basis;[119]
- Article 46 states that Member States shall ensure that policy makers, the FIU, law enforcement authorities, supervisors, data protection authorities and other competent authorities involved in anti-money laundering and combating terrorist financing have effective mechanisms to enable them to co-operate and co-ordinate domestically concerning the development and implementation of policies and activities to combat money laundering and terrorist financing. It seems that the provision is directed at cooperation at policy level – in particular the reference to 'co-ordinate' implies this. The provision does not specify whether this cooperation also extends to the exchange of relevant, individual (supervisory) information, or other forms of cooperation. It seems that this is left to the Member States' own discretion in implementing this provision.

As can be observed, not all changes and additions regarding supervision deal with the powers of the AML supervisors. More far-reaching, in my opinion, are the intended changes with respect to sanctioning. The proposal states that Member States must ensure that obliged institutions and professionals can be held liable for breaches of the national provisions adopted pursuant to the Directive and that the sanctions are effective, proportionate and dissuasive.[120] More specifically, it introduces the following changes:

115 Article 45(3) proposal and Amendment 115, 2013/0025(COD).
116 Article 45(4) and 45(5) proposal.
117 Article 45(6) proposal as amended by Amendment 117, 2013/0025(COD).
118 Article 45(7) and 45(8) proposal.
119 Article 45(10) proposal.
120 Article 55(1) proposal, as amended by Amendment 129, 2013/0025(COD).

- The proposal expands the power of administrative measures and sanctions to the AML supervisors of all categories of obliged institutions and professionals;[121]
- Member States are required to ensure that where obligations apply to legal persons, sanctions can be imposed on members of the management body or other individuals that are responsible for the breach. Whereas the Third Directive states in Article 39(3) under which circumstances a natural person can be held liable, the proposal refers to national legislation;[122]
- Article 55(4) obliges Member States to ensure that the supervisors have all the investigatory powers necessary for the exercise of their functions. In the exercise of sanctioning powers, AML supervisors are required to cooperate closely to ensure that administrative measures or sanctions produce the desired results and coordinate their action when dealing with cross-border cases;
- The proposal introduces a set of minimum principle-based rules to strengthen administrative sanctioning in case of non-compliance. It requires Member States to ensure that at least the following measures and sanctions can be taken or imposed: public statement ('if necessary and proportionate after a case-by-case evaluation'[123]); an order to cease conduct or desist from repetition of the conduct; revocation of a licence or withdrawal of authorisation; a temporary ban on exercising functions against managers who can be held responsible; administrative fines up to 10% of the total annual turnover of that legal person in the preceding business year (legal persons) or up to 5 million Euros (natural persons); administrative fines up to twice the amount of the profits gained or losses avoided;[124]
- Regarding the public statement, Member States must ensure that supervisors publish any sanction or measure imposed for a breach of the national provisions adopted in the implementation of this Directive, if necessary and proportionate after a case-by-case evaluation, without undue delay including information on the type and nature of the breach and the identity of persons responsible for this. Where publication would cause disproportionate damage to the parties involved, supervisors may publish the sanctions on an anonymous basis.[125] In considering this, they must take into account all kinds of circumstances that are stipulated in the proposal;[126]
- To ensure a consistent application and a dissuasive effect across the EU, EBA, EIOPA and ESMA shall issue guidelines addressed to the national AML supervisors on the types of administrative measures and sanctions and the level of fines applicable to credit and financial institutions;[127]
- Article 58 states that Member States shall ensure that supervisors establish effective mechanisms to encourage the reporting of breaches to the supervisors, which must include specific procedures for the receipt of reports on breaches and their follow-up; appropriate protection for the employees of institutions who report breaches committed within the institution, appropriate protection for the accused,[128] and the protection of personal data concerning both the reporter and the natural person who is allegedly responsible for a breach.

121 Article 55(2) proposal.
122 Article 55(3) proposal.
123 Amendment 130, 2013/0025(COD).
124 Article 56(2) proposal.
125 Amendment 132, 2013/0025(COD).
126 Article 57(1) and (2) proposal.
127 Article 57(3) proposal, as amended by Amendment 133, 2013/0025(COD).
128 Amendment 134, 2013/0025(COD).

2.3.4 Concluding remarks

This section presented requirements for supervision stemming from the Third Directive. As a minimum, Member States shall ensure that anti-money laundering supervisors (of banks, accountants and real estate agents) must at least have the power to compel the production of any information that is relevant to monitoring compliance, and to perform checks. For credit and financial institutions, these checks must be of an on-site nature. Supervisory authorities must also have adequate resources available. The supervision of accountants may be exercised by a professional association. Anti-money laundering supervision of the accountancy and real estate profession may be risk-based. Sanctions must be effective, proportionate and dissuasive. For financial and credit institutions, this means that supervisors must at least be able take administrative measures and sanctions against them. The Directive makes it obligatory that sanctions can be imposed against both legal and natural persons. Legal persons should also be held liable where a person with a leading position within a legal person causes the non-compliant behaviour, either individually or as part of the legal person, for the benefit of that legal person and when the lack of supervision or control by such a person has made possible the commission of infringements for the benefit of the legal person by any person under his authority. Section 2.3.3 discussed some expected changes in supervision and sanctioning with the adoption of the Fourth Directive. This new Directive is expected to be adopted in early 2015.

2.4 Completing the framework for effective supervision

The previous sections presented the more abstract requirements for effective AML supervision stemming from the notion of good governance and European law, more precisely from the principle of effectiveness in an enforcement context, and the minimum requirements for effective supervision stemming from the Third Directive. Building on the abstract and minimum requirements to complete the framework for effective supervision, inspiration was drawn from literature. Despite the different disciplines, backgrounds, and focuses, a common core of requirements can be identified in the literature.

The completion of the theoretical framework is based on academic literature, a variety of national studies on supervision in the Netherlands and the UK, principles formulated by the Basel Committee for Effective Banking Supervision and the World Bank study on effective AML/CTF supervision for banking supervisors, as well as some other related sources.

> The choice for the use of national studies from the Netherlands and the UK is determined by the great attention given to the matter of (regulatory) supervision and sanctioning in these countries. In the Netherlands, this interest has been present since the mid-1990s when the Government established the Committee on Administrative and Private Law Enforcement (the *Michiels Committee*), because it had concerns about the quality of supervision.[129] Interest grew with the Enschede (2000) and Volendam (2001) tragedies

129 Commissie Michiels (1998), *Handhaven op Niveau*, W.E.J. Tjeenk Willink: Deventer.

that were said to be (partly) the result of poor and ineffective supervision.[130] In this research special attention is given to the report of the Michiels Committee and the Framework Vision on Supervision issued by the Dutch Government.[131] This Framework Vision is a government document setting out the framework for the position and organisation of supervision at the national level in the Netherlands.[132] The UK Government has put efforts into improving regulation and enforcement. The first steps were taken with a White Paper, which addressed the potential negative effects of over-regulating on businesses.[133] In the 1990s the focus shifted to Better Regulation, which culminated in 1998 in the publication of the Principles for Better Regulation.[134] More recent studies focus on the effectiveness of regulation and enforcement. Particularly the Hampton and Macrory Reviews are used in this analysis.[135] Both reviews are concerned with effective regulation and sanctioning. The Hampton Review focuses on the relationship between regulators (supervisors) and the private sector. The Macrory Review is about the effectiveness of sanctions and the application thereof.

The Basel Core Principles for Effective Banking are included for two reasons.[136] Firstly, banking law is a well-developed and regulated policy field. In international and European initiatives aiming to strengthen financial stability, supervision and sanctioning occupy a central position. Banking law and the anti-money laundering policy historically have a close relationship. Back in the 1990s, the first anti-money laundering measures were addressed to banks and other financial institutions. Due to a high degree of regulation in the area and the experience with both banking law and preventive anti-money laundering legislation, the two have become interwoven in the day-to-day practice of banks. Secondly, the Basel Committee on Banking Supervision is a forum for cooperation on banking supervisory matters by national regulators. This means that the Core Principles have been developed by the supervisors themselves, which gives a practical viewpoint on effective supervision. This is a good addition to the academic literature on this point. The inclusion of the World Bank study in the research is self-evident, as it focuses on effective anti-money laundering supervision.

130 In 2000 a fireworks depot exploded. The depot was situated very close to a neighbourhood in the city of Enschede. The explosion killed 23 people and injured almost 1,000. Interestingly, a week before the disaster inspectors had carried out an on-site visit and had concluded that the company had met all the official safety regulations. In the town of Volendam, a bar burnt down during New Year's Eve after a sparkler set light to Christmas decorations on the ceiling. The bar was full of revellers and many teenagers died or were very badly injured. It turned out that the owner had been negligent in providing the necessary escape routes and had failed to inundate the Christmas decorations with a fire-resistant substance. Also there were too many people in the building at the time of the incident.

131 Ministerie van Binnenlandse Zaken en Koninkrijksrelaties (2005), *Kaderstellende Visie op Toezicht: Minder last, meer effect: Zes principes van goed toezicht*, Den Haag (in English: *Less burden, more effect: Six principles of good supervision*). Hereafter 'KVoT (2005)'.

132 Winter, H. (2013), 'Regulatory enforcement in the Netherlands: Struggling with Independence', in: Comtois, S. and De Graaf, K.J. (eds.), *On Judicial and Quasi-Judicial Independence*, Boom Juridische uitgevers: The Hague, pp. 157-166 at 158.

133 UK House of Commons (1985), *Lifting the Burden: White Paper*, Cmnd 9751.

134 OECD (2009), *Better Regulation in Europe: United Kingdom*, at 20, available at: <www.oecd.org/regreform/regulatory-policy/44912232.pdf>, last visited on 25 March 2014.

135 Hampton Review (2005), *Reducing Administrative Burdens: Effective Supervision and Enforcement*, Final Report; Macrory Review (2006), *Regulatory Justice: Making Sanctions Effective*, Final Report.

136 Basel Committee on Banking Supervision (2012), *Core Principles for Effective Banking Supervision*, available at: <www.bis.org/publ/bcbs230.pdf>, last visited on 25 March 2014.

Below the identified requirements are, for the sake of clarity, divided into three groups: legislative requirements, institutional requirements, and requirements with respect to the powers of supervisors and the way in which they apply these powers.

2.4.1 Legislative requirements

The first identified precondition for effective supervision is that the law must be of good quality. In general terms, the quality of the law is essential for the functioning of the legal order. Various legal principles are important for obtaining a good quality of the law. Most important are the legality principle and the principle of legal certainty. Above we saw that these are principles of proper administration which belong to the notion of good governance.[137]Although these principles primarily have a guarantee function (*waarborgfunctie*), as they aim to guarantee or protect the status and rights of citizens vis-à-vis Government, these are also interesting from a more instrumental perspective.[138] The legality principle essentially requires that actions of the executive power must be based on the law.[139] In other words there must be a legal basis on the basis of which the executive can act.[140] The power must be sufficiently clear and narrow. The executive may not go beyond the scope of the power assigned to it by the law, and it must act in accordance with such powers.[141] The principle of legality is therefore important for the positioning of (independent) supervisors, as well as their powers.[142] Although legal powers for supervisors are a matter that can be discussed in relation to the principle of legality, § 2.4.3 deals more specifically with the competences required for effective supervision.[143]

The legality principle is one of the cornerstones of Dutch constitutional and administrative law, and also in Spanish law it is found to be of great importance.[144] In the UK, the principle of legality is embedded in the wider notion of the rule of law.[145] The principle of legality

137 See § 2.2.1.2.

138 Ommeren, F.J. van (2010), 'Het legaliteitsbeginsel als hoeksteen van het staats- en bestuursrecht', *Ars Aequi*, September 2010, pp. 6-8. Cf. Schlössels. R.J.N. and Zijlstra, S.E. (2010), *Bestuursrecht in de sociale rechtsstaat*, Kluwer: Deventer, 6th edition, at 52 who state that within the instrumental function of the law, one should always keep in mind the legitimating and protective functions of the law as well.

139 Schlössels and Zijlstra (2010) at 44 et seq., who discuss the principle of legality in the framework of the legitimating function of administrative law.

140 Burkens, M.C, Kummeling, H.R.B.M., Vermeulen, B.P. and Widdershoven, R.J.G.M (2012), *Beginselen van de democratische rechtsstaat*, Kluwer: Deventer at 43; Lopéz Menudo, F. (1992), 'Los principios generales del procedimiento administrativo', *Revista de Administración Pública*, issue 129, Sept-Dec 1992, pp. 19-76 at 51-52.

141 Lopéz Menudo (1992) at 51 et seq.

142 Ottow, A.T. and De Cock Buning, M. (2013), 'Juridisch ruggengraat toezicht mag niet ontbreken', *Tijdschrift voor Toezicht*, vol. 4, issue 4, pp. 33-38 at 33-34.

143 See Ottow (2006) at 86 et seq., who gives an overview of the different dimensions of the principle of legality, including the legal powers for supervisors.

144 Van Ommeren (2010); Rivero Ortega, R. (1999), *El estado vigilante*, Editorial Tecnos, at 92-100.

145 Webley, L. and Samuels, H. (2012), *Complete Public Law: Text, Cases, and Materials*, Oxford University Press: Oxford, at 13 and 75, who explain the rule of law as a key principle of public law. The rule of law means that all are subject to law regardless of their status; in other words, no one is beyond the reach of the law even if he or she is a state official, and the state should not exercise its power in an arbitrary fashion; Cf. Bingham, T. (2007), 'The Rule of Law', *Cambridge Law Journal*, vol. 66, issue 1, pp. 67-85 at 69. It seems that the common law rule of law entails the legality principle but also applies to private persons.

also comes to the fore specifically in supervision and sanctioning cases. Widdershoven explains in this respect that the principle of legality as a criminal law standard also applies in the case of the imposition of administrative sanctions with a punitive character: ' (...) the principle of nullum crimen sine legem, the principle of nulla poena sine lege and the lex certa principle, are equally in force for the imposition of administrative fines'.[146] Altogether, this means that in the absence of a legal basis, the executive power cannot act.

Legal certainty is an established legal principle both in the civil law and common law systems. The principle of legal certainty, by Bingham considered as an 'ingredient' of the common law notion of the rule of law, requires that the law is transparent and accessible.[147] In delving deeper into the meaning and functions of legal certainty, there are various dimensions that can be identified. In his doctoral thesis, Oldenziel identified nine dimensions of the meaning of legal certainty, among which are stability and continuity (*bestendigheid*), foreseeability, clarity, honouring legitimate expectations, and non-retrospectivity.[148] From an instrumental perspective, it is important that persons are able to know and understand the law, and can understand the consequences of (non-) compliance with the law.[149] Legal certainty also concerns the predictability of the law. This means that the law must be clear and not be changed too easily as it could lose its predictability function.

The absence of a clear legal basis or a lack of legal certainty in legislation affects the enforceability of the norms in question. The enforceability of norms is important, because if norms are not enforceable, supervision can never be effective in the first place. Norms whose content or meaning is not sufficiently clear, foreseeable, or predictable are at least more difficult to enforce, because there can be discussions about the interpretation thereof.[150] In the literature, it is commonly understood that if the norms are unclear and impracticable, then consistent, effective and legitimate supervision is impossible.[151] In this respect, the Michiels Committee concluded that in cases of a low quality or ineffective enforcement in the Netherlands, one of the main factors causing this was the low quality of legislation and regulation: norms were often unclear, not practicable and unenforceable.[152] Furthermore, in his study on effective sanctions in the UK, Macrory also stated that from the outset 'it is evident that sensibly drafted and appropriate substantive law is

146 Widdershoven, R.J.G.M. (2002), 'Encroachment of criminal law in administrative law in the Netherlands', *Electronic Journal of Comparative Law*, vol. 6, issue 4, pp. 445-461 at 449. See § 5.6.3.1 for the distinction between reparatory and punitive sanctions in Dutch administrative law.

147 Bingham (2007) at 69-70.

148 Oldenziel, H.A. (1998), *Wetgeving en rechtszekerheid: een onderzoek naar* de *bijdrage* van het *legaliteitsvereiste aan* de *rechtszekerheid* van de burger, Kluwer: Deventer (doctoral thesis University of Groningen) at 14-24. Cf. Bingham (2007), at 69-70 and Webley and Samuels (2012) at 87.

149 Oldenziel (1998) at 17-19.

150 Aelen and Van den Broek (2014) at 17-20.

151 Cf. Duijkersloot, A.P.W. (2013), 'Handhaving door marktautoriteiten', in: Michiels, F.C.M.A. and Muller, E.R. (eds), *Handhaving*, Kluwer: Deventer, 2nd edition, pp. 341-360 at 358; Ottow (2006) at 77; Michiels, F.C.M.A. (2006), *Houdbaar Handhavingsrecht*, at 6-8; Hampton Review (2005) at 43; Markttoezichthoudersberaad (2011), *Effectief markttoezicht: bijdrage voor de herziening van de Kaderstellende Visie op Toezicht*, at 14-15, available at: <www.cbpweb.nl/downloads_med/med_20111114-effectief-toezicht.pdf>, last visited on 25 March 2014 (English: *Effective market supervision: for the revision of the Framework Vision on Supervision*).

152 Commissie Michiels (1998) at 43.

vital to the effectiveness of any regulatory system'.[153] Finally, the World Bank study also states that rules must be foreseeable and predictable. Insufficient clarity may undermine effective implementation, which in turn may lead to confusion and an uneven application of the norm and undermines the supervisor's ultimate objective, which is to stimulate compliance.[154]

Effective supervision requires that (substantive) legislation is clear, precise, foreseeable, predictable and enforceable.

2.4.2 Institutional requirements

The second set of requirements concern institutional requirements. Institutional requirements address the position and organisations of the supervisors as such. The institutional embedding and the relationship with other authorities and institutions may have an impact on the effectiveness of the supervisors, and hence on their activities in relation to supervision. Based on the literature, there are three core requirements: independence (§ 2.4.2.1), accountability and transparency (§ 2.4.2.2) and the availability of adequate resources (§ 2.4.2.3). In addition, it is of the utmost importance that supervisors have an adequate knowledge of the group of institutions or professionals for which they have supervisory responsibility (§ 2.4.2.4).[155] The institutional position can affect the information position of supervisors, and thus, the effectiveness of their supervision.[156]

2.4.2.1 Adequate level of independence from politics and the market

In recent years more weight has been given to the independence of market regulators and supervisors.[157] This can be observed for both the national and European level.[158]

153 Macrory Review (2006) at 14.

154 Chatain, P. et al. (2009), *Preventing Money Laundering and Terrorist Financing: A Practical Guide for Bank Supervisors*, World Bank: Washington DC, at 17. Hereafter 'World Bank (2009)'.

155 Note that this is not about the *expertise* of the supervisor, but rather about knowing the (size of) the group for which the authority has supervisory responsibility.

156 Please note that I do not refer to the *expertise* of the supervisors. I only refer to the question of whether the supervisor knows who it should supervise by having the possibility to access some basic information about the institution or professional.

157 For example: Aelen, M. (2014), *Beginselen van goed markttoezicht: Gedefinieerd, verklaard en uitgewerkt voor het toezicht op de financiële markten*, Boom Juridische uitgevers: The Hague (doctoral thesis Utrecht University), at 217-330; Duijkersloot (2013) at 358-359; Ottow, A. and Lavrijssen, S. (2012), 'Independent Supervisory Authorities: A Fragile Concept', *Legal Issues of Economic Integration*, vol. 39, issue 4, pp. 419-445; Quintyn, M., Ramirez, S., and Taylor, M.W. (2007), 'The Fear of Freedom: Politicians and the Independence and Accountability of Financial Sector Supervisors', *IMF Working Paper*, WP/07/25; Ottow (2006) at 76 et seq.; Goodhart, C. and Schoenmaker, D. (1998), 'Institutional Separation Between Supervisory and Monetary Agencies', in C.A.E., Goodhart (ed.), *The Emerging Framework of Financial Regulation*, Central Banking Publications: London, pp. 133–212; Basel Core Principle 2 and Essential Criterion 1 thereto, World Bank (2009) at 15-16.

158 At the national level one can see this in the following studies: Winter (2013); KVoT (2005); Hampton Review (2005) at 43. At the European level the discussion surrounds the so-called agencies: Busuioc, M. (2010), *The Accountability of European Agencies: Legal Provisions and Ongoing Practices*, Eburon: Delft (doctoral thesis Utrecht University); Vos, E. (2005), 'Independence, Accountability and Transparency of European Regulatory Agencies', in: Geradin, D., Muñoz, R. and Petit, N., *Regulation through Agencies in the EU: A new Paradigm of Governance*, Edward Elgar Publishing Ltd: Cheltenham, pp. 120-140; Busuioc, M.

Independence requirements for supervisors are strongly embedded at the European level. Particularly for utilities regulators and financial supervisors, European norms in relation to independence have at present 'a decisive function in the organisation of supervision' (*own translation, MB*).[159] The independence of supervisors comes down to the idea that their day-to-day activities should not be subject to any kind of undue external direction. It has been pointed out that the 'independence of a financial sector supervisor is one of the major factors affecting the effectiveness of supervision'.[160] The literature generally distinguishes between two 'types' of independence: political independence and independence from the market.[161] The literature does not refer to independence from the courts. This is logical, because (individual) decisions taken by supervisors are subject to review by the courts and/or tribunals. Likewise, independence never means *absolute* or *complete* independence.[162] As Ottow states: '[a]bsolute independence is not realistic and can conflict with the democratic principle of the Member States'.[163] For this reason, some prefer to call it autonomy.[164] Supervisors normally maintain relationships with politics and the market. In relation to politics, supervisors are obliged to abide by the general policy set by the Government. Aelen points at the fact that (market) supervisors are even expected to have a good, but not 'too good', relationship with the sector because supervisors are for the most part dependent on information provided by the sector itself (*own translation, MB*).[165]

When reference is made to independence or independent supervisors in this research, this should thus be understood as *relative* independence. It concerns the level of independence from politics and the market; i.e. the room for discretion for supervisors to take (individual) decisions without being (unduly) influenced by politics or the market.

Various reasons have been adduced to explain why supervisors must have a certain level of political and market independence. In relation to the market, it is submitted that independence should ensure that the market as a whole, individual market players, and the general public can trust the supervisor in that it will act in an *impartial* way and will create a level playing field.[166] A lack of independence may lead to a conflict of interest, meaning that the public interests that supervisors ought to consider are influenced by conflicting market interests, and even lead to regulatory capture. Regulatory capture is the

and Groenleer, M. (2014), 'The Theory and Practice of EU Agency Autonomy and Accountability: Early Day Expectations, Today's Realities and Future Perspectives, in: Everson, M., Monda, C. and Vos, E. (eds.), *European Agencies in Between Institutions and Member States*, Kluwer: Alphen aan de Rijn, pp. 175-200.

159 Aelen (2014) at 81-83.

160 Seelig, S. and Novoa, A. (2009), 'Governance Practices at Financial Regulatory and Supervisory Agencies', *IMF Working Paper*, WP/09/135, at 10; Dickson, J. (2013), 'Supervision: Looking Ahead to the Next Decade', in: Kellerman, A.J., De Haan, J. and De Vries, F. (eds.), *Financial Supervision in the 21st Century*, Springer Publishing, pp. 221-232 at 223.

161 Ottow (2006) at 62-66; Ottow, A.T. (2013), 'The different levels of protection national supervisors' independence in the European landscape', in: Comtois, S. and De Graaf, S.J. (eds.), *On Judicial and Quasi-Judicial Independence*, Boom Juridische uitgevers: The Hague, pp. 139-155 at 140-141.

162 Cf. Ottow and Lavrijssen (2012) at 420.

163 Ottow (2013) at 155. Cf. Winter (2013) at 166.

164 Cf. Busuioc and Groenleer (2014) at 185.

165 Aelen (2014) at 224.

166 Cf. Aelen (2014) at 219.

process by which regulators, which have been created to act in the public interest, become dominated by the market players that they were supposed to regulate and supervise in the first place.[167] Winter states that '(...) independence from the field is an absolute pre-condition for effective inspections'.[168]

> This argument may be relevant in this research, in particular with respect to situations where professional associations carry out AML supervision of their own members. There certainly is less independence from the market than can be expected from the Government or public authorities acting as supervisors. Critics may refer to 'chaps regulating chaps', where professional associations supervise their members.[169] A conflict of interest may arise between furthering the quality of the profession as a whole, and combating money laundering for the public interest. Therefore, in the context of the preventive AML policy it has been argued before that internal supervision alone is not sufficient, and that there must also be a form of external supervision.[170] See more about this in the next chapter.

The argument that supervisors should be free from any outside pressure in order to limit the risk of a conflict of interest as far as possible equally applies to political independence. Andersson et al. assert that '[a]voiding political capture is as important as not being captured by regulated firms, as the effects could be equally detrimental. Political capture may take different forms, but supervisors should have enough degree of freedom (...)'.[171] A conflict of interest may especially arise when politics has a certain interest in decisions that are taken by the supervisor. Examples are the telecommunications, energy, media and railway sectors, where Governments were for a long time a market player themselves in (partial) state-owned companies.[172] There are some additional arguments for political independence. Not only should it prevent political capture and a conflict of interest, political independence should also prevent short-term or inconsistent policy.[173] In the literature the continuity of policy is considered to be important, as this gives a signal to the markets and, thereby, creates a level of trust and confidence.[174] Yet in democracies where elections are held incidentally and periodically, and where Ministers can be replaced during Government periods, political influence may create unrest on the side of the supervisor. The European Commission also considered that short-term politics can lead to

---

167 Dal Bó, E. (2006), 'Regulatory Capture: A Review', *Oxford Review of Economic Policy*, vol. 22, issue 2, pp. 203-225 at 203; Aelen (2014) at 221-225. Regulatory capture is a theory associated with George Stigler who wrote in an influential paper that even where regulators have been set up to prevent monopolistic abuse, regulation can be captured by the industry: Stigler, G. (1971), 'The theory of economic regulation', *Bell Journal of Economics and Management Science*, vol. 2, issue 1, pp. 3-21.

168 Winter (2013) at 161.

169 Van den Broek (2014) at 81-82.

170 See Chapter 3; Tilleman, A.T.A (2009), 'Notariaat en Toezicht', *Ponder*, issue 27, at 17.

171 Andersson, M. Cerps, U. and Noréus, M. (2013), 'The Case for Analytical Supervision: The Swedish Perspective', in: Kellerman, A.J., De Haan, J. and De Vries, F. (eds.), *Financial Supervision in the 21st Century*, Springer Publishing, pp.33-46 at 45.

172 Ottow and Lavrijssen (2012) at 424; Ottow (2013) at 140.

173 Cf. Gilardi, F. (2005), 'The Formal Independence of Regulators: A Comparison of 17 Countries and 7 Sectors, *Swiss Political Science Review*, vol. 11, issue 3, pp. 139-167 at 140 and 144; Ottow (2013) at 141.

174 Ottow (2013) at 141; Aelen (2014) at 233.

uncertainty in the regulatory sphere.[175] A third argument for the political independence of supervisors is that they must be able to call on all their expertise in an effective or efficient way, without having to deal with the Government interfering with their activities.[176]

On the question of which aspects are concerned with independence, different views can be found in the literature. For central banks, literature generally distinguishes political or goal independence, on the one hand, and economic or instrument independence, on the other.[177] For regulators and supervisors, one can distinguish at the most abstract level *de facto* independence and *de jure* independence. De facto independence refers to the degree to which a regulator or supervisor can take day-to-day decisions without being influenced by instructions, threats or inducements from politics or the market, whereas de jure independence concerns the degree to which legislation ensures that it is not possible for the regulator or supervisor to be influenced by such instructions, threats or other inducements.[178] Specifically with regard to political independence, Ottow and Lavrijssen distinguish four aspects: legal (institutional), functional, staffing and financial independence.[179] In their view, institutional independence refers to the embedding of the position of supervisors in legislation and that they are distinct from any Ministry or Government body; functional independence concerns the extent to which supervisors have autonomous decision-making powers; staffing independence is about the degree of independence that staff have vis-à-vis politics and the market and the extent to which they may face pressure from outside; and financial independence is about the question whether supervisors can decide for themselves how to use their resources.[180] Quintyn and Taylor apply a somewhat different distinction, as they refer to regulatory, institutional, supervisory and budgetary independence.[181] Here, regulatory independence concerns the level of independence that the supervisor has in determining further rules and regulations for the supervisees; supervisory independence is related to licensing, supervision *sensu stricto*, sanctioning, and crisis management; institutional independence concerns the legal status of the supervisor in relation to the Government and the market; and budgetary independence refers to the role of the Government or politics in determining the supervisor's budget, including staffing and salary levels. Both categories show that true independence depends on many different aspects.

175 Ottow, A.T. and Lavrijssen, S.A.C.M. (2011), 'Het Europese recht als hoeder van de onafhankelijkheid van nationale toezichthouders', *Tijdschrift voor Toezicht*, vol. 2, issue 3, pp. 34-50 at 36.

176 Aelen (2014) at 234-235; Ottow and Lavrijssen (2012), at 425.

177 Grilli, V. Masciandaro, D. and Tabellini, G. (1991), 'Political and monetary institutions and public financial policies in the industrial countries', *Economic Policy*, vol. 6, issue 13, pp. 342-392; Debelle, G. and Fischer, S. (1994), 'How independent should Central Banks be?', *Conference paper Federal Reserve Bank of Boston*, pp. 195-225.

178 Henretty, C., Larouche, P., Reindl, A. (2012), *Independence, accountability and perceived quality of regulators: a CERRE Study*, Brussels, at 23, available at: <www.cerre.eu/sites/default/files/report_container.pdf>, last visited on 25 March 2014; Ottow (2013) at 14; Aelen (2014) at 217-218.

179 Ottow and Lavrijssen (2012) at 428. Cf. Scholten, M. (2011), 'Independent, hence unaccountable?', *Review of European Administrative Law*, vol. 4, issue 1, pp. 5-44, who also distinguishes institutional independence, personnel independence, financial independence and functional independence.

180 Ottow and Lavrijssen (2012) at 428-429.

181 Quintyn, M. and Taylor, M.W. (2003), 'Regulatory and supervisory independence and financial stability', *CESifo Economic Studies*, vol. 49, issue 2, pp. 259-294 at 267-277.

> What is actually decisive for concluding that there is (or is not) an adequate level of independence is difficult to say. Many observe that there is no 'one cap that fits all' model or a single legal concept of independence with a single set of applicable legal requirements.[182] The diversity between the different types of authorities that carry out supervision and differences between countries make it difficult to disentangle a common idea of what level of independence is adequate and what is not.

For this research the foregoing means that AML supervisors must have an adequate level of political and market independence, but that the level of independence may vary between the different supervisors. An adequate level of independence in any case prevents supervisors from being unduly influenced and ensures that they can exercise their tasks in an objective, neutral and professional way. Although the categorisations above show that actual independence depends on many aspects, this research cannot deal with all aspects related to independence as it is considered to be just one of the requirements for effective supervision. In order to make a useful analysis of independence that is feasible for this research, a distinction is made between *direct and indirect influence* from politics and the market on the (level of) the independence of supervisors. Direct influence refers to the institutional position of supervisors embedded within the law (institutional independence), and the discretion that the law affords to the supervisors in deciding how they apply their powers (operational independence).[183] This is done by looking at the powers that the Government, Parliament and/or the responsible Minister, on the one hand, and the market, on the other, have in relation to the supervisory authority. As was explained, supervisors must act within the general government policy insofar as this is not directly related to the day-to-day exercise of their tasks. However, the powers of politics or the market may not go as far as to influence the *individual* decision-making procedures and day-to-day practice within the supervisory authority. These aspects of independence are analysed and compared on the basis of the legal norms (*de jure* independence). This research does not pay attention to the indirect influence of politics or the market. Indirect influence can mostly be sought in relation to the staffing and funding of the authorities. Although these aspects are certainly a way to exert pressure 'via the back door', it will be impossible – due to the scope and focus of this research – to verify equally for all supervisors involved in this research how the staffing and funding policies are legally constructed and applied in practice. The only aspect that will be dealt with in this research is the question whether the AML supervisors have adequate resources for the performance of their tasks. This is a more factual question and will therefore be dealt with separately later in this chapter.

Independence does not stand alone as an institutional requirement for effective supervision. An adequate level of accountability and transparency functions as a counterbalance for independence.[184] The following sections deal with accountability and transparency.

182 Ottow and Lavrijssen (2012) at 431; Quintyn, M. (2009), 'Independent agencies: More than a Cheap Copy of Independent Central Banks?', *Constitutional Political Economy*, vol. 20, issue 3, pp. 267–295 at 268; Gilardi (2005) at 156; Henretty et al. (2012) at 14.

183 This can be compared with the legal and functional independence in Ottow and Lavrijssen's (2012) distinction.

184 Cf. § 2.2.1.2.

2.4.2.2 Accountability and transparency

Independence cannot be unlimited and therefore supervisors must be accountable for their actions.[185] It has been observed that independence and accountability are two sides of the same coin: '[a]rrangements for agency independence are not sufficient for effective regulation and supervision. Proper accountability measures are fundamental to reap the benefits of agency independence'.[186] On the one hand, an adequate level of independence must exist to guarantee objective, impartial and consistent decision-making, but on the other hand this cannot be effective without proper accountability mechanisms in place to ensure that the supervisors exercise their powers in accordance with the law.[187] In other words: accountability together with independence forces supervisors to act in an objective, neutral and professional way in carrying out their supervisory tasks effectively.

Accountability in relation to (effective) supervision does not only emerge prominently in the notion of good governance and in the literature, but also in (inter)national studies. Both the World Bank study and Basel Core Principle 2 refer to the necessity for accountability: supervisors must publish objectives and are accountable through a transparent framework for the discharge of their duties in relation to those objectives.[188] The World Bank study refers to the importance of accountability mechanisms in the building of trust between supervisors and the private sector that has to comply with the anti-money laundering obligations. The Dutch Framework Vision on Supervision places the independence of supervisors within the minimum limits of ministerial responsibility, while the Hampton Review places accountability as a balancing mechanism of independence.[189] The Dutch Market Supervisors' Forum places accountability even within the framework of effectiveness.[190] The Macrory Review considers accountability as a requirement for effective enforcement and states that regulators should justify their choice of sanctioning actions to stakeholders, Ministers and Parliament annually.[191] In addition, he recommended that supervisors should publish an enforcement policy, as this improves transparency and accountability towards the market and society as a whole.[192]

As explained in § 2.2.1.2, accountability concerns a relationship between two actors, whereby one actor gives account to the other. Governance literature distinguishes various types of accountability whereby questions such as who should give account, to whom,

185 Cf. Verhey, L.F.M. and Verheij, N. (2005), 'De macht van de marktmeesters: Markttoezicht in constitutioneel perspectief', in: Preadvies NJV, *Toezicht*, Kluwer, pp. 139-332 at 224-250; Aelen (2014) at 331 et seq.

186 Quintyn and Taylor (2003) at 261. Cf. Sijbrand, J. and Rijsbergen, D. (2013), 'Managing the Quality of Financial Supervision', in: Kellerman, A.J., De Haan, J., and De Vries, F. (eds.), *Financial Supervision in the 21st Century*, Springer Publishing, pp. 17-32 at 22-23.

187 Quintyn et al. (2007) at 6; Hüpkes, E.H.G., Quintyn, M. and Taylor, M.W. (2005), 'The Accountability of Financial Sector Supervisor: Principles and Practice', *IMF Working Paper*, WP/05/51; Scholten (2011); Ottow and Lavrijssen (2012) at 421.

188 Basel Core Principle 2 and Essential Criterion 3 thereto; World Bank (2009), at 16.

189 KVoT (2005); Winter (2013) at 163; Hampton Review (2005) at 43.

190 Markttoezichthoudersberaad (2013), *Criteria voor goed toezicht: visie markttoezichthoudersberaad*, 23 April 2013, available at: <www.afm.nl/~/media/Files/publicatie/2013/criteria-goed-toezicht-mtb.ashx>, last visited on 26 March 2014.

191 Macrory Review (2006) at 32-33 and 86-97.

192 Ibid., at 32.

about what, and how, play an important role.[193] In this research, accountability should be given by the AML supervisors. Concerning the question to which actors account must be given, Bovens distinguishes the following types of accountability: political accountability, legal accountability, administrative accountability, professional accountability and social accountability.[194] As a counterbalance to the political and market independence of supervisors, I consider political and social accountability to be the most relevant types here. By political accountability Bovens understands that authorities are accountable to their Minister, who must, in turn, render political account to Parliament. This is also known as (individual) ministerial responsibility.[195] Social accountability is observed as the process of giving account about the performance to other stakeholders, clients and the general public.[196]

Without doing away with its importance, this analysis does not include accountability vis-à-vis the judiciary here. Legal accountability structures via the courts and tribunals may be taken into account occasionally, but are in principle not within the scope of this research. Judicial review of decisions taken by supervisors is casuistic and concerns an individual and bottom-up approach, which does not coincide with the instrumental top-down perspective that this research takes. Moreover, judicial review is primarily an aspect of effective legal protection and for the reasons set out above, this is not included.

Supervisors must account for the exercise of the statutory tasks delegated to them. This is normally provided by informing, explaining and justifying conduct in relation to the (statutory) tasks assigned to the authority. The provision of information plays an important role. The submission of annual (supervision) plans and the publication of annual reports are particularly important for supervisors as this provides a structural accountability relationship.[197] This is also where the strong link with transparency comes into play.[198] In order to be held accountable, supervisors must be transparent about their activities, in particular about the necessity of supervision, supervisory choices, procedures and outcomes.[199] In discussing agencies and non-departmental public bodies in the UK, Craig also stated that accountability can be fostered by greater openness and that accountability can only be made a reality 'through proper regard for transparency'.[200] Other scholars link accountability with transparency requirements for supervisors as well.[201] Supervisors

193 Bovens, M. (2007), 'Analysing and Assessing Accountability: A Conceptual Framework', *European Law Journal*, vol. 13, issue 4, pp. 447-468 at 454.

194 Ibid., at 454-455. Other categorisations are certainly possible, cf. Henretty et al. (2012) at 37 who speak about accountability to (i) politicians, (ii) the market, (iii) the judiciary and (iv) relevant peer groups; cf. Busuioc and Groenleer (2014) at 192-193 who speak about managerial, political, judicial, extra-judicial and financial accountability obligations.

195 In Sweden, however, the basic rule under the Constitution is that the Government is accountable as a whole, known as collective responsibility. In exceptional cases there may be individual ministerial responsibility: Nergelius, J. (2011), *Constitutional law in Sweden*, Kluwer Law International, at 77-84.

196 Bovens (2007) at 457.

197 Henretty et al. (2012) at 37-38.

198 Cf. De Moor-van Vugt (2001) at 5-6, who explains that in the Netherlands transparency is immediately linked to ministerial responsibility. From an accountability perspective this is one of the types of accountability.

199 Aelen (2014) at 331-332; Duijkersloot (2013) at 358; Markttoezichthoudersberaad (2013) at 11.

200 Craig, P.P. (2012), *Administrative law*, Sweet & Maxwell: London, 7th edition, at 106; Cf. Aelen (2014) at 361.

201 Ottow and Lavrijssen (2012) at 421; De Moor-van Vugt (2001) at 5-7; Aelen (2014) at 331 et seq.

must explain why they carry out supervision, what their goals are, and they should make their choices in supervision visible.[202] This can be done via a supervision policy. Good supervisors are furthermore expected to actively publish information on the practices and (aggregated) results of inspections, and are accountable for the results achieved.[203] They should not only do this via the 'traditional channels of reporting to Government and Parliament, but also through transparency of supervisory assessments and actions for the market and for the public'.[204] They could, for example, publish annual (supervision) plans and reports. A degree of transparency is thus required for supervisors to give account and to be hold accountable. Nevertheless, at the same time it should be recognised that there are limits to the level of the transparency of supervisors. Particularly supervisors of the financial sector have to take into account a variety of confidentiality provisions, which makes it sometimes hard(er) for them to disclose information to the public.[205]

Effective supervision requires that AML supervisors must be accountable for the exercise of their supervision. In particular the political and social accountability structures are important and are part of the theoretical framework. Supervisors must at least be transparent as to the reasons for carrying out supervision, the supervisory goals, they must make visible the choices in supervision, and provide information about the procedures and results. Supervisors must thereby take into account the limits that confidentiality regimes may impose on them. This research particularly focuses on the legal embedding of accountability mechanisms for the supervisors: are they legally required to be accountable to stakeholders, the Minister, the Government, and Parliament, and if so, how should they do this and what are they required to report on? In order to get some understanding of the supervisors' practice, this research will also, to the extent possible, look at the practice of supervisors here: are they in practice accountable to stakeholders, the Minister, the Government) and Parliament? Do they actively publish information concerning supervision and, if so, which kind of information? Most important are the publication of annual (supervision) plans and annual reports, on which focus is placed. The availability of a public supervision policy comes more prominently to the fore at a later point in the theoretical framework.[206]

2.4.2.3 Adequate resources

The third institutional requirement for effective supervision is the availability of adequate resources: an authority must be financed in such manner that permits it to conduct effective supervision.[207] A lack of adequate resources may result in a situation where legislative goals are not attained, or where legislation is not applied in the way in which

202 Macrory Review (2006) at 32-33 and 86-97; Ottow (2006) at 77.
203 KVoT (2005) at 24-25.
204 Andersson et al. (2013) at 45.
205 Aelen (2014) at 358.
206 See § 2.4.3.3.
207 Basel Core Principle 2 and Essential Criterion 6 thereto; Commissie Michiels (1998) at 87-89; Viñals, J. and Fiechter, J. (2010), *The Making of Good Supervision: Learning to say 'no'*, IMF Staff Position Note, SPN/10/08 at 14; Dickson (2013) at 223 who states that 'to be an effective supervisor, adequate resources and appropriate mandates are necessary'.

it was foreseen. The availability of adequate resources safeguards the continuity of the supervisor and its activities. Capacity problems of supervisors can be found in all kinds of policy fields.[208] The availability of adequate resources is a requirement that directly stems from the Third Directive. Also other literature suggests the necessity of adequate resources as a requirement for effective supervision.[209] The World Bank study, for example, stated that supervisors should be provided with the financial, human and technical resources that they need.[210] Financial resources should correspond to the size, the level of risk and the quality of AML supervision, whereas human and technical resources require the appropriate training of supervisory staff.[211]

A way of dealing with limited resources is by exercising supervision on a risk basis. Under a risk-based approach, resources are allocated to those areas where the highest risks exist.[212] The Third Directive already considers this to some extent, where it stipulates that supervision for some entities could be performed on a risk-sensitive basis.[213] A risk-based approach to supervision was also recommended in the Hampton Review. It found that many regulators had a so-called 'tick-the-box mentality' towards supervision and did not allocate their scarce resources in an effective way. Hampton recommended that regulators should take a risk-based approach in their activities by allocating their resources to high-risk institutions or areas.[214] The Michiels Committee advised a similar approach, but named this shrewd supervision (*slim toezicht*). The Committee argued that supervision must not only take place on the basis of objective criteria, but that the experience with the sector must also play a role. This requires knowledge on the side of the supervisor about the group of institutions for which it has responsibility, and an alert attitude.[215] The Dutch Framework Vision on Supervision also considers supervision on the basis of risk, costs and benefits as being important, and refers to this as selective supervision.[216] And the financial crisis has taught financial regulators to act in a more risk-oriented way: '[t]he systemic crisis has underscored the importance of focusing supervisory resources on those issues and institutions that pose the greatest risk to the financial system, rather than on the observance of supervisory rules per se. This often implies changing the supervisory approach from compliance-oriented to risk-oriented.'[217]

208 E.g. Michiels (2006) at 22-23; Helsloot, I. and I.L. Haverkate (2013), 'Handhaving van brandveiligheid; een pars pro toto?', in: Michiels, F.C.M.A. and Muller, E.R. (eds.), *Handhaving*, Kluwer: Deventer, 2nd edition, pp. 461-482 at 474-476; Stouten (2012) at 287-290.

209 Hampton Review (2005); Commissie Michiels (1998) at 56 (a lack of financial resources as a factor of ineffective enforcement); Markttoezichthoudersberaad (2011) at 16; Voermans, W. (2005), 'De communautarisering van toezicht en handhaving', in: Barkhuysen, T., den Ouden, W. and Polak, M., *Recht realiseren: Bijdragen rond het thema adequate naleving van rechtsregels*, Kluwer: Deventer, pp. 69-88 at 75 and 77. In the context of environmental law supervision: Harding (1997) at 15-21; Blomberg, A. and Michiels, F.C.M.A. (1997), *Handhaven met effect*, VUGA, at 36 and 198; Demmke, C. (2001), 'Towards Effective Environmental Regulation: Innovative Approaches in Implementing and Enforcing European Environmental Law and Policy', *Jean Monnet Working Paper* 5/01, at 16-17.

210 World Bank (2009) at 18.

211 Ibid., at 18.

212 Ibid., at 19; Ross, S. and Hannan, M. (2007), 'Money laundering regulation and risk-based decision making', *Journal of Money Laundering Control*, vol. 10, issue 1, pp. 106-115.

213 The proposal for a Fourth Directive extends this to all AML supervisors, see: § 2.3.3.

214 Hampton Review (2005) at 27-34.

215 Commissie Michiels (1998) 84-85.

216 KVoT (2005) at 18-20.

217 Houben, A. (2013), 'Aligning Macro- and Microprudential Supervision', in: Kellerman, A.J., De Haan, J. and De Vries, F. (eds.), *Financial Supervision in the 21st Century*, Springer Publishing, pp. 201-220 at 210-211.

There are no general criteria that make an objective evaluation of the adequacy of resources possible. What exactly constitutes adequate resources is, therefore, to be observed in the circumstances applicable to each individual authority. Aspects that play a role in the decision as to whether or not adequate resources are in place may be the number of staff working on AML supervision, the budget for the supervisor or for anti-money laundering supervision specifically, if known, and the number of institutions and professionals for which a supervisor has responsibility. Any conclusions on the adequacy of resources in this research depend on the information available.

2.4.2.4 Adequate knowledge of supervisees

An adequate knowledge of the group of institutions for which an authority is the supervisor is of fundamental importance for the effectiveness of that supervision. This criterion is not primarily about the level of expertise of a supervisor, but about the factual question whether a supervisor knows the institutions and professionals for which it has supervisory responsibility. In particular the level of regulation of a profession is considered a preventive enforcement tool, because it may keep out the so-called 'bad apples'.[218] By regulating a profession or via licensing or registration requirements, it can be prevented that institutions or professionals withdraw from supervision. If a profession is not regulated at all or only to a limited extent, it is more difficult for a supervisor to know for which group of institutions and professionals it has supervisory responsibility. If a profession is regulated, a supervisor will generally have an overview of its supervisees.[219] Having a good informational position compared to supervisors of non-regulated professions, it will normally have a better understanding of the risks in the sector and of the general level of compliance by the institutions or professionals with the norms in place as well. Where a sector or profession is unregulated, the practical disadvantages may be limited where there are registration requirements for these institutions or professionals. If there is no register either, then an even greater effort must be made by the supervisory authority to find out which institutions and professionals fall under its supervision and, consequently, to formulate a proper risk-based supervision programme. It may result in the situation where a supervisor has to utilize a great deal of resources on this matter, which it can no longer use for actually carrying out the supervision.

To analyse whether authorities have an adequate knowledge of the institutions and professionals for which they have supervisory responsibility, I will verify whether and to what extent the banking sector and the accountancy and real estate professions are regulated in the Member States. If this is not the case, I will look at the existence of obligations for banks, accountants or real estate agents to be registered with their competent AML supervisors. The outcomes have an impact on the effectiveness of supervision and sanctioning.

218 Van den Berg, A. (2012), *Integriteitsbeoordelingen in advocatuur, notariaat en accountancy: een juridisch onderzoek naar informatiegebruik bij de bestrijding van integriteitsschendingen in de vastgoedsector*, Boxpress: 's-Hertogenbosch (doctoral thesis VU University Amsterdam), at 179 et seq.

219 Van den Broek (2014) at 76 and 80.

2.4.3 Competences and their effective application

The requirements for effective supervision in this part deal with the existence of adequate powers for supervisors and theories on how supervisors can apply these powers most effectively.

2.4.3.1 Adequate supervisory powers

For supervision to be effective, it is of paramount importance that supervisors have the legal powers to actually perform supervision.[220] In literature, the idea of adequate supervisory powers is widely embraced and a lack of powers is often considered to be a factor which reduces the effectiveness of supervision. A wide variety of sources refer to this aspect in relation to effective supervision.[221] Above I dealt with the minimum supervisory powers stemming from the Third Directive. The World Bank study also formulates powers that AML (banking) supervisors should specifically have. Firstly, they should have the power to compel banks to produce any information which is relevant to monitoring compliance with anti-money laundering requirements; this access must be (provided) in a timely manner and access to customer information should be granted without limitation and irrespective of the type of business, geography, customer category or the type of operation. Secondly, supervisors must have the power to make rules, regulations and to issue guidance. As we have seen earlier, the legislation must be sufficiently clear, foreseeable, or predictable before a supervisory authority can actually enforce those norms. In the case of norms that are more open-ended in nature, i.e. norms of which the content cannot be determined at an abstract level but depends on the circumstances under which the norms are applied, supervisors must be able to give more (binding) content to these norms. Thirdly, supervisors must have the power to carry out on-site visits and require access to suspicious transaction reports, as well as customer and related files. Supervisors should hereby avoid reliance on supervisees and, therefore, be able to obtain the relevant information themselves. The World Bank study considers that an effective AML supervisory system applies both to on-site and off-site supervision.[222] If off-site inspections were the only means of control, supervision would become superficial. In the field of environmental law, Blomberg considers that without on-site inspections, insufficient information can be gathered.[223] Therefore, it is of the utmost importance that not only the AML supervisors for financial and credit institutions, but all AML

220 Cf. Ottow (2006) at 86 et seq.

221 For example: Blomberg and Michiels (1997) at 36; De Moor-van Vugt, A.J.C. (2003), 'Europese criteria voor milieutoezicht', in: G.A. Biezeveld (ed.), *Handhaving van milieurecht vanuit Europees perspectief*, Boom Juridische uitgevers: The Hague, pp. 85-103; Voermans (2005) at 75; Blomberg (2008) at 61 and 79; Ottow, (2006) at 76; Commissie Michiels (1998) at 53 and 176-177; World Bank (2009) at 17-18; De Larosière (2009), *The High-Level Group on Financial Supervision in the EU*, 25 February 2009, available at: <http://ec.europa.eu/internal_market/finances/docs/de_larosiere_report_en.pdf>, last visited on 21 March 2014, at 23; Tijdelijke Commissie Onderzoek Financieel Stelsel (Commissie De Wit) (2010), *Verloren Krediet, Parliamentary Papers II*, 2009-10, 31 980, no. 4 (Commissie de Wit (2010)), recommendations 14 and 23; Basel Core Principle 1 and Essential Criterion 5 thereto; Markttoezichthoudersberaad (2011), at 4; Viñals and Fiechter (2010) at 14.

222 World Bank (2009) at 20.

223 Blomberg (2008) at 61.

supervisors have on-site supervision powers. This requirement thus goes beyond what the Third Directive requires.

In terms of the exercise of supervisory powers, the literature finds, in the first place, that these must be performed in a proportionate way.[224] The exercise of powers must not be disproportionate to the aims pursued. This means that the supervisor must always try to make use of the least intrusive powers where this is possible. Literature also demonstrates that supervisors must act with care: they must balance their own interests against those of the supervisees, taking all relevant circumstances into account.[225] In any case, there must always be a minimum level of supervision in practice. As stated in the context of financial supervision, 'it is critical that there be a "base-level" intensity of supervision for all financial institutions'.[226]

Here the general requirement that supervisors must have adequate supervisory powers provided by law is further coloured in by the (minimum) requirements from the Third Directive and literature that suggests how the supervisory powers must be exercised. This means that AML supervisors must have the power to compel the production of any information that is relevant to monitoring compliance, as well as the power to perform on-site checks. Supervisors, in particular those for financial and credit institutions, must also have the power to issue (binding) regulations. Supervisors must carry out inspections in practice, and do so in a proportionate and careful manner.

2.4.3.2 Adequate sanctioning powers

The existence of adequate sanctioning powers is of equally high importance. This could already be observed where the case law of the ECJ and the Third Directive established the requirement that sanctions should be 'effective, proportionate and dissuasive'. Especially in the UK, the Hampton and Macrory Reviews have stressed the importance of a wide sanctioning toolkit.[227] Other sources also refer to the necessity of adequate sanctioning powers.[228] In terms of the application of these sanctioning powers, it should again be observed that the powers must be applied in a proportionate and careful manner.[229] The application of sanctioning powers has received a great deal of attention in the academic debate. Scholars disagree about the way in which sanctions are most effectively addressed. In abstracto, two paradigms can be identified: while law & economics scholars tend to

224 De Moor-van Vugt (2003) at 95-97; Voermans (2005) at 77; Ottow (2006) at 77; Docters van Leeuwen, A.W.H. and Korte, H.W.O.L.M. (2006), 'Toezichtautoriteiten, in het bijzonder de AFM', in: Michiels, F.C.M.A. and Muller, E.R. (eds.), *Handhaving*, Kluwer: Deventer, pp. 335-355 at 348-349. See here the relationship with the principle of proportionality, falling under the notion of good governance: § 2.2.1.2.

225 Ottow (2006) at 77.

226 Yang Lim, A. and Lian Teo, S. (2013), 'Developments in Supervisory Enforcement', in: Kellerman, A.J., De Haan, J. and De Vries, F. (eds.), *Financial Supervision in the 21st Century*, Springer Publishing, pp. 103-110 at 105.

227 Hampton Review (2005) at 38-41; Macrory Review (2006) at 36-86.

228 Commissie De Wit (2010), recommendations 14 and 2; World Bank (2009) at 117 et seq.; De Larosière (2009) at 23; Basel Core Principle 11 and the Essential Criteria thereto, as well as Essential Criterion 6 to Principle 1.

229 Cf. World Bank (2009), at 122; Macrory Review (2006) at 31; Tridimas (2006) at 169-173; Ottow (2006) at 77.

argue in favour of a so-called deterrence style in which supervisors apply tough sanctions and act in a more formalistic way, criminologists and social scientists generally favour a more gradual response where supervisors first turn to the least intrusive means of intervention and will only as a last resort turn to formal sanctions. Both paradigms are briefly explained below, illustrated by Becker's theory on deterrence, on the one hand, and the theory of responsive regulation as developed by Ayres and Braithwaite, on the other.

> In the simplest picture two enforcement styles can be identified.[230] Literature often refers to 'enforcement', which has the same broad meaning as supervision in this research.[231] On the one hand, an enforcement style can be classified as a deterrence style whereby laws are applied strictly.[232] An important characteristic is 'the tendency to resort to formal legal methods and pay attention to the level of detail and complexity of the legislation'.[233] It is a confrontational style in the sense that it focuses on the violation and detection of violators. It can, however, also have preventive effects both against the violator who is punished, as well as in general for those who might have been tempted to violate the norms as well.[234] On the other hand, an enforcement style can be classified as a compliance style.[235] It focuses on the prevention of violations, remedying underlying problems, and interaction with the sector via advice, negotiations, meetings, and seminars.[236] Supervisors tend to turn to informal processes in striving for compliance. The formal powers are useful as a threat and are only used as a last resort.[237] This style presumes that non-compliance can also be the consequence of incompetence or unawareness on the side of the violator.[238] Along the dimensions of the degree of formalism and coercion, Winter and May have formulated the advantages and disadvantages of both paradigms: '[f]ormalism would be expected to provide greater certainty for the regulated in terms of what they are expected to do and thus help bring about social motivation to comply. However, after a point, formalism is likely to be perceived to be so picky that it backfires. Coercion would be expected to positively affect compliance, but only to a point. Inspectors must use the threat of sanctions once in a while to be taken seriously and to give credibility and certainty to their expectations and the consequences of not meeting them. However, as proved in earlier research, after a point increased threats of coercion will be perceived as overbearing and backfire'.[239]

Becker's deterrence theory

The economic literature on (criminal) law enforcement assumes that potential violators of the law behave rationally and consider both the advantages (benefits) and disadvantages

230 Hawkins, K. and Thomas, J.M. (1984), 'The Regulatory Process: Issues and Concepts', in: Hawkins and Thomas (eds.), *Enforcing Regulation*, Kluwer: Boston, pp. 3-23, at 12-14. Cf. Versluis, E. (2003), *Enforcement matters: Enforcement and compliance of European Directives in Four Member States*, Eburon: Delft (doctoral thesis Utrecht University) at 10-11.

231 See § 1.4 about the terminology applied in this research.

232 Also known as the legalistic, adversarial, coercive or vertical enforcement style.

233 Versluis (2003) at 10-11.

234 Hawkins and Thomas (1984), at 14.

235 Also known as the conciliatory, co-operative or horizontal enforcement style.

236 Hawkins and Thomas (1984) at 13.

237 Ibid., at 13; Versluis (2003) at 10.

238 Kagan, R.A. and Scholz, J.T. (1984), 'The "Criminology of the Corporation" and Regulatory Enforcement Strategies', in: Hawkins and Thomas (eds.), *Enforcing Regulation*, Kluwer: Boston, pp. 68-95, at 80 et seq.

239 Winter, S. and May, P.J. (2001), 'Motivation for Compliance with Environmental Regulations', *Journal of Policy Analysis and Management*, vol. 20, issue 4, pp. 675-698 at 679.

(costs) of violating the law. Potential violators are thought to make a conscious decision as to whether or not to comply with the law. This assumption was first brought forward by Gary Becker in 1968 in the sphere of criminal law enforcement and has been refined by other scholars.[240] Becker coined the theory that the decision to commit a crime should be looked at in the same way as other kinds of decisions and that people act in rational and utility-maximising ways, also with respect to crimes.[241] This means that in order to prevent potential violators from actually violating the law, the costs must be increased in order to deter them from violating the law. Enforcement plays an important role in increasing those costs to deter the violator. In the words of Suurmond and Van Velthuizen, enforcement holds the prospect of a certain risk of punishment.[242]

Understanding that enforcement is in itself a costly enterprise, the risk of punishment should be increased against the lowest costs possible.[243] How can the costs for potential violators be increased in such way that they are deterred from acting in a non-compliant manner with the law against the lowest possible enforcement costs? Becker's analysis is that a risk-neutral person is deterred from committing crime if his costs are higher than his benefits. The costs for violators can be increased by increasing the risk of punishment, which consists, on the one hand, of the probability of punishment or the risk of being caught and, on the other, of the scale of the punishment. The probability of punishment is higher where a supervisor increases its inspection activity. The scale of the punishment depends on the type of sanction in combination with the severity of that sanction, and the way in which it is effectuated. Economists widely prefer fines over imprisonment: fines are said to be free of costs because they are 'mere transfers of money', while imprisonment costs society money.[244] The probability and scale of punishment should be balanced in order to ensure a maximum risk of punishment. If the scale of punishment is high, the probability of punishment can be set at a lower level. However, if the scale of punishment is low then more resources should be devoted to supervision to increase the probability of punishment.

> The key question in the economic literature on (criminal) law enforcement is whether increasing the probability of punishment is a more effective deterrent than an equivalent increase in the scale of punishment. Stigler has pointed out that it would be less costly to increase the scale of punishment rather than to increase the probability of punishment. In the latter situation, scarce resources must be spent on enforcement, whereas increasing the sanction is in principle costless – especially where the sanction is a fine for the offender.[245] Empirical studies prove differently, however.[246]

240 Becker, G.S. (1968), 'Crime and Punishment: An Economic Approach', *Journal of Political Economy*, vol. 76, pp. 169-217. Cf. Polinsky, A.M. and Shavell, S. (2000), 'The Economic Theory of Public Enforcement of Law', *Journal of Economic Literature*, vol. 38, pp. 45-76.

241 Becker (1968) at 176.

242 Suurmond, G. en Van Velthoven, B.C.J. (2004): *Handhaven: eerst kiezen dan doen. Economische mogelijkheden en beperkingen (Interim Report IV)*, Expertisecentrum Rechtshandhaving, Ministerie van Justitie, at 20.

243 Suurmond and Van Velthoven (2004) at 12.

244 Polinsky and Shavell (2000) at 48.

245 Stigler, G. (1970), 'The Optimum Enforcement of Laws', *Journal of Political Economy*, vol. 78, issue 3, pp. 526-536 at 527.

246 See for an explanation of the criticisms of this theory: Faure et al. (2009) at 50.

Responsive regulation

Among criminologists and sociologists, responsive regulation has developed in the academic debate as the central theory of how to obtain compliance most effectively.[247] The basic presumption, first brought forward by Ayres and Braithwaite in 1992, is that enforcement should be attuned to the motives, behaviour and the possibilities of supervisees to comply with the norms, and that supervisors should always start with the compliance style. Ayres and Braithwaite argue that starting with a deterrence strategy is counterproductive, because punishment is expensive. It can result in a 'cat and mouse' game between the regulated sector and the supervisor and because in certain specific fields of law and policy, developments take place at such a great pace that (legal) norms cannot be kept up to date.[248] Braithwaite has also argued that starting with less coercive measures makes more coercive measures more legitimate and 'when regulation is seen as more legitimate, more procedurally fair, compliance with the law is more likely'.[249]

Responsive regulation prescribes a so-called tit-for-tat strategy. It comprehends in the first place enforcement by means of compliance strategies. Only in the case of persistent non-compliance does the application of more deterrent responses become justified. It means that where an institution is cooperating with the supervisor in order to attain compliance, the latter should refrain from a deterrent response. Yet where an institution misuses or abuses the cooperative behaviour offered by the supervisor, the latter should shift to a more deterrent approach. Where institutions show signs of moving towards compliance, forgiveness is the right way forward.[250] This strategy avoids the assumption that certain violators are incorrigible, but at the same time acknowledges that there are always some bad apples. It serves as a means to prevent the relationship between supervisee and supervisor from becoming locked in a negative spiral. Essential to this strategy is the so-called enforcement pyramid. This is a tool to examine which enforcement instruments should be applied in each layer of the pyramid.[251] Braithwaite is of the opinion that 'compliance is most likely when an agency displays an explicit enforcement pyramid'.[252] The supervisor should first turn to instruments that are available at the bottom of the pyramid, and should climb up the pyramid to escalate deterrence. Moving up the pyramid, the responses become more formal and punitive.

247 Van de Bunt, H., Van Erp, J. and Van Wingerde, K. (2007), 'Hoe stevig is de piramide van Braithwaite', *Tijdschrift voor Criminologie*, vol. 49, issue 4, pp. 386-399 at 386-387. This does not mean that this theory is widely accepted. Several (empirical) studies have identified its weaknesses: Mascini, P. and Van Wijk, E. (2009), *Responsive regulation door de Voedsel en Waren Autoriteit: Een empirisch onderzoek naar de theoretische veronderstellingen*, Boom Juridische uitgevers: The Hague; Baldwin, R. and Black, J. (2008), 'Really Responsive Regulation', *Modern Law Review*, vol. 71, issue 1, pp. 59-94; Lehmann Nielsen, V. (2006), 'Are Regulators Responsive?', *Law & Policy*, vol. 28, issue 3, pp. 395-416; May, P.J. and Wood, R.S. (2003), 'At the Regulatory Front Lines: Inspectors' Enforcement Styles and Regulatory Compliance', *Journal of Public Administration Research and Theory*, vol. 13, issue 2, pp. 117-139. See also the special issue of Regulation & Governance, vol. 7, issue 1, 2013 called *'Twenty Years of Responsive Regulation: An Appreciation and Appraisal'*.

248 Ayres, I. and Braithwaite, J. (1992), *Responsive Regulation: Transcending the Deregulation Debate*, Oxford University Press: New York at 26.

249 Braithwaite, J. (2002), *Restorative Justice and Responsive Regulation*, Oxford University Press: New York, at 33.

250 Ayres and Braithwaite (1992) at 21 and 33. See for similar reasoning: Kagan and Scholz (1984) at 86.

251 The enforcement pyramid can be different for each legal field and policy.

252 Ayres and Braithwaite (1992) at 35.

> It is assumed that at the bottom of the pyramid, institutions act as 'virtuous actors', both willing and having the capacity to take further steps to comply with the law. In such situations, persuasion, education or measures such as warning letters, suffice. Higher up, institutions are assumed to be 'rational actors', which have no wish to comply but after calculation do so. The threat of a fine or other penalty makes them comply with the law. At the top of the pyramid, institutions are 'incompetent or irrational actors', unable or unwilling to comply.[253] In such cases, supervisors should resort to severe punishment.

2

Crucial for the effectiveness of enforcement and a precondition for the enforcement pyramid and the tit-for-tat strategy is that supervisors have at their disposal a wide variety of responses, varying from active informal behaviour (advice, persuasion) to mild sanctions (warnings) and to more severe punishment (imprisonment, high fines, the revocation of licences). Ayres and Braithwaite call this last group of sanctions 'benign big guns'. Supervisors can allow themselves to speak softly, while actually carrying big sticks. The severe sanctions function as a threat towards potential violators.[254] After all, 'the bigger and the more various are the sticks, the greater the success regulators will achieve by speaking softly'.[255] The possibility of using severe sanctions against potential violators allows supervisors to operate more effectively. Severe sanctions, however, must not be the only type of sanction available to supervisors, because 'a regulatory agency with only a sanction that cannot politically or legally be used in a particular situation is unable to deliver a punishment payoff'.[256]

The one or the other, or both?

It seems that in many studies and in the practice of various supervisory authorities, the theory of responsive regulation is favoured over the deterrence style.[257] The influence of the theory of responsive regulation can be seen, for example, in the Dutch Framework Vision on Supervision. The vision includes the principle that supervision must be alert (*slagvaardig*): supervision should be soft where it is possible and 'hard' where it is necessary.[258] Supervisors are thus expected to stimulate the institutions for which they have supervisory responsibility where possible, but should intervene when there are no other options left. This strategy should be laid down in a supervision policy. Hence, just like responsive regulation prescribes, compliance should first be attempted through persuasion but where a supervisee is a persistent non-complier, then it should be punished. Hampton also recommends an advice-and-persuasion style, backed up by an effective sanctioning regime if this cooperative style would fail. An effective sanctioning regime underpins the regulator's advisory functions and also functions as a stick behind the door.[259] Likewise, Macrory stated that 'advice and incentives should play a key role in ensuring regulatory compliance, and should normally be the first responsive of regulators. Nevertheless, an effective sanction regime plays an equally vital role in a successful

253 Braithwaite (2002) at 31-33.
254 Ibid., at 35.
255 Ayres and Braithwaite (1992) at 19.
256 Ibid., at 36.
257 See: Van de Bunt et al. (2007).
258 KVoT (2005) at 21. It also requires that interventions are carried out quickly. This aspect is left out of the scope of this research.
259 It is close to the idea of Responsive regulation: first try to persuade, and only try to sanction when there is no other option left.

regulatory regime (…), its very existence will often act as an inducement to compliance without the need to invoke formal sanctions'. Sanctions can ultimately act as a deterrent to the non-complying institution and give a signal to the sector as a whole.[260] The World Bank study considers that besides the fact that sanctions must be deterrent, effective and proportionate, supervisors must also have a wide range of sanctions available. The study refers to the Basel Core Principles when it argues that supervisors must have a wide range of sanctions available, 'that allows supervisors to make a graduated response depending on the nature of the problems or the failure'.[261] Interesting is the fact that the European Court of Justice in its case law seems to prefer to explain its criterion of dissuasiveness along the lines of the deterrence theory. I already pointed out that Faure considers that the notion of dissuasiveness strongly resembles the notion of deterrence.[262] And according to Kokott in the *Berlusconi* case, the dissuasiveness of sanctions depends on 'the nature and level of the penalty but also the likelihood of its being imposed. Anyone who commits an infringement must fear that the penalty will in fact be imposed on him'.[263] These elements can also be found in Becker's deterrence theory. The foregoing shows that both theories are applied, although there seems to be a preference for the approach favouring a gradual response in which supervisors first turn to the least intrusive powers and will only as a last resort turn to formal sanctions.

Adequate sanctioning powers

It is important that the supervisors have adequate sanctioning powers available. There must be a wide range of sanctions, ranging from informal to formal sanctions, on the basis of which supervisors can escalate in the imposition of sanctions to ensure an effective and proportionate level of sanctioning. Supervisors should have more than one sanctioning power. They must speak softly where possible, and be hard where necessary. Ultimately, the sanctions must be able to deter potential violators, for which the nature and level of the penalty and the likelihood of it being imposed play a role. Therefore, supervisors must actually apply their powers in practice. As a minimum, the Third Directive requires that financial supervisors must at least have the power to impose administrative measures and sanctions for non-compliance with the preventive AML obligations and that Member States must ensure that both legal and natural persons can be held liable.[264]

2.4.3.3 Public supervision policies

It is important that supervisors issue supervision policies in which they make intelligible their supervisory and sanctioning choices and explain how they apply their discretion.[265] Such a policy should be publicly available.[266] This makes supervision by the supervisor

260 Macrory Review (2006) at 15.
261 World Bank (2009) at 122.
262 Faure (2010).
263 Joined Cases C-387/02, C-391/02, and C-403/02, *Berlusconi and Others* [2005], Opinion of AG Kokott, delivered on 14 October 2004, ECR I-3565, par. 89.
264 Cf. Basel Core Principle 11 and Essential Criterion 5 thereto.
265 Blomberg and Michiels (1997); Macrory Review (2006) at 32; De Moor-van Vugt (2003) at 101; KVoT (2005) at 21.
266 Macrory Review (2006) at 32; Commissie Michiels (1998) at 54.

transparent and more judge-proof.[267] In the words of Macrory, public supervision policies 'will improve transparency and accountability from regulators by signalling to business and society the kind of responses and standards they can expect from regulators in dealing with non-compliance'.[268] A public supervision (sanctioning) policy also demonstrates how supervisors apply their powers and, thus, creates a high(er) level of credibility. A supervision policy should contain an explanation of the legislative framework, the general supervision principles that the supervisor adheres to, the supervisory goals, the desired level of compliance (or supervision), and a general description of the procedures or methodology which must ensure that supervision is exercised thoroughly and consistently. It could also include norms or procedures with respect to cooperation with other relevant stakeholders. Any departure from a public supervision or public sanctioning policy requires justification.[269] Public supervision policies can partly be found in annual (supervision) plans.

2.4.3.4 Adequate cooperation powers

Great weight is attached to possibilities for cooperation, more specifically to legal gateways for information exchange.[270] Various international financial law standards pay attention to the matter of national and international cooperation between supervisors.[271] National studies also stress the importance of cooperation. The Michiels Committee noted in its report that insufficient cooperation between supervisors and between supervisors and law enforcement authorities was one of the main factors hampering effective enforcement.[272] One of the principles of the Dutch Framework Vision on Supervision is that supervisors must be cooperative: supervisors should exchange information with each other and make agreements on their supervision plans, as well as the form and extent of their cooperation. Cooperation can take various forms, for example via exchanging risk profiles of supervisees or carrying out supervision together or on behalf of the other.[273] Cooperation between supervisors ensures a consistent supervisory practice and a coherent and consistent explanation of legislation and regulations. This is important, because a consistent interpretation of rules and actions by supervisors can foster a sense of fairness among the supervisees, which in turn may enhance their compliance.[274] It has also been pointed out that cooperation can reduce administrative burdens for supervised institutions.[275] In relation to the AML policy specifically, the World Bank study observed that '[f]or the AML/CTF regime to be effective, a seamless flow of information between national and international agencies is of paramount importance'.[276] With respect to national cooperation in this policy, the World Bank distinguishes cooperation with the

267 Commissie Michiels (1998) at 54.
268 Macrory Review (2006) at 32.
269 Ibid.
270 E.g. Duijkersloot (2013) at 359-360; Stouten (2012) at 290-295.
271 World Bank (2009) at 9-10; Basel Core Principle 3 and Essential Criterion 1 thereto.
272 Commissie Michiels (1998) at 55-56.
273 KVoT (2005) at 22.
274 May, P.J. (2004), 'Compliance Motivations: Affirmative and Negative Bases', *Law and Society Review*, vol. 38, issue 1, pp. 41-68 at 46.
275 Hampton Review (2005) at 9.
276 World Bank (2009) at 147.

FIU, cooperation between supervisors, cooperation with reporting entities and with competent law enforcement authorities.

This research focuses primarily on cooperation between anti-money laundering supervisors and, to a certain extent, cooperation with the FIU and other relevant stakeholders – in particular professional or trade associations. From a supervisors' perspective, cooperation with the FIU is important, because an FIU can have data that the supervisor does not necessarily have.[277] For example, the FIU knows how many suspicion reports a particular institution has disclosed, the quality of these reports, and also has information in quantitative and qualitative terms as to what other similar institutions have reported in order to compare the performance of the institution. Such information is important for supervisory procedures, because it may say something about the individual institution's stance and its willingness to comply with anti-money laundering obligations. Having such information means that the supervisor can work through this in the formulation of its policy and annual (supervision) plans. The information strengthens the information position of the supervisor. Cooperation with other supervisors is also important, especially when it comes to issuing further regulations, or exchanging supervisory information. Likewise, cooperation is deemed important for supervisory consistency in order to ensure that norms are interpreted in the same way and are equally applied throughout the different sectors. The exchange of information between AML supervisors is also of great importance, because each of the supervisors may have a piece of supervisory information that, as such, does not point towards non-compliance or the criminal offence of money laundering, but in combination with other information it does do so. Supervisors may come across information that is relevant for other authorities as well. This is especially the case where various institutions are involved in financial transactions, like real estate agents, notaries and banks in real estate transactions.

By 'supervisory information' I understand specific individual information about an institution which possibly acts in contravention of its AML obligations or is otherwise involved in a money laundering transaction. Information can be the name of the institution, the directors or managers, the network to which it belongs, a description of the institution, the (potential) breaches and a description of the transaction and/or parties involved. The exchange of information is a delicate issue since it may include different types of business information or personal data for which different confidentiality regimes exist. This affects the legal possibilities for the exchange of information. In this light, this research focuses on the existence of legal bases in the AML legislation or legislation closely related thereto.

International cooperation is equally important for effective supervision.[278] Research has demonstrated that in the field of the AML policy international cooperation usually takes place between homologous institutions, meaning FIUs with FIUs, supervisors with supervisors, and so on.[279] This research pays no attention to this international aspect of supervision.

277 See Chapter 3.
278 Basel Core Principle 3 and Essential Criterion 2 thereto.
279 Deleanu and Van den Broek (2014) at 148.

All in all, AML supervisors must have adequate cooperation powers provided by law. They must in particular have the power to exchange supervisory information with each other, and with the FIU. Supervisors must also cooperate with each other and the FIU. This is analysed by looking at cooperation efforts, participation in projects and individual liaisons between supervisors, with the FIU and other relevant stakeholders. For the purpose of clarity a distinction will be made between cooperation on a policy level, and cooperation efforts by anti-money laundering supervisors on an operational level. Both types of cooperation are important for the effectiveness of AML supervision.

2.5 Concluding remarks

This chapter demonstrated the development of the theoretical framework for effective supervision as it will be applied in this research. The principle of effectiveness, both as a good governance principle and a principle of EU law, showed the legal embedding and meaning of effectiveness on a more abstract level. The Third Directive provided the minimum requirements with respect to supervision in the preventive AML policy. These minimum requirements were complemented by elements identified as important for effective supervision on the basis of a literature study. In mapping the legislative framework, the supervisors' institutional structures, their powers, the procedures and their application in practice, it is examined to what extent the requirements are complied with by the authorities in the respective Member States. The table below presents the theoretical framework that will be used throughout this research. If the requirements from this theoretical framework are complied with, then effectiveness is presumed.

Table 1 – Requirements for effective supervision

Legislative requirements	**Legislation must be clear, precise, foreseeable, predictable and enforceable**
Institutional requirements	**Anti-money laundering supervisors must be independent in their day-to-day activities from politics (Minister, Government, Parliament), as well as the market.** • For AML supervisors of financial and credit institutions there must be a high degree of independence • For other AML supervisors the degree of independence depends on whether it is an internal or external supervisor. However, a certain degree of independence must be maintained. **Anti-money laundering supervisors must be accountable for the exercise of their supervisory and sanctioning activities** • Accountability requires transparency. Supervisors must at least be transparent as to the reasons for carrying out supervision, the supervision goals, they must make visible the choices in supervision and sanctioning, and provide information about the results of supervision. Most important are the annual (supervision) plans and annual reports. **Anti-money laundering supervisors must have adequate resources** • AML supervisors must adjust their actions to the available resources ('shrewd' or selective supervision, risk-based supervision) **Anti-money laundering supervisors must have an adequate knowledge of supervisees** • AML supervisors must know the size of the group of supervisees and have some basic information on them. Regulation of the sector or profession, or licensing/registration requirements play an essential role.
Competences and their application	**Anti-money laundering supervisors must have adequate supervisory powers provided by law** • AML supervisors must have the power to compel the production of any information that is relevant to monitoring compliance and the power to perform checks, including on-site inspections • AML supervisors, in particular for supervisors of financial and credit institutions, must have the power to issue rules and regulations • AML supervisors must apply their supervisory powers in practice, and do so in a proportionate and careful manner **Anti-money laundering supervisors must have adequate sanctioning powers provided by law** • There must be a wide range of sanctions, ranging from informal to formal sanctions • AML supervisors must be able to apply sanctions against both legal and natural persons • AML supervisors of financial and credit institutions must at least be able to take administrative measures and impose administrative sanctions • AML supervisors must sanction in a proportionate and careful manner, and escalate in their sanctions. They must speak softly where possible, and be hard where necessary; ultimately the sanctions must be capable of providing a deterrent effect. **Anti-money laundering supervisors must have public supervision policies in place** • Supervision policies must contain an explanation of the legal framework, the goals, the desired level of enforcement (or compliance), and general principles of the supervisor for its activities, as well a general description of the procedures or methodology applied. **Anti-money laundering supervisors must have adequate powers provided by law to cooperate on an ongoing basis with other supervisors and the FIU** • AML supervisors must cooperate in practice on a policy and operational level

3 Supervisory architectures in the preventive anti-money laundering policy

3.1 Introduction

This chapter discusses the supervisory architectures of preventive anti-money laundering policies in the EU Member States.[1] Earlier studies observed that within AML prevention, procedural norms have primarily been left to the Member States' discretion.[2] This is not surprising given that European Union law is implemented, applied and enforced within the framework of the laws of the Member States, which means that national rules of procedure apply. The power of EU Member States to select competent authorities and determine applicable procedures is referred to as the principle of national procedural autonomy.[3] The result of this principle is, however, that procedures for enforcing (European) substantive norms differ from Member State to Member State.[4] This may create difficulties in supervision and sanctioning in cross-border situations where businesses and professionals operate in more than one Member State.[5] EU Member States' supervisory architectures under the preventive AML policy are influenced by factors such as national politics,

1 This chapter is a shortened version of Chapter 6 on AML/CTF Supervisory Architectures in the ECOLEF Final Report (2013, not published). An elaborated version of this chapter has been published in Unger, B, Ferwerda, J., van den Broek, M. and Deleanu, I. (2014) *The Economic and Legal Effectiveness of the European Union's Anti-Money Laundering Policy*, Edward Elgar Publishing Ltd: Cheltenham, pp. 62-86.

2 Deloitte (2011); Van den Broek (2014) at 62.

3 Jans et al. (2007) at 40-42.

4 The principle of procedural autonomy is limited by the principle of equivalence that requires that rules that govern a dispute with an EU law dimension may not be less favourable than those governing similar domestic disputes and the principle of effectiveness. This principle implies that the exercise of rights conferred by the Union legal order may not be rendered virtually impossible or made excessively difficult by rules of national procedural law. See: ECJ EU, Case 33/76, *Rewe* [1976] ECR-1989; ECJ EU, Case 45/76, *Comet* [1976] ECR-2043. See § 2.2.2.

5 As exemplified in the Jyske Bank judgment of the European Court of Justice: Case C-212/11, *Jyske Bank Gibraltar Ltd v Administración del Estado*, [2013] ECR I-0000. See on the matter of the allocation of supervisory responsibilities and reporting to the FIU in cross-border situations: European Commission (2011), *Commission Staff Working Paper on Anti-money laundering supervision of and reporting by payment institutions in various cross-border situations*, SEC(2011) 1178 Final; European Commission (2012), *Report from the Commission to the European Parliament and the Council on the application of Directive 2005/60/EC on the prevention for the use of the financial system for the purpose of money laundering and terrorist financing*, COM(2012) 168 final, at 12-13; European Commission (2012a), *Feedback Statement: Summary of comments on the report from the Commission to the European Parliament and the Council on the application of Directive 2005/60/EC*, at 11, available at <http://ec.europa.eu/internal_market/company/docs/financial-crime/072012_feedback_statement_en.pdf>, last visited on 14 March 2014.

culture, the legal system, the economy and finances. This leaves us with a 'patchwork' of AML supervisory architectures in the European Union.[6]

The primary aim of this chapter is to explain the selection of the countries studied in this research. The choice for Spain, the Netherlands, the United Kingdom, and Sweden is based on the models of AML supervisory architectures in the European Union. I have developed these models within the framework of the ECOLEF study.[7] The models present the supervisory architectures in a systematic way. The models demonstrate the main similarities and differences throughout the European Union. A brief explanation of the background of the modelling and the methodology applied for the design of the models is presented first (§ 3.2). This is followed by Section 3.3, which explains the four models of supervisory architectures based on their main characteristics.[8] Section 3.4 illustrates the models as they are implemented at the national level. Finally, this chapter ends with some concluding remarks.

3.2 Background of the modelling

3.2.1 Literature on financial supervision

The modelling of supervisory architectures is a topic to which particular attention is given in the field of financial law and regulation.[9] A central question here is the 'extent to which financial regulation as between different types of businesses should be integrated, and whether responsibility for financial regulation and supervision should be vested in a single agency'.[10] Normally three or four models of financial supervisory architectures are distinguished in the literature.[11] In a study by Goodhart et al., a supervisory architecture falls within one of these three models: the institutional/sectoral approach, the functional approach or the objectives-based approach.[12] Under the first approach, financial supervision focuses on the type of institution, meaning that there are separate supervisors for banks, insurance companies, and securities firms.[13] Supervision under the functional approach is directed at the type of products and services offered by the institutions. It does not matter which type of institution offers these products or services. Under the third approach, financial supervision is organised according to the objectives

6 I first coined this term in Van den Broek (2011a). Cf. Van den Broek (2014).

7 See § 1.7.

8 Van den Broek (2014) at 70-85 contains information on the potential strengths and weaknesses of the models, which were developed jointly with Member States' representatives during interviews and ECOLEF Regional Workshops.

9 See Wymeersch, E. (2007), 'The Structure of Financial Supervision in Europe: About Single Financial Supervisors, Twin Peaks and Multiple Financial Supervisors', *European Business Organization Law Review*, vol. 8, issue 2, pp. 237-306 who refers to numerous studies on this topic.

10 Llewellyn, D.T. (2006), *Institutional structure of financial regulation and supervision: the basic issues*, Paper presented at the World Bank seminar 'Aligning Supervisory Structures with country needs', Washington DC, 6-7 June 2006, at 4.

11 Goodhart, C.A.E., Hartmann, Ph., Llewellyn, D., Rojas-Suaréz, Weisbrod (1998), *Financial Regulation: Why, how and where now?*, London: Routledge; Wymeersch (2007); Group of Thirty (2008), *The structure of financial supervision: Approaches and challenges in a global marketplace*, Washington DC.

12 Goodhart et al. (1998) at 144 et seq.

13 Wymeersch (2007) at 252 also calls this the institutional or 'three-pillar' approach.

of supervision. A slightly different distinction can be found in a study on the structure of financial supervision from the Group of Thirty (G30).[14] The G30 distinguishes four principal models of financial supervision.[15] The first two are the institutional and the functional approach, which are identical to Goodhart's models. Yet, where Goodhart's third model is the objectives-based approach, G30 distinguishes the integrated approach and the 'twin-peaks' approach. Under the integrated approach there is one single authority that conducts both prudential and conduct-of-business supervision. Under the twin peaks approach there is one supervisor that performs conduct-of-business supervision, and another one that carries out prudential supervision. This last type of supervision focuses on safeguarding the solvency of financial institutions and the stability of the financial sector. Conduct-of-business supervision aims at ensuring orderly financial markets with proper relationships between market players, and the integrity and due care of financial institutions.

3

The studies do not explicitly state which elements are decisive for distinguishing between the different models of financial supervision. The key elements of the models seem, in my opinion, to be the following. In the first place, the *object of supervision* turns out to be of particular relevance for the distinction between the institutional and the functional approach. While the institutional approach focuses on the businesses, the functional approach takes the activities as its supervisory object. A second element is the *number of supervisors* involved.[16] The integrated approach in the G30's categorisation relies on one supervisor, whereas the other three approaches are characterised by the involvement of two or more supervisors. Thirdly, the *objectives or types of financial supervision* are of importance. Both the Goodhart and the G30 study pay attention to two types of financial supervision, namely conduct-of-business supervision and prudential supervision. While these are separated under the twin-peaks approach, no such separation exists in the other approaches.

The range and variety of supervisory models suggest that at this moment there is no consensus on which financial supervision model is best, most effective or optimal. In this context, it has been considered that '[m]any alternative models exist and they can be made to work effectively under normal circumstances. One might ask, however, whether all structures are equally effective and efficient under all circumstances, or more specifically, whether the organisational structure of financial supervision has a bearing on the efficiency and effectiveness of regulation and supervision in achieving the desired objectives'.[17] The

14 The G30 is 'a private, non-profit, international body composed of very senior representatives of the private and public sectors and academia. It aims to deepen understanding of international economic and financial issues, to explore the international repercussions of decisions taken in the public and private sectors, and to examine the choices available to market practitioners and policymakers.' Among its members are Jean-Claude Trichet (the current chairman), Jacques De Larosière (an emeritus member), and Alexandre Lamfalussy (a past member). Information available at: <www.group30.org>.

15 Group of Thirty (2008).

16 Llewellyn (2006) at 10.

17 Lumpkin, S. (2002), 'Supervision of Financial services in the OECD Area', *OECD Working paper*, at 4. Cf. Llewellyn (2006) at 7.

prevalent opinion seems to be that no single model can be considered as the optimal institutional model, as all of the models have their own advantages and disadvantages.[18]

3.2.2 Design of models in the preventive anti-money laundering policy

Supervision in the preventive AML policy is closely related to financial supervision. However, the first policy is not limited to financial law and institutions. It applies to a wide range of institutions and professionals – varying from large international financial conglomerates to jewellery shops – which results in the involvement of various different authorities.[19] A distinction between prudential and conduct-of-business supervision is absent in the preventive AML policy as well. Anti-money laundering supervision is a form of compliance supervision. The main objective of supervision is clear: to ensure compliance by the private sector with the obligations set by legislation in order to prevent them from being used or involved in money laundering and terrorist financing transactions. Where there is no voluntary compliance by the private sector this should be enforced through measures or sanctions. The type of supervision is thus a given fact and is the same throughout all EU Member States' preventive AML policies. This means that the identified models of financial supervision cannot be applied to the preventive AML policy as such.

This section presents the models for AML supervisory architectures as designed within the framework of the ECOLEF study. These models show the institutional design of supervision that can be identified in the preventive anti-money laundering policy in the European Union on the basis of selected elements. This modelling is largely inspired by the aforementioned models in financial supervision. The names of the models are indicative and, as such, are wider in content. Therefore, one needs to carefully read the description of the models to get a comprehensive understanding thereof. The models are, moreover, not meant to strictly demarcate the different supervisory architectures. Within the models there may be variations between Member States, and elements from one model may to some extent be present in other models as well.

3.2.2.1 Key elements

I have used two key elements to distinguish the models from one another. The first key element concerns the level of concentration of AML supervision in a particular Member State. In other words: the total number of authorities that are involved in the supervision of the preventive AML policy. This number will never be one, due to the wide range of institutions and professionals falling under the preventive policy. Therefore, I relate the number to the final responsibility for this supervision. The final responsibility for AML supervision is either explicitly assigned by law to a single authority or the total number of

18 Llewellyn (2006) at 7.

19 See Article 2 Third Directive for the minimum range of institutions and professionals. It appears that Member States have often extended the scope for various reasons: Van den Broek (2014a), 'Harmonization of substantive norms in preventive AML policy', in: Unger et al., *The Economic and Legal Effectiveness of the European Union's Anti-Money Laundering Policy*, Edward Elgar Publishing Ltd: Cheltenham, pp. 20-45 at 21-34.

supervisors involved, or this can be inferred from the legal provisions. In that case it is a matter of interpretation.

The second key element addresses the nature of the authorities. The question here is whether supervision is performed by external or internal supervisors, viewed from the perspective of the supervised institutions and professionals. External supervisors can be defined as those authorities that carry out supervision but which have no direct, professional relationship with the institutions or professionals it supervises. Generally, these are public (administrative) or government authorities. Internal supervisors, on the other hand, are professional associations that have a strong professional relationship with the members they oversee. This element is of particular relevance to AML supervision in relation to the designated non-financial businesses and persons that fall within the scope of the preventive policy, such as lawyers, civil-law notaries, accountants, auditors and tax advisors.

Without the intention of starting an in-depth, general and legal-political discussion at this point as to whether the preventive AML policy can best be regulated and supervised by or on behalf of the State or by professional associations, the reality is that in the EU professional associations can have a supervisory, and sometimes regulatory, role, although the extent of their involvement differs. Nevertheless, the following subsection does pay some attention to the matter of self-regulation and the question of who can combat money laundering best.

3.2.2.2 Who can combat money laundering best?

Against the background of the discussion on whether to have either external or internal supervisors perform supervision lies the fundamental question of whether combating money laundering (and terrorist financing), including the prevention thereof, is best dealt with by the State or can better be left to the professionals and their professional associations involved through self-regulation. Self-regulation can be defined as 'the situation of a group of persons or bodies, acting together, performing a regulatory function in respect of themselves and others who accept their authority'.[20] Self-regulation occurs in all kinds of legal fields varying from financial law, consumer law, and trade law to legislation regulating certain specific professions (lawyers, civil-law notaries, accountants). The exact meaning and shape of self-regulation differs among these legal fields.

Self-regulation has been advocated by authors from various research disciplines such as law, economics, sociology, and political science.[21] One of the reasons brought forward

20 Black, J. (1996), 'Constitutionalising self-regulation', *Modern Law Review*, vol. 59, pp. 24-55 at 27.
21 Cf. Black (1996) at 25-26.

by the proponents is that self-regulation can overcome problems of implementation and legitimisation associated with State regulation.[22] In the words of Streeck and Schmitter:

> '[b]y turning behavioural regulation into a matter of the organised self-interest of affected groups, it leaves the legitimation of regulatory interference to group representatives, who (....) can have recourse to more tangible group-specific norms and interest perceptions'.[23]

Various arguments can be brought forward in favour of self-regulation, most of which are based on expertise and efficiency. Self-regulation is said to ensure that the knowledge and expertise of all parties are used more effectively. Generally, practitioners have more knowledge about the markets, the profession and the technology than the Government and its authorities have.[24] Moreover, self-regulation is more flexible and adaptable than statutory regulation.[25] It is also said to impose lower regulatory burdens on firms and lower costs for the State, because the costs are borne by the industries or professions. Finally, self-regulation promotes commitment, pride and loyalty within a profession or industry and ensures that markets work better than they would under State regulation.[26]

The other side of the coin, however, is that the most obvious weakness of self-regulation is said to be the possibility of collusion and anti-competitive behaviour.[27] From a legal perspective weaknesses relate principally to the foreseeability and clarity of norms.[28] One can also look critically at the role of professional associations. Professional associations have close links to the professionals, because they are members of these associations. Furthermore, those working in professional associations are often professionals themselves. In general terms, the main objectives of professional associations are to further the particular profession as a whole, to protect the individual professionals, as well as to protect society or the public interest. Professional ethical norms play an important role in reconciling the three objectives and are often embodied in the professions' ethics codes. Professional associations might face a 'dichotomy between their role as advocates for a profession and the requirement that they perform a social good by regulating their members. (...) Short-term needs of current members may conflict with longer-term requirements of the profession overall. (...) Their relations with government are overtly political as they chart one course between acting as advisers and supplicants and another

22 Streeck, W. and Schmitter, P.C. (1985), 'Community, Market, State – and Associations? The Prospective Contribution of Interest Governance to Social Order', in: Streeck, W. and Schmitter, P.C. (eds.), *Private Interest Government: Beyond Market and State*, Sage: London, pp. 1-29 at 22-23. Cf. Birkinshaw, P., Harden, I., Lewis, N. (1990), *Government by moonlight: the hybrid parts of the state*, Unwin Hyman: London, at 8-9, who state in the British context that corporatism (*the attribution of public status to interest groups, MB*) may be one way in which the Government and Parliament may retain authority and legitimacy via the support of these organisations.

23 Streeck and Schmitter (1985) at 22.

24 Bartle, I. and Vass, P. (2005), 'Self-regulation and the regulatory State: A survey of policy and practice', *CRI Research report* 17, at 36; Streeck and Schmitter (1985) at 22.

25 Eijlander, Ph. (1993), *De wet stellen: Beschouwingen over onderwerpen van wetgeving*, Tjeenk Willink: Zwolle, at 182.

26 Bartle and Vass (2005) at 36-37. Eijlander (1993) at 182 speaks about a 'preparedness to comply' (*nalevingsbereidheid*).

27 Doyle, C. (1997), 'Self-Regulation and Statutory Regulation', *Business Strategy Review*, vol. 8, issue 3, pp. 35-42 at 36; Bartle and Vass (2005) at 8; Faure et al. (2009) at 18.

28 Eijlander (1993) at 183.

one between performing a lobbying role and acting as 'lesser governments'.[29] Frankel summarises this potential conflict as follows: '[s]hielding members from outside knowledge of their deviance also shields the profession from embarrassment, with its potential for precipitating a decline in public trust'.[30] A weakness of self-regulation thus also lies in the sphere of control and the enforcement of norms.[31] In order to balance the advantages and disadvantages of self-regulation, it seems that self-regulation nowadays operates mostly in a context in which it is backed with threats and sanctions by the regulatory state.[32] Alternatively, one can identify a relationship which is called mandated self-regulation (or regulated self-regulation[33]) whereby the profession or industry itself regulates detailed norms but where the general framework is set by the Government.[34] In any case it seems that where self-regulation is chosen, 'functions which relate to monitoring, transparency and accountability are often retained by the public authority or even enhanced'.[35]

Regarding the prevention of money laundering there is no answer (as yet) to the question which party can best fight this phenomenon, as literature presents diverging opinions. In this area, self-regulation refers to the regulation and supervision of legal and fiscal service providers, because internal supervision is only allowed for these professions.[36] Regarding the contradiction between advocating the profession and the performance of a social good, it has been pointed out that this dichotomy may also be present in the preventive AML policy:

> '[w]hile non-compliance with AML/CTF obligations sometimes requires robust action due to the severity of the breaches and to show other professionals that the professional association is taking the matter seriously, a high number of sanctions imposed by the professional association could lead to the impression that the professionals do not maintain a high quality standard. This, in turn, may lead to a decreased level of trust in the profession as a whole. Obviously this goes against to what the professional associations stand for, which is to further the quality of the profession. It may therefore not always be favourable for the professional associations themselves to actively verify compliance with AML/CTF obligations and impose sanctions.'[37]

This dichotomy becomes especially problematic where professionals, their professional associations and their members are not convinced of the need for and the importance of combating money laundering and, hence, where they consider the furthering of the profession as a whole or the protection of individual professionals to be more important. On the other hand, self-regulation can in certain cases be more advantageous than State regulation, especially where the regulation originates from the profession or the industry

29 Friedman, A. and Phillips, M. (2004), 'Balancing strategy and Accountability: A Model for the Governance of Professional Associations', *Nonprofit management and Leadership*, vol. 15, issue 2, pp. 187-204 at 188.
30 Frankel, M.S. (1989), 'Professional Codes: Why, How and with What Impact?', *Journal of Business Ethics*, vol. 8, pp. 109-115 at 113.
31 Eijlander (1993) at 183.
32 Bartle and Vass (2005) at 24 and 32.
33 Streeck and Schmitter (1985) at 22.
34 Black (1996) at 27.
35 Bartle and Vass (2005) at 40.
36 Cf. Article 37(5) Third Directive.
37 Van den Broek (2014) at 81.

itself and where clear incentives for professionals to comply exist.[38] The integrity and quality of professions is without doubt something that the AML policy touches upon, but the fact remains that these specific and detailed norms have been imposed top-down from organisations such as the FATF and the European Union, as well as national governments.

With respect to the AML supervision of civil-law notaries, lawyers, accountants and tax advisors in the Netherlands, research discusses the issue of internal or external supervision. In her dissertation, Stouten concluded that internal supervision under the preventive policy is valuable, but that this should be backed up by systematic oversight performed by an external supervisor to provide transparency and accountability to society. In this respect, she speaks about an urgent social need for external supervision in the preventive AML policy.[39] Alternatively, an independent organ within an association could be created to oversee the performance of AML supervision carried out by the professional association itself.[40] Other Dutch scholars have argued that the necessity of introducing external supervision has not been proven and that internal supervision does less damage to fundamental legal principles such as legal professional privilege, because the president of the Bar Association has his own legal privilege as well as a derived privilege from the lawyer.[41] In the UK, the Treasury has pointed to the enhanced understanding by professional associations of the way businesses operate, which may be beneficial for their AML supervision.[42]

3.3 Models of anti-money laundering supervisory architectures

This section presents the four models of AML supervisory architectures that can be identified based on the two elements outlined in the previous section. Sections 3.3.1 to 3.3.4 describe each supervisory model according to its main characteristics. Section 3.3.5 illustrates the differences between the models based on the comparative elements.

3.3.1 The FIU model

The main characteristic of the FIU model is that the financial intelligence unit (FIU) is the national authority with final responsibility for AML supervision. FIUs are (part of) national authorities that are primarily responsible for receiving, analysing and disseminating financial intelligence submitted through suspicion reports by obliged institutions or professionals. The institutional embedding of FIUs differs per country.[43] Because of the original functions of FIUs, they do not have direct, professional relationships with any of the obliged institutions or professionals. FIUs are thus external supervisors. Making the FIU ultimately responsible for AML supervision can be prompted by legislators' beliefs

38 Cf. Eijlander (1992) at 182-183.

39 Stouten (2012) at 377.

40 Stouten (2012) at 380-383 explains this for lawyers (*advocaten*) on the basis of Bills amending the Dutch Counsel Act.

41 Bannier, F.A.W. and Fanoy, N.A.M.E.C. (2010), *Visie leerstoel advocatuur op toezicht door BFT*, advies in opdracht van de NOvA. Cf. Stouten (2012) at 376.

42 HM Treasury, *Anti-Money Laundering and Counter Terrorist Finance Supervision Report 2010-11*, November 2011, at 6.

43 Egmont (2004), *Information Paper on Financial Intelligence Units and the Egmont Group*, September 2004; IMF (2004), *Financial Intelligence Units: An Overview*, Washington DC; Thony (1996).

that external supervision is most appropriate. Where an FIU has final responsibility, this does not necessarily mean that no other authorities are involved at all. In practice other supervisors may be involved, based on legislation or secondary regulations, or based on agreements concluded between the FIU and other authorities. Decisive, however, is the fact that final responsibility for the proper carrying out of supervision by other authorities in respect of the preventive AML policy remains with the FIU.

3.3.2 The external model

The term 'external' is used to indicate that external supervisors, which have no direct, professional relationship with the institutions and professionals they supervise, play an essential role in this model. The anti-money laundering legislation, or regulations drafted pursuant to this legislation, appoint the supervisory authorities in a Member State. Under the external model the final responsibility for supervision is shared among a number of external supervisors. This model, too, is most likely to be steered by legislators' beliefs that combating money laundering should be a matter of State regulation. The main characteristic of this model is that existing supervisory structures are used and that authorities designated for AML supervision usually already had supervisory tasks, possibly, but not necessarily, in this policy. Because of the nature of external supervisors, there is a certain distance between the supervisors and the institutions and professionals for which they have supervisory responsibility. Again, the general outline of this model does not disregard the fact that in practice the supervision or sanctioning of legal and fiscal service providers can also be (partially) performed by professional associations. This is either based on AML legislation or on supervisory arrangements between the external and internal supervisors.[44] These arrangements concern the situation that professional associations take over supervisory and sanctioning tasks from the external supervisors, and perform supervision or impose sanctions on behalf of the external supervisors or do so on a complementary basis. In that case external supervisors usually perform a kind of systematic oversight of the internal supervisors, although they retain the right to carry out AML supervision themselves.

3.3.3 The internal model

Within the internal model, AML supervision is mainly performed by professional associations. The guiding principle in this model is that where internal supervisors can perform supervision, they will be assigned as AML supervisors. This is presumably prompted by the national legislator's belief that professional associations are better capable of carrying out anti-money laundering supervision of their members than State or Government authorities. Only where professional associations have no jurisdiction, for example over unregistered professionals or dealers in goods, may other (external) authorities have supervisory competences. A characteristic of this model is that there are comparatively many supervisors, because each profession has its own professional body. Sometimes this number is even higher due to specialisations within the profession or

44 See § 3.4.2 and Chapter 5.

because of territorial competences. Under this model, all external and internal supervisors share ultimate responsibility for AML supervision.

In practice it will never be the case that a supervisory architecture in the preventive AML policy is solely composed of internal supervisors, because the supervision of financial and credit institutions and casinos is always performed by the State. Decisive for this model, however, is the extent of the presence of internal supervisors in a particular architecture. This is expressed either in scope, in the range of professionals, or in the factual number of internal supervisors. For example, due to the federal or decentralised structure of a Member State, there can be relatively many external supervisors compared to internal supervisors. Alternatively, due to the high level of self-regulation in a Member State, there can be a very high number of internal supervisors. Although both systems are different in their design, both can express the underlying idea of the internal model: where possible, internal supervisors are designated as AML supervisors for their members.

Where professional associations carry out AML supervision, the obligations for the professionals are often (implicitly) incorporated in the professional norms, or are at least referred to in the professions' codes. Likewise, AML supervision is mostly part of broader supervision programmes that concern the quality and the integrity of the professional.[45]

3.3.4 The hybrid model

The hybrid model combines elements of the three models mentioned before. The exact mixture differs per country and can have various gradations. Under this model there seems to be no explicit preference on the legislator's side for either internal or external supervisors.

Along the line of gradations, two extremes can be identified. The least hybrid variant concerns a combination of both internal and external supervisors. In relation to the internal model, the difference is the extent to which internal supervisors are involved in the supervision of designated non-financial businesses and professions. As explained, the principle under the internal model is that, where possible, professional associations are assigned as AML supervisors. Under this variant of the hybrid model, however, there is generally just one professional association involved, although many legal and fiscal service providers are member of a professional association. In the Member States that have been found to apply this model, the only professional association that is competent to perform AML supervision is the bar association. External supervisors supervise the other professions. The final responsibility for AML supervision is shared among the supervisors involved.

The most hybrid variant concerns a mixture of the three models. Final responsibility for AML supervision is shared between external and internal supervisors, as well as the FIU. Characteristic of this variant is the position of the FIU: it either serves as a so-called

45 Van den Broek (2014) at 67.

default supervisor for those professions or businesses that originally have no or a very weak supervisor, or it engages in the supervision of the entire range of obliged institutions and professions but with limitations as to the scope of its activities. In the latter case, the FIU can supervise a particular obligation only, for example the reporting obligation. The obliged institutions then also deal with AML supervisors that verify compliance with other obligations.

3.3.5 Positioning the different models

Based on the foregoing descriptions, the four models in the AML supervisory architecture can be illustrated as follows. The table demonstrates how the models are different from each other. The FIU model differs from the three other models, because one authority is ultimately responsible for AML supervision. Regarding the nature of the supervisors we can see three variations: under the FIU model and the external model external supervisors operate, while internal supervisors dominate the internal model. Under the hybrid model internal and external supervisors are mixed and their level of involvement varies from country to country. That is why the nature of supervisory authorities under this model is described as 'mixed'.

Table 2 – Supervisory architectures illustrated

	Number of authorities with final responsibility for AML supervision	**Nature of the supervisory authorities**
FIU model	1	external
External model	> 1	external
Internal model	> 1	internal
Hybrid model	> 1	mixed

3.4 The models exemplified

The ECOLEF study applied the models to the at that time 27 EU Member States based on the legislative texts of the Member States in the field of the prevention of money laundering (and terrorist financing).[46] Member States that belong to the FIU model are Bulgaria, the Czech Republic, Lithuania, Malta, Poland, Slovakia and Spain. The two Member States that fall under the external model are the Netherlands and Greece. The internal model appears to be present in a large group of Member States: Austria, Belgium, France, Germany, Ireland, Latvia, Luxembourg, Portugal and the United Kingdom. And, finally, Member States that belong to the hybrid model are Cyprus, Denmark, Estonia, Finland, Hungary, Italy, Romania, Slovenia and Sweden.[47] Brought together in a figure, this looks like the following. The dots represents the FIU model, the stripes represents the external model, the dark grey represents the internal model and the hybrid model is presented in light grey.

46 Van den Broek (2014) at 68-69. Due to the fact that the models were developed for the ECOLEF study, legislative changes after December 2012 have not been included in this modelling.

47 Van den Broek (2014) at 68-69.

Figure 1 – AML Supervisory Architectures in the European Union

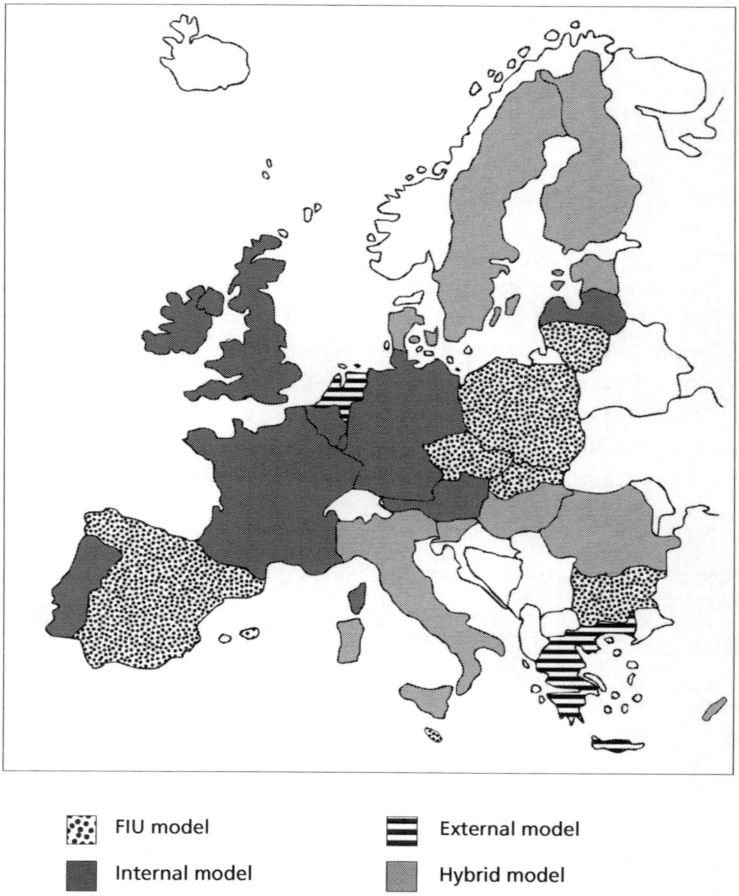

From the foregoing categorisation Spain, the Netherlands, the UK and Sweden have been selected for this research. Obviously, these Member States represent the four different models purveyed above. Spain is specifically included because it can be considered the purest form of the model it represents. In Spain, the FIU carries out supervision and has the least involvement by other authorities compared to other Member States applying this model. The UK is included because of the high level of professional associations present: out of a total of 28 supervisors, 22 are professional (and trade) associations. The Netherlands represents the external model and for reasons of practicality, linguistics and knowledge of the legal system, the Dutch supervisory architecture will be analysed in this research. Finally, Sweden is included in this research because of the fact that during the implementation of the Third Directive, the Swedish Government focused extensively on the matter of supervision.[48] This makes it an interesting country to analyse as well. The

48 Statskontoret (2008), *Tredje penningtvättsdirektivet – tillsyn och organisation*, 2008:2 (in English: *The Third Money Laundering Directive: compliance supervision and organisation in Sweden*).

following sections deal with a first outline of the supervisory architectures of the selected countries.

3.4.1 Spain

Spain exemplifies the FIU model. Supervision for the purpose of verifying compliance with preventive AML obligations is in Spain placed with the Spanish FIU: SEPBLAC (*Servicio Ejecutivo de la Comisión de Prevención del Blanqueo de Capitales e Infracciones Monetarias*). SEPBLAC is ultimately responsible for supervision with respect to the entire range of institutions and professionals that fall under the Spanish anti-money laundering legislation.[49]

The AML legislation empowers the Commission for the Prevention of Money Laundering and Monetary Offences (hereafter the 'Commission'), under whose authority SEPBLAC operates, to enter into arrangements with the three Spanish financial prudential regulators with the aim of coordinating and harmonising their AML inspections and supervisory activities with those carried out by SEPBLAC.[50] The Commission has entered into supervisory arrangements with all three regulators.[51] The general idea is that financial regulators include AML supervision in their general supervision programmes and send their supervision reports to the Commission Secretariat, another support body of the Commission. If breaches of the preventive obligations are identified, the Commission Secretariat can decide to start a sanctioning procedure. SEPBLAC, however, remains ultimately responsible for this supervision.

Chapter 4 is about the AML supervision of banks, real estate agents and accountants in Spain.

3.4.2 The Netherlands

The Netherlands demonstrates what the external model can look like at the national level. The supervision of compliance with obligations from the AML legislation is exercised by four supervisors that already had supervisory powers on the basis of other sectoral legislation.[52] The Ministers of Finance and Security & Justice appointed the following authorities: the Dutch Central Bank (*De Nederlandsche Bank, DNB*), the Netherlands Authority for the Financial Markets (*Autoriteit Financiële Markten, AFM*), the Financial

49 Section 47 in conjunction with Section 45(4)(f) *Ley 10/2010, de 28 de abril, de prevención del blanqueo de capitales y de la financiación del terrorismo, Boletín Oficial del Estado (BOE), no. 103, Sec. I, 37458-37499.* Hereafter: Act 10/2010.

50 Section 47 in conjunction with Section 44(2)(m) Act 10/2010.

51 The Commission concluded a memorandum with CNMV on 18 June 2003 and with DGSFP on 21 October 2004. The Memorandum with the Bank of Spain was last updated on 31 October 2013. See § 4.6.3.2.

52 Minister of Finance during deliberations in Parliament, *Parliamentary proceedings II*, no. 86, 21 May 2008, at 6084 (*Handelingen Tweede Kamer*).

Supervision Office[53] (*Bureau Financieel Toezicht, BFT*) and the Dutch Tax and Customs Administration/Bureau Supervision Wwft (*Belastingdienst/Bureau Toezicht Wwft, 'the Bureau'*).[54] The DNB and AFM are responsible for the supervision of financial and credit institutions, casinos and credit card companies both in the Netherlands and the overseas territories of the Netherlands, the so-called 'BES Islands'.[55] The Financial Supervision Office supervises lawyers (*advocaten*), (junior) civil-law notaries, registered accountants, accounting consultants and tax advisors. The Tax and Customs Administration/Bureau Supervision Wwft is the supervisor for real estate agents and dealers in high-value goods when they perform cash transactions of 15,000 Euros or more. Since the 10th of October 2010 it is the competent AML supervisor for all non-financial and credit institutions for the overseas territories of the Netherlands as well.

> For some years now, the Dutch Government has tried to transfer supervisory responsibility for lawyers from BFT to the Dutch Bar Association (*Nederlandse Orde van Advocaten*).[56] The Bill had not been adopted at the time of finalising this research, which means that BFT remains the formal supervisor under the Dutch AML Act.

In practice, professional associations are indirectly involved in the supervision. This is partly the result of the Dutch AML Act that states that where statutory disciplinary law systems apply, professionals subject to these disciplinary law systems cannot be sanctioned by means of the administrative sanctions under the AML Act.[57] Although the Dutch legislator finally opted for the Financial Supervision Office as the formal supervisor for legal and fiscal service providers, at the time of the enactment of the legislation it was considered that AML obligations were already embedded in the broader professional standards. Applying an administrative supervisory system to those professionals subject to statutory disciplinary law could possibly lead to concurrence between administrative and disciplinary sanctions, resulting in different courts having to adjudicate on the same

53 This is the English name that BFT uses on its own website: <www.bureauft.nl/Paginas/AboutBFT.aspx>, last visited on 9 October 2014. The Financial Supervision Office is also referred to as 'Bureau Financial Supervision'. Especially the FATF uses that name: FATF (2011), *Third Mutual Evaluation Report on the Netherlands*, 25 February 2011.

54 Section 24(1) of the *Wet ter voorkoming van Witwassen en Financieren van Terrorisme (Wwft), Stb. 2008, 303; Besluit aanwijzing toezichthouders Wet ter voorkoming van witwassen en financieren van terrorisme, Stcrt. 2008, 142* (in English: *Regulation on the appointment of supervisory authorities pursuant to the Dutch AML Act*). The Regulation was last amended via Stcrt. 2013, 35195.

55 On 10 October 2010 the Caribbean Islands of Bonaire, St. Eustatius and Saba, formerly part of the Netherlands Antilles that was dissolved with the Constitutional Reform of 2010, became special municipalities of the country of the Netherlands within the Kingdom of the Netherlands. Special AML/CTF legislation applies to the overseas part of the Netherlands, in which the Dutch financial supervisors have become anti-money laundering supervisors for the same financial and credit institutions in those overseas territories. See: Wet ter voorkoming van witwassen en financieren van terrorisme BES (Stb. 2011, 613); Besluit ter voorkoming van witwassen en financieren van terrorisme BES (Stb. 2012, 239); Besluit aanwijzing toezichtautoriteiten ex de Wet ter voorkoming van witwassen en financieren van terrorisme BES en mandaatverlening inzake handhaving en sanctionering van die wet, Stcrt. 2013, 223 as amended by Stcrt. 2013, 25564. This 'overseas' regime is not within the scope of this research. The focus is on the Netherlands' territory and the Dutch AML legislation.

56 At the time of writing, the fourth Government amendment to the Bill amending the Counsel Act and some other Acts had been presented: *Parliamentary Papers II*, 2013-14, 32 382, no. 18 (*Kamerstukken Tweede Kamer*).

57 Sections 26(2) and 27(2) Wwft.

matter, the Government concluded.[58] Likewise, BFT finds that the internal supervisors should be the first gatekeepers.[59] It has entered into supervisory arrangements with professional associations.

Since 2011, however, the Dutch Government has been trying to narrow down the role of disciplinary law enforcement in the field of the prevention of money laundering and terrorist financing. In 2011 the Ministry of Finance started a consultation procedure on a Bill to amend the AML Act. The Bill included provisions on the introduction of administrative law sanctions for those professions subjected to statutory disciplinary law systems, i.e. lawyers (*advocaten*), (junior) civil-law notaries and accountants.[60] The idea behind this proposal was that supervisors could choose between the imposition of administrative and disciplinary law sanctions and that the latter would have a particular added value where a professional should be (temporarily) banned from exercising his profession. In 2012, these specific provisions were transferred to the Bill amending the Counsel Act and some other Acts (*Wetsvoorstel herziening advocatuur*).[61] On the 22nd of January 2014, the fourth Government amendment to the Bill was presented, still upholding the introduction of administrative law sanctions for non-compliance with the AML obligations for lawyers and (junior) civil-law notaries, and indirectly for accountants.[62] At the time of finalising this research this Bill was not yet adopted, which means that the Dutch AML Act is still enforced via disciplinary law for these professions.[63]

Chapter 5 is about the AML supervision of banks, real estate agents and accountants in the Netherlands.

3.4.3 United Kingdom

With a total of 28 supervisors, the UK has by far the highest number of AML supervisors in the European Union. Besides the 22 professional (and trade) associations with supervisory competences under the preventive AML policy, there are six public bodies with supervisory responsibility. Pursuant to Regulation 23 Money Laundering Regulations 2007 (hereafter: MLR 2007 or 'the Regulations') these are the Financial Conduct Authority, the Office of Fair Trading, the Gambling Commission, Her Majesty's Revenue and Customs, the Department of Enterprise, Trade and Investment in Northern Ireland and the Secretary of State – in practice the Insolvency Service.[64] With the large presence of professional associations the UK is the best example of the internal model.

58 *Parliamentary Papers II*, 2004-05, 29 990, no. 3, at 9. For other arguments and presumptions, see: Faure et al. (2009) at 42-43.

59 FATF (2011) at 245.

60 Ministerie van Financiën, *Consultatie regeling 'Wijzigingswet Wet ter voorkoming van witwassen en financieren van terrorisme (WWFT)'*, available at: <www.internetconsultatie.nl/Wwft>, last visited on 17 March 2014.

61 *Parliamentary Papers II*, 2011-12, 32 382, no. 10 at 29-30.

62 *Parliamentary Papers II*, 2013-14, 32 382, no. 18.

63 See Faure et al. (2009) who studied the effectiveness of the disciplinary enforcement of the Dutch AML Act.

64 Cf. HM Treasury (2013), *Anti-Money Laundering and Counter Terrorist Finance Supervision Report 2012-13*, par. 7, available at: <www.gov.uk/government/publications/anti-money-laundering-and-counter-terrorist-finance-supervision-reports/anti-money-laundering-and-counter-terrorist-finance-supervision-report-2012-13>, last visited on 17 March 2014.

On the 1st of April 2013 the Financial Services Authority (FSA) was split into two new regulatory authorities. Whereas the FSA used to be the UK's integrated financial regulator, the Financial Services Act 2012 set out a new system for regulating financial services. It gave powers for prudential regulation and supervision to the newly established Prudential Regulatory Authority (PRA). The Financial Conduct Authority (FCA) regulates financial institutions that provide services to customers and is responsible for maintaining the integrity of the UK's financial markets. The FCA took over AML supervisory responsibility from the FSA.

As of the 1st of April 2014, the Office of Fair Trading has merged with the Competition Commission to become the Competition and Markets Authority (CMA). The CMA is established through the Enterprise and Regulatory Reform Act 2013 and has not taken over OFT's AML responsibility. The supervision of real estate agents has been transferred to Her Majesty's Revenue and Customs.[65] This means that the number of public bodies performing anti-money laundering supervision has diminished to five. The categorisation of the UK as falling under the internal model has not changed with this merger.

The underlying principle of the UK's preventive AML policy is that, where this is possible, professional associations include the verification of compliance with the Regulations in their overall supervisory efforts. Schedule 3 lists all professional (and trade) associations with supervisory competences in the preventive AML policy.[66]

Chapter 6 is about the AML supervision of banks, real estate agents and accountants in the United Kingdom.

3.4.4 Sweden

Sweden is an example of the hybrid model. With the implementation of the Third Directive, the Swedish Government considered the possibility and feasibility of assigning one supervisor for all institutions and professionals under the AML legislation. The Government ultimately decided, in accordance with recommendations from the Swedish Agency of Public Management, to keep the authorities that already had responsibilities under the previous legal regime and designated the county administrative boards of Stockholm, Västra Götaland, and Skåne as the supervisors for all institutions and professions that would become subject to the AML legislation with the implementation of the Directive.[67]

The following supervisors exercise AML supervision in Sweden: the Swedish Financial Supervisory Authority (*Finansinspektionen*) for all financial and credit institutions; the Gaming Board for casinos; the Swedish Bar Association for lawyers; the Supervisory Board of Public Auditors (*Revisorsnämnden*) supervises authorised and approved auditors and audit firms; and the Swedish Estate Agents Inspectorate (*Fastighetsmäklarinspektionen*)

65 HM Revenue & Customs, *April 2014: Supervision of Estate Agency Businesses by HMRC*, 31 January 2014, available at: <www.gov.uk/government/publications/april-2014-supervision-of-estate-agency-businesses-by-hmrc/april-2014-supervision-of-estate-agency-businesses-by-hmrc>, last visited on 17 March 2014.

66 Cf. Deloitte (2011), at 157-158.

67 Statskontoret (2008).

supervises real estate agents. The three country administrative boards supervise all other institutions, including dealers in high-value goods, trust and company service providers and other independent legal professionals, tax advisors, and accountants who are not authorised – provided that these professionals are registered at the Swedish Companies Registration Office (*Bolagsverket*).[68] Both the Financial Supervisory Authority and the Gaming Board are public authorities falling under the Swedish Ministry of Finance. The Ministry of Justice is the parent ministry of the Supervisory Board of Public Auditors and the Estate Agents Inspectorate. The county administrative boards are public authorities headed by county governors, who are appointed directly by the Government, and fall under the Ministry of Social Affairs. The only internal supervisor in this architecture is the Swedish Bar Association.

Chapter 7 is about the AML supervision of banks, real estate agents and accountants in Sweden.

3.5 Concluding remarks

This chapter introduced the supervisory architectures identified in the preventive AML policy within the European Union. Inspired by literature on financial law and regulation, the models developed for supervision under this policy are based on two key elements: the number of authorities with final responsibility for AML supervision and the nature of these supervisors (internal or external).

Four models can be identified. The first is the FIU model. This model's main characteristic is that the FIU is the national authority with final responsibility for AML supervision. The second model identified is the external model. Under this model only public administrative or Government authorities that have no direct or professional relationship with the supervisees formally perform supervision. These authorities share the final responsibility. The third model is the internal model. Apart from the supervision of financial and credit institutions and casinos, AML supervision is mainly carried out by professional associations. The principle is that where internal supervisors can perform AML supervision, they will be assigned with this task. All the supervisors are ultimately responsible. The last model is the hybrid model, which combines, in different gradations, different elements of the aforementioned models. So far, a mixture between internal and external supervisors, and a mixture between internal and external supervisors and the FIU can be identified. Here, too, final responsibility is shared between all the supervisors involved.

To establish the effectiveness of the architectures in the preventive AML policy at the national level, four Member States have been selected for this research. Each country represents one of the four models. Spain can be considered one of the purest examples of the FIU model. The Netherlands is chosen as an example of the external model. The UK,

68 The legislation concerning AML supervision is very fragmented in Sweden: Chapter 6, Section 1 *Penningtvättslag, SFS 2009:62* (AML Act). The county administrative boards derive their supervisory responsibility from Section 16 AML Regulation. See Chapter 7.

having 22 professional (and trade) associations carrying out AML supervision, represents the internal model, while Sweden is a country that belongs to the hybrid model. This chapter has provided a first description of the supervisory architectures of these four EU Member States. The following chapters contain a more in-depth analysis of the supervisory architectures in the Member States selected and the application thereof at the national level.

PART II

4 Anti-money laundering supervision of banks, real estate agents and accountants in Spain

4.1 Introduction

Spain is the country that represents the supervisory architecture named the FIU model.[1] Supervision for the purpose of verifying compliance with the preventive anti-money laundering obligations is assigned to the Spanish FIU named SEPBLAC (*Servicio Ejecutivo de la Comisión de Prevención del Blanqueo de Capitales e Infracciones Monetarias*).[2] This chapter offers an in-depth analysis of the supervisory system and practice in Spain regarding banks, real estate agents and accountants. The legislative, institutional and practical aspects that were identified as part of the theoretical framework of effective supervision are assessed in this chapter.

Section 4.2 starts by describing Spain's vulnerability for money laundering and the three groups of businesses specifically. Section 4.3 then outlines the legal framework for the prevention of money laundering. Both sections aim to purvey the context in which the fight against money laundering takes place in Spain. Section 4.4 deals with the institutional aspects of SEPBLAC. It must be sufficiently independent in the exercise of its supervision, and be accountable and transparent about its activities. Section 4.5 discusses the extent to which banks, real estate agents and accountants are authorised, regulated or required to register with SEPBLAC or other competent authorities. This section aims to answer the question whether SEBPLAC has, or can have, an adequate knowledge of all the institutions for which it has supervisory responsibility. Section 4.6 analyses the exercise of anti-money laundering supervision. It is verified whether SEPBLAC has adequate supervisory powers, and how it applies these in practice. Section 4.7 discusses the sanctioning regime. Unlike the other Member States included in this research, the imposition of sanctions is functionally separated from the supervision phase. The section pays attention to the doctrine of punitive administrative law and assesses the sanctioning powers, procedure and practice against banks, accountants and estate agents under the AML legislation. The last section (§ 4.8) deals with another aspect of effective supervision, namely the cooperation between AML supervisors, and with the FIU. Obviously, due to the fact that SEPBLAC is the single AML supervisor and the FIU at the same time, it is not a focal point like in the other country chapters.

1 Chapter 3.
2 Section 45 Act 10/2010.

4.2 Vulnerability of Spain for money laundering

In order to understand the context in which anti-money laundering supervision is exercised, it is relevant to have some ideas about the question whether money laundering is actually a problem in Spain. This section presents a number of studies that discuss the vulnerability for money laundering, or the scope of the problem, as well as the main predicate offences or sectors that are (considered to be) most at risk in Spain. Special attention is paid to the banking, real estate and accountancy sectors.

It appears that information about the scope of money laundering in Spain is largely absent and, where present, varies widely.[3] The ECOLEF study assessed the threat to all EU Member States, where threat is understood as 'the amount of money that could, or might, be laundered in a country if there were no barriers to laundering and there was no 'more attractive place' for the launderer to launder the money'.[4] The study ranked Spain as number 10 out of the EU Member States by estimated threat, with an estimation of 56,311 million Euros in 2009. In terms of estimated threat as a percentage of GDP in 2009, Spain was even listed relatively low as number 25 out of 27 Member States (5.4%).[5] By contrast, the US Department of State considers Spain to be a major European centre for money laundering activities and 'an important gateway for illicit narcotics entering Europe from Central and South America and North Africa'.[6] For this reason Spain is considered a country of primary concern. The amounts of money laundered or estimations thereof are not presented in this report. Even in the absence of hard figures, money laundering seems to be a point of attention for the Spanish Government. In its National Security Strategy 2013 the strengthening and improving of the investigation of money laundering is included as one of the main objectives within the fight against organised crime.[7] According to the INCSR 2014, money laundering in Spain is related mostly to drug trafficking and organised crime, as well as corruption, financial support for terrorism and tax evasion. Other important typologies concern ongoing investments in the real estate sector and other sectors (services, communications, cars, art and the financial sector), the smuggling of bulk cash, and informal money transfers to Latin America.[8] In 2006 the FATF already reported about international money transfers, organised VAT fraud, underground banking operations, drugs trafficking and smuggling, and corruption as

3 There is, although it has been required by the FATF since February 2012, no national risk assessment on money laundering in Spain which can provide reliable information on this point. Also, SEPBLAC's 2012 annual report does not refer to Spain's vulnerability for money laundering: SEPBLAC (2012), *Memoria Anual 2012.*

4 Unger and Ferwerda (2014) at 12.

5 Ibid., at 15-16.

6 US Department of State (2014), *International Narcotics Control Strategy Report: Volume 2 Money Laundering and Financial Crimes*, March 2014, at 186.

7 Spanish Government (2013), *The National Security Strategy: Sharing A Common Project*, NIPO 002130352, at 43.

8 US Department of State (2014) at 186-188.

the main predicate offences to money laundering in Spain.[9] In 2008 SEPBLAC identified correspondent banking and the real estate sector, plus a dozen other activities like cash and e-money, VAT carousels and money transfers, as the most commonly used techniques for money laundering.[10] For the real estate sector, the principal reasons mentioned were the fact that the valuation of property is very subjective and that the sector is highly sensitive to criminal behaviour like corruption and fiscal fraud.[11]

> The high level of corruption present in Spain is, for example, illustrated by the *Malaya* case. The Malaya case is one of the largest corruption scandals that Spain has ever faced. It revolved around the former mayor of Marbella, his ex-partner and ex-wife, as well as no less than 95 aldermen, lawyers, police officers, government officials and businessmen.[12] The corruption by the municipality of Marbella concerned a wide array of criminal offences varying from bribery to property fraud, and money was mainly laundered via the construction and real estate sectors. And although there are no formal figures on the spread of corruption in Spain, research also demonstrates that there have been around 814 corruption cases in the years 1996-2009.[13]

Scholars have also pointed at the vulnerability of the real estate sector for the purpose of money laundering while corruption cases in Spain have in common the use of this sector, in particular during the phases of re-zoning and development.[14] Paláez Martos summarises the vulnerability of the estate sector as follows: 'the reasons for which the real estate sector is susceptible to being used for money laundering are very diverse. A highlight is the fact that this sector is normally a value-stable sector, with great prospects of capital gains and a lack of transparency with respect to the valuation process, with a high-unit value

9 FATF (2006), *Third Mutual Evaluation Report on Spain*, 26 June 2006 at 11. Cf. Interview SEPBLAC, October 2011 in which representatives pointed at economic offences, tax crimes, organised crime and drug trafficking as the most common predicate offences, and to the vulnerability of the real estate sector. See also: Organización profesional de Inspectores de Hacienda del Estado (2007), *Fraude, Corrupción y Blanqueo de Capitales en España*, November 2007, at 1, available at <www.inspectoresdehacienda.org/attachments/Documento24.pdf>, last visited on 27 March 2014. This report lists the underground economy, financial fraud, urban and financial corruption as important money laundering typologies.

10 SEPBLAC (2008), *Tipologías de blanqueo de capitales*, available at <www.sepblac.es/espanol/ informes_y_publicaciones/informe_sobre_tipologias.pdf>, last visited on 27 March 2014.

11 Ibid., at 2; Peláez Martos, J.M. (2009), *Fraude Fiscal, Blanqueo de capitales y corrupción en el Sector Inmobiliario*, Kluwer España at 42 et seq.

12 Audiencia Provincial de Málaga, Sentencia no. 179/13, 16 April 2013; Audiencia Provincial de Málaga, Sentencia no. 535/2013, 4 October 2013. The Spanish media have reported widely on the *Malaya* case, for example: El País, *Isabel Pantoja condenada por blanqueo a 24 meses de prisión*, 18 April 2013; El País, *Maite Zalvídar declara que acusó a Julián Muñoz por despecho*, 15 October 2012; ABC Andalucía, *El cerebro del caso Malaya, Juan Antonio Roca, condenado a once años de cárcel*, 5 October 2013; El Mundo, *Corrupción en Marbella*, availabe at <www.elmundo.es/especiales/2006/04/espana/corrupcion_marbella/trama.html>, last visited on 27 March 2014.; RtvES, *El 'caso Malaya', la operación más importante en España contra la corrupción urbanística*, 2 October 2013.

13 Costas-Pérez, E., Solé-Ollé, A., and Sorribas-Navarro, P. (2012), 'Corruption scandals, voter information and accountability', *European Journal of Political Economy*, vol. 28, issue 4, pp. 469-484 at 472. Cf. Jerez Darías, L.M., Martín Martín, V.O. and Pérez González, R. (2012), 'Aproximación a una geografía de la corrupción urbanística en España', *Ería*, issue 87, pp. 5-18 at 12-14 who come to an estimation of 676 urban corruption cases at the municipal level in 2000-2010.

14 Peláez Martos (2009) at 43 and 349-356. Cf. Ferro Veiga, J.M. (2012), *Propriedad inmobiliairia: Blanqueo de capital y crimen organizado*, ECU: Alicante; Benito Sánchez, C.D. (2006), 'Blanqueo de capitales y fraude inmobiliario', in: Sanz Mulas, N. (ed.), *El Desafío de la Criminalidad Organizada*, Comares Editorial: Granada, pp. 95-129.

of goods and the habitual use of bearer shares as a means of payment' (*own translation, MB*).[15] In combination with the flourishing real estate market in the 1990s and early 2000s and a favourable quality-price ratio compared to neighbouring countries, this makes the Spanish real estate sector attractive for launderers. This was also mentioned in the country report of Spain to the EU Anti-Corruption Report 2014, wherein it was stated that '[w]hile high public spending on construction and urban development cannot be directly attributed to corruption, it contributes to an overall context which, jointly with weak supervision of decision-making at regional and local levels, increases the vulnerability of this sector to fraud and corruption'.[16]

Information about banks', accountants' or real estate agents' own involvement in money laundering operations is largely absent. Banks do not appear to have been recently involved in large money laundering scandals in Spain – although a number of banks have been sanctioned for non-compliance with the preventive obligations in the past few years.[17] Public information does not suggest any involvement by accountants in money laundering cases either. Above it was already suggested that the real estate sector is highly vulnerable to money laundering, most prominently due to its links with corruption. In addition, some real estate businesses have in the past been sanctioned for non-compliance with obligations stemming from the predecessor of Act 10/2010.[18]

4.3 Legal framework for the prevention of money laundering

This section presents the legal framework for the prevention of money laundering in Spain, from the legislative level to lower levels of regulation. It reveals a serious weakness in this framework.

The most significant piece of legislation in Spain is Act 10/2010 with regard to the prevention of money laundering and the financing of terrorism (hereafter Act 10/2010 or 'AML Act'), which is the result of the implementation of the Third Directive.[19] Spain exceeded the final implementation deadline for the Directive by 30 months. In October 2009 the ECJ already condemned Spain for not having implemented the Directive on time.[20] In March 2010 the European Commission started a second infringement procedure, but this was soon dismissed with the adoption of the AML Act in April of that year.[21] The Act has brought together in one act all norms that were previously laid down in a number of acts and royal decrees.[22] The Spanish Government considered that this situation was dysfunctional and decided to draft a new act to repeal the former anti-money laundering act, to expand the

15 Peláez Martos (2009) at 42.

16 European Commission (2014a), *Annex: Spain to EU Anti-Corruption Report 2014*, COM(2014) 38 final, at 11.

17 See § 4.7.4.

18 European Commission (2014a) at 11.

19 *Ley 10/2010, de 28 de abril, de prevención del blanqueo de capitales y de la financiación del terrorismo, Boletín Oficial del Estado (BOE), no. 103, Sec. I, 37458-37499*. Hereafter Act 10/2010 or AML Act.

20 ECJ EU, C-502/08, *Commission v Spain* [2009] ECR I-00161.

21 European Commission (2005), *Press Release: Commission takes action to ensure that 12 Member States implement EU rules*, IP/10/305, 18 March 2005.

22 The preamble to Act 10/2010 lists all the acts and royal decrees.

new act to the matter of terrorist financing and to limit the scope of Act 12/2003 to the blocking of terrorist funds once again.[23]

Together with the entry into force of the Act a new royal decree was pronounced, which should have entered into force in April 2011.[24] However, due to the announcement from the FATF that it would adopt new recommendations in February 2012, the procedure for drafting the decree was put on hold due to expected changes.[25] For this reason, Royal Decree 925/1995 (hereafter RD 925/1995) and the regulation (*reglamento*) that it approved under the former AML Act would remain in force until the new decree would be adopted.[26] More than two years after the publication of the new FATF Recommendations and four years after the entry into force of Act 10/2010, there is still no royal decree.[27] Until 30 September 2013, the draft text was open to public consultation.[28] Until the end of March 2014, no further information has been available about the progress of its adoption.[29] From a legal perspective, in particular the principles of legality and legal certainty, the absence of a royal decree issued under the current AML act is highly problematic. Because the royal decree was issued under the previous AML act that was repealed with the entry into force of the current act, the legal basis of the royal decree has formally disappeared. The first transitional provision to the AML Act does state that the former decree will remain in force until a new one is drafted. The question is how transitional are four years really? Can this provision still serve as the legal basis for the Royal Decree 925/1995? The situation is also inconvenient from a legal certainty point of view. The first transitional provision to Act 10/2010 states that the former decree applies 'insofar as it is not incompatible' with the new Act. In the absence of a clear list stating which provisions of the Decree should be considered (in)compatible with Act 10/2010, this situation results in uncertainty for obliged institutions and professionals, as well as for SEPBLAC. Obliged institutions and professionals now have to decide for themselves whether a particular provision should be considered (in)compatible and how this affects their obligations and internal control policies and procedures. There is a clear risk that provisions are interpreted and applied differently among the various institutions, and thus could cause an inconsistent application of the law. A conflict could also arise on the interpretation of norms between the obliged institutions and professionals, on the one hand, and SEPBLAC on the other. This clearly negatively affects legal certainty, as well as the enforceability of the norms.

4

23 Preamble to Act 10/2010.

24 FATF (2010), *Fourth Follow Up Report on Spain*, at 7.

25 Interview Ministry of Economy and Finance, November 2011.

26 First transitional provision to Act 10/2010. *Real Decreto 925/1995, de 9 de junio, por el que se aprueba el Reglamento de la Ley 19/1993, de 28 de diciembre, sobre determinadas medidas de prevención del blanqueo de capitales, BOE, no. 160, Sec. I, 6 de julio 1995, 20521-20528, modificado por Real Decreto 54/2005, de 21 de enero, por el que se modifican el Reglamento de la Ley 19/1993, de 28 de diciembre, sobre determinadas de prevención del blanqueo de capitales, aprobado por el Real Decreto 925/1995, de 9 de junio, y otras normas de regulación del sistema bancario, financiero y asegurador, BOE no. 19, Sec. I, 22 de enero 2005, 2573-2583.* Hereafter 'RD 925/1995'.

27 Verification via <www.boe.es>, last visited on 27 March 2014.

28 *Proyecto de Real Decreto por el que se aprueba el Reglamento de la Ley 10/2010, de 28 de abril, de prevención del blanqueo de capitales y de la financiación del terrorismo, Audiencia Pública hasta el 30 de septiembre de 2013*, available at <www.cpbc.tesoro.es/Novedades.PDF/Proyecto%20Reglamento%20Ley%2010%20 2010%20Audiencia%20P%C 3%BAblica.pdf>, last visited on 27 March 2014.

29 See § 1.8 where it was stated that the Royal Decree was eventually adopted in May 2014.

Finally, the situation is problematic as it appears that some obligations arising from the FATF Recommendations and the Third Directive are not (fully) implemented and that there are gaps in the Spanish legislation. The US Department of State commented in 2014 that in the absence of implementing regulations '(...) implementing regulations are not yet fully promulgated. Spain should take action to ensure such regulations are established in a timely manner'.[30] From the perspective of effective supervision, this view is to be fully supported.

The legislation in the field of the prevention of money laundering is complemented by a number of lower-level regulations issued by the competent ministries (*ordenes ministeriales*).[31] An important ministerial regulation is EHA/2444/2007 on requirements and guidance with respect to external experts that perform reviews of the internal policies and procedures of obliged institutions.[32] Like RD 925/1995, all ministerial regulations have been adopted under the previous legal regime. Likewise, the provisions of the ministerial regulations apply insofar as they do not conflict with the provisions of the AML Act. The difficulties arising from such a situation were discussed above. The last legal instrument in the preventive anti-money laundering policy is a resolution issued by the Treasury and Financial Policy General Directorate of the Ministry of Economy and Competitiveness, which publishes the agreement of the Commission for the Prevention of Money Laundering and Monetary Offences (*Comisión de Prevención del Blanqueo de Capitales e Infracciones Monetarias)* establishing the equivalent third countries to the Spanish AML/CTF policy.[33]

SEPBLAC has also issued guidance in order to support the obliged institutions and professionals in developing policies for the prevention of money laundering.[34] The guidance is neither legally binding nor enforceable against obliged institutions and professionals,

---

30 US Department of State (2014) at 188.

31 An overview of all regulations in force can be found at the website of the Commission for the Prevention of Money Laundering and Monetary Offences <www.cpbc.tesoro.es> or from SEPBLAC: <www.sepblac.es>. Over the years Government changes have led to the creation of new Ministries. The Ministry of Economy (ECO) was changed to the Ministry of Economy and Finance (EHA) and in November 2011 it was split into two Ministries: the Ministry of Economy and Competitiveness and the Ministry of Finance and Public Administration. The Treasury and Financial Policy General Directorate, responsible for the preventive anti-money laundering policy in Spain, was brought under the umbrella of the Ministry of Economy and Competitiveness. References to the Ministry of Economy and Finance (EHA) should be understood as references to the Ministry of Economy and Competitiveness.

32 See § 4.6.3. *Orden EHA/2444/2007, de 31 de julio, por la que se desarrolla el Reglamento de la Ley 19/1993, de 28 de diciembre, sobre determinadas medidas de prevención del blanqueo de capitales, aprobado por Real Decreto 925/1995, de 9 de junio, en relación con el informe de experto externo sobre los procedimientos y órganos de control interno y comunicación establecidos para prevenir el blanqueo de capitales, BOE no. 190, Sec. I, de 9 de agosto 2007, 34113-34118.*

33 *Resolución de 10 de agosto de 2012, de la Secretaría General del Tesoro y Política Financiera, por la que se publica el Acuerdo de 17 de julio de 2012, de la Comisión de Prevención del Blanqueo de Capitales e Infracciones Monetarias, por el que se determinan las jurisdicciones que establecen requisitos equivalentes a los de la legislación española de prevención del blanqueo de capitales y de la financiación del terrorismo, BOE no. 202, Sec. III, 23 de agosto 2012, 60331.*

34 SEPBLAC (2013), *Recomendaciones sobre las medidas de control interno para la prevención del blanqueo de capitales y de la financiación del terrorismo*, 4 April 2013.

but functions as a supporting tool for complying with the preventive obligations.[35] Legislation closely related to the legal framework for the prevention of money laundering is also present. Although this is not of direct importance for SEPBLAC's functioning as the supervisory authority, it is relevant for the obliged institutions and professionals that have to comply with this legislation. In § 4.5 attention is paid to the applicable legislation regarding the authorisation of banks, and the regulation of real estate agents and accountants.

4.4 SEPBLAC

This section deals with the institutional aspects of SEPBLAC. SEPBLAC's institutional embedding is first explained in section 4.4.1. This is followed by section 4.4.2 on SEPBLAC's (relative) political and market independence and the legal norms regulating its accountability. Attention is in particular paid to SEPBLAC's supervisory functions and less so to its FIU-related functions. This section ends with some concluding remarks (§ 4.4.3).

4.4.1 Institutional embedding

Section 45 Act 10/2010 introduces SEPBLAC and the Commission Secretariat as support bodies of the Commission for the Prevention of Money Laundering and Monetary Offences (hereafter also the 'Commission').[36] Because it is important for understanding SEPBLAC's institutional embedding, § 4.4.1.1 first discusses the organisation, the legal basis and the tasks of the Commission. Subsection 4.4.1.2 is on SEPBLAC itself.

4.4.1.1 Commission for the Prevention of Money Laundering and Monetary Offences

The Commission is an interministerial policy-making body in charge of the coordination of the prevention of money laundering. It is 'the public body which ultimately coordinates, directs and promotes the activities for the prevention of the use of the financial system or of enterprises of any other nature for money laundering, as well as for the prevention of monetary offences of a criminal nature and administrative infringements of the regulations on foreign economic transactions'.[37] The Commission should reflect an adequate representation of the public prosecutor's office, the ministries and other authorities with competences in this policy, the financial regulators and the autonomous communities with responsibility for protecting people and property and maintaining

35 Interview SEPBLAC, October 2013; Cf. SEPBLAC (2013) at 1.
36 The Commission Secretariat (*Secretaríat de la Comisión*) has responsibilities in the sanctioning procedure for breaches of preventive anti-money laundering obligations. See § 4.7.
37 García Sanz, J. and G. San Pedro (2007), 'Spain', in: Muller, W.H., C.H. Kälin and J.G. Goldsworth (eds.), *Anti-Money Laundering: International Law and Practice*, John Wiley & Sons Ltd., pp. 513-526 at 516.

public safety.[38] It convenes two to three times a year to discuss general policy matters, as well as international and European developments.[39]

The Commission's legal basis can be found in Section 44 of Act 10/2010. It is a dependent collegiate body (órgano *colegiado dependiente*).[40] Collegiate bodies are bodies that consist of representatives from the public administration as well as other organisations representing social interests, in order to coordinate, discuss and take decisions that strengthen particular public policies. The Public Administration, Authorities and Procedures Act (hereafter LPA) states that collegiate bodies are part of the public administration to which they belong, but do not, in principle, form part of their hierarchical structure.[41] Act 10/2010 states, however, that the Commission is subordinate (*dependiente*) to the Secretariat of State for Economy and Business Support which is part of the Ministry of Economy and Competitiveness. The Commission is also chaired by the Secretary of State for Economy and Business Support.[42] The Commission thus falls directly under this Ministry. This conclusion is strengthened by the fact that the Minister of Economy and Competitiveness is liable for the actions of the bodies of the Commission for the Prevention of Money Laundering and Monetary Offences under the terms established by the LPA.[43] This Act states that individuals are entitled to be compensated by the relevant competent public administration for any harm they suffer to any of their property and rights, except for cases of force majeure, provided that the harm is a result of the normal or abnormal functioning of public services.[44] This provision is drafted in a wide sense, applies to all types of public administration and all kinds of activities as well.[45] The Minister of Economy and Competitiveness can thus be held liable for activities undertaken by the Commission Secretariat and SEPBLAC.

> Next to leading and promoting activities for the prevention of money laundering, and violations concerning foreign economic transactions, the Commission's tasks are – inter alia – collaborating with law enforcement agencies and coordinating the investigation and prevention activities carried out by other bodies of the public administration that have competences in this policy; ensuring the most effective assistance to the courts, public prosecution and the criminal police; facilitating cooperation between the public administration and the professional organisations of institutions and professionals covered by the Act; and, finally, developing statistics on money laundering and terrorist

38 Section 44(3) Act 10/2010. Still awaiting the new royal decree, Section 20 RD 925/1995 contains an exact list of authorities and required positions that should be represented in the Commission.

39 Interview Ministry of Economy and Finance, November 2011.

40 Ministry of Economy and Competitiveness (2014), *Economía: Estructura y competencias*, available at <www.mineco.gob.es>, last visited on 27 March 2014.

41 Section 22 *Ley 30/1992 del Régimen Jurídico de las Administraciones Públicas y del Procedimiento Administrativo Común, modificado por Ley 4/1999, de 13 de enero 1999, de modificación de la Ley 30/1992, de 26 de noviembre, del Régimen Jurídico de las Administraciones Públicas y del Procedimiento Administrativo Común, BOE no. 12, Sec. I, 14 de enero 1999.* Title II, Chapter II LPA applies to collegiate bodies and contains rules determining the applicable legal regime, the tasks and powers of the President, the rights and duties of members, the appointment, removal, replacement and functions of the Secretary and the system of keeping minutes.

42 Sections 44(1) and 44(3) Act 10/2010.

43 Section 45(6) Act 10/2010.

44 Section 139(1) LPA.

45 Sections 139-144 LPA regulate the extra-contractual liability of the public administration in more detail.

financing.[46] The Commission is required by law to cooperate to the fullest extent possible with the Commission on Terrorist Financing Monitoring as well, which is a similar inter-ministerial working group functioning under the act that regulates the blocking of terrorist funds.[47] And it has a wide range of tasks and powers regarding SEPBLAC, which will be discussed in § 4.4.2.[48]

The Commission may act through its operational body called the Standing Committee (*Comité Permanente*). This Committee is composed of representatives of fewer authorities than those in the Commission and it convenes almost every two months.[49] A limited number of tasks that were originally assigned to the Commission can be performed by the Standing Committee. It may guide the actions of SEPBLAC and approve its organisational structure and operational guidelines, approve the annual supervision plans of SEPBLAC and the financial regulators to the extent that they carry out AML inspections of institutions and persons falling within the scope of Act 10/2010, and develop requirements for obliged institutions within the scope of the obligations of the Act. The Standing Committee can perform other tasks that are explicitly assigned to it by the Commission as well.[50]

4.4.1.2 SEPBLAC

SEPBLAC is a dependent body, both organically and functionally (órganica *y funcionalmente*), of the Commission for the Prevention of Money Laundering and Monetary Offences. It does not have its own legal personality.[51] The Bank of Spain (*Banco de España*) is in charge of SEPBLAC's economic, budgetary and hiring regime.[52] The most important tasks of SEPBLAC are to receive reports on suspicions of money laundering and terrorist financing and systematic reports, to analyse this information and to take the necessary actions in each case (the so-called 'FIU-related tasks'); to inform the public prosecution, criminal police and other competent administrative bodies of reasonable indications of crimes or administrative offences; and to supervise compliance with the anti-money obligations by obliged institutions and professionals.[53]

In 2013, 78 people were employed at SEPBLAC.[54] Staff from SEPBLAC are seconded from the Bank of Spain, the Tax Authority, the National Police and the Civil Guard.[55] SEPBLAC's overall budget for the past couple of years has been approximately 11 million Euros annually.[56] The task of supervision is carried out by the Supervision Department of

46 Section 45(2)(a-c) and (n) Act 10/2010.
47 Section 44(4) Act 10/2010.
48 Section 45(2)(d-g) Act 10/2010.
49 Section 21 RD 925/1995; Interview Ministry of Economy and Finance, November 2011.
50 Section 44(3), second paragraph, Act 10/2010. See more in § 4.4.2.
51 Interview SEPBLAC, October 2013.
52 Section Article 45(3) Act 10/2010. It means that payments for seconded staff are made through the Bank of Spain, and this is also the case for the use of buildings, IT systems and other facilities.
53 See for a full overview of all of SEPBLAC's tasks Section 45(4) Act 10/2010.
54 Interview SEPBLAC, October 2013.
55 Interview SEPBLAC, October 2011.
56 Deleanu, I. (2014), 'FIUs in the European Union – facts and figures, functions and facilities', in: Unger et al., *The Economic and Legal Effectiveness of the European Union's Anti-Money Laundering Policy*, Edward Elgar Publishing Ltd: Cheltenham, pp. 97-124 at 107.

SEPBLAC, which in 2013 consisted of 11 FTE (full-time equivalent).[57] The Supervision Department is small, especially in the light of the number of obliged institutions and professionals, which came to a total of 22,258 in 2012.[58] Therefore the Supervision Department receives support from the staff of two analytical units of SEPBLAC. In 2013 three members of staff from other departments supported the Supervision Department on a part-time basis.[59] These people can perform on-site inspections, although this is not the core function of their work.[60] The small number of staff for the exercise of supervisory tasks is worrisome. This was also pointed out by the FATF in 2006.[61] It remains to be seen in § 4.6 whether it allows SEPBLAC to have a sufficiently high supervision intensity in practice, with approximately 11 FTE (2011) to 14 FTE (2013) supervising 22,258 institutions (2012). This number includes 75 banks, 5,260 auditors, accountants and/or tax advisors, and 4,720 real estate agents or real estate businesses.[62] Even if this supervision is risk-based, it seems difficult – if not impossible – to carry out supervision in an effective manner.[63]

In sum, the authorities involved in the anti-money laundering policy in Spain can be illustrated in a simplified manner as follows.

57 Interview SEPBLAC, October 2013. Another 3 FTE were then said to be foreseen in the near future.

58 SEPBLAC (2012) at 24-25.

59 Interview SEPBLAC, October 2013.

60 Interview SEPBLAC, October 2011.

61 FATF (2006) at 112: 'Given the size and current structure of the financial sector and the small number of inspectors, the evaluators express some concerns on whether a proper and adequate AML/CFT supervision can take place in Spain, especially when considering the need to inspect all medium and smaller sized financial institutions (including the DNFBPs).'

62 SEPBLAC (2012) at 24-25.

63 Cf. Stouten (2012) at 287-290 for similar considerations in relation to the *Bureau Financieel Toezicht* (Financial Supervision Office). Although somewhat outdated, the FATF expressed the same concerns in 2006: FATF (2006), at 112: '(...) concerns on whether a proper and adequate AML/CFT supervision can take place in Spain, especially when considering the need to inspect all medium and smaller sized financial institutions (including the DNFBPs).'

Figure 2 – Institutional organisation of the preventive anti-money laundering policy in Spain

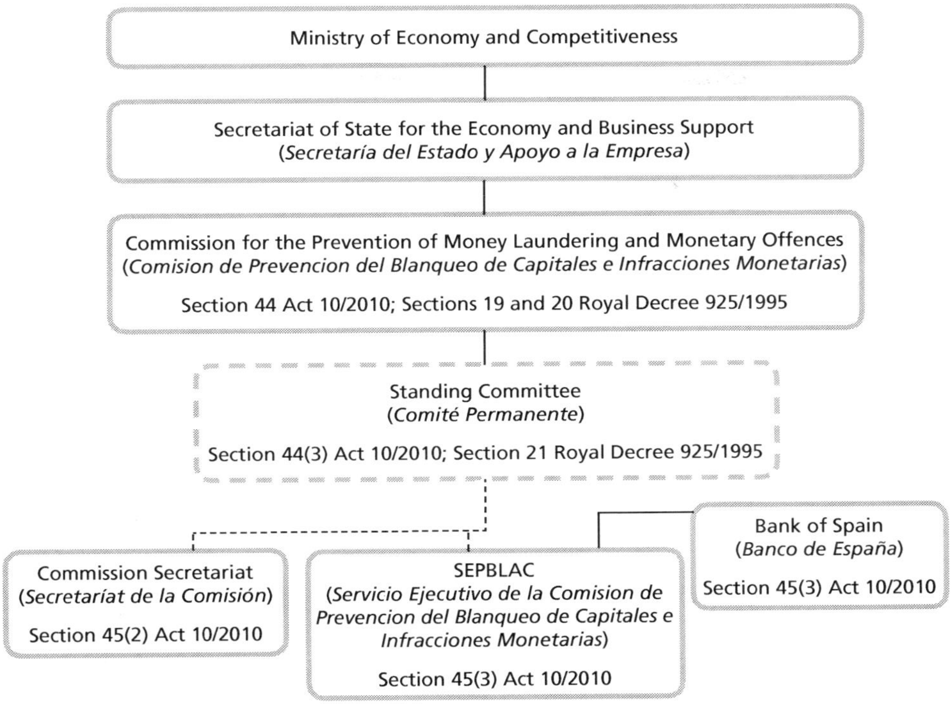

4

4.4.2 Independence and accountability

The previous section showed that SEPBLAC falls under the authority of the Commission for the Prevention of Money Laundering and Monetary Offences. The Commission has a number of tasks in relation to the functioning of SEPBLAC. Some of its tasks it can delegate to the Standing Committee.[64] The Commission:

- appoints the director of SEPBLAC subject to a proposal from the Chairman of the Commission, after consultation with the Bank of Spain;
- approves, after consultation with the Bank of Spain, the budget for SEPBLAC[65];
- enters into arrangements with any of the three financial regulators concerning the coordination of anti-money laundering supervision between SEPBLAC and themselves, to ensure that they carry out their duties efficiently;

64 Section 44(2)(f), 44(2)(g), 44(2)(h) and 44(3) Act 10/2010. No information has been made public as to whether the Commission has delegated other powers to the Standing Committee.

65 This budget is provided by the DG Treasury and Financial Policy, which falls under the Secretariat of State for the Economy and Business Support, to the Bank of Spain. The Bank of Spain has drawn up a separate account through which the funds for SEPBLAC are channelled in accordance with Section 45(5) Act 10/2010; Interview SEPBLAC, October 2011.

- provides ongoing guidance to the actions of SEPBLAC and approves its organisational structure and operational guidelines;
- approves SEPBLAC's annual supervision plans and, in case there are supervisory arrangements in place, those of the financial regulators.[66]

The powers which the Commission has vis-à-vis SEPBLAC are many and far-reaching. We have seen that for effective supervision an adequate level of independence is required. This means that the powers of politics (or the market) may not influence the individual decision-making procedures and day-to-day practice within the supervisory authority. The fact that the Commission falls directly under the Ministry of Economy and Competitiveness combined with the various powers of the Commission, especially the powers to formally approve SEPBLAC's operational guidelines and the annual supervision plans, shows that SEPBLAC cannot act independently without (the risk of) being unduly influenced. With regard to the annual supervision plans it can be pointed out that it is not uncommon that supervisory authorities draft their (annual) supervision plans in consultation with the organ under whose formal responsibility they operate, but formal approval as stipulated in Section 44, paragraph 2, under g Act 10/2010 is going, at least in my opinion, a step further. Admittedly, true independence depends on the content of the approval of the Standing Committee. That is, whether the approval is a mere yes or no decision, whether the Commission can influence the annual supervision plans on a general level or even an individual level, and whether approval can be made subject to certain conditions or standards that SEPBLAC must adhere to. SEPBLAC representatives have explained that the Standing Committee or the Commission can amend the proposals for annual supervision plans in any way they find suitable.[67] SEPBLAC may make proposals for annual supervision plans, but these can be fully amended and changed by the Commission or its Standing Committee. Therefore, one cannot speak of an adequate level of political independence on the side of SEPBLAC.

As regards obliged institutions and professionals, the AML Act or its regulations do not reflect any kind of formal relationship between SEPBLAC and this group. There are no panels with representatives from the sector at SEPBLAC, nor is there a financial relationship between the obliged institutions and professionals and SEPBLAC. The composition of the Commission for the Prevention of Money Laundering and Monetary Offences does also not indicate any relationship between the Commission and the obliged institutions and professionals.[68] Thus, no further remarks are to be made about SEPBLAC's market independence.

Having concluded that from the theoretical framework of effective supervision SEPBLAC does not have an adequate level of political independence and falls directly under the Secretariat of State of Economy and Business Support from the Ministry of Economy and Competitiveness, the picture becomes more diffuse when looking at the legal norms that regulate accountability. The AML Act only contains one explicit requirement for

66 Section 44(d-g) and (m) Act 10/2010.
67 Interview SEPBLAC, October 2013.
68 Section 44(3) Act 10/2010 in conjunction with Section 20 Royal 925/1995.

SEPBLAC to report to the Commission on the performance of its supervisory activities. It concerns the reporting on an annual basis to the Commission 'on actions that were included in the previous year's supervision plan but which were not able to be carried out, where applicable'.[69] Other than this, what I would call, negative form of accountability, there are no explicit norms that set the accountability from SEPBLAC to the Commission, or to the Secretariat of State of Economy and Business Support. Indirectly, SEPBLAC could be required to submit to the Standing Committee or the Commission any reports requested.[70] Whether this suffices as a general norm on which an ongoing accountability relationship can be based is doubtful. The norm is of a very open nature and there are no regulations that detail what kind of reports could be required from SEPBLAC, what should be included in the reports, when the reports should be submitted, and so on. In practice, there is some form of accountability by means of annual reports, but SEPBLAC has a poor practice here. While in 2007 and 2008 annual reports were published on its website, in the three years thereafter no such reports were published. Instead, SEPBLAC published some figures on its website during these years. The annual report for the year 2012 is the first report in years that SEPBLAC has published on its website. Unfortunately, and also very surprisingly, there is not a single reference to the supervisory activities undertaken by SEPBLAC during that year.[71] One still needs to rely on the one statistic placed on its website in that respect.[72]

4

Norms that oblige the Commission for the Prevention of Money Laundering and Monetary Offences to account for the activities performed are completely absent well. The AML Act does not state anything about this, nor does the LPA. Moreover, in practice it seems that the Commission is not actively seeking transparency in order to be accountable to the wider public. Its website does not contain any reports or other documents that give an insight into the meetings held, the activities performed and the results thereof, by the Commission and by its support bodies.[73]

4.4.3 Concluding remarks

This section has presented the complex institutional environment of Spain's supervisory authority, SEPBLAC. It not only has supervisory responsibility under the preventive anti-money laundering policy, but also functions as the FIU. This means that one of its most important tasks is to receive reports on suspicions of money laundering and terrorist financing and systematic reports, and to analyse this information. SEPBLAC falls under the Commission for the Prevention of Money Laundering and Monetary Offences, which is a dependent collegiate body falling under the authority of the Secretariat of State for the Economy and Business Support. This Secretariat belongs to the Ministry of Economy and Competitiveness. A wide variety of authorities are represented within

69 Section 48(1), third paragraph, Act 10/2010.
70 Section 45(4)(e) of Act 10/2010.
71 SEBPLAC (2012).
72 SEPBLAC (2012a), *Datos de actividad: Supervision – entidades inspeccionadas*, available at <www.sepblac.es/espanol/acerca_sepblac/estadisticas/2012/pdf/entidades_inspeccionadas.pdf>, last visited on 27 March 2014.
73 Website CPBCIM, <www.cpbc.tesoro.es>, last visited on 27 March 2014.

the Commission, which is chaired by the Secretary of State for Economy and Business Support. The Commission, possibly through its Standing Committee, has a wide range of far-reaching powers with respect to the functioning of SEPBLAC. Among these powers are the authority to appoint the director, to decide on SEPBLAC's budget, to guide its actions, and to formally approve its organisational structure, operational guidelines and annual supervision plans. From the theoretical framework of effective supervision, it can be concluded that SEPBLAC has an inadequate level of political independence. There are no issues with respect to SEPBLAC's market independence. Accountability norms for SEPBLAC are largely absent. There is one very general obligation in the AML Act to submit to the Commission any reports requested, but it is doubtful whether this can be used for an ongoing accountability relationship. Finally, this section has observed the small number of staff for the exercise of supervisory tasks.

4.5 The regulation of banks, accountants and real estate agents

This section verifies the extent to which banks, real estate agents and accountants are regulated sectors or professions in Spain. It gives an insight into the question whether the SEPBLAC has, or can have, an adequate knowledge of its supervisees.

4.5.1 Banks

Based on the EU directives on banking and the embedding in Section 149, first paragraph, under 11 Spanish Constitution 1978 (hereafter CE 1978), there are numerous laws and regulations in place in Spain that regulate the activities of banks.[74] Regarding the authorisation process for banks, however, the Discipline and Intervention of Credit Institutions Act (hereafter DICIA) and Royal Decree 1245/1995 on the formation of banks, cross-border activity, and other issues relating to the legal regime for credit institution, are the most important.[75] Banking activities have to be authorised, otherwise a credit institution is not allowed to carry out any banking activity in Spain.[76] This is only different for banks from other EU or EEA Member States which operate directly or through branches in Spain, and which have been granted a licence by their national financial regulator. This is due to the 'home state control principle', based on EU law.[77] The Bank of Spain is the responsible authority for the authorisation of banks.[78] It is obliged

74 Vega Serrano, J.M. (2011), *La Regulación Bancaria*, La Ley, at 83; Banco de España, *Bancos privados*, available at <www.bde.es/bde/es/secciones/normativas/Regulacion_de_En/Estatal/Bancos__privados.html>, last visited on 27 March 2014.

75 *Ley 26/1988, de 29 de julio, sobre Disciplina e Intervención de las Entidades de Crédito, BOE no. 182, Sec. I, 30 de julio 1988, 23524-23534; Real Decreto 1245/1995, de 14 de julio, sobre Creación de Bancos, actividad transfronteriza y otras cuestiones relativas al Régimen Jurídico de las Entidades de Crédito, BOE no. 181, 31 julio 1995, 23380-23389.*

76 Section 28(1) DICIA. Cf. Vega Serrano (2011) at 85-90 about the character of the banking authorisation.

77 Section 51-54 DICIA. The home state control principle is a means to facilitate passporting and based on European financial directives, in particular the banking directives. This system, however, is being abandoned step-by-step with the Europeanisation of financial supervision, i.e. the reforms for a new institutional framework of financial supervision in the EU. See: Ottow, A. (2011a), 'Het Europese toezicht op de financiële markten', *Regelmaat* 2011/4, pp. 202-212; Ottow (2014) at 123-143.

78 See about the Bank of Spain: Vega Serrano (2011) at 232-240.

to inform the General Secretariat of the Treasury and Financial Policy of the Ministry of Economy and Competitiveness of the opening of an authorisation procedure, and the processing and completion thereof.[79]

> The procedure commences with an application from a credit institution. Section 2 RD 1245/1995 establishes in a detailed fashion the requirements that banks must fulfil in order to obtain authorisation. One requirement is the establishment of an adequate internal control and communications procedure and a body in order to anticipate and prevent the performance of transactions related to money laundering. Other requirements concern the integrity and professional reputation of the shareholders, directors and management involved (the so-called fit and properness criteria), an initial capital of no less than 18 million Euros, the limitation of statutory purposes to the activities of a credit institution, the existence of a board of directors consisting of no less than five members, and more.[80] The application must be accompanied by a number of documents that can serve as proof of compliance with these requirements. The applying institution must provide drafts of the articles of association, demonstrate the programme of activities which contains the types of business activities envisaged, the soundness and adequacy of the administrative and accounting procedures and internal control procedures, as well as the procedure and internal control bodies to forestall and prevent operations related to money laundering, and a list of persons who will be on the board of directors, have a management function with detailed information on their professional and business reputation, training and professional activity and a declaration of their willingness to exercise good governance.[81]

Before deciding on the authorisation the Bank of Spain is obliged to request from SEPBLAC a report about the adequacy of the procedure and internal control bodies to forestall and prevent operations related to money laundering as foreseen in the applicant's programme of activities.[82] Banking authorisation must be refused by the Bank of Spain when the requirements are not complied with or the documentation is not provided. Authorisation is especially refused where – considering the need to guarantee the sound and prudent management of the future bank – the shareholders who are going to have a significant holding or percentage of voting rights or capital are not found suitable.[83] If none of the grounds for refusal laid down in Section 4 are present, the institution can be authorised for banking activities. Upon authorisation banks must register with the Commercial Companies Register (*Registro Mercantil*) and be included in the Special Register of the Bank of Spain.[84] This register is publicly available on the website of the Bank of Spain and can be consulted.[85] The bank must commence its banking activities within one year after the authorisation has been provided, otherwise the authorisation can be withdrawn.[86] The withdrawal of an authorisation is not considered to be a sanction, but rather an observation of non-compliance with the requirements.[87]

79 Section 1(1) RD 1245/1995.
80 Section 2(1) RD 1245/1995.
81 Section 3 RD 1245/1995.
82 Section 1 in conjunction with Section 3(b) RD 1245/1995; Vega Serrano (2011) at 94.
83 Section 4 RD 1245/1995.
84 Section 5(1) in conjunction with Section 1(3) and 1(4) RD 1245/1995; Vega Serrano (2011) at 95.
85 Banco de España Special Register, available at: <www.bde.es/bde/es/secciones/servicios/Particulares_y_e/Registros_de_Ent/>, last visited on 27 March 2014.
86 Section 57bis *Ley de Ordenación Bancaria, 31 de diciembre 1946, BOE no. 1, 1 de enero 1947, 110-121.*
87 Vega Serrano (2011) at 96 referring to STS 2456/1986, de 14 de mayo de 1986.

The AML Act does not refer specifically to banks falling under the scope of its application, but rather to the larger category of credit institutions.[88] Considering that banks are a type of credit institution, banks are fully covered by the AML legislation.[89]

4.5.2 Real estate agents

The real estate sector is a fully liberalised sector in Spain, which means that the profession is not regulated. Section 3 Act 10/2003 on urgent measures concerning the liberalisation of the estate agency and transport sectors stipulates that real estate functions can be exercised by licensed real estate agents or by any other natural or legal persons that are not in the possession of such a licence or a member of any professional association, but which are subject to the requirements that apply to these activities for the purpose of consumer protection.[90] This means there is no obligation for natural or legal persons that perform real estate activities to be licensed or to register themselves with the competent authorities. In principle any person can call himself an estate agent. Real estate agents are not required to become a member of a professional association either. Because of the unregulated nature of the profession, the AML Act applies a wide definition. Real estate agents are referred to as 'persons whose business activities include those of agency, commission or brokerage in the trading of real estate' (*own translation, MB*).[91]

There are associations that offer credentials and licences to real estate agents to which the first part of Section 3 refers. Licensed real estate agents are regulated by Royal Decree 1294/2007 that approves the General Statute of the Official Colleges of Real Estate Agents and their General Council.[92] The General Council of the Official Colleges of Real Estate Agents in Spain is a public law corporation established as a sovereign body of these colleges.[93] It represents the sector vis-à-vis the public administration and other branches of Government, in Community institutions and other foreign institutions. The Official Colleges are tasked to ensure compliance by their licensed members with the applicable legislation and professional norms in place, and to defend the rights of consumers.[94]

> When a real estate agent wants to become a member of an Official College, he must demonstrate that he has the right qualifications[95] or the licence that allows him to use the title API, which stands for *Agente de la Propiedad Inmobiliaria*. The licence is supplied by the Spanish Ministry of Development. To obtain this qualification, the estate agent needs to have a public university degree, to have followed a series of theoretical and practical training programmes and to have passed an examination to obtain the licence. Members

88 Section 2(1)(a) Act 10/2010.

89 See about credit institutions in Spain: Vega Serrano (2011) at 43-66.

90 *Ley 10/2003, de 20 de mayo, de medidas urgentes de liberalización en el sector inmobiliario y transportes, BOE no. 121, Sec. I., 21 de mayo 2003, 19255-19258.*

91 Section 2(1)(l) Act 10/2010 speaks about 'quienes ejerzan profesionalmente actividades de agencia, comisión o intermediación en la compraventa de bienes inmuebles'.

92 *Real Decreto 1294/2007, de 28 de septiembre, por el que se aprueban los Estatutos Generales de los Colegios Oficiales de Agentes de Propiedad Inmobiliaria y de su Consejo General, BOE no. 237, 3 de octubre 2007, 40196-40207*. Hereafter 'RD 1294/2007'.

93 *Consejo General de los Colegios Oficiales de Agentes de la Propiedad Inmobiliaria de España (COAPIS)*

94 COAPIS, *Consejo*, available at: <www.consejocoapis.org/consejo.php>, last visited on 27 March 2014.

95 Section 1(1)(b) RD 1294/2007.

of Official Colleges are included in the registers of the colleges, which can be publicly consulted.[96]

This obviously does not do away with the fact that there may be persons acting as an intermediary between sellers and buyers of estate property, but who are not members of the professional association or registered elsewhere.

4.5.3 Accountants

According to Cañibano and Ucieda, 'the model of accounting regulation adopted in Spain is legalistic with numerous sources of regulations on accounting for different kinds of business activity'.[97] Despite this wealth of legislation, the accountancy profession as such is not regulated and the title of accountant is not a protected title in Spain. Any natural person can call himself an accountant as no entry requirements or minimum qualifications are required by law. Professionals who or businesses that provide tax advice (*asesores fiscales*) or carry out bookkeeping, consultancy or other accountancy activities – generally referred to as *contables externos* – are not required to register themselves either. Accountants can, but are not required to, join a professional association in Spain.[98]

Auditing is the only accounting-related activity that is regulated in Spain.[99] The title of auditor does have statutory protection. The Audit Legislative Decree establishes the requirements that auditors and audit firms must comply with.[100] Upon obtaining authorisation, auditors are registered in the Official Registry of Auditors.[101] This register is publicly available and managed by the administrative authority that carries out the supervision of auditors: the Institute of Accounting and Audit (*Instituto de Contabilidad y Auditoría de Cuentas, ICAC*).[102] To become an authorised auditor in Spain a person must have obtained an official university degree; he must have completed the theoretical training courses; and he must have acquired practical training of at least three years and passed a professional proficiency examination organised and recognised by the State. The educational and practical training requirements are different for persons who can

96 For example, the website of the Colegio Oficial de Agentes de la Propiedad Inmobiliaria de la provincia de La Coruña: <www.coapicoruna.com/joomla/index.php?option=com_content&task=view&id=14&Itemid=35>, last visited on 27 March 2014.

97 Cañibano, L. and Ucieda, J.L. (2005), *Accounting and financial reporting in Spain*, Research Paper UAM, at 7, available at: <www.uam.es/personal_pdi/economicas/jlucieda/sci/canibano_ucieda_2005.pdf>, last visited on 27 March 2014.

98 This is the Accounting and Business Administration Association (*Asociación Española de Contabilidad y Administración de Empresas*). There are three professional associations for auditors. The largest is the Institute of Certified Public Auditors in Spain (*Instituto de Censores Jurados de Cuentas de España*). Membership is only open to statutory auditors listed in the Official Registry of Auditors and allowed to carry out statutory audits.

99 *Real Decreto Legislativo 1/2011, de 1 de Julio 2011, por el que se aprueba el texto refundido de la Ley de Auditoría de Cuentas, BOE no. 157, Sec. I, 2 de julio 2011, 70330-70372.* (In English: *Audit Legislative Decree 2011*).

100 Chapter II Audit Legislative Decree 2011.

101 Section 7 Audit Legislative Decree 2011.

102 Section 7(2) Audit Legislative Decree 2001. See about ICAC: Cañibano and Ucieda (2005) at 9-11.

demonstrate that they have the necessary certificates or studies required to be accepted at university and who have at least eight years of practical training.

The AML Act applies to auditors (*auditores de cuentas*), external accountants (*contables externos*) and tax advisors (*asesores fiscales*).[103]

4.5.4 Designating representatives to SEPBLAC

We have seen that banks in Spain are fully regulated, but that this is not the case for the professions of accountants and real estate agents. There are professional associations where natural or legal persons exercising accounting or estate agency activities can become a member, but this is not compulsory. The registers are available to SEPBLAC, but this may only contain a part of the professional population. It could lead to the conclusion that SEPBLAC cannot have an adequate oversight of accountants and estate agents. What makes SEPBLAC interesting, however, is that in theory it can have a full oversight of banks, accountants and estate agents via its function as a Financial Intelligence Unit, provided that all obliged institutions and professionals comply with the law.

As part of the internal control measures, obliged institutions and professionals are required to designate a director or manager in the business as a representative to SEPBLAC. Blanco Cordero refers to these representatives as compliance officers.[104] In the case of entrepreneurs or individual professionals, they themselves are the representative.[105] The obligation intends to ensure that the senior management of businesses are involved in the effective implementation of measures to prevent money laundering. A representative is the person within a business who is responsible for compliance with the reporting obligation in case of suspicions of money laundering and terrorist financing or the periodic reporting obligation. The representative is also the contact person for SEPBLAC and represents the business in any kind of administrative or judicial proceedings. SEPBLAC can make reasoned objections or reservations to the proposal of a representative, when for example it is of the opinion that a proposed representative does not have a relevant position or does not have adequate knowledge.[106] Non-compliance with the obligation to appoint a representative is considered to be a serious breach and can be sanctioned accordingly.[107]

> Section 12 RD 925/1995 details the requirements for representatives. In the case of legal persons, corporations or small-sized companies with more than 25 employees, the representative must be appointed by the board. The representative must demonstrate the professional behaviour that qualifies him as an adequate person for the position and, lastly, he must have adequate knowledge to exercise the functions of a representative. What is meant by professional behaviour or adequate knowledge is not further regulated and is left to the obliged institutions and professionals themselves. The proposed

103 Section 2(1)(m) Act 10/2010.

104 Blanco Cordero, I. (2009), 'Eficacia del sistema de prevención del blanqueo de capitales: estudio del cumplimiento normativo (compliance) desde una perspectiva criminológica', *Eguzkilore*, issue 23, pp. 117-138 at 122.

105 Section 26(2), first part, Act 10/2010.

106 Section 26(2) Act 10/2010.

107 Section 52(1)(n) in conjunction with Section 57 Act 10/2010. See more in § 4.7.

> appointment with the name of the representative as well as a detailed description of his professional career, and additional documentation, must be sent to SEPBLAC.[108] Supporting documentation that should accompany the form is the official appointment by the directorate of that person as the representative of the business, a photocopy of the passport or identity card, and documentation that demonstrates the professional skills of the proposed representative, such as a curriculum vitae.[109]

SEPBLAC keeps a register with the names and details of the representatives of obliged institutions and professionals and thus has an adequate overview. Although this database is primarily for FIU-related functions, all SEPBLAC employees are subject to the same confidentiality regime.[110] Therefore, SEPBLAC inspectors have access to all internal databases, including the database of representatives. The supervision department thus has access to the names of institutions and professionals subject to the AML Act. SEPBLAC annually publishes statistics on the number of obliged institutions and professionals on its website.[111] In 2012, SEPBLAC's register contained the following numbers: 75 banks, 5,260 auditors, accountants and/or tax advisors, and 4,720 real estate agents or agency businesses.[112]

4.5.5 Concluding remarks

Banking activities require an authorisation which is issued by the Bank of Spain. Upon authorisation, banks are included in the special register of the Bank of Spain. This register is publicly available and can be consulted by SEPBLAC. Moreover, before deciding on authorisation the Bank of Spain is obliged to consult SEPBLAC. The real estate sector is fully liberalised in Spain and there is no protection of title. Real estate agents are not required to register themselves with the competent authorities. A possibility to obtain the well-recognised API licence via membership of one of the Official Colleges exists, but is not compulsory. The registers of the Official Colleges can be accessed by SEPBLAC. Because of the unregulated nature of the profession, the Spanish AML Act applies a wide definition of real estate agents. The AML Act applies to auditors, external accountants and tax advisors. The title of accountant, with the exception of an auditor, is not protected in Spain. Membership of professional associations exists on a voluntary basis. The fact that the real estate and accountancy professions are not (fully) regulated becomes less problematic thanks to SEPBLAC's function as an FIU. All obliged institutions and professionals are required to designate a representative to SEPBLAC as a part of their internal control measures. The primary aim is to ensure an effective reporting regime, for which SEPBLAC keeps the names of the businesses and their representatives in a special register. Inspectors can use this information for supervision purposes, because all SEPBLAC staff fall under

108 Section 26(2), first part, Act 10/2010; SEPBLAC, *Form F-22*, available at <www.sepblac.es/espanol/sujetos_obligados/datos-representantes2.htm>, last visited on 27 March 2014.

109 SEPBLAC, *Sujetos Obligados y Expertos externos: Representante ante el Sepblac*, available at <www.sepblac.es/espanol/sujetos_obligados/datos-representantes2.htm>, last visited on 27 March 2014.

110 Section 49 Act 10/2010.

111 For 2011-2012: <www.sepblac.es/espanol/acerca_sepblac/estadisticas/2012/pdf/sujetos_a)_i).pdf> and <www.sepblac.es/espanol/acerca_sepblac/estadisticas/2012/pdf/sujetos_j)_y).pdf>, last visited on 27 March 2014. The statistics for 2010-2012 can also be found in its annual report: SEPBLAC (2012).

112 SEPBLAC (2012) at 24-25.

the same confidentiality regime. In 2012 the register included 75 banks, 5,260 auditors, accountants and/or tax advisors, and 4,720 real estate agents/businesses.

4.6 Anti-money laundering supervision by SEPBLAC

Formally, SEPBLAC is the only AML authority in Spain. SEPBLAC has no other supervision tasks and derives its powers solely from the AML Act. This section discusses the supervisory powers (§ 4.6.1) and supervision in practice (§ 4.6.2). In § 4.6.3 attention is paid to instruments that aim to strengthen SEPBLAC's supervision: the FIU functions, the use of external experts, and supervisory arrangements with the financial sector regulators, in particular with the Bank of Spain. This section ends with some concluding remarks.

4.6.1 Supervisory powers

The AML Act provides SEPBLAC with the power to perform on-site inspections.[113] On-site inspections by SEPBLAC are said to include the typical supervisory tools, 'such as the review of policies, procedures, books and records, and extend also to sample testing of customer files'.[114] A precondition for the use of this power is the existence of a supervision plan.[115] Obliged institutions and professionals, as well as their employees, directors and managers, are required to cooperate to the fullest extent possible with the staff of SEPBLAC, providing unrestricted access to as much information or documentation as required, including books, accounts, records, software, magnetic files, internal reports, minutes, official statements and any other related matters subject to inspection.[116] This broadly formulated cooperation duty implies that SEPBLAC inspectors have the power to compel the production of any information that is relevant to monitoring compliance.[117] On this basis SEPBLAC can perform off-site inspections in which it reviews the internal policies and procedures, or via which it assesses the reports from external experts.[118] Only lawyers can invoke legal professional privilege under the AML Act, and their obligation of professional secrecy in accordance with the legislation in force.[119] They can refuse to allow SEPBLAC to have access to files or refuse to forward information to it.[120] SEPBLAC does not have regulatory powers. This power rests with the Commission or its Standing Committee.

Section 4.7 shows that SEPBLAC does not have sanctioning powers, as in Spain a strict division between the inspection power and the power to sanction exists.[121] For now it is important to keep in mind that supervisory and sanctioning powers rest with two

113 Section 47(1) Act 10/2010.
114 FATF (2006) at 111.
115 García Ureta, A. (2006), *La potestad inspectora de las Administraciones públicas*, Marcial Pons, at 53. I will discuss the existence thereof in § 4.6.2.
116 Section 47(2) Act 10/2010. This provision is based on Section 39 LPA which establishes a duty of cooperation ('el deber de sujeción') for citizens. See also: García Ureta (2006) at 51 et seq.
117 Although outdated see FATF (2006) at 111.
118 § 4.6.3.3.
119 Section 22 Act 10/2010; Van den Broek (2014a) at 32.
120 Cf. FATF (2006) at 92.
121 García Ureta (2006) at 35-40.

different authorities: SEPBLAC carries out compliance supervision and the Commission Secretariat is responsible for sanctioning proceedings. Notwithstanding this, SEPBLAC inspectors do have the power to issue recommendations (*recommendaciones*) or to propose corrective measures (*medidas correctoras*) during or after a supervisory visit.[122] These measures do not do away with the possibility for the Commission Secretariat to initiate sanctioning proceedings. Recommendations are meant to improve the anti-money laundering procedures of an institution or professional, without the existence of an offence. Recommendations have a preventive function, and can be given after any inspection. In the absence of a legal basis, however, the recommendations that SEPBLAC inspectors give, lack legal force and cannot be enforced.[123] SEPBLAC can also propose corrective measures to the Standing Committee of the Commission, which can require obliged institutions to adopt these corrective measures to remedy deficiencies that are not severe enough to be considered as offences under the AML Act. The implementation of those corrective actions is monitored by the Standing Committee and its non-compliance is subject to sanctions.[124] Sanctions or measures imposed following the sanctioning procedure do have legal force as these are responses to identified breaches.

4.6.2 Anti-money laundering supervision: policy and practice

4.6.2.1 Supervisory policy

SEPBLAC's supervisory activities are based on annual supervision plans. These plans are prepared by SEPBLAC, but are adopted by the Standing Committee of the Commission for the Prevention of Money Laundering and Monetary Offences.[125] Unfortunately, the Act stipulates that these plans are privileged, which means that they cannot be consulted.[126] The annual supervision plans of SEPBLAC are discussed with the three financial regulators with which the Commission has entered into a supervisory arrangement, and their supervision plans with respect to the prevention of money laundering are geared to one another.[127] From interviews it became clear that the annual supervision plans that SEPBLAC prepares contain the alerts and risks for each specific sector. In the plans, prioritisations are made on a risk-based approach.[128] According to SEPBLAC representatives the annual supervision plans are very detailed. They state which obliged institutions are going to be inspected and may also include proposals made by the financial regulators.[129] The plans may be changed throughout the year by the Commission or Standing Committee and deviations from the annual supervision plan must be reasonably justified.[130]

122 Section 47(3) Act 10/2010. For recommendations, there is no legal basis: FATF (2010) at 15.

123 Interview SEPBLAC, October 2013. Cf. García Ureta (2006) at 37-40 who argues that the control of legality is what makes sanctions issued after the sanctioning proceedings different from measures taken during supervisory procedures, although in practice such a distinction is not always easy to make. He argues that it would be better for the legislator to distinguish between measures that inspectors take and sanctions imposed under sanctioning proceedings.

124 Section 51(1)(e) and section 52(1)(w) Act 10/2010.

125 Section 44(3) in conjunction with 44(2)(g) Act 10/2010.

126 Section 44(2)(g) Act 10/2010.

127 See § 4.6.3.2.

128 Interview SEPBLAC, October 2011.

129 Ibid.

130 Section 47(1) and 47(2) of Act 10/2010.

As regards SEPBLAC's general supervision policy or the risk-based approach to supervision, not much information is available. Having responsibilities only under the preventive AML policy, it is obvious that SEPBLAC focuses exclusively on compliance with the obligations stemming from the AML Act. How this is exercised, however, remains a matter of conjecture. We have already pointed out that SEPBLAC's annual report of 2012 does not include a single reference to (the exercise of) SEPBLAC's supervisory tasks.[131] SEPBLAC does not seem to have a general policy that indicates how inspections are carried out, and since the annual supervision plans are not publicly available, these can also not give any further information. The importance of a risk-based approach for AML supervision by SEPBLAC has been stressed in particular in light of the limited human resources available.[132] The only remark made by the FATF in 2006 about SEPBLAC's risk-based approach was the fact that '[a]s a supervisor, SEPBLAC uses a risk-based approach to AML/CFT supervision. In 2002 for instance, SEPBLAC focused its supervisory activity on bureaux de change and money transfer companies'.[133] In 2010, FATF found that SEPBLAC's supervision had become more risk-based. It stated that the annual supervision plans are based on the risk of the institution, to be determined by the alerts created by SEPBLAC with regard to the levels of reporting made by the obliged institutions and professionals as well as to the alerts provided by the financial regulators, and also by the risk of the sectors being abused for the purpose of money laundering (or terrorist financing).[134] Moreover, it pointed to the so-called money laundering risk map that would allow SEPBLAC to adopt a better focus within its supervisory efforts on banks and other financial institutions.[135]

> The money laundering risk map is a tool that is primarily meant as a means for creating awareness and providing guidance to the financial sector.[136] It is compiled of aggregated data from financial institutions based on the received suspicions of money laundering (or terrorist financing). The risk map gives general information about the underlying criminal activity for which suspicions were reported to the FIU by credit and financial institutions, the number and quality of the suspicion reports from the sector, and so on.[137] According to the FATF, the risk map allows credit institutions, in particular banks, to 'compare itself with other institutions of a similar size in terms of the kind of transactions that it is or is not reporting, the risk elements that it is taking into account, etcetera. Thus, the credit institution can detect its weaknesses in the detection and analyses of potentially suspicious transactions'.[138]

4.6.2.2 Supervision in numbers

Looking at the actual supervisory activities undertaken by SEPBLAC in the years 2010-2012, it can be observed that information made available by SEPBLAC and the Commission for the Prevention of Money Laundering and Monetary Offences – surprisingly –

131 See § 4.4.2 where this was mentioned as well.
132 FATF (2006) at 60 and 111-112; and FATF (2010) at 17 et seq.; Interview SEPBLAC, October 2011.
133 FATF (2006) at 81.
134 FATF (2010) at 17.
135 Ibid.
136 Interview SEPBLAC, November 2011.
137 FATF (2010) at 17.
138 Ibid., at 29.

diverges.[139] The numerical differences cannot be explained, because both sources of information do not contain information on how the statistics are compiled and what they mean. Based on information published on SEPBLAC's website ('SEPBLAC data'), we can see the following numbers.[140] It should be pointed out that the statistics only reflect on-site inspections as there is no information about the number of off-site inspections. In the year 2010, SEPBLAC undertook 27 on-site inspections, of which three were performed at credit institutions. These credit institutions may be, but are not necessarily banks. In 2011, SEPBLAC carried out 15 on-site inspections, none of which were at banks, accountants or estate agents. In 2012, SEPBLAC undertook 23 on-site inspections, of which 18 were at credit institutions. Again, these credit institutions may be, but are not necessarily banks. Unfortunately, SEPBLAC does not provide any further information. What this proves in any case is that banks may have been subject to AML inspections from SEPBLAC, but that accountants and real estate agents have never been supervised on-site since the entry into force of the AML Act. The Commission for the Prevention of Money Laundering and Monetary Offences states in its Statistical report 2010-12 that SEPBLAC performed 18 on-site inspections in 2010, 9 in 2011 and 3 in 2012. The statistical report does not give an insight into where these on-site inspections took place. In addition, the statistical report contains a table on the AML/CTF inspection activities *excluding* on-site inspections. The numbers reflected here are 122 in 2010, 238 in 2011 and 41 in 2012. Without information on what 'other inspection activities' means, I cannot draw any conclusion from this. The information from SEPBLAC is more detailed and will be illustrated and used hereafter.

4

Table 3 – On-site inspection activity by SEPBLAC (based on SEPBLAC data)

	Total inspections	Banks	Accountants	Real estate agents	Other
2010	27	3*	0	0	24
2011	15	0	0	0	15
2012	23	18*	0	0	5

** As explained the numbers given were for inspections at credit institutions. Credit institutions may be, but are not necessarily banks. The numbers, however, do not specify any further whether the inspections were with banks or other credit institutions.*

Based on SEPBLAC data, it performs on average 22 inspections annually on a total number of around 22,000 institutions.[141] This means that only an average of 0.1% of the total number of obliged institutions and professionals were supervised annually by SEPBLAC

139 SEPBLAC (2012a) and SEPBLAC (2011), *Datos de actividad 2011: Supervision – entidades inspeccionadas*, available at: <www.sepblac.es/espanol/acerca_sepblac/estadisticas/2011/pdf/entidades_inspeccionadas.pdf>, last visited on 27 March 2014; and Comisión de Prevención del Blanqueo de Capitales e Infracciones Monetarias (2013), *Memoria de Información Estadística 2010-12*, at 45-47 (*Statistical report 2010-12*). Hereafter referred to as: CPBCIM (2013).

140 SEPBLAC (2012a) and SEPBLAC (2011). Unfortunately data for 2013 were not published by the end of March 2014. There is also no other data available in relation to supervisory activities carried out by SEPBLAC. For example, the number of assessments of external review reports by SEPBLAC is unknown (see § 6.3.3).

141 The calculation is based on the average number of inspections (2010: 27, 2011:15, 2012: 23) and the average number of obliged institutions and professionals (in 2011: 20,416, in 2012: 22,258 – for simplification purposes the number is 22,000).

in the years 2010-2012.[142] The fact that this supervision intensity by SEPBLAC is so low seems to be primarily caused by the small size of the Supervision Department. In § 4.1.2 we could see that this is 11 FTE plus some help from other SEPBLAC staff. The resource constraints are serious and hamper effective supervision in practice. Already back in 2006, the FATF was of the same opinion and found that AML supervision by SEPLAC was not 'proper'.[143] Even if this supervision is based on a risk-based approach, it makes supervision by SEPBLAC practically non-existent. In relation to banks there is (presumably) some inspection activity, but accountants and real estate agents have never been inspected for their compliance with the preventive anti-money laundering obligations since 2010. This finding is worrisome in light of the fact that there are a considerable number of accountants and real estate agents in Spain: in 2012 SEPBLAC's register contained no less than 5,260 auditors, accountants and/or tax advisors, and 4,720 real estate agents.[144] It is even more worrisome, because both professions have a low record of reporting suspicious transactions to SEPBLAC: in 2011 accountants reported 8 cases and real estate agents 15 cases, which comes to 0.2% and 0.5% of the total number of disclosed suspicions to SEPBLAC in that year.[145] The years 2010 and 2011 provided similar results. Banks disclose far more suspicions to SEPBLAC: in 2012 banks reported 1,792 cases, which is 59% of all disclosed suspicions that year.[146]

A number of instruments are present in the Spanish AML Act that may enhance the effectiveness of the anti-money laundering supervision by SEPBLAC to a certain extent, or have a supportive function at least. The instruments will be discussed hereafter.

4.6.3 Instruments to strengthen SEPBLAC's supervision

This subsection deals with three instruments. In the first place it pays attention to SEPBLAC's functions as the national Financial Intelligence Unit. Due to its position as the FIU, SEPBLAC obtains a great deal of extra information and some extra powers which it can use for supervisory purposes as well. In the second place I pay attention to supervisory arrangements with financial regulators. We have seen that the Commission for the Prevention of Money Laundering and Monetary Offences can enter into arrangements with any of the three financial regulators on the matter of anti-money laundering supervision. This possibility takes away part of the supervisory work from SEPBLAC and avoids any 'double supervision' of the financial and credit institutions. In the third place, I look at external expert reviews. Institutions and professionals are required to have

142 The conclusion would be even more worrisome if this percentage would be calculated on the basis of the number of on-site inspections by SEPBLAC as in the Commission's Statistical report 2010-12. The average number of on-site inspections would be 10 (2010: 18, 2011:9 and 2012: 3) and the inspection rate for obliged institutions and professionals on an annual basis would then be 0.05%.

143 FATF (2006) at 134-135.

144 SEPBLAC (2012) at 24-25.

145 Ibid., at 15, 16 and 18; CPBCIM (2013) at 9, 11 and 13. The reporting numbers only concern suspicion reports and exclude the number of reports submitted through the systematic reporting system on the basis of Section 20 of Act 10/2010.

146 Ibid.

an annual review of their internal policies and procedures for the prevention of money laundering. These reviews should be performed by an external expert (*experto externo*).

It should be taken into account that these instruments can strengthen or enhance the effectiveness of SEPBLAC's supervision, and that they are not meant as tools to substitute it. SEPBLAC retains its own responsibility under Act 10/2010 to carry out its supervisory tasks effectively.

4.6.3.1 Function as a Financial Intelligence Unit

One of the advantages of including an FIU in AML supervision is that it can use data gathered under its FIU-related functions.[147] FIUs have a relatively rich information position. In relation to the designation of representatives as part of internal control measures this was discussed in § 4.5.4.

The register with designated representatives is not the only internal database that can be used. Because secrecy provisions under the AML Act apply equally to all SEPBLAC staff, there is no legal restriction for SEPBLAC inspectors to make use of SEPBLAC's databases with information on suspicions of money laundering and terrorist financing, as well as the reports that have been disseminated to SEPBLAC under the systematic reporting system.[148] This means that these databases can be used as a source for preparing the annual supervision plans, i.e. whether or not to include certain obliged institutions and professionals in the inspection cycle of a particular year, or as a preparation for an on-site inspection. SEPBLAC representatives have confirmed the use of internal databases for supervisory purposes.[149]

Next to the internal databases, SEPBLAC has access to other information that allows it to do analyses of incoming reports on suspicions of money laundering or terrorist financing as well. It has the power to request documentation and information from obliged institutions and professionals, which are required to supply all documentation and information requested.[150] A breach of this obligation is considered a very serious offence.[151] Secondly, FATF listed a wide number of external sources of information to which SEPBLAC has direct and immediate access.

> This included – inter alia – police information,[152] the companies register, tax databases, the land registry, and information from the financial sector regulators or from other bodies with supervisory competences.[153] SEPBLAC also had access to privately-owned

147 Van den Broek (2014) at 71.
148 The duty of secrecy is laid down in Section 49 Act 10/2010. The reporting obligations for institutions and professionals are laid down in Sections 18 and 20 of Act 10/2010 and Section 7 of RD 925/1995.
149 Interview SEPBLAC, October 2011.
150 Section 21 Act 10/2010.
151 Section 51(1)(b) Act 10/2010. See §7.2 on the categorisation of offences and corresponding sanctions.
152 National Police Force Database and the Guardia Civil Database (via Section 25(2) RD 925/1995); databases from the police forces of the Autonomous Communities (via Section 25(3) RD 925/1995).
153 FATF (2006) at 55.

> databases to which it subscribed.[154] The regime has changed somewhat with the entry into force of Act 10/2010, but SEPBLAC still has access to these databases and information.[155] Access to police and tax information is obtained via officials who work as liaison officers at SEPBLAC.[156] Section 48 lays down the access for SEPBLAC to information from the Bank of Spain, the National Securities Market Commission or the Directorate-General for Insurance and Pension Funds, the social security management bodies and the Treasury General of Social Security.

Moreover, Section 48 Act 10/2010 states that each authority or official that discovers facts that may constitute an indication or suspicion of money laundering or terrorist financing shall report such circumstance to SEPBLAC. This obligation extends to any information they are called upon to provide by the Commission for the Prevention of Money Laundering and Monetary Offences and its support bodies in the discharge of their powers.[157] That same provision also requires the Bank of Spain, the National Securities Market Commission, the Directorate-General for Insurance and Pension Funds, the Directorate-General for Registers and Notaries, the Institute of Accounting and Auditing, the professional associations and the competent state or autonomous bodies to provide such reports if they detect possible breaches of Act 10/2010 in the course of their own inspection or supervisory efforts. Judicial authorities are required to forward evidence to the Commission Secretariat, at the instruction of the public prosecutor´s office or upon their own motion, when they detect signs or indications of breaches of obligations under the AML Act that do not themselves constitute criminal offences.

Finally, Section 43 Act 10/2010 provides SEPBLAC with another opportunity to gather additional information that may benefit the analysis of suspicion reports, and possibly also its supervisory activities. This section requires credit institutions to report to SEPBLAC at periodic intervals on the opening or cancellation of current accounts, savings accounts, securities accounts and fixed-term deposits.[158] SEPBLAC is responsible for bringing together all this information into publicly-owned files called financial ownership files (FOF).[159] The responsibility for these FOFs rests with the Secretary of State for Economy and Business Support.[160] The FOF system functions more or less as a central bank account registry, although it is specifically designed for the prevention of money

154 Ibid. Examples are Dun & Bradstreet, Informa and World Check: Interview SEPBLAC, October 2011.

155 Interview SEPBLAC, October 2011.

156 Interview SEPBLAC, October 2011; FATF (2006) at 27. Section 49 of Act 10/2010 thereby states that the exchange of information between SEPBLAC and the tax authorities should preferably take place in the form determined by an arrangement between the Commission and the Spanish Tax Authority (*Agencia Tributaria*). However, on 27 March 2014, the websites and annual reports (2012) of SEPBLAC, the Commission for the Prevention of Money Laundering and Monetary Offences and the Spanish Tax Authority did not mention the existence of such a supervisory arrangement. The Official State Gazette (BOE) does not include any reference to (the existence of) a supervisory arrangement either.

157 Section 48(1) Act 10/2010.

158 Section 43(1) Act 10/2010.

159 In Spanish called *Fichero de Titularidades Financieras*. Hereafter FOF.

160 Section 43(2) Act 10/2010.

laundering (and terrorist financing).[161] SEPBLAC has direct access to the FOF data in the exercise of its powers.[162] The AML Act does not make a distinction between the FIU-related functions and the supervisory tasks of SEPBLAC. In March 2014 the system was still under development and not yet operational, which means that its practical relevance for SEPBLAC is still minor.[163]

> FOFs should include the names of holders, representatives or authorised persons, together with all other persons with withdrawal powers, the date of opening or cancellation, the type of account or deposit and the information identifying the reporting credit institution. It gives an insight into the existence of accounts operating from Spain, held by any person, be it domestic or foreign, resident or non-resident. It provides summary details of the account holder and the type of account, but does not provide SEPBLAC with access to the operations of the bank account.[164]

The internal databases, the access to external databases and information, the receiving of possible suspicions of money laundering and terrorist financing or of non-compliance with obligations from Act 10/2010 by authorities other than the obliged institutions and professionals, as well as the FOF system (once operational) are primarily meant for the FIU-related tasks of SEPBLAC. In the absence of provisions that prevent SEPBLAC from using these databases and information for its supervisory task, this means that SEPBLAC inspectors potentially have a wealth of data available. They do not only have to rely on information that they have collected during the supervision or on publicly available information. The FIU-related functions of SEPBLAC can thus raise the effectiveness of SEPBLAC's supervision, presuming that this information allows inspectors to better focus on particular sectors, individual institutions or professionals in planning and exercising inspections.[165]

4.6.3.2 Supervisory arrangements with the financial regulators

The Commission for the Prevention of Money Laundering and Monetary Offences is empowered to enter into arrangements with each of the three financial supervisors in Spain with the aim of coordinating and harmonising their AML inspections and

161 The Bank of Spain also keeps a Central Credit Register (*Central de Información de Riesgos*). This database, however, serves purposes other than the FOF system. It holds the credit records of natural and legal persons in order to facilitate institutions in their credit risk analysis. Information available at the Bank of Spain's website: <www.bde.es/bde/es/secciones/servicios/Particulares_y_e/Central_de_Infor/Central_de_Info_04db72d6c1fd821.html>, last visited: 27 March 2014.

162 Section 43(3) Act 10/2010. Also other law enforcement authorities can request to have access to the system, when they investigate matters on or related to money laundering or terrorist financing.

163 Interview SEPBLAC, October 2013; SEPBLAC (2012) at 35. See also: *Torres-Dulce recuerda que el Gobierno aún no ha desarrollado el Fichero de Titularidades Financieras*, 16 January 2014, available at: <www.elbuscadordeldetective.com/noticia.htm?id=1278>, last visited on 27 March 2014.

164 SEPBLAC (2012) at 38: 'Es necesario significar que en el citado Fichero de Titularidades Financieras no existirá información sobre saldos ni movimientos de las posiciones identificadas, sino exclusivamente la identificación de los productos y, lógicamente, la entidad de crédito de la que sean clientes sus titulares.'

165 It would be going beyond the focus of this research, however, to investigate the actual information that is available, and what is done with this information in practice.

supervisory activities with those carried out by SEPBLAC.[166] The Commission has made use of this possibility. The Commission is not allowed to enter into arrangements with professional associations or other authorities with supervisory responsibility for the large group of designated non-financial businesses and professionals. Back in 2006, the FATF commented on this narrow approach in light of SEPBLAC's limited resources.[167]

> Up-to-date information is absent due to the secrecy that surrounds (the conclusion of) these supervisory arrangements. The latest public information available tells us that the Commission entered into an arrangement with the National Securities Market Commission (*Comisión Nacional del Mercado de Valores, CNMV*) on 18 June 2003; with the Directorate General of Insurance and Pension Funds (*Dirección General de Seguros y Fondos de Pensiones, DGSFP*) on 21 October 2004 and that it updated its supervisory arrangement with the Bank of Spain on 29 February 2008.[168] The website of the Bank of Spain even refers to a new arrangement with SEPBLAC dated on 31 October 2013.[169]
>
> I here deal with the term (supervisory) arrangement. These are concluded between two parties, either both public administrative authorities or between the administration and the private sector, and concern agreements on the exercise of supervisory tasks. Other terms used to refer to these kinds of agreements are declarations of intention, memoranda of understanding, supervisory agreements, *convenanten* (Dutch) or *convenios* (Spanish).

None of these supervisory arrangements are publicly available, which means that what is agreed remains open to conjecture. From an accountability and transparency perspective, the importance of which was emphasised in Chapter 2, this is lamentable. From the scarce information available in FATF reports and obtained from interviews, it appears that in general these arrangements include an agreement on the inclusion of the verification of compliance with AML obligations in the prudential supervisory programmes of the three financial supervisors. They can opt to include it in regular supervisory procedures or carry out targeted AML supervision of their supervisees.[170] In any case, SEPBLAC remains ultimately responsible for this supervision and still has the right to carry out anti-money laundering supervision itself at the same time or after the inspections by the financial regulators ('follow up') at those institutions and professionals subject to the supervision of the Bank of Spain, CNMV and DGSFP.[171] AML supervision performed by the financial regulators should thus be considered as complementary to the supervision exercised by SEPBLAC. This is also why Section 44, second paragraph, sub g, Act 10/2010 states that the Commission is tasked to approve, on a proposal from SEPBLAC and, in case of agreement,

166 Cf. Section 44(2)(m) Act 10/2010. These three are independent regulatory agencies, which are to a large extent independent and have more powers than 'regular' administrative authorities. Cf. Fernández Rojas, G. (2005), 'Las Administraciones Independientes de Regulación y Supervisión en España', *Vniversitas*, issue 109, pp. 419-460; Betancor Rodríguez, A. (1994), *Las administraciones independientes*, Tecnos: Madrid; Magide Herrero, M. (2000), *Límites constitucionales de las administraciones independientes*, INAP: Madrid.

167 FATF (2006) at 135.

168 FATF (2006) at 110 and FATF (2010) at 16.

169 Banco de España (2014), *Acuerdos de colaboración en materia de supervisión*, available at <www.bde.es/bde/es/areas/supervision/funcion/acuerdos/Acuerdos_de_col_6814c51aafcd821.html>, last visited on 27 March 2014.

170 Interview SEPBLAC, October 2011.

171 FATF (2010) at 15.

the supervisors of the financial institutions, the annual supervision plan for institutions and professionals covered by that Act. The supervisory arrangements also include agreements on the exercise of joint inspections, where SEPBLAC inspectors accompany the prudential inspectors.[172] In 2011 the system of joint inspections was still of a recent nature and under development. Advantages mentioned were that it enabled SEPBLAC to obtain more information on the financial sector, and that SEPBLAC inspectors could train the prudential inspectors in AML matters. At that time, SEPBLAC had carried out some joint inspections with the CNMV and DGSFP, and one joint inspection with the Bank of Spain.[173]

> Some more information is available on the 2008 supervisory arrangement between the Commission and the Bank of Spain. It confirms the possibility for the Bank of Spain to perform anti-money laundering supervision, the possibility of joint inspections, the exchange of annual supervision plans and the establishment of a commission that should monitor the implementation of the supervisory arrangement.[174] As far as the information on the outcomes of inspections is concerned, representatives have indicated that where the Bank of Spain includes anti-money laundering aspects in its supervision it always sends the supervision report (*informe*) to the Commission Secretariat, which – if breaches are identified – can decide on the start of sanctioning procedures. SEPBLAC only receives a notification of the result (*resultado*) of the inspection carried out by the Bank of Spain. Jointly they can give recommendations to the respective bank, next to the possibility for the Commission Secretariat to initiate a sanctioning procedure in case of breaches.[175]

Regarding the supervision practice of the Bank of Spain, it is remarkable to observe that the 2011 and 2012 reports on banking supervision by the Bank of Spain do not include a single reference to the preventive anti-money laundering policy. This seems to suggest that in 2011 and 2012 no inspections were carried out which were aimed at or included the verification of compliance with AML obligations.[176] However, the Statistical Report 2010-2012 from the Commission states that the Bank of Spain carried out 5 (2010), 2 (2011) and 5 (2012) on-site inspections that included the verification of compliance with preventive obligations.[177] The report, however, does not provide any further information. The reports from the Bank of Spain or SEPBLAC do not indicate the exercise of any joint inspections in 2011 and 2012. This leads to the careful conclusion that the Bank of

172 FATF (2010) at 15.
173 Interview SEPBLAC, October 2011. FATF speaks about two joint inspections: FATF (2010) at 15.
174 FATF (2010) at 15-16.
175 Interview SEPBLAC, October 2013. The character of recommendations was explained in § 4.6.1.
176 Banco de España (2012), *Report on Banking Supervision in Spain 2012*, in particular Tables 1.1-1.3; Banco de España (2011), *Report on Banking Supervision in Spain 2011*, in particular Table 2.1 and 2.3. At the time of finalising this chapter, the 2013 report had not yet been published.
177 CPBCIM (2013) at 46.

Spain has not performed any AML supervision of banks, or at least hardly did so if the Commission's Statistical Report 2010-2012 is included.[178]

In sum, the supervisory arrangements have the potential to raise the effectiveness of SEPBLAC's supervision. The Commission may agree with the Bank of Spain regarding banks, and with the two other financial regulators that they primarily exercise the AML supervision of their supervisees. That would allow SEPBLAC, with its small team of inspectors, to focus more on the large group of designated non-financial businesses and professions for which it also has supervisory responsibility.[179] Nevertheless, in the absence of any transparency on the conclusion, the content and the legal safeguards that accompany these supervisory arrangements, nothing more can be said at this point about the effects of SEPBLAC's supervision. This conclusion is strengthened by the observation that the Bank of Spain's publicly available supervision statistics do not show any AML (-related) inspection of banks.

4.6.3.3 External expert reviews

The Spanish legislator has included in the AML Act a provision on external expert reviews of internal policies for the prevention of money laundering and terrorist financing.[180] Section 28 obliges all institutions and professionals, with the exception of individual entrepreneurs or professionals, to have the implementation and operational effectiveness of their internal policies reviewed annually.[181] These reviews should be carried out by so-called external experts. Ministerial Regulation EHA/2444/2007 details the content and the model of the external expert reviews.[182] The instrument of external reviews is not present in the Third Directive or in the FATF Recommendations and can be considered a gold-plating exercise by Spain.[183]

178 This could change in the future. In April 2013, the Bank of Spain announced the creation of a new division specifically in charge of anti-money laundering supervision and supervision on the remuneration of senior management and the marketing of financial products by banks to their customers. The creation of this new division, which should become active in 2014, was the result of rules imposed by the IMF, the European Commission and the European Central Bank after the euro crisis: El País, *El Banco de España refuerza el control de sueldos y blanqueo de capitales*, 4 April 2013.

179 See the concerns about this in § 4.4.1 and FATF (2006) at 112.

180 This was also present under the previous AML regime. Cf. Blanco Cordero (2009) at 122 who says that the obligation to have internal policies and controls is perhaps the most costly obligation for obliged institutions and professionals in Spain.

181 Section 28(4) Act 10/2010. In the two years after an external review the obliged institutions may replace the full examination with a follow-up report on the adoption of the identified breaches: Section 28(1) Act 10/2010.

182 The order was originally drafted on the basis of section 11(7) RD 925/1995. In 2011 SEPBLAC representatives stated that they had worked on detailed requirements for external experts that should be included or referred to in the new Royal Decree. In October 2013 representatives stated that this project had been put on hold and that the 2007 order was still in force: Interview SEPBLAC, November 2011; Interview SEPBLAC, October 2013. In March 2014 the 2007 order was still in force. No amendments are expected in the near future.

183 Gold-plating is a term that refers to the practice of national legislators exceeding the terms of EU Directives when transposing them into national law. Spain is not the only country that has such a system. See for example the German AML policy: FATF (2010), *Third Mutual Evaluation Report on Germany*, 19 February 2010, at 191-193.

An external expert is a natural person who has the right academic and professional profile to perform the task.[184] The meaning of this is not clear; until April 2014 no further requirements had been developed by the Spanish legislator, the Commission or SEPBLAC. The only requirement is that the person who is entrusted with the external review may not have provided any kind of paid service in the three years prior to the external review or three years after having performed the external review.[185]

> Most likely external experts are (trained and licensed) auditors, or persons with experience in business analysis, the prevention of money laundering and terrorist financing and/or audit procedures. There are private initiatives offering training and certifications for external experts.[186]

Those persons who want to act as an external expert must notify themselves to SEPBLAC before commencing review activities. The application form that must be filled in requires no more than some personal data of the external expert and the name of the legal person where the external expert is employed.[187] A curriculum vitae must accompany the application to demonstrate the candidate's professional experience. Applications by external experts are collected in a register at SEPBLAC.[188] The AML Act does not give SEPBLAC the power to make reservations to (or even to refuse) people who want to act as external experts, as it can do with representatives.[189] This makes it even more important to establish clear and concrete requirements for the person and professional experience of an external expert.

4

The outcome of external reviews must be written down in a report. The report should contain in detail the existing internal control measures, an assessment of their operational efficiency and, where necessary, any recommendations for corrections or improvements to remedy the deficiencies identified by the external expert.[190] The review should at least include a verification of the adequacy of the internal control measures associated with the risk management processes of money laundering, the theoretical rationale for the way in which the policy is designed and the way in which the policy and procedures are applied in practice.[191] The (annex to the) ministerial order states in more detail what should be included in the external review report and how the review should be performed.[192] Once the review is finished, the external expert must send the report to the board of directors

184 Section 28(1) Act 10/2010.
185 Section 28(2) Act 10/2010.
186 For example: Instituto de Expertos de Prevención de Blanqueo de Capitales y Financiación del Terrorismo (INBLAC), <www.inblac.org/>, last visited on 27 March 2014.
187 The application form can be found on SEPBLAC's website: *Form External Experts F22-7*, available at: <www.sepblac.es/espanol/sujetos_obligados/expertos.htm>, last visited on 27 March 2014.
188 Caro, M.A. (2010), 'La ley crea un registro de expertos externos en blanqueo', *Expansión, suplemento 'Asesores de Empresas'*, pp. 33-36 at 35, available at: <www.ciss.es/expansion/>, last visited on 27 March 2014.
189 See about the formulation of reservations with respect to representatives § 4.5.4.
190 Section 28(2) Act 10/2010. Cf. Section 2 Regulation EHA/2444/2007.
191 Section 4 Regulation EHA/2444/2007; Annex (*Examen externo sobre los procedimientos y* órganos *de control interno y comunicación establecidos para prevenir el blanqueo de capitales*) to Regulation EHA/2444/2007 for the specific details that the external expert is required to assess and include in the report.
192 Section 28(2) Act 10/2010 in conjunction with Section 1 Regulation EHA/2444/2007.

(or the management board) of the obliged institution within three months after the analysis has been concluded. The obliged institution must take necessary steps to remedy the deficiencies detected during the review.[193] External experts are required to disclose a list to SEPBLAC every six months demonstrating for which businesses he has reviewed internal policies.[194] Information on the name of the institutions and the corresponding identification data, the date on which the external review report was released and the date on which the external review was closed, must be provided. External review reports themselves must be made available to the Commission for the Prevention of Money Laundering and Monetary Offences, SEPBLAC and the Commission Secretariat for a period of five years following the date of issuance of the report.[195] The reference to 'must be made available' suggests that there is no obligation for external experts to automatically forward all external review reports to SEPBLAC, but only on request.

SEPBLAC can use the external review reports in various ways for the purpose of supervision. Firstly, it can use the data from external reviews and monitoring reports in the formulation of its annual supervision plans. One example would be that SEPBLAC can decide to carry out an on-site inspection at a specific obliged institution where the external review report has identified a number of serious deficiencies or where SEPBLAC – based on monitoring reports submitted by the obliged institution itself – is not certain or satisfied that appropriate measures have been taken. Another example is that SEPBLAC can decide to perform a number of thematic inspections – meaning inspections focussed on one particular (aspect of an) AML obligation – where it appears from various external expert reviews that in general some particular obligations are not complied with. Secondly, SEPBLAC inspectors can use the information in the external review report as preparation for their own on-site inspection. This allows SEPBLAC to focus specifically on certain obligations. Nevertheless, in 2006 the FATF found that even if this is a useful tool in theory, in practice it was considered insufficient to carry out AML supervision.[196] It should be considered that at that time SEPBLAC had only two FTE available for carrying out on-site supervision and the handling of these external review reports. In that respect, the situation has improved somewhat, although we have just seen that serious resource constraints still exist. Thirdly, SEPBLAC can decide to perform a number of off-site inspections by controlling the external review reports or monitoring reports on the implementation of corrective measures by the obliged institution alone.[197] Moreover, due to the formulation of Section 28 Act 10/2010 SEPBLAC should always *request* the external review reports from the obliged institutions or from the external expert. This takes time and effort on the side of SEPBLAC, which is already very constrained. It would be advisable to amend

193 Section 28(2) Act 10/2010.

194 Section 28(2) Act 10/2010. For the six-month update on reviewed institutions and professionals, the external expert must use form F22-8, available at: <www.sepblac.es/espanol/sujetos_obligados/expertos.htm>, last visited on 27 March 2014.

195 Section 28(3) Act 10/2010. The ministerial regulation still speaks about a term of six years and refers to the privileged character of the external review report: Section 6 Regulation EHA/2444/2007.

196 FATF (2006) at 135.

197 The Bank of Spain is said to include in its monitoring the advance in the implementation of the corrective measures required and the revision of external expert review reports in its off-site inspections: FATF (2010) at 16.

the law by clarifying that external experts and/or the reviewed institutions are required to forward the report to the Commission and SEPBLAC upon the issuance of the external review report or the monitoring report.

Because external experts are obliged to review the internal policies of obliged institutions in depth, it can be considered an instrument that increases the effectiveness of SEPBLAC's anti-money laundering supervision. External review reports can be used as a source for the annual supervision plan, as preparation for an inspection visit or be the subject of an off-site inspection (desk review). Because the annual inspection plans cannot be consulted, it is impossible to see how external review reports enhance SEPBLAC's supervision in this way. Unfortunately, no public data is available that proves whether and how SEPBLAC has performed off-site inspections in which it reviewed external review reports. Having concluded that SEPBLAC's own (on-site) supervision intensity is rather low, one must be extra careful with the use of external review reports for the purpose of supervision. After all, this instrument may not substitute the supervision exercised by SEPBLAC. The instrument of external expert reviews has the potential to raise the effectiveness of supervision even more when the identified legal flaws are rectified. The Act would benefit from more clarity on the aspects of the requirements for an external expert in terms of the person, education and experience, and the way in which the report must be made available to SEPBLAC. Legislation should state that external review reports must be submitted to SEPBLAC, preferably within a given time frame to be determined by the legislator or SEPBLAC.

4.6.4 Concluding remarks

This section has dealt with supervision by SEPBLAC. The AML Act provides SEPBLAC with adequate supervisory powers, with the exception of a regulatory power. Inspectors have the power to compel the production of any information that is relevant to monitoring compliance and the power to perform checks. SEPBLAC inspectors can perform both on-site and off-site inspections. SEPBLAC has no sanctioning powers. There is very little transparency as to how SEPBLAC exercises its AML supervision in practice. The fact that the annual report 2012 does not include a single reference to AML supervision is illustrative in this respect. The annual supervision plans cannot be consulted, there seems to be no general supervision policy and information on how the risk-based approach to supervision is implemented by SEPBLAC is largely absent. The inspection activity of SEPBLAC is very low, most likely caused by severe resource constraints. Banks may have been subject to AML inspections, but since the entry force of the AML Act accountants and real estate agents have never been supervised as to their compliance with the preventive obligations.

There are three instruments that can raise the effectiveness of SEPBLAC's supervision. These, however, may not substitute the supervision exercised by SEPBLAC. The instruments are SEPBLAC's FIU-related functions, the possibility for the Commission to enter into supervisory arrangements with the Bank of Spain and the two other financial regulators, and the obligation for institutions and professionals to have the internal policies for the prevention of money laundering and terrorist financing assessed by an external expert. Whereas the FIU-related functions, in particular the power to use and access a wide variety of internal and external databases, gives SEPBLAC a stronger information position, the other two instruments allow SEPBLAC to spend its limited resources more effectively. With respect to the supervisory arrangements it was, however, observed that they have a privileged character. Moreover, it appeared that Bank of Spain had not, or hardly, carried out any AML supervision of banks in the years 2011 and 2012. This gives rise to doubts about the practical effects of these arrangements. External review reports can be used by SEPBLAC as a source for the annual supervision plan, as preparation for an inspection visit or be the subject of an off-site inspection. How these are used in practice is not known. The external review system would nevertheless benefit from amendments to the law, in particular with respect to the person, education and experience of the external expert and the way in which the report must be made available to SEPBLAC.

4.7 Sanctioning for breaches of AML obligations

In Spain there is a strict separation between supervision and sanctioning. SEPBLAC is the authority responsible for AML supervision, but it cannot decide on the imposition of sanctions. Its task is to establish the facts upon an inspection, but an evaluation thereof rests with another authority. Sanctioning authority under the AML Act is given to the Council of Ministers, the Minister of Economy and Competitiveness and the Director-General for the Treasury and Financial Policy.[198] The Standing Committee of the Commission, upon a proposal from the Commission Secretariat, initiates and, where applicable, dismisses the sanctioning proceedings, and the Commission Secretariat carries out the preliminary investigation of these proceedings.[199] The division of competence depends on the seriousness of the breaches. The Council of Ministers, upon a proposal from the Minister of Economy and Competitiveness, has the power to impose a sanction in case of very serious breaches (*infracciones muy graves*), the Minister of Economy and Competitiveness has the competence – upon a proposal from the Commission for the Prevention of Money Laundering and Monetary Offences – in case of serious breaches (*infracciones graves*), whereas the Director-General for the Treasury and Financial Policy of the Ministry of Economy and Competitiveness – upon a proposal from the handling officer of the Commission Secretariat, is competent in case of minor breaches (*infracciones leves*).

This section analyses the sanctioning powers available for non-compliance with the anti-money laundering obligations, as well as the sanctioning procedure in practice in § 4.7.2 and 4.7.3. Before that, however, I will first pay attention to the doctrine of punitive administrative law in Spain, which is a popular topic among Spanish legal scholars.

198 Section 61(3) Act 10/2010.

199 Sections 61(1) and 61(2) Act 10/2010. See more in § 4.7.3.

4.7.1 The doctrine of punitive administrative law

The doctrine of punitive administrative law (*la potestad administrativa sancionadora*) attracts a great deal of attention in Spanish legal writing. The State's sanctioning power is considered to be one of the core administrative law principles in Spain. It is separate from the power to inspect (*potestad de inspección*).[200] The powers are considered to differ in character: while the inspection activity aims primarily at the prevention or the restoration of infringed legality, punitive administrative law rather searches for retribution and is always a direct response to an action or a failure to act. The most important general rules on punitive administrative law can be found in Sections 127 to 138 LPA.[201] This Act is complemented by Royal Decree 1398/1993 that approves the regulation on the general procedure for the exercise of sanctioning powers.[202] The LPA and the Decree only provide a general framework via principles and procedural rules. The administrative sanctioning procedures are regulated in sectoral legislation, depending on the context of the laws and regulations at stake.[203] An example of a special sanctioning regime is the tax sanctioning regime (*regimen sancionador tributario*), which is of a more repressive nature and provides less guarantees to offenders.[204] It should be pointed out that the LPA and the Decree not provide a definition of administrative sanctions, but since the doctrine of punitive administrative law searches for retribution and is a 'direct and deliberate response' to an action or failure to act, this notion excludes administrative measures aimed at avoiding future non-compliance or at the reparation of the consequences of the unlawful behaviour. Also sanctions that are not directly considered as a response to the non-compliant behaviour, for example the (temporary) revocation of licences, do not seem to fall under this doctrine, although there are discussions about this.[205] As Rebollo Puig et al. state: '(...) in practice, the line between administrative sanctions and other administrative decisions detrimental to the public cannot be clearly drawn. In fact, whether administrative decisions with the same detrimental effect are to be considered administrative sanctions or not, depends on their intention to punish'.[206]

> Until the Civil War Spain had a very legalistic approach: sanctioning by the public administration was in principle forbidden, although there were some exceptions to that rule.[207] After the Civil War (1936-1939), the number, depth and scope of administrative regulations expanded and punitive administrative law developed along with it. It is the

200 García Ureta (2006) at 35-36.

201 Supra, n. 41.

202 *Real Decreto 1398/1993, de 4 de agosto, por el que se aprueba el Reglamento del Procedimiento para el Ejercicio de la Potestad Sancionadora, BOE no. 189, 9 de agosto 1993, 24050-24056*. Hereafter 'RD 1398/1993'.

203 Rebollo Puig, M., Izquierdo Carrasco, M., Alarcón Sotomayor, L. and Bueno Armijo, A. (2013), 'Spain', in: Jansen, O.J.D.M.L (ed.), *Administrative sanctions in the European Union*, Intersentia: Antwerp, pp. 515-551 at 523.

204 *Ley 58/2003, de 17 de diciembre, General Tributaria, BOE no. 302, Sec. I, 18 de diciembre 2003, 44987-45056; Real Decreto 2063/2004, de 15 de octubre, por el que se aprueba el Reglamento general del régimen sancionador tributario, BOE no. 260, Sec. I, 28 de octubre 2004, 35598-35612*. Here it is stated that the sanctioning powers must be applied in accordance with the general principles, but 'with the specialties laid down in this Act'.

205 Rebollo Puig et al. (2013) at 515-517.

206 Ibid., at 517.

207 Santamaría Pastor, J.A. (2000), *Principios de Derecho Administrativo*, Volumen II, Editorial Centro de Estudios Ramón Areces, S.A., at 373-374.

predominant opinion in the legal literature that there is only a small difference between punitive administrative sanctions and criminal sanctions, and that both belong to the *ius puniendi* of the State.[208] From the 1960s onwards, the administrative sanctioning system was increasingly criticised for its failure to abide by minimum criminal law principles and guarantees, such as the presumption of innocence.[209] A general power for the administration to impose sanctions was included in the Spanish Constitution of 1978. The underlying reasons were, among other things, the desirability not to overburden the judicial system with minor crimes, the desirability to provide a more efficient and repressive reply to these types of offences and the desirability to act more quickly in respect of the punishable acts.[210] Section 25 CE 1978 allows the administration to impose sanctions, but prohibits administrative sanctions that (in)directly deprive the subject of liberty.[211]

The AML Act contains detailed provisions on the breaches and corresponding administrative sanctions and measures. These provisions occupy a central role and are supplemented by the general framework.

4.7.1.1 General principles underlying the administrative sanctioning system

As explained, there is a consensus among scholars that punitive administrative law and criminal law are much alike. Such reasoning can also be found in the case law of the Constitutional Court (*Tribunal Constitucional*).[212] Therefore, one can find criminal law principles in punitive administrative law, albeit adjusted to the distinct character of the latter.[213] The general principles regulate either the punitive administrative law *system as a*

208 Santamaría Pastor (2000) at 376-377; Nieto, A. (2002), *Derecho administrative sancionador,* 3rd edition, Tecnos: Madrid, at 80; Rebollo Puig et al. (2013) at 515; Bachmaier, L. and del Moral García, M. (2010), *Criminal Law in Spain*, Kluwer Law International: Alphen aan den Rijn, at 155; López Torralba, V. (2005), 'Breve estudio en torno al Procedimiento Administrativo Sancionador y sus garantías', *Revista Jurídica de la Comunidad de Madrid*, issue 22, September 2005, pp. 181-244 at § 1.2.

209 Santamaría Pastor (2000) at 375-376.

210 STC 77/1983 of 3 October 1983 (STC means *Sentencia de Tribunal Constitutional*).

211 Section 25(1) CE 1978 can be translated as follows: 'No one may be convicted or sentenced for actions or omissions which – when committed – did not constitute a crime, misdemeanour, or administrative infringement as established by legislation in force at that moment.' Section 25(3): 'The public administration may not impose sanctions which directly or indirectly imply a deprivation of liberty.'

212 STC 18/1981 of 8 June 1981, where the Constitutional Court considered: '[h]a de recordarse que los principios inspiradores del orden penal son de aplicación, *con ciertos matices*, al derecho administrativo sancionador, dado que ambos son manifestaciones del ordenamiento punitivo del Estado (…)'. This was confirmed in STC 54/2003 of 24 March 2003. Cf. Perelló Domenech, I. (1994), 'Derecho administrativo sancionador y jurisprudencia constitucional', *Jueces para la democracia*, issue 22, pp. 76-81 at 76, who refers to a number of other decisions where the Constitutional Court repeated this consideration.

213 Nieto (2002) at 170-174. Gallardo Castillo observes that it not so much the question whether criminal law principles apply to the punitive administrative system as there is no doubt about that, but rather to what extent, in which cases and how the principles should be applied. This is a difficult task, he argues, as administrative law lacks an established dogma as is applicable in criminal law which enables the construction of a stable sanctioning regime, and because of the tension in the coexistence of the heavily debated principles of legality and effectiveness in administrative case law: Gallardo Castillo, M.J. (2008), *Los Principios de la Potestad Sancionadora: Teoría y práctica*, Iustel: Madrid, at 20 et seq. Cf. Nieto (2002) at 167 who has the same line of reasoning.

whole, or are concerned with the *application* of the system.[214] Being general principles, these are also relevant for sanctioning activities under the AML Act. For a good understanding the principles will be discussed hereafter.

The first principle is the principle of legality. This principle has various meanings.[215] In the context of punitive administrative law legality entails that the sanctioning power of the administration only exists when it is explicitly attributed to it by means of legislation.[216] The Constitutional Court has outlined in its case law that the principle of legality requires a legal basis, but that this does not exclude the possibility that the legal norm contains references to regulations, provided that the regulations contain, in a sufficiently clear manner, the elements of the unlawful behaviour and the nature and limits of the possible sanctions. Such regulations must not be independent and be clearly subordinated to the law.[217] The second principle is the principle of non-retroactivity (*irretroactividad*). Non-retroactivity means that sanctioning provisions cannot change the legal consequences of actions committed or relationships that existed prior to the enactment of the law. This prohibition is embedded in Section 9, third paragraph, CE 1978 in which it is stated that the Constitution, among other things, guarantees 'the non-retroactivity of punitive provisions that are not favourable to or restrictive of individual rights'.[218] Retroactivity *in bonam partem* is, however, an obligation: 'sanctioning provisions shall have a retroactive effect provided they are favourable to the presumptive offender'.[219]

The specialty principle (*tipicidad*) is closely related to the principle of legality and legal certainty.[220] This principle obliges that conduct that can be sanctioned should be sufficiently and clearly laid down, in specific terms and not in general terms alone. The law should define as concretely as possible the elements of the punishable behaviour. On the basis of the case law Gallardo Castillo distinguishes three requirements: i) the definition of the conduct that is considered to constitute the offence; ii) the determination of the sanctions and, where appropriate, the scale of these sanctions and iii) a description of the necessary correlation between the offence and the corresponding sanctions, so that a potential offender can predict with sufficient certainty the type and degree of punishment that can be imposed.[221] This principle originally stems from the case law of the Constitutional Court and is laid down in Section 129 LPA which states that breaches must be classified as minor, serious or very serious.[222] The fourth principle, the principle of guilt (*culpabilidad*), means that the offence can be attributed to a legal or natural person.[223] Sanctions can only

214 Title IX of the LPA is divided into two chapters: Chapter I deals with principles of sanctioning powers (Sections 127-133), while Chapter II concerns the principles of the punitive administrative procedure. Cf. Santamaría Pastor (2000) at 383 and 387; Rebollo Puig et al. (2013) at 523; López Torralba (2005) at § 1.2.

215 Gallardo Castillo (2008) at 23-29.

216 Section 25(1) CE 1978; Section 127.1 LPA. Cf. Rebollo Puig et al. (2013) at 526-527.

217 See Gallardo Castillo (2008) at 28-29 who refers to a number of Constitutional Court judgments.

218 For the punitive administrative power it is reiterated in Section 25(1) CE 1978; Gallardo Castillo (2008) at 134.

219 Section 128 LPA.

220 Santamaría Pastor (2000) at 385; Gallardo Castillo (2008), at 87; Rebollo Puig et al. (2013) at 528.

221 Gallardo Castillo (2008) at 92.

222 Santamaría Pastor (2000) at 385.

223 Section 130(1) LPA. Cf. Rebollo Puig et al. (2013) at 530.

be imposed by the administration if non-compliant behaviour is committed willingly and with culpability. In the case of legal persons, intent or fault by the responsible natural persons must be proven.[224]

The principle of proportionality (*proporcionalidad*) requires that a sanction must be proportional to the offence. The decision as to the amount of the sanction must solely be made based on the severity of the offence and the characteristics of the offender. Most Spanish scholars do not consider this as a principle that attributes any substantive rights as such, but rather as a 'shield' that accompanies each right.[225] Santamaría Pastor points to three functions of the principle. In his opinion it serves as a rule of moderation, it limits the discretion of the administration in deciding on the sanction and allows for judicial review by the administrative courts.[226] The LPA provides general conditions that must always be taken into account in determining the sanction: the existence of intent or repetition and the nature of the damage caused.[227] In any case, administrative sanctions cannot lead to a deprivation of liberty. The sixth principle is the limitation principle (*prescripción*) that stipulates that there must be a time limit within which an illegal act must be sanctioned. It serves to ensure legal certainty on the one hand, and the effectiveness of the administration on the other.[228] The LPA states that the general limitation period for very serious offences is three years, for serious offences two years and for minor breaches six months.[229] The limitation period of the offences runs from the day on which the offence was committed. If no action is taken within this period, the administration can no longer act against the breach. There is also a limitation period for the execution or enforcement of the sanctions. These are three, two and one year for the three categories of breaches. The period starts to run from the day on which a final decision to impose a sanction has been made. If the sanction is not enforced within the prescribed time, the legal ground expires.[230]

Finally, the principle of *non bis in idem* is an important principle.[231] The Constitutional Court has inferred this principle from the principles of legality and specialty as laid down in Section 25, first paragraph, CE 1978.[232] It means that someone cannot be punished twice for the same act. This means that two administrative sanctions for the same act or a concurrence of an administrative and criminal sanction is not allowed.[233] The principle does not stand in the way of a combination between an administrative sanction and other administrative measures. As to the relationship between punitive administrative law and criminal law enforcement, there are systems in place to coordinate the two systems. The basic rule is that criminal law enforcement prevails: '[a]s long as an act is being dealt with within the criminal jurisdiction; the public authority must abstain from resolving the

224 Rebollo Puig et al. (2013) at 530.
225 Gallardo Castillo (2008) at 214.
226 Santamaría Pastor (2000) at 391.
227 Section 131(3) LPA.
228 López Torralba (2005) at § 2.5.
229 Section 132 LPA.
230 See about the limitation principle in theory and practice: Gallardo Castillo (2008) at 228-289.
231 Cf. Nieto (2002) at 398-455.
232 Santamaría Pastor (2000) at 393, who refers to judgments from the Constitutional Court.
233 Section 133 LPA. It has been commented that this provision is only a simplistic formulation and misses some fundamental elements that are very important in practice: Gallardo Castillo (2008) at 290 et seq.

matter. If this coordination fails and an administrative sanction is imposed, the criminal jurisdiction will still apply as it always prevails. If criminal proceedings conclude with a jurisdiction, prior administrative sanctions must be annulled in order to comply with the rule against double punishment'.[234]

4.7.1.2 The general administrative sanctioning procedure

There is no uniform administrative sanctioning procedure, but Section 134 LPA states that a legally established sanctioning procedure is required for the exercise of the sanctioning authority. This is called the principle of the required procedure.[235] There should be a separation between the authority that imposes the sanction and the so-called instructing authority (órgano *instructor*) that proposes the sanction. This separation is believed to provide a maximum guarantee to the citizen that an impartial and objective decision as to the imposition of the sanction is made. It resembles the classic criminal law principle that applies in Spanish law that states that magistrates (*jueces de instrucción*) who lead the criminal investigation do not decide on the content of the criminal case itself.[236]

> This formal separation, however, is not free from criticism. Santamaría Pastor comments on the fact that the employees entrusted with the task to propose the sanction often stand in a hierarchical relationship to the ones that finally impose the sanction. This makes the first group inclined to propose those sanctions 'that will prove favourable to the chief'. Moreover, he argues that the intervention of the political authority that decides on the sanction is often a pure formality, and in practice the same people that formulate the proposal, take the final decision on the sanction.[237]
>
> The foregoing also means that from the early stages of supervision to the last phase of sanctioning at least three authorities are formally involved: the supervisory, the instructing and, finally, the sanctioning authority. Although it aims to give a maximum guarantee to citizens that an impartial and objective decision is taken, such a strict standard also requires more from the authorities. After all, case files need to be assigned from the supervisory authority, to the instructing authority and, ultimately, to the sanctioning authority. It poses high demands in terms of communication and coordination between the different authorities, as the involvement of different authorities in different phases of the procedure could possibly entail a risk of information loss.

The LPA lays down some basic rights which are applicable in the procedure, such as the presumption of innocence, the rights of the accused, the possibility of interim measures and the fact that a sanctioning decision must be properly reasoned and that only those facts that have been established during the proceedings can be taken into account.[238] These principles follow from Section 24, second paragraph, CE 1978 and the Constitutional

234 Bachmaier and del Moral García (2010) at 155-156.
235 Rebollo Puig et al. (2013) at 532-533. López Torralba (2005) at § 2.1.1 calls it the guarantee of procedure.
236 Sections 103 CE 1978 and 134(2) LPA; Santamaría Pastor (2000) at 403-404; López Torralba (2005) at § 2.2.
237 Santamaría Pastor (2000) at 404.
238 Sections 135-138 LPA. See also STC 89/1995 of 6 June 1995 and STC 74/2004 of 22 April 2004.

Court has declared that these also apply in the field of punitive administrative law.[239] The regulation approved by RD 139/1993 under the LPA contains more detailed provisions concerning the sanctioning procedure, but only applies insofar as sectoral legislation does not regulate anything.[240]

4.7.2 Sanctioning powers under the AML Act

The AML Act describes the breaches and corresponding administrative sanctions and measures in a detailed manner. This high level of detail is interesting and can be explained by the above-mentioned doctrine. As required by Section 126 LPA, Section 50 Act 10/2010 states that the possible offences under this Act are categorised as very serious, serious or minor offences. Sections 51 to 53 set out in detail the behaviour that constitutes these offences and Sections 56 to 58 regulate the sanctions for each category of offences.

4.7.2.1 Very serious offences and corresponding sanctions

Very serious offences are those actions or omissions that are considered to undermine the goals of the preventive anti-money laundering policy. These are, for example, the failure to report to SEPBLAC when a director or employee of an obliged institution has internally revealed the existence of indications or certainty that an operation was related to money laundering or terrorist financing; the failure to cooperate with the Commission for the Prevention of Money Laundering and Monetary Offences, SEPBLAC and the Commission Secretariat; a breach of the tipping-off prohibition; and the obstruction of or resistance to inspections.[241] In the list of very serious offences, non-compliance with customer due diligence, internal policy or record-keeping requirements are not included, unless when for a serious offence a final sanction was imposed on the obliged institution or professional in the preceding five years for the same type of offence.[242] The following sanctions and measures can be imposed for very serious offences:

- a public warning *(amonestación pública)*. This measure basically entails a kind of naming and shaming procedure; once this sanction becomes binding in administrative proceedings, it shall be enforced in the manner established in the decision and always be published in the Official State Gazette (*Boletín Oficial del Estado, BOE*).[243]
- a fine ranging from a minimum of 150,000 Euros to a maximum amount that may be imposed up to the highest of these figures: either 5% of the net worth of the

239 For example: STC 13/1982 of 1 April 1982 and STC 14/1999 of 22 February 1999. Section 24(2) CE 1978 includes the right of access to the ordinary judge predetermined by law, to defence and assistance by an attorney, to be informed of the accusation made against them, to a public trial without delays and with all the guarantees, to utilise the means of proof pertinent to their defence, to refrain from self-incrimination, to refrain from pleading guilty, and to the presumption of innocence.

240 López Torralba (2005) at § 2.1.2.

241 The full list of very serious offences can be found in Section 51 Act 10/2010.

242 Section 51(1)(f) Act 10/2010.

243 Section 61(5), second sentence, Act 10/2010. Compare the naming & shaming powers in the Netherlands (Chapter 5) and the United Kingdom (Chapter 6).

institution or professional covered by Act 10/2010, twice the economic substance of the transaction, or 1,500,000 Euros.
- in case of institutions that require an administrative authorisation before the performance of their operations, the withdrawal of this authorisation (a licence withdrawal).

The Act determines that a fine is a compulsory sanction in all events, and *must* be combined with either the public warning or the licence withdrawal.[244] The legislator has thus clearly determined that that the public warning and licence withdrawal are not to be considered administrative sanctions. Rather, they should be seen as complementary administrative measures to the fine. Sanctions may also be imposed on the directors or managers of the institutions who were responsible for the offence.[245] Each manager or director can be ordered to pay a fine of between 60,000 and 600,000 Euros, can be ordered to be removed from office and be forbidden to hold an administrative or management position in the same institution or any institution covered by Act 10/2010 for a maximum period of ten years.[246] The fine is a compulsory sanction and *may* be simultaneously imposed with the other sanctions.

4

4.7.2.2 Serious offences and corresponding sanctions

The category of serious offences is the largest in the AML Act.[247] Some of the facts that are considered a serious offence are: a failure to comply with formal identification obligations; a failure to comply with the record keeping obligation; a failure to comply with the obligation to approve in writing and to implement adequate internal control procedures including the written approval and implementation of an explicit policy for customer admissions; a failure to comply with the obligation of external review; and the entering into or continuing business relationships or the execution of prohibited transactions.[248] Unless there are indications of the certainty of money laundering and terrorist financing non-compliant behaviour with respect to some customer due diligence requirements can be classified as a minor offence, when this offence can be considered as merely occasional or isolated based on the percentage of incidents in the sample of compliance.[249] The following sanctions can be imposed:

- a private warning (*amonestación privada*) – the offender receives a warning, but contrary to a public warning, this is not published;
- a public warning;
- a fine ranging from a minimum of 60,001 Euros and a maximum amount that may be imposed up to the highest of these figures: 1% of the net worth of the institution covered by the Act, the sum of the economic substance of the transaction plus 50%, or 150,000 Euros.

244 Section 56(1), last sentence, Act 10/2010.
245 Section 54 Act 10/2010.
246 Section 56(2) Act 10/2010.
247 Section 52 Act 10/2010.
248 The full list can be found in Section 52(1), 52(3), 52(4) and 52(5) Act 10/2010.
249 Section 52(2) Act 10/2010.

Again the fine is a compulsory sanction and *must* be combined with the private or public warning.[250] At the same time sanctions can also be imposed on the directors or managers of the institution who were responsible for the offence.[251] These sanctions are a private warning, a public warning, a fine for each person of between 3,000 and 60,000 Euros, or temporary suspension from office for a maximum period of one year. Here too, the fine is a compulsory sanction and should be combined with one of the other sanctions.[252]

Finally, non-compliance with the obligation to declare cash with a total value of 10,000 Euros or more is sanctioned with a minimum fine of 600 Euros and with a maximum of up to twice the value of the non-declared money.[253]

4.7.2.3 Minor offences and corresponding sanctions

The AML Act does not provide a list of minor offences, which means that all other offences not mentioned as a very serious or serious offence are to be considered as minor next to those that can be considered a minor offence on the basis of Section 52, second paragraph, of Act 10/2010.[254] Minor offences can be sanctioned by means of a private warning and/or a maximum fine of 60,000 Euros.[255] There is no provision in place concerning sanctions for directors or managers of the institutions who were responsible for the offence.

4.7.2.4 Limitation of the offences and sanctions

In accordance with the limitation principle, Section 60 Act 10/2010 provides the limitation periods for the offences and sanctions. Very serious and serious offences shall have a limitation period of five years, and minor offences a period of two years, from the date on which the offence was committed.[256] In the case of ongoing non-compliance, the limitation period runs from the termination of the activity or the last act with which the offence was committed. In case of a failure to comply with customer due diligence obligations, the limitation period begins on the date of the termination of the business relationship, and for the record keeping obligation, on the expiry of the statutory record keeping period. The limitation period is interrupted by any action by the Commission, SEPBLAC or the Commission Secretariat carried out with the formal knowledge of the obliged institution or professional, leading to the inspection, monitoring or control of all or part of the obligations herein. It is also interrupted by the initiation, with the knowledge of those concerned, of administrative sanctioning proceedings or criminal prosecution for the same facts or for other facts that cannot be separated from those punishable under the AML Act. In line with the LPA, the sanctions imposed have a limitation period of three

250 Section 57(1) Act 10/2010.
251 Section 54 Act 10/2010.
252 Section 57(2) Act 10/2010.
253 Section 57(3) in conjunction with Section 43 Act 10/2010. This obligation, however, is not something that banks, accountants and real estate agents have to comply with. The supervisory role of SEPBLAC is here also limited. Therefore, this obligation is outside the focus of this research.
254 Section 53 Act in conjunction with Section 52(2) Act 10/2010.
255 Section 58 Act 10/2010.
256 This is longer than the general prescription period laid down in Section 132 LPA.

years (very serious offences), two years (serious offences), and one year (minor offences), starting on the date of the notification of the sanctioning decision. The limitation period for sanctions is interrupted when an administrative or judicial agreement suspends the execution of the decision.[257]

4.7.3 The sanctioning procedure under the AML Act

When SEPBLAC finishes an inspection, it draws up an inspection report which it sends to the Commission Secretariat.[258] According to Section 61 Act 10/2010 the Standing Committee of the Commission is empowered to initiate and dismiss sanctioning procedures, upon a proposal from the Commission Secretariat.[259] The third transitional provision to the AML Act, however, decides that the power to initiate sanctioning proceedings shall continue to be exercised by the Commission Secretariat.[260] In its role as an instructing authority it carries out the preliminary investigations of the sanctioning procedures and proposes, via a so-called *propuesta de resolución*, sanctions to the authorities with the power to impose sanctions.[261] The proposal must as a minimum contain the facts that are considered proven and their legal qualification, the possible breach and the name of the person responsible for this, a proposal for the sanction to be imposed and an explanation of the temporary measures that have been adopted, or alternatively, if applicable, propose the decision that there is no breach or responsibility by the person in question. The actual sanctioning power rests, as explained, with the Council of Ministers, the Minister of Economy and Competitiveness and the Director-General for the Treasury and Financial Policy for very serious, serious and minor offences.[262] The entire sanctioning procedure may take a maximum of one year, starting from the date of notification of the commencement of the proceedings.[263] The expiry of this time limit leads to the expiry of the sanctioning procedure and a new decision to initiate proceedings must be taken. This must, of course, be done within the limitation period for the offences.[264] Once a sanction is imposed and has become final, the Commission Secretariat is responsible for the implementation of the sanctioning decision in administrative proceedings.[265] In particular, where a public warning is imposed and this decision has become final, it is responsible for the publication in the Official State Gazette.

257 Section 60(2) Act 10/2010.

258 The Commission Secretariat's staff come from la *Secretaría del Tesoro y Política Financiera, Subdirección General de Inspección y Control de Movimientos de Capitales* of the Ministry of Economy and Competitiveness. This division falls under the *Secretaría de Estado de Economía y Apoyo a la Empresa*. See: *Real Decreto 345/2012, de 10 de febrero, por el que se desarrolla la estructura orgánica básica del Ministerio de Economía y Competitividad, BOE no. 36, Sec. I, 11 de febrero 2012, 12607-12633* (in English: *Royal Decree concerning the organic basic structure of the Ministry of Economy and Competitiveness*). See about the inspection report: FATF (2006) at 111.

259 The power to initiate or conclude the dismissal of the punitive proceedings for a breach of the obligation to declare under Section 34 rests with the Commission Secretariat.

260 See § 4.3 on the consequences of the absence of a Royal Decree under Act 10/2010.

261 See Section 18 RD 1398/1993.

262 See § 4.7.

263 Section 61(4) Act 10/2010.

264 See § 4.7.2.

265 Section 61(5) Act 10/2010.

In line with the doctrine of punitive administrative law, the AML Act states that the offences and corresponding sanctions shall be without prejudice to the acts and omissions described as crimes in the Penal Code or special criminal laws.[266] There can be no simultaneous punitive administrative and criminal proceedings with respect to the same person on the same facts. In that case the latter takes precedence.[267] Only if the public prosecutor's office decides not to start criminal proceedings, may the Commission Secretariat continue the sanctioning proceedings.[268]

In determining the amount or severity of the sanction(s), the Commission Secretariat and the competent sanctioning authority are obliged to take into account various aggravating and mitigating circumstances that are laid down in Section 59 of Act 10/2010. The general idea is that the sanction must be scaled in such way that the commission of the offence is not more beneficial than compliance. On the other hand, the sanction must be proportionate to the offence committed. Three indicators that should be taken into account in determining the sanction are the sum of the transactions or the proceeds that are the result of the offence, the circumstance of having acted or failing to act to remedy the breach on one's own initiative, and the existence of sanctions imposed for offences under the AML Act against the same institution or professional in the preceding five years.[269] The determination whether or not to impose sanctions on the managers and directors of the institutions, as well as the amount of the sanctions, depends on the degree of responsibility or intention of the person concerned, his past conduct in connection with the AML obligations, the nature of his representation, and his financial situation when the sanction is a fine.[270] In addition, the provisions stipulating the sanctions for the categories of offences mostly oblige the sanctioning authority to combine the imposition of a fine with another sanction. For the imposition of sanctions for very serious or serious offences on financial institutions or institutions which require authorisation, the Commission Secretariat must request from the sectoral supervisor a report on the potential impact of the proposed sanction(s) on the stability of the institution concerned.[271]

4.7.4 Sanctioning in practice

There is no publicly available sanctioning policy that can be consulted. According to SEPBLAC representatives, the public warning is not extensively used due to the reputation damage it can cause to the institution concerned. The most commonly used sanction is the fine (*multa*).[272] This is not surprising since the AML Act designates the fine as the standard sanction for non-compliance, which in most cases must be combined with another sanction.[273] Sanctioning decisions made under the AML Act are in principle not

266 Section 62 Act 10/2010.

267 When it becomes apparent during the sanctioning procedure that an act can also be considered a criminal offence, the Commission Secretariat shall report this to the public prosecutor's office and suspend the proceedings until it becomes clear whether criminal proceedings will be instituted or not.

268 Section 62(4) Act 10/2010.

269 Section 59(1) Act 10/2010.

270 Section 59(2) Act 10/2010.

271 Section 61(3), second part, Act 10/2010.

272 Interview SEPBLAC, October 2013.

273 See § 4.7.2.

published in any form, with the exception of public warnings.[274] Once a public warning has become final, this sanction is published in the Official State Gazette.

The only source of data available with respect to sanctions imposed under Act 10/2010 is the Statistical Report 2010-12 from the Commission. This report states that in 2010 six economic sanctions *(sanciones económicas)* were imposed, of which three were against financial institutions, two against non-financial institutions and one against a manager or director *(administrador)*. In 2011 the total number of sanctions was seven, of which three were against financial institutions, two against DNFBPs and two against managers or directors. In 2012 thirteen sanctions were imposed, of which five were against financial institutions, six against non-financial institutions and two against managers or directors. The total amount of all economic sanctions in 2012 was 3.2 million Euros.[275] The fact that the report speaks about economic sanctions allows us to presume that the statistics only concern fines. The report, however, does not provide information about other types of sanctions imposed, the non-compliant behaviour for which the sanctions were imposed, the seriousness of these offences, and so on. Moreover, it does not distinguish any further as to against which type of obliged institutions or professionals the sanctions were imposed, other than the distinction between financial and non-financial institutions. Based on this data we cannot therefore conclude whether banks, accountants or real estate agents have been sanctioned for non-compliance with the preventive obligations in the years 2010-12. In the absence of (on-site) inspections of accountants and real estate agents during these years, however, it seems highly unlikely that professionals from these two groups were sanctioned.

Further insight into sanctioning practice could be provided by the Official State Gazette and the case law of the Spanish Supreme Court.[276] A look at the publications in the Official State Gazette since 1 April 2010 provides four cases of non-compliance in which a public

274 Interview SEPBLAC, October 2013.

275 CPBCIM (2013) at 47. The exact amount is 3,242,010 Euros.

276 For the context and aim of this research, it is not possible to analyse *all* case law of *all* competent courts in Spain. To give an impression of the sanctioning activity under the preventive AML regime, the case law of the Supreme Court is pertinent – being the highest competent court dealing with sanctions imposed under this piece of legislation. Search in the database on: <www.poderjudicial.es/search/>. Reference period: 1st of September 2009 until the 28th March 2014. Search terms: 'blanqueo', 'blanqueo de capitales', 'blanqueo de dinero', 'SEPBLAC', 'Ley 19/1993', 'Ley 10/2010'. Cases concerning the (non-)declaration of cash were left out of this analysis, because these cases do not result from supervision by SEPBLAC or sectoral supervisors.

warning was imposed.[277] One of the sanctions was imposed against a money remittance institution. The other three public warnings concerned very serious offences committed by banks, two under the predecessor of Act 10/2010 and one under Act 10/2010. Two banks, Jyske Bank Gibraltar and HSBC Bank Plc., were fined for offences committed in the years 2007 and 2002 respectively.[278] The resolution on Banco Espírito Santo does not indicate when the offences were committed, but refers to the current AML Act. In all three cases public warnings were combined with fines, as required by the AML Act. The fines varied from 1.11 million Euros in the case of Banco Espírito Santo, to 1.7 million Euros against Jyske Bank and even up to 2.1 million Euros against HSBC Bank. In all three cases, various fines were imposed and the amounts attached to each individual fine were added up, explaining why the total amounts are higher than the statutory caps provided in the AML Act. The case law of the Supreme Court (*Tribunal Supremo*) demonstrates that sanctions for non-compliance with preventive anti-money laundering obligations have been imposed, but the facts of all of these cases date from (far) before the entry into force of Act 10/2010.[279] Notwithstanding this, in all these cases fines were combined with a private warning. For example, in a case against a Spanish construction company, offences were subject to a fine of between 1000,00 and 300,000 Euros and all fines were accompanied by a private warning.[280] It is interesting to observe that in all but two Supreme Court cases, estate agency businesses and banks were involved in these cases.[281] So far, sanctions imposed under the current regime have not yet ended up at the Supreme Court.

277 Search in database on <www.boe.es/buscar/>. Reference period: 1st of April 2010 – 28th of March 2014. Search terms used 'blanqueo', 'blanqueo de capitales', 'Ley 19/1993', 'Ley 10/2010'. Results: Resolution 7232 of 26 April 2010 against Jyske Bank Gibraltar Limited (*Resolución de 26 de abril de 2010, de la Dirección General del Tesoro y Política Financiera, por la que se publica las sanciones impuestas a Jyske Bank Gibraltar Limited por infracciones muy graves de la Ley 19/1993, de 28 de diciembre, sobre determinadas medidas de prevención del blanqueo de capitales*), BOE no. 110, 6 May 2010, 40285-40286; Resolution 6575 of 13 May 2013 against HSBC Bank Plc (*Resolución de 13 de mayo de 2013, de la Secretaría General del Tesoro y Política Financiera, por las que se publican las sanciones impuestas a HSBC Bank Plc, Sucursal en España, por infracciones muy graves de la Ley 19/1993, de 28 de diciembre, sobre determinadas medidas de prevención del blanqueo de capitales*), BOE no. 144, 17 June 2013, 45771-45771; Resolution 7465 of 27 June 2013 against Moneygram Payments Systems Spain SA (*Resolución de 27 de junio de 2013, de la Comisión de Prevención del Blanqueo de Capitales e Infracciones Monetarias, por la que se publica el Acuerdo del Consejo de Ministros de 2 de noviembre de 2012, por el que se sanciona a Moneygram Payments Systems Spain SA, por infracción muy grave de la normativa sobre prevención del blanqueo de capitales*), BOE, no. 162, 18 July 2013, 50828-50828; Resolution 3166 of 24 February 2014 against Banco Espírito Santo (*Resolución 3166 de 28 de febrero 2014 de la Secretaría de la Comisión de Prevención del Blanqueo Capitales e Infracciones Monetarias, por la que se publica el Acuerdo del Consejo de Ministros de 3 de mayo de 2013, por el que se sanciona a Banco Espírito Santo, SA, Sucursal en España, por infracciones muy graves de la normativa sobre prevención de blanqueo de capitales*), BOE, no. 71, 24 March 2014, 26340.

278 The Spanish Supreme Court even referred the case against Jyske Bank to the European Court of Justice, which gave a ruling in April 2013: Case C-212/11, *Jyske Bank Gibraltar Ltd against Spain* [2013] ECR I-00000.

279 STS 6457/2009 of 4 November 2009; STS 2028/2010 of 23 April 2010; STS 4812/2011 of 18 July 2011; STS 7085/2011 of 8 November 2011; STS 7055/2012 of 6 November 2012; STS 529/2013 of 5 February 2013; STS 1338/2013, of 12 March 2013; STS 2174/2013 of 21 April 2013; STS 1996/2013 of 29 April 2013; STS 4808/2013 of 30 September 2013 and STS 5917/2013 of 17 December 2013.

280 STS 2174/2013 of 21 April 2013 (*Vallehermoso División Promoción, S.A.U.*).

281 In STS 4808/2013 it concerned an insurance company and in STS 7085/2011 a currency exchange office. All other cases referred to in footnote 277 concerned either estate agency businesses – including construction companies offering housing – and banks – including savings banks, so-called *cajas de ahorros*.

In sum, it seems unlikely that accountants and real estate agents have been sanctioned for non-compliance with the AML Act since 2010, since they have not been inspected. Statistical data proves that fines have been imposed on financial institutions, but does not specify whether banks were involved. Analyses of the Official State Gazette and the case law of the Supreme Court do prove that dissuasive sanctions are imposed in practice and that fines are always combined with either a private or public warning. The Official State Gazette shows that the combination of a fine and a public warning has been imposed on three occasions against banks since the entry into force of the AML Act – although in two cases the breaches took place before that time. The case law of the Supreme Court also shows that in most cases estate agency businesses and banks were involved. However, because the facts of these Supreme Court cases mostly took place (far) before the entry into force of Act 10/2010, this data does not allow us to say something about the sanctioning practice since 2010.

4.7.5 Concluding remarks

The doctrine of punitive administrative law is very important in the Spanish legal system and is also strongly reflected in the sanctioning of non-compliance under the preventive anti-money laundering legislation. A strict separation between supervision, to be exercised by SEPBLAC, and sanctioning exists. This power rests with the Council of Ministers, the Minister of Economy and Competitiveness and the Director-General for the Treasury and Financial Policy, depending on the seriousness of the breaches. In the sanctioning procedure, the Commission Secretariat plays an important role as the instructing authority. The Spanish AML Act distinguishes in great detail the type of offences (very serious, serious or minor), the corresponding sanctions and the limitation periods. There is a wide range of sanctions varying from private warnings to relatively high fines and public warnings, as well as the revocation of licences. This allows the sanctioning authority to scale up the sanctioning action where it is of the opinion that the circumstances so require. Sanctions can be imposed on the non-complying institutions and professionals, as well as their managers or directors who are responsible for the breaches.

Although the AML Act provides indications of how the sanctioning powers should be used, there is no publicly available sanctioning policy that makes visible the exercise of sanctioning powers. That is, which circumstances play a role, the desired level of enforcement or compliance, the sanctioning goals and so on. Another complicating factor is the fact that sanctions are in principle not published anywhere. Some statistical data from the Commission for the Prevention of Money Laundering and Monetary Offences is available and states how many fines were imposed in the years 2010-2012. We can conclude from this data that there is some sanctioning activity, but not whether banks, accountants or real estate agents have been sanctioned for non-compliance with the preventive anti-money laundering obligations. Given the fact that no inspections have taken place with accountants and estate agents in these years, it seems unlikely that they have been sanctioned. By way of the Official State Gazette and the case law of the Spanish Supreme Court it was attempted to provide some more insight into AML sanctioning practice. It seems that most cases date from (far) before the entry into force of the AML

Act, although the Official State Gazette shows that since the entry into force of the Act, three banks have been publicly warned and fined for acting in breach of the preventive AML obligations. What the cases of the Supreme Court demonstrate is that in the past banks and estate agents have been sanctioned for non-compliance. Accountants, so it seems from this data, have not been sanctioned at all.

4.8 Supervisory cooperation for the prevention of money laundering

SEPBLAC is the only AML supervisor and the FIU at the same time. Above we saw that all SEPBLAC staff operate under the same secrecy provisions and that FIU-related data can thus be used for supervisory purposes as well.[282] We have also seen that the Commission for the Prevention of Money Laundering and Monetary Offences is empowered to enter into arrangements with the three financial regulators, in which aspects of AML supervision and cooperation can be further regulated.[283] These arrangements, however, are privileged and it is thus impossible to analyse whether and to what extent the exchange of supervisory information between SEPBLAC and the financial regulators, in particular the Bank of Spain, is allowed. The AML Act or RD 925/1995 do not contain provisions on the exchange of (individual) supervisory information.

282 Section 49 Act 10/2010. See § 4.5.4.
283 See § 4.6.3.3.

5 Anti-money laundering supervision of banks, real estate agents and accountants in the Netherlands

5.1 Introduction

The Dutch supervisory architecture in the preventive anti-money laundering policy belongs to the external model.[1] This chapter provides an in-depth analysis of the supervisory system and practice in the Netherlands with respect to banks, accountants and real estate agents. The legislative, institutional and practical aspects that were identified as part of the theoretical framework of effective supervision are assessed in this chapter.

Section 5.2 starts by describing the Netherlands' vulnerability for money laundering and the vulnerability of banks, real estate agents and accountants specifically. Section 5.3 then outlines the legal framework for the prevention of money laundering. Both sections aim to purvey the context in which the fight against money laundering takes place in the Netherlands. Section 5.4 deals with the institutional aspects of the AML supervisors. These are the Dutch Central Bank (*De Nederlandsche Bank*, hereafter DNB) for banks, the Bureau Supervision Wwft of the Dutch Tax and Customs Administration (*Belastingdienst/Bureau Toezicht Wwft*, hereafter 'DTCA/Bureau Supervision Wwft') for real estate agents[2] and the Financial Supervision Office (*Bureau Financieel Toezicht*, hereafter BFT) for accountants. The authorities must be sufficiently independent in the exercise of their supervisory tasks, and be accountable and transparent about their activities. Section 5.5 discusses the extent to which banks, real estate agents and accountants are authorised, regulated or required to register with their supervisors or other competent authorities. This section aims to answer the question whether the supervisors have, or can have, an adequate knowledge of all these businesses for which they have supervisory responsibility. Sections 5.6-5.8 are about AML supervision as exercised by the three authorities. It is verified whether they have adequate supervisory and sanctioning powers, whether they apply it in a proportionate and careful manner, and escalate their actions where necessary. Finally, section 5.9 deals with another aspect of effective supervision: the cooperation between AML supervisors under this policy, and to a certain extent with the FIU. There must be no legal barriers to the exchange of information between AML supervisors, and with the FIU.

1 § 3.4.2.
2 For simplicity purposes real estate intermediaries are included in the use of the term 'real estate agent' in this research.

5.2 Vulnerability of the Netherlands for money laundering

In order to understand the context in which anti-money laundering supervision is exercised, it is relevant to have some ideas about the question whether money laundering is actually a problem in the Netherlands. This section presents a number of studies that discuss the vulnerability for money laundering, or the scope of the problem, as well as the main predicate offences or sectors that are (considered to be) most at risk in the Netherlands. Special attention is paid to the banking, real estate and accountancy sectors.

The Netherlands is considered an attractive country for money launderers. In 2006, Unger et al. studied the amount of money laundering in the Netherlands and calculated that on an annual basis around 18.5 billion Euros are laundered in and through the Netherlands, of which 80% of the proceeds stem from crimes committed outside the Netherlands.[3] Researchers concluded that this is due to the attractive financial and tax climate in the Netherlands, particularly for foreign investors. Likewise, the FATF referred to the Netherlands as being vulnerable to money laundering, due to 'its large financial center, the openness to trade and the size of criminal proceeds'.[4] Applying the same method of research as Unger et al., the Dutch National Police Force estimated in 2012 that 17 billion Euros are laundered annually in the Netherlands.[5] The ECOLEF study ranked the Netherlands as number five in the list of the most threatened EU Member States in 2009, with an estimated threat of 94,121 million Euros.[6] In its INSCR 2014, the US Department of State included the Netherlands in its countries of primary concern. The foregoing indicates that, although there seems to be agreement on the vulnerability of the Netherlands, the numbers are scarce and diverge widely. Drugs and fraud seem to be the main predicate offences in the Netherlands.[7] The INSCR referred to the sale of cocaine, cannabis or synthetic and designer drugs, such as ecstasy, as well as financial fraud.[8] In its analysis, the Dutch National Police Force discussed – among other things – loan-back constructions, the use of cash, ABC transactions and leasing as money laundering methods.[9] It indicated that trade-based money laundering (TBML), the use of associations and new methods of payment are likely to be the new money laundering trends.[10] There appears to be a low level of corruption, hence this is not considered a big problem in the Netherlands.[11] The EU Anti-Corruption Report even commended the Netherlands on its

---

3 Unger, B. et al. (2006), *The amounts and effects of money laundering*, Report for the Ministry of Finance; Unger, B. (2006a), 'De omvang en effecten van witwassen', *Justitiële Verkenningen*, vol. 32, issue 2, pp. 21-33.

4 FATF (2011) at 8, 19-25.

5 KLPD (2013), *Criminaliteitsbeeldanalyse 2012: witwassen*, at 165.

6 As noted in Chapter 4, this threat is understood as 'the amount of money that could, or might, be laundered in a country if there were no barriers to laundering and there was no 'more attractive place' for the launderer to launder the money'. This is something different from estimations of the money actually laundered: Unger and Ferwerda (2014) at 12-16. In terms of the estimated threat as a percentage of GDP, the Netherlands is ranked in 17th place (14%).

7 Unger et al. (2006) at 48; FATF (2011) at 24.

8 US Department of State (2014) at 163.

9 KLPD (2013) at 26-75.

10 Ibid., at 164.

11 FATF (2011) at 19-20.

approach in preventing corruption: '[t]he integrated approach to preventing and detecting corruption both at central and local level could serve as a model elsewhere in the EU'.[12]

> The Netherlands was one of the first countries worldwide to undertake a national threat assessment on money laundering in 2010-11.[13] The outcomes are not publicly available, which is lamentable. The Ministers of Finance and Security & Justice reported in February 2014 that the information from the threat assessment, together with the FATF guidance on national money laundering and terrorist financing risk assessments (February 2013) is used to develop a national risk assessment on money laundering and that the first results are expected in 2015.[14]

Banks play an important role in the prevention of money laundering and terrorist financing. Due to the high level of sophistication of the Dutch financial sector and the attractive financial and tax climate, banks operating in the Netherlands are always vulnerable to money laundering. The Netherlands has no history of major money laundering cases or scandals involving banks. Nevertheless, two recent high-profile money laundering cases in the United States of America included Dutch banks (see below). Looking at the reporting numbers of banks to the Dutch FIU it appears that banks have had a good overall level of reporting, although in terms of numbers banks' performance is slightly decreasing. In 2011, banks disclosed 6,469 unusual transaction reports (UTR) to the FIU, excluding reports concerning money transfers.[15] This made up 30% of the total number of UTRs received by FIU-NL excluding the reports filed in relation to money transfers.[16] In 2012, the number decreased to 4,822 UTRs, making up 19% of the total number of non-money transfer-related UTRs.[17] With this decrease, the banking sector was no longer the sector reporting most to the FIU, as dealers, money transfers and Government authorities reported more in that year.[18] The percentage of the number of UTRs from banks declared suspicious by FIU-NL diminished from 25% to 16%.[19] Nevertheless, the number of banks that actually make the disclosures has increased since 2010. In that year, 28 banks disclosed their suspicions to the FIU. In 2011 this was 31 and in 2012 this increased to 38 reporting banks.[20] Compared to other financial and credit institutions banks perform well. The FATF indicated that Dutch banks perform much better than other financial and credit institutions, and especially reporting by life insurance companies was considered to be 'practically non-existent'.[21] It did comment on the time of completion for the reports of

12 European Commission (2014b), *Annex: Netherlands to EU Anti-Corruption Report 2014*, COM(2014) 38 final, at 9.
13 Algemene Rekenkamer (2014), *Bestrijding witwassen: stand van zaken 2013*, March 2014, at 9.
14 Ministerie van Veiligheid & Justitie, *Bestuurlijke reactie op rapport over bestrijding witwassen*, kenmerk 478752, 4 februari 2014.
15 The Dutch FIU distinguishes reports on money transfers from the rest of the UTRs, since this covers 88% of the total number of UTRs received by the FIU. Banks have also reported 12,830 UTRs in relation to money transfers in 2011 and 11,511 UTRs in 2012: FIU Nederland (2012), *Jaaroverzicht 2012*, at 48 (in English: *Annual report 2012*).
16 Ibid., at 44.
17 Ibid., at 48.
18 Ibid., at 48.
19 Calculations are based on the number of suspicious transactions divided by the non-money transfer-related unusual transactions reports disclosed to the FIU in one year: FIU Nederland (2012) at 48 and 55.
20 Ibid., at 49.
21 FATF (2011) at 174-175.

banks, which was calculated at 34 days starting from the day of the transaction. The FATF indicated that this would cause too much delay and that it could limit the law enforcement possibilities of seizure and confiscation.[22]

> The two Netherlands-based banks that were involved in high-profile money laundering cases in the United States of America are ABN AMRO Bank N.V. and ING Bank N.V. In 2005, the US authorities and DNB found – among other things – that ABN AMRO Bank lacked adequate risk procedures, that it did business with shell companies, that it failed to report suspicious transactions to the competent authorities and, most importantly, that the bank enabled other banks and individuals from countries recorded on US sanctions regulations (Iran, Libya) to channel money through the financial system of the USA for a period of more than ten years.[23] ABN AMRO Bank agreed to pay 80 million US dollars to US federal and state regulators and in 2010 the bank agreed to pay another 500 million US dollars in exchange for escaping formal prosecution in relation to the affair.[24] In June 2012 ING Bank was required to pay to the US authorities a fine of 619 million US dollars, a record at that time. ING Bank was found to have breached US sanctions regulations against Iran and Cuba by transferring more than 1 billion US dollars illegally through banks in the USA between 1990-2007, thereby concealing the origin and nature of the transactions. A Caribbean subsidiary of ING Bank played a key role in this process.[25]

We have heard a lot about the real estate sector recently, in particular about the commercial real estate sector.[26] The commercial real estate sector refers to property which is primarily used for commercial purposes. Criminal investments in the real estate sector have been identified as one of the principal money laundering methods in the Netherlands.[27] Large criminal organisations and fraud schemes were discovered and brought to justice in recent years, as illustrated by the *Klimop* case.[28] This case involved fraudulent property sales for a period of at least thirteen years and concerned the sale and development of property by the Philips pension fund and the development company called *Bouwfonds*. Research has also demonstrated that estate agents in the Netherlands are vulnerable to criminal activity and, hence, money laundering. Ferwerda et al. even observed that 'real estate agents (...) are primarily led by financial gain'.[29] They concluded that the removal of title protection for estate agents and the liberation of the market, in combination with the growing size of this market and the fact that real estate agents themselves are sometimes involved in criminal

22 Ibid., at 176.

23 See about this case: Unger (2007), *The scale and impacts of money laundering*, Edward Elgar Publishing Ltd: Cheltenham, at 1-4.

24 Financial Times, *ABN Amro admits sanctions breach*, 10 May 2010; The Telegraph, *Tax-payer owned RBS pays $500m to settle ABN money laundering case*, 11 May 2010.

25 US Department of Justice, *ING Bank N.V. Agrees to Forfeit $619 Million for Illegal Transactions with Cuban and Iranian Entities*, 12 June 2012, available at: <www.justice.gov/opa/pr/2012/June/12-crm-742.html>, last visited on 16 September 2014.

26 Kruisbergen, E.W., Van de Bunt, H.G. and Kleemans, E.R. (2012), *Georganiseerde criminaliteit in Nederland: vierde rapportage op basis van de Monitor Georganiseerde Criminaliteit*, research commissioned by the Dutch Ministry of Security & Justice, at 134 et seq.

27 Unger et al. (2006) at 69, 72 and 77; KLPD (2008), *Witwassen: Verslag van een onderzoek voor het Nationaal dreigingsbeeld 2008*, October 2008, at 72-104.

28 Van de Bunt, H. et al. (2011), *Bestuurlijke rapportage vastgoedfraudezaak 'Klimop'*, Final Report, June 2011.

29 Ferwerda, H. et al. (2007), *Malafide activiteiten in de vastgoedsector: Een exploratief onderzoek naar aard, actoren en aanpak*, research commissioned by the Dutch Ministry of Justice, at 125.

activity, has led to a decay in integrity norms in this profession.[30] Because of the strong competition in the market, real estate agents sometimes feel obliged to fulfil the demands of their customers, even when their customers want something illegal, researchers asserted.[31] The media regularly report on estate agents and property developers who have been involved in participation in criminal organisations, and sometimes in money laundering specifically.[32] Due to the high risks and various wrongs in the real estate sector, the Dutch Central Bank gave supervisory priority to the commercial estate sector in 2012, and also in 2013 attention was paid to the estate sector.[33] This proves that the Dutch real estate sector thus bears a relatively high risk of money laundering. It is in this light interesting to observe that the level of reporting from estate agents to FIU-NL is very low, something which the Dutch National Police Force concluded as well.[34] In 2011 and 2012 the number of reports from estate agents amounted to only 0.1% of the total number of non-money transfer-related UTRs.[35] The number of UTRs from real estate agents that were declared suspicious by the FIU did increase from 9% in 2011 to 28% in 2012, and the amount of money involved in these suspicious transactions increased from 19,000 Euros to nearly 8.2 million Euros.[36] Likewise, the number of real estate agents reporting to the FIU increased from 6 in the years 2010 and 2011, to 23 in 2012.[37] Nevertheless, in 2011 other designated non-financial businesses and professionals such as accountants, civil-law notaries and tax advisors all reported more than real estate agents, albeit in 2012 the difference with tax advisors was minimal.[38] This is the context in which the supervisory activities for the prevention of money laundering should be seen.

> It should be clarified at this point that although the DNB has supervisory responsibility for financial and credit institutions operating in the commercial estate sector, in particular on project development, the financing of development projects and investments in the commercial estate sector, the Dutch Tax and Customs Administration/Bureau Supervision Wwft is appointed as the AML supervisor for real estate agents (see § 5.4.2).

30 Ibid., at 125.

31 Ibid., at 125.

32 Examples are: NRC Handelsblad, *Hoofdverdachte vastgoedfraude betaalt miljoenenschikking*, 28 October 2010; De Volkskrant, *Vastgoedhandelaar Joep J. met gezin opgepakt*, 21 juni 2011; De Telegraaf, *Malafide makelaar gepakt*, 10 May 2012; Dagblad De Limburger, *Zaak Van-Rey: Invallen bij Van Pol en makelaar*, 28 January 2013; Het Financieele Dagblad, *Reeks vastgoedbonzen fêteerde Hooijmaijers*, 12 October 2012; RTV Oost, *Gevangenisstraf voor makelaar Enschede*, 16 October 2012, available at: <www.rtvoost.nl/nieuws/default.aspx?nid=152101>, last visited on 3 April 2014; Trouw, *Opsporingsdiensten pakken witwassen via makelaar aan*, 7 July 2013.

33 DNB (2012), *Thema's DNB toezicht 2012*, January 2012 at 10-11; DNB (2013), *Thema's DNB toezicht 2013*, January 2013 at 12-13 and 18-19.

34 KLPD (2013) at 87.

35 Calculations are based on the number of UTRs disclosed by real estate agents divided by the total number of non-money transfer-related UTRs: FIU Nederland (2012), *Jaaroverzicht 2012*, at 74. The calculations exclude UTRs on money transfers, as these are based on a comparatively low objective threshold, leading to very high numbers of reports of this kind (88% of the total numbers of reports received in 2012).

36 Ibid. at 74 and 76.

37 Calculations are based on the number of suspicious transactions divided by the non-money transfer-related unusual transaction reports disclosed to the FIU in one year: FIU Nederland (2012), *Jaaroverzicht 2012*, at 74.

38 Ibid., at 74.

With regard to accountants, there is no evidence that points at a high level of vulnerability for money laundering. Although accountancy firms that perform statutory audits in the Netherlands have been prominent in the media in recent years, aspects of the prevention of money laundering did not play a direct role in these cases. The media exposure was caused by strong action taken by the Netherlands Authority for the Financial Markets (*Autoriteit Financiële Markten, AFM*), the Government supervisor of audit firms. In 2012 and 2013, it imposed fines on – inter alia – KPMG, Deloitte and Ernst & Young (now: EY) for non-compliance with the Audit Firms Supervision Act (*Wet toezicht accountantsorganisaties*).[39] The case law on the involvement of accountants in criminal cases involving money laundering only exists in relation to the abovementioned *Klimop* case, where two former registered accountants were convicted. One of the registered accountants was sentenced to two years and six months imprisonment for money laundering, participation in a criminal organisation, bribery and a number of other criminal offences.[40] The Dutch National Police Force states, however, that accountants can be used as a financial facilitator in order to create a paper trail, strengthening this position by presenting an example of a case.[41] Accountants do relatively well in reporting unusual transactions to the Dutch FIU: of all non-financial institutions, the accountancy sector reports most after the civil-law notaries. In 2011 the sector disclosed 325 UTRs. In 2012 this slightly decreased to 322 UTRs.[42] The ratio of UTRs that were declared suspicious by the FIU is also relatively high: 20% in 2011 and 28% in 2012.[43] And also the amount of money involved in these transactions increased from 41 million Euros in 2011 to 94.5 million Euros in 2012.[44] This, the FIU explained, primarily had to do with one big case involving around 50 million Euros.[45] Compared to real estate agents, this is a large amount of money. The total number of accountants actually reporting to FIU-NL decreased from 87 in 2011 to 83 in 2012, but compared to other designated non-financial businesses and professionals, this is a high number of reporting professionals. The FATF concluded in its evaluation on the Netherlands that 'the reporting system appears quite effective for civil-law notaries and accountants'.[46]

---

39 AFM, *Boetebesluit Deloitte*, 15 February 2012, available at: <www.afm.nl/~/media/files/boete/2012/deloitte.ashx>, last visited on: 3 April 2014, AFM, *Boetebesluit KPMG*, 21 February 2011, available at: <www.afm.nl/~/media/files/boete/2013/kpmg/primair-boetebesluit-kpmg-art8-lid-1-bta.ashx>, last visited on: 3 April 2014, AFM, *Boetebesluit KPMG II*, 21 February 2011, <www.afm.nl/~/media/files/boete/2013/kpmg/primair-boetebesluit-kpmg-art8-lid-2-bta.ashx>, last visited on 3 April 2014, Rb. Rotterdam, ROT12/1391, 30 May 2013, AFM, *Boetebesluit Ernst & Young*, 9 November 2011, last visited: <www.afm.nl/~/media/files/boete/2012/ernst-young-compliance.ashx>, last visited on 3 April 2014.

40 Press release, *Gevangenisstraffen tot 4 jaar in vastgoedfraude "Klimop"*, 27 January 2012, available at: <www.rechtspraak.nl/Organisatie/Rechtbanken/Noord-Holland/Nieuws/Pages/Gevangenisstraffentot4jaarinvastgoedfraudeKlimop.aspx>, last visited on 3 April 2014.

41 KLPD (2013) at 122-123 and 127.

42 FIU Nederland (2012), *Jaaroverzicht 2012*, at 74.

43 Calculations are based on the number of UTRs disclosed by accountants divided by the total number of non-money transfer-related UTRs: FIU Nederland (2012), *Jaaroverzicht 2012*, at 74. The calculations exclude UTRs on money transfers.

44 Ibid., at 76.

45 Ibid., at 76.

46 FATF (2011) at 12.

5.3 Legal framework for the prevention of money laundering

The Netherlands' first legal instrument regarding the prevention of money laundering dates back to 1993 after the implementation of the First Directive.[47] The central piece of preventive legislation is the Money Laundering and Terrorist Financing Prevention Act (*Wet ter voorkoming van witwassen en financieren van terrorisme*, hereafter AML Act or 'Wwft').[48] The Act was considerably revised on the 1st of January 2013. It was, among other things, clarified that forensic accountancy services fall entirely under the scope of the Act and it provided an explicit legal basis for the exchange of supervisory information between the AML supervisors.[49]

At the level below the Act various regulations are in force. In the first place, the Wwft Decree (*Uitvoeringsbesluit Wwft*) details the scope of the AML Act and contains a list of indicators that give rise to the unusual nature of transactions which may point at money laundering or terrorist financing, on the basis of which obliged businesses and professionals must disclose a report to the Dutch FIU.[50] In the second place, the Wwft ministerial regulation (*Uitvoeringsregeling Wwft*) provides more details on provisions from the AML Act, for example with regard to equivalent third countries.[51] In the third place, the Decree on the appointment of Wwft supervisors (*Besluit aanwijzing toezichthouders Wwft)* in which the Ministers of Finance and Security & Justice appoint the four AML supervisors.[52] The Act, Decree and ministerial regulations are supplemented by a wealth of guidance documents

47 Council Directive 91/308/EEC of 10 June 1991 on prevention of the use of the financial system for the purpose of money laundering, OJ L-166 of 28 June 1991.

48 *Wet ter voorkoming van witwassen en financieren van terrorisme,* Stb. 2008, 303.

49 *Wet van 20 december 2012 tot wijziging van de Wet ter voorkoming van witwassen en financieren van terrorisme en de Wet ter voorkoming van witwassen en financieren van terrorisme BES in verband met de implementatie van aanbevelingen van de Financial Action Task Force*, Stb. 2012, 286. Cf. FIU Nederland (2013), *Information sheet on changes in the Wwft, effective from 1 January 2013*, available at: <http://en.fiu-nederland.nl/sites/www.fiu-nederland.nl/files/u3/1978%2013%20Informatieblad%20FIU%20English%20v2.pdf>, last visited on 3 April 2014; Snijders-Kuiper, B. and Tilleman, A.T.A. (2013), 'Nieuwe witwaswetgeving! Overzicht van de belangrijkste wijzigingen voor de notariële praktijk', *Weekblad voor Privaatrecht, Notariaat en Registratie*, issue 6972; Kolkman, D.S. and Reckweg, C.A. (2012), 'WWFT wijzigingen 2013', in: Bureau Financieel Toezicht, *Nieuwsbrief Toezicht*, vol. 8, issue 2, winter edition, pp. 8-11. The last amendments to the Act entered into force on the 1st of August 2014: Stb. 2014, 253. See § 1.8.

50 *Besluit van 15 juli 2008, houdende bepalingen met betrekking tot de reikwijdte van de Wet ter voorkoming van witwassen en financieren van terrorisme, het vaststellen van indicatoren en het overdragen van bevoegdheden in het kader van de Wet ter voorkoming van witwassen en financieren van terrorisme (Uitvoeringsbesluit Wet ter voorkoming van witwassen en financieren van terrorisme)*, Stb. 2008, 305. Last amended on: 6 December 2013, Stb. 2013, 537.

51 *Regeling van de Minister van Financiën en de Minister van Justitie van 23 juli 2008, nr. FM 2008-1792 M, Generale Thesaurie, Directie Financiële Markten, Afdeling Integriteit, tot vaststelling van regels ter uitvoering van de Wet ter voorkoming van witwassen en financieren van terrorisme (Uitvoeringsregeling Wet ter voorkoming van witwassen en financieren van terrorisme)*, Stcrt. 2008, 142. Last amended on 1 January 2014: Stcrt. 2013, 35195.

52 See § 3.4.2. *Besluit van de Minister van Financiën en de Minister van Justitie van 18 juli 2008, nr. FM 2008-01794 M, Directie Financiële markten, Afdeling Integriteit, tot aanwijzing van personen die zijn belast met het toezicht op de naleving van de Wet ter voorkoming van witwassen en financieren van terrorisme gestelde regels (Besluit aanwijzing toezichthouders Wet ter voorkoming van witwassen en financieren van terrorisme)*, Stcrt. 2008, 142. Last amended on 1 January 2014: Stcrt. 2013, 35195.

issued by the Ministry of Finance,[53] the AML supervisors[54] and various professional associations[55]. In addition, the Dutch FIU (*FIU-Nederland*, hereafter 'FIU-NL' or FIU) publishes information brochures on its website.[56]

The Dutch AML Act is closely related to various other pieces of legislation that together form the entire preventive framework, such as the Sanctions Act 1977 (*Sanctiewet 1977*), the Financial Supervision Act (*Wet op het financieel toezicht, Wft*), the Supervision of Trust Offices Act (*Wet toezicht trustkantoren, Wtt*), and the Dutch Notaries Act (*Wet op het notarisambt, Wna*). Related norms are important for the obliged institutions and professionals, as well as for the supervisors. Where necessary, these pieces of legislation will be discussed throughout this chapter.

5.4 The AML Supervisors: institutional aspects

This section provides an analysis of the institutional aspects of the supervisors, most notably their independence and accountability regimes. The focus rests with the (relative) political and market independence and corresponding accountability structures, in particular regarding the AML policy.[57] This section aims to provide an insight into how AML supervision plays a role within the organisations of the Dutch Central Bank (§ 5.4.1), the Dutch Tax and Customs Administration/Bureau Supervision Wwft (§ 5.4.2), and the Financial Supervision Office (§ 5.4.3). This section ends with some concluding remarks in § 5.4.4.

53 *Algemene leidraad Wet ter voorkoming van witwassen en financiering van terrorisme (Wwft) en Sanctiewet (SW)*, 17 January 2014, available at: <www.rijksoverheid.nl/documenten-en-publicaties/richtlijnen/2011/02/21/algemene-leidraad-wet-ter-voorkoming-van-witwassen-en-financieren-van-terrorisme-Wwft-en-sanctiewet-sw.html>, last visited on 3 April 2014 (in English: *General guidance document on the AML Act and Sanctions Act*). Hereafter 'Algemene leidraad Wwft en SW'.

54 *DNB Leidraad Wwft en SW*, 9 January 2014; *AFM Leidraad Wwft*, 15 August 2013; *BFT Specifieke leidraad naleving WWFT voor accountants, belastingadviseurs, administratiekantoren en alle overige instellingen zoals genoemd in artikel 1 lid 1 letter a sub 11, 12 en 13 WWFT*, 1 April 2011; *BFT Specifieke leidraad naleving WWFT voor accountants, belastingadviseurs, administratiekantoren en alle overige instellingen zoals genoemd in artikel 1 lid 1 letter a sub 11, 12 en 13 WWFT*, 1 April 2011; *BFT Specifieke leidraad naleving WWFT voor (kandidaat-)notarissen en overige instellingen zoals genoemd in artikel 1 lid 1 letter a sub 12 en 13 WWFT*, 1 April 2011; *Belastingdienst/Bureau Toezicht Wwft, Leidraad Wwft: Richtlijnen voor Makelaars in onroerende zaken*, 12 September 2013; *Belastingdienst/Bureau Toezicht Wwft, Leidraad Wwft: Richtlijnen voor Taxateurs van onroerende zaken*, 12 September 2013; *Belastingdienst/Bureau Toezicht Wwft, Leidraad Wwft: Richtlijnen voor Verkopers van goederen*, 12 September 2013; *Belastingdienst/Bureau Toezicht Wwft, Leidraad Wwft: Richtlijnen voor Domicilieverlening*, 12 September 2013.

55 *Nederlandse Orde van Advocaten, Richtsnoeren voor advocaten voor de naleving van de verplichtingen uit de Wet ter voorkoming van witwassen en financieren van terrorisme (Wwft)*, March 2013; *Nederlandse Beroepsorganisatie van Accountants, Handreiking 1124 – Richtsnoeren ter voorkoming van witwassen en financieren van terrorisme (WWFT) voor belastingadviseurs en accountants*, February 2014.

56 FIU Nederland, *Informatiebladen*, available at: <www.fiu-nederland.nl/content/informatiebladen-0>.

57 See § 2.4.2.1 and 2.4.2.2.

5.4.1 Dutch Central Bank (*De Nederlandsche Bank*)

5.4.1.1 Institutional embedding

The Dutch Central Bank is a limited liability company. Its one share is held by the Dutch State. DNB contributes to the soundness of the European monetary policy and the smooth functioning of payment systems, and is a member of the European System of Central Banks (ESCB) and the Eurosystem. Besides its role as a Central Bank, it is one of the two financial regulators in the Netherlands. With the introduction of the Financial Supervision Act in 2007 (hereafter 'Wft') the Netherlands introduced the twin-peaks model.[58] The DNB was designated as the prudential supervisor and the AFM was assigned the exercise of conduct-of-business supervision.[59] Regarding its role as a prudential financial regulator, the DNB is an independent administrative authority (*zelfstandig bestuursorgaan*).

The term 'zelfstandig bestuursorgaan' was first coined in the 1970s.[60] Independent administrative authorities are Government bodies that do not fall directly under the authority of a Ministry.[61] They do not operate under full political responsibility from the Minister and the latter has, in principle, no powers to give instructions on individual matters to those authorities.[62] The Minister can have other powers, such as the power to appoint board members, to issue general instructions and to approve the budget. The exact powers of the Minister with respect to each single independent administrative authority (hereafter ZBO) are regulated when the authority is set up or brought under the scope of the Autonomous Administrative Authorities Framework Act (*Kaderwet Zelfstandige Bestuursorganen*, hereafter AAAFA[63]). At present not all ZBOs fall under the scope of this Act.[64] Various different reasons can underlie the creation of ZBOs, one of which is the belief that a separation between policy (Minister) and implementation (ZBO) is necessary for the exercise of certain Government tasks.[65] ZBOs carry out a wide range of tasks. In general, they are assigned supervisory tasks, or tasks related to the certification or the payment of benefits. In May 2013, there were 118 ZBOs in the Netherlands.[66]

Independent administrative authorities are not an uncontested phenomenon: in 2012 the Dutch Government agreed to review their position. The coalition agreement shows that the Government wants to diminish the number of independent administrative authorities,

58 Kremers, J. and Schoenmaker, D. (2010), 'Twin Peaks: Experiences in the Netherlands', *LSE Financial Markets Group Paper Series*, Special Paper 196, December 2010; Grundmann-van de Krol, C.M. (2012), *Koersen door de Wet financieel toezicht*, Boom Juridische uitgevers: The Hague, at 13-14. See for a general description of financial supervision models: Wymeersch (2007); Llewellyn (2006).

59 Grundmann-van de Krol (2012) at 683-687.

60 Scheltema, M. (1974), *Zelfstandige bestuursorganen*. Groningen: Tjeenk Willink.

61 Section 1a of the AAAFA.

62 Zijlstra, S.E. (2009), *Bestuurlijk organisatierecht*, Kluwer: Deventer, at 81-82.

63 *Wet van 2 november 2006, houdende regels betreffende zelfstandige bestuursorganen*, Stb. 2006, 587.

64 For ZBOs that were already in place before the AAAFA entered into force in 2007, a special Act approved by Parliament is required. The Netherlands Court of Audit provides various reasons for not including a ZBO under the scope of the Act: Algemene Rekenkamer (2012), *Rapport Kaderwet zbo's: reikwijdte en implementatie*, June 2012, at 12.

65 Section 3 AAAFA. See Zijlstra (2009) at 82-84 for a distinction between different types of ZBOs and the motives for setting these up.

66 De Leeuw, J. (2013), *Onderzoek naar de herpositionering van ZBO's*, research commissioned by the Ministry of Interior Affairs and Kingdom Relations, May 2013, at 15.

preferring public tasks to be performed by agencies (agentschappen) which act more directly under a Minister.[67] The main reason for this is said to be the lack of democratic control by Parliament, as ministers only have responsibility for the functioning of ZBOs to a certain extent.[68] Research commissioned by the Ministry of Interior Affairs and Kingdom Relations assessed the status of all ZBOs in the Netherlands. For the two ZBOs included in this research, DNB and BFT, it advised to keep these authorities as ZBOs.[69]

The DNB has been appointed as the AML supervisor for credit institutions (including banks), life insurance companies, payment service providers, money exchange officers, trust offices, leasing companies and casinos.[70] AML supervision is, in the first place, integrated in regular supervisory procedures. For banks this is performed by special banking teams of the DNB from its Banking Supervision Division (*Toezicht banken*). Secondly, AML supervision can be part of thematic integrity supervision. This type of supervision is carried out or led by the Expert centre on culture, organisation and integrity.[71] When supervisory cases end in sanctioning procedures, the Expert Centre on Intervention and Enforcement becomes involved.[72] There is no single division within the DNB that carries out targeted AML supervision, which makes it difficult to identify how many staff are involved and what the budget for the AML supervision of banks is. Data from the FATF third mutual evaluation report appears to be outdated.[73]

In accordance with Section 1:107 Wft, the DNB keeps a public register of banks that operate in the Netherlands. At the end of March 2014, the banking sector was comprised of 71 Dutch banks, 5 non-EU/EEA banks with branches in the Netherlands and 39 EU/EEA banks with branches in the Netherlands.[74] Furthermore, a high number of foreign credit and financial institutions from other EU or EEA Member States directly provide banking services in the Netherlands.[75] Under the Wft, the DNB does not supervise those banks from other EU Member States which operate directly or through branches in the Netherlands and which have been granted a licence by their national financial regulator. This is due to the 'home state control principle' stemming from EU law.[76] Under the Dutch AML Act, however, no such restriction applies, as we will see in § 5.5.1.1. Representatives

67 Coalition agreement VVD – PvDA, *Bruggen slaan*, 29 October 2012, at 42-43 available at: <www.rijksoverheid.nl/documenten-en-publicaties/rapporten/2012/10/29/regeerakkoord.html>, last visited on 4 April 2014.

68 De Leeuw (2013) at 5.

69 De Leeuw (2013) at 96-97 and 143.

70 Section 24(1) Wwft and Section 1(a) Decree on the appointment of Wwft supervisors.

71 In Dutch: *Expertisecentrum Cultuur, organisatie en integriteit.*

72 In Dutch: *Expertisecentrum Interventie en Handhaving.*

73 FATF (2011) at 200-201. The data are all for the year 2010. The interview held with the DNB in May 2013 made it clear that the numbers have changed considerably since that year.

74 Data based on the Wft register available via <www.dnb.nl>. For 'Dutch banks' the number of institutions with a licence based on Sections 2:12(1) and 2:13(1) Wft are included; Section 2:20(1) Wft for 'branches of non-EU banks' and Section 2:14 Wft for 'branches of EU banks'. It is also possible, however, that foreign banks operate directly, without a branch in the Netherlands (for example, on the basis of Section 2:18 Wft). These are not included in the figures.

75 Data based on the Wft register available via <www.dnb.nl>. For banks from the EEA without a branch in the Netherlands this occurs on the basis of Section 2:18 Wft. This number is 552.

76 See § 4.5.1.

stated that the DNB was responsible for the supervision of approximately 100 banks in 2013.[77]

5.4.1.2 Independence and accountability

Political independence and accountability

As an independent administrative authority the DNB exercises its activities under a high degree of independence. It is not attached to a Ministry. Nevertheless, ministerial responsibility for the functioning of the DNB and the proper functioning of the financial system rests with the Minister of Finance. This responsibility concerns the overall functioning of financial supervision, and not the tasks of the DNB as a central bank under the monetary policy. Regarding the ministerial responsibility for the Minister of Finance, the Explanatory Memorandum to the Financial Supervision Act stated that:

> '[t]he supervisors are independent in the manner in which they exercise supervision. The supervisors are required to operate within their specific expertise and legal framework. The **Minister of Finance is responsible at a distance**. This responsibility concerns the quality of regulation, the responsibility for an adequate framework of supervisory powers, and the appointment and dismissal of directors of the supervisors. The assumption that supervisors are independent in the exercise of their supervision means that the minister will only carry out an investigation where his responsibility at a distance so requires. However, the foregoing does not lead to the conclusion that the independence of supervisors is unlimited. The Minister needs to oversee the exercise of legislation concerning supervision and be able to form an opinion about the way in which the supervisor exercises or has exercised the Act. The minister needs to be able to take action in case a supervisor does not operate in the way in which the minister and Parliament had in mind when they assigned the supervisory task to the supervisor.'[78] *(Own translation and emphasis added, MB).*

5

The Minister derives his formal oversight powers most prominently from the Wft, the Banking Act 1998, and the AAAFA.[79] Aside from these formal powers, the Minister and DNB participate in (expert) meetings on a more informal basis. In the vision document 'Oversight at a distance 2011', the Minister of Finance set out how he intends to use his oversight powers without unduly limiting the independence of the DNB and AFM.[80] Without entering into the full specifics of each of the Minister's powers, the whole idea is that the Minister can in general terms exert influence on the supervision policies of the financial supervisors, but is not allowed to mingle in individual cases and decisions of the financial supervisory authorities.[81] This is different from former times, when the Banking Act 1948 provided the Minister with the power to provide instructions requiring the DNB

77 FATF (2011) at 29; confirmed in: Interview De Nederlandsche Bank, May 2013.

78 *Parliamentary Papers II*, 2003-04, 29 708, no. 3, pp. 14-15.

79 The AAAFA is applicable to DNB, but with some important exceptions: see Section 1:30 Wft.

80 Ministerie van Financiën (2011), *Toezicht op afstand: de relatie tussen de minister van Financiën en de financiële toezichthouders De Nederlandsche Bank (DNB) en de Autoriteit Financiële Markten (AFM) 2011-2016*, February 2011 (in English: *Vision document Oversight at a distance: the relationship between the Minister of Finance and the financial supervisors DNB and AFM 2011-2016*).

81 See Annex I to Vision document Oversight at a distance, which lists all the powers of the Minister, varying from soft to hard instruments.

to take action in individual cases. Although never applied in practice, this was considered to be too intrusive on the independent position of the financial supervisors.[82] The power to give instructions was turned into a right for the minister to require information, currently laid down in the AAAFA and the Financial Supervision Act.[83] Worth mentioning is the power to set general policy rules with regard to the exercise of the supervisory tasks of the DNB and AFM.[84] Since February 2012 the Minister of Finance has this power in relation to two parts, 1.2 and 1.3, of the Financial Supervision Act, which concern institutional aspects and cooperation. The financial supervisors can still can make their own decisions within this framework. Moreover, this power is limited compared to powers that some Ministers have in relation to other independent administrative authorities.[85] The Minister should always first consult the financial supervisors before he makes use of this policy-making power.[86] The Minister can also take over the tasks of the DNB or transfer them to another authority if he is of the firm belief that the DNB is severely neglect its tasks; he can appoint, dismiss or suspend the President and/or directors of the DNB, or he can decide not to agree with the estimates, the annual (accounts) report or (amendments to) the articles of association of the DNB. These are far-reaching powers and should, therefore, be used only as a last resort.[87] The Minister of Finance, the DNB and AFM have in place an agreement that further elaborates the use of these powers by the Minister vis-à-vis the DNB and AFM and that provides safeguards for the financial supervisors' independence.[88]

The DNB is obliged to report annually about the exercise of its financial supervision (*ZBO-verantwoordingen*). These reports contain explanations of the supervisory policy that the DNB has exercised in a particular year, and the effects this has had on financial stability and on the sector. Annual reports are submitted to the Ministers of Finance and Social Affairs, as well as to the Senate (*Eerste Kamer der Staten-Generaal*) and Parliament (*Tweede Kamer der Staten-Generaal*).[89] The reports are also published on

82 Zijlstra, S.E. (2009a), 'Toezichthouders', in: Huizink, J.B. and Schoenmaker, D. (eds.), *Leerboek Wft*, Maklu, pp. 87-109 at 100.

83 Section 20 AAAFA and Section 1:42 Wft.

84 Section 1:25 Wft.

85 Cf. the Netherlands Authority for Consumers and Markets (*Autoriteit Consument en Markt, ACM*) where the Minister has the power to approve policy rules set by the Authority as well as to annul general decisions made by the ACM: Parliamentary Papers II, 2012-13, 33 662, no. 2 at 4. Cf. Section 22 AAAFA which entails powers for Ministers to annul decisions from ZBOs. This section does not apply to the DNB.

86 *Parliamentary Papers II*, 2010-11, 32 782, no. 3.

87 For example in relation to taking over tasks from the DNB or transferring powers to another authority (Section 23 AAAFA), the Minister should first have exhausted all other powers to come to an improvement of the situation. Only if there is no prospect of any improvement may he apply this power. See: *Parliamentary Papers II*, 2000-01, 27 426, no. 3, at 28.

88 *Toezichtarrangement aangaande de toezichthouders op de financiële markten*, december 2012, available at: <www.rijksoverheid.nl/bestanden/documenten-en-publicaties/kamerstukken/2012/12/18/toezichtarrangement-financiele-toezichthouders/toezichtarrangement-financiele-toezichthouders.pdf>, last visited on 15 March 2014. (In English: *Agreement concerning the supervisors of the financial markets*). On 3 April 2014, the Minister of Finance laid before Parliament an updated version of the agreement, in order to align it with the decision to include the financial regulators within the scope of the AAAFA: *Parliamentary Papers II*, 2013-14, 32 648, no. 5. This updated version is not analysed within the framework of this research.

89 Section 18 AAAFA. The Minister of Finance is responsible for the functioning of the financial system, whereas the Minister of Social Affairs has ministerial responsibility for the tasks of the DNB related to the pensions system.

the DNB's website. Secondly, account must be given to Parliament or the Senate when they decide to establish parliamentary investigation committees. The most intrusive type of investigation is the parliamentary inquiry.[90] The DNB has been subject to various parliamentary investigations in recent years. For example, the Parliamentary Committee on the financial sector ('Commissie-De Wit') carried out a parliamentary investigation on the structural problems in the financial sector and the financial crisis. It also investigated in a parliamentary inquiry the aid measures taken by the Government to support individual banks. Both the parliamentary investigation and the inquiry discussed the role of the DNB.[91] The DNB invoked its confidentiality obligations during the investigation and the inquiry.[92] This was later criticised by Duijkersloot and Kummeling, who argued that the DNB had interpreted Dutch legislation too strictly. They considered that the European Directive on which Dutch legislation is based leaves room for a more lenient interpretation, as practice in other EU Member States demonstrated.[93] Ultimately, the DNB did give an account to the parliamentary committee although it did so 'behind closed doors'.[94] The same problem was encountered by the Netherlands Court of Audit (*Algemene Rekenkamer*), which evaluates, on an annual basis, the central records of the National Treasury, the financial statements by the Central Government and the Central Government's trial balance.[95] The Senate or Parliament can request the Court of Audit to start an investigation.[96] The Court of Audit was requested to investigate the effectiveness of the DNB's supervision of banks in 2011. In practice it encountered the problem that it had insufficient powers to do so as the DNB refused to grant access to information based on the strict confidentiality regime.[97] Duijkersloot and Kummeling found this interpretation, that was supported by the Minister of Finance and the Council of State, to be unnecessary and undesirable for the reasons set out above.[98]

With regard to accountability for the exercise of AML supervision specifically, it appears that the annual reports of the DNB contain some information in relation to the exercise of thematic integrity supervision. The annual report of 2011 reported on research focussing on compliance with the customer due diligence obligations by banks. The DNB identified some serious weaknesses and reported on the imposition of some 'formal measures'.[99]

90 Section 70 *Wet op de parlementaire enquête* (in English: *the Dutch Constitution and the Parliamentary Inquiry Act 2008*).
91 Commissie De Wit (2010). This report was followed up in 2012: Parlementaire Enquêtecommissie Financieel Stelsel (Commissie de Wit) (2012), *Verloren Krediet II – De balans opgemaakt, Parliamentary Papers II*, 2011-12, 31 980, no. 61 (Commissie de Wit 2012).
92 Duijkersloot, T. and Kummeling, H. (2012), 'Onnodig en onwenselijk: de geheimzinnigheid van DNB', *Nederlands Juristenblad*, 2012/5.
93 Duijkersloot, T. and Kummeling, H. (2012a), 'Parlement en geheime toezichtinformatie', in: Kummeling, H.R.B.M., de Morree, P.E., Nehmelman, R., Ortlep, R. and Widdershoven, R.J.G.M. (eds.), *De samengestelde Besselink: Bruggen bouwen tussen nationaal, Europees en internationaal recht*, Wolf Legal Publishers, pp. 75-82 at 77-80.
94 Ibid., at 81.
95 Sections 82 and 83 *Comptabiliteitswet 2001* (in English: *Government Accounts Act)*. Hereafter Cw 2001.
96 Section 90 Cw 2001.
97 Algemene Rekenkamer (2011), *Toezicht van DNB op de stabiliteit van banken*, November 2011, at 5; De Moor-Van Vugt, A.J.C. et al. (2012), *Gegevensuitwisseling door Toezichthouders*, WODC: The Hague, research commissioned by the Ministry of Security & Justice, at 48 et seq.
98 Duijkersloot and Kummeling (2012); Cf. De Moor-Van Vugt et al. (2012), at 35.
99 DNB (2011), *ZBO-verantwoording 2011*, at 18-19 (in English: *Annual report 2011*).

Thematic supervision in that year also focussed on compliance with the AML obligations on correspondent banking relations.[100] While the annual report of 2012 does not refer to AML supervision, the 2013 report gives an account of the exercise of thematic AML supervision, and the results and action taken.[101] In the parliamentary investigations involving the DNB, AML supervision was not a point of discussion. It is interesting to observe that despite the difficulties that the Court of Audit encounters in relation to the DNB's prudential supervision of banks, this does not seem to apply to the DNB's AML supervision. In 2008 and 2013, the Court of Audit investigated the effectiveness of the fight against money laundering and terrorist financing in the Netherlands, in which the role of the DNB was assessed on a more abstract level.[102] It appears that the DNB accounts for the exercise of its AML supervision, although it is unsatisfactory that nowhere is any mention made of its integration into the regular supervision of banks.[103]

Market independence and accountability

The DNB's relationship with the market is mostly of a financial nature. Since January 2013, the fees are regulated by the Financial Supervision (Funding) Act (*Wet bekostiging financieel toezicht*).[104] Costs for DNB's financial supervision, including the Financial Supervision Act and the AML Act, are shared by the Government and the market.[105] The Government's objective is to decrease the Government contribution to 0 Euros in 2015.[106] The costs for financial supervision must from then onwards be entirely borne by the sector itself. In 2013, the Government contribution to the DNB was 13%, whereas the sector itself was responsible for 87% of the funding.[107] The DNB's estimates should be approved by its Supervisory Board (*Raad van Commissarissen*) and the Ministers of Finance and Social Affairs.[108] The Act requires the DNB to organise meetings with a representative panel of institutions subject to the DNB's supervision twice a year.[109] Representatives of the Ministries also attend these meetings and the DNB may also invite other parties, like the Dutch banking association. The meetings provide the sector with an opportunity to influence the DNB's financial plans, and indirectly its supervisory policy as well. This input from the representative panel can provide the DNB with useful insights into the administrative burdens and costs of compliance for the private sector.[110] The panel can

100 Ibid., at 27.

101 DNB (2013a), *ZBO-verantwoording 2013*, at 14 (in English: *Annual report 2013*).

102 Algemene Rekenkamer (2008a), *Bestrijden witwassen en terrorismefinanciering, Parliamentary papers II*, 2007-08, 31 477, no. 1-2; Algemene Rekenkamer (2014).

103 More about this in § 5.6.2.2.

104 *Wet van 24 mei 2012, houdende regels met betrekking tot de financiering van het toezicht op de financiële markten*, Stb. 2012, 250; *Besluit van 20 september 2012, houdende nadere regels inzake de financiering van het toezicht op de financiële markten*, Stb. 2012, 451.

105 DNB (2013a) at 32-33. See for all pieces of financial legislation that fall under the Financial Supervision (Funding) Act: Section 1(c) Wbft.

106 Coalition agreement VVD – PvDA, *Bruggen slaan*, 29 October 2012, available at: <www.rijksoverheid.nl/documenten-en-publicaties/rapporten/2012/10/29/regeerakkoord.html>, last visited on 4 April 2014.

107 De Leeuw (2013) at 96.

108 Section 5 Wbft and Section 3(1) Wbft. The agreement between the Minister of Finance and the financial supervisors sets out the criteria based on which the Minister will evaluate the estimate: supra, n. 88, at 11.

109 Section 9 Wbft.

110 *Huishoudelijk reglement Adviserend panel DNB*, 24 April 2008 (in English: *Advisory Panel DNB Regulations*), which was applicable under the former legal basis (1:39 Wft); Ministerie van Financiën (2011) at 24.

provide advice that the DNB and the Ministries must take into consideration and respond to, but there is no obligation to follow it. At the end of each financial year, the DNB is accountable for its expenditures via the publication of annual reports.[111] The Ministers should give their formal approval for the annual financial statement, but no such approval is required from the sector. The agreement sets out how the annual financial statement is evaluated by the Ministers.[112] The market can thus influence the DNB's financial plans via the representative panel, through which it can indirectly influence the supervisory policy as well. The DNB must respond to the advice, but is not obliged to follow it. It gives account through annual reports. The DNB has an adequate level of market independence.

5.4.2 Dutch Tax and Customs Administration/Bureau Supervision Wwft (*Belastingdienst/Bureau Toezicht Wwft*)

5.4.2.1 Institutional embedding

The Dutch Tax and Customs Administration (hereafter DTCA) is an executive organ of the Ministry of Finance.[113] The organisation consists of four large divisions – Taxes (*Belastingen*), Customs (*Douane*), Benefits (*Toeslagen*), and the Fiscal Information and Investigation Service (*Fiscale Inlichtingen- en Opsporingsdienst, FIOD*) – as well as a number of additional divisions.[114] The DTCA's most prominent tasks are the levying and collection of taxes; the paying out of income-related benefits regarding child care, health care and rent; and the supervision of the import, export and transit of goods and compliance with tax laws and regulations.[115] The FIOD, an investigation division with links to the Public Prosecution Service, is responsible for the detection of financial, economic and fiscal fraud.

5

111 Sections 5-8 Wbft.

112 Section 5(2) Wbft in conjunction with Section 34 AAAFA. The agreement between the Minister of Finance and the financial supervisors sets out the criteria based on which the Minister will evaluate the financial statements: Supra, n. 88 at 14-15.

113 Section 2 Uitvoeringsregeling Belastingdienst 2003 (in English: *Tax and Customs Administration Executive Regulation 2003*); Cf. Feteris, M.W.C. (2009), *Formeel belastingrecht*, Kluwer: Deventer, at 18.

114 *Uitvoeringsregeling Belastingdienst 2003*, Stcrt. 2002, 247. Last amended on 1 January 2014, Stcrt. 2013, 36216.

115 Cf. *Algemene wet inzake Rijksbelastingen 1959* (State Taxes Act); *Wet inkomstenbelasting 2001* (Income Tax Act), *Wet op de loonbelasting 1964* (Wages and Salaries Tax Act), *Wet op de vennootschapsbelasting 1969* (Corporate Tax Act), *Douanewet 2008* (Customs Act) are some of the Acts for which the Tax and Customs Administration levies and collects taxes.

Figure 3 – Organisation of the Dutch Tax and Customs Administration[116]

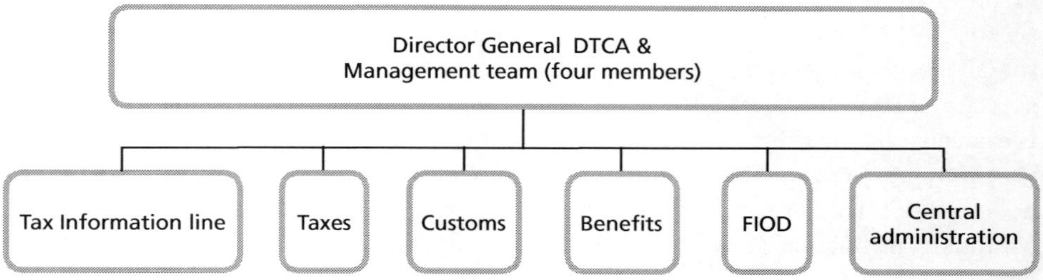

The Bureau Supervision Wwft (hereafter also 'the Bureau') of the Dutch Tax and Customs Administration is the AML supervisor of dealers or intermediaries in the sale of vehicles, ships, works of art, antiques, precious stones, precious metals, jewellery insofar as they receive cash payments amounting to 15,000 Euros or more, real estate agents (including estate intermediaries), valuers of real estate (*taxateurs onroerend goed*), as well as virtual offices (*domicilieverleners*).[117] Since 2010 it is also responsible for the AML supervision of the non-financial institutions of the overseas regions of the Kingdom of the Netherlands: Saba, St. Eustatius and Bonaire.

The Bureau Supervision Wwft is part of the Taxes division, and falls under the formal authority of the director of the subdivision Large Businesses (*Belastingdienst/Grote ondernemingen*).[118] The Bureau supervised approximately 70,100 businesses in the Netherlands in 2011, of which 8,500 were real estate agents, and around 50 businesses in the overseas BES islands.[119] In April 2013 the number of estate agents had slightly increased to a total of 9,138.[120] In 2013, the Bureau had 41 FTE available for AML supervision. Representatives estimated that on average 10 FTE are spent on the supervision of real estate agents. The Bureau's budget is fully integrated in the DTCA's payment system and is therefore not publicly available. An estimation was once made in 2009 when it was estimated to be around 1.5 million Euros.[121] Since then, however, staff have increased considerably. Staff work from different DTCA offices throughout the country.

> The number of institutions subject to the Bureau's supervision is not entirely clear and varies from one year to another. This has to do with the fact that any person in the Netherlands can call himself a real estate agent or estate intermediary, the fact that the DTCA's database is not always completely accurate, and the fact that dealers in goods are

116 Own simplified figure based on: Belastingdienst, *Organisatieschema*, available at: <www.belastingdienst.nl/wps/wcm/connect/bldcontentnl/standaard_functies/prive/organisatie/onze_organisatie/organisatieschema/organisatieschema>, last visited on 8 April 2014.

117 Section 24(1) Wwft and Section 1(d) Decree on the appointment of Wwft supervisors.

118 *Besluit van de Minister van Financiën en de Minister van Veiligheid en Justitie van 6 september 2013, kenmerk: FM 2013/1120M, tot wijziging van een ministeriële regeling en een aantal ministeriële besluiten op het terrein van het voorkomen van witwassen en terrorismefinanciering, in verband met een aanpassing van de organisatie van de Belastingdienst*, Stcrt. 2013, 25564.

119 FATF (2011) at 244.

120 Interview Belastingdienst/Bureau Toezicht Wwft, April 2013.

121 FATF (2011) at 244.

only subject to the AML obligations when they accept cash payments of 15,000 Euros or more. For other transactions they fall outside the scope of the Act.

5.4.2.2 Independence and accountability

Political independence

As mentioned, the Bureau Supervision Wwft belongs to the Dutch Tax and Customs Administration. The DTCA is headed by the Directorate General of the Tax and Customs Administration. This DG, in turn, falls under the authority of the Secretary General and, ultimately, the Minister of Finance. Being an executive organ of the Ministry of Finance, the DTCA falls under his full ministerial responsibility vis-à-vis Parliament. As it is part of the Ministry of Finance, this means that the DTCA is not independent (institutional independence). The DTCA is not a purely supervisory authority, like the DNB or the Financial Supervision Office, and the aspect of independence is where the DTCA differs from these authorities the most.[122]

Figure 4 – Organisation of the Ministry of Finance[123]

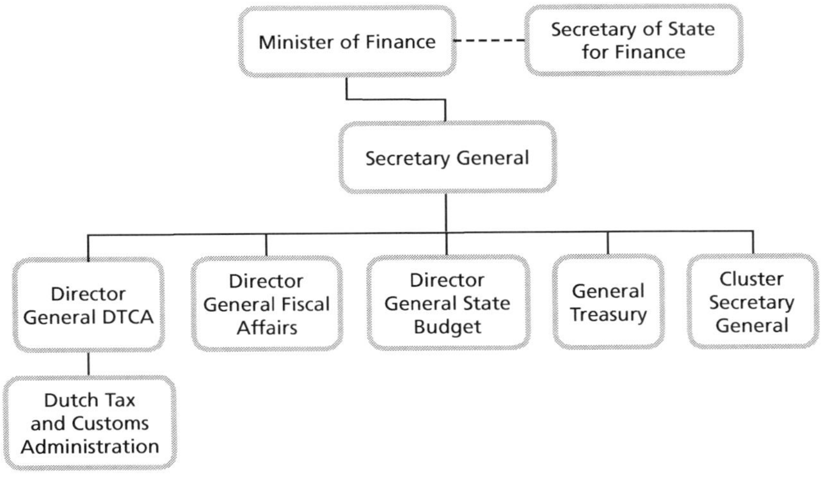

The Bureau is fully embedded within the organisation of the DTCA. We have already seen that the director of the subdivision Large Businesses is formally in charge of the Bureau. Moreover, the Bureau depends on the DTCA's infrastructure in terms of budgeting, salaries, declarations of expenses, the purchase of office supplies, and IT facilities. In terms of supervisory policy and the exercise of AML supervision, the situation is more complicated. According to representatives, the Bureau Supervision Wwft's primary discussion partner is the Directorate Financial Markets (DFM) which belongs to the General Treasury of

122 Commissie Horizontaal Toezicht Belastingdienst (2012), *Fiscaal toezicht op maat: Soepel waar het kan, streng waar het moet*, Den Haag, at 22 and 24.

123 Own figure based on: Ministerie van Financiën, *Organogram*, available at: <www.rijksoverheid.nl/ministeries/fin/organisatie/organogram>, last visited on: 8 April 2014.

the Ministry of Finance.[124] The General Treasury (*Generale Thesaurie*) is, among other things, responsible for financial economic policy in the Netherlands. Besides being the primary discussion partner, the DFM determines and provides the budget of the Bureau to the DTCA. The head of the Bureau Supervision Wwft drafts annual supervision plans and annual reports that, after consultation with and approval from the director of Large Businesses (hereafter 'director LB'), are sent to and discussed with DFM.[125] This means that not only the director LB from the DTCA can influence the annual supervision plans and reports, but that also the DFM from the General Treasury has an opportunity to provide insights into these plans and reports. If the DFM does not agree with the plans, the Bureau Supervision Wwft and the DFM enter into a dialogue. In practice, representatives stated, the Bureau wishes to maintain a good working relationship and is generally willing to take into account the insights from the DFM if there are good arguments to make certain changes.[126] Based on laws, regulations or other public information, it cannot be said which formal powers the DFM and the director LB have if they disagree with the Bureau on the annual supervision plans, the annual reports, the supervision or sanctioning policy under the AML Act. This seems to be fully embedded within the organisational structure of the Ministry of Finance and DTCA.

An aspect that provides the Bureau with some further operational independence within the DTCA concerns the possibility of having access to databases. The Bureau has access to the DTCA's information databases.[127] However, no other divisions and subdivisions – not even the subdivision Large Businesses – have access to the Bureau's database that contains supervisory information. This is not allowed because Section 22 Wwft states that any party that performs, or used to perform, any duty for the purpose of the application of this Act or of decisions taken pursuant to this Act shall be prohibited from making any further or other use of data or information provided or received by virtue of this Act, and from publicising such data and information in any further or other way than is required for the performance of that party's duties or than is required pursuant to this Act. An exception is made for the exchange of information between the four formal AML supervisors.[128] This means that there is a one-way information flow from the DTCA to the Bureau Supervision Wwft.

> There is one minor exception, which stems from Section 25 Wwft. Under this provision, AML supervisors are obliged to notify FIU-NL, where necessary in derogation from the applicable statutory confidentiality provisions, when they discover facts in the course of their duties that may be an indication of money laundering or terrorist financing. During the exercise of its AML supervision, the Bureau Supervision Wwft may come across circumstances that point to (fiscal) fraud. If the Bureau finds that these circumstances give rise to indications of money laundering (or terrorist financing), it makes a disclosure to the FIU in accordance with Section 25 Wwft. After the FIU-NL's own analysis of this disclosure, it can decide to share this information with the FIOD or

124 Interview Belastingdienst/Bureau Supervision Wwft, April 2013.

125 Interview Belastingdienst/Bureau Supervision Wwft, April 2013.

126 Interview Belastingdienst/Bureau Toezicht Wwft, April 2013.

127 Section 67 State Taxes Act in conjunction with Section 43c(1)(t) Executive Regulation to the State Taxes Act 1994.

128 See § 5.9.

other law enforcement authorities. The FIU can forward the information to the FIOD through its permanent liaison officers.[129] This means that information submitted by the Bureau Supervision Wwft to the FIU in accordance with the AML Act can ultimately end up with the FIOD for further criminal investigation. This, however, is a decision (to be) made by the FIU and not by the Bureau Supervision Wwft or the FIOD.

Despite the fact that in terms of having access to databases the Bureau seems to be given some more independence within the DTCA, this does not do away with the conclusion that the Bureau Supervision Wwft has an inadequate level of political independence. Particularly the fact that the Bureau does not only require approval from the director LB but that the DFM, which belongs to another part of the Ministry of Finance, can also exert influence on the Bureau's annual supervision plans and reports is decisive for this finding.

Accountability

Finding that the level of political independence is inadequate, accountability and transparency become even more important to counterbalance this lack of independence. Unlike the DNB which is legally obliged to publish annual reports (*ZBO-verantwoordingen*), legislation does not contain an obligation for the Bureau to account for the exercise of its AML supervision, for example through the publication of annual reports.[130] In theory, the Bureau's work may be investigated by the Court of Audit, or parliamentary investigations or inquiries. The latter instrument has never been used in relation to the Bureau Supervision Wwft. As regards investigations by the Court of Audit, it was just mentioned that it investigated the effectiveness of the fight against money laundering and terrorist financing in the Netherlands in 2008 and 2013. In this investigation, the role of the Bureau Supervision Wwft was assessed only at an abstract level.[131] Although the Bureau Supervision Wwft is not obliged to publish annual reports, it is still remarkable that there is not a single public document in which account is given about the exercise of AML supervision. The DTCA's annual report for the year 2011 does not mention the activities of the Bureau Supervision Wwft.[132] The overall annual reports for the years 2011 and 2012 of the Ministry of Finance do not make any references to its activities either. The 2011 annual report of the Ministry of Finance mentions the AML policy by presenting the sanctioning activities of the DNB and the AFM, as well as the number of unusual transactions reported to the FIU on the basis of subjective indicators.[133] Interestingly, no mention is made of the activities of the Bureau Supervision Wwft. The annual report for the year 2012 of the Ministry of Finance remains silent about any supervisory activity under

129 Regioplan Beleidsonderzoek (2012), *Naar een beleidsmonitor bestrijding witwassen*, WODC: The Hague, research commissioned by the Dutch Ministry of Security & Justice, at 25.

130 While the Bureau Supervision Wwft derives all its powers from the Dutch AML Act and regulations, this would be the most logical place to include such an obligation. None of the instruments in the preventive AML policy, however, contains such an obligation.

131 Algemene Rekenkamer (2008a); Algemene Rekenkamer (2014).

132 Belastingdienst (2011), *Beheerverslag 2011*, *Parliamentary Papers II*, 2011-12, 33 000-IXB, no. 24. From the year 2012 onwards, the DTCA's annual reports are incorporated in the annual report of the Ministry of Finance: Ministerie van Financiën, *Beantwoording Kamervragen beheersverslag Belastingdienst*, kenmerk DGB/2013/4527, 17 September 2013.

133 Ministerie van Financiën (2011a), *Jaarverslag en slotwet 2011*, *Parliamentary Papers II*, 2011-12, 33 240 IXB, no. 1, at 50-51.

the preventive AML policy.[134] The Bureau Supervision Wwft, as we have just seen, makes annual supervision plans and annual reports. However, these are not publicly available. This means that although internally the Bureau Supervision Wwft forwards these documents to the DFM, which can hold the Bureau accountable internally, no such opportunity exists for the institutions and professionals for which it has supervisory responsibility and for the general public. There are no legal provisions that stand in the way of the publication of the annual supervision plans or annual reports, or to include the data from these reports in the overall annual reports of the DTCA or the Ministry of Finance. From interviews it became clear that the Bureau Supervision Wwft is considering making annual plans and annual reports publicly available in the future in order to increase the visibility of the Bureau as an independent division within the DTCA, as well as to improve understanding and awareness on the side of the supervised population and the wider public.[135] Until the first quarter of 2014, the Bureau had not published any documents. Transparency and, therefore, accountability are not adequately embedded within the Bureau Supervision Wwft. More openness should be about the activities foreseen and performed, in order to be held accountable. The publication of the annual reports seems to be the most logical option in this respect.

Market independence

Panels with representatives from the private sector are not present at the Bureau Supervision Wwft, and no financial relationship exists either between the two. The Bureau Supervision Wwft, therefore, has an adequate level of market independence. Regarding accountability to the institutions for which the Bureau has supervisory responsibility, it would be advisable to at least make the annual reports publicly available and to exercise a higher degree of transparency than is currently the case.

5.4.3 Financial Supervision Office (*Bureau Financieel Toezicht*)

5.4.3.1 Institutional embedding

The Financial Supervision Office is an independent administrative authority established by the Dutch Notaries Act.[136] Set up in 1993 by the Ministry of Justice as the authority responsible for monitoring the third-party bank accounts of notaries, its task was extended in 2001 to third-party bank accounts of court bailiffs. The Financial Supervision Office (hereafter also 'BFT') supervises the integrity of these professionals, the quality of their work and their financial position. Since 2003 the BFT is responsible for the AML supervision of lawyers (*advocaten*), (junior) civil-law notaries, registered accountants, accounting consultants, tax advisors and other independent legal advisers.[137]

134 Ministerie van Financiën (2012), *Jaarverslag en slotwet 2012*, *Parliamentary Papers II*, 2012-13, 33 605 IXB, no. 1.

135 Interview Belastingdienst/Bureau Toezicht Wwft, April 2013.

136 Section 110 Dutch Notaries Act (*Wet op het notarisambt*, Stb. 2011, 417). On the 1st of January 2013, when amendments to the Act entered into force, the BFT was brought under the scope of the AAAFA. See § 5.4.3.2.

137 Its task is now laid down in Section 24(1) Wwft in conjunction with Section 1(c) Decree on the appointment of Wwft supervisors.

As mentioned in Chapter 3, a Bill amending the Counsel Act and some other Acts (*Wetsvoorstel herziening advocatuur*) has been pending before Parliament since 2010. The Bill includes a proposal to remove the anti-money laundering supervision of lawyers from the BFT and to assign it to (a body of) the Dutch Bar Association (*Nederlandse Orde van Advocaten*).[138] This foreseen transfer of supervisory responsibility has, on the one hand, been influenced by the broader discussion on the supervision of lawyers, in particular by a report from Docters Van Leeuwen who gave various recommendations to strengthen the supervision of lawyers.[139] On the other hand, this has also been influenced by the fact that the BFT does not have the power to carry out on-site inspections and to control lawyers' administration due to the principle of legal professional privilege.[140] This has led to *de-facto* no AML supervision of lawyers.[141]

AML supervision is carried out by the 'Wwft team'. In 2012 a total of 41.3 FTE worked at the BFT and the Wwft team was comprised of 12 FTE.[142] In 2013 the Wwft team consisted of 13 FTE.[143] The total budget of the authority was a little more than 6.2 million Euros.[144] The number of staff working in the BFT's Wwft team stands in stark contrast to the total number of professionals for which it has supervisory responsibility: around 30,000 businesses, with a total of approximately 50,000 professionals.[145] At the end of 2012, the BFT had supervisory responsibility for 17,648 accountants.[146] The BFT acknowledges that it is a small organisation, with a small capacity and limited resources, and that it is challenging to supervise such a high number of professionals.[147] Since 2008 the BFT's capacity for AML supervision has hardly changed.[148]

The BFT has faced considerable organisational changes. In April 2013, the two BFT directors were laid off by the Board and replaced by an interim director.[149] Members of Parliament asked questions to the Minister of Security & Justice on this matter.[150] There appeared to be a disagreement between the directors on the execution of the

138 See also: Algemene Rekenkamer (2014) at 6; FATF (2014b), *Second Follow Up Report: Mutual Evaluation on the Netherlands*, February 2014, at 37.
139 Docters van Leeuwen, A. (2010), *Het bestaande is geen alternatief: een verkenning naar verbeteringen in het toezicht op de advocatuur*, NSOB.
140 Hof van Discipline 11 September 2009, ECLI:NL:TAHVD:2009:YA0027. See also: Faure et al. (2009) at 118-119; Stouten (2012) at 298 and Bannier, F.A.W. et al. (2008), *Heeft de lokale deken een geheimhoudingsplicht en een verschoningsrecht?*, advies in opdracht van de Algemene Raad van de Nederlandse Orde van Advocaten, at 5.
141 Algemene Rekenkamer (2008a) at 16; Docters Van Leeuwen (2010), at 16; Stouten (2012) at 269-270.
142 Bureau Financieel Toezicht (2012), *Jaarverslag 2012*, at 50 (in English: *Annual Report 2012*).
143 Algemene Rekenkamer (2014) at 6.
144 Bureau Financieel Toezicht (2012) at 37.
145 Ibid., at 26; FATF (2011) at 245; Stouten (2012) at 279.
146 Nederlandse Beroepsorganisatie van Accountants (2012), *Jaaroverzicht 2012*, at 5 (in English: *Annual report 2012*). The total number of accountants was 21,418. The Wwft is not however applicable to internal or government accountants (1,489) and post-active accountants (2,281). At the time of finalising this chapter the annual report for the year 2013 had not yet been published.
147 Bureau Financieel Toezicht (2013), *Nieuwsbrief Toezicht*, no. 1, winter edition, at 2.
148 Algemene Rekenkamer (2014) at 6.
149 Bureau Financieel Toezicht (2013a), *Oosterloo waarnemend directeur Bureau Financieel Toezicht*, available at <www.bureauft.nl/Documents/OOSTERLOO%20WAARNEMEND%20DIRECTEUR%20BUREAU%20FINANCIEEL%20TOEZICHT.pdf>, last visited on 7 April 2014.
150 *Parliamentary Papers II*, 2012-13, Vragen, 2013Z11110.

> BFT's supervision programmes.[151] In December 2013 a new director was appointed.[152] According to the Minister Security & Justice, the organisational struggles did not influence the exercise of the BFT's AML supervision.[153]

Although the Government has appointed the BFT as the formal AML supervisor for the legal and fiscal service providers, initiatives from professional associations have led to the development of internal supervision systems within which compliance with AML obligations is incorporated.[154] The BFT engages with those associations that (wish to) include AML aspects into their wider quality controls and is of the opinion that professional associations must be the first gatekeeper in the prevention of money laundering and terrorist financing.[155] According to Stouten, this form of internal supervision should be seen as complementary to the work of the BFT as it has a more cooperative and supportive character than AML supervision exercised by the BFT.[156] With respect to accountants, the supervisory arrangement with the Dutch Association of Registered Accountants and Accounting Consultants (*Samenwerkende Registeraccountants en Accountants-administratieconsulenten, SRA*) is of direct relevance.[157] This supervisory arrangement states that the SRA is primarily responsible for the AML supervision of its members. More about this indirect involvement of professional associations in the AML supervision follows in § 5.8.2.

5.4.3.2 Independence and accountability

Political independence and accountability

Being an independent administrative authority (*zelfstandig bestuursorgaan*) the BFT is positioned at a distance from the political arena.[158] Ministerial responsibility for its functioning rests with the Minister of Security & Justice. The main piece of legislation is the Autonomous Administrative Authorities Framework Act, which applies to the BFT since January 2013.[159] It was primarily brought under the scope of this Act to better ensure that it can carry out its tasks independently without undue influence from politics.[160] It

151 Minister van Veiligheid en Justitie, *Beantwoording Kamervragen over het bericht dat twee directieleden van het BFT zijn opgestapt*, 24 June 2013, Kenmerk 395729.

152 Bureau Financieel Toezicht (2013), *Thieu Coffeng nieuwe directeur Bureau Financieel Toezicht*, 11 December 2013, available at: <www.bureauft.nl/publiek-pers/nieuws-publicaties/Documents/Persbericht%20benoeming%20de%20heer%20mr%20%20M%20E%20%20Coffeng.pdf>, last visited on 7 April 2014.

153 Minister van Veiligheid en Justitie, *Beantwoording Kamervragen over het bericht dat twee directieleden van het BFT zijn opgestapt*, 24 June 2013, Kenmerk 395729. Cf. Interview Bureau Financieel Toezicht, June 2013.

154 Stouten (2012) at 278.

155 FATF (2011) at 245.

156 Stouten (2012) at 278-279.

157 Bureau Financieel Toezicht (2012) at 27.

158 See § 5.4.1.1.

159 Section 110(9) Wet op het notarisambt, as introduced in Stb. 2011, 470.

160 Section 3(1)(a) AAAFA; *Parliamentary Papers II*, 2007-08, 25 268, no. 60, at 3.

seems that AAAFA applies to the BFT in full.[161] The Minister has a range of powers to oversee its functioning. He is competent to:

- appoint, suspend or dismiss the directors of the BFT (Section 12);
- request information which he needs to perform his oversight activities – even confidential information. In that case the Minister has a derived duty of secrecy (Section 20);
- draft general policy rules for the exercise of the BFT's functions (Section 21);
- annul individual decisions from the BFT (Section 22);
- take over or transfer the activities of the BFT to another authority if he is of the opinion that the BFT is neglecting its tasks (Section 23).

All powers are, in principle, ways for the Minister to oversee the functioning of the BFT. The Minister can set the framework for supervision by formulating general policy rules, but within this framework the BFT is allowed to take its own decisions. Nevertheless, the last two powers for the Minister can highly affect individual decision-making on the side of the BFT. Section 10:35 of the General Administrative Law Act, however, provides that individual decisions of independent administrative authorities may only be nullified in case of a conflict with the law or the public interest.[162] A second legal safeguard is that ZBOs should first be given an opportunity to discuss the matter with their Minister before the latter resorts to the use of this instrument.[163] Ministers may only use this power as a last resort and should use it with great restraint.[164] Likewise the power to transfer or take over the activities of the BFT is an *ultimum remedium*. The Minister should first have exhausted all other powers to come to an improvement of the situation. Only if there is no prospect of any improvement may he apply this power.[165] The Minister has no power to give instructions to the BFT in exceptional (individual) circumstances. With the powers purveyed above, as well as powers in relation to the financing of the BFT and the continuous periodic meetings with the BFT's Board, this power was not considered desirable or necessary.[166] There are enough safeguards to prevent the Minister from limiting the (political) independence of the BFT. Therefore, it has an adequate level of political independence.

The BFT is legally required to send annual reports about the activities performed and the policy pursued before the 15th of March of each calendar year to the Minister of Security & Justice, the Senate and Parliament.[167] In practice, the BFT publishes its annual reports on

161 *Parliamentary Papers II*, 2009-10, 32 250, no. 7, at 11-12; *Besluit van 1 december 2011, houdende de vaststelling van het tijdstip van inwerkingtreding van enkele artikelen, of onderdelen daarvan, van de wet van 29 september 2011 tot wijziging van de Wet op het notarisambt naar aanleiding van de evaluatie van die wet, alsmede regeling van enkele andere onderwerpen in die wet en wijziging van de Wet op het centraal testamentenregister en van de Wet ter voorkoming van witwassen en financieren van terrorisme (Stb. 470)*, Stb. 2011, 587; De Leeuw (2013) at 143.

162 Cf. *Parliamentary Papers II*, 2000-01, 27 426, no. 3, at 27.

163 Section 10:41 Awb.

164 *Parliamentary Papers II*, 2000-01, 27 426, no. 3, at 27.

165 Ibid., at 28.

166 *Parliamentary Papers II*, 2010-11, 29 911, no. 47, at 3.

167 Section 18 AAAFA and Section 4:80 Awb.

its website as well.[168] They contain a separate section in which it accounts for the exercise of its AML supervision. Aside from this direct form of accountability, the Minister of Security & Justice has the obligation to investigate the effectiveness and efficiency of the BFT every five years and to send a report thereon to the Senate and Parliament.[169] In 2009, when this obligation for the Minister was still based on the old Notaries Act, this resulted in a report in which the tasks and position of the BFT were assessed by an evaluation committee whose members were appointed by the Minister.[170] Other forms through which the BFT may be held accountable is through parliamentary investigations or inquiries, or investigations by the Dutch Court of Audit. In 2008 and 2013, the Court of Audit investigated the effectiveness of the fight against money laundering and terrorist financing in the Netherlands, in which the role of the BFT was assessed at a more abstract level.[171]

Market independence

The BFT's governance has no panels or other means through which the institutions and professionals subject to its supervision can exert an influence on its supervisory policy and activities. To a certain extent there is a financial relationship with the professionals. As of 2014 the BFT should be subsidised by the institutions which it supervises.[172] This financing should be regulated under the new Notaries Act and the Dutch Bailiffs Act, and will not apply to the AML Act. This means that the Ministry of Finance remains the sponsoring body for AML supervision exercised by the BFT.[173] To date, there are no further elaborated plans on how this change in funding should take place. It is thus not clear whether the private sector will be represented in the BFT via panels of institutions in order to hold BFT accountable, other than the publication of annual reports in which it accounts for its expenditures and activities.

5.4.4 Concluding remarks

This section dealt with the institutional aspects of the Dutch Central Bank (DNB), the Dutch Tax and Customs Administration/Bureau Supervision Wwft and the Financial Supervision Office (BFT). Both the DNB and BFT are independent administrative authorities (*zelfstandige bestuursorganen, ZBO*). The Autonomous Administrative Authorities Framework Act partly applies to the DNB, and in full to the BFT. The fact that both authorities are ZBOs means that they are set at arm's length from the responsible Minister, but that the latter has powers to oversee their work. In the case of the DNB, the Minister of Finance has signed an agreement determining how and at what times the Minister makes use of his intervention powers. Both the DNB and BFT are legally

168 Jaarverslagen Bureau Financieel Toezicht, available at: <www.bureauft.nl/publiek-pers/nieuws-publicaties/Paginas/jaarverslagen.aspx>, last visited on 7 April 2014.

169 Section 39 AAAFA.

170 Evaluatiecommissie Bureau Financieel Toezicht (2009), *Toezicht en inzicht: Een helder denkraam*, August 2009.

171 Algemene Rekenkamer (2008a) and Algemene Rekenkamer (2014).

172 At the end of 2013 it became clear that this was not manageable; the current expectation is that the BFT will be (partly) funded by institutions starting in 2015.

173 Interview Bureau Financieel Toezicht, June 2013.

required to draft annual reports and to send these to the responsible Minister, Parliament and the Senate. In practice, they publish these reports on their websites as well. The reports include information about the exercise of AML supervision. Accountability can also be provided through political investigations or inquiries, or through investigations by the Court of Audit. Both authorities have an adequate level of political independence. The DNB has the most involvement from the private sector by the representative panel. Both authorities have an adequate level of market independence.

The foregoing is different for the Bureau Supervision Wwft. It has an inadequate level of political independence, especially due to the position of the DTCA as an executive organ of the Ministry of Finance. In light of the theoretical framework that for effective supervision an adequate level of political independence is required, it would be advisable to remove the Bureau Supervision Wwft from the organisation of DTCA and to make it an independent administrative authority or, alternatively, to assign another authority that is positioned more at a distance from the political arena as the AML supervisor, as is the case for the DNB and BFT. If the Bureau Supervision Wwft remains as the AML supervisor, it is advisable to at least create a more independent position within the DTCA for the Bureau in a law or regulation. The lack of an adequate level of political independence is accompanied by the absence of a legal obligation in the AML Act or lower-level regulations for the Bureau Supervision Wwft to account for the exercise of its AML supervision. In practice, the Bureau and the DTCA should become more transparent as well. The annual reports from the Ministry of Finance and the DTCA do not mention its work at all. And annual supervision plans and reports from the Bureau itself are internal documents. The most logical option to increase transparency would be to publish these annual reports from the Bureau Supervision Wwft.

5.5 The regulation of banks, real estate agents and accountants

This section verifies the extent to which banks, accountants and real estate agents are regulated sectors or professions in the Netherlands. It gives an insight into the question whether the supervisory authorities have, or can have, an adequate knowledge of their supervisees. This section pays attention to the definition of banks, real estate agents and accountants under the AML Act where this differs from other legislation.

5.5.1 Banks

The Financial Supervision Act (hereafter also: Wft) defines a bank as 'a party whose business it is to obtain repayable funds outside a restricted circle (*besloten kring*) from (legal) persons that are not professional market parties, and to grant loans for its own account' (*own translation, MB*).[174] In the Netherlands no person may undertake financial service activities without a licence. Section 2:11 Wft prohibits banks from acting as such without having obtained a licence from the DNB, provided that no exemptions apply or a dispensation has been granted by the DNB. Section 3:7 Wft prohibits any other institution

174 This definition changed a bit with the entry into force of the EU Capital Requirements Regulation and the implementation of the EU Capital Requirements Directive in Dutch national legislation: see § 1.8.

than a licensed credit institution from using the word bank or translations or forms thereof in its name or in the conduct of its business, unless this is done in a context which clearly shows that it does not operate on the financial markets. Foreign banks established in the EEA are not required to obtain a banking licence from the DNB and may operate directly or through a branch in the Netherlands when the DNB is accordingly notified by the home state regulator.[175] Section 2:12 Wft contains the requirements for (Dutch) institutions that wish to obtain a banking licence.[176] Credit institutions must complete an application form to demonstrate that all requirements are met.[177] With this application they must, amongst other things, submit a business plan, statements testifying that the directors and members of the supervisory board are fit and proper persons for such a position, the internal policies of the firm, and information concerning the firm's liquidity and capital.

Banks must comply with the obligations stemming from the Wft and the Prudential Rules under the Wft Decree.[178] Institutions must, inter alia, demonstrate that those people who are responsible for the day-to-day policy of the institution, i.e. managers, directors and persons sitting on supervisory boards, are fit and proper.[179] In determining their trustworthiness and suitability, the DNB takes into account criminal records, as well as supervisory, financial, fiscal-administrative or other precedents, as well as the intentions and actions of the persons in question.[180] Typically, the DNB requires those persons to demonstrate a strong track record in the banking sector. This test normally takes place at the moment on which the person takes on a position in the financial sector for the first time. A re-examination may take place when there are signs of changed or new antecedents in relation to this person. Furthermore, the institution must demonstrate that it has an adequate policy that ensures the sound exercise of the business.[181] It must describe the type of activities that it pursues with the associated risks, and show how it intends to manage, mitigate and control those risks. The institution must, among other things, also demonstrate that it has a transparent control structure that allows for an adequate exercise of supervision thereover and that it has a sound operational structure.[182] Where it is a subsidiary of a third-country credit institution, it must provide information that it is under sufficient consolidated supervision in the country where the latter institution has its registered office.[183] Finally, the institution must demonstrate that it has sufficient capital and that it is solvent and liquid.[184] The DNB verifies whether the capital adequately reflects

175 See Section 3:7(2)(b) Wft, Sections 2:14-2:19 Wft.

176 Section 2:13 Wft contains requirements for banks that also want to perform investment activities.

177 See Section 8 Market Access of Financial Undertakings under the Wft Decree (*Besluit van 12 oktober 2006, houdende regels ter uitvoering van de Wet op het financieel toezicht met betrekking tot de reikwijdte en toegang tot de financiële markten*, Stb. 2006, 506). The Market Access of Financial Undertakings under the Wft Decree was last amended in July 2014: Stb. 2014, 303.

178 *Besluit van 12 oktober 2006, houdende prudentiële regels voor financiële ondernemingen die werkzaam zijn op de financiële markten*, Stb. 2006, 519. Last amended in July 2014: Stb. 2014, 303.

179 Sections 3:8 and 3:9 Wft.

180 Sections 5 and 6 Prudential Rules under the Wft Decree. Section 7 contains the sources of information to which the DNB has access for verifying the trustworthiness of those persons.

181 Sections 3:10 Wft in conjunction with Sections 10-16 Prudential Rules under the Wft Decree.

182 Sections 3:16 and 3:17 Wft.

183 Section 3:31 Wft.

184 Sections 3:53, 3:57 and 3:63 Wft and Chapters 9-11 of the Prudential Rules under the Wft Decree.

the type of business, risks, the business model and operations the bank intends to carry out in the Netherlands.

5.5.1.1 Banks under the AML Act

Under the Wft, the DNB's supervisory competence with regard to banks is limited due to the 'home state control principle'.[185] Banks with a licence granted by a supervisor of another EU or EEA Member State, that intends to act as such in the Netherlands directly or through a branch office, are exempted from the obligation to apply for a licence. They may rely on the licence from their home state regulator pursuant to a European passport and are only required to follow the notification procedure. Accordingly, sole supervisory responsibility rests with the home state regulator. If the foreign bank operates through a branch in the Netherlands, the DNB's supervisory responsibility is limited to monitoring the liquidity of the branch operating in the Netherlands.[186] Such limitation, however, does not apply under the AML Act. The scope of the AML Act is not limited to banks operating with a licence from the DNB. For the thematic integrity supervision exercised by the DNB, this means that AML supervision can be performed on Dutch branches of those banks that have obtained a licence in another EU/EEA Member State. This is, presumably, done where a supervision project is specifically aimed at verifying AML compliance.

5.5.2 Real estate agents

The title of real estate agent is not a protected title in the Netherlands and the profession is not regulated. Every person, whether professionally qualified or not, can call himself a real estate agent and provide estate agency activities – the most prominent being the selling, leasing and managing of real estate and to act as an intermediary for the sale thereof. No distinction is made between residential and commercial real estate agents.

> Between 1967 and 2001 the title of real estate agent was protected via the Dutch Commercial Code (*Wetboek van Koophandel*). The activities of a real estate agent were not protected. Everybody could act as an intermediary in the sale or purchase of property, but the title real estate agent could only be used by those who were sworn in by a district court. The title protection was abandoned in 2001, in line with the at that time prevailing thoughts of *deregulation*. A report dating from 1998 on the functioning of the free market system, deregulation and the quality of legislation in relation to the estate agency profession recommended abolishing the legal protection for real estate agents.[187] More transparency on the quality of the services provided by real estate agents and other intermediaries was said to be necessary for the benefit of consumers. It was argued that the protected title only offered some information about the professionalism, integrity and independence of real estate agents and not of other intermediaries in the sector as such. Moreover, it did not say anything about the actual quality of the estate agent as

185 This is likely to change in the near future: see § 1.8.

186 That this may lead to problems is demonstrated by the Icesave debacle that took place in the Netherlands in 2008. See for a detailed analysis of the case: De Moor-Van Vugt, A.J.C., Du Perron, C.E. and Krop, P.J. (2009), *De bevoegdheden van De Nederlandsche Bank inzake Icesave*, research commissioned by the Dutch Ministry of Finance; Aelen and Van den Broek (2014a) at 21.

187 Van Dijkhuizen, C. et al. (1998), *Rapport van de MDW-werkgroep makelaars*, Ministerie van Economische Zaken: The Hague.

the title was based on a single examination on the professionalism of the estate agent. Because of the high level of organisation and the dynamics of the markets within which real estate agents operated, the authors of the report considered it more appropriate to introduce a certification framework, drafted by the private sector itself – i.e. professional associations, consumer authorities and other organisations with an interest in the profession.[188] The Ministers of Economic Affairs and Justice also wanted to create an equal level playing field and decided, in line with the recommendations, to deregulate the profession.

Real estate agents can, but are not obliged to, follow a certification study offered to estate agents in the Netherlands. Various institutions offer certification studies and all have their own entry requirements in terms of a university degree or a higher vocational education degree, as well as requirements for permanent education. Likewise, real estate agents can become members of any of the three professional associations for estate agents in the Netherlands: the Netherlands Association of Estate Agents (*Nederlandse Vereniging van Makelaars, NVM*), the Netherlands Property Mediation Association (*Vereniging Bemiddeling Onroerend Goed, VBO*) and VastgoedPro. Not all real estate agents are members of these associations.[189] Two of the three professional associations (NVM and VBO) have entry and licensing requirements and a Code of Ethics or Code of Conduct.[190] Members of the NVM and VBO who act in violation of these Codes can become liable to disciplinary action by their respective associations. These are not statutory disciplinary systems, as is the case for accountants, lawyers and civil-law notaries in the Netherlands. Rules of procedure vary between the two associations. Vastgoedpro does not have such a procedure. In the literature, the professional associations in the estate agency sector have been criticised. In their study, Ferwerda and others found that the internal control systems of the professional associations generally seem to have more of a symbolic value than actually preventing fraudulent activities concerning speculation with regard to premises.[191] Moreover, these professional associations are not subject to external oversight.

NVM is the largest professional association and requires its members to have successfully followed three certification studies at the SVM (*Stichting Vakopleiding Makelaardij*[192]), regarding the residential, commercial and agrarian sectors. Its Code of Ethics consists of ten articles, all of which deal with the level of independence, objectivity, reliability and expertise of the members. For example, if an NVM member enters into negotiations with more than one candidate for a certain property, then he is obliged to inform the parties involved accordingly (article 4). Moreover, a real estate agent may not have any direct or indirect interest in real estate (article 6), nor participate in unfair competition (article 7). This Code of Ethics does not explicitly refer to matters like (the prevention of) fraud, money laundering or other criminal activities. Based on the membership regulations (*Reglement Lidmaatschap & Aansluiting*), the NVM Board is empowered to

188 *Parliamentary Papers II*, 1997-98, 24 036, no. 82.

189 FATF (2011) at 31.

190 NVM, *Erecode*, available at: <www.nvm.nl/over_nvm/nvm_lidmaatschap/erecode.aspx>, last visited on 9 April 2014 (in English: *NVM Disciplinary Regulations*); VBO, *Beroeps- en gedragscode Vereniging VBO Makelaar*, available at: <www.vbomakelaar.nl/makelaars-taxateurs/kwaliteitsborging>, last visited on 9 April 2014.

191 Ferwerda et al. (2007) at 122.

192 This is one of the institutions that can issue the certification diplomas in accordance with Government requirements.

impose fines of between 5,000 and 15,000 Euros on its members (article 24) and can exclude a member (article 25) where it is of the opinion that it does not comply with the NVM regulations or obligations. An appeal is possible at the disciplinary councils or the highest disciplinary organ of the NVM (*Centrale Raad van Toezicht*). According to the disciplinary regulations of the NVM (*Reglement tuchtrechtspraak NVM*) they can issue a reprimand, a private fine of a maximum of 50,000 Euros to be paid to the association, temporary exclusion from NVM membership for a maximum period of one year, or permanent exclusion.[193]

One can observe that the profession is only regulated to a limited extent and is, therefore, fragmented. Anyone can call himself a real estate agent, whether professionally qualified or not. There are possibilities for certification and for membership of professional associations. There is no single register containing all the names and business information of real estate agents. Due to the fragmented nature of the profession, the DTCA/Bureau Supervision Wwft runs the risk of not having an accurate knowledge of the group of real estate agents for which it has supervisory responsibility.

5.5.2.1 *Real estate agents under the AML Act*

Aside from the lack of regulation of the estate agency profession, the AML Act itself does not require estate agents to register themselves with the AML Supervisor. In addition, the Act poses some legal difficulties in relation to estate agents. One of the legal problems concerned the fact that the AML Act obliged real estate agents to perform customer due diligence only on their clients. The new FATF Recommendations from February 2012, however, require Member States to oblige real estate agents to perform customer due diligence on both their clients and the other party. This incompatibility with the international standards was removed on the 1st of January 2014.[194] Other problems still exist. Hereafter we will delve deeper into valuation activities and the question whether real estate businesses fall under the scope of the Act.

Valuation activities by estate agents

Before 2013 real estate agents only fell under the scope of the AML Act when they acted as an intermediary in the establishment and conclusion of agreements on real estate (*onroerend goed*) and rights attached to this property.[195] With the amendments to the AML Act that entered into force on the 1st of January 2013, another important task of estate agents – valuation (*taxatie*) – was brought under the scope of the Act. The AML Act defines valuers as 'natural or legal persons who, in the exercise of a profession or business, perform valuations of real estate and rights to which the real estate is subjected'.[196] A valuation is an objective evaluation of the value of real estate, usually for the purpose of

193 Section 31 of the NVM Disciplinary Regulations.

194 *Wijziging van de Wet op het financieel toezicht en enige andere wetten (Wijzigingswet financiële markten 2014)*, Stb. 2013, 487. The obligation is now laid down in Section 3(12) Wwft. See: FATF (2014b) at 32.

195 Section 1(14) Wwft; Section 62 Dutch Commercial Code.

196 Section 1(1)(a)(24) Wwft.

mortgage loans.[197] Based on a valuation report, banks or other lenders can decide on the amount of a mortgage loan. Valuation reports are sometimes used in purchase or selling decisions as well. The valuation of real estate is always done by a real estate agent other than the one involved as an intermediary in the selling or buying of real estate.

> Valuation is not a regulated activity. Valuers can work in a real estate business, or act as independent professionals. Valuers can also be estate agents, but this is not necessarily the case. Contrary to the estate agents' activity of mediation that is fully liberalised, some requirements must be fulfilled in order to perform valuation activities.[198] Valuers must have successfully completed certification studies, be registered in one of the two valuation registers and be a member of one of the three professional associations. To be included in the valuation register, one must have liability insurance and a declaration of professional competence. Valuers must thus comply with higher standards in terms of certification and registration with professional associations.

The Dutch Government considered that valuers of real estate can be faced with unusual transactions that give rise to suspicions of money laundering. A valuer can observe that there have been price fluctuations with respect to the property that cannot be explained or he can be requested by the client to value the property higher or lower than the actual value, which is a form of price manipulation. The FATF Recommendations and the Third Directive do not (explicitly) require that valuation activities are brought under the scope of the AML policies of Member States. However, in light of the particular AML risks in the estate sector in the Netherlands, the Dutch Government found it necessary to partly include valuers under the scope of the AML Act. As a result of the partial inclusion, they are only required to report unusual transactions to FIU-NL and to retain the data they have used in the disclosure.[199] They are excluded from customer due diligence, the record keeping of documents in relation to customer due diligence, and training obligations.

> During the discussions on the amendments to the AML Act in the Senate, Senators asked the Government why it had decided not to include valuers in full under the AML Act.[200] They observed that valuers could become aware of unusual circumstances related to the property particularly because of checks on clients and their backgrounds. They considered that customer due diligence could increase the quality of the reports to the FIU. The Senators also argued that the law would be clearer and more comprehensible if valuing would fall in full under the scope of the Act, especially since a considerable number of estate agents perform valuation activities. The Government responded to the Senate that it had not included valuation fully as a result of a 'careful balance of interests'. Unusual circumstances would mostly not arise from the client, but from the assignment given to the valuer. The Government stated, moreover, that the relationship between

197 Please note that valuation activities concern establishing the value of buildings or property, and not the wider activity of surveying. Surveying is a more thorough examination of the conditions of a building, which goes beyond the determination of the value alone. It entails a comprehensive technical assessment of the property's current condition with detailed guidance on any repairs required and future maintenance.

198 Nationale Hypotheek Garantie (2010), *Brancheverenigingen stellen normen vast voor taxateurs en taxatierapporten en de controle erop ten behoeve van financieringen met NHG-garantie*, available at: <www.nhg.nl/fileadmin/user_upload/Documenten/PDF/Branchebrede_normering_NHG.pdf>, last visited on 7 April 2014.

199 Section 16(1) in conjunction with section 16(3) Wwft, and Section 34 Wwft.

200 *Parliamentary Papers I*, 2012-13, 33 236, C, at 8.

> the valuer and the client is usually of short duration and that in many cases there is no physical contact between the two parties. This would make the identification of the client and possibly the ultimate beneficial owner too cumbersome and costly.[201]

Because the activity of valuation is only subject to the reporting obligation, valuers of real estate have a somewhat different reporting obligation than other obliged institutions and professionals. Since valuers of real estate are not obliged to perform customer due diligence on their clients, they will not (in all cases) have this information available. Therefore, the AML Act states that valuers only have to report the kind of information that they possess. Furthermore, upon reporting valuers must provide a description of the property concerned.[202]

The partial inclusion of valuation activities under the scope of the AML Act can be considered a step forward in light of the vulnerability of the real estate sector for money laundering, but at this point the law is not sufficiently clear and comprehensible. It may not be fully clear to estate agents performing both mediation and valuation when they have to comply in full with the AML obligations, or when they are required to partially do so. Moreover, they might have to develop two different internal policies for the two different tasks exercised by the estate agents. In practice, perhaps, larger real estate businesses where both activities are performed will voluntarily comply in full with the AML Act, although they are not required to do so. This, however, does away with the intention of the Government, which is to avoid higher costs and such (sometimes lengthy) procedures. The argument that in most cases the unusual circumstances do not arise from the client but from the assignment fails in my opinion. In order to determine whether circumstances or an assignment are/is really unusual and should be reported to the FIU, the valuers of real estate often need background information. This could include information about the client: who is the client (is he perhaps a criminal?), what is his position vis-à-vis the property (is he the owner?) and what are his motives behind the valuation? Such information gives content to the possible unusual nature of transactions or assignments. Partial inclusion in the AML Act can, therefore, not be upheld. In the absence of more clarity regarding the applicable AML regime for estate agents who perform both mediation and valuation activities, the norms are less enforceable for the Bureau Supervision Wwft.

Real estate businesses

It is not clear whether the Bureau Supervision Wwft has supervisory responsibility for real estate businesses (*makelaarskantoren*). While the Dutch AML Act, for example, states that it applies to a '*natural person, legal person or company* providing advice or assistance as a lawyer, civil-law notary or junior civil-law notary' (*emphasis added, MB*), no such mention is made in relation to real estate agents. The AML Act applies to an 'intermediary as referred to in Section 62 of the Dutch Commercial Code, insofar as this intermediary provides brokerage services in the establishment and conclusion of

201 *Parliamentary Papers I*, 2012-13, 33 236, C, at 8.
202 Section 16(1)(3) Wwft.

agreements on immovable property and rights attached to immovable property'.[203] Section 62 Commercial Code states that an intermediary is someone who:

- makes it his business to provide mediation in the negotiation and conclusion of agreements to the order and in the name of persons with whom he is not in a fixed relationship;
- is a managing partner of a firm or director of a body corporate that makes it its business to conduct such negotiations;
- is under a contract of employment with a person, firm or body corporate, and carries out the actions referred to in this article in the name of his or her employer.[204]

This provision suggests that an intermediary is always a natural person. The first paragraph refers to sole traders, the second paragraph to partners of a firm or the director of a body corporate, and the third paragraph concerns employees. Representatives of the Bureau Supervision Wwft have indicated that in supervisory activities no distinction is made between natural and legal persons and that this has never led to discussions with the private sector. The Bureau Supervision Wwft has never sanctioned a real estate business. Rather, upon establishing non-compliant behaviour it sanctions the natural person (the real estate agent) himself, or attributes his behaviour to the managing partner or a director of the body corporate or firm. Nevertheless, in the absence of a clear reference in the AML Act to real estate businesses, the Bureau Supervision Wwft's supervisory responsibility may be a point of discussion. It may particularly result in a situation where the Bureau Supervision Wwft encounters a situation where the real estate business, with a number of estate agents working for it, has no or an inadequate policy for the prevention of money laundering to which the employees must adhere. In these circumstances it might be more appropriate to sanction the business and not the individual estate agents working for the business, the managing partner or director.[205] It is at this point remarkable that in defining valuers of real estate, the AML Act does refer to 'natural and legal persons', as could be seen above. This, again, causes confusion and legal uncertainty for real estate businesses where estate agents perform both mediation and valuation activities. At the same time it makes supervision by the Bureau Supervision Wwft more complicated, in particular where it concerns the question on whom to impose a sanction. It would therefore be advisable to explicitly include real estate businesses under the scope of the AML Act, as the legislator has recently done for accountancy firms (see § 5.5.3.1). This would increase the decisiveness – and possibly the effectiveness – of the Bureau Supervision Wwft in terms of sanctioning.

203 Section 1(1)(a)(14) Wwft.

204 *Own translation of the Dutch Commercial Code, MB.*

205 See § 5.6.2.4, however, which proves that currently the Dutch AML Act does not oblige institutions and professionals to develop internal procedures and policies for the prevention of money laundering and terrorist financing, as required by the Third Directive.

5.5.3 Accountants

In the Netherlands the accountancy profession is a regulated profession. In 1963 and 1972 the Dutch legislator decided that the titles registered accountant (*registeraccountant*) and accounting consultant (*accountant-administratieconsulent*) required legal protection and drafted legislation thereon.[206] The Dutch legislator primarily aimed to regulate the integrity and professionalism of the profession and to end uncertainty with respect to who could call himself an accountant and who could not.[207] On the 1st of January 2013, the two Acts merged into the Accountancy Profession Act.[208] This Act aimed at merging the two former professional associations in place under the former Acts into a single professional association, the Dutch Institute of Chartered Accountants, and at establishing a single accountants' register.[209] The titles of registered accountant (RA) and accounting consultant (AA) remained the same, although the Act aimed to better demarcate both types of accountants.[210]

> The Dutch Institute of Chartered Accountants (*Nederlandse Beroepsorganisatie van Accountants*, hereafter also the 'NBA') is the successor of the Royal Netherlands Institute of Registered Accountants (NIVRA) and the Netherlands Order of Accounting Consultants (NOvAA).[211] The NBA is a body established and governed by public law.[212] It represents around 21,000 professionals working in public accountancy practice, at government agencies, as internal auditors or in organisational management. The four statutory tasks are to further the good exercise of the profession by accountants via the issuance of internal professional norms; to represent the common interest of accountants; to take care of the reputability of the profession as well as the practical education.[213] NBA fulfils these tasks by the issuance of professional norms, supervising the compliance of members with legal norms, managing the accountants' register and taking responsibility for the practical education of accountants.[214] The NBA is thus responsible for the regulation of the profession within the legal framework set by the Dutch legislator. The Minister of Finance is responsible for the functioning of the NBA.[215]

The legal framework for accountants is complemented by the Audit Firms Supervision Act.[216] This Act was introduced after major bookkeeping affairs at the beginning of the 21st century.[217] It applies to audit firms (*accountantsorganisaties*) and, as explained, it introduced the AFM as the supervisor. Accountants working at audit firms are only allowed to perform

206 Via the *Wet op de Registeraccountants*, Stb. 1962, 258 (in English: *Registered Accountants Act*) and the *Wet op de accountant-administratieconsulenten*, Stb. 1972, 748 (in English: *Accounting Consultants Act*).

207 *Parliamentary Papers II*, 1959, 5519, no. 3, at 4 and 11; *Parliamentary Papers II*, 1968-69, 9935, no. 3, at 9-10; Van den Berg (2012) at 53-54 and 190.

208 *Wet van 13 december 2012, houdende bepalingen over het accountantsberoep, de Nederlandse beroepsorganisatie van accountants en de Commissie eindtermen accountantsopleiding*, Stb. 2012, 680. Hereafter 'Wab'.

209 *Parliamentary Papers II*, 2011-12, 33 025, no. 3, at 1.

210 Ibid., at 2.

211 About the predecessors, see: Van den Berg (2012) at 60-63.

212 Section 134 of the Dutch Constitution (*Grondwet*).

213 Section 3 Wab.

214 *Parliamentary Papers II*, 2011-12, 33 025, no. 3, at 4.

215 *Parliamentary Papers II*, 2011-12, 33 025, no. 3, at 13.

216 *Wet van 19 januari 2006, houdende het toezicht op accountantsorganisaties*, Stb. 2006, 70. Hereafter 'Wta'.

217 Van den Berg (2012) at 54-55.

statutory auditing tasks if their firm has obtained a licence issued by the AFM.[218] Audit firms that have obtained a licence to carry out statutory audits are incorporated in a public register.[219] The last Act which is relevant for individual accountants is the Accountants Disciplinary Law Act (*Wet tuchtrechtspraak accountants, Wtra*).[220] Individual accountants are liable to disciplinary action when they act in breach of the Accountancy Profession Act or in any other way endanger the good exercise of the profession.[221]

The Accountancy Profession Act requires accountants to be registered in the Dutch accountants' register in order to use the title of registered accountant or accounting consultant.[222] Applicants automatically become members of the NBA if their registration is accepted.[223] Upon registration the applicant must provide certification from which it appears that he has successfully completed the education required, or submit a declaration of professional competence instead.[224] Registration can be refused by the NBA if the accountant does not meet the education requirements, cannot provide a certificate of good conduct (*verklaring omtrent het gedrag*), if he is bankrupt or under conservatorship (*onder curatele*), if there is a court judgment against him on the right to exercise the accountancy profession or if, based on the antecedents of the applicant, there exists a reasonable fear that the applicant will breach the legal requirements or that his registration will harm the reputability of the profession in any other way.[225] If there are no grounds to refuse registration, the accountant is registered. The register is open to the public free of charge.[226] The register can be consulted online, data can be requested by telephone, or parties can consult the register in writing. Section 37, second paragraph, Wab states that the NBA should provide a copy of the accountants' register free of charge to (the authorities of) the Dutch public administration or EU. This allows the Financial Supervision Office to receive a copy of the register. This means that, in principle, it has a complete overview of the group of accountants for which it has supervisory responsibility under the AML Act.

> The accountants' register contains the surname, the first name(s), the date of birth, the private address and the address of the firm where the accountant is employed, the date of registration, the title (RA or AA), and the member group to which the accountant belongs.[227] Furthermore, it contains a remark when the education of the accountant satisfies the requirements for the exercise of statutory audits. If disciplinary action has been taken against the accountant, the register contains information concerning this

218 Section 11 Wta sets out the requirements which must be fulfilled in order to be eligible for an audit licence. These requirements are detailed in a number of Decrees and ministerial regulations.

219 Autoriteit Financiële Markten, *Public database audit firms*, available at: <www.afm.nl/en/professionals/registers/alle-huidige-registers.aspx?type={B5D6C574-90DE-4E1C-A997-5D84E5086C6B}>, last visited: 9 April 2014.

220 *Wet van 27 juni 2008, houdende nieuwe regels inzake tuchtrechtspraak ten aanzien van accountants*, Stb. 2008, 324. Hereafter also: Wtra.

221 Section 42(1) Wab.

222 Section 41(1) Wab.

223 Section 2(3) Wab.

224 Section 54 Wab. Sections 46-53 stipulate the education requirements for RAs and AAs.

225 Section 38(1) Wab.

226 Section 37 Wab.

227 Section 36 Wab.

disciplinary action (type, date, duration).[228] If an accountant has stopped practising or is (temporarily) prohibited from providing accountancy services, the date of the annulling of the registration is included in the register.

It should, however, be pointed out that the coverage of accountants under this Act is not clear concerning all points. We will now discuss some of the main difficulties.

5.5.3.1 Accountants under the AML Act

Both registered accountants and accounting consultants fall under the scope of the AML Act. The AML Act makes no exceptions as to the type of services accountants provide. In the past, there have been some difficulties concerning the definition of accountants as used in the AML Act.

External accountants

In line with the Third Directive, the AML Act employs the term 'external accountant'.[229] The Act, however, does not define what an external accountant is. It was, however, generally understood to apply to all accountants with the exception of internal accountants (in-house) and government auditors.[230] Nevertheless, the Audit Firms Supervision Act and the Financial Supervision Act – which already existed when the AML Act entered into force – use the term external accountant to refer to a natural person employed at or affiliated with an audit firm and who is responsible for the performance of a statutory audit.[231] This is a much more limited definition. Because of the different meanings of external accountant in the different pieces of legislation, Stouten recommended in her doctoral thesis to avoid the use of the term external accountant under the AML Act.[232] From a legal certainty perspective, it is indeed advisable to avoid as much as possible terms that are applied differently in different pieces of legislation. This is even more so where different pieces of legislation apply to the same group of professionals or in related areas of the law, as this may easily lead to confusion and misunderstandings. The 2013 amendments to the AML Act have not changed this, which means that this recommendation still stands.

Forensic accountants

For years it was not clear whether forensic accountants fell under the scope of the AML Act. Forensic accountants are experienced auditors or accountants who are hired to investigate possible suspicions of fraudulent activity within a business. Forensic accounting can be understood as a specialist domain of accountancy, within which accountants collect, control, refine, work on, analyse and report on information for the purpose of the

228 Section 36(3) Wab stipulates that the record of disciplinary actions is deleted after ten years from the date on which the action was taken. If the disciplinary action is a temporary deletion from the register, the record remains in the register until five years after the end of the temporary deletion: Section 36(4) Wab.

229 Section 1(1)(a)(11) Wwft; Article 2(1)(3)(a) Third Directive.

230 Cf. Stouten, M. (2012), *De witwasmeldplicht: Omvang van handhaving van de Wwft meldplicht voor juridische en fiscale dienstverleners*, Boom Juridisch uitgevers: The Hague (doctoral thesis Utrecht University) at 212.

231 See Section 1(f) Wta and Section (1)(1) Wft.

232 Stouten (2012) at 495-496 and 502.

maintenance of law and order.[233] Although it was originally believed that they fell under the scope of the AML Act, a judgment by the Trade and Industry Appeals Tribunal from 2009 raised doubts in this respect.[234] With the 2013 amendments to the AML Act, it was clarified that forensic accountants or those professionals performing forensic accountancy provisions indeed fall under the scope of the Act.[235] The Government considered this to be a codification of existing practice.[236]

Accountancy firms

As just raised with respect to real estate businesses, a similar discussion existed for accountancy firms as well. With the 2013 amendments, it was clarified that the Act applies to both individual accountants and to firms. This means, most importantly, that the BFT can take action not only against individual accountants via disciplinary law, but is also empowered to apply sanctions against firms. This enhances the decisiveness, and possibly the effectiveness, of the BFT, considering that disciplinary procedures against individual accountants might take a long time.[237]

Multiple reporting obligations for accountants: how to reconcile them?

Accountants have multiple reporting obligations. The different reporting obligations stem from the AML Act, the Audit Firms Supervision Act, and the Financial Supervision Act.[238] These regimes are different and may be difficult to comply with at the same time in practice.[239] A particular complication applies to accountants working at audit firms.[240] The reporting obligation under the AML Act requires accountants to disclose unusual transactions to the FIU-NL upon identifying already conducted or intended transactions, without limitations as to the type of activities the accountant performs.[241] Accountants are not allowed to inform other parties of this disclosure and are obliged to observe confidentiality in respect of the fact that this disclosure or information may give rise to further investigations. This is called the tipping-off prohibition or the prohibition of disclosure.[242] Under the Audit Firms Supervision Act, however, accountants working at firms that perform statutory audits are required to report suspicions of material fraud to the police. At the same time, this might have to be reported to the AFM as an incident.[243] This Act, however, requires that accountants working at audit firms must first enter into

233 Pheijffer, M. (2000), *De forensisch accountant: het recht meester*, Koninklijke Vermande: The Hague (doctoral thesis Leiden University), at 49; Stouten (2012) at 244-247.

234 CBb 23 November 2009, ECLI:NL:CBB:2009:BK4209, *AB 2010/117* annotated by M. Stouten; Stouten, M. (2011), 'Een ongebruikelijke uitleg van de witwasmeldplicht: Tijd voor een wetswijziging', *Nederlands Juristenblad*, issue 31, pp. 2020-2025; Stouten (2012) at 228-238.

235 Section 1(1)(a)(11) Wwft.

236 *Parliamentary Papers II*, 2011-12, 33 238, no. 3, at 7.

237 Faure et al. (2009) at 140.

238 Stouten (2012) at 213.

239 Diekman, P. (2010), 'Meldplichten voor accountants: Complex Spoorboekje', *De Accountant*, March 2010, at 20-23; Stouten (2012), at 392-393. See for a different opinion: Van Onzenoort, D. (2013), 'Meldplicht ongebruikelijke transacties', *Accountancynieuws*, no. 14, August 2013, pp. 22-24.

240 Faure et al. (2009) at 105.

241 Section 16 Wwft.

242 Section 23 Wwft.

243 Section 26 Wta and Chapter 9 Besluit Wta (*Audit Firms Supervision Decree*); Section 32(4) BWta.

dialogue with the client and give the client the possibility to repair the consequences of the fraud identified, before they must report and decline the assignment.[244] This means, however, that they have to inform the client about the identified fraud, which may be at odds with the tipping-off prohibition.[245] Various Dutch scholars observe that this is a particular problem where an accountant identifies a possible suspicious situation upon performing a statutory audit for a client. It is then up to the accountant to decide whether the situation is exclusively an unusual transaction that should be reported without delay to the FIU-NL, or whether it is a case of fraud for which he must enter into discussions with the client in order to solve the problem.[246] At present this situation with conflicting obligations for accountants still exists. Stouten considered that the Third Directive and the FATF Recommendations leave little room for the Dutch legislator to create a 'reparation obligation' in the AML Act, by analogy with the Audit Firms Supervision Act.[247] Nevertheless, for the sake of legal certainty and the enforceability of the norms, the legislator should step in and clarify how the two situations should be balanced and how accountants should act when faced with such a conflict. This gives more certainty to both accountants and the supervisors under the respective pieces of legislation.

5.5.4 Concluding remarks

The DNB has a good overview of the banks it supervises. It knows exactly which banks operate in the Netherlands and due to the licensing procedure it also has (access to) a considerable amount of information on those institutions. Upon licensing the DNB verifies whether the members of the management and supervisory boards are fit and proper for such a position, and banks must demonstrate that they have an adequate policy which ensures a sound exercise of the business. The DNB keeps a (public) register of banks that operate in the Netherlands. The real estate profession is not regulated and the title of a real estate agent is not protected in the Netherlands. Real estate agents can, but are not obliged to, follow a certification study offered to estate agents in the Netherlands. Likewise, they can become a member of a professional association. Due to the fragmented nature of the profession, the DTCA/Bureau Supervision Wwft runs the risk of not having an accurate knowledge of the group of professionals for which it has supervisory responsibility. A complicating factor is the inclusion of valuation activities under the scope of the AML Act. Although, in light of the vulnerability of the sector, it can be considered a step forward in the fight against money laundering, the law is not sufficiently clear and comprehensible on this point. Moreover, real estate businesses do not seem to fall under the scope of the AML Act. This requires an amendment to the Act in order to allow the supervisor to act more decisively. The accountancy profession is a regulated profession and the titles registered accountant and accounting consultant are protected. Accountants must be included in the accountants' register of the Dutch Institute of Chartered Accountants in order to use their titles. This public register can be accessed by the Financial Supervision Office. The inclusion of accountants under the scope of the AML Act provides some difficulties, in

244 See in particular Section 37 BWta; Diekman (2010) at 21.
245 Faure et al. (2009) at 105.
246 Ibid., at 105; Stouten (2012) at 393.
247 Stouten (2012) at 393.

particular regarding the use of the term 'external accountants' and the conflicting reporting obligations for accountants under the AML Act and the Audit Firms Supervision Act.

5.6 Dutch Central Bank (*De Nederlandsche Bank*)

5.6.1 Supervisory powers

5.6.1.1 Supervisory powers stemming from the AML Act

The DNB derives its AML supervisory powers via the AML Act from the General Administrative Law Act (*Algemene wet bestuursrecht*, hereafter: Awb).[248] While the AML Act originally contained an explicit link to the General Administrative Law Act, stating that 'the provisions of Chapter 5, Part 5.2 of the General Administrative Law Act shall apply *mutatis mutandis* to persons responsible (…) for supervising compliance (…) under this Act', this provision became lost with the amendments made to the AML Act in 2012 and 2013. Based on the legislative proposals and the explanatory memoranda to these Acts, I believe that this was never the intention of the legislator, but was caused due to various amendments to the provision.[249] In practice, however, this most likely caused a minimal effect because title 5.2 Awb (see below) is applicable to every person who complies with the definition of 'supervisor' in Section 5:11 Awb.[250] Nevertheless, this does not do away with the fact that the Dutch legislator previously found it important to regulate the matter in the AML Act and has now – without any further explanation – removed the provision regulating the explicit link between the AML Act and the General Administrative Law Act.

The General Administrative Law Act is an act that governs the activities of administrative authorities or the Government, most prominently decision-making procedures by the administration and judicial review by the administrative courts. It also contains a chapter on administrative law supervision that includes provisions on supervisory powers.[251] It has a strong procedural character and, therefore, substantive administrative law is normally

248 Section 24 Wwft.

249 With the Financial Markets Amendments Act 2012 (*Wijzigingswet financiële markten 2012*, Stb. 2011, 610) there was a renumbering of paragraphs due to the insertion of another paragraph in Section 24. Originally being Section 24(4) Wwft, the link to the General Administrative Law Act now became Section 24(5) Wwft. In the large-scale 2013 revisions, Section 24(5) was amended (*Wet van 20 december 2012 tot wijziging van de Wet ter voorkoming van witwassen en financieren van terrorisme en de Wet ter voorkoming van witwassen en financieren van terrorisme BES in verband met de implementatie van aanbevelingen van de Financial Action Task Force*, Stb. 2012, 286). I believe, however, that the legislator made a mistake, as the text of the proposal clearly referred to Section 24(3) Wwft at that time. Nevertheless, this has resulted in an amendment to Section 24(3) Wwft as proposed, but at the same time it led to the removal of Section 24(5) Wwft.

250 Section 5:11 Awb: "Supervisor' means a person who is charged by or pursuant to law with monitoring compliance with the rules laid down by or pursuant to any provision of law' (*own translation, MB*).

251 Cf. Seerden, R. and Wenders, D. (2011), 'Administrative law in the Netherlands', in: Seerden, R. (ed.), *Administrative law of the European Union, its Member States and the United States: A comparative analysis*, Intersentia, pp. 101-175.

laid down in special legislation. Title 5.2 Awb provides the following relevant powers to supervisors:[252]

- Section 5:15: the power to enter premises
- Section 5:16: the power to demand the provision of information
- Section 5:16a: the power to demand to see a person's identity card
- Section 5:17: the power to inspect business information and documents, to make copies thereof or to take the information and documents.

On the basis of Section 5:20, first paragraph, Awb everyone is obliged to fully cooperate with a supervisory authority. This means, for example, that upon the request of a supervisor a person must provide access to certain (digital) records. However, not everyone is always required to cooperate. Section 5:13 Awb requires that an inspector may only exercise his powers to the extent that it is reasonably necessary for the performance of his duties. Not only does this mean that the inspector may not go beyond what is reasonably necessary for the inspection and should exercise his powers in the least onerous way for the person concerned, it also means that in practice there must be a certain connection between a person and the activities over which supervision is exercised.[253] And those who are bound to secrecy by virtue of their office or profession or by law may refuse to cooperate if this follows from their duty of secrecy.[254] The Dutch Supreme Court (*Hoge Raad*) has ruled that this exemption also applies to professionals with a derived duty of secrecy.[255] Obviously there are a number of limitations to the use of these supervisory powers. The power to enter premises is a far-reaching power, because it does not require consent from the person involved. Especially in relation to premises that function as homes (as well), this is a delicate matter.[256] Therefore, for entering homes on the basis of Section 5:15 Awb a number of additional requirements apply to the supervisory authorities, one of which is the requirement of consent.[257] Section 5:15 Awb does not allow supervisors to search through offices by, for example, opening drawers, as such a search is restricted to looking around in the office.[258] Inspectors must also identify themselves before entering premises and explain the reason for their visit.[259]

252 Sections 5:18 Awb (inspect and measure goods, take samples, open packages or to take them along) and 5:19 Awb (stop and inspect means of transport that are subject to supervision, the cargo thereon, the related documents) are not considered to be relevant in the context of anti-money laundering supervision.

253 Blomberg, A. (2013), 'Handhaving en toezicht', in: Michiels, F.C.M.A. and Muller, E.R. (2013), *Handhaving*, Kluwer: Deventer, 2nd edition, pp. 33-62, at 55.

254 Section 5:20(2) Awb. This concerns lawyers, civil-law notaries, medical staff, and clergymen. See further § 5.8.1.

255 HR 29 March 1994, ECLI:NL:HR:1994:ZC9693, *NJ 1994/552* annotated by A.C. 't Hart; HR 12 March 1997, *BNB/1997/146c*, annotated by P.J. Wattel; HR 12 February 2002, ECLI:NL:HR:2002:AD4402, *NJ 2002/440* annotated by Y. Buruma.

256 Jansen, O.J.D.M.L (2013), 'The Netherlands', in: Jansen, O.J.D.M.L. (ed.), *Administrative Sanctions in the European Union*, Intersentia, pp. 317-465.

257 See Blomberg (2013) at 43-44; Bröring, H.E. (2005), *De bestuurlijke boete*, Kluwer: Deventer, at 90-97.

258 Blomberg (2013) at 46-47; Bröring (2005) at 92.

259 Section 5:12 Awb in conjunction with Section 1 of the General Act on Entry into Dwellings (*Algemene Wet op het binnentreden*); Bröring (2005), at 93. This last Act is a *lex specialis* of Section 5:12 Awb, containing stricter requirements for specific circumstances.

Section 5:16 Awb provides the power to demand the provision of information. This means that AML supervisors can ask specific questions to the supervisees in writing or orally, who are required to truthfully answer these questions, as we could see above. The inspector must make clear to the supervisee that he is making use of the power under Section 5:16 Awb and that it is not a matter of informal questioning. The supervisor must also be able to explain why he is asking such questions and the scope and nature of the questioning must be clear to the supervisee.[260] However, when questions are asked by the supervisor with a view to the imposition of a punitive sanction on the supervisee,[261] the latter is not required to make statements concerning the violation for this purpose. Moreover, if the supervisee concerned is questioned with a view to the imposition of a punitive sanction on him, the supervisor must caution him that he is not required to answer.[262] Section 5:17 Awb gives supervisors the power to inspect business information and documents. The power is limited to business information, which means that private correspondence may not be part of the supervision. A difference with the power to demand the provision of information is that the exercise of this power is not required to be as specific as the questions pursuant to Section 5:16, although there must be some direction as to the kind of documents the supervisor wants to check. So-called 'fishing expeditions' are in breach of Section 5:13 Awb.[263] Another difference is the fact that this power always relates to existing and recorded data, which is not necessarily the case when supervisors demand the provision of information. Institutions are required not only to provide data carriers to the supervisor, but also to provide real access to the data itself.[264] Copies of documents can be made by the supervisor himself, if this is necessary for carrying out the supervision.[265] Copies means hard-copy prints, but also includes the copying of data to data carriers like USB sticks or CDs. Finally, in applying the powers assigned to them, administrative authorities must abide by the principles of proper administration, which are partly codified in the General Administrative Law Act.[266]

5.6.1.2 Reliance on the Financial Supervision Act

The DNB relies heavily on the Financial Supervision Act (Wft) in the exercise of anti-money laundering supervision.[267] The Wft is an act which brings together nearly all norms and conditions which apply to the financial markets and the supervision thereof.[268] The supervisory powers that the DNB has under the Wft also stem from Title 5.2 Awb and are thus the same as the supervisory powers laid down in the AML Act.[269] The only difference

260 Bröring (2005) at 97.
261 See about the distinction between reparative and punitive administrative sanctions: § 5.6.3.1.
262 Section 5:10a Awb.
263 Blomberg (2013) at 48.
264 Bröring (2005) at 103.
265 Section 5:17(2) Awb; Bröring (2005) at 103.
266 E.g. Sections 3:2 (duty of care), 3:4 (proportionality) and 3:46 (reasoning) Awb. See about these principles: § 2.2.1.2.
267 FATF (2011) at 197.
268 See: Grundmann-van de Krol (2012) at 2-14 for the development of financial regulation in the Netherlands until the Wft.
269 Section 1:74(2) Wft; Leliveld, J.T.C. (2007), 'De toezichtbepalingen van de Wft', *Tijdschrift voor Financieel Recht*, issue 7-8, pp. 216-220.

is that the Wft provides regulatory powers to the DNB too, which means that the DNB can issue general binding regulations on the basis of the Wft.[270]

The DNB interprets the Wft as leaving room to integrate the verification of compliance with anti-money laundering obligations entirely within the broader supervisory tasks of the Wft, namely via the activities in relation to integrity supervision. Upon drafting the AML Act, the Government acknowledged the close relationship between the prevention of money laundering and the safeguarding of integrity under the Wft as well. It considered that both pieces of legislation create more or less the same obligations for banks and other financial and credit institutions.[271] The DNB's AML Guidance from January 2014 contains numerous references to the Wft, being the backbone for integrity norms, and it states that integrity risks are understood, among other things, as the risk of money laundering and the risk of terrorist financing.[272] Interviews clarified that the DNB often bases its thematic integrity supervision primarily on the integrity norms stemming from the Wft, but that the AML Act gives the DNB the opportunity to bring more nuance to the exercise of integrity supervision. The AML Act is used to 'colour in' the obligations from the Wft with respect to the norms on the sound conduct of business, compliance, employees, training and client identification requirements.[273]

> The Wft provides a fully elaborated framework concerning the soundness of conducting business (*integere bedrijfsvoering*).[274] It includes integrity as an explicit norm of financial supervision. Sections 3:10 and 3:17 Wft, as well as the Prudential Rules under the Wft Decree, provide a legal basis for integrity supervision by the DNB on banks and other financial and credit institutions. These provisions are not explicitly linked to AML matters but are implicitly extended to them via the obligation in Section 3:10 Wft to have measures in place that ensure compliance with any law. Financial and credit institutions are obliged to have an adequate policy that safeguards controlled and sound business operations. This means, among other things, that they are obliged to have measures to prevent the commission of offences or other transgressions of the law that could damage confidence in the institution or in the financial markets, as well as measures to prevent confidence in the institution or in the financial markets from being damaged because of its clients.

5

Apart from the argument of nuance, capturing AML supervision within the exercise of thematic integrity supervision is convenient for two other reasons as well. Firstly, this interpretation remedies the legislator's omission in the AML Act to implement Section 34 Third Directive (and FATF Recommendation 18) concerning internal controls (§ 5.6.2.4) and provides the DNB with a wider palette of sanctioning powers (§ 5.6.3.2).

According to the FATF, the DNB's supervisory powers 'are sufficient to obtain all relevant documents, records and other information relating to accounts, other business

270 Sections 1:28-1:29a Wft; Cf. Grundmann-van de Krol (2012) at 710-713.

271 Yet it did point out that the AML Act has a more specific objective: *Parliamentary Papers II*, 2007-08, 31 328, no. 3, at 5-6.

272 *DNB Leidraad Wwft en SW*, 9 January 2014, at 4.

273 Interviews De Nederlandsche Bank, June 2010 and May 2013.

274 *DNB Leidraad Wwft en SW*, 9 January 2014, at 4.

relationships, transactions and the internal policies of the institution'.[275] The FATF did point out that there is a difference in scope between the Wft and AML Act in terms of the coverage of financial and credit institutions. The AML Act has a wider scope of application, which makes reliance on the Wft difficult for some specific institutions, such as collective investment schemes.[276] Banks, however, are covered by both the Wft and AML Act, which means that no such problem exists vis-à-vis this group of institutions. Throughout the following subsections, we will see how the above-mentioned relationship between the Wft and AML Act is given shape in both the supervisory and sanctioning procedures of the DNB.

5.6.2 Anti-money laundering supervision in practice

5.6.2.1 The 'two-track' approach to anti-money laundering supervision

As was briefly explained in § 5.4.1, the DNB exercises its AML supervision via two tracks. It is integrated in the regular supervisory procedures for banks, which are performed by special teams of the Banking Supervision Division (*Divisie Toezicht banken*). Not in all supervisory procedures are AML obligations verified, but only when there is a reason to do so. This is for example the case after the bank has reported an incident to the DNB, on the basis of compliance or management reports forwarded to the DNB, because there is a change in the internal policy of a bank, or because of reports in the media.[277] At the same time, AML supervision is included in the thematic supervision that focuses on integrity.

5.6.2.2 Inclusion of anti-money laundering supervision in regular supervisory procedures

The DNB bases its general supervisory activities on the so-called FOCUS! system. This is a methodology on the basis of which banks and other financial and credit institutions receive a risk score card. It includes five categories (T1-5), for which different risk analyses exist. In general, the higher the impact of the problems at an institution, the more intense the risk analysis and supervision will be.[278] Money laundering risks are included in the risk assessments on three levels: they can follow from a particular sector (macro), the type of services provided by a financial or credit institution (meso), or the lack of an internal policy for the prevention of money laundering (micro). For low-risk institutions, the DNB only includes the money laundering risk at the macro level. The risk analyses for the two highest risk categories (T4-5) always include individual integrity risk assessments, which means that the money laundering risk at the meso and micro level are included. On the basis of these risk analyses, the DNB categorises banks into four supervisory regimes for the purposes of its regular supervision: low, neutral, high or urgent.[279] Neutral supervision is the basic regime of regular supervision. For the high or urgent supervisory

275 FATF (2011) at 204.
276 FATF (2011) at 185-186.
277 Interview De Nederlandsche Bank, May 2013.
278 DNB (2012a), *FOCUS! De vernieuwde toezichtaanpak van DNB*, April 2012, at 13.
279 DNB (2012a) at 20.

regimes, the DNB prepares individual risk mitigation projects for the institutions. The DNB's supervisory style depends on the risk category within which a financial institution finds itself. In the intensified level of supervision, the DNB will act in a stricter fashion by providing concrete instructions or by applying sanctions, whereas under the low risk regime it will act more as an adviser.[280]

The DNB does not have general annual supervision plans or AML supervision plans for the exercise of regular, prudential supervision. In line with the FOCUS! approach, the DNB designs supervision plans for each individual institution. Anti-money laundering checks may, or may not, play a role in these supervisory procedures. The exercise of regular supervision on banks is done via periodic, on-site meetings between DNB inspectors of the banking teams and compliance officers of the banks (*toezichtgesprekken*). These meetings can be regarded as a form of ongoing monitoring. Within this monitoring, inspectors look at the seven elements of sound business governance (*integere cultuur*), which the DNB expects financial institutions to adopt within their business culture.

> The seven elements are: (i) the balancing of interests and balanced actions; (ii) consistent actions; (iii) openness to discussion; (iv) leading by example; (v) feasibility; (vi) transparency; and (vii) enforcement. A document entitled 'The Seven Elements of an Ethical Culture Strategy and approach to behaviour and culture at financial institutions' presents the DNB's strategy on the issue of behaviour and culture. It describes the background and the reasons as to why it is important to include ethical behaviour and culture in supervision, sets out the legal framework for doing so, and explains what the current situation is, both within institutions and in the exercise of supervision by the DNB.[281] It is remarkable to observe that in the explanation of the legal framework for supervision or elsewhere in the document, no single mention is made of the AML Act.[282]

If there are signals to suggest that more in-depth supervision is required, inspectors may decide to start an on-site supervisory inspection (*toezichtonderzoek*). Signals, also called incidents, can be changes in internal policy, management or procedures, media reporting, non-compliance with the seven elements mentioned above, a bad risk score from FOCUS!, and so on. Supervisory inspections are a more in-depth and focused form of supervision. Besides meeting with compliance officers, DNB inspectors talk to (the board of) directors, management and staff and they assess transaction and client files in a more in-depth manner.[283] The verification of AML obligations may be discussed and looked at in these periodic supervision meetings and supervisory inspections, but this is not the case in each meeting or inspection. When integrity issues arise during the exercise of regular supervision, inspectors may ask the staff of the Expert centre on culture, organisation and integrity for advice or may ask them to participate in a supervisory meeting or inspection.[284]

280 DNB (2009), *The Seven Elements of an Ethical Culture Strategy and approach to behaviour and culture at financial institutions 2010-2014*, November 2009, at 9.

281 Ibid., at 2.

282 Ibid., at 4-6.

283 Interview De Nederlandsche Bank, May 2013.

284 Ibid.

Concerning the actual inclusion of anti-money laundering supervision in regular supervision procedures, it should be observed that this is invisible. The DNB does not keep, or at least it does not publish, statistics on the number of inspections in regular supervisory procedures, let alone on the inclusion of AML supervision therein. As a consequence, nothing can be said about the inclusion of the verification of compliance with the Dutch AML Act in regular supervisory procedures on banks. From the perspective of the theoretical framework of effective supervision more information should be published.

5.6.2.3 Thematic anti-money laundering supervision

Thematic supervision has become increasingly important for the DNB. It is, among other things, the result of a critical report issued by the temporary Parliamentary Committee on the financial sector ('Commissie De Wit') on the financial system and the role of the Dutch Government.[285] The verification of AML compliance can be included in thematic integrity supervision. This is mostly exercised by the Expert centre on culture, organisation and integrity. It is not carried out on the basis of a risk-based approach as in regular supervisory procedures. Rather, external signals that reach the DNB via the media or the institutions themselves, or results from regular supervision may be the starting point for the selection of themes for supervision. Each year, the DNB publishes the themes for supervision on its website.[286] This can be seen as an annual supervision plan. The outcomes from thematic supervision are incorporated in the thematic register of the FOCUS! system, so thematic supervision 'feeds' the risk-based approach for general supervisory procedures.[287] One can observe the interplay between regular and thematic supervision.

The annual supervision plans for thematic supervision indicate that compliance with the AML Act has been a focal point in the DNB's supervision in the years 2012, 2013 and 2014. Regarding banks specifically, the annual plans demonstrate that compliance with the AML obligations by banks was a focal point in the DNB's thematic integrity supervision in 2012. In that year the DNB verified whether banks were involved in business relations with citizens coming from jurisdictions subject to the FATF's blacklists, or were undertaking transactions with institutions from other high-risk jurisdictions.[288] DNB requested information from banks, analysed the information and carried out on-site visits. The number of banks involved in the thematic research is not known. The DNB stated that it would share the findings with the sector. The results, presumably, have been shared with the institutions for which the DNB has supervisory responsibility via newsletters, but they have not been made public on the website, in thematic reports or the annual report for 2012.[289] From the perspective of transparency and accountability, this is lamentable. Outcomes could be made public in a general fashion through inclusion in the annual report or by the publication of thematic reports on good and bad practices.

285 Supra, n. 91.

286 DNB (2014a), *Thema's DNB toezicht 2014*, January 2014; DNB (2013); DNB (2012).

287 DNB (2012a) at 17.

288 DNB (2012) at 17.

289 DNB (2012b), *ZBO-verantwoording 2012* (in English: *Annual report 2012*).

In 2013 banks were subjected to thematic integrity supervision focussing on compliance with specific AML obligations. Ongoing due diligence under the preventive AML policy was one of the cross-sectoral thematic supervision topics in that year.[290] Earlier investigations at financial institutions had shown a large number of deficiencies in relation to client identification, risk classifications, the ongoing monitoring of clients and transactions. An interview clarified that the deficiencies were diverse in nature, for example the ongoing due diligence had a (too) low interval, too little information was gathered for the ongoing due diligence or there was no policy in place at all.[291] The DNB concluded from this that the awareness and analyses with regard to integrity risks are insufficient, and that therefore the institutions are not able to manage integrity risks continuously and on an adequate basis, in particular the risk of money laundering.[292] In the thematic supervision plan for 2013 the DNB announced that it would select a number of banks, insurance companies and trust offices. The DNB thereby aimed to include a representative part of the sectors, including high-risk institutions, institutions on which the DNB does not have sufficient knowledge (e.g. no previous supervisory experience), requests from regular supervision teams, and 'ad random' selected institutions.[293] The first part of the research consisted of requesting information from the selected institutions via questionnaires, followed by a benchmark. The second part of the research consisted of on-site inspections.[294] In its annual report for 2013, the DNB reported that it included more than 75 banks, life insurance companies and trust offices in this supervision project. The DNB carried out around 30 on-site visits at these institutions.[295] How many of those were banks is not further specified. Likewise, the DNB's report does not share the main findings and outcomes of the project. These might have been shared with the supervised institutions via newsletters, but it is not certain whether this happened.[296] Particularly from an accountability perspective, the DNB should think about publishing the results of these visits. For the year 2014, the supervision plan shows a cross-sectoral supervision project regarding transactions with institutions from other high-risk jurisdictions.[297] Banks are not specifically mentioned, but could be included. Another cross-sectoral supervision project concerns new methods of payment, in which the DNB aims to assess the management of integrity risks at banks and other payment institutions which are working with new methods of payment.[298] The annual supervision plan states that it is the intention to combine off-site and on-site supervision methods.

The foregoing indicates that banks are included in thematic supervision projects that focus on AML compliance. The numbers of banks inspected, or the findings of the projects, however, are not publicly available.

290 DNB (2013) at 24-25.
291 Interview De Nederlandsche Bank, May 2013.
292 DNB (2013) at 25.
293 Interview De Nederlandsche Bank, May 2013.
294 DNB (2013) at 33.
295 DNB (2013a) at 14.
296 Cf. DNB (2013a) at 10.
297 DNB (2014a) at 35.
298 Ibid., at 36.

5.6.2.4 Focus on internal policies and governance and the Dutch AML Act

In all of its supervisory activities the DNB strongly focuses on internal policy, the processes, the management and overall business governance.[299] Thereby the DNB aims to verify whether a financial institution is capable of adequately complying with the Wft, the AML Act and other relevant legislation containing norms on integrity and sound business management. Unlike other Dutch AML supervisors, supervision focusses less on the level of transaction and client files. The focus on business governance and behaviour does not mean that no transactions files or client files are assessed at all; this is always done to check the real functioning of internal processes.[300] It is not surprising that the DNB focuses more strongly on the existence of an internal policy compared to other AML supervisors. This is caused by the legislator's omission to implement Section 34 Third Directive and FATF Recommendation 18 and concerning internal controls in the AML Act.[301]

> FATF Recommendation 18 states that financial institutions should be required to implement programmes against money laundering and terrorist financing and that financial groups should be required to implement group-wide programmes, including policies and procedures for sharing information within the group for AML/CFT purposes. Section 34 Third Directive requires Member States to oblige institutions and persons covered by the Directive to establish adequate and appropriate policies and procedures of customer due diligence, reporting, record keeping, internal control, risk assessment, risk management, compliance management and communication in order to forestall and prevent operations related to money laundering or terrorist financing. The Directive goes beyond the FATF Recommendation by requiring this for all obliged institutions and professionals.

Section 35 Wwft only refers to training requirements for staff. It states that an institution must ensure that the employees are familiar with the obligations laid down in the Act and that they are trained to recognise an unusual transaction. There is no reference in the AML Act to the obligation to have an internal policy for the prevention of money laundering and terrorist financing. In the general AML Guidance, however, the Ministry of Finance states that an important component of AML supervision is verifying whether the institutions have an adequate internal organisation and controls.[302] It is strange to observe that no such obligation is present in the AML Act, but that the Ministry interprets the current provisions as including this obligation. Likewise, it can be observed that AML supervisors have the power to instruct the institutions for which they have supervisory responsibility, which may concern the implementation of internal procedures and controls to prevent money laundering and terrorist financing.[303]

The DNB's focus on internal policies is based on its reliance on the Wft. Unlike the AML Act, the Wft requires financial and credit institutions to have internal controls, compliance, audit and training requirements. In interpreting the Wft provisions on integrity as

299 DNB (2010), *Visie op Toezicht 2010-2014*, March 2010, at 22-23.
300 Interview De Nederlandsche Bank, May 2013.
301 FATF (2011), at 184 et seq.
302 *Algemene leidraad Wwft en SW*, 17 January 2014, at 17.
303 Section 32 Wwft.

including AML aspects, the authorities are of the opinion that the Wft already embodies the obligation to have an internal policy.[304] The DNB consequently checks whether the institutions have an internal policy for the prevention of money laundering, and turn to the use of sanctions when this is not the case. For institutions and professionals outside the financial sector, the obligation to have an internal policy can only be inferred from the AML Guidance from the Ministry of Finance and the above-mentioned possibility for supervisors to give an instruction under the AML Act. The general AML Guidance, however, is not a legally binding instrument and the authority to issue instructions can only be used at the moment when non-compliant behaviour is identified by the competent supervisor.[305]

Although the situation may not cause problems for the DNB in the exercise of its supervision due to its reliance of the Wft, it will be impossible, or at least very difficult, for the other Dutch AML supervisors to enforce this in the absence of a norm establishing such as an obligation for institutions and professionals. Therefore, the Dutch AML Act is not in line with the Third Directive and needs to be amended. This could, for example, be done by broadening the formulation of Section 2a, second paragraph, Wwft. This provision states that obliged institutions and professionals must take adequate measures to prevent the risks of money laundering and terrorist financing which can be caused by the use of new technologies. The legislator could require that obliged institutions and professionals must take adequate measures, at least by establishing appropriate policies and procedures of customer due diligence, reporting, record keeping, internal control, risk assessment, risk management, compliance management and communication, in order to prevent the risks of money laundering and terrorist financing, including the risks that can be caused by the use of new technologies in business practices. Alternatively, the legislator could draft a separate provision.

5.6.3 Sanctioning powers

The DNB derives its sanctioning powers primarily from the Dutch AML Act (§ 5.6.3.1). Alternatively, it can resort to the use of sanctioning powers given to it via the Financial Supervision Act (§ 5.6.3.2). Section 5.6.3.3 discusses the relationship between the two sets of sanctioning instruments. Finally, section 5.6.3.4 demonstrates some other powers that the DNB can turn to in case of non-compliance.

5.6.3.1 Sanctioning powers under the AML Act

The AML Act provides the Minister of Finance with the power to impose incremental penalty payments (*last onder dwangsom*[306]) and administrative fines (*bestuurlijke boete*) and provides the power to give instructions (*aanwijzing*) directly to the AML supervisors. The Minister has delegated his sanctioning powers to the DNB, the AFM and the Financial

304 FATF (2011) at 184 et seq.

305 *Algemene leidraad Wwft en SW*, 17 January 2014, at 1.

306 Other translations into English that are used for this type of sanction are 'order under penalty' or 'order under coercive sum'.

Supervision Office, and mandated these powers to (the staff of) the Bureau Supervision Wwft.[307] The incremental penalty payment and administrative fine can be imposed on legal persons as well as on natural persons, provided that they have either ordered the offence or had actually controlled the forbidden act. In practice, the natural persons are usually *de facto* managers (*feitelijk leidinggevenden*), such as the managers and directors of a legal person.[308]

Section 26 Wwft provides the power to impose incremental penalty payments. An incremental penalty payment is a reparatory sanction that contains an order to remedy a breach in whole or in part, and the obligation to pay a sum if the order is not carried out within the timeframe provided.[309] Section 26 stipulates for which offences penalty payments can be imposed. This varies, inter alia, from not (adequately) performing customer due diligence and the reporting obligation, to tipping-off, to not keeping adequate records, and to not cooperating with the supervisor. The authority determines the maximum amount above which no further sums will be forfeited. The amount must be proportionate to the gravity of the interest violated and to the intended effect of the sanction.[310]

The power to impose administrative fines is laid down in Section 27 Wwft. The first paragraph stipulates for which offences a fine can be imposed.[311] The administrative fine is a punitive sanction. The statutory cap in the AML Act for a single breach is 4 million Euros or twice the amount of money the breach has yielded, if the gain from the breach is more than 2 million Euros.[312] In the case of repetitive behaviour, meaning that the same breach occurred within five years after the first breach and for which the institution or professional was fined, the amount of the fine for the second breach should be doubled.[313] Somewhat comparable to the Spanish system, the Dutch AML Act provides for a categorisation of offences and corresponding administrative fines. Minor offences belong to the first category, serious offences to the second category, and the most serious offences to the third category. Pursuant to Section 28 Wwft, offences belonging to the first category should be fined with a maximum of up to 10,000 Euros. Second category offences can be fined with a maximum of up to 1 million Euros. And offences belonging to the third category

307 For the incremental penalty payment and administrative fine: Section 31 Wwft in conjunction with Section 5 of the Wwft Decree (*Uitvoeringsbesluit Wwft*) for the DNB, AFM and BFT. Powers may not be delegated to subordinates (Section 10:14 Awb), hence the Minister should mandate the power to the Dutch Tax and Customs Administration/ Bureau Supervision Wwft: *Besluit van de Minister van Financiën van 27 november 2009, nr. FM/2009/3373, betreffende bekendmaking mandaatverlening handhaving en sanctionering Wet ter voorkoming van witwassen en financieren van terrorisme*, Stcrt. 2009, 18645. This regulation was amended on the 1st of January 2013: Stcrt. 2013, 25564. For the power to issue instructions which pertains to all AML supervisors: Section 32 Wwft in conjunction with Section 24(1) Wwft and the Decree on the appointment of Wwft supervisors.

308 Section 5:1(3) Awb in conjunction with Section 51 Dutch Criminal Code.

309 See: Van Buuren, P.J.J., Jurgens, G.T.J.M. and Michiels, F.C.M.A. (2011), *Bestuursdwang en dwangsom*, Kluwer: Deventer.

310 Section 5:32b(3) Awb.

311 This is the same list as Section 26 Wwft provides, with the exception of Section 16. Only non-compliance with Section 16(1) and 16(2) Wwft can be sanctioned with an administrative fine.

312 Section 28(2) and 28(4) Wwft.

313 Section 28(2) Wwft.

can be fined with the statutory cap of a maximum of 4 million Euros. The categorisation of offences is more specifically regulated in the Financial Sector Administrative Fines Decree. All offences under the AML Act are categorised as either first or second category offences, which means that fines for non-compliance under the AML Act cannot exceed 1 million Euros per breach.[314] Also the breaches of sections 3:10 and 3:17 Wft, which provide the legal basis for integrity supervision by the DNB, are categorised in the second category.[315] The starting amount for fines for second category offences is 500,000 Euros. The supervisor can decide to raise or lower the amount of the fine taking into account the severity or duration of the breach, the degree of culpability on the side of the offender, as well as the offender's means to pay (*financiële draagkracht*).[316] The system is the same for administrative fines that the DNB can impose under the Financial Supervision Act.

Supervisors can instruct obliged institutions or professionals to follow a certain line of conduct. This power used to be formulated very strictly.[317] Supervisors could only impose an instruction for two specific offences and the lines of conduct could only concern the development of internal procedures and the training of employees. In 2012-13 this was a point of discussion at the AML coordination meeting.[318] On the 1st of January 2014 the power was widened.[319] The Government considered that supervisory practice had demonstrated the usefulness of instructions and that the broadening was aimed at creating the possibility to give an instruction for all offences that can also be sanctioned with an administrative fine.[320] Not complying with an instruction results in the possible imposition of an incremental penalty payment or administrative fine.[321]

> It is not easy to typify the character of an instruction, because instructions can be given without a prior offence taking place or after the identification of an offence.[322] Under the AML Act, the instruction is a reaction to non-compliant behaviour, hence it seems that it should be considered as a sanction, even though non-compliance with an instruction itself can be sanctioned with an incremental penalty payment or administrative fine. When the instruction follows non-compliant behaviour, the aim of an instruction is not to punish an offender and is, like the incremental penalty payment, a reparatory sanction.

314 *Besluit bestuurlijke boetes financiële sector,* Stb. 2009, 329; Section 5:46(3) Awb.

315 This changed with the amendments made to the AML Act in August 2014, hence after the period studied for this research. The first paragraphs of both section 3:10 Wft and 3:17 Wft are now third category offences. See § 1.8.

316 Section 2 Financial Sector Administrative Fines Decree.

317 Section 32 was originally formulated as follows (*own translation, MB*): 'When an institution fails to fulfil its obligations under Sections 16 or 17(2), the person designated under Section 24(1) may, by issuing an instruction, order the institution to adhere to a particular line of conduct within a period specified by the person designated under Section 24(1) regarding (i) the development of internal procedures and controls to prevent money laundering and terrorist financing; and (ii) the training of employees as laid down in Section 35.'

318 Interview Bureau Financieel Toezicht, June 2013.

319 *Wijziging van de Wet op het financieel toezicht en enige andere wetten (Wijzigingswet financiële markten 2014)*, Stb. 2013, 487.

320 *Parliamentary Papers II*, 2012-13, 33 632, no. 7 at 24.

321 Sections 26 and 27 Wwft.

322 Duijkersloot, A.P.W. (2007), *Staats- en Bestuursrecht: Toezicht op gereguleerde markten*, Ars Aequi Libri, at 65-66; Grundmann-Van de Krol (2012) at 724-729.

A combination of sanctions?

Dutch administrative law makes a distinction between *reparatory* and *punitive* sanctions based on the aim of the sanction.[323] Administrative law enforcement in the Netherlands was originally restricted to the use of reparatory sanctions like interim penalty payments and administrative enforcement orders (*last onder bestuursdwang*). With these sanctions, 'the reparation of the infringement of the legal order is the primary goal, not punishment'.[324] This changed in 1989, when traffic violations were transferred from the criminal law realm to administrative law, leading to the introduction of administrative fines.[325] Administrative fines are punitive sanctions, because the primary aim is to punish the offender. The distinction between reparatory and punitive sanctions is relevant in Dutch administrative law, due to the applicability of Article 6, second paragraph, of the European Convention on Human Rights to punitive administrative sanctions and criminal sanctions on the basis of the 'criminal charge' criterion.[326] From this doctrine it follows that the administration cannot impose two or more punitive administrative sanctions at the same time for the same facts.[327] A concurrence between two reparatory sanctions, or concurrences between a criminal sanction and a punitive administrative sanction, is not possible either.[328] However, a combination between a punitive administrative sanction and a reparatory administrative sanction, or between a criminal sanction and a reparatory administrative sanction, is possible. This means, for example, that the incremental penalty payment can be combined with an administrative fine.

5.6.3.2 Reliance on the Financial Supervision Act

Also in terms of sanctioning the DNB relies on its powers stemming from the Financial Supervision Act (Wft). The Wft offers the DNB a wider palette of sanctions that are more diverse and include the most dissuasive sanction: the revocation of a (banking) licence. The Wft provides the following sanctioning powers, which to a certain extent overlap with the powers from the AML Act:[329]

- The power to issue instructions (Section 1:75 Wft)
- The power to appoint a trustee (Section 1:76 Wft)
- The power to impose an incremental penalty payment that must be announced publicly (Section 1:79 in conjunction with 1:99 Wft)
- The power to impose an administrative fine that must be announced publicly (Section 1:80 Wft in conjunction with 1:97/1:98 Wft)

323 Van Wijk/Konijnenbelt & Van Male (2014) at 447-450; Rogier, L.J.J. (1992), *Strafsancties, administratieve sancties en het una-via beginsel*, Gouda Quint (doctoral thesis Erasmus University Rotterdam); Verhey and Verheij (2005) at 261-262; Jansen (2013) at 320-324.

324 Widdershoven (2002), § 2.2.

325 See for the development of the administrative fine in the Netherlands: Jansen (2013) at 332-353.

326 See for the most important consequences of the application of Art. 6 of the Convention for the Protection of Human Rights and Fundamental Freedoms: Van Wijk/Konijnenbelt & Van Male (2014) at 457-461.

327 Cf. Section 5:43 Awb.

328 For reparatory sanctions this is laid down in Section 5:6 Awb.

329 FATF (2011) at 205.

- The power to issue a public warning (Sections 1:94-1:96 Wft)
- The power to amend, revoke (in full or partly), or restrict a licence (Section 1:104 Wft)

I will first pay attention to the powers that are similar to the AML Act, and then to the other sanctioning powers. The power to instruct under the Wft can contain any kind of instruction and can be imposed on any kind of breach of the Wft or the regulations issued pursuant to that Act. This Wft power of instruction can, therefore, be considered a sanction.[330] Under the Wft, the DNB can impose an instruction on a legal person which entails that a de facto manager (*feitelijk leidinggevende*) or a person involved in the policy-making (*beleidsbepaler*) of that legal person is no longer allowed to exercise the management or policy function. This instruction can follow after a re-examination of the trustworthiness and suitability of managers, directors and persons sitting on the supervisory board.[331] If an instruction is not complied with within a reasonable period of time, the DNB can resort to other sanctions.[332] Until January 2014, the power to give an instruction pursuant to the Wft had a wider remit than the instruction power stemming from the AML Act, but now they are similar.

The power to impose an incremental penalty payment or administrative fine is similar to the powers from the AML Act as well, with the exception that under the Wft these decisions must be made public. Incremental penalty payments must be published once the timeframe has expired and publication does not contravene the interests and aim of the supervision exercised by the supervisor. Administrative fines imposed pursuant to the Wft are to be published when they have become final – meaning that they can no longer be contested before the courts – unless this publication is or could be contrary to the aim of supervising compliance with the norms stemming from the Wft.[333] In some (serious) cases the decision to impose an administrative fine should even be published before it has become final.[334] In that case, the parties involved must be given a five-working days term to start a preliminary injunction proceeding, which results in the suspension of the publication until the court has delivered its decision on the preliminary injunction.[335] The Wft provisions on publication in title 1.5.2 Wft suggest that publication is an obligation for the financial supervisors. According to Doorenbos, this formulation leaves no discretion to the financial supervisors and publication is required in all cases, and Grundmann-van de Krol speaks of a restrained power (*gebonden bevoegdheid*).[336] Publication can only be refused when it is or could be contrary to the aim of supervising compliance with the norms stemming from the Wft.[337] At the time of its introduction, however, the Government considered that the DNB could exercise restraint in the publication of decisions in the light

330 Duijkersloot (2007) at 65.
331 Cf. § 5.1.1.
332 See: DNB, *Aanwijzingsbevoegdheid*, available at: <www.toezicht.dnb.nl/2/50-202170.jsp>, last visited on 15 April 2014.
333 Section 1:98 Wft.
334 See Section 1:97 Wft.
335 Section 1:97(2) and 1:97(3) Wft.
336 Doorenbos, D.R. (2007), *Naming & Shaming*, Serie Onderneming en Recht, no. 38, at 81; Grundmann-Van de Krol (2012) at 755.
337 Section 1:97(4) Wft.

of its role as a prudential supervisor and that it can often rely on the exception ground.[338] The DNB does not normally publish sanctions. When the DNB does report on the imposition of an administrative fine, it publishes the name of the company and, where relevant, the names of the directors or other persons with an interest, followed by an explanation of the offences identified and the amount of the fine imposed. The decisions are published on its website. From a legality perspective one may wonder why the legislator has opted for this publication regime. The DNB's current practice, which seems to be mostly based on the Minister's interpretation of the Act, erodes the legal obligation or the restrained power for both financial supervisors to publish their sanctioning decisions. Of course, the Act itself provides the exception and the DNB may have well-founded reasons to abstain from publication in most cases, but it is remarkable that in practice the exception has become the norm. I wonder why the legislator has not opted for more tailored publication regimes for the DNB and the AFM, in light of their distinctive roles within financial supervision. Next to the publication provisions in case of the imposition of an incremental penalty payment or administrative fine, the Wft also provides the DNB (and the AFM) with the power to issue a public warning. This power is formulated as a discretionary power and serves to protect the parties operating in the financial markets and to further the adequate functioning of these markets.[339] Grundmann-van de Krol observes that the supervisor must balance the interest of warning the public, on the one hand, and the interest and possible consequences for the party involved, on the other.[340]

> The publication of a warning, or the publication of decisions imposing administrative fines or incremental penalty payments, can be considered sanctions.[341] They are known as 'naming & shaming'. In Dutch literature the use of the power to publish has led to the question whether publication should be seen as a punitive sanction or not. If that were the case, Article 6 ECHR would apply including the 'ne bis in idem' principle, meaning – among other things – that publication cannot be combined with other punitive administrative sanctions or criminal sanctions for the same offence.[342] Upon introducing this power in the Wft, the Dutch Government was very succinct about this and stated, contrary to its earlier considerations, that publication is not a punitive sanction.[343] Some scholars argue, however, that the publication of a decision to impose an administrative fine has most prominently the aim to punish an offender because it causes severe reputation damage to the (potential) offender.[344] They find that, notwithstanding

338 *Parliamentary Papers II*, 2005-06, 29 708, no. 19, at 421; cf. Tillema, A.J.P. and Doets, C.A. (2007), 'Bestuursrechtelijke handhaving', in: Busch, D. et al., *Onderneming en financieel toezicht*, Serie Onderneming en Recht, no. 40, Kluwer: Deventer, pp. 493-545 at 533.

339 Sections 1:94-1:96 Wft; *Parliamentary Papers II*, 2005-06, 29 708, no. 19, at 417.

340 Grundmann-Van de Krol (2012) at 756.

341 Sauvé, A.M.P.J.H. (2010), *Naming and Shaming: Een onderzoek naar de juridische mogelijkheden en beperkingen voor de Arbeidsinspectie om op het terrein van de Arbeidsomstandighedenwet, de Arbeidstijdenwet, de Wet arbeid vreemdelingen en de Wet minimumloon en minimumvakantiebijslag haar inspectiegegevens te openbaren en haar boetebeschikkingen te publiceren*, Uitgeverij Paris, at 31 et seq.; Doorenbos (2007) concludes this for publication under the Wft, at 86, where he speaks about the applicability of Article 6 ECHR.

342 See § 5.6.3.1. Cf. Doorenbos (2007) at 86-91.

343 *Parliamentary Papers II*, 2005-06, 29 708, no. 19, at 302. See for criticism of this turn in the reasoning: Doorenbos (2007) at 76-86.

344 Doorenbos (2007) at 86 and 94-96 and 101; Michiels, F.C.M.A. (2007), '"Naming and Shaming" in het markttoezicht', *Nederlands Tijdschrift voor Bestuursrecht* 2007-3, pp. 85-95.

> the other goals that publication may have,[345] this does not do away with the fact that one's reputation is at stake and is damaged. Therefore, naming & shaming must be seen as a punitive sanction.[346] For publications in relation to incremental penalty payments the situation is somewhat more complicated, because publication can here be considered as supporting the reparatory character of the sanction.[347] Dutch scholars acknowledge that naming & shaming is a potential powerful and effective sanction for supervisors.[348] At the same time there are serious critical voices in relation to legal protection for the parties involved.[349]

As observed, the power to impose an incremental penalty payment or administrative fine in the AML Act is not accompanied by a power or duty to publish. The Government considered that the publication of imposed fines and incremental penalty payments related to the preventive AML policy would only have limited added value.[350] It did not provide well-founded reasons for this statement. In the absence thereof, it is difficult to see why naming & shaming would not have preventive and repressive effects in the preventive AML policy as well. Stouten found that the possibility of publication was removed too easily under the AML Act and concluded that it should be reintroduced.[351] Although at present the Dutch Public Access to Government Information Act (*Wet openbaarheid van bestuur, Wob*) may serve as a legal basis to publish these decisions, Stouten provided various convincing arguments showing that this is not an adequate basis for the publication of sanctioning decisions under the AML Act. She recommended to include a publication regime in the AML Act itself.[352] Also from the perspective of effective supervision the introduction of a publication power is very welcome. It makes the range of sanctions available to AML supervisors wider and more dissuasive; two important elements in the theoretical framework. In light of the requirement that sanctions should also be proportionate and to avoid a similar situation as the DNB currently faces under the Financial Supervision Act, the publication of sanctions should be formulated as a discretionary power. Supervisors can reserve this power for the most serious cases of non-compliance.

The Wft also provides the power to appoint a trustee (*curator*), which means that all or certain organs or representatives of a financial institution, such as a board of directors, can only exercise their tasks after approval by one or more appointed trustees, with due regard for the assignments of the trustees.[353] Therefore, it has been said that this measure is a far-

345 Van Erp, J. (2009), *Naming en shaming in het markttoezicht*, Boom Juridische uitgevers: The Hague, at 20-22, distinguishes four perspectives, or aims of publication: the consumer perspective (protection and information), the punitive perspective, the prevention perspective (i.e. to prevent repetitive non-compliant behaviour) and the legitimacy perspective on the side of the supervisory authority.
346 Doorenbos (2007) at 86-96; Michiels (2007), at 88.
347 Michiels (2007) at 88.
348 Sauvé (2010) at 13; Michiels (2006) at 39-41.
349 Doorenbos (2007), at 96-97; Michiels (2006) at 39-41. See different: Sauvé (2010) at 61-78.
350 *Parliamentary Papers II*, 2007-08, 31 328, no. 3, at 34.
351 Stouten (2012) at 433-434.
352 Ibid., at 433-434.
353 Grundmann-van de Krol (2012) at 737-740.

reaching instrument and takes away financial institutions' autonomy.[354] Before imposing this measure, the supervisor must give the financial institution a reasonable period of time to bring forward its views in writing.[355] The measure can be imposed for a maximum period of two years, with the possibility to prolong this by a year each time.[356] Finally, the Wft provides the DNB with the possibility to amend, revoke or restrict a licence. This is a far more dissuasive sanction than the sanctioning powers under the AML Act, as it can ultimately result in the temporary or final closure of financial or credit institutions. As explained in § 5.5.1, banks cannot operate in the Netherlands without a licence.

5.6.3.3 Applying Wft sanctions for non-compliance with the preventive AML obligations?

The DNB uses its Wft sanctioning powers to enforce compliance with the AML Act. Although in the majority of cases this will most likely not result in any problems, the Wft powers cannot always be used, in my opinion. Chapter 2 demonstrated that supervisors must act on the basis of the law and that in relation to sanctioning, particularly the imposition of punitive administrative sanctions such as administrative fines, and the principle of *nulla poena sine lege* (no sanction without a law) applies.[357]

Where a single AML offence is identified, the AML Act itself provides the corresponding sanctions that supervisors are allowed to impose. Admittedly, the Wft and AML Act are so interrelated that in practice it will often be the case that an AML offence is accompanied by an offence under the Wft, or is actually at the same time a Wft offence as well. The line of reasoning followed by the DNB is that its supervision efforts are primarily based on the integrity norms stemming from the Wft, which are further 'coloured in by' the obligations from the AML Act.[358] Consequently, a breach of the AML Act is almost always at the same time a breach of a Wft obligation concerning integrity as well. The question is whether the DNB can always sanction the offence under the AML Act via the Financial Supervision Act? One could say that this is indeed possible, thereby arguing that the offence under the AML Act could be taken into account as an aggravating circumstance for the Wft offence and is sanctioned by DNB on the basis of the more general provision in the Wft. Under this interpretation, the Wft sanction essentially captures the offence of the AML Act. From a strict legality perspective there is no problem, since the DNB has been given Wft sanctioning powers. On the other hand, one could argue that the legislator, upon drafting the AML Act, has deliberately not made a connection to the Wft or this situation, and has provided AML supervisors with a separate set of sanctions under the AML Act. The Government did pay attention to the relationship between the AML Act and Wft in the Explanatory Memorandum to the AML Act, but limited itself to stating that the objective and scope of the Wft is wider than those of the AML Act, and that financial institutions could fit the requirements stemming from the Wft and AML Act together in their internal

354 Roth, G.P. (2008), 'De stille curator in de Wet op het financieel toezicht: Een kritische verkenning van een buitenissige rechtsfiguur', *Tijdschrift voor financieel recht*, issue 9, pp. 289-298.
355 Section 1:47(2) and 1:47(1) Wft.
356 Section 1:76(5) Wft.
357 See § 2.4.1; Widdershoven (2002) at 449.
358 Interview De Nederlandsche Bank, May 2013.

organisations.[359] From this it can be argued that the legislator had the opportunity to legally connect the AML Act and the Wft, but explicitly decided not to do so and that this choice should not be overridden by importing the Wft sanctioning powers into AML matters. In addition, the AML Act can be considered a more specific act in relation to the Wft, because the AML Act has a more specific objective than the Wft.[360] On the basis of the Latin proverb *lex specialis derogate legi generali,*[361] which Dutch administrative courts apply, it could be argued that the DNB should sanction offences under the AML Act with the powers that are most specifically assigned to it for this purpose. Understanding that the legislator designed a set of sanctions in the AML Act itself, these should be used for sanctioning non-compliance with AML obligations primarily.

The last two arguments are supported by the fact that the financial supervisors themselves, in particular the AFM, seem to have (had) doubts about the possibility to invoke Wft sanctioning powers for offences under the AML Act. During the FATF evaluation, the AFM indicated that in one case it felt that it had to impose the most dissuasive sanction, namely the removal of a licence, for a breach of the AML Act. However, '[i]n that case, the AFM did not feel able to use the power in Article 1:104 Wft to withdraw a licence from a regulated financial entity for failing to implement adequate CDD measures, since they did not think the connection between the Wft integrity provisions and the Wwft were sufficiently robust to survive an appeal (...)'.[362] Although there is no further case law on this matter – after all, which bank would appeal against a less dissuasive sanction under the Wft than it would have faced under the AML Act[363] – the AML Act is unclear and unforeseeable on this point, with a negative effect on legal certainty. The legislator should step in and either make a connection between the Wft and AML Act, opt for a combination of the two Acts, or explicitly state that this practice is not allowed. The connection between the AML Act and the Wft could be made by stating in the AML Act that the DNB and AFM are required to use the sanctioning powers from the Wft where a breach of the AML Act coincides with, or is accompanied by a Wft breach.

5

5.6.3.4 Other sanctions

The DNB can also decide to make use of informal measures before resorting to the imposition of sanctions. It can, in case of identified non-compliance, arrange a signalling meeting with the institution (*normoverdragend gesprek*) or give a written, informal warning. Those kinds of instruments are aimed at persuading the institutions to comply with legislation before turning to the imposition of formal sanctions. Informal instruments

359 *Parliamentary Papers II*, 2007-08, 31 328, no. 3, at 5-6.
360 Ibid., at 5.
361 It refers to a doctrine within which it is believed that where two laws govern the same factual situation, a law governing a specific subject matter (*lex specialis*) overrides a law which only governs general matters (*lex generalis*).
362 FATF (2011) at 185.
363 As was the case until the 1st of January 2014: the DNB relied on its instruction power under the Wft to sanction breaches of AML legislation. Since that date the Dutch AML Act contains a similar instruction power to the one in the Wft: see § 5.6.3.2.

play a very important role in DNB practice.[364] At the same time it can be pointed out that in the most serious cases of non-compliance with AML obligations, AML supervisors can decide to file a criminal complaint. Non-compliance with a wide range of anti-money laundering obligations, varying from the CDD and reporting obligations to the tipping-off prohibition and the record keeping obligation, is criminalised via Section 1(2) of the Economic Crimes Act.[365] This Act is a so-called framework act, listing a wide range of economic crimes and misdemeanours. The maximum sanction is two years' imprisonment, community service (*taakstraf*) or a criminal fine with a cap of 20,250 Euros.[366]

5.6.4 Sanctioning policy and practice

5.6.4.1 Duty to sanction (beginselplicht tot handhaving)

Whereas legislation provides Dutch administrative authorities with the *power* to impose sanctions, Dutch legal doctrine has developed in such a way that it is now sometimes suggested that a so-called *duty* to sanction (*beginselplicht tot handhaving*) exists.[367, 368] This general administrative law doctrine has been developed by the administrative courts, particularly in the context of condoning illegal behaviour in spatial planning law. The standard considerations in the case law of the Administrative Jurisdiction Division of the Council of State, one of the Netherlands' highest general administrative law courts, demonstrates that only in exceptional circumstances such as foreseen legalisation in the near future, disproportionality, or legal certainty, can an administrative authority decide not to act against an illegal situation.[369] This means that, as a principle, administrative authorities, including supervisors, must enforce when non-compliant or illegal behaviour is identified. Administrative authorities may have sanctioning policies in place which gives the possibility for the authority to issue warnings before it prepares a sanctioning decision.[370] This policy, however, may not result in a situation where low priority offences are not sanctioned at all.[371]

364 See § 5.6.4.2.

365 Sections 2, 3(1), 4(1), 5(1), 5(3), 8, 16, 17(2), 23(1), 23(2), 33 and 34 Wwft; *Wet van 22 juni 1950, houdende vaststelling van regelen voor de opsporing, de vervolging en de berechting van economische delicten (Wet op de Economische Delicten, WED)*, Stb. 1950, K258.

366 Section 6(1)(2) WED.

367 Pursuant to Section 1:1(1) Awb administrative authorities are (i) an organ of a legal person governed by public law, or (ii) any other person or body vested with public authority. A number of authorities are excluded via Section 1:1(2) Awb. The three supervisors included in this research are administrative authorities.

368 E.g. Van Wijk/Konijnenbelt & Van Male (2014) at 442-444; Vermeer, F.R. (2001), 'De beginselplicht tot handhaving en de ruimte om te gedogen', *JBPlus* 2001, pp. 76-85; Ottow (2006) at 288 et seq. However, this is not agreed by all: Cf. Blomberg, A.B. (2000), *Integrale handhaving van milieurecht*, Boom Juridische uitgevers: The Hague, at 79-80; Verhey and Verheij (2005) at 286-288.

369 For example: ABRvS 2 February 1998, ECLI:NL:RVS:1998:ZF3176, *AB 1998/181* annotated by F.C.M.A. Michiels; ABRvS 30 June 2004, ECLI:NL:RVS:2004:AP4683, *JB 2004/293* annotated by C.L.F.G.H. Albers.

370 See for example in the field of competition law: Ottow (2006) at 290-291.

371 Most recently: ABRvS 4 June 2014, ECLI:NL:RVS:2014:1982; ABRvS 25 June 2014, ECLI:NL:RVS:2014:2303. Cf. Van Wijk/Konijnenbelt & Van Male (2014) at 443.

In the literature, there are different opinions on the question whether this duty also applies to market supervisors, such as DNB.[372] Before 2010, it seemed that the highest administrative court handling cases against the DNB and other market regulators, the Trade and Industry Appeals Tribunal (*College van Beroep voor het bedrijfsleven, CBb*), denied the application of this duty to market regulators.[373] In 2011, however, the CBb confirmed the existence of the duty to sanction in a case against the Dutch telecommunications market regulator.[374] It followed the exact considerations of the Administrative Jurisdiction Division of the Council of State. A year before this decision the CBb had already, though more covertly, dealt with the duty to sanction vis-à-vis the regulator in the field of competition law.[375] Although there are no cases in relation to the DNB on this point, there are various reasons to suggest that the duty to enforce also applies to the Dutch financial regulators, hence, to the DNB.[376] The DNB also seems to assume this, as can be seen in the joint sanctioning policy with the AFM, which I will discuss hereafter.[377]

5.6.4.2 Sanctioning policy

The DNB has a joint sanctioning policy (*handhavingsbeleid*) with AFM, which is publicly available.[378] Although the policy does not deal specifically with AML supervision, finding that this supervision is for a large part embedded within the regular supervision procedures and thematic integrity supervision, this policy is applicable to AML supervision too. This interpretation is confirmed in the DNB's AML Guidance from January 2014.[379] The sanctioning policy stipulates that the main goal is compliance with the applicable norms.[380] The starting point is that every institution voluntarily complies with the norms, and that supervisory efforts contribute to this behaviour. Where supervision does not have the effect of creating compliant behaviour, the DNB can resort to the use of formal sanctioning instruments in order to enforce compliant behaviour. Sanctions by the DNB depend on the content and purpose of the norm breached. Actions are taken once a breach has come to the supervisor's knowledge and in an effective way. Finally, the DNB acts in accordance with the principles of proper administration.[381] Not every breach of the applicable norms will result in the use of formal sanctioning instruments. A signalling meeting between the supervisor and supervisee (*normoverdragend gesprek*) or an informal warning plays an important role in the supervisory activities.

372 Ibid., at 289-290.

373 Duijkersloot (2007) at 67; who refers to CBb 10 November 2005, ECLI:NL:CBB:2005:AU6169, *JOR 2006/47* annotated by R.H. Maatman.

374 CBb 15 June 2011, ECLI:NL:CBB:2011:BQ8708, *JB 2011/182* annotated by G. Overkleeft-Verburg.

375 CBb 20 June 2010, ECLI:NL:CBB:2010:BN4700, *AB 2010/242* annotated by I. Sewandono.

376 Aelen (2014) at 200-203.

377 *Handhavingsbeleid van de Autoriteit Financiële Markten en De Nederlandsche Bank*, Stcrt. 2008, 132, at 30, par. 3c.

378 *Handhavingsbeleid van de Autoriteit Financiële Markten en De Nederlandsche Bank*, Stcrt. 2008, 132, at 30. The policy is also available on the websites of the DNB and AFM.

379 *DNB Leidraad Wwft en SW*, 9 January 2014, at 2.

380 Although it is a joint sanctioning policy, I omit references to the AFM hereafter.

381 *Handhavingsbeleid van de Autoriteit Financiële Markten en De Nederlandsche Bank*, part 3 'Uitgangspunten'.

From the annual reports it becomes clear that the DNB prevents the use of formal sanctions as much as possible and relies, to a large extent, on informal sanctioning instruments. It thereby states that signalling meetings with supervisees are an effective means to come to the main enforcement goal of compliant behaviour.[382] In 2011, the DNB had over a thousand of these discussions with banks and on only three occasions did the DNB have to resort to the imposition of a formal sanction.[383] In the annual report for the year 2012 the DNB noted that the mere notice of an *intention* to impose a formal sanction on non-complying institutions resulted in practice becoming conscious of the severity of the breach and the ending of the breach by the non-compliant institutions.[384] In the annual report for the year 2013, the DNB reported on the conclusion of 'enforcement plans' (*handhavingsplannen*) as a means to overcome non-compliant behaviour in a more informal way.[385] This approach has been commented upon by the IMF, which supported a greater use of formal sanctions by the DNB.[386]

The sanctioning policy contains a number of factors that the DNB should take into account when it considers imposing a sanction. The first is that administrative law is preferred over criminal law enforcement. In principle, the DNB uses its administrative law sanctioning powers in case of non-compliance. Only in the most severe cases does it consider filing a criminal complaint.[387] This happens after deliberation with the Dutch Fiscal Information and Investigation Service (FIOD) and the public prosecutor.[388] Aspects that play a role in the decision are the complexity of the breach, the concurrence with other crimes, culpability, the public interest, and the balance between the expected effects of administrative law or criminal law enforcement. The second factor concerns the ending of the breach. If the breach is of an ongoing nature, then action should in any case be taken in order to bring the breach to an end. At the same time, the imposition of a punitive sanction should be considered. The third factor concerns the publication of public warnings and imposed sanctions. Public warnings will be published if this is in line with the purpose of the norms breached. Decisions on sanctions imposed and which have become final must as a principle be published, unless this conflicts with the supervisory objectives.[389] The fourth factor is that supervisors resort sooner to the use of formal instruments and more dissuasive instruments against institutions that are (willingly) not complying with market entry requirements and do not have a licence or registration. The last factor is that supervisors must take into account all relevant circumstances in their choice whether or not to apply a sanction and if so, which sanction. The enforcement policy lists a number of factors that should play a role in this decision.[390] This list is not

382 DNB (2011) at 17.

383 Ibid., at 17.

384 DNB (2012b) at 9.

385 DNB (2013a) at 11.

386 IMF (2011), *Financial Sector Assessment Program Update: Kingdom of the Netherlands-Netherlands*, June 2011, at 14-15.

387 Cf. § 5.6.3.4.

388 Based on an agreement with these authorities: *Convenant bestuurlijke boeten en strafrechtelijke sancties*, Stcrt. 2000, 4 at 9. (In English: *Agreement on administrative fines and criminal sanctions*).

389 Please note that the restrained power of publication is not laid down in the AML Act. See § 5.6.3.1 and 5.6.3.2.

390 These are further elaborated in an explanation of the policy: DNB, *Hoe beslissen de AFM en DNB over een maatregel na een overtreding?*, 17 May 2011, available at: <www.dnb.nl/nieuws/nieuwsoverzicht-en-archief/nieuws-2011/dnb252194.jsp>, last visited 28 April 2014.

exhaustive, nor imperative in nature. The explanation that is attached to the policy makes clear that the behaviour surrounding the breach as such is taken into account, but also the wider internal business culture. The DNB aims to be as transparent as possible about the application of the formal sanctioning instruments in its annual reports and the publication of sanctioning decisions.[391]

In practice, the DNB hardly ever publishes its sanctions. In 2013, it imposed 49 incremental penalty payments and 4 administrative fines on financial and credit institutions. None of these decisions were published.[392] In 2012, the DNB imposed 54 incremental penalty payments and 1 administrative fine. Likewise, these sanctioning decisions were not published.[393] It is slightly different for financial and credit institutions acting illegally, as here the DNB seems to be somewhat more proactive in terms of publication (2 publications in 2013 and 3 in 2012).[394]

5.6.4.3 Sanctioning in practice

In terms of sanctioning for non-compliance with obligations stemming from the AML Act, the annual reports do not contain specific information that allows one to say how many times the DNB has undertaken formal action against banks. The DNB publishes the number and type of sanctions it has imposed on banks, but it does not indicate for which breaches. In general, the DNB has taken the following actions against banks subject to its supervision:

Table 4 – DNB formal sanctions against banks (overall)[395]

	2011	2012	2013
Incremental penalty payment	0	0	0
Administrative fine	1 (0 Euro)	0	1 (27,225 Euro)
Instruction	4	2	2
Other	0	0	0

In addition, the annual reports contain some anecdotal information about the results of thematic integrity supervision. In the 2013 report, the DNB stated that it had included 75 banks, insurance companies and trust offices in off-site supervision, resulting in 30 on-site inspections, and finally, against 8 institutions the DNB had resorted to the use of sanctioning measures.[396] However, the DNB does not provide information on how many banks were specifically included, how many on-site inspections took place at banks, which offences were identified, and against which institutions the formal measures were taken. From interviews it has become clear that the DNB relies heavily on its informal powers,

391 Please note again that the publication of sanctions is not possible under the AML Act.
392 DNB (2013a) at 41 (Table 5).
393 DNB (2012b) at 34 (Table 4).
394 DNB (2013a) at 41 (Table 6).
395 Own table based on DNB (2011) at 28 (Table 7 'Maatregelen bij onder toezicht staande instellingen'); DNB (2012b) at 34 (Table 4 'Maatregelen bij onder toezicht staande instellingen); and DNB (2013a) at 41 (Table 5 'Maatregelen bij onder toezicht staande instellingen').
396 DNB (2013b) at 14.

in particular the signalling meetings with banks. DNB representatives also reported that it has imposed formal sanctions, most prominently the power to issue an instruction from the Wft in order to (also) remedy identified AML breaches. The reliance on the Wft for the power to issue instructions had mostly to do with the fact that until January 2014 the instruction power under the AML Act had a very limited formulation. Representatives also clarified that until May 2013 the DNB had never used the power to impose an administrative fine or to revoke or amend a licence due to a failure to comply with the AML Act.[397] After this period, the DNB supposedly imposed an administrative fine for non-compliance with the AML Act for the amount of 27,225 Euros. The media reported, since the DNB did not publish the sanction, that the DNB had fined ABN AMRO Bank for not having adequately performed customer due diligence with regard to the treasurer of the largest Dutch housing association as a private client.[398] Had the bank carried out a more thorough investigation against him, it would have known that the treasurer possessed remarkably high capital. This treasurer is now a suspect in a criminal investigation concerning money laundering, tax avoidance, and corruption.[399] His actions were part of a major scandal which almost led to the bankruptcy of the housing association.[400] The fine of 27,225 Euros is comparatively low, considering that the DNB has the power to impose administrative fines of up to 1 million Euros per breach. One of the reasons for this may have been the fact that ABN AMRO Bank voluntarily reported the matter to the DNB.[401] It is not known whether the DNB used its power from the AML Act or the Wft.

5.6.5 Concluding remarks

The DNB has adequate supervisory powers provided by the AML Act. It has the power to compel the production of information relevant to the monitoring of compliance and to carry out on-site inspections, as required by the Third Directive. Via the Financial Supervision Act, the DNB has regulatory powers regarding integrity, which may include AML-related aspects as well. In practice, the anti-money laundering supervision of banks is embedded within the DNB's regular supervision of banks and thematic (integrity) supervision. For the regular supervision procedures on banks it is impossible to say to what extent verification with preventive AML obligations is included in the supervisory procedures and practice. This differs per risk category, per institution, and the DNB does not keep statistics thereon. More information could, and in the light of the theoretical framework of effective supervision should, be published. The annual plans for thematic supervision for the years 2012, 2013 and 2014 do demonstrate that the thematic AML supervision of banks is exercised by the DNB. The procedures differ per investigation. Unfortunately, the results of these investigations are not published on the DNB's website or in the annual reports. For transparency and accountability reasons, as well as the provision

397 Interview De Nederlandsche Bank, May 2013.

398 Het Financieele Dagblad, *DNB beboet ABN om Vestia-fout*, 19 August 2013; NRC Handelsblad, *ABN-Amro boete van DNB om Vestia-fout*, 19 August 2013.

399 Het Financieele Dagblad, *OM houdt treasurer van corporatie Vestia aan*, 16 April 2012; Het Financeele Dagblad, *DNB beboet ABN om Vestia-fout*, 19 August 2013.

400 See about this scandal: Commissie Kaderstelling en Toezicht Woningcorporaties (2012), *Eindrapportage*, 17 December 2012, at 27-30, *Parliamentary Papers II*, 2012-13, 29 453, no. 286.

401 Het Financieele Dagblad, *DNB beboet ABN om Vestia-fout*, 19 August 2013.

of guidance to banks and financial and credit institutions in general, the DNB should think about publishing the results of these visits. This can be done in an aggregated fashion, for example through thematic reports on good and bad practices. In its supervision the DNB strongly focuses on the existence of adequate internal policies and procedures. The AML Act does not contain provisions that oblige institutions to have adequate internal policies and procedures for the prevention of money laundering and terrorist financing, other than training for employees. It can bring this focus into its supervision via the Wft.

The DNB's sanctioning powers are adequate. The AML Act provides the power to impose incremental penalty payments, administrative fines or instructions. The Wft brings about more sanctioning powers for the DNB, especially the restrained power to publish sanctioning decisions in the case of fines and incremental penalty payments and public warnings (naming & shaming), and the power to amend, revoke, in full or partly, or restrict a licence or registration may be dissuasive sanctioning powers. However, the legislator should provide for a connection between the AML Act and the Wft as the current practice can under certain circumstances be considered as a breach of the principle of legal certainty. The DNB has a public joint sanctioning policy with the AFM, which from the theoretical framework of effective supervision is a good thing. The policy contains the enforcement goals and principles, and explains which factors the DNB should take into account when applying its powers. Currently, it cannot be said how many times banks have been sanctioned for non-compliance with preventive AML obligations on the basis of information from the DNB itself. The DNB publishes information regarding sanctions imposed on banks in general statistics. Nevertheless, it could and, in light of the theoretical framework of effective supervision, should make its information more intelligible which would allow others to see which financial and credit institutions have been sanctioned and for which breaches. In any case, based on other information it appears that the DNB speaks softly vis-à-vis banks as it has (presumably) imposed only one, rather low administrative fine for non-compliance with the AML Act since the entry into force of that Act.

5.7 Dutch Tax and Customs Administration/Bureau Supervision Wwft (*Belastingdienst/Bureau Toezicht Wwft*)

5.7.1 Supervisory powers

The Bureau Supervision Wwft derives its supervisory powers via the AML Act from the General Administrative Law Act (*Awb*).[402] The powers were already described in § 5.6.1. For the exercise of AML supervision, inspectors from the Bureau Supervision Wwft have the power to carry out on-site inspections and to request information, records and other documents that are necessary for the exercise of supervision. There is no other piece of legislation that gives (additional) supervisory powers to the Bureau Supervision Wwft. The Bureau does not have regulatory powers.

402 Section 24(1) Wwft.

5.7.2 Anti-money laundering supervision in practice

The Bureau Supervision Wwft performs focused AML supervision and does not integrate this supervision in wider supervisory programmes. Supervisory activities are planned in annual supervision plans, and accountability is given internally through annual reports. We have seen in § 5.4.2.2 that these reports are not publicly available. Nevertheless, representatives have provided annual reports for the years 2010-13 for research purposes, and these allow one to say more about AML supervision and sanctioning on real estate agents in practice.[403] It appears that the DTCA/Bureau Supervision Wwft bases its supervisory efforts on a risk-based approach resulting in two tracks of supervision: individual supervision based on specific risk signals and project-based supervision. This means that the Bureau Supervision Wwft plans supervisory visits on the basis of individual risk-based signals, either composed internally or received from other authorities or the media, or that it decides to focus on particular sectors. Besides, it devotes a considerable amount of attention to the creation and raising of awareness among the professionals for which it has supervisory responsibility.[404]

5.7.2.1 Risk-based approach to anti-money laundering supervision

The Bureau Supervision Wwft understands risk primarily as the risk that an unusual transaction is not reported to the FIU, although the circumstances require this.[405] In the absence of information on this specific risk factor, the Bureau Supervision Wwft aims to include in its assessments those sectors, types of activities or customers where it considers that this risk of money laundering is higher. The Bureau has applied a risk-based approach in its supervision since 2009.[406] The implementation of a risk-based approach appears to be a difficult task. The main problem seems to be the relatively weak information position of the Bureau Supervision Wwft regarding the population for which it has supervisory responsibility, and the fact that the size of the population, particularly dealers in goods, is not clear and varies from one year to another.[407] In relation to real estate agents, the difficulty seems to be caused primarily by the fact that the profession is unregulated and that not all estate agents are members of professional associations. A single register or database which contains information on all real estate agents operating in the Netherlands is not available.[408] In addition, real estate agents who exclusively perform valuation activities only fall partially under the scope of the AML Act. For them the risks are different than for real estate agents who act as an intermediary in the sale or purchase of real estate (as well).

The Bureau Supervision Wwft derives its internal information on the professionals for which it has supervisory responsibility most prominently from the tax database. This database

403 I have been allowed to use and refer to these reports for the purposes of this research: Interview Belastingdienst/Bureau Toezicht Wwft, April 2013.

404 Belastingdienst Holland-Midden/Unit MOT-Ordening (2009), *Visiedocument "Waarheen... waarvoor...?" Handhaving in de jaren 2009-2012,* 6 January 2009 at 11-12.

405 Interview Belastingdienst/Bureau Toezicht Wwft, April 2013.

406 FATF (2011) at 244.

407 See § 5.4.2.1.

408 See § 5.5.2.1.

is held and maintained by other divisions of the Tax and Customs Administration.[409] It includes all information on tax payers, which is information on businesses and the natural persons involved that is relevant for fiscal purposes.[410] The Netherlands uses a system of classifying businesses based on their economic activity. Thereby, businesses are provided with sectoral codes (standard industrial classifications, SBI) based on their principal economic activity. The classifications and codes are used by, among others, the Dutch Chamber of Commerce and the Tax and Customs Administration for registration purposes.[411] Real estate agents and intermediaries have their own sectoral codes. For the identification of the group of real estate agents for which it has supervisory responsibility and the performance of risk assessments, the Bureau Supervision Wwft uses these codes in tax database searches.[412] The use of this database for the purpose of AML supervision brings about some difficulties. There is, for example, a risk of the 'contamination' of the tax database. Businesses receive their sectoral codes upon registration with the Dutch Chamber of Commerce, which forwards the information to the Dutch Tax and Customs Administration. The latter authority again classifies the businesses according to its own system. Whereas the Chamber of Commerce and the Tax Authority used to apply the same standard industrial classifications, they have started to diverge over the years and are no longer entirely the same.[413] A second difficulty may arise when a business does not only provide services as a real estate agent. As just explained, the sectoral codes are provided for the principal economic activity. Theoretically, this means that if a real estate agent has another principal activity, such as project development, he will be given another sectoral code. A third difficulty concerns the fact that valuers of real estate do not have their own separate sectoral code and are therefore more difficult to identify in the tax database. And lastly, section 5.5.2.1 already pointed to the lack of clarity as to whether real estate businesses actually fall under the scope of the AML Act in the first place. The use of the tax database also requires quite an effort on the side of the Bureau to get a full picture of the group of supervisees, since it has to carry out searches for all (groups of) institutions and professionals for which it has supervisory responsibility. Although the information from the tax database may be an adequate starting point for the Bureau Supervision Wwft, the information in the tax database does not give indications of potential money laundering risks. Because of this, external information is needed to create adequate risk profiles.

The Bureau Supervision Wwft tries to acquire additional (risk) information through the receiving of external risk signals from authorities such as the FIU-NL, law enforcement agencies, other AML supervisors, professional associations and the media. In practice, however, it appears that the Bureau hardly receives any signals from these authorities.[414]

409 The Tax database is called Beheer van Relaties (BvR): Interview Belastingdienst/Bureau Toezicht Wwft, April 2013.

410 Interview Belastingdienst/Bureau Toezicht Wwft, April 2013.

411 Centraal Bureau voor de Statistiek, *Het aantal bedrijven in Nederland volgens het CBS*, available at: <www.cbs.nl/nl-NL/menu/themas/bedrijven/links/2007-beschrijving-bedrijven-1.htm>, last visited on 2 May 2014.

412 Interview Belastingdienst/Bureau Toezicht Wwft, April 2013.

413 Centraal Bureau voor de Statistiek, *Het aantal bedrijven in Nederland volgens het CBS*, available at: <www.cbs.nl/nl-NL/menu/themas/bedrijven/links/2007-beschrijving-bedrijven-1.htm>, last visited on 2 May 2014; Interview Belastingdienst/Bureau Toezicht Wwft, April 2013.

414 No quantitative data is available, but this was made clear during the interview: Interview Belastingdienst/Bureau Toezicht Wwft, April 2013.

For AML supervisors the possibility to exchange supervisory information has only existed since the 1st of January 2013.[415] And the FIU-NL can only provide general reporting trends to the Bureau Supervision Wwft.[416] Only the police are said to report to the Bureau Supervision Wwft, but only intermittently. These signals are included in the risk assessment. In the absence of external risk signals, the Bureau Supervision Wwft must profile the risks itself. In relation to estate agents, it applies three techniques. Firstly, it looks at its own supervisory experiences concerning real estate agents.[417] Real estate agents which have been found non-compliant in the past are considered to bear a higher risk of money laundering. Secondly, there is the general feeling, backed by the literature and specific studies, that the commercial real estate sector faces a higher risk of being involved in money laundering schemes, although the Bureau's own activities during the past few years have been too limited to statistically prove this assumption.[418] Thirdly, the Bureau Supervision Wwft cross-checks the information from the tax database with information coming from other sources. Information from other sources may, for example, include the Dutch Chamber of Commerce, the Land Registry (*Kadaster*), professional associations, or the internet. Cross-checking may result in unusual patterns that can indicate a high(er) risk of money laundering. Understanding that the profession is unregulated, that not all real estate agents are members of professional associations, and that apart from the database on real estate valuers there are no public registers with information on these professionals, makes cross-checking a difficult technique in relation to estate agents.[419]

5.7.2.2 Project-based supervision

With project-based supervision there is a (relatively) greater focus on a particular group of professionals during a particular year, or on specific aspects or activities of those professionals. The projects are chosen on the basis of perceived risks or because the Bureau wishes to obtain more information on a market or specific sector. Projects can also be chosen on the basis of requests from other authorities. In the years 2011 and 2012 real estate agents were subject to project-based supervision. This can be seen as a direct result of the FATF evaluation in which the FATF recommended the Bureau Supervision Wwft to focus more on this sector. In the years 2011-12, the number of supervisory visits on real estate agents was considerably higher than on the other professionals for which the Bureau has supervisory responsibility.[420] In total, 436 (2011) and 491 (2012) inspections

415 See § 5.9.

416 Section 13(g) Wwft. The Police Data Act (*Wet politiegegevens, Wpg*) prohibits the FIU from sharing information from suspicious transaction reports with third parties, including the competent AML supervisor. More about this in § 5.9.

417 FATF (2011) at 244.

418 Cf. § 5.2. Belastingdienst/Bureau Toezicht Wwft (2011), *Jaarverslag 2011* (not publicly available); Belastingdienst/Bureau Toezicht Wwft (2012), *Jaarverslag 2012* (not publicly available).

419 For other professionals subject to its supervision, this may be a successful technique. For car dealers, for example, the Bureau Supervision Wwft can cross-check its information with the register of licensing plates kept by the Government Road Transport Agency (*Rijksdienst voor het Wegverkeer*). This authority monitors the environmental and safety aspects of Dutch road transportation.

420 Belastingdienst/Bureau Toezicht Wwft (2011); Belastingdienst/Bureau Toezicht Wwft (2012).

took place with regard to real estate agents. In 2011 this concerned 286 real estate agents or businesses, and in 2012 some 325 real estate agents or businesses.[421]

5.7.2.3 *Individual supervision*

Individual supervision takes place on the basis of individual risk signals stemming from the Bureau Supervision Wwft's risk assessment, or is the result of a follow-up inspection (*hercontrole*). When, for example, the police provide information to the Bureau that particular real estate agents are named in a criminal investigation, this may be a reason to verify their compliance with the preventive AML obligations as well. Also the cross-comparison between internal databases as well as earlier supervision results may play a role in deciding to carry out an on-site inspection. The annual reports 2011 and 2012 do not provide the number of individual inspections of real estate agents specifically. Nevertheless, we could see that in those years real estate agents formed a considerable part of the Bureau's project-based supervision. The annual report for 2013 mentions that the Bureau Supervision Wwft performed 462 inspections of estate agents, involving an estimated 300 real estate agents or businesses.[422]

Looking at the project-based supervision and individual supervision together, this means that on average 3.3% of all estate agents (businesses) have been subject to AML supervision annually in the years 2011-13.[423] Acknowledging that this number may not be completely accurate, it does give an indication of the likelihood that a real estate agent or business can receive an AML inspection from the Bureau Supervision Wwft. This is a comparatively high intensity of supervision.[424]

5

5.7.2.4 *Supervisory procedure*

Supervision by the Bureau is always of an on-site nature. Inspectors follow the internal code of practice which describes the procedure for supervisory visits. During interviews it was made clear that the Bureau Supervision Wwft distinguishes between the supervision of smaller businesses and larger businesses. Large businesses are businesses that for their fiscal activities fall under the competence of the division *Belastingdienst/Grote ondernemingen*. This can be due to the nature of the business, the internal scope of its activities, its profits from the business, and so on. Real estate businesses can sometimes be a large business.[425] The Bureau Supervision Wwft always verifies compliance with all AML obligations. In relation to smaller businesses, it focusses on dossiers on a transaction and

421 Although this could be inferred from the numbers, it should be pointed out that real estate businesses were not inspected twice in one year: the difference in numbers stems from the use of the term 'entity' and the system that the Belastingdienst/Bureau Toezicht Wwft applies.

422 Belastingdienst/Bureau Toezicht Wwft (2013), *Jaarverslag 2013* (not publicly available), at 2.

423 This calculation is based on the last available number of estate agents – 9,138 (Interview Belastingdienst/Bureau Toezicht Wwft, April 2013) – and on the average number of estate agents visited in 2011 (286), 2012 (325) and 2013 (300*).

424 Though difficult to compare and without drawing final conclusions from this indication: see § 4.6.2.2 where on average 0.1% of all institutions was supervised annually.

425 Interview Belastingdienst/Bureau Toezicht Wwft, April 2013.

client level. This means that it can decide to assess all transaction files and see whether the CDD obligations have been performed adequately, whether or not a suspicion report should have been disclosed to the FIU and whether the records are adequately kept. The Bureau can also decide to select a few dossiers and run some sample testing. Specifically for real estate agents, it not only looks at completed transactions but also at dossiers where assignments were withdrawn.[426] In relation to larger businesses, the Bureau focusses on internal policies and procedures. It checks whether there is an adequate internal policy in place, which includes the handling of customer due diligence, reporting and record-keeping obligations under the AML Act. It verifies whether staff are regularly trained or updated on typologies and trends, and assesses dossiers on a transaction level but less intensely than for smaller businesses. The aim is to verify whether the internal policies enable the business to comply with the AML obligations in an adequate manner.

From a supervisor's perspective this distinction in the supervisory approach is logical. However, we have previously seen that the AML Act does not explicitly oblige institutions and professionals to have internal policies and controls for the prevention of money laundering in place.[427] Unlike the DNB, which relies on the Wft for this obligation, the supervisory powers of the Bureau only stem from the AML Act. This means that if it finds that there are no internal controls or policies for the prevention of money laundering, the Bureau Supervision Wwft cannot act against any breaches in relation to internal controls by the large businesses. It might be able to find dossiers in which customer due diligence was not exercised properly, or where suspicions were not reported to FIU-NL, but the effort that the Bureau must make in that respect concerning larger businesses is enormous. Introducing a self-standing obligation in the AML Act on internal policies and controls would make the distinction in the exercise of AML supervision meaningful and make the Bureau more decisive and effective.

I have already previously explained that the partial inclusion under the AML Act of valuation activities by real estate agents may give rise to difficulties in terms of clarity and legal certainty. From the supervisor's perspective I had doubts about the enforceability of the norms and showed the inequality between the inclusion of valuers of real estate and real estate agents under the AML Act. While the AML Act refers to valuers of real estate as natural and legal persons, for real estate agents it only refers to Section 62 of the Dutch Commercial Code, which only concerns natural persons. As a consequence, real estate businesses performing valuation activities could be sanctioned as such, where this is not the case for real estate businesses that only perform mediation activities. It also seems that the current supervisory procedure of the Bureau must be amended. Notwithstanding the size of the business, which is currently decisive for the way in which the Bureau exercises AML supervision, it should also start making a differentiation in its supervision between 'pure' estate agents, estate agents that also act as a real estate valuers, and 'pure' valuers. For the group of estate agents that also act as real estate valuers, the development of a supervisory procedure seems most challenging. In 2013 the Bureau did not carry out on-site inspections of valuers of real estate as it decided to fully focus on the creation of

426 Interview Belastingdienst/Bureau Toezicht Wwft, April 2013.
427 See § 5.6.2.4.

awareness among this group of professionals.[428] The partial inclusion of valuers of real estate under the AML Act makes supervision for the Bureau Supervision Wwft in relation to real estate agents performing valuation activities unnecessarily complicated.

5.7.2.5 *Creation of awareness*

Finally, the Bureau Supervision Wwft invests a great deal of effort in the creation and raising of awareness among its supervisory population. It has drafted detailed guidelines for specific categories of professionals, organises and attends seminars and meetings, and enters into dialogue with partners, such as the professional associations for real estate agents.[429]

5.7.3 Sanctioning powers

The Bureau Supervision Wwft derives its sanctioning powers from the AML Act and lower-level regulations. As explained in § 5.6.3.1, all AML supervisors have the power to impose incremental penalty payments, administrative fines and to issue instructions. In the most serious cases the Bureau can decide to file a criminal complaint as well.[430] As explained, the AML Act does not provide a power to the AML supervisors to publish their sanctioning decisions. Although at present the Dutch Public Access to Government Information Act may serve as a legal basis to publish these decisions, it would be more robust if the AML Act contains a similar publication regime to the Financial Supervision Act.[431] The Bureau can turn to informal measures like a signalling meeting (*normoverdragend gesprek*) or informal warnings. Those measures are aimed to persuade real estate agents to comply with legislation before applying more stringent sanctions. The use of informal measures appears to be a common tool for the Bureau, as shown in the next section.

It should be pointed out that because of the lack of clarity as to whether real estate businesses fall under the scope of the AML Act, it is also questionable whether they can be sanctioned. This may be a more theoretical discussion, as § 5.5.2.1 demonstrated that the Bureau Supervision Wwft has never sanctioned a real estate business. Rather, it attributes the behaviour of the business to the managing partner or a director of a body corporate or firm. Nevertheless, the Third Directive clearly obliges Member States to ensure that both natural and legal persons can be held liable for acting in breach of the preventive AML obligations, which is another argument for explicitly bringing real estate businesses within the scope of AML legislation.

5.7.4 Sanctioning policy and practice

The general administrative law doctrine concerning the duty to sanction applies to the Bureau Supervision Wwft. The Bureau has no sanctioning policy in which it sets out its

428 Belastingdienst/Bureau Toezicht Wwft (2013) at 2.
429 Belastingdienst Holland Midden/Unit MOT-Ordening (2009) at 11-12.
430 See § 5.6.3.4.
431 See § 5.6.3.2.

enforcement goals, the desired level of compliance, the general principles it applies to sanctioning and the sanctioning procedure. The Vision document 2009-2012, which is still considered to be applicable, states that with the exercise of supervision the Bureau strives to create a positive effect on compliance. It does not however refer to the sanctioning powers of the Bureau and the way in which it intends to apply these powers in order to create this 'positive effect'.[432] The theoretical framework of effective supervision states that it is important that supervisors issue policies in which they make intelligible their choices and explain how they will apply their discretion in using the available supervisory and sanctioning powers, so it is advisable that the Bureau Supervision Wwft drafts such policy and makes this publicly available. The policy should at least include an explanation of the legal framework, the Bureau's vision and goals, the desired level of enforcement (or compliance), and general principles which the supervisor uses for its activities, as well as a general description of the procedures or methodology applied. During interviews representatives stated that the Bureau Supervision Wwft aims for a cooperative enforcement style.[433] It only resorts to formal sanctions where there is a clear sign of culpability or non-cooperative behaviour on the side of the estate agents. Repetitive or ongoing non-compliance were said to be indications of such behaviour.

Based on the data stemming from the non-public annual reports,[434] it appears that until 2013 real estate agents had never been sanctioned with an incremental penalty payment or administrative fine for non-compliance with the preventive AML obligations.[435] This is remarkable in light of the fact that the level of compliance by real estate agents in 2011 was lower than 50%. In 3% of the cases it resulted in a signalling meeting or informal warning, and in 0.2% this actually resulted in the announcement of an intended sanction (*sanctievoorstel*). No sanctions were imposed. In 2012 the level of compliance was only 30%. This is low, although the Bureau did report that from all cases in which non-compliant behaviour was identified, 67% of the cases concerned minor offences that could be attributed to unawareness on the side of the real estate agents. The breaches identified mostly concerned an inadequate or non-timely performance of customer due diligence or record-keeping. In that year, 3% of the cases resulted in a signalling meeting, informal warning, or the announcement of an intended sanctioning. Again, no sanction was imposed. In 2013, the Bureau noted that in the 8,800 dossiers checked during the 462 inspections, in more than 3,000 dossiers it identified breaches. In total, 65 real estate agents exceeded the margin of breaches of 75% or higher. It also identified suspicious transactions that should have been reported to the FIU in 21 dossiers. In 19 cases the real estate agents still disclosed the suspicion report after the inspection. In the two other cases the estate agents refused to disclose information to the FIU. One real estate agent received an incremental penalty payment and another estate agent is currently being prosecuted

432 Belastingdienst Holland-Midden/Unit MOT-Ordening (2009) at 3.

433 Interviews Bureau Toezicht Wwft, April 2010 and April 2013.

434 See § 5.7.2. I have been allowed to use and refer to these reports for the purposes of this research: Interview Belastingdienst/Bureau Toezicht Wwft, April 2013.

435 Interview Belastingdienst/Bureau Toezicht Wwft, April 2013.

by the Public Prosecution Service for not having disclosed reports to the FIU.[436] After the incremental penalty payment was imposed on the real estate agent, he decided to comply with the order from the Bureau to report a transaction to FIU-NL. The prosecution is the result of a cooperative effort called 'Non-reporters' ('Niet-melders').[437] This is a project that started in mid-2012 within which the FIU-NL, the Public Prosecution Service, the Fiscal Intelligence and Investigation Service (FIOD), the National Police Force, the Financial Supervision Office and the Bureau Supervision Wwft cooperate in order to stimulate compliant reporting behaviour.[438]

Chapter 2 discussed that supervisors must sanction in a proportionate and careful manner, and escalate their sanctions. They must speak softly where possible, and be hard where necessary; ultimately the sanctions must be capable of providing a deterrent effect. Based on the data described above, I conclude that the Bureau Supervision Wwft indeed speaks softly, but that it fails to be hard where necessary. Various arguments play a role here. Firstly, the AML Act has been in force since 2008 and has applied to real estate agents for some time. Considering the awareness-raising efforts on the side of the Bureau, for example by the publication of AML guidance and the organisation of seminars, estate agents should have become familiar with this legislation. One would expect that this can be seen in the activities of the supervisory authority too: while in the first years it can be expected that the supervisor adopts a cooperative style, once there is more experience with the legislation it could adopt a more formal approach. In this sense, one can indeed observe a difference between the year 2013 and preceding years, albeit minimally.[439] Secondly, the Bureau Supervision Wwft includes real estate agents in its project-based supervision and gives this group of professionals a high supervisory priority. This seems to be instigated by the risk of money laundering in this sector and may be related to the low reporting levels of estate agents as well.[440] In the third place, the Bureau Supervision Wwft has now identified a high percentage of non-compliant behaviour for at least three years in a row. Although in the majority of cases this concerned minor offences in relation to inadequate or non-timely customer due diligence, the Bureau Supervision Wwft also identified a number of cases in which the estate agent did not comply with the reporting obligation. This is a very serious offence, because not reporting unusual transactions completely undermines the Dutch system for the prevention of money laundering. In the years 2011-2013 the Bureau Supervision Wwft agreed with 5 (2011), 10 (2012) and even 19 (2013) estate agents to still report these transactions to the FIU after it had completed

436 Belastingdienst/Bureau Toezicht Wwft (2013) at 2, Openbaar Ministerie (2013), *OM, FIOD en Politie pakken niet-melden ongebruikelijke transacties aan*, 7 October 2013, available at: <www.om.nl/onderwerpen/fraude/@161598/fiod-politie-pakken/>, last visited on 2 May 2014.

437 Openbaar Ministerie (2012), *Zes strafrechtelijke onderzoeken naar niet-melden ongebruikelijke transacties*, 4 July 2012, available at: <www.om.nl/actueel-0/nieuws-persberichten/@159102/zes-strafrechtelijke/>, last visited on 2 May 2014; Openbaar Ministerie (2012), *Acht strafrechtelijke onderzoeken naar niet-melden ongebruikelijke transacties*, 21 November 2012, available at: <www.om.nl/onderwerpen/verkeer/@159817/acht/>, last visited on 2 May 2014.

438 Algemene Rekenkamer (2014) at 8; Bureau Financieel Toezicht (2013) at 15.

439 After all, in the year 2013 the Bureau Toezicht Wwft for the first time imposed a formal sanction on an estate agent.

440 See § 5.2.

supervised dossiers on these estate agents.[441] When the real estate agents complied with the agreement, the Bureau would not sanction them. In the years 2011 and 2012, these agreements made up 22% and 26% of the total number of reports received by the FIU-NL.[442] Only those estate agents that refused to cooperate were sanctioned in 2013: the Bureau Supervision Wwft imposed an incremental penalty payment on one estate agent and it was decided to prosecute another real estate agent.[443]

5.7.5 Concluding remarks

The Bureau Supervision Wwft has adequate supervisory powers insofar as this concerns inspections: it can compel the production of information relevant to the monitoring of compliance and it can perform on-site inspections. The AML Act, however, does not provide it with regulatory powers. The non-public annual reports from the Bureau, which have been provided by representatives for the purpose of this research, show that AML supervision by the Bureau is not integrated in wider supervisory programmes. The Bureau applies a risk-based approach. It exercises its supervision based on individual risk signals and project-based supervision. Supervisory activities are planned in annual supervision plans. As concluded in section 5.4, the annual reports from the Bureau should be published in order to be transparent and to account for the exercise of AML supervision. The implementation of a risk-based approach appears to be a difficult task. The main problem is the relatively weak information position of the Bureau Supervision Wwft regarding the population for which it has supervisory responsibility and the fact that the number of professionals subject to its supervision, particularly dealers in goods, is not clear and varies from one year to another. In relation to real estate agents the main reasons seem to be the unregulated nature of the profession and the fact that real estate agents perform valuation activities that fall only partly under the AML Act. Nevertheless, real estate agents have been given supervisory priority in recent years resulting in a high inspection intensity. In the exercise of its supervision, the Bureau distinguishes between smaller and larger institutions. For smaller institutions it focusses on dossiers on a transaction and client level. For larger institutions, it verifies whether there are adequate internal policies and controls. However, in the absence of such an obligation in the AML Act, it cannot enforce this obligation. Introducing a self-standing obligation in the AML Act on internal policies and controls would make the distinction in the exercise of AML supervision meaningful and make the Bureau more decisive and effective. The partial inclusion of valuers of real estate makes the supervision of estate agents performing valuation activities unnecessarily complicated as well.

The Bureau Supervision Wwft has adequate sanctioning powers, although the legislator should provide for a publication regime for sanctioning decisions similar to the regime laid down in the Financial Supervision Act and clarify that real estate businesses can be sanctioned as well. The Bureau has no (public) policy in which it sets out its enforcement

441 Belastingdienst/Bureau Toezicht Wwft (2011), Belastingdienst/Bureau Toezicht Wwft (2012), Belastingdienst/Bureau Toezicht Wwft (2013).

442 FIU Nederland (2012) at 74. Cf. § 5.3: at the time of writing, the annual report 2013 has not been released.

443 Belastingdienst/Bureau Toezicht Wwft (2013).

goals, the desired level of compliance, general principles applicable upon sanctioning and the sanctioning procedure. It should publish such policy in order to be transparent and accountable about the exercise of its AML supervision. Its practice does not comply with the requirement that sanctions must ultimately be capable of providing a deterrent effect. Until 2013 the Bureau had never imposed an incremental penalty payment or an administrative fine, although in a large number of inspections it had identified breaches of customer due diligence, record keeping and even the reporting obligations. The Bureau Supervision Wwft's cooperative style is adequate concerning the identification of minor offences. However, this policy is applied even in cases of very serious offences, such as non-reporting. Real estate agents are given the opportunity to overcome a breach without any consequences or directly backed by a formal measure. Under certain circumstances this may be understandable, but it should certainly not be standard procedure. The Bureau Supervision Wwft has adequate sanctioning powers available, and should start applying these powers in the case of serious infringements in order to show the sector that it takes the matter seriously and to deter future non-compliance.

5.8 Financial Supervision Office (*Bureau Financieel Toezicht*)

5.8.1 Supervisory powers

Like the two previous AML supervisors, the Financial Supervision Office obtains its supervisory powers via the AML Act from the General Administrative Law Act.[444] These powers were already described in § 5.6.1. BFT inspectors have, in principle, the power to carry out on-site inspections and to request information, records and other documents that are necessary for the exercise of AML supervision. The BFT does not have regulatory powers. In recent years the BFT has encountered serious problems in relation to the application of supervisory powers, to which I will now pay attention.

5.8.1.1 Application of supervisory powers by the Financial Supervision Office

Having supervisory responsibility for the group of legal and fiscal service providers, the fundamental principle of legal professional privilege has affected the BFT's supervision in practice.[445] As will be shortly explained, persons who are bound to secrecy by virtue of their office or profession, or by law, may refuse to cooperate if this follows from their duty of secrecy. In practice, this meant that civil-law notaries and lawyers could refuse to provide the BFT with access to their files.[446] Since January 2013 civil-law notaries can no longer invoke their privilege against the BFT.[447] In light of the fact that the AML supervision of lawyers is supposed to be transferred to the Dutch Bar Association, this legal hindrance is

444 Section 24(1) Wwft and title 5.2 of the General Administrative Law Act.
445 See Stouten (2012) at 75-90 and 298-301.
446 Section 5:20(2) Awb is considered to apply to civil-law notaries, lawyers, physicians, and the clergy: Van Buuren, P.J.J. and Borman, T.C. (eds.) (2009), *Tekst en Commentaar Algemene Wet Bestuursrecht*, Kluwer: Deventer, 6th edition, at 357. See also Bannier, F.A.W., Duijst-Heesters, W. and Fanoy, N.A.M.E.C. (eds.) (2008a), *Beroepsgeheim en verschoningsrecht: handboek voor de advocaat, medisch hulpverlener, notaris en geestelijke*, Sdu Uitgevers, at 12 who call these the 'classic' privileged professions.
447 Section 111a (new) Dutch Notaries Act.

also solved.[448] Accountants do not have self-standing professional privilege, although they have been given a so-called informal professional privilege in tax-related cases against the DTCA.[449] Accountants cannot invoke legal professional privilege under the General Administrative Law Act and are thus in principle bound to cooperate.[450] Nevertheless, legal professional privilege may affect the BFT's supervision in relation to accountants.[451] Via two ways accountants can (argue that they) fall within the scope of legal professional privilege. Firstly, accountants might fall under the legal professional privilege exemption of the AML Act specifically when they give advice or are involved in procedures on tax-related matters. Secondly, they can invoke a derived duty of secrecy when they act under the assignment of a lawyer. Both options are discussed hereafter, whereby I point to some legal difficulties and practical challenges.

5.8.1.2 The legal professional privilege exemption and tax advice under the AML Act

Section 1(2) Wwft stipulates that the Act shall not apply to tax advisors, lawyers, or (junior) civil-law notaries, insofar as they perform activities for a client in relation to the determination of the latter's legal position, representation and defence before the courts, the provision of advice before, during and after legal proceedings, or the provision of advice about instituting or avoiding legal proceedings. This provision should be seen as the implementation of the legal professional privilege exemption from the Third Directive.[452] The consideration of 'determining the client's legal position' should be interpreted restrictively: only the first introductory meeting falls under this exemption.[453] The procedure-related exemption has no such restriction.

It is not clear whether it has been the legislator's intention to exclude accountants from the scope of Section 1(2) Wwft. Stouten observes that the Act or the Explanatory Memorandum thereto do not mention accountants at all.[454] Based on arguments of equivalence, legal certainty and the fact that accountants can render legal assistance in tax-related proceedings as well, she reasons that accountants sometimes perform the same role as tax advisors and that in these cases the exemption should apply to accountants.[455] In fact, accountants will often be or act as tax advisors as well, thus resulting in a wide application of the privilege to accountants. The application of the legal professional privilege exemption under the AML Act is more complicated, because the profession of tax advisor in the Netherlands is

448 See § 3.4.2.

449 Møller, L.H.E. (2005), 'Hoe ver reikt het zogenoemde 'informele verschoningsrecht?', *Weekblad Fiscaal Recht*, 6606, pp. 3-8; Stouten (2012) at 202.

450 Møller (2005); Bannier et al. (2008a) at 12-14; Stouten (2012) at 2012. See differently Van den Berg (2012) at 144 who is of the opinion that accountants can invoke legal professional privilege via section 5:20(2) Awb, and are not required to provide information that falls under their duty of secrecy. Case law on this point: HR 25 October 1983, ECLI:NL:HR:1983:AG4685, *NJ 1984/132* annotated by A.C. 't Hart; HR, 14 June 1985, ECLI:NL:HR:1985:AC9068, *NJ 1986/175* annotated by W.L. Haardt; HR 6 May 1986, ECLI:NL:HR:1986:AB9404, *NJ 1986/813* annotated by W.L. Haardt.

451 Cf. Van den Berg (2012) at 145 speaks about a weak information position of the BFT in relation to accountants' involvement in real estate criminality.

452 Article 23(2) Third Directive.

453 Stouten (2012) at 136.

454 Ibid., 206.

455 Ibid., at 206-207.

not regulated like the accountancy profession. In principle, any person can call himself a tax advisor. It could, therefore, be the case that accountants invoke the legal professional privilege against the BFT directly on the basis of Section 1(2) Wwft when they perform activities similar to tax advisors in relation to legal proceedings.

As an aside, it should be pointed out that the legal professional privilege exemption in the Dutch AML is more lenient than the exemption from the Third Directive.[456] Because the Directive is an instrument of minimum harmonisation – which allows Member States to take stricter, but not more lenient measures – this is not allowed. The exemption under the Directive only refers to an exemption from reporting obligations.[457] The consideration 'shall not apply' in the Dutch Act suggests that invoking legal professional privilege results in the entire inapplicability of all AML obligations, including customer due diligence and the record-keeping obligations. The Government has confirmed this interpretation in the Explanatory Memorandum to the Act.[458] It finds a full exemption appropriate because 'after all, it is unnecessary to collect information for cases in which no report has to be disclosed' (*own translation, MB*). This reasoning is rather odd. After all, the professional himself must determine whether or not the situation at hand falls under his legal professional privilege and for this he obviously needs a certain amount of information allowing him to make a proper and well-balanced decision. This conflict between national and EU law could potentially result in an infraction procedure from the European Commission, although it will be unlikely given that the Act has been in force since 2008.[459]

Interviews made clear that in circumstances where accountants provide services similar to tax advisors and can invoke legal professional privilege, the BFT accepts the privilege of accountants. It does perform a marginal check to verify whether the accountant justifiably invokes his privilege under the AML Act.[460] As explained, the advice exemption only applies to the first introductory meeting. Therefore, it will be unlikely that accountants justifiably invoke the legal professional privilege exemption for this circumstance. Regarding the procedure-related exemption, the BFT requests accountants to provide an anonymised copy of appeal letters. If an accountant can produce the document, the BFT accepts that this falls under his legal professional privilege and will not supervise that specific dossier.[461]

5.8.1.3 Derived legal professional privilege for accountants

Accountants can also invoke legal professional privilege, when they perform their services on a contractual basis with a professional who has a duty of secrecy and the right to legal professional privilege. This is called a derived professional privilege.[462] This derived

456 Van den Broek (2014a) at 42.
457 Article 23(2) Third Directive refers to an exemption from the application of the reporting obligation; article 9(5) Third Directive refers to an exemption from the consideration to make a report to the FIU in accordance with Section 22 Third Directive when CDD cannot be completed. Cf. FATF (2014b) at 32.
458 *Parliamentary Papers II*, 2006-07, 31 238, no. 3, at 15.
459 The Netherlands is not the only country that goes beyond the exemption in the Third Directive: Van den Broek (2014a) at 42.
460 Interview Bureau Financieel Toezicht, June 2013.
461 Interview Bureau Financieel Toezicht, June 2013.
462 Bannier et al. (2008a) at 14.

privilege prevents information that would normally be privileged from becoming public, simply because the information is not primarily collected or processed by the person with a duty of secrecy and corresponding professional privilege. As just explained, in the Netherlands civil-law notaries and lawyers are among those with such privilege, although notaries can invoke this against the BFT.[463] Accountants can still invoke this against the BFT when they are retained by a lawyer. This is particularly important for forensic accountants, but holds true for accountants in general as well.[464]

As explained in § 5.5.3.1, forensic accountancy activities were explicitly brought under the scope of the AML Act in 2013. This means that when forensic accountants become acquainted with an unusual transaction from a client or a third party on behalf of a client, they are obliged to notify the FIU. They are also obliged to cooperate with the BFT and to provide access to relevant files. However, soon after inclusion within the scope of the AML Act, questions were raised about the extent to which forensic accountants could invoke a derived professional privilege and, hence, would not need to report unusual transactions to the FIU and could refuse to provide the BFT with access to documents. In February 2013, two lawyers wrote that businesses hiring forensic accountants for fraud investigations, but did not want them to report to the FIU, could evade this 'problem' by having forensic accountants operating under an assignment from a lawyer.[465] This resulted in discussions in the media and questions in Parliament. In order to establish a proper balance between the reporting obligation, on the one hand, as well as the derived legal professional privilege, on the other, Stouten had earlier already advised to exclude forensic accountancy activities in the framework of annual accounts controls, or preventive forensic accountancy activities from the exemption from reporting – hence, to allow the reporting obligation to 'revive' – and to keep other forensic accountancy activities under the exemption.[466] This recommendation was not followed: the AML Act makes no distinction between the types of forensic accountancy activities. The Minister of Security & Justice replied to Parliament that forensic accountants can indeed be discharged from their obligation to report to the FIU when they perform a fraud investigation pursuant to an assignment from lawyers.[467] In order to prevent supervision from becoming illusory because misuse is made of the derived professional privilege, the Minister stated that the exemption from reporting to the FIU under the AML Act must be interpreted restrictively and that for each individual assignment the role and function of lawyers must be explained. The lawyer must be in charge of the fraud investigation. From the Minister's statement, I infer that the role of the lawyer must be documented in writing. When a lawyer carries out an activity which is not subject to the legal professional privilege exemption, such as mediation, then the (forensic) accountant also has no derived duty of secrecy either.[468]

463 This means that when accountants are hired by civil-law notaries to deliver specific services, they also can no longer invoke a (derived) professional privilege against the BFT.

464 See Brouwer, D. (2013), 'De forensische accountant als Paard van Troje?', *Accountancynieuws*, issue 3, 15 February 2013; *Parliamentary Papers II*, 2013-14, Vragen, 2013Z02294; Letter from the Minister of Security & Justice, 28 February 2013, ref. no. 2013Z02294.

465 Het Financieel Dagblad, *Maak advocaten leidend bij fraude*, 4 February 2013.

466 Stouten (2012) at 496.

467 Letter from the Minister of Security & Justice, 28 February 2013, ref. no. 2013Z02294.

468 Ibid.

In principle, the BFT has no problems in accessing accountants' files.[469] Where a (forensic) accountant acts on his own, he must cooperate with the BFT. The question of course remains how a derived duty of secrecy and legal professional privilege works through with respect to supervision carried out by the BFT on accountants that (also) perform forensic accountancy activities under assignment from a lawyer. Can forensic accountants refuse to allow the BFT to have access to certain files? It seems a reasonable explanation that where a forensic accountant can invoke the derived privilege under the AML Act, he may (or even must) refuse to allow the BFT to have access to these documents. Where he cannot invoke this right, because the lawyer's activities do not fall under the professional privilege – this is to be decided by the lawyer himself – then he must also cooperate and provide the BFT with full access to the documents. The question whether or not a particular activity is privileged must be interpreted restrictively. How this must be realised in practice, though, seems very challenging. Think, for example, about the situation where a forensic accountant (also) performs other accountancy services at the same time or in relation to the same business. Can he, supported by his derived professional privilege, then refuse full access to all files or must he give BFT partial access to his files? This is a delicate question, because the legal professional privilege of the lawyer and the derived professional privilege of the accountant must be safeguarded, while at the same time AML supervision should not be disproportionately hampered. The BFT's current practice is that it asks for a copy of the lawyer's assignment to the forensic accountant, in which the role and function of the lawyer is explained and how the lawyer falls under the legal professional privilege exemption. This, too, concerns a marginal check to verify whether the accountant justifiably invokes the (derived) legal professional privilege.[470] If the BFT is of the opinion that the lawyer has only been brought in to by-pass the reporting obligation, then there is an abuse of the derived duty of secrecy and the reporting obligation revives. In those cases, however, the BFT must make a reasonable case that there is actually an abuse.[471]

5.8.2 Anti-money laundering supervision in practice

In 2009 the Financial Supervision Office was evaluated. This was required under the (old) Dutch Notaries Act and was further justified by political concerns with regard to the effectiveness and efficiency of the BFT's functioning.[472] The Evaluation Committee was critical on the exercise of AML supervision by the BFT. It observed, for example, that stakeholders had doubts about the depth of the inspections carried out by the BFT.[473] In relation to accountants, the committee considered that the BFT, due to its severe capacity and resource problems, could not *de facto* perform AML supervision and that as

469 Stouten (2012) at 228-229.
470 Interview Bureau Financieel Toezicht, June 2013.
471 This is included in the updated version of AML guidance by the Dutch Institute of Chartered Accountants: *Nederlandse Beroepsorganisatie van Accountants, Handreiking 1124 – Richtsnoeren ter voorkoming van witwassen en financieren van terrorisme (WWFT) voor belastingadviseurs en accountants*, February 2014, at 16.
472 *Instellingsbesluit Evaluatiecommissie Bureau Financieel Toezicht*, Stcrt. 125/2008.
473 Evaluatiecommissie Bureau Financieel Toezicht (2009) at 28.

a consequence only an 'appearance of supervision' was created.[474] This was also concluded in a report by the Dutch Court of Audit, which calculated in 2008 that lawyers and accountants had on average a 0.6% chance of being inspected by the Financial Supervision Office.[475] The Evaluation Committee recommended to transfer AML supervision to the AFM, which already performs supervision of a large number of audit firms pursuant to the Audit Firms Supervision Act.[476] This recommendation was not followed by the Dutch legislator. The BFT's risk-based approach for AML supervision was also a specific point of criticism. An integral approach to risk-based analyses was lacking and there was no systematic overview of the risks and conduct of the supervisory population as a whole.[477] Only for notaries was this different, due to the fact that the BFT also performs financial supervision of this group and thus had more information available.[478] The absence of adequate risk-based analyses was caused by the weak legal information position of the BFT, the weak factual cooperation between the various organisations involved in AML supervision in terms of the exchange of information, and the focus of the BFT on client files instead of the business culture.[479] This led to the researchers' conclusion that the supervision was still at a pioneering stage.

Despite the criticism, the Financial Supervision Office has continued to apply the same three-track approach in its AML supervision that it had in place since the mid-2000s.[480] In the first track, it aims to increase awareness and familiarity with the applicable legislation and regulation and typologies of money laundering. Inspectors attend seminars, answer questions from the supervisory population, and organise meetings with professional associations and the sectors. In the second track, the BFT aims to improve the self-regulation of the professions via the conclusion of (supervisory) arrangements. In these arrangements it is agreed that the professional associations perform AML supervision, and that BFT only oversees the work of those associations. In the third track, it carries out risk-based and regular supervision.[481] The regular supervisory visits are selected on an ad random basis, primarily with the aim of obtaining an oversight of the profession as a whole. The risk-based visits are selected because of the higher perceived risk of money laundering, or because the BFT has received external or internal signals indicating a higher risk for specific individuals or for a group of professionals. This is where the risk-based approach comes into play.

474 Ibid., at 37.

475 *Parliamentary Papers II*, 2007-08, 31 477, nos. 1-2.

476 Evaluatiecommissie Bureau Financieel toezicht (2009) at 37. See § 5.5.3.

477 Smits, J., Struiksma, N. and Van den Heuvel, M. (2009*), Systeem in zaken: een evaluatie van de effectiviteit en doelmatigheid van het Bureau Financieel Toezicht*, research commissioned by the Ministry of Justice, at 54.

478 Smits et al. (2009) at 54.

479 Ibid., at 44.

480 Cf. Faure et al. (2009) at 112-113; Bureau Financieel Toezicht, *Werkwijze*, available at : <www.bureauft.nl/wwft/werkwijze-toezicht/Paginas/Werkwijze.aspx>, last visited on 29 April 2014; Bureau Financieel Toezicht (2008), *Jaarverslag 2008*, at 30 where the BFT states that it continued the three-track policy that it had started 'years ago'. Interestingly, in recent annual reports the BFT applies a somewhat different categorisation, where it brings the conclusion of arrangements under the first pillar concerning the raising of awareness and where it splits the regular supervisory procedures and risk-based supervisory procedures: Bureau Financieel Toezicht (2012) at 27-28.

481 Evaluatiecommissie Bureau Financieel Toezicht (2009) at 24.

Hereafter, I will first discuss the third track of AML supervision as exercised by the BFT first, considering that this should be the core of the BFT's compliance supervision (§ 5.8.2.1). I pay attention to the risk-based approach, the existence of (annual) supervision plans and the extent to which AML supervision is carried out on accountants. I then continue by discussing the outsourcing of AML supervision to professional associations particularly for the accountancy sector in § 5.8.2.2. In section 5.8.2.3 some attention is paid to the awareness-raising activities.

5.8.2.1 Supervision by the Financial Supervision Office

Risk-based approach

It has been observed that the BFT's AML supervision has become more and more risk-oriented in recent years, and that the BFT considers this an important point of departure.[482] Stouten observed that for the BFT, in light of its limited resources, it is far more effective to perform risk-based supervision. Another reason is that the professional associations already perform general quality checks on their members, which may to a certain extent include compliance with the AML Act.[483] Since the criticism from the Evaluation Committee in 2009 on the absence of an adequate risk-based approach, the legal information position from the BFT in relation to accountants has not changed. For its risk-based supervision of this group, it is still highly dependent on external signals. The BFT has invested in cooperation with other authorities that may have important signals for its supervision. In 2012, for example, the BFT entered into an arrangement with the DTCA as part of a project on 'bad accountants'.[484] With this arrangement the DTCA committed itself to sharing files with the BFT upon the identification of certain AML offences, such as insufficient identification of the ultimate beneficial owner or not duly reporting.[485] The BFT can also receive signals from the Public Prosecution Service, the FIOD, the National Police Force, the other AML supervisors, the professional associations and the media.[486] With some of these authorities the BFT liaises within the project 'Non-reporters'.[487] External signals are picked up by the Planning & Control Division, where analysts process the signals and carry out a first analysis of the signals in order to identify the urgency with which the signal must be picked up through a risk-based visit.[488] Regular visits can also lead to specific risk signals and, thus, to risk-based supervision visits. These are so-called internal signals. In its annual report for 2011 the BFT stated that within its regular supervision it aims to be more risk-based by looking at the type of

482 See FATF (2011) at 245; Stouten (2012), at 282 et seq.
483 Stouten (2012) at 282-284.
484 *Convenant inzake de samenwerking bij het tegengaan van ontoelaatbaar gedrag van accountants tussen de Belastingdienst en het Bureau Financieel Toezicht*, Stcrt. 2012, 12056 (hereafter 'DTCA Arrangement'). Please note that this arrangement has not been concluded with the division within the DTCA (the Bureau Supervision Wwft) that carries out anti-money laundering supervision.
485 Section 3 DTCA Arrangement.
486 Regarding the professional associations to the BFT: see § 5.8.2.2.
487 See § 5.7.4.
488 Interview Bureau Financieel Toezicht, June 2013. As of the 1st of January 2014, these functions may have been taken over by the Team on development and risk-based visits (the TOBO team): Bureau Financieel Toezicht (2013) at 6.

customers for which the professionals provide their services.[489] Finding that some types of customers may be more sensitive to money laundering, professionals who provide services to these types of customers may be considered as high(er) risk. This concerns, for example, accounting consultants who provide services to 'coffee shops' (shops which sell cannabis).[490] According to the FATF, the BFT's risk focus until 2010 had rested mostly with forensic accountants and similar business providers.[491]

Supervision plans and policy

The BFT drafts annual supervision plans that are not publicly available. The plans accompany the estimates that are sent to the Ministry of Security & Justice.[492] The estimates contain budgetary requests for all of the BFT's tasks under the Dutch Notaries Act, the Bailiffs Act and the AML Act. In the annual plans the BFT indicates the number of contemplated AML visits for a particular year. These are not specified for specific groups of professionals, or the names of professionals to be inspected.[493] The BFT reserves time and resources for the performance of risk-based visits as well. Because the risk-based approach is largely dependent on external signals that mostly come to its attention throughout the year, risk-based visits cannot be planned far in advance. The BFT therefore drafts annual supervision plans mostly regarding regular inspections. Plans may also contain a number of inspections surrounding a theme or project.[494] Supervision plans as part of the estimates are discussed with the Ministry of Security & Justice, and with representatives of the Ministry of Finance.[495] The Ministries can request the BFT to amend the annual supervision plans. Because these plans accompany the estimates which require formal approval via the subsidy letters, they also form part of this procedure. In light of the theoretical framework of effective supervision, in which it was stated that there must be an adequate level of independence from politics and the market, this practice is debatable. Nevertheless, considering that this concerns a potential *indirect* influence on the BFT's political independence in the determination of its budget, I do not elaborate on this any further.[496] Next to the annual plans, BFT inspectors also draft quarterly plans in which they plan their regular visits more specifically. Since January 2014, the team on development and risk-based visits (*Team Ontwikkeling en Bijzondere Onderzoeken*) is responsible for the planning of risk-based visits.[497]

Traditionally, the BFT's AML supervision has mostly focused on civil-law notaries.[498] This is not surprising, given that the BFT has most information available for this group. It has, for example, access to information from the Land Registry that can point at possible

489 Bureau Financieel Toezicht (2011), *Jaarverslag 2011*, at 25.
490 Ibid., at 25.
491 FATF (2011) at 246.
492 Interview Bureau Financieel Toezicht, June 2013.
493 FATF (2011) at 245.
494 Interview Bureau Financieel Toezicht, June 2013.
495 FATF (2011) at 245.
496 See § 2.4.2.1 where I explain why I do not deal with the indirect influence on the independence of supervisors.
497 Bureau Financieel Toezicht (2013) at 6.
498 Faure et al. (2009) at 116; FATF (2011) at 246; Stouten (2012) at 288.

ABC transactions involving civil-law notaries. Moreover, before January 2013 the BFT spent considerable time on performing supervision upon request from the notarial disciplinary tribunals, thereby allowing the BFT to carry out the AML supervision of civil-law notaries without being hampered by the legal professional privilege exemption that notaries could invoke against the BFT regarding access to their files.[499] These supervisory visits placed a considerable burden on the BFT's resources.[500] And since January 2013 the BFT is the integral supervisor of civil-law notaries. It took over the integrity and quality-related supervision from the notarial disciplinary tribunals. BFT now carries out financial supervision, quality and integrity supervision, and the AML supervision of the notarial profession. Altogether this demonstrates that the BFT has a better information position on notaries than for the other professionals under its AML supervision. During interviews BFT representatives have indicated that the BFT focusses more and more on accountants. This is a consequence of the FATF evaluation, which concluded that there were effectiveness issues in relation to the monitoring of accountants.[501] For the year 2013, the BFT planned to exercise on-site inspections at several accountancy firms.[502] This can be seen as a similar project to the one conducted in 2009, when the BFT performed a number of risk-based supervision visits on forensic accountants.[503] The BFT also planned 50 regular visits to accountancy firms, besides the AML audits that the SRA carries out on its members.[504]

Supervision in practice

The BFT has pointed out that it aims to carry out AML supervision in a lenient manner where possible, and dissuasive where necessary (*terughoudend waar het kan en doortastend waar het moet*).[505] Inspectors are required to follow an internal code practice that ensures consistency in the supervisory visits. Regular visits are exercised by BFT inspectors, which each have a geographical responsibility.[506] Regular visits are performed by a single BFT inspector, whereas risk-based visits are usually performed by two or more BFT inspectors.

The numbers available in terms of the exercise of regular and risk-based supervision show that the regular visits outnumbered the BFT's risk-based visits in the years 2010-2012. This gives the impression that the BFT's risk-based approach in relation to AML supervision is rather reactive and plays a limited role in its supervision in practice. In 2010, the BFT concluded 29 regular visits, with another nine pending at the end of that year. The BFT did not report on which group(s) of professionals the regular visits were performed. It also

499 Stouten (2012) at 288; Faure et al. (2009) at 117 have called this the 'U-turn construction'.
500 Bureau Financieel Toezicht (2010), *Jaarverslag 2010*, at 23: '(…) De onderzoeken in opdracht van de Kamers van Toezicht overstijgen qua problematiek vaak het standaard onderzoekswerk. Ze kosten veel tijd en hebben niet altijd een puur financieel of WWFT-gerelateerd karakter'.
501 FATF (2011) at 245; Cf. FATF (2014b) at 37 in which the FATF stated that the Netherlands did not provide any data concerning accountants on the basis of which the FATF could verify whether effectiveness issues are still present.
502 Bureau Financieel Toezicht (2013) at 2.
503 FATF (2011) at 247.
504 See about the AML-audits by the SRA: § 5.8.2.2.
505 Bureau Financieel Toezicht (2012) at 29.
506 Interview Bureau Financieel Toezicht, June 2013.

concluded 15 risk-based inspections, and it had another 12 pending at the end of the year. It stated that the risk-based visits focused particularly on forensic accountants and civil-law notaries.[507] In 2011, the BFT concluded 36 regular visits with another seven pending at the end of the year, against six risk-based visits, with another eight pending.[508] Lamentably, the BFT did not state on which types of professionals the regular supervisory visits were carried out. Most of the risk-based visits were carried out on notaries, after a request from the notarial disciplinary tribunals on the basis of the Dutch Notaries Act.[509] In 2012, the BFT concluded 43 regular supervisory visits, with 5 pending at the end of the year. Of the regular visits, 19 took place at accountancy firms.[510] It concluded 13 risk-based visits, and at the end of that year it had another ten inspections pending. From the explanation for the risk-based visits, it appears that again most took place with civil-law notaries.[511] The numbers for the year 2013 were not yet available at the time of finalising this chapter. This is pitiful, because BFT itself indicated that in 2013 it would focus on accountants. It appears that until 2013 accountants were included in regular and risk-based supervision by the BFT concerning their compliance with the AML obligations. Nevertheless, the inspection intensity until 2013 appears low in light of the high number of accountants that fall under the scope of the AML Act: 17,648 at the end of 2012. An explanation for this could be found in the limited resources available to the BFT. In § 5.4.3.1, we saw that the 12 FTE working in the BFT's Wwft team stands in stark contrast to the total number of professionals for which it is responsible.[512]

Table 5 – BFT's general inspection numbers 2010-2012[513]

	Regular supervision (pending at the end of the year)	Risk-based supervision (pending at the end of the year)
2010	29 (9)	15 (12)
2011	36 (7)	6 (8)
2012	43 (5)	13 (10)

The finding of the low intensity of the AML supervision of accountants by the BFT may be compensated by the conclusion of supervisory arrangements with associations active in the accountancy sector. The BFT has entered into one such arrangement with an organisation representing accountancy businesses working for small and medium-sized businesses, which I will discuss in the next subsection. I will also pay attention to the indirect role of the Dutch Institute of Chartered Accountants, the leading professional association for the accountancy profession.[514]

507 Bureau Financieel Toezicht (2010) at 19.
508 Bureau Financieel Toezicht (2011) at 26.
509 Ibid., at 26.
510 Bureau Financieel Toezicht (2012) *Jaarverslag 2012*, at 28.
511 Ibid., at 28.
512 Compare with § 4.4.2.1.
513 Own table based on Bureau Financieel Toezicht (2010) at 19; Bureau Financieel Toezicht (2011) at 26 and Bureau Financieel Toezicht (2012) at 28.
514 See § 5.5.3 about the Dutch Institute of Chartered Accountants (NBA).

5.8.2.2 Outsourcing of supervision to professional associations

As part of its three-track approach the BFT engages with associations that (wish to) include AML aspects into their wider quality controls. It is of the opinion that professional associations must be the first gatekeepers in the prevention of money laundering and terrorist financing.[515]

> As indicated in Chapter 4, I use the term supervisory arrangements. These are agreements made between two parties, either both public administrative authorities or between the administration and the private sector, in this research on the exercise of supervision. Other terms used to refer to these kinds of agreements are declarations of intention, memoranda of understanding, supervisory agreements, *convenanten* (Dutch) or *convenios* (Spanish).[516] The BFT is somewhat ambiguous in the use of its own terminology. It refers to both supervisory arrangements and 'covenants'. According to representatives there is no difference in their legal character. The only difference is that the BFT considers that with 'covenants' the other contracting party acts on an equal level with the BFT, whereas supervisory arrangements imply an ultimate responsibility of and a final say for the BFT.[517] This research does not make such a distinction.

Various reasons can underlie the conclusion of (supervisory) arrangements. One is that they can serve as an attempt to experiment with new administrative relations. In that role they stimulate learning and growing processes.[518] An advantage is that parties can lay down their own commitments and that such arrangements do not need to be very detailed.[519] Alternatively, they can be seen as a further elaboration of public policy and be chosen as an alternative to legislation.[520] The two viewpoints do not necessarily exclude each other: a learning process could eventually result in the adoption of a (formal) legal instrument.[521]Arrangements can also be concluded to further detail the possibilities for cooperation and coordination. The legal character of (supervisory) arrangements is difficult to qualify in general, as their content can diverge widely.[522] They do bind the signing parties, most importantly from a moral viewpoint. The legal enforceability of arrangements is different for each specific situation. Some argue that they are not legally enforceable, but others state that this depends on the situation and the content of the agreement.[523] Supervisory arrangements do not necessarily require a legal basis, because they concern agreements between two (or more) parties. It is however generally accepted that public law powers cannot be (fully) transferred via the use of arrangements. In practice, they are concluded between public authorities and are normally published in

515 FATF (2011) at 245.
516 Van Wijk/Konijnenbelt & Van Male (2014) at 253.
517 Interview Bureau Financieel Toezicht, June 2013.
518 Van der Jagt, J.A.E. (2006), *Milieuconvenanten gehandhaafd: Een juridisch onderzoek naar handhaafbaarheid en handhaving van Nederlandse milieuconvenanten en in het bijzonder van klimaatconvenanten in het licht van de democratische rechtsstaat*, Boom Juridische uitgevers: The Hague (doctoral thesis Utrecht University), at 74.
519 Ibid., at 74.
520 Ibid., at 75; Scheltema, M.W. and Scheltema, M. (2003), *Gemeenschappelijk recht: Wisselwerking tussen publiek- en privaatrecht*, Kluwer: Deventer, at 178-179.
521 Van der Jagt (2006) at 75.
522 Ibid., at 127; Van Wijk/Konijnenbelt & Van Male (2014) at 253.
523 Scheltema and Scheltema (2003) at 179.

the Government Gazette (*Staatscourant*). Arrangements between public administrative authorities and the private sector can be published, but this is not always the case.

Turning to the conclusion of supervisory arrangements by BFT specifically, the Evaluation committee observed in 2009 that the outsourcing of AML supervision to professional associations was necessary for an effective and efficient supervisory practice and recommended the conclusion of more supervisory arrangements.[524] This was partially influenced by the fact that the BFT had inadequate resources and capacity in relation to all the professionals for which it had supervisory responsibility under the AML Act.[525] The supervisory arrangements between the BFT and the professional associations should contain, according to the Evaluation Committee, agreements made in relation to the exercise of AML supervision, the embedding thereof within the quality audits by the professional associations, and contain a clear demarcation between the respective responsibilities of the professional associations and the BFT. It seems that the recommendations were aimed mostly at the conclusion of arrangements with professional associations for civil-law notaries and lawyers.[526] And they were also mostly directed towards cooperation with professional associations that are established and regulated by law. Since the evaluation, the BFT has concluded various supervisory arrangements. In its annual report for 2012 it considered that: '[b]ased on so-called (supervisory) arrangements the KNB, NFB, SRA, CKO and the Dutch Bar Association have performed supervision of their own members.[527] These quality-improving visits varied per group of professionals and coverage. In some cases the BFT receives the actual names of non-complying professionals, while in other cases the associations only provide the aggregate findings to the BFT. Important is that the respective professional association shows societal engagement and confirms the importance of (compliance with) the preventive anti-money laundering legislation to its members' (*own translation, MB*).[528] In early 2014 two supervisory arrangements were still in force.[529]

Supervisory arrangement with the SRA

In June 2012 the BFT entered into a supervisory arrangement with the Association of Registered Accountants and Accounting Consultants (*Samenwerkende Registeraccountants en Accountants-administratieconsulenten*, SRA). It entered into force on the 1st of October 2012.

524 Evaluatiecommissie Bureau Financieel Toezicht (2009) at 29 and 37-38.

525 Cf. Faure et al. (2009) at 112-113.

526 Evaluatiecommissie Bureau Financieel Toezicht (2009) at 37-38.

527 KNB = Royal Dutch Association of Civil-law Notaries; NFB = Netherlands Federation of Tax Advisors, CKO = Quality Audit College (part of one of the two former professional associations in the accountancy sector). The CKO ceased to exist in January 2013 when the Dutch Institute of Chartered Accountants came into existence. See § 5.5.3. I will discuss the SRA in the next subsection.

528 Bureau Financieel Toezicht (2012) at 26.

529 Besides the supervisory arrangement with the SRA, the BFT has had an arrangement in place since 2008 with the Register Belastingadviseurs (Register of Tax Advisors, RB). This was updated on 17 June 2011. The supervisory arrangement is not publicly available. See: *Het Register: Vakblad van het Register Belastingadviseurs*, vol. 2, issue 11 (November 2011), at 41.

> Unlike the Dutch Institute of Chartered Accountants, the SRA is a private network association founded in 1989.[530] Around 370 accountancy firms with around 20,000 professionals, including accountants, tax advisors, and other professionals, are SRA members. Members are accountancy firms that perform their tasks particularly in the small and medium-sized business sector or in the agricultural sector.[531] SRA membership is not regulated or protected by law, although being an SRA member is said to indicate a high degree of quality.[532] SRA has an internal disciplinary system, which is not statutory in nature. Within the SRA an independent review committee performs monitoring and quality audits of the accountancy firms.[533] The SRA's internal auditing system was accredited by the professional associations NIVRA/NOvAA when these professional associations started to perform internal quality audits as well.[534] The current accreditation from the NBA allows the SRA to supervise its own members. The NBA does not in principle do reviews of individual accountants who are employed with an accountancy firm that is an SRA member.[535] The SRA has also concluded an arrangement with the AFM concerning supervision on the quality of statutory audits performed by audit firms pursuant to the Audit Firms Supervision Act, as well as with the DTCA on fiscal matters.[536]

The arrangement between the BFT and SRA covers around 20% of the total number of accountancy firms. It cannot be estimated how many individual accountants are involved.[537] The arrangement is not based on legislation, because the AML Act does not contain any provisions on this point. The supervisory arrangement lays down that it is complementary to the powers from the BFT stemming from the AML Act and explicitly states that it does not replace these powers. There is no transfer of public law powers from the BFT to the SRA. The SRA exercises supervision based on its own internal norms.[538] Lamentably, the arrangement is not publicly available even though there are no legal restrictions on its publication.[539] The choice of the BFT to outsource a part of its AML supervision of accountants is an important aspect within its supervisory approach and should, in light of the requirements of transparency and accountability stemming from the theoretical framework, be publicly available.

The supervisory arrangement lays down that the SRA bears its own responsibility for the exercise of the AML supervision of its members in terms of depth and scope, but that it must

530 In Dutch: *Vereniging*. Interview SRA, May 2013.

531 Article 4 of the SRA Articles of Association, available at: <www.sra.nl/over-sra/lid-worden-van-sra/statuten-van-sra>, last visited on 28 April 2014.

532 Interview SRA, May 2013.

533 Section 2 *Reviewreglement SRA* (in English: *SRA Review Regulations*), available at <www.sra.nl/kantoorondersteuning/review/reviewreglement>, last visited on 28 April 2014.

534 Interview Nederlandse Beroepsorganisatie van Accountants, June 2013.

535 Ibid.; Raad voor Toezicht NBA (2012), *Verslag van werkzaamheden 2012*, at 16.

536 *Convenant tussen de Stichting Autoriteit Financiële Markten en de vereniging voor Samenwerkende Registeraccountants en Accountants-administratieconsulenten inzake samenwerking op het gebied van toezicht op accountantsorganisaties*, Stcrt. 2012/4462.

537 Nederlandse Beroepsorganisatie van Accountants (2012) at 5.

538 Section 2 SRA Review Regulations.

539 This was last verified on 28 April 2014 on the websites of the Financial Supervision Office and the SRA. The supervisory arrangement was, however, made available to me during the interview with the SRA for research purposes. I have been allowed to use and to refer to the supervisory arrangement for the purposes of this research: Interview SRA, May 2013.

report on a periodic basis to the BFT, as well as immediately upon the identification of a breach which is not minor in nature.[540] Whether or not sanctions are required is ultimately to be decided by the BFT.[541] The SRA is required to subject at least 10% of its members annually to a specific AML audit or to general quality audits within which attention is paid to compliance with the AML Act.[542] The BFT oversees this activity and does not carry out regular AML inspections on SRA member firms and accountants working at such firms. The BFT may still carry out risk-based visits. The arrangement leaves it to the SRA's discretion which members it will subject to AML supervision. The names of members subject to AML(-related) audits must be reported to the BFT. The latter can request the SRA to visit specific members. SRA AML(-related) audits are always on-site in nature.[543] During the audits the SRA is obliged to verify whether the member has a procedure for the exercise of customer due diligence and whether any disclosures were made to FIU-NL. The SRA must always perform checks on a number of client and/or transaction files to see if the procedures are followed in practice. The BFT and SRA have jointly created a detailed list which contains all aspects that the latter must assess during an audit.[544] After the audit, SRA reviewers must lay down their findings in writing. The findings must be tested on the basis of an evaluative framework which has been established by the BFT.[545] This results in five possible scores. When the SRA concludes that a firm is to be awarded one of the two lowest scores, it should immediately report this to the BFT. In other cases, the SRA can allow the SRA member to overcome the breaches without reporting directly to the BFT.

The supervisory arrangement states that the BFT is at all times allowed to request all information contained in the AML files from the SRA and that the SRA must comply with this request.[546] At the same time, however, the arrangement states that SRA members cannot invoke legal professional privilege against SRA reviewers, and that before an AML audit the members are requested to sign a declaration in which they allow the SRA reviewer to disclose any information obtained during the review to the BFT. Above we have seen in which situations accountants could invoke a (derived) legal professional privilege against the BFT.[547] The text of the supervisory arrangement suggests that upon request from the BFT, the SRA is obliged to forward the privileged information that it has obtained during the reviews to the BFT.[548] This undermines the professional privilege of the accountants and creates an unequal level playing field with accountants that are directly subject to BFT supervision. The text of the arrangement should be amended so that SRA reviewers are not allowed or obliged to share privileged information received from SRA members during an audit with the BFT. In the last place, the arrangement deals with aspects like the training of SRA reviewers by the BFT, the reporting of findings of AML audits to the SRA

540 Section 4(1) and Sections 7 and 9(5) BFT-SRA Supervisory Arrangement (hereafter 'Supervisory Arrangement').
541 Section 9 Supervisory Arrangement.
542 Section 2(1) Supervisory Arrangement.
543 Section 2(6) Supervisory Arrangement.
544 Annex 2 to the Supervisory Arrangement.
545 Section 5(1) Supervisory Arrangement.
546 Section 11(2) in conjunction with Section 6(4) Supervisory Arrangement.
547 See § 5.8.1.2 and 5.8.1.3.
548 The BFT does not share this view: Interview Bureau Financieel Toezicht, June 2013.

members themselves, the costs in relation to the exercise of supervision pursuant to the supervisory arrangement and some other aspects.[549]

> An interesting aspect that arises from the supervisory arrangement is the question whether the BFT is allowed to exchange supervisory information that it has obtained from the SRA with other AML supervisors. This will be discussed in § 5.9.

How many times the SRA has performed AML, or related audits within the general 10%-obligation, and how many times it has identified offences cannot be said.[550] The SRA does not publish any information on this and at the time of finalising this chapter the annual report for 2012 is the last available report from the BFT. Considering that the arrangement entered into force in 2012, information on this should be found in the annual report for 2013. Hence, at this moment in time nothing can be said about the functioning of the arrangement in practice.

The informal role of the NBA

The BFT and the Dutch Institute of Chartered Accountants (NBA) have not entered into a supervisory arrangement.[551] It is also unlikely that in the near future such an arrangement will be entered into.[552] Back in 2012 the Supervisory Council of the NOvAA was of the opinion that there was no legal basis on the basis of which results from internal audits could be communicated to the BFT.[553] The NIVRA and NOvAA did have this power on the basis of the Registered Accountants and the Accountant Consultants Acts with respect to the AFM. This has now been laid down in Section 24 Accountancy Profession Act which regulates cooperation with the AFM insofar as this is required under the Audit Firms Supervision Act. In her research Stouten recommended to amend the Acts, or to create a legal basis for an information gateway from the professional associations (now the NBA) to the BFT in the Accountancy Profession Act.[554] This recommendation has not been followed. The NBA's current opinion is that it cannot share with the BFT any individual results of quality audits performed by the NBA. Therefore, it only forwards its general annual reports with respect to the activities carried out by the Council for Supervision to the BFT.[555]

> As regards the informal involvement of the predecessors of the NBA in AML supervision and sanctioning, the NIVRA and NOvAA, Stouten concluded in 2012 that although there are common grounds between the quality controls on the basis of internal professional norms and the supervision of compliance with obligations on the basis of the AML Act, both professional associations did not pay attention to compliance with this Act. The NOvAA did not consider supervision with regard to AML compliance to be part of its

549 Sections 3, 6, 12-14 Supervisory Arrangement.

550 The SRA applies a six-year inspection cycle and supervision on a risk-oriented basis: Interview SRA, May 2013.

551 Stouten (2012) at 406.

552 Interview Bureau Financieel Toezicht, June 2013; Interview Nederlandse Beroepsorganisatie van Accountants, June 2013.

553 Stouten (2012) at 404.

554 Ibid.

555 Interview Nederlandse Beroepsorganisatie van Accountants, June 2013.

tasks, while NIVRA's internal quality controls did not actively include the verification of compliance with anti-money laundering obligations.[556]

The NBA sees an important role for itself in providing advice and guidance on AML compliance to accountants and accountancy firms on its website.[557] To that effect, it has published a guidance document on its website which NBA members can follow.[558] Compliance with the AML Act is also an aspect that is always assessed in internal quality audits performed by the Council for Supervision of the NBA.[559] Before NBA reviewers go on-site for a quality audit, firms are required to complete a questionnaire concerning their internal system of quality assurance.[560] Parts of the questionnaire concern compliance with the AML Act: the questionnaire in relation to assurance services contains 14 questions on the AML Act, and the questionnaire for assurance-related services includes 13 questions. The FATF mentioned that the predecessors of the NBA had peer review mechanisms in place which included on-site visits to accountants every six years and that 'the time dedicated to the implementation of the AML/CFT was estimated to be approximately 30 minutes'.[561] The annual report on the activities of the Council for Supervision of the NBA states that one of the most common grounds for providing an instruction with respect to the improvement of the internal quality assurance systems of accountancy firms relates to compliance with the AML Act.[562] This, however, is the only reference to the AML Act and leaves a lot of room for guesswork.[563] It is, for example, not clear how many times such an instruction has been issued or in which cases disciplinary complaints have been filed in relation to this non-compliance. In any case, there are more and more disciplinary actions against accountants by the NBA and its predecessors for (also) not complying with preventive AML obligations. For the period of January 2008 until April 2014, I was able to find seven disciplinary cases initiated by the NBA that included non-compliance with the AML Act, against one disciplinary case initiated by the BFT.[564]

556 Stouten (2012) at 392-406.

557 Interview Nederlandse Beroepsorganisatie van Accountants, June 2013.

558 *Nederlandse Beroepsorganisatie van Accountants, Handreiking 1124 – Richtsnoeren ter voorkoming van witwassen en financieren van terrorisme (WWFT) voor belastingadviseurs en accountants*, February 2014.

559 Interview Nederlandse Beroepsorganisatie van Accountants, June 2013.

560 These are so-called 'oriëntatievragenlijsten'.

561 FATF (2011) at 233.

562 Raad voor Toezicht NBA (2012) at 15.

563 Ibid.

564 Search in the database on <www.tuchtrecht.nl>. Reference period: 1st of January 2008 – 31st of March 2014. Search terms: 'BFT', 'Bureau Financieel Toezicht', 'witwassen', 'Wwft', 'Wet melding ongebruikelijke transacties', 'Wet identificatie bij dienstverlening'. Altogether, I was able to find a total of ten disciplinary cases: seven were initiated by NBA, one by BFT, one by the Public Prosecution Service and one anonymous complainant: Case 10/1991 Wtra AK, 9 May 2011, ECLI:NL:TACAKN:2011:YH0167; Case 12/1168 en 12/1169, 8 February 2013, ECLI:NL:TACAKN:2013:YH0342; Case 12/1955 Wtra AK, 1 July 2013, ECLI:NL:TACAKN:2013:2; Case 12/2450 Wtra AK, 30 September 2013, ECLI:NL:TACAKN:2013:47, Case 12/2338 Wtra AK, 30 September 2013, ECLI:NL:TACAKN:2013:45; Case 13/852 Wtra AK, 11 November 2013, ECLI:NL:TACAKN:2013:64; Case 13/1145 Wtra AK, 2 December 2013, ECLI:NL:TACAKN:2013:67; Case 13/1476 Wtra AK, 20 December 2013, ECLI:NL:TACAKN:2013:75; Case 12/2337 Wtra AK, 20 December 2013, ECLI:NL:TACAKN:2013:78; and Case 13/2415 Wtra AK, 14 March 2014, ECLI:NL:TACAKN:2014:24.

Considering that the NBA is the professional association for the accountancy sector established and regulated by public law, that all individual accountants are included in its register, and in light of the fact that the NBA seems to be more active in starting disciplinary cases that include non-compliance with the AML Act than the BFT, it is disappointing that there is very little to no cooperation with the BFT. The results of quality audits could help to diminish the resource problems that the BFT seems to face. It can at the same time provide input for its risk-based supervision and, thus, make the BFT's supervision more effective. It is important that the Dutch legislator creates a legal basis for cooperation between the NBA and BFT and that both authorities are convinced of the need for cooperation on this point. The conclusion of a supervisory arrangement that is, in terms of its content, similar to the one concluded with the SRA would increase the effectiveness of the BFT's AML supervision of accountants.

5.8.2.3 Awareness-raising activities

Finally, the BFT pays a lot of attention to the creation of awareness in relation to the AML obligations. It appears that it undertakes a wide variety of activities, including presentations, its website, interviews, publications, the training of auditors and active support for the relevant professional associations.[565] The BFT considers that an important part of its awareness-raising activities concerns the continuation and maintenance of relationships with all relevant stakeholders. All BFT activities under this pillar have the aim of increasing knowledge among the supervised population and their professional associations concerning AML obligations, as well as the importance of compliance.

5.8.3 Sanctioning powers

5.8.3.1 Sanctioning powers stemming from the AML Act

The Financial Supervision Office also derives its sanctioning powers from the AML Act and lower-level regulations. The three administrative sanctioning instruments available are the incremental penalty payment, the administrative fine and instructions, and were explained in § 5.6.3.1. The lack of the power to publish sanctioning decisions in the AML Act was discussed before.[566] Like the other two supervisors, the BFT can first turn to more informal instruments such as a signalling meeting with the professional in question, or an informal warning. Those measures are aimed at persuading the non-complying institution or professional to comply with the legislation in force before applying more stringent sanctions. In the most severe cases the BFT can decide to file a criminal complaint.[567] The BFT can use these sanctioning powers against accountancy firms only. It cannot impose the incremental penalty payments or the administrative fines against individual accountants, because for them a statutory disciplinary law regime applies.[568]

565 Bureau Financieel Toezicht (2012) at 26.
566 See § 5.6.3 and 5.7.3.
567 See § 5.6.3.4.
568 Sections 26(2) and 27(2) AML Act.

5.8.3.2 Sanctioning via disciplinary law

Individual accountants should be sanctioned via disciplinary law for acting in breach of the AML Act. When the BFT considers that an individual accountant should be sanctioned, it must file a complaint with the Accountants' Chamber (*Accountantskamer*) and on appeal with the Trade and Industry Appeals Tribunal in The Hague.[569] It is in this case not the AML supervisor itself that imposes a sanction, but the disciplinary tribunal. The Accountants Disciplinary Law Act provides the Accountants' Chamber with the following disciplinary sanctions:[570]

- warning (*waarschuwing*)
- reprimand (*berisping*)
- disciplinary fine of a minimum of 3 and a maximum of 8,100 Euros[571]
- temporary exclusion from the accountants' register for a maximum period of one year
- permanent exclusion from the accountants' register

The range of sanctions against accountants under the disciplinary law system is wider than in the AML Act. Both the warning and reprimand are a caution, but the difference is that a reprimand contains a clear reproach on the negligent behaviour of the accountant concerned. A warning rather highlights the incorrectness of certain behaviour in light of the proper exercise of the accountancy profession, and is milder in nature. The Accountants Disciplinary Law Act provides for the possibility to combine the fine with the other available sanctions.[572] The maximum amount of the fine is 8,100 Euros; however, this is much lower than under the AML Act (a cap of 1 million Euros[573]) which can question the dissuasiveness of the disciplinary fine. On the other hand, contrary to the AML Act, the Act provides for the publication of the judgement in which the sanctions are imposed.[574] This could be regarded as some type of naming & shaming like the DNB's power under the Financial Supervision Act.[575] In practice, however, it appears that the judgments are usually published in an anonymised fashion. The sanctions under the Accountants Disciplinary Law Act give the impression that these are more aimed at restoration, rather than on real punishment. This fits the character of a disciplinary sanctioning system, but may not in all cases be equivalent to the administrative law sanctioning regime under the AML Act as was just outlined for the fine.

Nevertheless, although disciplinary law and administrative law sanctioning are mutually exclusive under the AML Act, the BFT can decide to take action both against the accountancy firm and individual accountants at the same time, if the circumstances of the

569 The Accountants' Chamber is based in Zwolle and is part of the District Court of Zwolle-Lelystad. Its composition varies, but is always dominated by members of the judiciary, supplemented by one or more members of the accounting profession. See for more information: <www.accountantskamer.nl>.

570 *Wet tuchtrechtspraak accountants* (in English: *Accountants Disciplinary Law Act, ADLA)*: Section 2(1) ADLA.

571 Section 5 ADLA in conjunction with Section 23(4) Dutch Criminal Code.

572 Section 2(2) ADLA.

573 See § 5.6.3.1.

574 Section 2(3) ADLA.

575 See § 5.6.3.2.

case so require. This means that it can impose administrative sanctions on the accountancy firm and file a disciplinary complaint against individual accountants at the Accountants' Chamber. Likewise, disciplinary law and criminal law enforcement do not exclude one another.

5.8.3.3 Discussion about disciplinary law sanctioning

Opinions on the preference for either disciplinary law or administrative law sanctioning in the Netherlands diverge. At the time of the introduction of the AML Act, the Government was of the opinion that compliance with the anti-money laundering obligations would be part of the professional norms of legal and fiscal service providers. It considered that administrative law sanctioning could lead to concurrence whereby both the administrative courts and disciplinary tribunals would have to adjudicate (part of) the professional's behaviour.[576] Professional associations would be the first gatekeeper in verifying compliance with the AML obligations. The Evaluation Committee of the BFT was also of the opinion that in principle disciplinary law is preferred over administrative law. It considered that disciplinary tribunals can view the actions of the non-compliant professional as a whole and, where necessary, take into account other aspects of professionalism which can lead to less stringent or heavier disciplinary actions.[577] Moreover, it preferred this type of sanctioning in light of BFT's limited resources and capacity.[578]

However, research from Faure et al. proved that disciplinary law enforcement under the AML Act has been limited in quantitative terms. Empirical research demonstrated that the pace and dissuasiveness of the disciplinary interventions are questionable, and that disciplinary law sanctioning does not live up to the expectations that the Government had upon drafting the legislation.[579] In her research also Stouten had reservations about the use of disciplinary law for enforcing compliance with the Dutch AML Act. She concluded, among other things, that the reliance on disciplinary law was at odds with the principle of equivalence, because of the limited possibility to publish disciplinary sanctions (particularly with respect to lawyers and civil-law notaries), the absence of the power to impose an incremental penalty payment or to impose provisional sanctions, and because of the absence of the power to impose a fine more or less equal to the power under the AML Act.[580] This made disciplinary fines a non-dissuasive power. On the other hand, Faure et al. observed that within the accountancy profession, there is the opinion that outsiders focus too much on the repressive side of disciplinary law. Proponents of the system argued that disciplinary actions against accountants can bring about severe reputational damage, and that in this context a warning or reprimand can already have severe consequences.[581]

576 *Parliamentary Papers II* 2004-05, 29 990, no. 3, at 9.
577 Evaluatiecommissie Bureau Financieel Toezicht (2009) at 47.
578 Ibid., at 35.
579 Faure et al. (2009) at 153-155.
580 Stouten (2012) at 438.
581 Faure et al. (2009) at 142.

Chapter 3 discussed the current legislative developments regarding the role of disciplinary law in the enforcement of the Dutch AML Act. Already since 2011 the Dutch Government has been trying to narrow down the role of disciplinary law by introducing the possibility of administrative law sanctions against lawyers, (junior) civil-law notaries and accountants. This confirms a shift in the belief that professionals should exclusively be sanctioned via statutory disciplinary law systems. At the time of finalising this chapter, the Bill has not yet entered into force, which means that until the moment of adoption individual accountants can only be sanctioned via disciplinary law.

5.8.4 Sanctioning policy and practice

The general administrative law doctrine concerning the duty to sanction applies to the BFT. It has a sanctioning policy, but this is not publicly available.[582] In June 2013, representatives stated that the Financial Supervision Office was working on a revision of its policy under the AML Act and that it aimed to publish this on its website.[583] The current information on the BFT's website only refers to the sanctions that it can impose, but not how it intends to use these powers.[584] In light of the theoretical framework of effective supervision, it is advised that the BFT publishes this policy on its website. The policy should at least include an explanation of the legal framework, the BFT's vision, the enforcement goals,[585] the desired level of enforcement (or compliance), the supervisory principles underlying the activities, as well as a general description of the procedures or methodology applied. It should, moreover, contain information on how the Financial Supervision Office acts when non-compliant behaviour is identified by professional associations under a supervisory arrangement with the BFT. This increases the BFT's transparency towards the supervised population and the general public. As explained, the BFT aims to perform AML supervision in a lenient manner where possible, and acts more dissuasively where necessary.[586] Representatives explained that the BFT in general applies a somewhat more lenient approach after regular supervisory visits, where the BFT mostly aims to create awareness, and to give guidance and education in order to comply with the AML Act. The BFT acts in a harder fashion after risk-based visits, since these are often the result of external signals that already identify potential non-compliant behaviour.[587]

With regard to the accountancy firms and individual accountants that are members of the SRA, the supervisory arrangement lays down that the BFT is responsible for the sanctioning of non-compliant behaviour.[588] The arrangement establishes a matrix with five categories. Highly compliant accountancy firms receive a score of 5, minor breaches result in scores of 4-3, whereas scores 2 and 1 indicate highly non-compliant behaviour.[589]

582 Cf. Stouten (2012) at 280.
583 Interview Bureau Financieel Toezicht, June 2013. See also: Bureau Financieel Toezicht (2012) at 11.
584 Bureau Financieel Toezicht, *Handhaving*, available at: <www.bureauft.nl/wwft/werkwijze-toezicht/Paginas/Handhaving.aspx>, last visited on 1 May 2014.
585 Inspiration can be drawn from: Smits et al. (2009) at 39.
586 Bureau Financieel Toezicht (2012) at 29.
587 Interview Bureau Financieel Toezicht, June 2013.
588 Section 9 SRA-BFT Supervisory Arrangement.
589 Annex I ('Normering van bevindingen') to the SRA-BFT Supervisory Arrangement.

When SRA reviewers give the member a score of 3 or 4, the SRA member is given the opportunity to still comply with the AML Act. Three months after the first visit, the member should inform the SRA whether it complies with the legislation and the reviewer can decide to carry out a follow-up visit.[590] In the case of scores 1 or 2, the SRA should directly inform the BFT in order to impose sanctions on the accountancy firm and/or to start disciplinary proceedings.

The Dutch Institute of Chartered Accountants (NBA) adopts an informal role in verifying AML compliance. When it establishes non-compliance with the AML legislation, it does not inform the BFT directly thereof.[591] Rather, it can give recommendations to accountancy firms on how to establish adequate internal procedures in order to comply with customer due diligence, reporting and record-keeping obligations, or decide to take disciplinary action against individual accountants. When it does so, the NBA embeds this non-compliant behaviour fully into the professional standards concerning the integrity and professional behaviour of the accountant.[592]

Regarding the sanctioning activity of the Financial Supervision Office against accountants, it appears that the information in the annual reports is not intelligible. In the reports, the BFT only reports on the total number of sanctions imposed for non-compliance with the AML Act for all professionals for which it has supervisory responsibility. Based on annual reports for the years 2010-2012, the BFT has imposed the following sanctions.

Table 6 – Administrative sanctions imposed by the BFT (overall)[593]

	2010	2011	2012
No sanction	-	6	-
Signalling meeting	12	8	2
Warning with an obligation to report on the progress	9	10	2
Warning without an obligation to report on the progress	4	2	5
Instruction	-	-	5
Intention to impose an incremental penalty payment	1	1	4
Incremental penalty payment	-	-	1
Intention to impose an administrative fine	-	-	3
Administrative fine	-	1	1
Disciplinary complaint	-	-	1
Unfinished sanctioning procedures	-	7	6

590 Section 9(2), 9(3), and 9(4) SRA-BFT Supervisory Arrangement.
591 See § 5.8.2.2.
592 For example: Case 12/2450 Wtra AK, 30 September 2013, par. 4.7 and Case 13/852 Wtra AK, 11 November 2013, par. 4.8. In both cases reference was made to the Professional Code for Accountants, particularly Article B1-210.3 VGC (acceptance of clients).
593 Own table based on data from Bureau Financieel Toezicht (2010) at 22; Bureau Financieel Toezicht (2011) at 28 (Table 8) and Bureau Financieel Toezicht (2012), at 29.

The table suggests that the BFT's sanctioning activity has increased during the years 2010-2012. Unfortunately, the numbers presented do not allow one to disentangle the sanctioning activity from the BFT on accountants specifically. Presumably, the sanctioning activity has not been very high in this period, because until 2013 the BFT's own supervision focussed mostly on civil-law notaries. A second reason for this presumption is that until January 2013 the BFT could only take (disciplinary) action against individual accountants. This changed with the inclusion of accountancy firms under the scope of the AML Act.[594] Thirdly, information on sanctioning activity following from the supervisory arrangement between the SRA and BFT is not (yet) included, because the arrangement only entered into force in October 2012.

For formal action taken against individual accountants, the database with disciplinary cases heard by the Accountants' Chamber reflectss a total of ten disciplinary cases against accountants that include non-compliance with the AML Act.[595] It was already pointed out that seven of these cases were brought forward by the NBA.[596] This shows the important role that the NBA plays in ensuring compliance with preventive AML obligations by accountants. Non-compliance with the AML Act formed part of the broader complaints and in all cases accountants were sanctioned. Sanctions varied from a reprimand to exclusion from the accountants' register. In one case the BFT successfully followed the disciplinary procedure against two accountants.[597] In February 2013, two accountants were sanctioned for, inter alia, not identifying the client according to the standards of the Dutch AML Act and not reporting unusual transactions. In this case concerning possible VAT fraud, the BFT filed a disciplinary complaint after a risk-based visit which was instigated as the result of a signal received from the Public Prosecution Service.[598] The Accountants' Chamber decided that the accountants had not identified their client in the way they ought to have done and that the accountants should have been aware of the incorrect VAT declarations for which they should have filed an unusual transaction report to the FIU. Both accountants were sanctioned with a reprimand. The case has been published in an anonymised manner. Altogether the procedure took eight months. According to BFT representatives, more disciplinary law cases against accountants are currently pending.[599]

5.8.5 Concluding remarks

The Financial Supervision Office has adequate supervisory powers in relation to accountants, although it lacks regulatory powers and there are some delicate issues in relation to legal professional privilege. Accountants may, under certain circumstances, invoke professional privilege via Section 1(2) Wwft. Accountants, in particular forensic

594 See § 5.5.3.1.

595 Supra, n. 565. Reference period: 1st of January 2008-31st of March 2014. Search terms: 'BFT', 'Bureau Financieel Toezicht', 'witwassen', 'Wet melding ongebruikelijke transacties', 'Wet identificatie bij dienstverlening'.

596 See § 5.8.2.2.

597 Case 12/1168 en 12/1169, 8 February 2013, ECLI:NL:TACAKN:2013:YH0342. This is the one disciplinary complaint as laid down in Table 6 above.

598 Interview Bureau Financieel Toezicht, June 2013.

599 Interview Bureau Financieel Toezicht, June 2013.

accountants, may also invoke a derived privilege and a duty of secrecy when they perform activities under the assignment of lawyers. The law is not sufficiently clear on how, particularly, the derived privilege and the duty of secrecy work through with respect to the supervision performed by the Financial Supervision Office. It has now developed a way through which it can marginally check whether an accountant justifiably invokes the (derived) privilege and secrecy. When it finds an abuse, however, the BFT must make a reasonable case that there is actually an abuse. Moreover, the AML Act should be amended on the matter of legal professional privilege, because it conflicts with the Third Directive.

The BFT applies a three-track approach in its AML supervision: the raising of awareness, the conclusion of supervisory arrangements with professional associations and the exercise of regular and risk-based supervision. Regarding the exercise of supervision, the BFT has internal, annual supervision plans. Risk-based supervision by the BFT is mostly the result of external signals from the police, the DTCA, the Public Prosecution Service, other AML supervisors, professional associations and so on. In practice, it appears that regular supervision outweighs risk-based supervision. This gives the impression that the BFT's risk-based approach in relation to AML supervision is rather reactive and plays a limited role in its supervision. It appears that until 2013 accountants were included in regular and risk-based supervision by the BFT but that the inspection intensity was low in light of the total number of accountants that fall under the scope of the AML Act. Resources issues could be an explanation for this. The outsourcing of AML supervision to professional associations may be used to strengthen the BFT's AML supervision in practice. The Financial Supervision Office has entered into a supervisory arrangement with a private professional association called the SRA. This arrangement is not publicly available, but it should be published in light of the theoretical framework of effective supervision. The arrangement covers around 20% of the total number of accountancy firms and it entered into force in October 2012. The arrangement states clearly what the SRA must do and what the role of the BFT is. The arrangement should, however, be amended on one point. The text of the arrangement suggests that upon a request from the BFT, the SRA is obliged to forward the privileged information that it has obtained during the reviews to the BFT. This undermines the professional privilege of the accountants and creates an unequal level playing field with other accountants. Unfortunately, no data is available as yet on the practical implementation of the arrangement. The BFT has no supervisory arrangement with the Dutch Institute of Chartered Accountants (NBA) in place. Considering that NBA is the professional association for the accountancy sector established and regulated by public law, that all accountants are included in its register, and in light of the fact that the NBA has been more active than the BFT in starting disciplinary cases that include non-compliance with the AML Act, it is unfortunate that there is little to no cooperation between the two organisations. The results of the NBA's quality audits could help to diminish the resource that the Financial Supervision Office seems to face and at the same time provide input for its risk-based supervision. It is important that the legislator steps in by creating a legal possibility for the NBA to forward individual supervisory information to the BFT and that both authorities are convinced of the need for cooperation on this point.

The BFT has adequate sanctioning powers in relation to accountancy firms, although the legislator should also provide for a discretionary power for AML supervisors to publish sanctioning decisions. For individual accountants, the BFT must (still) resort to the use of disciplinary law. Disciplinary law sanctioning is the task of the Accountants' Chamber, which has, in principle, a wide range of sanctions available. In terms of the dissuasiveness of the individual disciplinary sanctions, however, there may be some reservations. Particularly the low maximum amount of a disciplinary fine compared to the fines that can be imposed under the AML Act, and the fact that judgments, if published, are published in an anonymous fashion, are not particularly dissuasive. The BFT has no public sanctioning policy in which it describes its vision, enforcement goals and the desired level of compliance in the preventive AML policy, the general principles and procedure applied, or information on how the BFT acts when non-compliant behaviour is identified by professional associations under a supervisory arrangement. It should publish such policy in order to be transparent and accountable. In practice, it appears impossible to give a full outline of the sanctions imposed against accountancy firms. Data in the BFT's annual reports is not intelligible. For various reasons it is presumed that the BFT's own sanctioning activity has not been very high in the period 2010-12. Regarding the use of disciplinary law, it could be observed that the NBA has been far more active than the BFT. The NBA started seven disciplinary cases which included non-compliance with the AML Act, compared to one case initiated by the BFT. This is another reason why a supervisory arrangement between the BFT and the NBA should be concluded.

5.9 Supervisory cooperation for the prevention of money laundering

The theoretical framework of effective supervision requires adequate possibilities for cooperation between the supervisors, and between supervisors and other stakeholders. It is important that relevant supervisory information can be, and is shared with the relevant partners. In its mutual evaluation report, the FATF concluded that the bodies established for cooperation were not all used effectively.[600] The Dutch Court of Audit had already reported about a poor exchange of information between stakeholders in the anti-money laundering policy back in 2008.[601] The AML Act and other mechanisms have allowed the creation of various forums for cooperation between the AML supervisors themselves, and with other stakeholders like the FIU. This section focuses on the domestic cooperation efforts between AML supervisors and, to an extent, between AML supervisors and the FIU. First I pay attention to the more institutionalised forums for AML cooperation, followed by an exposition of some individual liaisons of the DNB, Bureau Supervision Wwft and BFT.

5.9.1 Institutionalised forums for AML cooperation on a policy and operational level

Four institutionalised cooperative efforts are particularly relevant to the anti-money laundering supervisors. This first is the AML coordination meeting. The second effort concerns the Financial Expertise Centre (*Financieel Expertise Centrum, FEC*) and the third

600 FATF (2011) at 271.
601 Algemene Rekenkamer (2008a) at 22-23.

is the National Task Force on Tackling the Misuse of Real Estate (*Nationale Regiegroep Aanpak Misbruik Vastgoed).* The fourth forum is the Committee on the duty to disclose unusual transactions. There are various other initiatives as well involving some AML supervisors and law enforcement authorities, but these are excluded here because these initiatives do not include all AML supervisors.[602]

5.9.1.1 AML coordination meeting (Wwft Toezichthoudersoverleg)

The AML coordination meeting is the primary forum for cooperation between the supervisors on a policy level. All four AML supervisors participate in this meeting, as well as the FIU. Meetings take place every two months and during these meetings the supervisors and the FIU share information of general interest, such as general supervisory information, legislative developments, trends and typologies. The FATF considers that the meetings have 'an open agenda. The FIU reports that the supervisors (and especially the DNB) play an active part in this process. (...) The group discusses risks arising from different entities'.[603] During various interviews it was confirmed that the meetings take place regularly, around 4-5 times a year, and that the AML supervisors find that it is a useful forum for cooperation.[604] This forum is not used for the exchange of supervisory information between the individual AML supervisors, which means that for now I only deal with the legal possibilities for an information gateway from the FIU to the AML supervisors and the other way around.

5

Information from the FIU to the AML supervisors

The AML coordination meeting is particularly important for the exchange of relevant information between AML supervisors and the FIU. During the meetings the FIU can give feedback on the quality of the reports it has received, pursuant to Section 13(g) AML Act. This provision allows the FIU to provide intelligence to the AML supervisors on the disclosure behaviour of obliged institutions and professionals. The FIU can share the information on its own motion within the AML coordination meeting or with the individual AML supervisors, when the FIU is of the opinion that institutions do not (fully) comply with the reporting obligation. The AML supervisors can subsequently on the basis of this information verify compliance and take measures where necessary. The supervisors can also request the FIU for this kind of information upon performing or after a supervisory visit. Section 13(g) AML Act allows the FIU to provide general feedback to the AML supervisors on reporting trends – both in quantitative and qualitative

602 An example is the 'Vastgoed Intelligence Centre', a cooperative effort between the DTCA, the Public Prosecution Service, the police and FIU-NL in the field of commercial real estate: FIU Nederland (2009), *Jaarverslag 2009*, at 28. Another example is the 'Markttoezichthoudersberaad', an informal cooperative effort by the market regulators in the Netherlands. Both the DNB and the AFM participate in this initiative. See: Intentieverklaring Markttoezichthoudersberaad, March 2009, available at: <www.dnb.nl/binaries/intentieverklaring_markttoezichthoudersberaad_tcm46-251000.pdf>, last visited: 2 May 2014.

603 FATF (2011) at 270.

604 Interview Financial Intelligence Unit Nederland, June 2013; Interview Bureau Financieel Toezicht, June 2013.

terms[605] – but not about the content of individual disclosures or the subjects mentioned in the disclosure. In the Explanatory Memorandum to the Act, the Government stated that the information from the FIU to the AML supervisors cannot, in principle, contain information on the content of the disclosures. The Government considered that information on the content of UTRs would not be necessary for verifying compliance with the reporting obligation or for the development of the supervisors' supervision policies.[606] Arguments for this statement are not given which is lamentable, because in my opinion that kind of information would actually allow the AML supervisors to compare records and files obtained from the obliged institutions themselves with the disclosures as received from the FIU.[607] Allowing the AML supervisors to compare information from different sources, instead of relying fully on the documentation of the obliged institution alone, makes this information more reliable and useful for the verification of compliance with the preventive anti-money laundering obligations.

It should be pointed out that an even more stringent regime applies to unusual transaction reports that after initial research have been declared suspicious by the FIU. The Police Data Act (*Wet Politiegegevens, Wpolg)* applies to information stemming from UTRs that have been declared suspicious by the Dutch FIU (and by that have become suspicious transaction reports). The Police Data Act only allows the sharing of police information insofar as this is required for the purposes mentioned in the Police Data Act and that the information is only processed by police staff which have been authorised.[608] The Act and Decree issued under the Act do not provide for the provision of police data, i.e. the UTRs that have been declared suspicious, to the AML supervisors.[609]

A possibility for the FIU to provide information on the content of disclosures, especially of unusual transaction reports, would in particular be beneficial to the Bureau Supervision Wwft since its information position is relatively weak and its supervisory activities with respect to smaller businesses are mostly focused on a transaction or client-file level.[610] Representatives from the DNB and the Bureau Supervision Wwft indicated during interviews that receiving information from the FIU on the content of individual disclosures made to the FIU would increase the effectiveness of their AML supervision.

605 E.g. the number of disclosed reports to the FIU by a particular sector; the number of disclosed reports by individual institutions or professionals; the number of reports based on objective or subjective thresholds.

606 *Parliamentary Papers II*, 2007-08, 31 238, no. 3, at 26.

607 Cf. Van den Broeke, P.J. and Hoff, R.J. (2008), *Memo Wet ter voorkoming van witwassen en financieren van terrorisme*, Kluwer: Deventer, at 101-102.

608 Sections 3 and 6(1) *Wet houdende regels inzake de verwerking van politiegegevens (Wet politiegegevens)*, Stb. 2007, 300.

609 With *intervention from the Public Prosecution Service*, police data may be shared with the DNB (and the AFM) under very strict conditions (*emphasis added, MB*). For the DNB: Section 4:3(2) Police Data Decree. One of the purposes for which police data may be shared with the DNB is the control on the level of compliance with Sections 3:10 and 3:17 Wft which, as we have already seen in this chapter, are (also) used as the starting point of the DNB's AML supervision. Whether this means that the DNB can use this information for its AML supervision is, however, extremely doubtful. Neither the Act nor the explanatory memorandum discusses this matter. From an equivalence perspective, however, it could be argued that it should not be the case that the DNB can receive this type of information, whereas the other AML supervisors do not have such a possibility.

610 See § 5.7.2.4.

The representatives from the Financial Supervision Office considered that they already have an adequate relationship with the FIU.[611] The FIU is considering whether to provide each individual AML supervisor, periodically and on its own initiative, with analytical reports on the reporting behaviour of obliged institutions and professionals per category. In that way, the supervisors should get more insight about the money laundering trends and typologies and the behaviour of their supervisory population than before.[612]

Information from the AML supervisors to the FIU

In the flow of information from the AML supervisors to the FIU, the AML Act obliges the supervisors to inform the FIU when they, in the course of their supervisory activities, discover facts that may be an indication of money laundering or terrorist financing.[613] This can, in situations, even override the statutory secrecy regimes applicable to them.[614] The supervisors can inform the FIU during the AML coordination meetings, or directly. Often, however, AML supervisors agree with the supervisees that they will still make the disclosure themselves.[615]

*5.9.1.2 Financial Expertise Centre (*Financieel Expertise Centrum*)*

The Financial Expertise Centre (hereafter FEC) is a network of seven partners: the AFM, the DTCA, the DNB, the FIU-NL, the Fiscal Intelligence and Investigation Service of the DTCA (*FIOD*), the Public Prosecution Service and the National Police Force.[616] The basis for cooperation within the FEC is an agreement and the FEC information protocol 2014 (*Informatieprotocol FEC 2014*).[617] The FEC is governed by a Board (*FEC-raad*), which consists of representatives of the FEC partners on the administrative level. The Board meets at least three times yearly and decides, by consensus, on the activities of the FEC and gives direction to the FEC Unit (*FEC-eenheid*).[618] This Unit consists of staff from each of the seven FEC partners, who are seconded to this forum. Representatives of the Ministry of Security & Justice and the Ministry of Finance attend meetings of the FEC

611 Interview Bureau Financieel Toezicht, June 2013.

612 Interview Financial Intelligence Unit Nederland, June 2013.

613 Section 25 Wwft.

614 Section 25 Wwft states: 'zo nodig in afwijking van de toepasselijke wettelijke geheimhoudingsbepalingen'.

615 See for example § 5.7.4.

616 FIU-NL became a partner with the new agreement and until the new agreement the Dutch General Intelligence and Security Service (AIVD) was a FEC partner too. See about the development and institutional aspects of the FEC: Luchtman, M.J.J.P. Vervaele J.A.E. and Jansen, O.J.D.M.L (2002), *Informatie-uitwisseling in het kader van het Financieel Expertise Centrum*, research commissioned by the Ministry of Finance; Wagemakers, M. (2005), 'Verscherpt integriteittoezicht in de financiële sector', *Tijdschrift voor Financieel Recht*, issue 7, pp. 185-189; Van den Broek (2011b), 'Effectiviteit, publieke verantwoording en transparantie van het Financieel Expertise Centrum', *Tijdschrift voor Compliance*, issue 4/5, pp. 230-238; Van den Broek, M. and Popping, D. (2012), 'De governance van het Financieel Expertise Centrum', in: Nederlands Compliance Instituut, *Jaarboek Compliance 2013*, NCI, pp. 143-165.

617 *Convenant houdende de afspraken over samenwerking in het kader van het Financieel Expertise Centrum*, Stcrt. 2014, 2351. (This Agreement replaced the FEC Agreement from 2009, Stcrt. 2009, 71); *Informatieprotocol FEC 2014*, Stcrt. 2014, 7155 (this Information Protocol replaced the FEC Information Protocol 2011).

618 Sections 1(1) and 4(1), 4(5), 4(6), and 4(7) FEC Agreement 2014.

Board as an observer.[619] The FEC operates from the DNB's premises, but is not part of the DNB.[620] The overall objective of the FEC is to strengthen the integrity of the financial sector by encouraging, coordinating and expanding mutual cooperation between the partners through the exchange of information and the sharing of insights, knowledge and skills.[621] Cooperation within this forum takes places on both policy and an operational level, and its scope is wider than the preventive anti-money laundering policy alone. More specifically, the FEC is assigned three tasks:

- to create conditions for a structural exchange of information between the FEC partners;
- to set up a joint knowledge centre from, for and by the FEC partners in the (for the FEC) relevant areas; and
- to support and execute projects with the objective of obtaining concrete and, from an operational perspective, useful results.[622]

Regarding the exchange of information within the FEC, it is important to highlight the fact that there is no single legal framework and that the agreement also does not regulate anything on this matter. Therefore, the legal frameworks of the individual FEC partners apply.[623] Within the FEC, information is not always shared with all FEC partners. On the one hand, the law does not allow all FEC partners to share information amongst themselves, while, on the other hand, safeguards have been established via the FEC information protocol 2011 (now: FEC information protocol 2014) within the working process of the FEC.[624] In short, the procedure works as follows. FEC partners can bring their (personal) information to the FEC Unit. Upon disclosing this information, they must indicate for which specific aim the information can be processed and which other FEC partners may not receive this information. This is followed by a joint analysis of the information and a continuous dialogue between the FEC Unit and the FEC partner bringing in the information as how to process this information. Only after advice from the FEC is the information exchanged with the (selected) partners.[625]

Within the FEC, (the prevention of) money laundering is an important matter.[626] The 2012 annual report indicates that the FEC partners undertook a national threat assessment on money laundering.[627] In addition, the FEC also started some research projects within which attention was paid to money laundering.[628] In 2008, the Court of Audit found that within the AML/CTF policy the exchange of information between all relevant stakeholders

619 Section 4(3) FEC Agreement 2014.

620 Although the DNB gives account of the FEC in its annual reports, e.g. DNB (2012b) at 30. This is somewhat odd in light of the legal form of the FEC and gives the impression it is a part of the DNB.

621 Section 2 FEC Agreement 2014.

622 Section 3 FEC Agreement 2014.

623 Cf. Luchtman et al. (2002); Van den Broek (2011).

624 *Informatieprotocol FEC 2011 and toelichting bij het informatieprotocol*, both available at: <www.fec-partners.nl>. See also: Van den Broek (2011); Van den Broek and Popping (2012) at 151-153.

625 See: Van den Broek and Popping (2012) at 151-153. This system was introduced with the Information Protocol 2011 and is, with some changes, pursued by the FEC Information Protocol 2014.

626 FATF (2011) at 269-270.

627 Financieel Expertise Centrum (2012), *Jaarverslag 2012-2014 voor het jaar 2012*, at 14.

628 Ibid., at 20.

was insufficient, for which money laundering could not be combated effectively.[629] The Court of Audit therefore recommended to make the exchange of information in relation to combating money laundering an explicit task of the FEC, and that all AML supervisors, the FIU and authorities from the criminal law enforcement chain should participate in the forum.[630] At present, two AML supervisors participate in the FEC. The participation of the AFM and DNB is most prominently based on the provisions from the Financial Supervision Act, and a number of related sectoral acts.[631] On the basis of a thorough analysis of the respective legal frameworks of the FEC partners on the exchange of information, I concluded in earlier research that the legal basis in the Financial Supervision Act for a systematic exchange of information within the FEC was too weak and that it was doubtful whether the AFM and DNB could exchange information with all other FEC partners.[632] In 2013, the Dutch Government proposed to amend the Financial Supervision Act in order to better regulate the exchange of information within the FEC.[633] However, the Council of State commented in its advice on the uncertain formal-legal status of this cooperative network.[634] The Government retained the provision in the Bill, but made some changes in the formulation of the provision in light of recommendations from the Council of State. The comment on the formal-legal status of the FEC, however, was ignored.[635] This demonstrates that the FEC is not an uncontested forum for cooperation, despite its own claims on the effectiveness of the cooperative network.[636] On the 1st of January 2014, the Bill entered into force introducing an explicit legal basis for the DNB and the AFM for the exchange of information with their FEC partners as well as with the Financial Supervision Office.[637]

The Bureau Supervision Wwft and the Financial Supervision Office are not FEC partners. Theoretically, the Bureau Supervision Wwft is a FEC partner as it formally belongs to the DTCA, but since it cannot forward intelligence to other divisions of the DTCA, it does not participate in the FEC in practice.[638] An important reason for their absence is that until January 2013, AML supervisors were subject to strict confidentiality regimes that did not allow them to share supervisory information at all. As a result, it appeared that the BFT could receive information but not, or hardly, disclose information itself to other relevant authorities.[639] The FATF considered that the exchange of information between supervisors pursuant to the AML Act could only be interpreted implicitly from the text of the Act,

629 Algemene Rekenkamer (2008a) at 22.
630 Ibid., at 22.
631 Section 5 Information Protocol FEC 2014.
632 Van den Broek (2011). This publication was the result of my master's thesis written in 2010 under the Legal Research Master's Programme: Van den Broek, M. (2010), *New Governance: The exchange of information within the Dutch Financial Expertise Centre from a Good Governance Perspective*, Research Master's thesis, Utrecht University: August 2010 (not published, available upon request).
633 *Parliamentary papers II*, 2012-13, 33 632, no. 2, at 4.
634 *Parliamentary papers II*, 2012-13, 33 362, no. 4, at 18-19.
635 Ibid., at 19.
636 FEC (2012) at 10.
637 *Wijziging van de Wet op het financieel toezicht en enige andere wetten (Wijzigingswet financiële markten 2014)*, Stb. 2013, 487.
638 See § 5.4.2.2.
639 Stouten (2012) at 295; Algemene Rekenkamer (2008a) at 22.

but that challenges about the disclosure of confidential information to other supervisors could arise.[640]

The 2013 amendments to the AML Act created an explicit basis for the exchange of information between the statutory AML supervisors, as well as foreign supervisors.[641] Supervisors can exchange information on request or do so on their own initiative. The Government considered that this change was necessary in the light of effective AML supervision and in order to comply with the FATF observation on this point.[642] Section 22, second paragraph, Wwft is inspired by the formulation of Section 1:90 Wft, which allows for the provision of information by the DNB and the AFM to other supervisors pursuant to that Act.[643] Section 22 Wwft allows the AML supervisors to exchange information with other national and foreign AML supervisors provided that the aim for which the information is given is sufficiently prescribed, the intended use of the information concerns anti-money laundering supervision, the provision of information does not conflict with Dutch law or public policy, and that the confidentiality of the information is adequately safeguarded. Moreover, the provision of information must not conflict with the interests which the Dutch AML Act aims to protect and the information may not be used for a goal other than that for which the information was provided.[644] If the information which the Dutch supervisor intends to share originates from a foreign counterpart, the AML supervisor must obtain explicit approval for the onwards sharing of this information.[645] Where foreign counterparts wish to use the information for other purposes, there are limited grounds based on which AML supervisors can give their consent.[646]

The provision is an improvement compared to the old situation, which left no formal cooperation powers to the supervisors acting under the AML Act and affected the BFT and the Bureau Supervision Wwft in particular.[647] Nevertheless, the provision insufficiently acknowledges the involvement of the professional associations in the anti-money laundering supervision exercised by the Financial Supervision Office. In the Explanatory Memorandum, the Government explained that the professional associations were excluded from the scope of Section 22 Wwft to do justice to the special position of lawyers and notaries in Dutch society.[648] By doing that, however, it also excluded – intentionally or not – the professional and trade associations involved in the AML supervision of the accountancy sector. Considering the important role of the NBA and

640 FATF (2011) at 156.

641 Section 22(2)-22(6) Wwft. As an aside, I am somewhat sceptical about the reference to a 'supervisor' in Section 22(6) Wwft as it refers the authorities to which the Minister of Finance delegated powers under Section 31 Wwft. However, that section in itself refers to Section 24 Wwft which is the actual legal basis for the appointment of supervisory authorities. In my opinion it would be more appropriate to refer to Section 24 Wwft.

642 *Parliamentary Papers II*, 2011-12, 33 238, no. 3, at 19.

643 Ibid., at 19.

644 Section 22(2)(a-f) Wwft.

645 Section 22(3) Wwft.

646 Section 22(4) Wwft.

647 The Government gives an example on these two supervisors: *Parliamentary Papers II*, 2011-12, 33 238, no. 3, at 19. See also: Stouten (2012) at 295; Algemene Rekenkamer (2008a), § 2.3.3.

648 *Parliamentary Papers II*, 2011-12, 33 238, no. 3, at 19-20.

the fact that the Financial Supervision Office has outsourced a part of its AML supervision of accountants to the SRA, the information gateway may be difficult to apply in practice. We have seen that the supervisory arrangement between the SRA and BFT regulates that, at any time, the BFT may request access to files regarding AML(-related) audits performed by SRA reviewers, including the supervision report drafted by SRA reviewers.[649] The SRA is obliged to comply and to forward this information to the BFT. Not only does this cause problems in relation to legal professional privilege, as outlined in § 5.8.2.2, the supervisory arrangement also does not regulate what the BFT can subsequently do with this information. It is thus not certain whether the BFT can share the information that it has received from the SRA with the other AML supervisors, if the situation so requires. The NBA does not share the results of its quality audits with the BFT in the absence of a legal basis, so no problems are expected here.[650]

The amendments to Section 22 Wwft may give rise to discussions as to whether or not the BFT and the Bureau Toezicht Wwft should join the FEC too, as was recommended by the Court of Audit in 2008.[651] If the Bureau Supervision Wwft and Financial Supervision Office would become FEC partners, however, the current legal framework would only allow them to exchange information with each other and the DNB and the AFM. They would not be allowed to share information with the other FEC partners; although they could perhaps receive information from these partners.[652] With the current formulation of the AML Act there is at present little added value for the Bureau Supervision Wwft and the BFT to join the FEC, considering that they already cooperate with the other AML supervisors and the FIU in the AML coordination meeting, and can exchange relevant supervisory information on an operational basis.

5.9.1.3 *The National Task Force on Tackling the Misuse of Real Estate* (Nationale Regiegroep Aanpak Misbruik Vastgoed)

This task force focuses on the real estate sector. It was established in 2009 after a number of investigations and publications on the vulnerability of the sector for criminal activity, including money laundering.[653] The task force meets three times a year and has as its main task to formulate an action programme against misuse in the real estate sector. This action programme must be monitored and evaluated. Within this task force the DTCA, DNB and BFT are represented. As with the FEC, the Bureau Supervision Wwft is not represented or somehow involved with the task force.[654] This is remarkable, since it is the AML supervisor on real estate agents and valuers of real estate and may deliver a valuable contribution to tackling misuse in the real estate sector. Information exchanged within the task force may be beneficial to the Bureau's risk assessments and, thus, its information position. It

649 Section 6(4) SRA-BFT Supervisory Arrangement.
650 Interview NBA, June 2013. See also § 5.8.2.2.
651 Algemene Rekenkamer (2008a) at 22.
652 This depends on the legal framework in place for the other individual FEC partners: Section 5 Information Protocol FEC 2014.
653 *Instellingsbesluit Nationale Regiegroep Aanpak Misbruik Vastgoed,* Stcrt. 2012, 10502. This decision replaced the former one: Stcrt. 2009, 70.
654 Interview Belastingdienst/Bureau Toezicht Wwft, April 2013.

would be advisable to allow the Bureau Supervision Wwft to join the task force, although at the same time the Bureau should respect Section 22 Wwft which allows it to exchange information only with the other AML supervisors.

5.9.1.4 Committee on the duty to disclose unusual transactions (Commissie inzake de meldingsplicht ongebruikelijke transacties)

Section 21 Wwft establishes the Committee on the duty to disclose unusual transactions. This Committee consists of representatives of the Ministry of Finance, the Ministry of Security & Justice, the private sector, all four AML supervisors, the FIOD, the Public Prosecution Service and the police.[655] It is obliged to hold periodic consultations with the representatives of the Ministries of Finance and Security & Justice with regard to the structure and execution of the reporting duty, as well as the determination of the objective and subjective reporting indicators. These indicators, as explained in § 5.3, give rise to the unusual nature of transactions which may point at money laundering or terrorist financing, on the basis of which the obliged institutions and professionals must disclose a report to the Dutch FIU. Although all four AML supervisors are represented within this Committee, due to its focus and activities, this forum is of less relevance for the exercise of AML supervision and cooperation between the AML supervisors as such.

5.9.2 Cooperation efforts by the AML Supervisors on an operational level

Next to the possibility for AML supervisors to exchange individual supervisory information pursuant to Section 22 Wwft, the following operational liaisons are in place. It should be pointed out that there is no data available that can demonstrate that information is actually exchanged within these operational liaisons. Likewise, none of the AML supervisors report about the number of times information is exchanged based on Section 22 Wwft. Therefore, I will only briefly describe the operational liaisons that give an indication of cooperation efforts by the AML supervisors on an operational level.

Concerning the exercise of regular supervision, the DNB liaises with the AFM on the basis of an arrangement – also outside the scope of the FEC. Understanding that the verification of compliance with AML Act is incorporated within the regular supervisory procedures, at least at the DNB, the arrangement could also function as a basis on which supervisory information concerning AML Act is exchanged directly between the two supervisors.[656] This is most likely to be done when the information is not related to a specific individual person or legal entity, but on more general supervisory matters relevant to the anti-money laundering policy.[657] Based on public information, it seems that the Bureau Supervision Wwft has no agreements or arrangements with other AML supervisors in place. If the Bureau feels that information needs to be shared with (one of the) other AML supervisors,

655 Section 5 Wwft ministerial regulation (*Uitvoeringsregeling Wwft*).

656 *Convenant inzake de samenwerking en coördinatie op het gebied van toezicht, regelgeving en beleid, (inter) nationaal overleg en andere taken met een gemeenschappelijk belang, laatst gewijzigd 28 maart 2013*, Stcrt. 2013, 9996.

657 Interview De Nederlandsche Bank, May 2013.

it can do so directly on the basis of Section 22 Wwft. Especially the Financial Supervision Office could be a partner with which information is likely to be exchanged, as both carry out AML supervision on professionals acting in or closely related to the real estate sector. In particular the strong link between real estate agents and civil-law notaries during the sale and purchase of real estate may lead to information flows between the two authorities. Interviews made clear that the Bureau Supervision Wwft and the Financial Supervision Office were in the process of drafting an arrangement which should provide more clarity on the use of the powers of both supervisors on the basis of Section 22 Wwft. Until this arrangement is formalised, they will not exchange signals although they formally have the power to do so.[658] Until April 2014, such an arrangement had not been published. Both the BFT and the Bureau Supervision Wwft participate in the project on 'Non-reporters' ('Niet-melders'). This is a project which started in mid-2012 within which the FIU-NL, the Public Prosecution Service, the Fiscal Intelligence and Investigation Service (FIOD), the National Police Force, the Financial Supervision Office and the Bureau Supervision Wwft cooperate in order to stimulate compliant reporting behaviour. Above I already pointed out some of the successes of this project.[659]

5.9.3 Concluding remarks

Cooperation between AML supervisors, and with the FIU, take place via different forums for cooperation. On a policy level, four efforts are of direct or indirect importance for supervisory cooperation in relation to the preventive anti-money laundering policy: the AML coordination meeting, the Financial Expertise Centre (FEC), the National Task Force on Tackling the Misuse of Real Estate, and the Committee on the duty to disclose unusual transactions.

Within the AML coordination meeting supervisors and the FIU share information of general interest, such as general supervisory information, legislative developments, trends and typologies. The AML Act allows the FIU to give general feedback on reporting levels and trends to the supervisors. It cannot share information about the content of individual disclosures or the subjects mentioned in the disclosure. Especially information on unusual transaction reports that have been declared suspicious by the FIU after investigation cannot be shared with the supervisors. Such information, however, would increase the effectiveness of AML supervision. The AML Act obliges the supervisors to inform the FIU when they, in the course of their supervisory activities, discover facts that may be an indication of money laundering or terrorist financing. The second effort is the Financial Expertise Centre. The FEC is a network comprising of various authorities in which information regarding the integrity of the financial sector is exchanged. Money laundering is an important matter for the FEC. The DNB participates in this network, but the Financial Supervision Office and the Bureau Supervision Wwft do not. The lack of a legal basis for the sharing of information used to be the main reason for these authorities not participating. Since the 1st of January 2013, however, AML supervisors are allowed to share individual, subject-specific supervisory information with each other, as well as with

658 Interview Bureau Financieel Toezicht, June 2013.
659 § 5.7.4.

their foreign counterparts on the basis of Section 22 Wwft. Nevertheless, the provision insufficiently acknowledges the involvement of the professional associations in the AML supervision exercised by the BFT. And although the BFT and the Bureau Supervision Wwft now have more legal possibilities for exchanging information than before, participation in the FEC will have no more than a little added value for these organisations. Regarding the National Task Force on Tackling the Misuse of Real Estate, in which the DNB and BFT already participate, it is advised that the Bureau Supervision Wwft also joins this task force. All AML supervisors participate in the Committee on the duty to disclose unusual transactions, but due to its focus and activities, this forum is of less relevance.

AML supervisors can exchange individual supervisory information with each other based on Section 22 Wwft. Data concerning the application thereof is, unfortunately, not available. This does not allow one to say something about the question whether the AML supervisors cooperate with each other on an operational level. There are indications, however, that the AML supervisors have created other operational liaisons for cooperation as well, like the project 'Non-reporters' for the Financial Supervision Office and the Bureau Supervision Wwft.

6 Anti-money laundering supervision of banks, real estate agents and accountants in the United Kingdom

6.1 Introduction

The supervisory architecture in the preventive anti-money laundering policy in the United Kingdom belongs to the internal model.[1] This chapter provides an in-depth analysis of the supervisory system and practice in the UK with respect to banks, real estate agents and accountants. The legislative, institutional and practical aspects that were identified as part of the theoretical framework of effective supervision are assessed in this chapter.

Section 6.2 starts by describing the UK's vulnerability for money laundering and the three groups of businesses specifically. This is followed by an outline of the legal framework for the prevention of money laundering (§ 6.3). Both sections aim to purvey the context in which the fight against money laundering takes place in the UK. Subsequently, Section 6.4 deals with the institutional aspects of the anti-money laundering supervisors. The AML supervision of banks, estate agents and accountants is carried out by the Financial Conduct Authority (hereafter FCA), the Office of Fair Trading[2] (hereafter OFT or 'the Office') and various professional associations. This research focuses on two of these associations: the Institute of Chartered Accountants in England and Wales (hereafter also ICAEW) and the Association of Accounting Technicians (hereafter also AAT). The authorities must be sufficiently independent in the exercise of their supervisory tasks, and be accountable and transparent about their activities. A discussion on the extent to which banks, estate agents and accountants are authorised, regulated or required to register with their supervisors or other competent authorities follows in § 6.5. This section aims to answer the question whether the supervisors have, or can have, an adequate knowledge of all these businesses for which they have supervisory responsibility. Sections 6.6 to 6.9 are about AML supervision exercised by the four selected supervisors. It is verified whether they have adequate supervisory and sanctioning powers, whether they apply these in a proportionate and careful manner in practice, and whether they escalate their actions where necessary. Finally, Section 6.10 deals with another aspect of effective supervision:

1 § 3.4.3.

2 As mentioned in § 1.8 the Office of Fair Trading was the AML supervisor of real estate agents until the 1st of April 2014. On that day, AML supervisory responsibility for real estate agents was transferred to Her Majesty's Revenue and Customs. Because this research compares the systems between different Member States until the 31st of March 2014, the developments after that date are only mentioned where it matters most. More about this in § 6.4.2.3 and 6.7.

the cooperation between AML supervisors under this policy, and to an extent with the FIU. There must be no legal barriers to the exchange of information between these supervisors, and with the FIU.

6.2 Vulnerability of the United Kingdom for money laundering

In order to understand the context in which anti-money laundering supervision is exercised, it is relevant to have some ideas about the question whether money laundering is actually a problem in the UK. This section presents a number of studies that discuss the vulnerability for money laundering, or the scope of the problem, as well as the main predicate offences or sectors that are (considered to be) most at risk in the United Kingdom. Special attention is paid to the banking, real estate and accountancy sectors.

The UK has a large, stable and sophisticated financial sector, which makes it a highly attractive country for money launderers.[3] Different sources stress the vulnerability of the UK for money laundering, although estimations about the actual amounts of money laundered are scarce and available numbers diverge widely. The National Crime Agency stated in 2014 that '[m]any hundreds of billions of pounds of international criminal money is almost certainly laundered through UK banks, including their subsidiaries, each year'.[4] This proves not only the vulnerability for money laundering of the UK as a whole, but particularly the banking sector. The ECOLEF study ranked the UK as the most threatened EU Member State, with an estimated threat of 282,004 million Euros annually.[5] And in 2007, HM Treasury estimated that 10 billion GBP (roughly 12.1 billion Euros[6]) was laundered through the regulated sector, meaning all institutions and professionals subject to the preventive AML policy.[7] Particular vulnerable sectors through which laundering may take place are considered to be banks, wire transfer companies, money service businesses (MSBs) and cash-rich businesses.[8] Direct AML risks for the financial sector are considered to be e-money issuers and cybercrime.[9] Challenges are also posed by the money service businesses' sector, digital currencies (such as Bitcoins) and alternative banking platforms, i.e. institutions providing banking services without being authorised to do so.[10] In terms of major sources of illegal proceeds in the UK, the US Department of State refers to drugs crimes but at the same time points at the increasing importance of financial fraud, internet fraud, credit/debit card fraud, the use of cash, the purchase

3 US Department of State (2014) at 203 which includes the UK in its list of countries of primary concern.

4 National Crime Agency (2014), *National Strategic Assessment of Serious and Organised Crime 2014*, at 12.

5 As noted in Chapter 4, this threat is understood as 'the amount of money that could, or might, be laundered in a country if there were no barriers to laundering and there was no 'more attractive place' for the launderer to launder the money'. This is something different than estimations of the actual money laundered: Unger and Ferwerda (2014) at 12-16. In terms of the estimated threat as a percentage of GDP, the UK is ranked at number 18 (13.3%) out of 27.

6 The exchange rate on 5 March 2014 was 1 GDP = 1.21 Euros. This exchange rate will be used throughout this chapter.

7 Rietbroek, S. (2013), 'De Zeven AML Zonden van HSBC', *Tijdschrift voor Compliance*, issue 1, pp. 56-59; Rietbroek, S. (2013a), 'De Zeven Anti-Money Laundering Zonden van HSBC', *Tijdschrift voor Compliance*, issue 2, pp. 168-170.

8 National Crime Agency (2014) at 12.

9 FCA (2013), *Anti-money laundering annual report 2012/13*, July 2013, at 14-15.

10 Ibid., at 15.

of high value assets, the smuggling of people and goods and the use of underground banking systems such as hawala.[11] This is similar to considerations of the FATF at the time of the mutual evaluation in the UK. The FATF concluded that the use of cash was the most prominent laundering technique and common underlying predicate offences were drug trafficking, immigration crime, VAT fraud, smuggling and the counterfeiting of goods.[12] Corruption does not seem to be a big problem in the UK.[13] As obliged by the FATF Recommendations and in order gain more insight into the scope and extent of money laundering, the UK Government undertook a national risk assessment on money laundering in the first half of 2014.[14]

The banking sector seems to face a particularly high money laundering threat. This is mostly due to high volumes of money circulating in the British financial sector, but also because they are used for popular money laundering techniques in the UK. The vulnerability of British banks for being used by launderers, in particular when there is a lack of compliance on the side of the banks, is illustrated by the *HSBC* case.[15] The largest British bank was found guilty of laundering money for organised crime in the United States.[16] The FCA and its predecessor the Financial Services Authority (hereafter FSA) also started to act very strongly against banks for not complying with AML obligations in the UK. In January 2014, for example, the FCA imposed a 7.6 million GBP fine on a bank for failures in the prevention of money laundering.[17] In terms of reporting, the banking sector is the largest reporting sector to UKFIU. On average banks reported between 75-80% of the total number of disclosures in the years 2011-2013.[18]

The real estate sector in the UK does not seem to have a particularly high money laundering vulnerability. It is not mentioned as one of the sectors with the highest AML vulnerability, and the fact that estate agents in the UK normally do not handle clients' money also lowers their direct vulnerability. Nevertheless, in 2009 UKFIU considered that

11 US Department of State (2014) at 203.

12 FATF (2007a), *Third Mutual Evaluation Report on the United Kingdom of Great Britain and Northern Ireland*, at 14.

13 European Commission (2014c), *Annex United Kingdom to the EU Anti-Corruption Report*, COM(2014) 38 final.

14 National Crime Agency (2013), *Suspicious Activity Reports (SARs) Annual Report 2013*, at 28.

15 BBC News, *HSBC to pay $1.9bn in US money laundering penalties*, 11 December 2012; The Guardian, *HSBC pays record $1.9bn fine to settle US money-laundering accusations*, 11 December 2012; USA Today, *HSBC will pay $1.9 billion for money laundering*, 11 December 2012.

16 The *HSBC* case is not a self-standing case, as other British banks have been hit by AML fines in the USA as well. Lloyds TSB Group PLC was forced to pay 350 million US dollars in January 2009 and another 217 million US dollars in December 2009. Barclays settled its case by agreeing to pay 298 million US dollars to avoid further prosecution. In short, both banks had breached US sanctions regulations by performing client transactions for Iranian and Sudanese clients and clients from other territories under US sanctions for a number of years, thereby concealing the origin and nature of the transactions. For Barclays: US Department of Justice, *Barclays Bank PLC Agrees to Forfeit $298 Million in Connection with Violations of the International Emergency Economic Powers Act and the Trading with the Enemy Act*, 18 August 2010, available at: <www.justice.gov/opa/pr/2010/August/10-crm-933.html>, last visited on 16 September 2014.

17 *FCA Decision Notice: Standard Bank Plc*, Ref. no. 124823, 22 January 2014.

18 National Crime Agency (2013) at 8; Serious Organised Crime Agency (2012), *Suspicious Activity Reports Regime: Annual Report 2012*, at 14; Serious Organised Crime Agency (2011), *Suspicious Activity Reports Regime: Annual Report 2011*, at 14.

'[a] high proportion of serious organised criminals invest criminal proceeds in private and commercial property. It is reasonable to assume that estate agents are involved in the transactions at some point'.[19] The use of cash as (part) consideration for the purchase of property is particularly considered a risk for the sector. Moreover, real estate agents themselves are sometimes convicted in the UK for taking part in money laundering schemes.[20] In the *Pattison* case, for example, an estate agent was convicted of money laundering after having bought a house with a large undervalue from a client of his, who was arrested for drug trafficking.[21] The reporting numbers of estate agents are very low: in the period October 2012 to September 2013 estate agents' reports only amounted to 0.07% of the total received by UKFIU.[22] This is in line with previous years and makes it the sector that discloses the least reports.[23]

The accountancy sector bears a considerable risk for money laundering. As in many other jurisdictions, accountants can, wittingly or unwittingly, give financial or tax advice which is in fact a scheme to conceal the proceeds of crime. Yet it appears that accountants in the UK are largely compliant with the preventive obligations. HM Treasury's AML Supervision Report 2012-13 indicates that '[a]ll accountancy sector supervisors reported that the risk of non-compliance was low among their members; based on their monitoring activity, the training and support available to the firms they supervise'.[24] Nevertheless, accountants have been included in large money laundering schemes themselves. One high-profile case from 1990 is the *AGIP v Jackson* case, a civil case in which the High Court concluded that accountants were involved in money laundering.[25] The role of ICAEW and other regulatory bodies was criticised later because, despite the High Court judgment, ICAEW concluded that there was insufficient evidence to justify bringing a disciplinary case against the members involved.[26] More recently, in 2012 a former accountant was imprisoned and more than 2 million GBP was confiscated from him. He was convicted of fraud by submitting several thousand fraudulent self-assessment repayments, failures to declare Income Tax, and non-payments of VAT.[27] And in 2010 a former accountant, who was already excluded from the profession by ICAEW after not being willing to cooperate with

19 Serious Organised Crime Agency (2009), *Estate Agents – Identifying Risks to your Business and Reporting Suspicious Activity*, at 2.

20 On 28 February 2014, a Northern Irish real estate agent was sentenced to 12 months imprisonment for participating in a mortgage fraud and money laundering arrangement. See: *Court sentences trio for bogus loans and mortgages: summary of judgment*, available at: <www.courtsni.gov.uk/enGB/Judicial%20Decisions/SummaryJudgments/Documents/Court%20sentences%20trio%20for%20bogus%20loans%20and%20mortgages/j_j_Summary%20of%20judgment%20-%20R%20v%20Brassil,%20Creegan%20and%20Mallon%2028%20Feb%2014.htm>, last visited on 20 May 2014.

21 *R v Pattinson* [2007] EWCA Crim 1536, [2008] 1 Cr App R (S) 51. See for an explanation of the case by the Supreme Court: *R v Waya* [2012] UKSC 51, par. 59.

22 National Crime Agency (2013) at 8.

23 Cf. Serious Organised Crime Agency (2011) at 14 where estate agents reported only 0.05% of the total.

24 HM Treasury (2013), Anti-*Money Laundering and Counter Terrorist Finance Supervision Report 2012-13*, par. 5.1, available at: <www.gov.uk/government/publications/anti-money-laundering-and-counter-terrorist-finance-supervision-reports/anti-money-laundering-and-counter-terrorist-finance-supervision-report-2012-13>, last visited on 8 May 2014.

25 *AGIP (Africa) Limited v Jackson & Others* [1990] 1 Ch. 265.

26 Mitchell, A., Sikka, P., Willmot, H. (1998), *The Accountants' Laundromat*, Monograph, Southgate Publishers.

27 Serious Organised Crime Agency (2012) at 28.

the UK Inland Revenue, was sentenced to eight years imprisonment for a similar offence.[28] Not only have accountants been involved in money laundering schemes themselves, they have also been convicted of tipping-off their clients.[29] In the years 2011-2013, accountants reported between 1.71% (2013) and 2.44% (2011) of the total number of suspicious activity reports to UKFIU annually.[30] In the period October 2012 to September 2013, accountants disclosed 5,428 SARs.[31] The reporting numbers of accountants have declined somewhat, but compared to other designated non-financial businesses and professionals they do relatively well. For example, lawyers report roughly 1.5 % to UKFIU annually, whereas we just saw that estate agents only reported 0.07% of all SARs in 2013.

6.3 Legal framework for the prevention of money laundering

The prevention of money laundering is embedded in two core pieces of legislation and regulation, namely the Proceeds of Crime Act 2002 (hereafter POCA 2002) and the Money Laundering Regulations 2007 (hereafter MLR 2007 or 'the Regulations').[32] Unlike what we could see for Spain and the Netherlands so far, the preventive AML policy in the UK is, at least from a legislative perspective, separated from the preventive combating of terrorist financing policy as they operate under distinct legal regimes.[33] POCA 2002 contains the substantive criminal offences of money laundering and imposes reporting obligations on the regulated sector.[34] The other preventive requirements are laid down in the MLR 2007, which is the direct result of the implementation of the Third Directive.[35] The Regulations were amended in October 2012 in order to make them more effective, as well as to make them more proportionate to the businesses by allowing more flexibility in complying with their obligations.[36] With respect to supervision the amendments included extra sanctions for the AML supervisors, as well as a legal basis for the exchange of information between them.[37]

28 *R v Charalambous* [2010] Blackfriars Crown Court. See: HM Revenue and Customs, *Accountant jailed in 11£m tax fraud*, 30 June 2010, available at: <www.mynewsdesk.com/uk/pressreleases/hm-revenue-customs-accountant-jailed-in-11m-tax-fraud-432337>, last visited 20 June 2014.

29 *R v Doshi* [2011] EWCA Crim 1975.

30 National Crime Agency (2013) at 8; Serious Organised Crime Agency (2012) at 14; Serious Organised Crime Agency (2011) at 14.

31 National Crime Agency (2013) at 8.

32 Proceeds of Crime Act 2002 (c.29), last amended by: S.I. 2013/3115 (9th of December 2013); The Money Laundering Regulations, S.I. 2007/2157. Last amended by: S.I. 2014/506 (5th of March 2014).

33 Formally the CTF policy is regulated in, among other things, the Terrorism Act 2000, last amended by: S.I. 2013/3172 (12th of December 2013). However, in practice, they are applied jointly. Due to its broad wording and advantageous regime for financial investigators and law enforcement agencies in terms of (the collection of) evidence, POCA 2002 can be and has been applied to terrorism and terrorist financing cases as well.

34 POCA 2002 (and TA 2000) have been amended with the implementation of the Third Directive by the Terrorism Act 2000 and the Proceeds of Crime Act 2002 (Amendment) Regulations 2007, S.I. 2007/3398.

35 HM Treasury (2007), *Implementing the Third Money Laundering Directive: Draft Money Laundering Regulations 2007*, January 2007; Burrell, P. and Meakin, K. (2007), 'United Kingdom', in: W.H. Muller, C.H. Kälin and J.G. Goldworth, *Anti-Money Laundering: International Law and Practice*, John Wiley & Sons Ltd., 2007, pp. 369-380, at 371.

36 The Money Laundering (Amendment) Regulations, S.I. 2012/2298. Cf. HM Treasury (2011b), *Consultation on proposed changes to the Money Laundering Regulations 2007: summary of responses*, November 2011, at 3.

37 See about cooperation between AML supervisors: § 6.10.

POCA 2002 and the Regulations are supplemented by guidance documents. Under Regulations 42 and 45 MLR 2007, as well as Sections 330 and 331 POCA 2002, HM Treasury is competent to authorise AML guidance issued by professional or trade associations or the supervisors. AML supervisors are not obliged to issue guidance documents, but in practice they do so.[38] The best known and most used guidance document, however, is issued by the Joint Money Laundering Steering Group, which consists of representatives from trade associations across the financial services industry.[39] Despite the fact that this guidance document stems from a private initiative, its importance can be seen by the fact that the FCA endorses the Guidance in its own Handbook for those aspects that concern the prevention of money laundering.[40] HM Treasury has further approved the AML guidance documents of, inter alia, the Combined Committee of Accountancy Bodies,[41] the Gambling Commission, HM Revenue and Customs and the Law Society of England and Wales.[42]

> Besides the possibility for HM Treasury to check the quality and consistency of guidance documents, the authorisation also has a more formal role as a possible defence in court. A court must take the authorised guidance documents into account for those money laundering prosecutions that involve persons or businesses to which the guidance documents apply.[43] If it appears that the person or business has fully complied with these documents, he may raise this as a legal defence in court. In criminal prosecutions and civil actions under common law, this is a way to avoid criminal or civil liability.

The legislative and regulatory framework in the preventive AML policy is complemented by other pieces of legislation, regulations and professional norms, such as the Financial Services and Markets Act 2000 and the Estate Agents Act 1979. The related norms are important for both the obliged institutions and professionals, as well as their AML supervisors. Where relevant, these norms will be mentioned in the following subsections.

6.4 The AML Supervisors: institutional aspects

This section provides an analysis of the institutional aspects of the supervisors, most notably their independence and accountability regimes. The focus rests on the (relative) independence from politics and the market, and corresponding accountability structures

38 HM Treasury (2013), par 5.5.

39 For information about JMLSG, see: <www.jmlsg.org.uk/>.

40 FCA Handbook, SYSC, Rule 6.2.5 [G]: 'The FCA, when considering whether a breach of its rules on systems and controls against money laundering has occurred, will have regard to whether a firm has followed relevant provisions in the guidance for the United Kingdom financial sector issued by the Joint Money Laundering Steering Group'. The letter [G] is given to the Rule, which indicates guidance given under Section 139B of the Financial Services and Markets Act 2000, as amended by the Financial Services Act 2012. The Handbook is available at: <http://fshandbook.info/FS/html/FCA/>.

41 The CCAB is a group of the six chartered accountancy bodies in the UK: ICAEW, ICAS, ACCA, ICAI and CIMA. See for more information: <www.ccab.org.uk/>.

42 HM Treasury, *HM Treasury Approved AML/CTF Guidance*, available at: <www.gov.uk/government/uploads/system/uploads/attachment_data/file/200701/aml_hmt_approved_guidance.pdf >, last visited on 8 May 2014.

43 FATF (2007a) at 109-110.

to counterbalance the level of independence, in particular regarding the AML policy.[44] This section aims to provide an insight into how AML supervision plays a role within the organisations of the Financial Conduct Authority (§ 6.4.1), the Office of Fair Trading (§ 6.4.2), the Institute of Chartered Accountants in England and Wales and the Association of Accounting Technicians (§ 6.4.3 and 6.4.4). Some concluding remarks can be found in § 6.4.5.

The accountancy sector in the UK has a total of 11 AML supervisors, constituting nearly half of all AML supervisors in the UK.[45] As explained in the introduction, I have specifically chosen for ICAEW and AAT, because these professional associations are different from each other in terms of age, size and jurisdiction. Together they reflect the variety that is present among the different professional associations performing AML supervision.[46]

It should be pointed out that the Office of Fair Trading ceased to exist on the 1st of April 2014.[47] In light of the fact that AML supervisory responsibility for real estate agents has been transferred to HM Revenue and Customs, some attention will be paid to this development as well.

6.4.1 Financial Conduct Authority

6.4.1.1 Institutional embedding

The Financial Conduct Authority is a non-departmental public body whose statutory powers are set by the Financial Services and Markets Act 2000, as amended by the Financial Services Act 2012 (hereafter 'FSMA 2000' and 'FSA 2012').[48] It is formed as one of the two successors of the Financial Services Authority, which was the single statutory regulator of financial services in the UK.[49] Since 2010, the Government had been trying to reform the financial supervisory and regulatory structure into the 'twin-peaks' model.[50] The financial crisis had made the UK aware of its shortcomings in financial regulation and supervision: '[p]erhaps the most significant failing is that no single institution had responsibility, authority or powers to oversee the financial system as a whole'.[51] The Turner Review had already acknowledged that FSA's supervisory approach, called the 'light touch' regulation, had failed and that more attention should be paid on macroeconomic regulation and the scrutiny of individual businesses.[52] In order to make its financial regulatory structure more effective, the Government decided to adopt a new approach, with an important

44 § 2.4.2.1 and 2.4.2.2.
45 HM Treasury (2013), par. 7. If one would include the number of professional associations for tax advisors as well, one would come to 17.
46 See § 1.3.
47 See § 1.8.
48 Financial Services Act 2012, c 21.
49 Section 2(2) Financial Services and Market Act 2000 (hereafter FSMA 2000).
50 Cf. Chapters 3 and 6.
51 HM Treasury (2011a), *White Paper: A new approach to financial regulation – the blueprint to reform*, Cm8083, at 5.
52 FSA (2009), *The Turner Review: a regulatory response to the global banking crisis*, March 2009.

role for judgment and expertise at the heart of regulation.[53] The FSA 2012 brought about four institutional changes. Firstly, it established the Financial Policy Committee as a committee of the Court of the Bank of England with responsibility for macro-prudential regulation. Secondly, the Act created the Prudential Regulation Authority (hereafter PRA) as a subsidiary of the Bank of England with responsibility for micro-prudential regulation and supervision. Thirdly, it created the FCA as the independent conduct-of-business regulator with responsibility for the proper functioning of the markets, the integrity of the financial system, consumer protection and competition. And, finally, the Act made the Bank of England responsible for the regulation of recognised clearing houses. The new framework came into full effect on the 1st of April 2013.

The FCA is structured as a private company limited by guarantee, the one share being owned by HM Treasury.[54] It is governed by a Board, which consists of executive and non-executive directors that are appointed by HM Treasury.[55] The Board is responsible for setting the overall policy of the Authority, but day-to-day decisions and staff management are the responsibility of the Executive Committee.[56] The FCA's statutory objective is to ensure that the relevant markets function well. This strategic objective is divided into three operational objectives: to secure an adequate degree of consumer protection, to protect and enhance the integrity of the UK financial system, and to promote effective competition.[57] Under the Regulations, the FCA is the AML Supervisor for FSMA-authorised institutions, including banks, as well as for so-called 'Annex I financial institutions'.[58] These institutions conduct one or more listed activities, such as lending, financial leasing, the provision of payment services, and money broking, but do not require authorisation under the FSMA.[59] The FCA's AML policy is part of its efforts to tackle financial crime. The FCA does not have a self-standing objective to tackle financial crime, but reducing the extent to which firms are vulnerable for financial crime is brought under the objective to protect and enhance the integrity of the UK financial system. That explains why the FCA's AML efforts are placed within the operational objective of the protection of the integrity of the UK financial system.[60] For authorised firms, AML supervision is carried out by firm supervisors and the specialist financial crime supervision team.[61] For Annex I financial institutions, this is exercised by the specialist team only.[62] The firm supervisors carry out the regular conduct-of-business supervision that may or may not include money laundering aspects depending on the supervisor's view, whereas the specialist team carries out targeted AML supervision and supports the firm supervisors when this is reasonable in the light of the complexity of the firm or a higher risk of money laundering.[63] In 2014,

53 Ibid., at 7.
54 FCA (2013a), *Corporate Governance at the Financial Conduct Authority*, April 2013, at 3.
55 Section (2)(1) in conjunction with 2(2) of Schedule 1ZA FSMA 2000, as amended by FSA 2012.
56 The role of the Board is further detailed in the Corporate Governance document: FCA (2013a) at 4-5.
57 Section 1B(3) FSMA 2000, as amended by FSA 2012.
58 Regulation 23(1)(a) MLR 2007 in conjunction with Schedule 1 MLR 2007.
59 Regulation 3(3) MLR 2007 in conjunction with Schedule 1 MLR 2007.
60 FCA (2013) at 6.
61 Ibid., at 7.
62 Interview Financial Services Authority, April 2012; Interview Financial Conduct Authority, May 2014.
63 More about this in § 6.2 of this chapter.

the FCA had responsibility for over roughly 50,000 firms.[64] More specifically with respect to banks, in February 2014 there were 157 UK banks, 80 non-EEA banks with branches in the UK and 75 EEA banks with branches in the UK.[65] Overall numbers concerning staff and budget reserved for AML supervision are not available, although the FCA had 22 staff working at the specialist financial crime supervision team at the end of 2013.[66] In the first quarter of 2014, this number had increased to 27.[67]

6.4.1.2 Political independence and accountability

Political independence

Because the FCA is a non-departmental public body (hereafter NDPB), it exercises its activities under a high degree of independence from the UK Government. In general, an NDPB is defined as 'a body which has a role in the process of national government but is not a government department, or part of one, and which accordingly operates to a greater or lesser extent at arm's length from Ministers'.[68] The FCA is not attached to any Government Department or public authority, and has no financial relationship with the Government or Parliament either. The FCA is not to be regarded as acting on behalf of the Crown and its member officers and staff are not to be regarded as Crown servants.[69]

> The term non-departmental public body is not an undisputed one. In the literature, NDPBs have been referred to as quangos: quasi-autonomous non-governmental organisations. Quango is a term that was coined in the 1970s, but until now there has never been a single definition.[70] The definitional imprecision led to a situation where the term became a 'catch-all phrase to describe a wide range of bodies' that were associated with the Government but did not form a constituent part of any Government Department.[71] The term NDBPs was a response by the UK Government to the definitional imprecision and with the distinction of types of NDPBs it aimed to shed more clarity on this issue.[72] At present, the UK Cabinet Office distinguishes four types of NDPBs: executive, advisory, tribunal NDPBs and the Independent Monitoring Board of Prisons, Immigration

6

64 FCA, *Regulating*, 31 March 2014, available at: <www.fca.org.uk/about/what/regulating>, last visited on 8 May 2014.

65 Bank of England (2014), *List of banks as compiled by the Bank of England as at 28 February 2014*, available at: <www.bankofengland.co.uk/pra/Documents/.../banklist1402.xls>, last visited on 8 May 2014.

66 FCA (2013) at 7.

67 Interview Financial Conduct Authority, May 2014.

68 Pliatzky, L. (1980), *Report on Non-departmental Public Bodies*, CMND 7797: 1980.

69 Section 16, Schedule 1ZA FCMA 2000 as amended by FSA 2012.

70 See Flinders, who defines quangos as 'any body that spends public money to fulfil a public task but with some degree of independence from elected representatives': Flinders, M.V. (1999), 'Setting the Scene: Quangos in Context', in: Flinders, M.V. and Smith, M.J. (eds.) (1999), *Quangos, Accountability and Reform*, MacMillan Press Ltd, pp. 3-16 at 4; Cf. Greve, C., Flinders, M. and Van Thiel, S. (1999), 'Quango's: What's In A Name?: Defining Quango's from a Comparative Perspective', *Governance: An International Journal of Policy and Administration*, vol. 12, issue 2, pp. 129-146.

71 Cole, M. (2005), 'Quangos: The Debate of the 1970s in Britain', *Contemporary British History*, vol. 19, issue 3, pp. 321-352 at 322-323; Gay, O. (1996), 'The Quango Debate', *Research Paper* 96/72, House of Commons Library, at 5.

72 Although Craig demonstrates that also this term has some flaws on its own too: Craig, P.P. (2012), *Administrative Law*, Sweet & Maxwell: London, 7th edition, at 98.

Removal Centres and Immigration Holding Facility.[73] The predecessors of the FCA have sometimes been referred to as quangos.

The FCA is positioned at a distance from its so-called parent department, HM Treasury, and has considerable freedom in its operational activities.[74] Of course, this independence is not unlimited and would not be effective without proper accountability mechanisms in place. In 2001 the Chancellor, Gordon Brown, wrote that 'the FSA is independent of government, but it is important that the FSA and its Board can be called to account by both the Government and Parliament, and fully recognises the interests of all its stakeholders'.[75] The Government has various ways to hold the FCA accountable, usually through HM Treasury.[76] Legislation provides for a range of accountability mechanisms, which will be discussed below. HM Treasury has, however, no powers whatsoever to interfere with the FCA's operational activities or decisions in individual cases. Treasury Ministers are not allowed to give instructions to the FCA: not with respect to the FCA's policies, nor individual decisions. Nevertheless, HM Treasury can indirectly exert influence on the FCA, because it has the power to appoint the Board members, and to dismiss them on grounds of incapacity or serious misconduct, or on the ground that the personal or financial interests of the appointed member have a material effect on the functions of the member.[77]

There used to be some serious critical voices as to the accountability of the FSA. In 2011 the Treasury Select Committee of the UK Parliament announced that it would start an inquiry into the accountability of the (at that time) future Financial Conduct Authority. The Committee considered that better accountability can improve the quality of regulation, but that '(...) the scope for effective challenge is, in practice, limited under current arrangements and this may have contributed to poor regulatory performance both before and during the financial crisis'.[78] It therefore recommended that the Government should amend the Financial Services Bill. The Committee recommended that the board of the FCA should publish the minutes of each meeting, that the Chief Executive is to be subject to pre-appointment scrutiny by the Treasury Select Committee, that legislation provides that the Board should be responsible for responding to requests for factual information and papers from Parliament, and that the legislation provides that Parliament may request retrospective views of the FCA's work.[79]

73 Cabinet Office (2012), *Public Bodies 2012*, at 1-2. Cf. Craig (2012) at 99-101.

74 As pointed out by the IMF as well: IMF (2011a), *United Kingdom: Basel Core Principles for Effective Banking Supervision Detailed Assessment of Compliance*, IMF Country Report No. 11/233, July 2011, at 15 and 38-39.

75 HM Treasury (2001), *An Independent And Accountable FSA*, available at: <http://webarchive.nationalarchives.gov.uk/+/www.hm-treasury.gov.uk/newsroom_and_speeches/press/2001/press_144_01.cfm>, last visited on 13 May 2014.

76 See about the general accountability procedure for NDPBs: Craig (2012) at 105.

77 Section 2(2) and 2(4)(1) of Schedule 1ZA FSMA 2000, as amended by FSA 2012. As explained in Chapter 2, I will not elaborate on the indirect influence on supervisors' independence. See for this: Craig (2012) at 102-103.

78 House of Commons – Treasury Committee (2012), *Financial Conduct Authority*, 26th Report of Session 2010-12, January 2012, par. 64.

79 Ibid., par. 80.

Annual report and annual public meeting

The Financial Services Act 2012 reflects a move towards greater transparency and accountability. It addresses transparency as a regulatory principle and widens the accountability mechanisms that were established under FSMA 2000. The FCA is accountable for its actions to HM Treasury, and through the Treasury to Parliament. At least once a year it must report to HM Treasury. This annual report should include information about a wide range of matters. The FCA is obliged to report on:

- the discharge of its functions;
- the extent to which the FCA feels it has advanced its operational objectives (consumer protection, integrity, competition);
- the extent to which the FCA feels it has acted compatibly with its strategic objective (ensuring that the relevant markets function well);
- how, in its opinion, it feels it has complied with the duty, so far as is compatible with acting in a way which advances the consumer protection objective or the integrity objective, to discharge its general functions in a way which promotes effective competition in the interests of consumers;
- its considerations of the matter mentioned in section 1B(5)(b), which is about taking action intended to minimise the extent to which it is possible for a business to be used for a purpose connected with financial crime;
- its consideration of the principles of good regulation – which since 2012 include two principles relating to transparency;[80]
- how it has complied with the duty to ensure a co-ordinated exercise of functions with the PRA;
- any direction received from the PRA to refrain from certain actions,[81] or the power of the PRA in relation to with-profits policies during the period to which the report relates;[82]
- how it has complied with its duty to co-operate with others outside the UK who have functions similar to the FCA or in relation to the prevention of financial crime;[83]
- such other matters as HM Treasury may from time to time direct.

Information whose publication would in the opinion of the FCA be against the public interest, should not be included in the annual report. The report must be accompanied by a statement of the remuneration paid to the appointed members of the Board of the FCA during the period to which the report relates and such other reports or information,

80 As laid down in Section 3B FSMA 2000 as amended by FSA 2012. The two 'transparency principles' are: (g) the desirability in appropriate cases of each regulator publishing information relating to persons on whom requirements are imposed by or under this Act, or requiring such persons to publish information, as a means of contributing to the advancement by each regulator of its objectives; and (h) the principle that the regulators should exercise their functions as transparently as possible'.

81 See about this 'veto power': House of Commons, HC 721-i, Session 2012-13, 6 November 2012 (Oral evidence taken before the Treasury Committee, 'Accountability on the Financial Conduct Authority', Witness John Griffith-Jones).

82 Sections 3I and 3J FSMA 2000 as amended by FSA 2012.

83 Section 354A FSMA 2000 as amended by FSA 2012.

prepared by such persons, as the Treasury may from time to time direct.[84] HM Treasury is obliged to lay copies of the report, statement and other documents before Parliament. The Financial Secretary to the Treasury is responsible for the overall functioning of the FCA, but it is the Commercial Secretary to the Treasury who is responsible for the matters of asset freezing and financial crime, including the AML policy.[85] These secretaries are junior Treasury Ministers.[86] Ultimately, the Chancellor of the Exchequer has responsibility for the FCA and the Treasury Secretaries.[87] According to De Lange, ministers in the UK are 'individiually and collectively responsible and accountable towards Parliament'.[88] Hence, the FCA, through HM Treasury, is accountable to Parliament via the publication of annual reports. Within three months following the publication of the annual report, the FCA must organise an annual public meeting. This meeting should enable a general discussion of the contents of the report which is being considered and give a reasonable opportunity for those attending the meeting to put questions to the FCA about the way in which it has discharged, or has failed to discharge, its functions during the period to which the report relates.[89] These meetings can be attended by market representatives, other stakeholders, and the wider public.

Independent inquiries

HM Treasury may also launch independent statutory inquiries where it appears to the Treasury that events have occurred in relation to a collective investment scheme or a person who is, or was at the time of the events, carrying on a regulated activity, or listed securities or an issuer of listed securities, which posed or could have posed a serious threat to the stability of the UK financial system or caused or risked causing significant damage to the interests of consumers.[90] It may also require this where those events have not occurred or where the risk or damage has been reduced, but for a serious failure in the system established by FSMA 2000, or by any previous statutory provision, for the regulation of such schemes, or of such persons and their activities, or the listing of securities, or the operation of that system.[91] Likewise, the Treasury can launch an independent statutory inquiry if events have occurred in relation to recognised clearing house or a recognised inter-bank payment system.[92] The mechanism of statutory inquiries can be used in the case of possible serious regulatory failures on the side of the FCA as well.

84 Section 11(3) of Schedule 1ZA FSMA 2000 as introduced by FSA 2012.

85 *Commercial Secretary to the Treasury*, available at: <www.gov.uk/government/ministers/commercial-secretary-to-the-treasury>, last visited on 27 May 2014.

86 De Lange, R. (2014), 'The United Kingdom of Great Britain and Northern Ireland', in: Besselink, L., Bovend'Eert, P., Broeksteeg, H., De Lange, R. and Voermans, W. (eds.), *Constitutional Law of the EU Member States*, Kluwer: Deventer, pp. 1651-1693 at 1665.

87 Cabinet Office (2013), *List of Ministerial Responsibilities: Including Executive Agencies and Non-Ministerial Departments*, December 2013. Cf. De Lange (2014) at 1665 who explains that the term Chancellor of the Exchequer is an ancient title for the Minister of Finance.

88 De Lange (2014) at 1666.

89 Section 12 of Schedule 1ZA FSMA 2000 as introduced by FSA 2012.

90 Section 68 FSMA 2000, as amended by FSA 2012.

91 Section 68(2) FSMA 2000, as amended by FSA 2012.

92 Section 68(3) FSMA 2000, as amended by FSA 2012.

If HM Treasury considers that it is in the public interest to have an independent inquiry into the events and the circumstances surrounding them, they may also appoint an independent person to conduct an inquiry.[93] It may, through a direction to the appointed person, control the scope of the inquiry, the period during which it is to be held, the conduct of the inquiry and the making of reports.[94] This power is broader than the provision under its preceding Act, where the Treasury could appoint an independent person to conduct a review of the economy, efficiency and effectiveness with which the FSA has used its resources in discharging its function.[95] If the FCA refuses access to any documents or information, the person holding the inquiry can forward the matter to the High Court, which can decide whether the failure to release the documents or information is an act in contempt of court, were the inquiry to be held in court.

Investigations of regulatory failure

New is Section 73, which obliges the FCA to investigate and report on a possible regulatory failure on its own initiative. The FCA must carry out an investigation into the events and the circumstances surrounding them and report to HM Treasury on the result of the investigation if events have occurred in relation to a regulated person or collective investment scheme which comprised any of the three operational objectives of the FCA. It can also be required to carry out such an investigation when the events have not occurred, or the failure or adverse effect might have been reduced, but for a serious failure in the system established by FSMA 2000 for the regulation of authorised persons and their activities, for the listing of securities or for the regulation of collective investment schemes, so far as it relates to the functions of the FCA, or the operation of that system, so far as it relates to those functions (the 'regulatory system'). HM Treasury can also oblige the FCA to carry out such an investigation where it appears to the Treasury that it is in the public interest that such an investigation is undertaken and where the FCA has not started an investigation.[96]

> The procedure of the investigation, on its own initiative or directed by HM Treasury, is in principle form-free and it is for the regulator to decide how it will carry out the investigation, provided that he complies with the norms stemming from Section 78 FSMA 2000, as amended by FSA 2012. The FCA has published a document online in which it sets out its thinking on the conduct of such investigations, what it considers to be regulatory failures, which thresholds apply, examples as well as a procedural outline of the investigations.[97] The Treasury may decide to direct the regulator in terms of the scope of the investigation, the period during which the investigation is to be carried out, the conduct of the investigation and the making of reports.[98] In principle the reports from the statutory inquiries or investigations must be published in full by the Treasury and be laid before Parliament. In certain circumstances the Treasury may decide to withhold

93 Section 69 FSMA 2000, as amended by FSA 2012.
94 The powers and procedure are laid down in Section 70 FSMA 2000, as amended by FSA 2012.
95 Section 12 FSMA 2000 (old).
96 Section 77 FSMA 2000, as amended by FSA 2012.
97 FCA (2013b), *How the Financial Conduct Authority will investigate and report on regulatory failure*, April 2013.
98 Section 78(5) FSMA 2000, as amended by FSA 2012.

information.[99] If HM Treasury withholds all or part of the material in the report from publication, it must publish and lay before Parliament a statement of the reasons for not publishing the report in full. Publication may take place in any form which the Treasury thinks fit.[100]

Publication of full records of Board meetings, annual accounts and Select Committees

FSA 2012 introduced the obligation for the FCA to publish the full records of meetings of the Board, as was recommended by the Treasury Select Committee.[101] Since 2004, the Board has already voluntarily published the summary minutes on its website.[102] Regarding the FCA's accounts and audit, the Treasury may require the FCA to comply with any provisions of the Companies Act 2006 about accounts and their audit which would not otherwise apply to it, or direct that any provision of that Act about accounts and their audit is to apply to the FCA with such modifications as are specified in the direction, whether or not the provision would otherwise apply to the FCA. The FCA must send a copy of its annual accounts to the Comptroller and Auditor General (National Audit Office), which has the responsibility for examining these accounts.[103] The Treasury must lay the copy of the certified accounts and the report before Parliament. Finally, we could observe that accountability is secured through the Treasury Select Committee.[104] This committee of the House of Commons in the UK Parliament has powers to examine the expenditure, administration and policy of the Treasury, including its agencies and associated authorities such as the FCA.

All the foregoing legal instruments are means by which the Government, and indirectly Parliament, can hold the FCA to account for the exercise of its functions. These are general instruments, but may be used in the context of the preventive AML policy as well. In practice, however, this happens to a limited extent.[105] More importantly, in the context of AML supervision a voluntary accountability mechanism applies.

Voluntary accountability mechanism under MLR 2007

In relation to the performance of the FCA's tasks under the Regulations, the FCA is accountable to HM Treasury. Although it is not an obligation under the MLR 2007, all AML supervisors submit special annual reports on their AML activities to the Treasury for this purpose. This is why it is said to be a 'voluntary' accountability mechanism. The FCA also publishes its own annual AML report online. The Treasury collects the submissions from all AML supervisors and publishes an aggregated report on its website. The idea behind this initiative is to increase the effectiveness of the supervisory efforts by improving transparency and accountability, and illustrating good practices. Because this is a voluntary regime, the Treasury has no formal powers to give instructions to the AML

99 See 82(3-5) FSMA 2000, as amended by FSA 2012.
100 Section 82(7) FSMA 2000, as amended by FSA 2012.
101 Section 10 Schedule 1ZA FSMA 2000 as amended by FSA 2012.
102 FCA (2013c), *Transparency*, Discussion Paper DP13/1**, March 2013, at 14.
103 Sections 14 and 15 Schedule 1ZA FSMA 2000 amended by FSA 2012.
104 Cf. in general about select committees as a form of accountability: Craig (2012) at 105.
105 In FSA's annual report for 2012-13, for example, only half a page was devoted to the FSA's activities under the AML policy: FSA (2013), *Annual report 2012-13*, at 76.

supervisors or to (dis)approve of the submissions. For the period 2012-13, for example, one AML supervisor did not submit its annual report on AML supervision. The reason for this was not disclosed in the Treasury report.[106] It appears that the information contained in HM Treasury's reports remains rather abstract and is sometimes even non-intelligible. For example, in the 2013 report, the Treasury stated that the AML supervisors in the accountancy sector performed 2,059 visits.[107] How this was calculated, which associations carried out the most visits and which ones performed the least, whether the visits were targeted AML visits or integrated into broader monitoring activity, were not explained. From an effective supervision perspective, it would be advisable to consider embedding this voluntary accountability regime in the Regulations. Some minimum powers could be given to the Treasury to ensure that all AML supervisors are accountable and transparent about their AML supervision in practice, and at the same time it may allow the Treasury to publish aggregated AML supervision reports that contain intelligible information and are meaningful for the general public as well.

In any case, a combination of the Treasury's annual AML supervision report and its own annual AML report that is publicly available leads to the conclusion that the FCA is highly transparent about and accountable for the exercise of its AML supervision within the voluntary regime.

6.4.1.3 Market independence and accountability

The FCA has a strong relationship with the regulated sector. It is entirely funded by the firms it regulates through fees in order to meet its expenses.[108] The FCA's AML policy must be self-funding. This means that for authorised businesses, part of their payable fees includes a fee for the verification of compliance with MLR 2007. Businesses that are not authorised by the FCA but need to be registered with it under the Regulations ('Annex I financial institutions') need to pay an amount of 100 GBP upon registration. This is a fixed fee.[109] The FCA cannot under-collect and is not allowed to over-collect.[110] Whereas the income used to be partially based on the fines it imposed on obliged institutions under the MLR 2007, since 2013 the FCA is obliged to pay to HM Treasury any amounts received by way of penalties imposed after deducting amounts that the FCA has applied towards expenses incurred by it in carrying out its functions under the Regulations.[111] This is a welcome change as it avoids the potential criticism that the regulator simply imposes high penalties to increase its own income.

106 HM Treasury (2013), par. 4.2.
107 Ibid., par. 5.2.
108 Section 23 Schedule 1ZA FSMA 2000 as amended by FSA 2012.
109 FCA, *Application for registration as an Annex I financial institution*, available at: <www.fca.org.uk/your-fca/documents/forms/application-for-registration-as-an-annex-i-financial-institution>, last visited on 13 May 2014.
110 Regulation 35(2) MLR 2007.
111 Regulation 35(4) MLR 2007 as amended by the Payment to Treasury of Penalties Regulations 2013, S.I. 2013/429.

The FCA is not required to give accountability specifically to the firms it regulates on how the funds are spent, although the principles of good regulation oblige the FCA to consider the need to use its resources in the most efficient and economical way as well as to be transparent about the exercise of its functions.[112] We have just seen that the FCA must give account through the publication of annual reports, as well as the organisation of annual public meetings. These meetings can be attended by market representatives. Financial services panels are also available to the regulated sector. These panels belong to the system that the FCA has to set up to make and maintain effective arrangements for consulting practitioners and consumers on the extent to which the FCA's general policies and practices are consistent with its general duties.[113] The four statutory panels are the FCA Practitioner Panel, the Smaller Businesses Practitioner Panel, the Markets Practitioner Panel and the Consumer Panel.[114]

> The FCA Practitioner Panel is composed of senior representatives from the financial services industry. The main objective is to represent the interests of practitioners and to provide input to the FCA from the industry in order to help it in meeting its statutory objectives and the principles of good regulation.[115] The Smaller Businesses Practitioner Panel operates in more or less the same way as the Practitioners Panel. It represent the views and interests of smaller regulated firms and provides advice to the FCA on its policy. According to the FCA, 'eligible practitioners for the Smaller Business Practitioner Panel are practitioners representing firms of small or medium size within their sector – whether by market capitalisation, funds under management, size of balance sheet and employees etc.'[116] The Chair of this Panel is also a member of the Practitioner Panel. Members of the Market Practitioner Panel 'are chosen as senior level representatives of sectors participating in financial markets'.[117] It overlaps to an extent with the Practitioner Panel. Finally, the Consumer Panel works 'to advise and challenge the FCA from the earliest stages of its policy development to ensure they take into account the consumer interest'.[118] This panel cooperates with other consumer organisations and reviews the FCA's policies and rules in relation to (the effectiveness of) consumer protection.

The panels provide different inputs to the FCA by representing the interest of consumers and different types of practitioners. Members of these panels are appointed by the FCA, but the panels express their views independently. The panels can only give advice to the FCA. The FCA is not obliged to follow this advice, although it must regularly publish its responses to the representations. This kind of participation has been called 'accountability from the bottom'.[119]

112 Section 3B FSMA 2000 as amended by FSA 2012.
113 Section 1M FSMA 2000 as amended by FSA 2012.
114 Sections 1N-1Q FSMA 2000 as amended by FSA 2012.
115 FCA, *Statutory Panels*, available at: www.fca.org.uk/about/governance/who/statutory-panels>, last visited 13 May 2014.
116 Ibid.
117 Ibid.
118 Financial Services Consumer Panel, *What is the Panel?*, available at: <www.fs-cp.org.uk/about_us/what_is_the_panel.shtml>, last visited on 13 May 2014.
119 Craig (2012) at 105.

6.4.2 Office of Fair Trading

6.4.2.1 Institutional embedding

The Office of Fair Trading is the UK's main consumer and competition authority established by the Enterprise Act 2002 as a statutory corporation. It is a non-ministerial department of the UK Government. The OFT's mission is to make markets work well for consumers and to contribute to economic development. It aims to have competitive, efficient, innovative markets which are responsive to consumer demands. It also ensures a high level of consumer protection, empowers consumers and ensures that they are confident in making decisions.[120] The Board is ultimately responsible for strategic direction, policy priorities and performance monitoring. The Board may authorise any (sub-)committee to perform the tasks, pursuant to paragraph 12 of Schedule 1 Enterprise Act. Board members and appointed non-Board members operate in four committees: the Audit and Risk Assurance Committee, Executive Committee, Policy Committee and Remuneration Committee. Each committee has its own terms of reference.

Under the Regulations, the Office of Fair Trading is the competent supervisor for non-FSA (FCA) authorised consumer credit financial institutions and for (residential and commercial) real estate agents.[121] AML supervision is carried out by the consumer credit and anti-money laundering division, more specifically by the Anti-Money Laundering Unit.[122] This Unit is subdivided into two divisions: the compliance and registration division and the business support division.[123] The AML Unit reports on a monthly basis to the Board on its progress and risks. In 2012, an estimated 11.5 FTE worked on AML supervision. OFT Representatives clarified that the AML Unit may have some additional staff around the time of fee collection.[124] The budget for the Unit was 1.1 million GBP, roughly 1.4 million Euros, in 2012.[125] The AML Unit is relatively small in relation to the total of number of institutions which the OFT supervises under the Regulations. In 2012, there were 12,323 institutions, of which little more than a half were estate agents (6,601).[126]

6.4.2.2 Political independence and accountability

Being a non-ministerial government department (NMGD), the OFT is an authority with a relatively high level of independence. Non-ministerial departments are Government departments 'in their own right – but they do not have their own minister. They are

120 OFT (2013), *Annual Report and Accounts 2012-13*, OFT1490, at 13.
121 Consumer credit financial institutions are businesses that are engaged in consumer credit lending requiring a standard licence. These do not need to be authorised by the FCA or be supervised by HMRC as a money service business.
122 The Consumer Credit and Anti-Money Laundering Division is divided into the Consumer Credit Group and Anti-Money Laundering Unit. The CCG is responsible for administering the Consumer Credit Act 2006; while the AML Unit carries out its activities under the MLR 2007.
123 OFT (2011), *Anti-Money Laundering Annual Report to HM Treasury 2010-11*, June 2011, at 24.
124 Interview Office of Fair Trading, April 2012.
125 OFT (2012), *Annual Report and Accounts 2011-12*, OFT1347, at 47.
126 Interview Office of Fair Trading, April 2012; OFT (2011) at 5.

usually headed up by a statutory board'.[127] They belong to the wider group of executive agencies.[128] The political independence of NMGDs in general is assured by being given the status of a government department, but only require accountability to Parliament (and the judiciary). It has been observed that the OFT 'constitutes a classic example of institutional depoliticization by completely excluding ministers from the controversial and highly political process of competition decisions and merger control'.[129] Although it acts under a high level of independence from the Government, the OFT has a less independent position than the FCA. Unlike the FCA, the OFT belongs to the Government.[130] Indirect influence can be exercised by the Secretary of State for Business, Innovation & Skills, through the appointment of the Chairman of the Office of Fair Trading and at least four Board members.[131] He must consult the Chairman before appointing a Board member.[132] The terms of members' appointments are determined by the Secretary of State, but may not exceed five years.[133] The Secretary of State has no powers to influence day-to-day or individual decisions made by the OFT.

The OFT itself stresses its independence from any Minister, and states that it is 'accountable to the public through Parliamentary scrutiny'.[134] It is by law obliged to publish annual plans and reports. The plans should contain a statement of the main objectives and priorities for the year and be preceded by a public consultation on its proposals.[135] The report should include at least a general survey of developments in respect of matters related to the OFT's functions, an assessment of the extent to which the main objectives and priorities have been met, a summary of significant decisions, investigations or other activities, as well as a summary of the allocation of the financial resources and, finally, an assessment of the OFT's performance and practices in relation to its enforcement functions.[136] Through its annual reports the OFT accounts for its overall policy and activities, but not for the individual decisions taken throughout the year. These are only included in a summarised fashion in the annual report when they are considered 'significant'. In practice, the OFT annual reports include limited information on AML supervision.[137] Nevertheless, the voluntary accountability mechanism under the Regulations, as was outlined above for the FCA, applies to the OFT as well. For this purpose the OFT sends a special report on its AML activities to HM Treasury. The Treasury has no formal powers to give instructions directly or indirectly or to formally (dis)approve of the annual AML reports from the OFT.

127 Cabinet Office (2012) at 9.
128 Craig (2012) at 101.
129 Wilks, S. (2007), 'Boardization and Corporate Governance in the UK as a Response to Depoliticization and Failing Accountability', *Public Policy and Administration*, vol. 22, issue 4, pp. 443-460 at 448.
130 Section 1 (2) Enterprise Act 2002 stipulates that the functions of the OFT are carried out on behalf of the Crown. The staff are civil servants.
131 The Secretary of State for BIS is the Minister with overall responsibility for the Department.
132 Section 1 Schedule 1 Enterprise Act 2002.
133 Section 3(1) of Schedule 1 Enterprise Act 2002.
134 OFT, *Accountability*, available at: www.oft.gov.uk/about-the-oft/oft-structure/accountability/#.U3IpWPlPzzQ, last visited on 7 January 2014.
135 Section 3 Enterprise Act 2002.
136 Section 4 Enterprise Act 2002.
137 For example: OFT (2013) at 24.

From an effective supervision perspective, in particular transparency and accountability, it is unfortunate that the OFT only published its 2010-11 report on its website.[138]

6.4.2.3 Market independence and accountability

Under the Regulations the relationship between the OFT and the market is of a financial nature. In general the OFT is partially funded by the Government, and partially by the application of a fee system for the institutions subject to OFT's supervision under the Consumer Credit Act 1974 and MLR 2007.[139] AML supervision, however, is required to be fully self-funding.[140] Therefore, the OFT requires the institutions and professionals for which it has supervisory responsibility to pay registration and annual fees. For the OFT it is also prohibited to over-collect.[141] The amounts of the fees are set annually and reviewed at the end of each year. If the OFT has spent less money on its AML activities than it has received through the fees, the institutions will be refunded through a discount the following year.[142]

> This occurred in 2011. At the end of the year, the OFT considered that: '[f]ees are based on OFT's best estimates of costs for the financial year. However, the OFT's costs have been less than were originally estimated. Although the number of businesses registering has been in line with initial forecasts, the total income received from those businesses has exceeded expectations, due to a higher than expected number of premises per business and also because the AML team has carried a number of vacancies. As a result, for the financial year 2010/11 the OFT's AML regime had an unintended surplus of £633,000'.[143] The OFT remedied this by giving a discount for the annual fee for the following year.

The supervised population cannot influence how the OFT spends its AML budget. The Office is required to present the overall Accounts to Parliament annually.[144] The accounts are audited by the National Audit Office.

6.4.2.4 Transfer of the AML supervision of estate agents to HM Revenue and Customs as of April 2014

In 2012 it became clear that the UK Government intended to create a new Competition and Markets Authority (hereafter CMA). In May 2012, the Government presented the Enterprise and Regulatory Reform Bill that included the creation of the CMA. The Government considered that the UK's competition policy posed challenges, particularly because two authorities – the Office of Fair Trading and the Competition Commission – were responsible for the enforcement of that policy, leading to a duplication of and

138 OFT (2011), available at: <www.oft.gov.uk/shared_oft/AML/oft1345.pdf>, last visited on 7 January 2014.
139 OFT (2013) at 43 et seq.
140 Regulation 35 MLR 2007.
141 Regulation 35(2) MLR 2007.
142 OFT (2011a), *OFT Anti-Money Laundering Registration Policy*, OFT1104, at 9-10.
143 OFT (2011) at 7.
144 Section 6(4) Government Resources and Accounts Act 2000.

inefficiency in the work.[145] The CMA was supposed to become the UK's principal competition authority and would assume most of the functions of the OFT and the CC. The Government considered that: '[t]he Competition and Markets Authority will provide greater coherence in competition enforcement and a more streamlined approach to decision making. Processes will be faster and less burdensome for business. A single strong centre of competition expertise will provide national and international leadership'.[146] The CMA was established in October 2013 and took over the functions of the Office of Fair Trading and the Competition Commission on the 1st of April 2014. Both authorities were abolished on that date.

The Government decided to transfer the OFT's responsibility under the Money Laundering Regulations to the FCA and Her Majesty's Revenue and Customs (hereafter 'HMRC'). On the 1st of April 2014, the FCA became the AML supervisor for consumer credit financial institutions and HMRC for real estate agents. The AML supervision of real estate agents would preferably go to the professional bodies in the real estate sector but since this is not allowed under the Third Directive, the UK Government decided to transfer this responsibility to HMRC. HMRC was considered to be the most appropriate authority due to its supervisory experience under the MLR 2007 in relation to a wide range of businesses.[147] HMRC is the UK's Tax Authority. Like the OFT, it is a non-ministerial department. It is established by the Commissioners for Revenue and Customs Act (CRCA) 2005.[148] Being a non-ministerial department means that it is a Government department without its own minister. Under the Regulations, HMRC acts as a so-called default supervisor. It supervises high-value dealers, money service businesses and trust and company service providers, as well as auditors, accountants and tax advisers that are not members of any of the professional associations appointed as AML supervisor.[149] Since 2009, it also has AML supervisory responsibility for bill payment service providers and telecommunication, digital and IT payment service providers that are not supervised by the FCA.[150] Anti-money laundering supervision is exercised by the AML Supervision Unit (AMLS). Around 150 people work in this Unit, of which an estimated 20-30 people become involved in the AML supervision of estate agents.[151] The budget for the Unit entirely consists of the fees it collects under the registration system. In 2013, this was 7.5 million GBP.[152]

145 Department for Business, Innovations & Skills (2013), *Enterprise and Regulatory Reform Act 2013: Policy Paper*, June 2013, at 14.
146 Ibid., at 15.
147 Interview HM Revenue and Customs, May 2014; Interview HM Treasury, May 2014.
148 Commissioners for Revenue and Customs Act (CRCA) 2005, c.11, last amended by S.I. 2014/834 (26th of March 2014).
149 Regulation 23(1)(d) MLR 2007.
150 Schedule 6 of the Payment Service Regulations 2009, S.I. 2009/209.
151 Interview HM Revenue and Customs, May 2014.
152 HM Revenue and Customs (2013), *Annual report and accounts 2012-13*, at 121.

The OFT's powers under the Estate Agents Act 1979 will move to Powys County Council.[153] This Welsh Council will run the National Trading Standards Estate Agents Team (NTSEAT) and takes on, inter alia, the power to decide whether estate agents are fit to carry out their work in the terms of the Act. The Council carries out the work on behalf of the National Trading Standards Board pursuant to a three-year contract. Local trading standards officers throughout the UK will conduct investigations into possible breaches of the Estate Agents Act 1979 and will take whatever action they deem appropriate. The approval of codes of practice for estate agents moves to the Trading Standards Institute which operates a successor scheme to the OFT's Consumer Codes Approval Scheme. Consumers can complain about estate agents at Citizens Advice Bureaus.

6.4.3 Institute of Chartered Accountants in England and Wales

6.4.3.1 Institutional embedding

The Institute of Charted Accountants in England and Wales is one of the oldest professional associations in the accountancy sector in the UK, founded by Royal Charter in 1880. The Charter recognises the ICAEW's 'pre-eminence, stability and permanence, as well as defining its public interest remit'.[154] Members are allowed to use the title of chartered accountant. This, however, does not provide a legal position which is different from other accountants.

ICAEW has a wide range of missions varying from the advancement of the theory and practice of accountancy, finance, business and commerce in all their aspects, to the preservation of the professional independence of accountants and the maintenance of high standards of practice and professional conduct by all its members.[155] The Council is responsible for the management and oversight of ICAEW's activities. It decides on the strategy and budget and is allowed to delegate some powers to other bodies within ICAEW.[156] The maximum number of members of the Council is 85 elected members, 20 co-opted members, and 15 members appointed ex officio.[157] The main body to which the Council has delegated powers is the Board. The Board is comprised of a maximum of 15 members.[158] It acts in accordance with the strategy and budget approved by the

153 Schedule 2 of The Public Bodies (Abolition of the National Consumer Council and Transfer of the Office of Fair Trading's Functions in relation to Estate Agents etc.) Order 2014, S.I. 2014/631.

154 ICAEW, *Who we are*, available at: <www.icaew.com/en/about-icaew/who-we-are>, last visited on 9 May 2014.

155 See for the full mission statement: Article 1(a)(i)-(v) ICAEW Supplemental Charter 1948 to Royal Charter 1880.

156 Clause 2 of the ICAEW Supplemental Charter 1948; Principal Bye-law 49. Principal Bye-laws made under Clause 15 of the Supplemental Charter 1948.

157 Principal Bye-law 32. An elected member is a member chosen by ICAEW members (Bye-law 33). A co-opted member is appointed by the Council. This person shall not be appointed for a term exceeding four years and may not be older than 70 years. A co-opted member is eligible for another term (Bye-law 36). Ex-officio members of the Council are those members that have a particular function, such as President, Deputy-President and Vice-President. During their term of office, they are considered ex-officio members (Bye-law 36a). Other holders of offices within ICAEW who are not a Council member can also become an ex-officio Council member (Bye-law 36b).

158 ICAEW, *Formal Scheme of Delegations*, available at: <www.icaew.com/en/about-icaew/who-we-are/committees/scheme-of-delegations >, last visited on 9 May 2014.

Council. The Board's responsibility lies with the development and implementation of ICAEW strategy, policy and operational plans, and the resources. It is supported by five Departmental Boards.[159] Each of these Departmental Boards is accountable to the Board, which in turn is accountable to the Council. In all Committees, the majority is composed of ICAEW members, with a minority of non-accountant members.

AML supervision within ICAEW is the responsibility of the Professional Standards Board (hereafter PSB). It comes in with the application of members to the Practice Assurance Scheme (hereafter PAS or 'the Scheme') and the monitoring thereof, which is the responsibility of the Practice Assurance Committee (hereafter PAC).[160] The Scheme is a framework that sets quality assurance principles for member firms and practising certificate holders (PC holders[161]), and offers practice support and advice, together with monitoring visits that aim to review the efficiency and competence of members. The PAC is responsible for all operational matters relating to the Practice Assurance monitoring process and is directly accountable to the PSB.[162] The actual monitoring is done by the Quality Assurance Department (hereafter QAD). This department operates under the responsibility of the PAC and is directly accountable it. The PAC 'considers important practical issues arising from visits, gives guidance to QAD reviewers and makes policy recommendations to the ICAEW's Professional Standards Board'.[163] In early 2014, the QAD was comprised of approximately 40 field-based reviewers with the task of monitoring firms under the Scheme and 15 staff in management and administrative functions. Hence, in total roughly 55 staff have direct responsibility for AML supervision. ICAEW supervises over 13,000 member firms and 23,000 PC holders under the PAS and, hence, for AML purposes.[164] Additionally, ICAEW supervises a number of firms on a contractual basis. These firms are non-member firms and are usually not subject to a scheme that is similar to ICAEW's PAS or are firms that provide services that do not require a practising certificate.[165] A contract is offered to an accountancy firm where at least one principal of the firm is an ICAEW member. There were approximately 200 such contracts with non-member firms at the beginning of 2014. As with ICAEW member firms, AML supervision is included within the PAS monitoring contract.[166]

159 The Commercial Board, Professional Standards Board, Learning and Professional Development, Member Services and the Technical Strategy.

160 See about ICAEW membership and monitoring under the Practice Assurance Scheme: § 6.5.5.

161 A practising certificate holder is a principal in an accountancy firm and who has been certified to act in public practice. This means that they have become a principal of an accountancy firm or independently offer accountancy services to the public. PC holders must comply with the practice assurance regulations. More about this in § 6.5.5.

162 ICAEW *Formal Scheme of Delegations*, Appendix 12.7 (Practice Assurance Committee).

163 ICAEW (2012), *Effective AML/CTF Supervision 2011*, submitted in May 2012 by ICAEW to HM Treasury, at 3. This report is not a publicly available report, but has been provided to me during the interview with ICAEW for research purposes. I have been allowed to use and refer to the report for the purposes of this research: Institute of Chartered Accountants in England and Wales, May 2014. More about the tasks of PAC, see § 6.8.4.

164 ICAEW (2012) at 5; Interview Institute of Chartered Accountants in England and Wales, May 2014.

165 It is possible, for example, that a firm is owned and managed by a majority of accountants that are members of a professional association that does apply membership and monitoring to firms. See: ICAEW (2012) at 5.

166 Interview Institute of Chartered Accountants in England and Wales, May 2014.

6.4.3.2 Independence and accountability

Political independence and accountability

ICAEW is a private supervisor and is independent from the Government in terms of its activities and funding. To a certain extent, however, it is accountable to the Financial Reporting Council (hereafter FRC). The FRC is the UK's independent regulator responsible for promoting high quality corporate governance and reporting in order to foster investment. The Council operates under the authority of the Department for Business, Innovation and Skills (BIS) and undertakes a wide range of tasks.[167] Relevant for this research is the oversight of the regulation of statutory auditors by the recognised supervisory and qualifying bodies.[168] This task is exercised by the FRC's Conduct Committee and supporting committees. When the FRC is of the opinion that a professional association has not fulfilled its tasks properly in the statutory field of auditing, it can take action. The FRC also has the non-statutory task of independent oversight of the regulation of the accountancy profession by the professional associations beyond the regulated activity of auditing. This is based on voluntary agreements with the six chartered professional associations, including ICAEW.[169] These associations have agreed to consider FRC recommendations in relation to the unregulated accountancy activities as well. In this oversight role, the FRC can only make recommendations on how activities of the associations might be improved. The professional associations can decide to implement the recommendations within a reasonable period of time or can decide not to implement the recommendations. In that case, the associations must provide reasons for this decision.[170] The FRC cannot enforce its recommendations.

The FRC's non-statutory oversight has in the past included the monitoring procedures of the professional associations.[171] Anti-money laundering, however, was not a focal point of attention. Nevertheless, we have seen before that a more or less voluntary accountability regime applies to the AML supervisors. This accountability regime was already described under the accountability structures of the FCA and OFT above and applies in a similar fashion to ICAEW. ICAEW does not publish these annual returns to HM Treasury on its own website. In light of the theoretical framework, particularly from the accountability and transparency requirements, it is advised to publish these annual returns.

167 See the website of the Financial Reporting Council for more information: <www.frc.org.uk>.

168 Sections 1228 and 1229 Companies Act 2006 in conjunction with the Statutory Auditors (Amendment of Companies Act 2006 and Delegation of Functions etc.) Order 2012.

169 The Institute of Chartered Accountants in England and Wales (ICAEW), The Institute of Chartered Accountants of Scotland (ICAS), The Institute of Chartered Accountants in Ireland (ICAI), The Association of Chartered Certified Accountants (ACCA), The Chartered Institute of Management Accountants (CIMA), and The Chartered Institute of Public Finance and Accountancy (CIPFA). For more information: Financial Reporting Council, *Oversight of the accountancy profession*, available at: <www.frc.org.uk/Our-Work/Conduct/Professional-oversight/Oversight-of-the-accountancy-profession.aspx>, last visited on 9 May 2014.

170 See for example: FRC Professional Oversight Board (2010), *Review of the Monitoring Arrangements by the UK Professional Accountancy Bodies of Their Members Who Practise Non-Regulated Accountancy Services*, May 2010, at 2.

171 FRC Professional Oversight Board (2010).

Market independence

The downside of a close relationship between professional associations and members is that there may be a risk that professional associations are not adequately independent from their members.[172] In the 1990s criticism was voiced with regard to the role of professional and trade associations in the accountancy sector in the UK. It was stated, inter alia, that the associations were not at all independent from the members and, as a result, they aimed to 'sweep things under the carpet'.[173] In the *AGIP v Jackson* affair, mentioned above, ICAEW's role was heavily criticised.[174] This strong criticism has resulted in a less benign regulatory environment in the UK.[175]

Throughout the organisation, members seem to have a great deal of influence through their majority presence in Committees, the Board and, ultimately, the Council.[176] This is also the case for AML supervision. The QAD, which carries out the AML monitoring, consists of ICAEW staff only. This prevents members, at least in the monitoring phase, from monitoring one another. The PAC, responsible for the decision whether or not a case is forwarded to the investigation and disciplinary stage, however, consists of ten members, of which eight are ICAEW members and two are non-accountants.[177] Other committees involved in the supervision and sanctioning procedure are the Investigation Committee and the Disciplinary Committee. The Investigation Committee and the Disciplinary Committee both consist of at least fourteen members of whom a quarter must be independent non-accountants.[178] It is ultimately the Disciplinary Tribunal, consisting of two ICAEW members and one non-accountant member from the Disciplinary Committee, that decides whether and if so, which, disciplinary sanction should be imposed.[179] The three committees and the Tribunal have an important role in AML supervision and sanctioning. The independent non-accountant members are part of the Committees to ensure independence, as the FATF also outlined in 2007.[180] Nevertheless, from the perspective of effective supervision this does not seem to be sufficient. Chapter 2 pointed out that there should be an adequate level of independence from the market. Through their majority presence in all three committees, with a balance of approximately 75% against 25%, ICAEW members play a crucial role throughout the entire disciplinary process. It would be advisable to create a more even balance, or even to decide that the Disciplinary Committee and the Tribunal become entirely independent from the members. This avoids (the appearance of) any lack of independence on the side of ICAEW and, thus, criticism in that respect.

172 See § 2.4.2.1 and 3.2.2.2.

173 Mitchell, A., Sikka, P., Willmot, H. (1998a), 'Sweeping it under the carpet: The role of accountancy firms in money laundering', *Accounting, Organizations and Society*, vol. 23, issue. 5/6, pp. 589-607.

174 Ibid., at 602-603.

175 Friedman and Phillips (2004) at 188.

176 This, too, has been criticised: Friedman and Phillips state that such traditional governance 'seems unsuited to a context of complexity and change': Friedman and Phillips (2004) at 189.

177 ICAEW *Formal Scheme of Delegations*, Appendix 12.7 (Practice Assurance Committee).

178 ICAEW, *Professional Standards Committees*, available at: <www.icaew.com/en/about-icaew/who-we-are/committees/professional-standards-committees>, last visited on 12 May 2014.

179 Ibid. Please note that this Tribunal does not form part of the UK's tribunal system managed by the Tribunals Service.

180 FATF (2007a) at 225.

ICAEW and its members have a financial relationship as well. Members must pay a fee according to the extent to which they make use of the services offered by ICAEW. The membership fee in 2012-13 was around 150 GBP per year. In addition, members must pay an extra fee if they need training, have to be supervised under the Practice Assurance Scheme, if they want to join an interest group, and so on. The costs for enforcing ICAEW's AML supervision are borne by the members. Accordingly, members must apply and pay for AML supervision separately. There is no standard fee-scale. ICAEW gives a rough indication of 310 GBP (plus VAT) per year for firms with one ICAEW principal and one non-ICAEW member principal.[181] The Council is competent in deciding how the budget is spent. Accountability for the choices made in relation to expenditures is provided through the financial review that accompanies ICAEW's annual report.

6.4.4 Association of Accounting Technicians

6.4.4.1 Institutional embedding

The Association of Accounting Technicians was founded in 1980 and is partly registered as a charity and partly as a company limited by guarantee.[182] It has no Royal Charter; its founding norms are the Articles of Association. AAT members, or those qualified by AAT, can use the title accounting technician. They are not allowed to call themselves chartered accountants, although they can perform exactly the same tasks as most chartered accountants, with the exception of the statutory activities of insolvency and audit.[183] AAT has two main missions. It aims to advance public education and promote the study of the practice, theory and techniques of accountancy. And the AAT aims to prevent crime and promote the sound administration of the law for the public benefit by promoting and enforcing standards of professional conduct amongst those engaged in accountancy and monitoring and supervising their compliance with money laundering legislation.[184]

> AAT is associated with four professional associations: the Chartered Institute of Public Finance and Accountancy (CIPFA), the Institute of Chartered Accountants in England and Wales (ICAEW), the Chartered Institute of Management Accountants (CIMA), and the Institute of Chartered Accountants of Scotland (ICAS). These associations are called Sponsoring Bodies as they recognise AAT qualifications and offer accounting technicians a short route towards becoming a chartered accountant. Sponsoring bodies can each appoint up to three members in the AAT's Council and by that they contribute to the development and expertise of AAT. Although the name may suggest so, sponsorship is non-financial.[185]

The AAT's primary body is the Council. The Council consists of a President, ex-officio members of Council, nominated members of Council, elected members of Council and

181 ICAEW, *Anti-money laundering supervision*, available at: <www.icaew.com/en/technical/legal-and-regulatory/money-laundering/anti-money-laundering-supervision>, last visited on 12 May 2014.

182 AAT (2013), *Annual report and financial statements of the group for the year ending 31 December 2013*, at 36.

183 See § 6.4.3.1.

184 Article 4 AAT Articles of Association.

185 AAT (2013) at 38.

co-opted members of Council.[186] The size of the Council is variable and its tasks are broadly to decide on the strategy, policy and budget of AAT. It may approve policies; alter, revoke or add to rules, regulations and bye-laws relating to AAT and its affairs; determine the requirements and qualifications for membership; set the amount of fees; keep a list of members and it may discipline members for misconduct by making regulations on what is considered to be misconduct, the disciplinary procedures and sanctions.[187] The Council may delegate its tasks to Boards.[188] The Boards operate within the framework set by the Council, decide on how the allocated resources are spent specifically, and are directly accountable to the Council.[189] Below the level of the Boards various panels, steering groups, committees and sub-committees with specific assignments operate. In the context of disciplinary action, the AAT's Investigations Committee and Disciplinary Committee play an important role.[190]

Pursuant to Schedule 3 MLR 2007, AAT is an AML supervisor for its members. Compliance with AML legislation is even an explicit mission of AAT. Supervision is embedded within the general monitoring process under the responsibility of the Regulation and Compliance Board (hereafter 'RCB'). The RCB only deals with the regulatory policy and has no powers to influence the monitoring work.[191] This is the responsibility of the Conduct & Compliance Team (hereafter 'CCT'), which operates under the RCB. However, the actual monitoring is carried out by ICAEW under a contract.[192] AAT has approximately 130,000 members worldwide.[193] AAT does not carry out AML supervision on all members. Student members and members based outside the UK are not supervised by AAT under the Regulations.[194] In early 2014 AAT supervised approximately 3,367 members under the MLR 2007.[195] As we will see in § 6.5.6, AAT members are always individuals, but AAT may supervise firms whose partners are all member of one of the AML Supervisors listed in Schedule 3 of the

186 Article 41(1) AAT Articles of Association. Ex-officio Members are members who are members of Council by virtue of their office. These are the President, the Vice-President, and former Presidents until two years after they ceased office (Article (41(2)). Nominated members are persons who are nominated by each of the Sponsoring Bodies to become a nominated member of the Council. Each Sponsoring Body may nominate up to three persons (Article 42(1)). Elected members are AAT members chosen among AAT's members to represent their interests within the Council. There is a maximum of 18 elected members in the Council (Article 45(1)). Co-opted members are members who are appointed by the Council. There is a maximum number of four co-opted members (Article 46(1)). All members have the same rights.

187 See for the full list of tasks and powers the AAT's Articles of Association.

188 Article 59 AAT Articles of Association.

189 The following Boards operate within AAT: Learning and Development Board (LDB), the Members' Services Board (MSB), the Regulation and Compliance Board (RCB), the Resources Board (RB), and the Audit and Assurance Board (AAB).

190 AAT 2012 Disciplinary Regulations, 15 March 2012.

191 Interview Association of Accounting Technicians, May 2014.

192 More details about this procedure in § 6.9.2.

193 AAT (2013) at 13.

194 Members based outside the UK are not supervised because they fall outside the AAT's jurisdiction, as licences only apply within UK territory. Student members are not supervised because they are not yet qualified AAT members. If they already perform accountancy tasks, they have to register with HMRC in order to be supervised under the MLR 2007.

195 Interview Association of Accounting Technicians, May 2014.

MLR 2007 unless the partners' activities are confined to providing administrative support to the firm.[196]

6.4.4.2 Independence and accountability

Political independence and accountability

AAT is a private supervisor and is independent from the Government in terms of its activities and funding. Unlike ICAEW, there is no statutory or contractual oversight of regulation from the FRC's Conduct Committee. AAT members do not perform the statutory tasks of audit, insolvency or investment business, and the non-statutory oversight of the regulation of the accountancy profession by the FRC applies to the six chartered professional associations only. There are thus no formal accountability mechanisms in place between AAT and the Government, either directly or indirectly. Nevertheless, it appears that AAT engages with the FRC when it comes to consultations and advice.[197] In the context of AML supervision, I have already dealt with the accountability regime under the Regulations. This regime applies to AAT in the same fashion as for the other AML supervisors. AAT does not publish its annual returns to HM Treasury online. In light of the theoretical framework, particularly from the accountability and transparency requirements, it is advised to publish these annual returns.

Market independence

Throughout AAT's governance, members play an important role. They are represented in the AAT Council, as well as the various Boards and Committees. The CCT, however, consists solely of AAT staff. Based on (perceived) risks, this team selects the members that should be monitored in a particular year. Later in the disciplinary procedure important roles are played by the Investigations Committee and the Disciplinary Committee. The Investigations Committee consists of five AAT Council members.[198] Its task is to oversee the investigation conducted by the CCT of any misconduct against a member. One Council member from the Investigations Committee and one CCT staff member jointly form an 'Investigations Team'. The Council member can be actively involved in the investigation, direct the CCT staff member to carry out a further investigation and monitor the progress of further investigations, if they are needed. The Investigations Team ultimately decides whether or not the case should be forwarded to the Disciplinary Committee. If the Council member and the CCT staff member do not agree, the former has a casting vote.[199] The Disciplinary Committee is entirely independent from the AAT Governance structure in the sense that no Council members take a place in this Committee. The Committee consists of twelve people and they are either AAT members (but not Council members) and independent lay persons who are not professional accountants.[200] Usually these are people who have worked at other professional associations or are solicitors. The AAT Council

196 AAT, *MIP Guidance*, available at: <www.aat.org.uk/mip-guidance>, last visited on 18 June 2014.

197 E.g. AAT (2011), *Annual report and financial statements of the group for the year ending 31 December 2011*, at 9.

198 AAT 2012 Disciplinary Regulation 4a.

199 More details about this procedure in § 6.9.4.

200 AAT 2012 Disciplinary Regulation 4b.

has no powers to influence the Disciplinary Committee and this Committee is thus fully separated from the Council, and the RCB. Three selected people from the Disciplinary Committee – one AAT member and two independent lay persons – form the Disciplinary Tribunal.[201] The Tribunal decides whether and which sanction to impose. In light of the theoretical framework of effective supervision, this demonstrates an adequate level of market independence. Monitoring is the responsibility of the CCT, which fully consists of AAT staff. AAT members do play a role throughout the disciplinary procedure, but unlike the case for ICAEW, they do not represent the majority. Particular decisive factors are the fact that the Disciplinary Committee is independent from the AAT Governance structure and the Disciplinary Tribunal consists of a majority of independent lay members.

AAT does not receive any Government funding and its activities are entirely funded from membership fees and licences. In January 2014 AAT required a general admission fee of 45 GBP from members. On top of that, AAT requires members to pay for trainings (accounting qualifications are divided into different levels), registrations, and assessments.[202] AAT requires its members to apply for AML supervision separately and to pay an additional fee on top of the basic membership fee. For the year 2013-14 this fee was 80 GBP per partner or director who provides professional services to clients. A reduction in the fee applies to members with a gross fee income below 7,000 GBP. No fees had to be paid by members with a gross fee income below 1,000 GBP. The Council is competent in deciding how the AAT budget is spent. Accountability for the choices made in relation to the expenditures is provided through the financial review that accompanies AAT's annual report. There are no ways for members to influence AAT's spending of its budget.

6.4.5 Concluding remarks

This section presented the institutional aspects of the AML Supervisors. It is interesting to observe that the AML supervisors in the UK are different from each other in terms of independence and accountability. AML supervision is partly exercised by public bodies. Comparing the FCA and OFT it can be observed that most independence, and at the same time most accountability obligations to counterbalance this independence, is given to the FCA. At the same time is AML supervision exercised by professional associations as well. These do not form part of the UK's system of public bodies, but even between the professional associations the level of independence from the Government and the accountability obligations differ. AAT seems to be positioned at the greatest distance from the Government in terms of independence, and interestingly, also in terms of accountability. Contrary to the FCA, where the high level of independence is counterbalanced by a wide variety of accountability mechanisms embedded in the law, only the voluntary accountability mechanism to HM Treasury applies to AAT to account for the exercise of the public task of AML supervision.

201 Please note that this Tribunal does not form part of the UK's tribunal system managed by the Tribunals Service.

202 AAT, *AAT Fees*, available at: <www.aat.org.uk/qualifications/aat-fees>, last visited on 12 May 2014.

Under the Regulations, the FCA is the AML Supervisor for FSMA-authorised institutions, including banks, as well as for some other financial institutions. AML supervision is carried out by firm supervisors and a specialist financial crime supervision team. In 2014, the FCA had responsibility for over roughly 50,000 firms, of which over 300 are UK banks and branches. Being a non-departmental public body, the FCA is highly independent and this status is laid down in legislation. At the same time, a wide range of legal mechanisms counterbalance this independence. Recent years have demonstrated an increased attention for accountability mechanisms of the FCA. Currently, the FCA can be held to account through the following means: annual report, public annual meeting, independent inquiry (possibly exercised by an independent person), the newly established obligation for the FCA to carry out investigations on regulatory failure on its own initiative or under the direction of HM Treasury, the publication of full records of Board meetings, annual accounts and through questions from the Treasury Select Committee. HM Treasury must lay down some of the aforementioned reports before Parliament. These mechanisms can be used to account for the FCA's AML supervision. However, a more or less voluntary accountability mechanism applies. In relation to the performance of the FCA's tasks under MLR 2007, the FCA is accountable to HM Treasury. AML supervisors send, on a voluntary basis, an annual report on their AML activities to the Treasury. The FCA publishes this report online. The Treasury gathers all reports and publishes a report with aggregate findings as well. The FCA is fully funded by fees and has, therefore, a strong relationship with the market. The market is represented via statutory panels that give advice to the FCA from the consumer and practitioner perspective. The FCA is obliged by law to maintain effective arrangements for consulting practitioners and consumers on the extent to which the FCA's general policies and practices are consistent with its general duties. Accountability is given via the annual report and annual public meeting. It appears that the FCA's statutory independence is adequately counterbalanced by a large number accountability mechanisms.

The Office of Fair Trading is the UK's main consumer and competition authority. Under the Regulations, it supervises non-FCA-authorised consumer credit financial institutions and real estate agents. Supervision is exercised by the AML Unit. This unit is small in relation to the total of number of institutions which the OFT supervises under the Regulations: in 2012, OFT supervised 12,323 institutions, of which 6,601 were real estate agents. The OFT is a non-ministerial government department, and is positioned under the Department of Business, Innovation and Skills (BIS). The Secretary of State for the Department of BIS has no powers to exert any influence on day-to-day and individual decisions. The OFT is accountable to the public through Parliamentary scrutiny and is obliged by law to publish annual plans, subject to consultation, and annual reports. The OFT accounts for its overall policy and activities, but not for the individual decisions taken throughout the year. In practice, the OFT hardly uses the reports to account for its AML supervision. Accountability is rather given to the Treasury through the voluntary mechanism. Under the Regulations the relationship between the OFT and the market is of a financial nature. The supervised population cannot influence how the OFT spends its AML budget and it accounts for the spending in its annual report. There are no issues in relation to the OFT's market independence. As of the 1st of April 2014, AML supervisory responsibility for estate agents has moved to HMRC. The OFT has now been abolished as it has merged with the Competition Commission to form the Competition and Markets Authority.

ICAEW and AAT supervise their members. Within ICAEW, AML supervision comes with members applying to the Practice Assurance Scheme and the monitoring thereof. ICAEW supervises 13,000 member firms and 23,000 PC holders. It also has around 200 supervisory contracts with non-member firms that are supervised by ICAEW under the MLR 2007. Within AAT, AML supervision is embedded within the general supervisory process under the authority of the Regulation and Compliance Board. AAT has responsibility for AML supervision for 3,367 members. Monitoring is exercised by the Conduct & Compliance team, which has outsourced the actual monitoring to ICAEW staff. Both ICAEW and AAT are private supervisors and operate largely without Government influence, although there is a difference between the two professional associations as ICAEW has more connections with the Government than AAT has. Indirectly, the Government can hold ICAEW accountable as there is statutory (auditing) and the contractual oversight of regulation from the Financial Reporting Council. No such formal relationship applies to AAT. The voluntary accountability regime under the MLR 2007 applies to both associations. Both associations do not publish their own annual AML reports online. From the perspective of effective supervision, in particular accountability and transparency, it is recommended to publish these reports. In terms of market independence, the two differ. Within ICAEW members play a crucial role during the disciplinary procedure. They have a large majority in the committees that are responsible for deciding whether to start disciplinary proceedings and to impose a sanction. A better balance should be created, or ICAEW should make the Disciplinary Committee and the Tribunal entirely independent from the members. This avoids (the appearance of) any lack of independence. Within AAT, members do play a role throughout the disciplinary procedure, but unlike the case of ICAEW, they do not represent a majority in the relevant committees. Both ICAEW and AAT's AML supervision is required to be self-funding. They collect the budget for the exercise of AML supervision through the levying of fees. Members cannot influence any budgetary decisions, and both associations account for the spending of the budget in their annual reports. In sum, it appears that AAT has an adequate level of market independence, whereas from the perspective of effective supervision ICAEW should diminish the role of its members during the disciplinary procedure.

In relation to the voluntary accountability mechanism that applies to all four AML supervisors included in this research, it was observed that HM Treasury's reports sometimes remain rather abstract and even non-intelligible. From an effective supervision perspective, it would be advisable to consider embedding this voluntary accountability regime in the Regulations. Some minimum powers could be given to the Treasury to ensure that all AML supervisors are accountable and transparent about their AML supervision in practice, and at the same time it may allow the Treasury to publish aggregated AML supervision reports that contain intelligible information and are meaningful for the general public as well.

6.5 The regulation of banks, real estate agents and accountants

This section verifies the extent to which banks, accountants and real estate agents are regulated sectors or professions in the United Kingdom. It gives an insight into the question whether the supervisory authorities have, or can have, an adequate knowledge of the institutions and professionals for which they have supervisory responsibility. This section pays attention to the definition of banks, real estate agents and accountants under the AML Act where this differs from other legislation.

Before turning to the specific institutions individually, attention is first paid to the rather unique obligation to register. It is unique in the sense that such is not required by the FATF Recommendations or by the Third Directive. Although other EU Member States have some registration obligations, no other Member State has such an extensive registration obligation specifically under the preventive AML policy. This could therefore be seen as a gold-plating exercise by the UK legislator.[203] The duty or power to keep registers for some supervisors in combination with the obligation to register for the regulated sector is not a new feature in the UK, though. The previous regime already contained elements of this in relation to money service operators and high value dealers.

6.5.1 Obligation to register under MLR 2007

The duty or power to keep registers under the Regulation applies to HMRC, the FCA and the OFT. It does not apply to the professional and trade associations that supervise their members. The default supervisor HMRC is partly assigned the *duty* to maintain registers for high value dealers, money service businesses and trust or company service providers, bill payment service providers and telecommunication, digital and IT payment service providers, for which it has supervisory responsibility.[204] In addition, it has been given the *power* to keep registers for accountants, auditors or tax advisors which are not members of a professional association.[205] HMRC has made use of this discretion, which means that these professionals should also register themselves with HMRC. HMRC may keep the register in any form it thinks fit and may publish or make available for public inspection all or part of the register.[206] Regulation 32 provides the FCA and the OFT with the power to maintain a specific AML register. Both supervisors have decided to make use of this possibility, which means that institutions that fall under their supervisory responsibility are obliged to apply for AML registration and pay fees accordingly.[207] For the FCA the

203 Gold-plating is a term that refers to the practice of national legislators exceeding the terms of EU Directives when transposing them into national law. Cf. Chapter 4 with regard to the external expert review system.

204 Regulation 25(1) MLR 2007. Sub-paragraphs (d) en (e) were inserted by the Payment Services Regulations 2009, S.I. 2009/209.

205 Regulation 32(4) MLR 2007.

206 Regulation 25(2) and 25(3) MLR 2007. See for the FCA and OFT: Regulations 32(6) and 32 (7) MLR 2007.

207 Regulation 33 MLR 2007. The registration policy is published on the FCA's website: FCA, *Application for registration as an Annex I financial institution*, available at: <www.fca.org.uk/your-fca/documents/forms/application-for-registration-as-an-annex-i-financial-institution>, last visited on 13 May 2014; OFT (2011a) (also published online).

obligation to register only applies to the so-called Annex I financial institutions.[208] For authorised institutions, like banks, the more stringent authorisation requirements of the FSMA 2000 apply. The OFT maintains an AML register with respect to both consumer credit financial institutions and estate agents.[209]

It seems that the main rationale behind the registration system is to enable Government authorities that act as AML supervisors to obtain a clear picture of the group of institutions and professionals for which they have supervisory responsibility in terms of their population and the presence of specific money laundering risks. The system enables them to collect and retain certain basic information on their supervisees, as well as to develop a solid risk-based approach. A second rationale seems to be the fact that Government authorities acting as supervisors under the MLR 2007 have to be self-funding. This means that the obliged institutions must pay their supervisors for their registration and for their AML supervision. The registration system allows HMRC, the FCA and the OFT to obtain funds through registration fees and annual supervision fees. As explained, these fees may not exceed the expenses reasonably incurred by the supervisors under the Regulations.[210]

Because the regimes for HMRC, the FCA and the OFT coincide to a very large extent, I limit myself to a description of the regime that applies to HMRC. Where the registration regime of the FCA and the OFT diverges, this is explained. The institutions subject to HMRC's AML supervision must be registered. If these institutions do not register themselves, they are not allowed to act as such.[211] Regulation 27 sets out in detail how the institutions must apply for AML registration. Information that must at least be provided concerns the applicant's name and, if different, the name of the business; the nature of the business; and the name of the nominated money laundering reporting officer (if any).[212] In addition, money service businesses and trust and company service providers must provide information regarding the name of the person who effectively directs or will direct the business and any beneficial owners of the business, as well as information needed by HMRC to decide whether the applicant, the person who effectively directs the business or service provider, the beneficial owner of the business or service provider and the nominated officers are fit and proper persons with regard to the risk of money laundering or terrorist financing.[213] If any of these persons in relation to money service business or trust or company service provider fails the fit and proper test, the business cannot be registered. Such fit and proper tests do not apply to the other institutions that should register with HMRC. For the registration systems of the FCA and OFT, there is no requirement regarding 'fit and proper' either.

HMRC may ask for additional information if it reasonably considers that it needs this information to come to a decision on the application. The applicants must provide this requested information within 21 days running from the date on which the request was

208 Regulation 32(2) in conjunction with Regulation 22 MLR 2007.
209 Regulation 32(3) MLR 2007.
210 See § 6.4.1.3 and 6.4.2.3. Cf. Regulation 35(2) MLR 2007.
211 Regulation 26 MLR 2007.
212 Regulation 27(2)(a-c) MLR 2007. For the OFT and FCA regime: Regulation 34(2) MLR 2007.
213 Regulation 28 details which aspects HMRC must consider in performing the fit and proper test.

made.[214] Applicants are required to inform HMRC when there are material changes affecting any matter contained in the information provided to HMRC, originally or later on request, or where it becomes apparent to the business that the information contains a significant inaccuracy. It is not certain what is meant by a significant inaccuracy as it seems to bring along a certain threshold. HMRC seems to interpret it as any change or inaccuracy in relation to the registration.[215] HMRC must be informed within thirty days beginning on the date of the occurrence of the change, the discovery of the inaccuracy or at a time agreed with HMRC.[216]

HMRC may refuse to register an applicant only if any of the application requirements have not been complied with, where it appears that the information provided is false or misleading, or where the applicant has failed to pay the registration fee or the annual fee.[217] In my opinion the word 'only' considerably limits HMRC's discretion in determining whether or not to register an institution as it precludes other situations that may be a ground for refusal, but in practice it does not seem to be problematic.[218] The registration of money service businesses or trust or company service providers must in any case be refused by HMRC where the businesses, directors, beneficial owners and nominated officers are not found to be fit and proper with regard to the risk of money laundering or terrorist financing.[219] Where no grounds of refusal are present, HMRC is obliged to include the institution or professional as soon as possible in the relevant AML register.[220] HMRC is furthermore obliged to cancel a registration where in relation to money service businesses or trust or company service providers it is satisfied that the fit and proper requirements are no longer satisfied.[221] HMRC may cancel a registration where any of the grounds mentioned above are not met at any time after the registration, or if the registered institution or professional has failed to comply with a notice under Regulation 37.[222, 223]

Although the HMRC, the OFT and FCA regimes function in principle the same, interesting terminological differences exist between the registration systems of HMRC, on the one hand, and those of the OFT and FCA, on the other, particularly where the applicant does not agree with the refusal or cancellation of a registration. These differences are caused by the different regulatory and appeal procedures already in place for HMRC, the FCA and

214 Regulation 27(3) MLR 2007.

215 HM Revenue and Customs, *How to report changes or cancel your MLR registration*, available at: <www.hmrc.gov.uk/mlr/changes/index.htm>, last visited on 20 May 2014.

216 Regulation 27(4) and 27(5) MLR 2007.

217 Regulation 29 MLR 2007. See for the FCA and OFT regime: Regulation 34(3) MLR 2007.

218 Interview HM Treasury, May 2014.

219 Regulation 28 MLR 2007.

220 Regulation 29(3) MLR 2007. See for the OFT and FCA registration system: Regulation 34(4) MLR 2007.

221 Regulation 30(1) in conjunction with Regulation 28 MLR 2007.

222 This last ground for cancellation was inserted with the 2012 amendments to MLR 2007: S.I. 2012/2298. Regulation 37 provides a general power for AML supervisors to request information or require the production of recorded information from the obliged institutions or professionals or connected persons, or require attendance before it to answer questions, by means of a notice. The notice should specify which information is requested, which recorded information must be produced, or at which time and place the obliged institution or professional is required to answer questions.

223 For the FCA and OFT the same grounds for refusal and cancellation apply: Regulation 34(3) and 34(7) MLR 2007.

the OFT in other contexts as there is no general arrangement of dispute resolution by the administration in the UK.[224]

6.5.2 Banks

Banks are financial institutions that were already required to authorise themselves under FSMA 2000.[225] Banks undergo a more extensive procedure than most institutions that only need to register pursuant to the Regulations, because the authorisation procedure includes, among other things, a fit and proper test. Both authorised and registered institutions are incorporated in the FCA register, which is accessible to the public.[226] The relevant Act for the authorisation of banks is FSMA 2000, which totally reorganised the UK's regulatory regime with respect to banking, insurance and investment services. FSMA 2000 itself was largely amended with the entry into force of the Financial Services Act 2012.

Section 19 FSMA 2000 prohibits persons from carrying out a regulated activity unless they are authorised or exempted from this.[227] Any contravention of this general prohibition is a criminal offence punishable by two years' imprisonment and an unlimited fine.[228] Pursuant to Section 31 FSMA 2000 an authorised person is – among other things – a person who has a Part 4A permission to carry on one or more regulated activities.[229] An activity is a regulated activity if it relates to an investment of a specified kind, if it is specified and carried on in relation to property, if it relates to information about a person's financial standing or the setting of a specified benchmark.[230] It is only a regulated activity, however, if it is exercised by way of business.[231] What constitutes a regulated activity is set out in an order.[232] Authorisation is the responsibility of the Prudential Regulation Authority (PRA) and the FCA. The law makes a distinction between PRA-regulated activities and FCA-regulated activities.[233]

224 Langbroek, Ph., Buijze, A. and Remac, M. (2012), *Designing Administrative Pre-Trial Proceedings*, Eleven International Publishing, at 12.

225 Cf. Regulation 32(2) MLR 2007.

226 Financial Services Register, available at: <www.fca.org.uk/register/>, last visited on 18 May 2013.

227 Section 418 FSMA 2000 defines what can be considered as carrying on regulated activities in the United Kingdom.

228 Section 23(1) FSMA 2000.

229 Three other categories of authorised persons, but that are not relevant in the framework of this research, are: (i) EEA firms that qualify for authorisation under Schedule 3; (ii) Treaty firms that qualify for authorisation under Schedule 4; (iii) persons otherwise directly authorised under the Act.

230 Section 22(1) and 22(1A) FSMA 2000 as amended by FSA 2012.

231 Concerning the business test, the broad intention is to filter out those persons who carry out a financial services activity on a non-professional or non-profit basis. They do not require authorisation. Section 419 FSMA 2000 gives order-making power to the Treasury to decide in which circumstances a person should not be regarded as carrying on a regulated activity by way of business. This has been done by means of the Financial Services and Markets Act 2000 (Carrying on Regulated Activities by Way of Business) Order 2001, S.I. 2001/1177. Last amended by: The Financial Services and Markets Act 2000 (Regulated Activities) (Amendment) (No. 2) Order 2013, S.I. 2013/1881.

232 The Financial Services and Markets Act 2000 (Regulated Activities) Order 2001, S.I. 2001/544. Last amended by: S.I. 2013/1881. Hereafter 'RAO 2001'.

233 Sections 22A and 55A(2) FSMA 2000, as amended by FSA 2012, in conjunction with The Financial Services and Markets Act 2000 (PRA-regulated activities) Order 2013, S.I. 2013/556.

The regulated activity for which banks require authorisation is the accepting of deposits. It is a specified activity if money received by way of deposit is lent to others, or any other activity of the person accepting the deposit is financed wholly, or to a material extent, out of the capital of or interest on money received by way of deposit.[234] Deposits are sums of money, paid on terms under which it will be repaid, with or without interest or a premium, either on demand or at a time or in circumstances agreed by or on behalf of the person making the payment and the person receiving it and which are not referable to the provision of property (other than currency) or services or the giving of security. Banks that want to carry out this activity in the UK should thus obtain permission pursuant to Part 4A FSMA 2000. The leading regulator for banking authorisation is the PRA, although the authorisation of a firm to carry out the activity of deposit-taking will not be granted unless both the PRA and the FCA agree that the applicant satisfies and continues to satisfy the threshold conditions.[235]

The threshold conditions are laid down in Schedule 6 under FSMA 2000 and both regulators have the power to draft threshold condition codes.[236] Threshold conditions are 'the minimum conditions that a firm must satisfy to be granted and retain permission to carry on regulated activities. In setting these standards a balance has to be struck between ensuring that new entrants do not pose undue risks to consumers or to financial stability, and the benefits that ease the entry and increased competition are expected to deliver'.[237] In its approach to banking supervision, the PRA explains the threshold conditions that fall under its responsibility. Applicants must ensure that a firm's head office is in the UK if it is incorporated in the UK; that a firm's business is conducted in a prudent manner, which means particularly that it should have appropriate resources; that it is fit and proper and appropriately staffed; and that the group to which it belongs is capable of being effectively supervised by the PRA.[238] The PRA has also detailed what is required under these threshold conditions.[239] While the PRA is the leading regulator for banking authorisation, the (Threshold Conditions) Order 2013 states which threshold conditions continue to apply to the FCA.[240] Firstly, it should still verify links with other institutions: if the applicant has any close links with other financial institutions or persons those must not prevent the FCA from performing effective supervision of the applicant. Secondly, the FCA should look at the adequacy of non-financial resources. Thirdly, the FCA should look at the suitability of the applicant.[241] The fourth threshold condition concerns the business model, which must be suitable for carrying out the regulated activities, having regard to

234 Section 5(1) RAO 2001.
235 Section 55B FSMA 2000, as amended by FSA 2012.
236 Section 137O FSMA 2000, as amended by FSA 2012.
237 Bank of England and FSA (2013), *A review of requirements for firms entering into or expanding in the banking sector*, March 2013, at 12.
238 Prudential Regulation Authority (2013), *The Prudential Regulation's Approach to banking authorisation*, at 8.
239 Ibid., at 11 (Box 1).
240 The Financial Services and Markets Act 2000 (Threshold Conditions) Order 2013, S.I. 2013/555. Hereafter 'TCO 2013'.
241 This means that the FCA checks the connection with other persons, the nature of any regulated activity that the applicant carries on or seeks to carry on, whether it is performed in an appropriate manner particularly in relation to consumer protection and integrity, whether its managers are fit and proper, etc.

the FCA's operational objectives.[242] The FCA has published guidance on these conditions in its Handbook.

> The split in authorisation that came about with the Financial Services Act 2012 also led to a new procedure for application. This now consists of a pre-application, assessment, and (for some applicants) mobilisation stage.[243] Pre-application is meant as a means to help the prospective applicant to understand the authorisation procedure and to increase the likelihood that a complete application will be submitted. Applicants for banking authorisation must provide a substantial amount of information to the PRA and FCA to enable them to verify whether all threshold conditions are met and whether permission can be granted. One can think of the application form, a detailed regulatory business plan, ownership and governance structure, the internal policies of the firm including information about compliance and internal audits, information about the liquidity and capital of the firm, and so on.[244]

When all threshold conditions are met, the PRA can, with the consent of the FCA, give permission for the applicant to carry on the deposit-taking activity or activities to which its application relates or such of them as may be specified in the permission.[245] When banks obtain permission to carry out the activity of accepting deposits, they will be included in so-called lists of banks that are published, on a monthly basis, on the website of the Bank of England.[246] Banks are also included in the aforementioned FCA register.[247] The register incorporates information on all authorised firms, but also those firms that are registered pursuant to – inter alia – the Money Laundering Regulations 2007 (as outlined above), the Payment Services Regulations 2009 and the Electronic Money Regulations 2011.

6.5.3 Real estate agents

The title of estate agent is not a protected title in the UK: anyone can set themselves up as an estate agent. No (entry) qualifications are required, with the exception of surveyors.[248] Surveyors may also act as estate agents. Section 22 Estate Agents Act 1979 includes the power for the Secretary of State to issue regulations to ensure that estate agents satisfy minimum standards of competence, but this power has not been used.[249] At present, a person is an estate agent if he does things in the course of a business, pursuant to instructions from another person (the client) who wishes to dispose of or acquire an interest in land for the purpose of, or with a view to, effecting the introduction to the client of a third person who wants to acquire (or dispose) of such interest, and who after

242 Sections 3B-E of Schedule 6 to FSMA 2000, as amended by TCO 2013.
243 Bank of England and FSA (2013) at 37.
244 See for a detailed list of the documents required: Bank of England and FSA (2013) at 41 et seq.
245 Section 55F FSMA 2000, as amended by FSA 2012.
246 Prudential Regulation Authority, *Banks & building societies lists*, available at: <www.bankofengland.co.uk/pra/pages/authorisations/banksbuildingsocietieslist.aspx>, last visited on 28 May 2014.
247 Financial Services Register, available at: <www.fca.org.uk/register/>, last visited on 18 May 2013.
248 Surveyors are licensed professionals who in relation to property determine, locate and define the boundaries of land, and who examine the conditions of land and assets. The licence is provided by the Royal Institution of Chartered Surveyors. See for more information the website of the RICS: <www.rics.org>. Cf. Shears, P. (2008), 'Hang your shingle and carry on: estate agents – the unlicensed UK profession', *Property Management*, vol. 27, issue 3, pp. 191-211.
249 Shears (2008) at 203.

such an introduction has been effected in the course of that business, for the purpose of securing the disposal (or acquisition) of that interest in the UK and Ireland.[250] Simply put: '(...) an estate agent is someone whose job is to help people buy and sell houses and property'.[251] A person cannot act as an estate agent if he is banned from the profession or has been declared bankrupt.[252]

The Regulations state that estate agents can be firms or sole practitioners performing the activities under Section 1 Estate Agents Act 1979. Since 1 October 2012, however, the MLR 2007 contains a wider understanding of real estate agent, in order to include estate agents dealing in overseas properties. Regulation 3(11A) reads that estate agency work is to be read in accordance with Section 1 of the Estate Agents Act 1979, but that for references in that section to disposing of or acquiring an interest in land it needs to include these activities *outside the UK* where that estate or interest is capable of being owned or held as a separate interest.[253] Nevertheless, the foregoing means that real estate agents, when performing other activities such as valuation, surveying (if licensed), planning advice or property management, do not fall under the scope of the Regulations.

Estate agents can become members of the Royal Institute of Chartered Surveyors (RICS), which is a professional association for estate agents and surveyors, or the National Association of Estate Agents (NAEA), which is a trade body for estate agents.[254] Membership, however, is not compulsory. In 2007 between 70-75% of the total number of estate agents belonged to a professional body.[255]

It has for some time been discussed whether the profession should be regulated.[256] In 2010, the OFT dealt with the question whether a regulatory regime for estate agents was required. In its report *Home buying and selling: A Market Study* it expressed the view that 'there is not a strong case for introducing more regulatory structures and rules in this sector'.[257] The OFT rather recommended a strengthening of the enforcement regime. This view was not shared by other stakeholders, including the Law Society and the National Association of Estate Agents.[258] The RICS, too, calls for greater regulation of estate agents.[259] And back in 2007, the FATF observed that '[t]he private sector confirmed the sector is vulnerable to money laundering, and the system would be better served with

6

250 Section 1 Estate Agents Act 1979.
251 Shears (2008) at 192.
252 Sections 3 and 23 Estate Agents Act 1979. Cf. FATF (2007a) at 19-20.
253 S.I. 2012/2298.
254 FATF (2007a) at 28.
255 Ibid., at 206; Shears (2008) at 203.
256 The Carsberg Review, for example, called for an active registration system: Carsberg Review (2008), *Review of residential property*, Final Report, June 2008, at 9-13.
257 OFT (2010), *Home buying and selling: A Market Study*, OFT1140b, at 10.
258 See: The Law Society Gazette, *Regulation of Estate Agents 'Unnecessary', says OFT*, 22 February 2010; The Guardian, *Regulation of estate agents ruled out after OFT inquiry*, 18 February 2010, which quoted Peter Bolton King, the chief executive of the National Association of Estate Agents, '[o]nce again the OFT has categorically failed to see that better regulation of the home-buying and selling market is required. Buying a home is often the largest single transaction of a person's life and it is disappointing that the OFT has not thought it appropriate to acknowledge that a robust and appropriate level of consumer protection is needed'.
259 The Guardian, *Rics calls for estate agents tests*, 4 May 2013.

requirements for licensing, standards of integrity, and requirements for CDD relating to the buyer of real estate in addition to the seller'.[260]

We just saw that estate agents are subject to the registration system under the Regulations. The registration requirement does not apply to solicitors who provide estate agency services as they are supervised by the Solicitors Regulation Authority (SRA) on behalf of the Law Society. The OFT handles a system with registration and annual supervision fees, which are calculated according to the size of the real estate businesses.[261] All estate agents registered with the OFT are included in its public register, which '(...) contains the name of the business, any name under which it trades and the addresses at which the estate agency work (…) is carried out, as supplied by the business at the point of registration'.[262] The fact that the register is public allows third parties to notify the OFT in case estate agents are not registered while they should be.[263] The registration requires minimum information on the side of estate agents. According to the OFT, '[t]here is no fitness test and therefore no questions about convictions, insolvencies relating to the business or individuals involved in the business'.[264] Information that must be submitted to the OFT concerns information like the name, size, location, number of premises of the business and so on, information on the money laundering reporting officer, and information on the activities performed or pursued.[265]

In light of the fact that the estate agency profession is an unregulated profession, that no integrity or quality checks are performed on this sector, and that estate agents in the UK bear a certain AML vulnerability, the OFT's AML supervision becomes more effective by introducing the requirement to demonstrate the fitness and properness of estate agents working at a firm or sole practitioners. A more in-depth registration obligation, as is in place for HMRC in relation to money service businesses and trust and company service providers, enhances the OFT's information position on the market and allows the system to have preventive effects as well. After all, requesting information concerning whether estate agents are fit and proper may lead to businesses not registering themselves, or possibly result in the the OFT banning an estate agent under the Estate Agents Act 1979. Finally, this information can be used by the OFT as input for its AML risk assessments. This recommendation would also apply to HMRC when it takes over the AML supervision of estate agents. Apart from the fee application, HMRC's registration system for estate agents will function in the same way as the OFT system. Estate agents that are already registered with the Office of Fair Trading do not need to reregister again.[266] They are automatically included in HMRC's public supervised businesses register. People can enter the name of an estate agent and the area in which he is working to see if he is registered with HMRC.[267]

260 FATF (2007a) at 219.

261 This was briefly dealt with in § 6.4.2.3.

262 HM Treasury (2012), *Anti-Money Laundering and Counter Terrorist Finance Report 2011-12*, at 16.

263 Ibid.

264 OFT (2011a) at 6.

265 OFT, *Anti-Money Laundering Registration Form*, available at: <www.oft.gov.uk/shared_oft/business_leaflets/general/Anti-money_laundering_regis1.pdf>, last visited on 13 January 2014.

266 HM Revenue and Customs (2014), *Guidance: Supervision of Estate Agency Businesses by HMRC*, January 2014.

267 Interview HM Revenue and Customs, May 2014.

6.5.4 Accountants

In the UK the accountancy profession is not a regulated profession and the title of accountant is not protected. Any individual, whether professionally qualified or not, can enter the profession and offer a wide range of accountancy services.[268] Yet there are three reserved areas for which minimum qualifications and training are required by law: audit, insolvency and investment business.[269] For these areas the Government has established the regulatory framework through legislation.

> Accountants that carry out auditing must be qualified by one of the Recognised Qualifying Bodies and they and the firm they work for must be supervised by one of the five Recognised Supervisory Bodies. Accountants and firms that perform insolvency activities must be qualified and licensed by Recognised Professional Bodies for the regulation of insolvency practitioners.[270] Businesses that carry out the regulated activity of investment business must either be authorised by the FCA where they perform 'mainstream' investment business or be licensed by a designated professional body. Designated professional bodies are all chartered professional associations in the UK.[271]

For accountants who provide non-statutory accountancy services – such as bookkeeping, accounts preparation, payroll, and the provision of tax advice – professional associations play the most important role in the regulatory framework. Professional associations have regulatory and supervisory responsibility for their members in order to maintain professional standards and to further the accountancy profession. Sometimes members can be firms and individuals, other times associations only provide membership to individuals. Accountants are not obliged to become members of a professional association. Individuals or firms that provide accountancy services but that are not members of any professional association are, however, required to register with HMRC. The AML registration system as purveyed above applies to them.[272] This is, for example, the case for the student members of professional associations who are not yet fully qualified but already provide accountancy services. In 2007, the FATF estimated that this was a group of around 40,000 accountants.[273] Hereafter, I will look closely at the requirements for membership at ICAEW and AAT.

268 Paterson, I., Fink, M. and Ogus, A. (2003), *Economic impact of regulation in the field of liberal professions in different Member States: Regulation of Professional Services*, Study for the European Commission DG Competition, at 38.

269 The Acts regulating these services are: The Companies Act 2006 (audit); the Insolvency Act 1986; and the Financial Services and Markets Act 2000 (investment business).

270 Part XIII Insolvency Act 1986.

271 The Institute of Chartered Accountants in England and Wales, The Institute of Chartered Accountants of Scotland and the Institute of Chartered Accountants in Ireland (2004), *Designated Professional Body Handbook 2004*, updated until 1 April 2013, available at: <www.icaew.com/~/media/Files/Members/Regulations-standards-and-guidance/dpb%20handbook/DPB_handbook.pdf>, last visited on 17 June 2014.

272 HM Revenue and Customs, *Accountancy Service Providers and Money Laundering Regulations*, available at: <www.hmrc.gov.uk/agents/mlr/laundering.htm>, last visited on 28 May 2014.

273 FATF (2007a) at 225.

6.5.5 Membership of ICAEW

ICAEW registers individual members when they qualify as chartered accountants as well as member firms. In principle, a firm is considered to be an ICAEW member firm if at least 50% of the firm is owned and managed by ICAEW members. If a firm is an ICAEW member firm and it provides accountancy services in public practice, it is automatically subject to the ICAEW's Practice Assurance Scheme (PAS). All accountancy services provided by a member firm, whether provided individually by ICAEW member or members of another accountancy body, are monitored by ICAEW.[274] All ICAEW member firms subject to the PAS are automatically registered by ICAEW for AML supervision. All ICAEW members (individuals) who are providing accountancy services in public practice and are principals, whether in ICAEW member firms or other firms, are required to have a Practising Certificate (PC). The term principal includes an individual in sole practice, a salaried or equity partner, a member of a limited liability partnership and a director of a company; or any individual who is held out as being a principal (such as a manager). PC holders fall under the PAS as well and are also supervised under the Regulations. Member firms and PC holders must comply with the laws, regulations and standards that are relevant to the services they provide, including ICAEW's regulations, standards and guidance.[275]

> Regulation 5 of the Practising Certificate Regulations lists the requirements that must be fulfilled by individual members to obtain a practising certificate. An individual must have been an ICAEW member for two years; be compliant with the requirements regarding the ongoing professional development and the individual must understand the fundamental principles set out in the Code of Ethics (...). Moreover, he must comply with the Council's Professional Indemnity Insurance Regulations; be a fit and proper person to hold a practising certificate; have submitted an application in such form as prescribed including the payment of set application fees; and have passed an aptitude test if relevant.

As explained, ICAEW supervises non-member firms on a contractual basis as well. They also have to comply with ICAEW's regulations, standards and guidance.[276] On its website, ICAEW sets out what kind of information and forms these firms have to provide.[277] This may include an application form (with information on the business, its office, individuals with beneficial interests in the entity applying for supervision, and connected firms, as well as the name and contact details of the money laundering reporting officer), a separate fit and proper declaration completed by every principal, the nominated money laundering reporting officer and shareholder who is not an ICAEW member, and an ownership and control form.

274 Interview Institute of Chartered Accountants in England and Wales, May 2014.

275 Cf. Regulation 1 of the Practice Assurance Regulations.

276 See § 6.4.3.1.

277 ICAEW, *How to apply for AML supervision*, available at: <www.icaew.com/en/technical/legal-and-regulatory/money-laundering/anti-money-laundering-supervision>, last visited on 28 May 2014.

6.5.6 Membership of AAT

AAT applies different levels of membership.[278] In order to provide accountancy, taxation or related consultancy services to the public, AAT members must join the AAT's Scheme for Members in Practice (hereafter MIP). The MIP scheme provides AAT's framework to regulate members, to provide support and ensure that members are committed to high ethical and professional standards. The framework includes monitoring checks. Only full or fellow members are eligible for the MIP scheme. There are two types of MIPs: registered and licensed members. A registered member is an individual who holds the AAT qualification,[279] but who has never practised the accounting profession before. After one year, when the individual has gained experience and has followed sufficient training, he can apply for full membership and become a licensed member. A licensed member is a member who holds a practising licence. Regulation 6 MIP Regulations lays down the requirements for licensed members. Interesting is that applicants must demonstrate that they have successfully completed the AAT's anti-money laundering diagnostic tests.[280] These online tests are said to ensure that AAT members have a sufficient understanding of their duties under the Regulations. It furthermore enables the AAT to determine the level of technical competence of their members. Lastly, it is stated that the risk of non-compliance is reduced.[281]

AAT members who wish to become a registered member in practice, must provide considerable information about the business, and the services provided or pursued including the number and type of customers. The application form includes a section on the MLR 2007. Other information that must be submitted are details on professional experience, continuing professional development records, as well as a copy of the Professional Indemnity Insurance cover.[282] AAT members that wish to become licensed members in practice must provide more information, for example on their working experience, a statement of suitability from a professional referee, and evidence that certain AAT tests, including the AML diagnostic tests, have been completed successfully.[283] Licensed members must renew their licence every year for which up-to-date information must be provided.

AAT members are always individuals, but AAT may supervise firms whose partners are all member of one of the AML Supervisors listed in Schedule 3 MLR 2007 unless the partners' activities are confined to providing administrative support to the firm.[284] According to the

278 AAT distinguishes between: student membership, affiliate membership, full membership, fellow membership, and self-employed members: AAT, *AAT Membership*, available at: <www.aat.org.uk/membership>, last visited on 28 May 2014.

279 Or a qualification of another professional association that is considered of an equivalent level.

280 AAT MIP Regulation 7. The MIP Regulations are available at: <www.aat.org.uk/sites/default/files/assets/Regulations-and-guidelines-for-members-in-practice.pdf>, last visited on 28 May 2014.

281 HM Treasury (2012) at 10.

282 See for the full set of information that must be provided upon registration: AAT MIP Regulation 4.

283 See for the full set of information that must be provided to apply for a licence: AAT MIP Regulation 6.

284 Interview Association of Accounting Technicians, May 2014.

AAT, it 'has agreed policies with other supervisory authorities to guide members with concurrent memberships to elect just one supervisory authority for their practice'.[285]

6.5.7 Concluding remarks

Notwithstanding the level of regulation of the banking sector and the real estate and accountancy professions, the Regulations provide for a registration system. This is a rather unique feature of the Regulations, considering that it is not required by the the Third Directive (or the FATF Recommendations). The main rationale behind this system is to enable the Government authorities that act as AML supervisors to obtain a clear picture of the group of institutions and professionals for which they have supervisory responsibility in terms of its population and the presence of specific money laundering risks, in particular for non-regulated sectors. The registration system applies to (some) institutions and professionals subject to AML supervision by the FCA, the OFT and HMRC. Information that must be provided upon registration is rather minimal and concerns the name of the applicant and, if different, the business, the nature of its activities and the name of the nominated money laundering reporting officer. Money service businesses and trust and company service providers must provide more information to HMRC upon registration, in order to allow HMRC to determine the fit and proper suitability of the applicant, the person who effectively directs the business or service provider, the beneficial owner of the business or service provider and the nominated officers.

Banks are subject to a more extensive authorisation procedure under the FSMA 2000, as amended by FSA 2012. The regulated activity for which banks require authorisation from the PRA and the FCA is the accepting of deposits. Banks that want to carry out this activity in the UK should thus obtain permission pursuant to Part 4A FSMA 2000 and comply with the so-called threshold conditions. For that they have to provide a great deal of information including information about the (activities of) the business, internal policies, liquidity and solidity. Upon authorisation, banks are included in both the Bank of England's register of banks as well as the FCA register.

The real estate profession is not a regulated profession and there is no title protection. Anyone can call himself an estate agent and provide these services, as no entry requirements exist. Membership of professional or trade associations is on a voluntary basis. Real estate agents are subject to the AML registration obligation and, upon registration, they are incorporated in the OFT's public register. The OFT requests a minimum level of information. In light of the fact that the profession is an unregulated profession, that no integrity or quality checks are performed on this sector, and that estate agents in the UK bear a certain AML vulnerability, the OFT's AML supervision becomes more effective by introducing the requirement to demonstrate the fitness and properness of estate agents working at a firm or sole practitioners. More information would have to be provided to the OFT, which would benefit its information position and risk assessments. This would

285 AAT (2008), *Guidance on anti-money laundering legislation*, October 2008, at 44.

also hold true for HMRC, when it takes over the AML supervision of real estate agents in April 2014.

The accountancy profession is an unregulated profession in the UK. Any individual, whether professionally qualified or not, can enter the profession and offer a wide range of accountancy services with the exception of three reserved areas for which minimum qualifications and training are required by law: audit, insolvency and investment business. For the purpose of AML supervision, however, all accountants and accountancy firms are registered. This may occur through membership of a professional association that is appointed as an AML Supervisor, such as ICAEW and AAT. There is, however, no obligation to become a member of a professional association. Individuals or firms that provide accountancy services but that are not members of any professional associations designated as an AML supervisor are required to register with the default supervisor HMRC.

In sum, it can be concluded that despite the fact that the real estate and accountancy professions are unregulated sectors, the Regulations overcome this problem through the introduction of a registration obligation for (some) institutions and professionals that are under the AML supervision of the FCA, the OFT and HMRC. A stringent authorisation procedure applies to banks, within which the FCA plays an important role. The four AML supervisors included in this research have an adequate knowledge of their supervisees, although from an effective supervision perspective the OFT's regime would benefit from more in-depth registration requirements for real estate agents.

6.6 Financial Conduct Authority

6.6.1 Supervisory powers

6.6.1.1 Money Laundering Regulations 2007

Regulation 37 MLR 2007 allows officers of the FCA (as well as the OFT and HMRC) to require information from and the attendance of relevant and connected persons. Relevant persons are persons to whom the Regulations apply or used to apply. Connected persons are those persons connected to a relevant person or has at any time been, in relation to the relevant person, a person listed in Schedule 4 to MLR 2007.[286] This Schedule refers to natural persons with certain positions in bodies corporate, partnerships, unincorporated associations and persons who have been an employee or agent of the relevant person. Through a notice, the FCA is allowed to request information from the institutions for which it has supervisory responsibility and the connected persons. The officers can also order the institution or connected person to produce such recorded information as specified, or to attend before an officer at a time and place specified in the notice. This power may only be used if it is reasonably necessary for the exercise of the FCA's functions under the Regulations.[287]

286 Regulation 37(2) MLR 2007.
287 Regulation 37(3) MLR 2007.

The Regulations also provide authorised officers of the FCA (as well as the OFT and HMRC) with the power to enter premises, inspect them, observe the carrying on of business or professional activities by the institution, inspect any recorded information found on the premises, and to require any person on the premises to provide an explanation of any recorded information or to state where it may be found. They may also take copies or make extracts from any recorded information found on the premises.[288] Premises exclude those premises that are solely used as a home.[289] Again it is required that the use of these powers is reasonably necessary for the exercise of the FCA's functions under the Regulations.[290] In certain circumstances it may be necessary for an FCA inspector to enter the premises under a warrant issued by a justice. This power is laid down in Regulation 39 MLR 2007 and is normally used in situations where the institution concerned has not fully complied with the notice to provide information, where there is a high risk of the removal, the tampering or destroying of relevant information, or where an institution has obstructed the FCA inspectors in the exercise of their powers under Regulation 38.[291]

6.6.1.2 Financial Markets and Services Act 2000

When AML supervision is integrated in wider supervisory programmes, FCA inspectors can (also) use the supervisory powers stemming from FSMA 2000. An important task under FSMA 2000 for the FCA is tackling financial crime as part of protecting the integrity of the UK's financial system. Financial crime is widely defined and interpreted as including fighting money laundering. Under Section 1L FSMA 2000 the FCA must maintain arrangements for supervising authorised persons that allow it to check compliance under FSMA 2000. In relation to authorised firms, including banks, the FCA has the following supervisory powers: request (the production of) specific information, on-site inspections, meetings with management or other representatives of authorised firms, transaction monitoring, reviews and analysis of periodic returns and notifications, reviews of past business, use of auditors or skilled persons and liaisons with other authorities or regulators.[292]

The MLR 2007 do not provide regulatory powers. For the FCA, this power is laid down in Section 137A FSMA 2000. This provision states that the FCA may make such rules applying to authorised persons with respect to the carrying on by them of regulated

288 Regulation 38(1)(a)-(e) and Regulation 38(2) MLR 2007. An exemption applies to professionals who can invoke legal professional privilege: Regulation 38(3) MLR 2007.

289 Regulation 38(5) MLR 2007. This stems from Article 8 of the European Convention and Human Rights and the Court's interpretation in the Colas Est judgment of the definition of "home": ECtHR, *Société Colas Est and others v France* [2002], app. no. 37971/97. See for an inventory of the case law on Article 8 ECHR: Mowbray, A. (2007), *Cases and Materials on the European Convention on Human Rights*, Oxford University Press: Oxford, at 485-585.

290 Regulation 38(4) MLR 2007.

291 Regulation 39(2) and 39(4) MLR 2007.

292 Part XI FSMA 2000, as amended by FSA 2012. See also: SUP 1A.4.5 FCA Handbook, available at: <http://fshandbook.info/FS/html/FCA/SUP/1A/4>, last visited on 10 June 2014. See also for the use of these supervisory powers: FCA Enforcement Guide 3.1-3.31. The Enforcement Guide is available alongside the FCA Handbook: <http://media.fshandbook.info/Handbook/EG_FCA_20140401.pdf>, last visited on 13 June 2014.

activities, or with respect to the carrying on by them of activities which are not regulated activities, as appear to the FCA to be necessary or expedient for the purpose of advancing one or more of its operational objectives. It is a broad power, as it may apply to authorised persons even though there is no relationship between the authorised persons to whom the rules will apply and the persons whose interests will be protected by the rules.[293] The regulations must always be in writing, consulted with the PRA and be brought to the attention of the public.[294] Considering that tackling financial crime is a key part of the FCA's remit, the FCA may also issue regulations on financial crime and, thus, include money laundering aspects.[295]

6.6.2 Anti-money laundering supervision in practice

6.6.2.1 The 'two-track' approach to anti-money laundering supervision

Anti-money laundering supervision of banks is integrated into the regular supervisory procedures, which are carried out by specialist supervision teams, the so-called firm supervisors. In the second track AML supervision is carried out by a specialist financial crime supervision team. The vast majority of the FCA's AML supervision is exercised by this team.

6.6.2.2 Inclusion of anti-money laundering supervision in regular supervisory procedures

Anti-money laundering supervision is integrated in regular supervisory procedures. Compliance with the Regulations may be taken into account by supervisors during the conduct supervision of banks. The inclusion of AML supervision in conduct supervision is not obligatory, and the extent to which firm supervisors include this is left to their own discretion. The risk category of the bank, as well as the perceived risk of money laundering or financial crime, affects the inclusion of AML supervision. If supervisors come across particular AML aspects that in their opinion require further attention, they can approach the specialist financial crime supervision team for help or assistance.[296]

The FCA's general risk-based approach divides its supervisory population into four risk categories varying from C1 (high) to C4 (low). The annual Risk Outlook gives an idea of the type of risks on which the FCA focuses in a particular year. For the year 2013, the drivers of conduct risk were divided into inherent risk, structure and behaviours risk and environmental risk.[297] The FCA identifies a number of cross-market risks as well. Money laundering plays a role in this last risk category. The FCA considers money laundering in relation to unsustainable strategies to attract funding, which may promote risky

293 Section 137A(3) FSMA 2000, as amended by FSA 2012.
294 Section 138G and 138I FSMA 2000, as amended by FSA 2012.
295 In fact, the part 'SYSC: Senior Management Arrangements, Systems and Controls' in the FCA's Handbook contains various general rules and references to anti-money laundering obligations for authorised businesses. Available at: <http://fshandbook.info/FS/html/FCA/COND/2>, last visited on 28 May 2014.
296 Interview Financial Conduct Authority, May 2014.
297 FCA (2013d), *Risk Outlook 2013*, March 2013, at 50.

behaviour including a higher exposure to financial crime. Money laundering risks also come about with over-reliance on, and an inadequate oversight of, payment and product technologies as institutions may not be able to recognise money laundering structures.[298] The supervisory regimes are adjusted to the risk category in which a financial or credit institution is placed. Institutions belonging to C1 and C2 are managed on a relationship basis by named firm supervisors; the other two categories are supervised by specialist teams.

The FCA does not keep statistics on activities under the general supervisory procedures. In its annual reports, the FCA provides a number of examples of activities it has undertaken in that year, but numbers are not mentioned. No mention is made of the extent to which AML supervision is included either. Consequently, nothing more can be said about the inclusion of the verification of compliance with the MLR 2007 in regular supervisory procedures on banks.

6.6.2.3 Specialist financial crime supervision team

The specialist financial crime supervision team's supervision of banks can be divided into three core activities, all of which are exercised on a risk-based approach. Firstly, the team exercises proactive AML supervision of banks through the Systematic Anti-Money Laundering Programme (SAMLP). Secondly, the team performs thematic reviews focussing on specific AML obligations.[299] Thirdly, the team exercises event-driven supervision. This can either consist of assisting firm supervisors with the financial crime aspects, or even taking over cases with a (serious) money laundering concern from them.

Systematic Anti-Money Laundering Programme: SAMLP

The intensive SAMLP is an example of the FCA's proactive AML supervision. It has been running since early 2012 and covers 14 major retail and investment banks operating in the UK.[300] These banks are chosen for the money laundering risks they pose, considering factors such as turnover, the services they provide and their customer base. They generally fall within the two highest risk categories within the FCA (C1 and C2).[301] In 2014-15, the FCA will also include some smaller firms that present high levels of money laundering risk.[302] The reviews are in depth and involve the testing and interviewing of key staff responsible for the bank's business, the implementation of AML procedures and controls, as well as the review of selected files (sample testing).[303] During the programme, a team from the FCA specialist team focuses on the bank's functioning over a longer period of time – normally up to six months. The team drafts an internal report which is discussed with the responsible management and Board of the bank for the implementation of any FCA recommendations. If non-compliant behaviour is identified and sanctions should be

298 Ibid., at 55.
299 FCA (2013) at 7-8.
300 Ibid., at 7.
301 Interview Financial Conduct Authority, May 2014.
302 FCA (2014), *Business Plan 2014/15*, March 2014 at 5.
303 FCA (2013) at 7.

applied, the team forwards the file to the enforcement division for further consideration. The SAMLP investigations are not limited to banks operating in the UK and may involve visits to overseas branches and subsidiaries.[304] Until July 2013, the FCA had done SAMLP reviews for five UK banks. For three of these banks it conducted overseas supervision as well.[305] The FCA is considering whether to make SAMLP an ongoing programme with a four-year cycle where each institution will have different units examined at each cycle, and to publish the results of the SAMLP assessments.[306]

Thematic AML reviews

Thematic reviews are a means for the specialist financial crime supervision team to zoom in on specific obligations and to get a better understanding of the institutions' level of compliance and understanding of their obligations. At the same time the thematic reports serve as guidance to the supervised institutions as the reports contain examples of good and poor practice. The specialist team usually carries out two thematic reviews annually.[307] Themes are chosen based on perceived high risks in particular sectors or for particular activities. Within the sample of firms, the FCA selects firms using a risk-based approach as well as giving a representative view of the sector. Thematic reviews always include desk reviews and on-site visits. Information is first gathered from the institutions, after which a team goes on-site for interviews with management and key staff and to review a selected number of files and documents.[308] The FCA has already undertaken various thematic studies on AML obligations and banks have been included in these reviews regularly.

In 2011 the FSA published a report on banks' management of high-risk money laundering situations.[309] Within this study, FSA inspectors performed 35 visits on 27 banking groups in the UK, of which 8 were large banks and 19 were medium and smaller-sized banks.[310] The main conclusion was that around three quarters of banks in the sample, including the majority of the major banks, did not always manage high-risk customers and PEP relationships effectively. This study resulted in five follow-up actions by the FSA.[311] In July 2013 the FCA presented a thematic report on banks' control of money laundering, terrorist financing and sanctioning risks in trade finance. For this study a team visited 17 banks in the UK and the overseas branches of three major banks.[312] The FCA concluded that: '[...] policies, procedures and controls to counter money laundering risk were generally weak and most banks had inadequate systems and controls over dual-use goods'.[313] Problems were mostly found in relation to the absence of policies or procedures

304 Interview Financial Conduct Authority, May 2014.
305 FCA (2013) at 7.
306 FCA (2013e), *Business Plan 2013/14*, March 2013, at 41.
307 Interview Financial Conduct Authority, May 2014.
308 Interview Financial Conduct Authority, May 2014.
309 FSA (2011), *Banks' management of high money-laundering risk situations: How banks deal with high-risk customers (including politically exposed persons), correspondent banking relationships and wire transfers*, June 2011.
310 Ibid., at 8.
311 Interview Financial Supervisory Authority, April 2012. See for sanctions: § 6.6.4.
312 FCA (2013f), *Banks' control of financial crime risks in trade finance*, TR13/03, at 7-8.
313 FCA (2013f), at 4.

on how to deal with specific trade-based money laundering risks and the absence of knowledge and information about financial crime risks in trade finance business. Other relevant thematic reviews focussed on banks' defences against investment fraud and AML and anti-bribery and corruption systems and controls by asset management firms.[314] In the report on defences against investment fraud, the then FSA had serious concerns about banks' customer due diligence measures: risk assessments on existing customers were not updated and there was insufficient attention for the ongoing monitoring of existing clients. It stated that '[t]hese findings are relevant to banks' anti-money laundering measures more generally, so they raise serious concerns'.[315]

Event-driven supervision

Even-driven supervision concerns individual cases of money laundering risks or serious identified weaknesses in institutions' AML controls. The specialist team receives information from firm supervisors, who ask for their advice or assistance, or from other sources of intelligence.[316] The specialist team cannot act on all signals and it selects cases for further investigation based on the money laundering risk perceived.[317] In 2012-13, the specialist team picked up around 100 cases for investigation (not only concerning banks).[318]

6.6.3 Sanctioning powers

Under the Regulations, the FCA has only one sanctioning power available. The Regulations provide the FCA, OFT, HMRC (and in relation to credit unions in Northern Ireland: the DETI) with the power to impose a civil penalty in case of non-compliance with the preventive obligations, or in the case of a failure to comply with a notice given under Regulation 37.[319] A civil penalty is a financial penalty (a fine) imposed by a Government authority in reaction to a failure to comply with or wrongdoing concerning regulations or administrative law. Understanding that criminal law takes a prominent role in enforcing administrative law breaches in the UK, civil sanctions can be seen as a means to 'complement the existing system of criminal sanctions but with a more tailored and flexible approach to ensure effective regulation'.[320] The term 'civil' as used in this context is, unlike what it may suggest, not the same as private fines as can be found in civil law countries. Rather, it is comparable to the instrument of the administrative fine, as mentioned in the two previous chapters.

314 FSA (2012), *Banks' defences against investment fraud: detecting perpetrators and protecting victims*, June 2012; FCA (2013g), *Anti-Money Laundering and Anti-Bribery and Corruption Systems and Controls: Asset Management and Platform Firms*, TR13/09.

315 FSA (2012) at 4.

316 FCA (2013) at 7.

317 Interview Financial Conduct Authority, May 2014.

318 FCA (2013) at 7.

319 Regulation 42 MLR 2007. Regulation 42(1) thereby refers to breaches of Regulations 7(1), (2) or (3); 8(1) or (3); 9(2); 10(1); 11(1); 14(1); 15(1) or (2); 16(1), (2), (3) or (4); 19(1), (4), (5) or (6); 20(1), (4) or (5); 21, 26, 27(4), or 33.

320 Cf. McEldowney, J. (2013), 'United Kingdom', in: Jansen, O.J.D.M.L. (ed.), *Administrative Sanctions in the European Union*, Intersentia: Antwerp, pp. 585-604 at 586, who stated this in the context of environmental law.

Under the Regulations, a civil penalty may be imposed on a 'person who fails to comply with any requirement (...)'. The Regulation or other regulations do not say what is understood by a person, although presumably this means the institution for which the FCA has supervisory responsibility under the MLR 2007 (the relevant persons) and connected persons thereto.[321] In the context of the AML policy, these connected persons are usually (senior) management, directors, or the money laundering reporting officer. There is no statutory cap on the amount of the fine, but the sanctions must be appropriate. Appropriate means 'effective, proportionate and dissuasive'.[322] A civil penalty cannot be imposed where there are reasonable grounds to be satisfied that the person has taken all reasonable steps and exercised all due diligence to ensure that the requirement would be complied with. Where the FCA intends to impose a penalty on a PRA-authorised person – as is normally the case for banks – then the FCA must consult the PRA beforehand.[323] In principle the FCA is obliged to publish its penalty decisions.[324] Only when publication would be unfair to the person with respect to whom the action was taken (or was proposed to be taken) in the opinion of the FCA, be prejudicial to the interests of consumers, or be detrimental to the stability of the UK financial system, may the FCA not publish these decisions.[325] Considering that decisions on non-compliance with the Regulations are either final or decision notices, the FCA in practice publishes these decisions.[326] This can be regarded as a form of naming & shaming. In addition to this sanctioning power under the Regulations, the FCA states that it uses a range of more informal tools for enforcing AML compliance: '[t]hese include; seeking attestations from senior management that weaknesses have been remediated; using a Skilled Person to test systems and controls, identify weaknesses, and, in some cases, remediate the weaknesses identified (...)'.[327]

FSMA 2000 provides the FCA with a large variety of sanctioning powers.[328] Considering that banks are authorised firms and that money laundering falls under the operational goal of tackling financial crime and protecting the integrity of the UK financial system, the FCA can in most cases also decide to resort to sanctioning powers under FSMA 2000 for enforcing AML compliance. Examples of sanctioning powers under this Act include the decision to publicly censure a firm (a public warning), to impose a financial penalty or to suspend the permission of an authorised person or impose a restriction in relation to the carrying on of a regulated activity by an authorised person for up to twelve months.[329] In

321 See § 6.6.1 about the meaning of relevant and connected persons.

322 Regulation 42(1C) MLR 2007.

323 Regulation 42(4A) MLR 2007.

324 Section 391(4) FSMA 2000, as amended by FSA 2012. Although it is not an obligation under the Regulation, considering that the Enforcement Guide applies to this policy as well, the duty of publication is also considered to apply here. This is detailed in the FCA's Enforcement Guide 6.8 and 6.9. See for the actual publications: *FCA Final Notices*, available at: <www.fca.org.uk/your-fca/list?ttypes=Final+Notice&>, last visited on 11 June 2014; and *FCA Decision Notices*, available at: <www.fca.org.uk/your-fca/list?ttypes=Decision+notice&ssearch=>, last visited on 11 June 2014.

325 Section 391(6) FSMA 2000, as amended by FSA 2012.

326 Decision notices: Section 388 FSMA 2000; Final Notices: Section 390 FSMA 2000. Differences: DEPP 1.2.2.

327 FCA (2013) at 12.

328 Cf. McEldowney (2013) at 596-598.

329 Sections 205-206A FSMA 2000, as amended by FSA 2012. See the FCA Enforcement Guide 7.2 that explains on which institutions and persons the FCA can impose these powers.

more serious cases, the FCA may also decide to cancel a firm's authorisation or impose a requirement on this authorisation.[330] As just explained, the FCA is in principle obliged to publish its final and decision notices.[331]

The FCA can also decide to take enforcement action through the courts. For example, the FCA may seek an injunction. This is a court order issued by the High Court that prohibits a person from doing or continuing to do a certain act or requires him to carry out a certain act.[332] According to the FCA's Enforcement Guide, 'the court may make three types of order under these provisions: to restrain a course of conduct, to take steps to remedy a course of conduct and to secure assets.'[333] Likewise, the FCA may apply to the courts for a restitution order.[334] Finally, the FCA has the power to prosecute a wide range of criminal offences.[335] Section 402 FSMA 2000 thereby explicitly states that the FCA may institute proceedings for an offence under the prescribed regulations relating to money laundering.[336]

The FCA also has sanctioning powers against natural persons working at the institutions. It may prohibit an individual from operating in financial services, declare that the individual is not fit and proper (anymore), and/or decide to prohibit an individual from undertaking specific regulated activities.[337] The final and decision notices must, in principle, be published.

6.6.4 Sanctioning policy and practice

6.6.4.1 Sanctioning policy

The FCA has a general enforcement policy laid down in the Enforcement Guide (hereafter 'EG') which exists alongside the FCA Handbook.[338] The EG contains information on the supervisory, sanctioning and criminal prosecution powers available to the FCA when acting as a supervisor under Part IV FSMA in relation to authorised firms. A number of enforcement goals underlie the FCA's approach. These are maintaining an open and co-operative relationship with those which the FCA regulates, transparency, proportionality, responsiveness and consistency, fair treatment when exercising enforcement powers, bringing about behavioural changes and to deter future non-compliance by others, to eliminate financial gain and to remedy the harm caused by the non-compliance.[339] The

330 Section 55J and 55L FSMA 2000, as amended by FSA 2012.See Enforcement Guide 8.1.
331 Section 391(4) FSMA 2000. See for supervisory notices: Section 391(5) FSMA 2000. Warning notices are in principle not published: Section 391(1ZB) FSMA 2000. See also: Enforcement Guide 6.6 and 6.7.
332 Section 380 FSMA 2000. See Enforcement Guide Chapter 10.
333 Enforcement Guide 10.2.
334 See Enforcement Guide Chapter 11.
335 Under Sections 401 and 402 FSMA 2000, the FCA may prosecute a range of offences; Enforcement Guide Chapter 12.
336 Section 45 MLR 2007 states which breaches are criminal offences.
337 Sections 56 and 63 FSMA 2000. See Enforcement Guide Chapter 11.
338 FCA Enforcement Guide, available at: <http://media.fshandbook.info/Handbook/EG_FCA_20140401.pdf>, last visited on 13 June 2014.
339 Enforcement Guide 2.2.

ultimate objective of the FCA's enforcement is to achieve 'credible deterrence'.[340] The procedures for imposing some specific sanctions – statutory notices, financial penalties and the conducting of interviews to which a direction under Section 169(7) FSMA 2000 has been given – are further detailed in the Decision Procedure and Penalties Manual (hereafter 'DEPP'), aiming to guarantee the proportionality of enforcement action by the FCA. Different from the EG, the DEPP is a module in the FCA's Handbook. Although DEPP 1.1.1 only refers to the FCA's policy on the imposition and amount of penalties under FSMA 2000, representatives have indicated that this is applied in the context of the Regulations as well.[341] Individual DEPP provisions support this interpretation.

Considering that the Regulations essentially only provide the FCA with the power to impose a civil penalty, although sometimes it can turn to other sanctioning powers under FSMA 2000 as well, I will now briefly describe how the FCA makes use of this power. The DEPP provides a non-exhaustive list of factors which the FCA takes into account in determining whether to impose a financial penalty or not. The factors relate to the nature, seriousness and impact of the suspected breach (deliberate or reckless behaviour, the duration and frequency of the breach, systematic weakness in internal control systems, etc.), the conduct of the person after the breach (brought to the attention of the FCA, cooperative behaviour, remedial steps already taken, etc.), the previous disciplinary record and compliance history, as well as FCA guidance and other published materials.[342] Specifically with regard to the AML policy, DEPP 6.2.3 states that the FCA will also consider whether a firm has followed the JMLSG Guidance.

In determining whether to impose a financial penalty (fine) or rather to choose for public censure, DEPP 6.4 states that the FCA will consider all relevant factors of a case. This shows that proportionality is taken into account. It may include the question whether deterrence may be effectively achieved by issuing a public censure, the seriousness of the breach (the more serious, the more likely is a fine), the compliance history (a poor history may be a factor in favour of a fine), and the impact on the person concerned. When the FCA decides to impose a fine, the following enforcement principles apply: disgorgement, discipline and deterrence. Disgorgement means that a firm or individual should not benefit from any breach. Discipline means that a firm or individual should be sanctioned for wrongdoing and, finally, deterrence means that the imposition of a penalty should deter the firm or individual who committed the breach, and others, from committing further or similar breaches.[343] A five-step framework for deciding the amount of the financial penalties applies.[344] With regard to firms, the FCA takes the following steps hereunder. For individuals these steps are the same, but within the steps different criteria apply.[345] The five steps are intended to ensure a proportionate response to the breach. However, the

340 FSA (2013a), *Enforcement Annual Performance Account 2012/13*, at 5.
341 Interview Financial Conduct Authority, May 2014.
342 DEPP 6.2.1.(1)-(3).
343 DEPP 6.5.2.
344 All steps are detailed in DEPP 5.5A.1 – DEPP 5.5A.5.
345 Detailed in DEPP 5.5B.1 – DEPP 5.5B.5.

FCA still reduces the amount of the fine if it would cause the firm or individual concerned serious financial hardship.[346]

Step 1 – Removal of the financial benefit derived directly from the breach.
Step 2 – Determination of a figure reflecting the seriousness of the breach.
Step 3 – Adjusting the figure downwards or upwards by taking into account any aggravating and mitigating circumstances.
Step 4 – Adjusting the figure upwards, where appropriate, to ensure a deterrent effect.
Step 5 – Consider the application of a settlement discount (up to 30% of the penalty).

It should be pointed out that the FCA stated in its annual AML report 2012/13 that within the AML policy it is moving more and more to an early intervention approach. This means that the FCA is making increasing use of early interventions, such as ordering a temporary prohibition of the firm's business when there are serious concerns with regard to AML compliance, until the deficiencies are addressed.[347] According to the FCA, '[s]uccessful early intervention cases will often not produce public outcomes, as the outcome is frequently swift remedial action without necessarily involving any immediate publicity'.[348] The imposition of a penalty is still possible after the use of such early intervention mechanisms.

6.6.4.2 Sanctioning in practice

Regarding the FCA's sanctioning practice for non-compliance with the preventive obligations by banks, the following can be observed. In 2011 the FSA did not impose any formal sanctions in relation to non-compliance with MLR 2007.[349] In 2012, 2013 and early 2014 the FSA/FCA imposed a total of six financial penalties on banks for non-compliance with the Regulations.[350] In addition, it imposed one civil penalty of 17,500 GBP on a money laundering reporting officer working for one of these banks.[351] All penalties were published. The amounts of the fines vary considerably: the lowest fine was imposed on Turkish Bank (UK) Ltd (294,000 GBP), whereas Coutts & Company was fined 8.75 million GBP. The average amount of the six financial penalties on banks in these years was 3.66 million GBP, approximately 4.5 million Euros. Out of the six penalties, three followed from the thematic review of banks' management of high-risk money laundering situations of 2011.[352]

346 What constitutes serious financial hardship and how the FCA deals with this is explained in DEPP 6.5D.
347 FCA (2013) at 13; Interview Financial Conduct Authority, May 2014.
348 FSA (2013a) at 13.
349 Interview Financial Services Authority, April 2012.
350 *FSA Final Notice: Coutts & Company*, Ref. no. 122287, 23 March 2012; *FSA Final Notice: Habib Bank AG Zurich*, Ref. no. 113991, 4 May 2012; *FSA Decision Notice: Turkish Bank (UK) Ltd*, Ref. no. 204566, 2 August 2012; *FSA Final Notice, EFG Private Bank Ltd*, Ref. no. 144036, 28 March 2013; *FCA Final Notice: Guarantee Trust Bank (UK) Limited*, Ref. no. 466611, 8 August 2013; *FCA Decision Notice: Standard Bank Plc*, Ref. no. 124823, 22 January 2014.
351 *FSA Final Notice: Mr Syed Itrat Hussain*, Ref. no. SIH 01010, 4 May 2012.
352 See § 6.6.2.3.

> In the Coutts & Company case, for example, the (then) FSA concluded that Coutts had failed to take reasonable care to establish and maintain effective AML systems and controls in relation to high risk customers. In particular Coutts had failed to assess adequately the level of money laundering risk posed by prospective and existing high risk customers. This included failures to properly identify and record all politically exposed persons, to consistently apply appropriate ongoing monitoring and to carry out adequate reviews of its AML systems and controls for high risk customers. FSA inspectors reviewed more than a hundred high risk customer files and found breaches in more than 70% of the files.[353]

This proves that the FCA's enforcement practice is dissuasive. In addition, the FCA has reported that it made use of its early intervention approach with four banks, one of which was still sanctioned afterwards in the financial year 2012-13. One of the interventions concerned an agreement between the FCA and the bank that the latter would not open new accounts for customers that are high-risk politically exposed persons, until it had corrected the identified AML breaches.[354] According to representatives, the FCA applied this power six times for non-compliance with the Regulations until early 2014.[355] Other informal sanctions were also taken. One can think of sending out warning letters or agreeing on action plans. These measures are, however, not published. Only from the Treasury's AML annual supervision report for 2012-13 can one deduce that the FCA varied one permission.[356] Whether this was a bank's permission cannot be derived from this report.

6.6.5 Concluding remarks

Both the Regulations 2007 and FSMA 2000 provide the FCA with adequate supervisory powers. The FCA is empowered to compel (the production of) information, as well as to enter and inspect premises and any recorded information found on the premises. The MLR 2007 do not provide FCA regulatory powers, but via FSMA 2000 the FCA can make general rules as appear necessary or expedient to it for the purpose of advancing one or more of its operational objectives, through which money laundering is indirectly covered. The FCA exercises its AML supervision via two tracks. On the one hand, it integrated this in the regular supervisory procedures and, on the other hand, a specialist financial crime supervision team carries out AML supervision. On a risk-based approach, which takes into account the money laundering risk, regular supervisors may decide to include the verification of AML compliance into their supervision of banks. The extent to which they do so depends on their discretion. In the absence of information as to how and to what extent the verification of compliance with MLR 2007 is integrated, nothing more can be said about the actual integration of AML supervision in regular supervisory procedures. More information could, and in the light of the theoretical framework of effective supervision should be published. Quite some information is available about the AML supervision of banks by the financial crime supervision team. It carries out a large number

353 *FSA Final Notice: Coutts & Company*, Ref. no. 122287, 23 March 2012, par. 6.
354 FCA (2013) at 13.
355 Interview Financial Conduct Authority, May 2014.
356 HM Treasury (2013), par. 5.4.

of on-site inspections and investigations on banks annually, in particular through the ongoing Systematic Anti-Money Laundering Programme and thematic studies on banks' compliance with AML obligations. It also carries out event-driven AML supervision on a risk-based approach, where firm supervisors or other intelligence bring concerns about a firm's AML compliance to the team.

Under the Regulations, the FCA only has the power to impose a civil penalty (a fine). There is no statutory cap on this fine. It seems that the requirement stemming from the theoretical framework of effective supervision, concerning the wide range of sanctions, is not complied with. Nevertheless, due to the close relationship between the MLR 2007 and FSMA 2000, the FCA may in most cases also make use of its enforcement powers under this last Act. These include: public censures (warnings), financial penalties, the suspension of or a restriction on authorisation, withdrawal of a firm's authorisation or the imposition of requirements on this authorisation, as well as enforcement action through the civil and criminal courts (e.g. injunctions or restitution orders) and prosecution. The FCA can also prohibit an individual from operating in financial services, declare that the individual is not fit and proper (anymore), and/or decide to prohibit an individual from undertaking specific regulated activities. Enforcement decisions laid down in final or decision notices are, in principle, always published by the FCA, which can be seen as an additional sanction. The FCA has a detailed public supervision policy, which from the theoretical framework of effective supervision is very good. The policy contains the enforcement goals and principles, and explains how the FCA makes use of its different supervisory and sanctioning powers. For the application of specific sanctions this is further detailed in the Decision Procedure and Penalties Manual (DEPP), which should ensure proportionality in its enforcement actions. In practice the FCA has been active in terms of imposing sanctions on banks that do not comply with AML obligations, showing the dissuasiveness of its policy as well. In the period from 2011 until early 2014, the FCA fined six different banks, as well as one money laundering reporting officer. The average amount of the fines on banks was approximately 4.5 million Euros. In addition, the FCA made use of early interventions against banks at least four times, and also applied various informal measures against banks.

6.7 Office of Fair Trading

6.7.1 Supervisory powers

The Office of Fair Trading derives its supervisory powers directly from the Regulations. These powers have been explained in § 6.6.1.1 for the FCA. This means that the Office has the power to request (the production) of information or to require attendance by an institution for which it has supervisory responsibility, or a connected person. Moreover, it has the power to perform on-site inspections, either directly or under a warrant issued by a justice. The Regulations do not provide the OFT with regulatory powers, although it may issue a Guidance that is to be approved by the Treasury.[357]

357 See § 6.3.

6.7.2 Anti-money laundering supervision in practice

The AML supervision of real estate agents is based on two tracks. The first track consists of risk-based AML supervision exercised by the OFT itself. The second track consists of the exercise of AML supervision by officers of Local Authority Trading Standard Services (hereafter 'LATSS') on behalf of the OFT. I will now pay attention to both tracks.

6.7.2.1 Supervision by the Office of Fair Trading

AML supervision by the OFT is a separate supervisory regime and is not integrated into wider supervisory programmes.[358] AML supervision always focuses on *all* AML obligations. OFT inspectors have not performed inspections in which they focussed on one single (aspect of) an AML obligation. The OFT's AML supervision is based on a risk-based approach.[359] The risk assessment is primarily based on information that is submitted by estate agents upon registration, the OFT's visiting history, and intelligence gathered and analysed by the OFT on the sector. Other available information that the OFT's AML Unit collects concerns industry trends, media messages, previous or running complaints about the estate agent, registration for the Consumer Redress Scheme and whether action is taken against a real estate agent in any other way.[360] The AML Unit may also receive intelligence from other AML supervisors or enforcement partners under its other statutory duties, such as the LATSS. Customer and geographical risks are included in the risk assessment. The OFT prepares annual supervision plans, which are not available to the public. OFT representatives indicated that annual plans include the number of inspections and activities planned and an indication of the businesses that will be visited. Factors that are taken into account in drafting the annual supervision plans are the risk, the size of the businesses, the annual turnover and the geographical location. The majority of the institutions to be inspected are considered high risk, but the OFT always selects a benchmark group from lower-risk categories on an ad random basis ('random inspections').[361] The size of the businesses to be inspected also varies from large businesses to sole traders. The group that the OFT inspects annually should preferably also have a wide range in annual turnovers and geographical locations.[362]

The AML Unit carries out AML supervision in four ways: telephone contact, letters seeking details of estate agents' details of AML policies and procedures, questionnaires, and on-site visits.[363] In practice AML supervision is a combination of off-site and on-site inspections. Originally, the OFT intended to use off-site inspections on a self-standing basis for a part of its supervisory activities. However, in the first years of the OFT's practice, it appeared that businesses generally did not provide sufficient information to adequately determine

358 OFT (2011b), *Money Laundering Regulations 2007: The OFT's approach to penalties*, OFT1326, at 4.
359 OFT (2013a), *OFT Anti-Money Laundering Enforcement Principles: Money Laundering Regulations 2007*, May 2011 (updated May 2013), OFT1094, at 9-10.
360 OFT (2011c), *Visits to businesses under the Money Laundering Regulations 2007: Code of Practice*, OFT1386, at 6.
361 OFT (2013a) at 10.
362 Interview Office of Fair Trading, April 2012.
363 OFT (2013a) at 10.

their level of compliance.[364] One of the main reasons for this seems to be the fact that the Regulations do not require that internal AML policies are kept in writing. Although the OFT clearly brought this to the attention of the Treasury during the consultation procedure for the 2012 amendments to MLR 2007, the wide range of amendments that entered into force did not include any changes in this regard.[365] Regulation 20 MLR 2007 only requires that obliged institutions establish and maintain appropriate and risk-sensitive policies and procedures. Obviously, supervisors have interpreted this as written policies and have attempted to guide the obliged institutions and professionals.[366] The OFT does not mention anything of this kind in its Core Guidance, but in the Code of Practice it refers to information that officers are likely want to review 'in the form of written documentation' including AML policies and procedures.[367] In 2011, the OFT found that 93% of the inspected institutions for which it has supervisory responsibility had no or very poorly written internal procedures and policies. All that the OFT could do was to advise these institutions to record the policies and procedures.[368]

The OFT's Code of Practice provides detailed information which aspects OFT inspectors will include in their reviews during on-site visits. This is, inter alia, information in the OFT register, the estate agent's business model, the risk assessment of the estate agent's customers, internal policies, and the implementation of procedures and training opportunities for staff, and transaction files. Moreover, officers will talk to staff about their AML awareness and are available to answer questions that the estate agent has about AML legislation.[369] At the end of each inspection, inspectors discuss the results with the business concerned. The Code of Practice lays down that together with the supervised business, OFT inspectors will discuss a timetable for improvements and answer any questions that the business has. In case of breaches of MLR 2007, the steps that must be taken and the timeframe are explained, as well as the consequences for a failure to comply with these points. This demonstrates that the OFT gives businesses the necessary time to correct their non-compliant behaviour, before it resorts to the use of sanctions.

Information about the exercise of AML supervision in practice is scarce. In the year April 2010 to April 2011, the OFT carried out 12 on-site visits on estate agents and consumer credit financial institutions, and 9 off-site inspections.[370] From April 2011 to April 2012, the OFT increased its inspection activity by carrying out 22 on-site visits on estate agents.[371] In light of the number of real estate agents in 2012 (6,601), the inspection numbers are

364 Interview Office of Fair Trading, April 2012.

365 OFT (2011d), *The Money Laundering Regulations 2007: OFT Response to HM Treasury's Review*, OFT1362, at 7-8.

366 E.g. Gambling Commission (2011), *Money laundering: the prevention of money laundering and combating the financing of terrorism. Guidance for remote and non-remote casinos*, 2nd edition, at 5, makes it seem like an obligation to have written AML internal policies; HM Revenue and Customs (2010), *Anti-money laundering guidance for high value dealers*, July 2010, at 5 states that particularly larger businesses may find it useful to have written policies.

367 OFT (2009), *Money Laundering Regulations 2007: Core Guidance*, OFT954 at 14; OFT (2011c) at 14.

368 OFT (2011d) at 8.

369 OFT (2011c) at 12-13.

370 OFT (2011) at 11.

371 Interview Office of Fair Trading, April 2012.

very low: only approximately 0.3% of estate agents were supervised by the OFT in 2012.[372] Acknowledging that this number may not be fully accurate, it does give an indication of the likelihood that a real estate agent could receive an AML inspection from the OFT during that year. The OFT acknowledged in 2011 that '[t]he reactive inspections carried out are not statistically significant because they are focused on businesses about which we have received information indicating a likelihood of non-compliance'.[373] Unfortunately, for the years 2012 and 2013 no inspection numbers are available as the OFT has not published special annual AML reports anymore and the general annual reports and accounts do not provide these numbers either. The OFT should become more transparent about this.

6.7.2.2 Outsourcing of supervision to LATSS

The Regulations allow the OFT to enter into arrangements with local weights and measures authorities (in practice the LATSS), allowing LATSS' officers and officers from the Department of Enterprise, Trade and Investment for Northern Ireland, to exercise the supervisory powers under Regulations 37-39 MLR 2007.[374] Everything these officers do or omit shall be treated as having been done or omitted to be done by an OFT officer, with the exception in the case of criminal proceedings against the relevant officer.[375] LATSS officers are not allowed to disclose the information obtained during the supervision to any other authority than the OFT, unless the latter has given its approval or there exists a (statutory) duty to disclose the information.[376]

> LATSS play an important role in relation to the OFT's tasks in the field of fair trading and consumer protection. There are more than 200 LATSS in the UK. They are funded by and accountable to local authorities.[377] LATSS enforce a wide range of legislation and their role is to promote and maintain fair trading and to protect consumers on a local level.[378] They have legal responsibility varying from enforcing weights and measures legislation to regulations in relation to food standards and the safety of goods. Part 8 Enterprise Act 2002 gives the OFT the responsibility to lead and coordinate enforcement with other authorities, including LATSS. In 2005 the OFT took on responsibility for strategic leadership and support to LATSS in relation to the fair trading aspects of work shared by them.[379]

The Regulations do not stipulate what the arrangements between the OFT and the LATSS should comprise of and how the arrangements should be concluded and maintained. It is, for example, not clear whether the arrangement should entail a specific methodology

372 The calculation is a rough calculation based on the number of on-site visits that took place between April 2011-April 2012 (22) divided by the number of estate agents in the year 2012 (6,601).
373 OFT (2011) at 10.
374 Regulation 41(1) in conjunction with Regulation 36 MLR 2007.
375 Regulation 41(2) and (3) MLR 2007.
376 Regulation 41(4) MLR 2007.
377 National Audit Office (2008), *Effective inspection and enforcement: implementing the Hampton vision in the Office of Fair Trading*, March 2008 at 11; Audit Commission (1999), *Measure for measure: the best value agenda for Trading Standard Services*, December 1999, at 23.
378 Audit Commission (1999) at 16-18.
379 Office of Fair Trading and Local Authority Trading Standards Services-programme of joint action, June 2006.

for on-site AML inspections. Nor is it clear whether LATSS can themselves decide which estate agents (or consumer credit financial institutions) they visit, and if so, whether these decisions are based on a risk-based approach. Likewise, it is not clear whether LATSS would include AML supervision as an aspect of wider supervisory programmes or whether the visits should focus on compliance with MLR 2007. It could also be the case, however, that the OFT provides a list of which real estate agents must be visited during the year. Finally, there is also no obligation that arrangements must be concluded in writing. One of the few things that is clear is that the OFT is fully responsible for the AML inspections performed by the LATSS officers, as was just explained. LATSS can carry out AML supervision on behalf of the OFT, but the OFT is directly and legally responsible for any supervisory actions by LATSS. The OFT's Code of Practice speaks little about the performance of AML inspections by LATSS as well. It explains that on some occasions a LATSS officer may wish to accompany the OFT and that, when this is the case, the business concerned will be notified of the fact, and the name of the LATSS officer and the reason why he wishes to attend will be provided.[380] It furthermore states that the OFT has the power to enter into arrangements with LATSS and that the powers under the Regulations are shared. In the absence of such arrangements, the OFT will still work together with LATSS by, for example, providing them with a copy of the letter that the OFT sends to the business for their information.[381]

From the viewpoint of transparency and accountability, as well as legality and legal certainty, formal, written arrangements between the OFT and LATSS should be concluded. These arrangements should also regulate in more detail the relationship under the AML regime between the authorities. Furthermore, the arrangement should seek to set out a clear methodology that deals with the performance of AML supervision by LATSS. The OFT's Code of Practice can serve as a source of inspiration in the design of AML supervisory procedures for LATSS. Based on the theoretical framework of effective supervision it would be advisable to publish the arrangements and communicate the essence of these arrangements to the real estate agents and consumer credit financial institutions that are under the OFT's AML supervision. This would create awareness and understanding on the role of LATSS in the AML regime. At the same time it enables obliged institutions and the public to know with which LATSS the OFT has an arrangement and with which ones it does not.

In practice, AML supervision by LATSS officers is still in its infancy. Until 2011 the OFT took sole responsibility for AML supervision, although in the year 2010-11 LATSS carried out 20 AML on-site visits as part of a pilot project and after receiving adverse signals from the OFT.[382] This is more than the number of on-site visits by OFT itself (12) in that year.[383] In 2011-12 the OFT carefully started to make use of the possibility to outsource AML supervision.[384] In this period one informal agreement with a LATSS existed, which was

380 OFT (2011c) at 10.
381 Ibid., at 15-16.
382 OFT (2011) at 11.
383 Ibid.
384 OFT (2011e), *FAQ on MLR 2007 Supervision by OFT: Version 7*, at 14-15.

mainly about input by means of intelligence from LATSS to the OFT's risk assessments for AML supervision, and the performance of on-site inspections on behalf of the OFT.[385] In 2012, the OFT aimed to conclude a more formal supervisory arrangement with a LATSS under MLR 2007. The formal arrangement should include agreements on the number of inspections to be performed by the LATSS, the training of LATSS officers by the OFT and the costs of supervision. The costs of supervision performed by LATSS are to be borne by the OFT, which, once again, implies that it is responsible for the work carried out by LATSS.[386] There is no evidence that proves that the arrangements were formalised in the years thereafter. Unfortunately, statistics or information about the exercise of AML supervision by LATSS have not been published anywhere and data for the years 2012 and 2013 is not available.

6.7.3 Sanctioning powers

Also the OFT's AML sanctioning regime is separate from other regulatory regimes for which the OFT has responsibility, which means that it will only use the sanctioning powers it has been provided with under the Regulations.[387] As explained in § 6.6.3 for the FCA, Regulation 42(1) provides some AML supervisors with the power to impose a civil penalty on a person who fails to comply with obligations under the MLR 2007, ranging from a failure to comply with aspects of customer due diligence measures, to developing internal AML policies and appointing a money laundering reporting officer, or who fail to comply with a notice given under Regulation 37. As explained, no maximum amount is attached to the fine as long as it is considered to be appropriate by the supervisor and that for this purpose appropriate is to be understood as effective, proportionate and dissuasive. Unlike the FCA, the OFT has prosecutorial powers under the Regulations for almost the same list of obligations as for which a civil penalty can be imposed.[388] Prosecution can take place against the obliged institution of professionals as such, or, where such a body is a body corporate, a partnership or unincorporated association, against any person who commits the breach with the consent or connivance (tacit approval) of an officer of the body corporate, the association or a partner, and the offence must be attributable to neglect on their part.[389] In that case both the officer[390] as well as the body corporate, the partner and partnership, or the officer[391] and the association are guilty of an offence and are liable for prosecution. Again, a person is not guilty if he took all reasonable steps and

385 Interview Office of Fair Trading, April 2012.
386 Interview Office of Fair Trading, April 2012.
387 OFT (2011b) at 4. It will, for example, normally use its power to ban real estate agents as it can do under the Estate Agents Act 1979 when it is of the opinion that an estate agent is unfit to carry out estate agency work. Section 3(1) Estate Agents Act 1979 lists the grounds on which such an order may be made.
388 Regulation 46(1) in conjunction with Regulation 47 MLR 2007. The only difference is a breach of Regulation 11(1)(d) – the consideration of reporting – which is not liable for prosecution but for which a civil penalty can be imposed.
389 Regulation 47(1), (2) and (3) MLR 2007.
390 Regulation 47(9)(a) MLR 2007 states that an officer means a director, manager, secretary, chief executive, member of the committee of management, or a person purporting to act in such a capacity.
391 Regulation 47(9)(b) states that officer means any officer of the association, or any member of its governing body, or any person purporting to act in such a capacity.

exercised all due diligence to avoid committing the offence.[392] If ultimately convicted, a natural person is liable to be sentenced to a term of imprisonment for a period up to two years and/or an unlimited (criminal) fine. Where a legal person is prosecuted and found guilty, it will be sentenced to pay a fine. No concurrence between a financial penalty and prosecution for breaches under MLR 2007 is allowed. This would be contrary to the *ne bis in idem* doctrine, in common law also known as double jeopardy, which prohibits a person from being sanctioned twice for the same fact.[393]

> With the consultation of HM Treasury on the 2012 amendments, a debate on the criminal sanctions under the AML policy was started. Especially the Law Society lobbied for the removal of criminal sanctions, arguing that these were unlikely to stimulate effective compliance.[394] The threat of facing criminal sanctions would undermine the risk-based approach that applies to the preventive regime, because institutions would be far more concerned with avoiding criminal liability rather than looking at the true risks of being used for the purpose of money laundering in the first place, the Law Society argued.[395] A second argument was that even in very serious cases AML supervisors tended to resort to the power to impose a financial penalty, rather than prosecuting the business and its principals for non-compliance.[396] Other stakeholders did not agree and opposed the removal of the criminal sanctions under the Regulations. Respondents saw the criminal sanctions, even when not or seldom used, as a powerful deterrent and enforcement tool. Moreover, they demonstrate the dedication of the UK Government to fighting money laundering. The removal of the criminal sanctions could be regarded as a decrease in this dedication and send out a wrong signal.[397] Ultimately, criminal sanctions were not removed.

As an aside it should be pointed out that the LATSS also have prosecutorial powers under MLR 2007. LATSS carry out many investigations into fraud and may decide, as part of the investigation, to prosecute businesses or persons responsible for the breach. This will particularly be done in relation to trust and company service providers. It is, however, not excluded that this will not happen with estate agents in the future.[398] When LATSS decide to prosecute an estate agent, they should notify the OFT of the intended prosecution, together with the facts on which the charges are founded. They must also notify the OFT of the outcome of the proceedings after they are finally determined.[399] In this context, it is difficult to understand why LATSS have not been given the possibility to impose civil penalties for breaches under the Regulations. This could lead to the suggestion that LATSS can either opt to persuade institutions to comply or start a prosecution in case of non-

392 Regulation 45(4) MLR 2007.

393 Regulation 45(5) MLR 2007; Hunter, J. (1984), 'Development of the Rule against Double Jeopardy', *Journal of Legal History*, vol. 5, issue 1, pp. 1-19 at 3-4.

394 Law Society of England and Wales (2011), *Response to the HM Treasury Consultation on the Money Laundering Regulations 2007*, August 2011, at 4.

395 Law Society of England and Wales (2009), *The costs and benefits of anti-money laundering compliance for solicitors: Response by the Law Society of England and Wales to the call for evidence in the Review of the Money Laundering Regulations 2007*, December 2009 at 7.

396 Ibid., at 8.

397 HM Treasury (2011b), *Consultation on proposed changes to the money laundering regulations 2007: Summary of Responses*, November 2011, at 5-6.

398 Interview HM Revenue and Customs, May 2014.

399 Regulation 46(4) and 46(5) MLR 2007.

compliance. There is no middle course for breaches that require a sanction but that are not sufficiently severe for a criminal prosecution. Such a black and white picture does not reflect sanctioning reality where supervisors must have adequate sanctions.

6.7.4 Sanctioning policy and practice

6.7.4.1 Sanctioning policy

The OFT is very transparent about its sanctioning policy under the Regulations. It has published three documents that jointly demonstrate its policy: the OFT's approach to penalties under the MLR 2007, its AML enforcement principles, and its interim penalty policy.[400] The AML enforcement principles and the OFT's approach to penalties deal with the AML sanctioning regime in general, whereas the interim penalty policy concerns the steps which the OFT takes in determining whether to impose a penalty and the amount thereof. Representatives indicated that the OFT would finalise its penalty policy once the first cases had successfully passed through the system.[401] Until the end of 2013, however, no such policy had been published. With its sanctioning policy, the OFT seeks to change the behaviour of the offender, to eliminate any financial gain or benefit from non-compliance, to be responsive and to consider what is appropriate for the offender and the breach, to be proportionate to the nature of the breach and the resulting vulnerability to being used for money laundering, and to deter future non-compliance.[402] In order to attain these goals, the enforcement principles state that actions under the AML policy must be proportionate, consistent, targeted, transparent, and accountable.[403] These principles are the same as the statutory principles of good regulation, but adjusted to the OFT's AML regime.[404]

For the imposition of proportionate sanctions under the Regulations the OFT lists a range of factors that it takes into account, including the seriousness of the breach, the available sanctions, the duration of the breach, and the compliance history.[405] In principle the OFT first turns to the least formal means to ensure compliance – such as guidance, advice (general or individual level), or education – unless there are special circumstances that immediately require more formal enforcement actions. The OFT states that it hopes to perform its supervision through the use of guidance and advice. It will, however, consider direct formal action when the case at hand so requires. Examples where the OFT may do so are where it appears that a business has not taken, or taken very limitedly, steps towards compliance; where there is a serious risk of money laundering; where there is a serious breach or where breaches have been continuing for a long period of time.[406] This

400 OFT (2011b); OFT (2013a); OFT (2011f), *Money Laundering Regulations 2007: Interim Penalty Policy*, OFT1271.
401 Interview Office of Fair Trading, April 2012. Cf. OFT (2011b) at 1.
402 OFT (2013a) at 12-13; OFT (2011b) at 3.
403 OFT (2013a) at 15.
404 The statutory better regulation principles apply to all UK regulators and can be found in Part II of the Legislative and Regulatory Reform Act 2006 and Part IV of the Regulatory Enforcement and Sanctions Act. The principles are the result of the Hampton and Macrory reviews, to which attention was paid in Chapter 2.
405 See for the full list: OFT (2013a) at 15-16.
406 OFT (2013a) at 17-18.

is a departure from the previous enforcement principles, where the OFT stated that it would not escalate the sanctions unless dialogue is failing and the business has a history of non-compliance.[407] Part of the OFT's consistent and targeted AML enforcement regime is working together and sharing information with other AML supervisors, HM Treasury, the Serious Organised Crime Agency and LATSS.[408] Finally, the OFT aims to be transparent and accountable. It will notify the business concerned of the reasons for its enforcement action and make known the right of appeal. Moreover, the OFT will, where possible and appropriate, publish its sanctions or the court proceedings.[409] This may serve as an extra deterrent for non-complying business and a means of guidance for other estate agents. Part of accountability and transparency also entails full cooperation with the FATF and HM Treasury in reviewing the effectiveness of the OFT's sanctioning regime.[410]

> To exemplify its enforcement policy, in particular the element of proportionality, the OFT has provided an enforcement diagram that to a certain extent reflects the enforcement pyramid of the responsive regulation theory.[411] At the bottom of the pyramid one can find actions such as the provision of guidance, advice and education, whereas at the top, one can find civil penalties or prosecution and appeal.[412] What is different from the enforcement pyramid as illustrated in the responsive regulation theory is that the OFT's pyramid includes elements that are not, strictly speaking, enforcement action. The OFT, for example, places inspections in one of the lower levels of the pyramid. Inspections, however, are not a means to ensure compliance but in the first place, but rather a means to verify the levels of compliance.[413] This is a tool that stands at the heart of the supervisory process and, strictly speaking, it does not form part of the OFT's enforcement armoury.[414] It is interesting to observe that the OFT places financial penalties and prosecution at the same level in its pyramid. The reason for this is not clear, particularly because representatives have indicated that prosecution should be used only as a last resort in light of its more punitive nature.[415] In fact, until the end of 2013, the OFT had never used its prosecutorial powers under the Regulations.[416] In the enforcement pyramid of the responsive regulation theory, criminal penalties are thought to be more formal and deterrent than civil penalties.[417]

If the OFT decides to impose a civil penalty, the interim penalty policy explains in detail how the procedure commences and which steps are followed.[418] It also gives an indication

407 OFT (2011g), *Anti-Money Laundering Enforcement Principles: Money Laundering Regulations 2007*, May 2011, OFT1094, at 12.
408 More about cooperation with other AML supervisors in § 6.10.
409 OFT (2013a) at 19-20.
410 Ibid., at 20.
411 Compare with § 2.4.3.2.
412 OFT (2013a) at 17.
413 This does not do away with the possibility that the threat of an inspection or a compliance visit may have the effect that businesses will comply with the requirements.
414 Obviously, it also depends on how enforcement is defined by the OFT. Yet in the wider context of the OFT's AML regime, virtually all OFT policy documents make a clear distinction between supervision and enforcement (sanctioning).
415 Interview Office of Fair Trading, April 2012.
416 Until the end of 2013, the OFT only mentioned imposed penalties: OFT, *Anti-money laundering enforcement*, available at: <www.oft.gov.uk/OFTwork/aml/AML-enforcement/#named8>, last visited on 9 March 2014.
417 Cf. § 2.4.3.2.
418 OFT (2011f) at 6-7.

of how the OFT calculates the amount of the penalties. In case of non-registration, the OFT uses a fixed-penalty approach, with a starting point of 2,000 GBP. The penalty is adjusted to the size of the business, for every additional premises an additional 1,000 GBP, and the existence of any aggravating or mitigating circumstances.[419] Financial penalties for direct breaches of AML obligations are calculated differently. The OFT then calculates the amount of the fine by following four steps. In the first step, the OFT decides the percentage of the relevant turnover as a penalty. What the relevant turnover is in the case of estate agents is a matter to be decided in each individual case.[420] The OFT takes 5%, 10% or 15% of the relevant turnover as the starting point for the financial penalty, depending on the seriousness of the breach. For example, the OFT applies 15% of the relevant turnover as a starting point for the financial penalty where the business intentionally facilitated a breach. It will most likely use 5% as a starting point where there is no evidence that the breach indicates a widespread problem within the business.[421] The amount that the OFT calculates is subsequently adjusted for the duration of non-compliance (step 2) and the existence of aggravating and/or mitigating factors (step 3).[422] In the fourth step, the OFT reviews whether the amount of the financial penalty calculated is appropriate for that business. The level of the financial penalty should be sufficiently dissuasive for both the offender and the wider market, but also be proportionate. How the OFT assesses this is not laid down in the penalty policy.

From the theoretical viewpoint on effective supervision, the public documents on the OFT's AML sanctioning policy are very good. They provide detailed information on how the OFT approaches sanctioning under the AML policy and the interim penalty policy also shows with a great level of detail how the OFT makes use of the power to impose a civil penalty under MLR 2007. It provides the steps, the relevant factors, and non-exhaustive examples, where appropriate. Unfortunately, however, there is no policy in which the OFT sets out how it intends to make use of its prosecutorial powers under the Regulations. Likewise, it is lamentable that the policy does not address the role of LATSS considering that they, too, have prosecutorial powers under the MLR 2007. In light of the fact that the OFT intends to involve these authorities more and more in its AML supervision, the policy should provide clarity as to the respective sanctioning roles of both and their cooperation. Particularly their mutual relationship should be clarified. That the exercise of AML supervision by LATSS is considered as having been done or omitted to be done by officers of the OFT, implies that the OFT is responsible for LATSS' AML supervision. In the context of sanctioning, however, LATSS are given prosecutorial powers and are only required to notify the OFT of intended proceedings for breaches of MLR 2007 and the outcomes. This suggests that LATSS can use their discretion in deciding to commence a prosecution and on how to deal with AML breaches. In light of the fact that the OFT is the formal AML supervisor of estate agents and seeks proportionate and consistent enforcement, it would advisable to determine that the OFT is also the authority which is

419 Ibid., at 8-9.
420 Ibid., at 11. The OFT prefers to use actual figures for the relevant turnover during the period of non-compliance. If figures are not available, the OFT will use the best available proxy.
421 OFT (2011f) at 12-13.
422 Ibid., at 13-14.

ultimately responsible for enforcement under the Regulations with respect to real estate agents (and consumer credit financial institutions).

6.7.4.2 Sanctioning in practice

In terms of the use of sanctioning powers by the OFT, more information is available than about its inspection activity. Representatives stated that until May 2012 the OFT had imposed five fines on estate agents, all of which were for trading without being registered at the OFT. The total value of the penalties was 15,500 GBP.[423] For the financial year that ran from April 2011 to April 2012, the OFT furthermore stated that it had concluded 30 AML enforcement cases.[424] It cannot be said, apart from the five fines for acting without being registered, if, and if so, which informal measures were taken or sanctions were imposed, whether these were against estate agents or consumer credit financial institutions, whether these were imposed for non-compliance with the obligation to register or the other preventive obligations, or what the amount of the fines was. For the following financial year, the OFT's annual report made mention of four closed enforcement cases under the AML policy, with a total value of 567,215 GBP.[425] Again, no further information was provided apart from the fact that one fine of 544,505 GBP was imposed on a payday lender (and not on an estate agent).[426] The annual report furthermore stated that eight AML cases were still pending at the enforcement stage.[427] The OFT started to publish its AML sanctions on its website in January 2013 in the form of press releases. From that month until April 2014, the OFT published eleven financial penalties: ten were imposed on real estate agents or businesses, and one penalty was imposed on a consumer credit financial institution (a payday lender), as just mentioned above.[428] The online publications of the actions taken under the Regulations include the name of the offender, the breach for which he was sanctioned and the amount of the penalties in question.

Based on the foregoing data it can be observed that over the years the OFT's sanctioning activity has moved in two directions. In the first place its sanctions have become more and more dissuasive: whereas until May 2012 it had fined various estate agents with a total value of 15,500 GBP, the amounts of the last three fines which the OFT imposed in March 2014 varied between 29,000 and 169,652 GBP, approximately 35,000 to 205,000 Euros.[429] Moreover, since January 2013 the OFT has started to publish information about the sanctioning activity, which can be considered as a form of naming & shaming. The first

423 Interview Office of Fair Trading, April 2012.

424 OFT (2012) at 17

425 OFT (2013) at 24.

426 Ibid., at 24.

427 Ibid., at 16.

428 OFT, *Anti-money laundering enforcement*, available at: <www.oft.gov.uk/OFTwork/aml/AML-enforcement/#named8>, last visited on 9 March 2014; OFT, *OFT fines three estate agents a total of £246,665 for breaching money laundering regulations*, Press release 28 March 2014, available at: <http://webarchive.nationalarchives.gov.uk/20140402142426/http://oft.gov.uk/news-and-updates/press/2014/24-14>, last visited 7 April 2014.

429 OFT, *OFT fines three estate agents a total of £246,665 for breaching money laundering regulations*, Press release 28 March 2014, available at: <http://webarchive.nationalarchives.gov.uk/20140402142426/http://oft.gov.uk/news-and-updates/press/2014/24-14>, last visited 7 April 2014.

direction is most likely related to the second direction. Whereas the OFT's fines used to be applied mostly for acting without being registered at the OFT, recent fines demonstrate that it has actually started to sanction estate agents for breaching other preventive AML obligations.

It seems that the OFT has never made use of its power the start criminal proceedings for non-compliance with MLR 2007. There are no numbers available for AML prosecutions started by LATSS against real estate agents for non-compliance with MLR 2007. Information on the use of informal measures by the OFT is also not available.

6.7.5 A look ahead: AML supervision by HMRC as of April 2014

As explained, HMRC has taken over the AML supervision of estate agents from the OFT. Within HMRC the AML Supervision Unit (AMLS) exercises the supervision of all institutions for which it has supervisory responsibility under the Regulations. The AMLS falls under the Enforcement and Compliance Directorate General.[430] This Unit will also take on board the AML supervision of estate agents. This means that the AML supervision of estate agents will remain a separate supervisory regime. AML supervision by HMRC is risk-based. Risk assessments are primarily done by AMLS's risking team, which analyses trends, signals and risks in relation to the institutions for which HMRC has supervisory responsibility both on an individual and sectoral level. On-site visits are carried out by the AMLS Unit's compliance team, which has a sectoral approach.[431] This means that within the Compliance team, a special team supervises estate agents. Because the institutional shift from the OFT to HMRC takes place at the moment of finalising this research it makes it impossible to carry out in-depth research on HMRC's future activities and the further design of the supervision of estate agents. Nevertheless, there are two important aspects that HMRC should take into account in order to build and strengthen its AML supervision in general, as well as of estate agents specifically.

The first aspect concerns the level of transparency that the OFT applies in its AML supervision. The OFT has been highly transparent about the way in which it exercises its desk reviews and on-site visits (OFT Code of Practice), as well as about the functioning of its sanctioning policy in case of identified non-compliance (the OFT's approach to penalties under the MLR 2007, AML enforcement principles, and the interim penalty policy). From the theoretical framework of effective supervision, we could see the importance of transparency both in relation to accountability and in relation to explaining the public supervision policies in order to prepare the supervised population for AML visits. Looking at HMRC's website, however, similar documents in relation to the institutions and professionals for which it already has AML supervisory responsibility cannot be found. HMRC has a specific AML strategy, but this is not a public document.[432] It seems a less open organisation in terms of providing institutions and the wider public with information on its own policy, strategy and activities under the MLR 2007. It would

430 Interview HM Revenue and Customs, May 2014.
431 Interview HM Revenue and Customs, May 2014.
432 Interview HM Revenue and Customs, May 2014.

however be advisable, however, from an effective supervision perspective, to be(come) more transparent and open, as estate agents were accustomed to in relation to the OFT.

The second aspect concerns the (level of) cooperation with Local Authority Trading Standards Services. Understanding that the situation will become somewhat different, it remains of great importance to have good cooperation with the LATSS. The situation will be different in that the OFT has always shared its powers under the Estate Agents Act 1979 with the LATSS, whereas after the 1st of April 2014 Powys County Council in Wales will run the National Trading Standards Estate Agents Team (hereafter NTSEAT) with full powers under the Estate Agents Act 1979. HMRC will not have any powers under this Act. Despite the fact that the different and more distanced positions of the two organisations presumably leads to a situation where joint inspections under the MLR 2007 are less obvious than is the case for the OFT and the LATSS, a proper legal basis for the exchange of information will be equally important. This is especially the case, because the LATSS will still have prosecutorial powers under the Money Laundering Regulations 2007 and NTSEAT in particular with regard to estate agents. At present a legal basis for the exchange of information under the Regulations does not seem to exist; they do not allow HMRC to enter into supervisory arrangements with the NTSEAT, nor are other legal bases adequate for the provision of information from HMRC to NTSEAT in MLR 2007, as we will see in § 6.10.

6.7.6 Concluding remarks

The OFT lacks regulatory powers under the Regulations. Apart from this, it can request (the production of) information or require attendance by an institution for which it has supervisory responsibility, or a connected person. Moreover, the OFT has the power to carry out on-site inspections, either directly or under a warrant issued by a justice. AML supervision by the OFT is a separate supervisory regime based on risk. The risk assessment is based on information submitted by estate agents upon registration, visiting history, and intelligence gathered and analysed by the OFT on the sector, as well as industry trends, media messages, complaints about the estate agent, registration for the Consumer Redress Scheme and whether action is taken against a real estate agent in any other way. Based on the risk assessment, the OFT prepares annual supervision plans that are not publicly available. In practice AML supervision is a combination of off-site and on-site inspections. Off-site inspections on a self-standing basis appeared impossible for the OFT because of the fact that the Regulations do not require that internal AML policies are kept in writing. Requiring this would enhance the enforceability of the norm. The OFT's Code of Practice provides detailed information on the aspects that OFT inspectors will review during on-site visits and how they will proceed. Information about AML inspections in practice is scarce and when available, the intensity seems rather low in light of the total number of real estate agents active in the UK. The Regulations allow the OFT to enter into arrangements with LATSS, allowing LATSS officers to exercise AML supervision as well. The Regulations do not stipulate what the arrangements should comprise of and how these arrangements should be concluded and maintained. The only thing that is clear is that the OFT is fully responsible for the AML inspections performed by the LATSS officers. From the viewpoint of transparency and accountability, as well as legality and legal certainty, formal, written arrangements between the OFT and LATSS should be concluded. These arrangements should also regulate in more detail the relationship under the AML regime between the authorities. AML supervision by LATSS seems to be in its infancy: LATSS carried out some on-site visits as part of a pilot project and the OFT concluded one informal agreement with a LATSS. Information about the exercise of AML supervision by LATSS in practice is not available either.

In terms of sanctioning, the Regulations provide the OFT with the power to impose a civil penalty (no statutory cap) and prosecutorial powers. This is not a wide range of sanctions, but allows the OFT, to a limited extent, to scale up enforcement action if necessary. Both sanctions can be imposed against legal and natural persons. Concurrence between the two sanctioning powers is not allowed. The OFT is transparent about its sanctioning policy. It has published three documents that jointly demonstrate its policy. The AML enforcement principles and the OFT's approach to penalties deal with the AML sanctioning regime in general, whereas the interim penalty policy concerns the steps which the OFT takes in determining whether to impose a penalty. The OFT strives for a number of enforcement goals, including a change of behaviour by the offender, the elimination of financial gain or benefits from non-compliance, and general preventive effects. In order to attain these goals, the OFT strives to be proportionate, consistent, targeted, transparent, and accountable. The documents provide a number of factors that are taken into account when applying the enforcement principles in individual cases. The internal penalty policy sets out how financial penalties are calculated by the OFT. Nevertheless, the OFT's sanctioning policy lacks an explanation of when and how the OFT makes use of its prosecutorial powers. Likewise, information on the use of prosecutorial powers by LATSS and the relationship with enforcement action taken by the OFT under the AML policy is lacking as well. These two elements should still be integrated into its sanctioning policy. In practice the OFT has made use of the power to impose financial penalties on real estate agents on various occasions. It appears that its sanctions have become more dissuasive over the years in terms of the amount of the fines and the publication of the sanctions on the OFT website, and that the OFT has moved from imposing sanctions for acting in breach of the registration obligation to imposing sanctions for breaches of the wider range of preventive AML obligations. It seems that the OFT has never prosecuted an estate agent; but information about the use of prosecutorial powers under the Regulations by either the OFT or the LATSS is not available. Information on the use of informal measures by the OFT is not available either.

The OFT's AML supervision of estate agents was taken over by HMRC on the 1st of April 2014. The AML supervision of estate agents will remain a separate supervisory regime and be based on (perceived) levels of risk. Two important aspects should be taken into account by HMRC. The first is the high level of transparency that the OFT applied by publicly displaying its supervisory and sanctioning policy under the Regulations. HMRC seems less open, but from an effective supervision perspective it is important to be(come) more transparent and open like the estate agents were accustomed to in relation to the OFT. Cooperation, though in a different form, with the NTSEAT will be of equally high importance. Because of the prosecutorial powers that the NTSEAT has under the MLR 2007 and which may be applied against real estate agents, there should be a proper legal basis for the exchange of relevant supervisory information between HMRC and NTSEAT. At present, this basis seems to be lacking in the Regulations.

6.8 Institute of Chartered Accountants in England and Wales

6.8.1 Supervisory powers

ICAEW has been appointed as the AML supervisor under the Regulations and 'must effectively monitor the relevant persons for whom it is the supervisory authority and take necessary measures for the purpose of securing compliance'.[433] This means that professional associations are expected to embed AML supervision into their professional norms and procedures. Being a professional association, ICAEW obviously has regulatory powers. AML supervision is conducted as part of the Practice Assurance Scheme. The Practice Assurance Regulations (hereafter PAR) set out how this scheme operates and provide ICAEW with its supervisory powers. These are not formulated as powers, but rather as obligations for member firms and practise certificate holders. Member firms and PC holders are required to cooperate with ICAEW, its staff and any committee that carries out functions under the PAS.[434] ICAEW, in practice QAD, also has the power to request information from member firms and PC holders: member firms and PC holders must provide any information requested under the PAS, whether in the annual return or otherwise, promptly and in accordance with the terms specified.[435] This power allows ICAEW to do desk reviews. Seemingly, there are no limitations as to the kind of information ICAEW can request. It can decide to carry out on-site inspections (visits) as well.[436] Regulation 10 PAR states that ICAEW will notify a member or PC holder not less than thirty business days in advance of a visit. During those visits, ICAEW must be provided with appropriate facilities to enable the visiting reviewer to carry out his functions during the visit.[437] This includes that reviewers must have access to all information, books, records and documents in hard-copy or electronic form, indicated in the visit notice or not, which ICAEW considers necessary to perform the monitoring.[438] Being a professional association, members cannot invoke their professional secrecy against ICAEW.[439]

433 Regulation 24(1) MLR 2007.
434 Practice Assurance Regulation 4.
435 Practice Assurance Regulation 8.
436 Practice Assurance Regulation 10.
437 Practice Assurance Regulation 13.
438 Practice Assurance Regulation 14(c).
439 It should be pointed out that UK law distinguishes legal professional privilege that applies to solicitors, their employees, barristers and in-house lawyers (and notaries), and the legal privilege exemption that also applies to relevant professional advisers such as auditors, accountants and tax advisers (privileged circumstances). LPP is a wider concept than the legal privilege exemption, as the latter exemption only applies to money laundering reporting under the terms of the Proceeds of Crime Act 2002 and does not extend LPP to relevant professional advisers in any other circumstances. A UK Supreme Court judgment delivered on 23 January 2013 confirmed that LPP does not extend to professionals other than lawyers, even when providing similar advice: *R (on the application of Prudential plc and another) (Appellants) v Special Commissioner of Income Tax and another (Respondents)* [2013] UKSC 1. Cf. Van den Broek, M. (2014a) at 32 and in particular the accompanying online appendix 3.2.

6.8.2 Anti-money laundering supervision in practice

AML compliance is assessed as part of the PAS, because ICAEW believes that this 'enhances the effectiveness, relevance, proportionality and, therefore, the value of our risk-based AML assessments and any resulting recommendations'.[440] Supervisory activities do not only cover the verification of compliance with AML obligations but concern a wide range of professional, ethical (and sometimes statutory) obligations for member firms and PC holders. ICAEW is not obliged to include AML supervision in all of its monitoring activities under the PAS, although in practice it generally does so. Besides the integrated approach, ICAEW may also decide to carry out thematic visits that focus on (specific obligations under) the MLR 2007. In addition, ICAEW provides members with assistance and guidance on how to comply with their obligations through helplines, news items on the website, help sheets, attendance at events and monthly alerts sent out to the members.[441]

6.8.2.1 Risk-based approach

ICAEW applies a four to eight-year cycle for its monitoring, 'depending on the size and risk of the firm and reflecting the fact that we have now visited our firms at least once'.[442] The monitoring is based on this periodic cycle, as well as on the basis of the risk. Because AML supervision is embedded in the PAS monitoring, the risk assessment goes beyond AML risk. ICAEW carries out inspections on the largest member firms annually, as well as a number of other member firms that have a higher risk profile or a poor visiting history. ICAEW also adjusts the 'extent of any additional desk top monitoring, and the timing, length and frequency of visits, according to the size and risk profile of the firm' to the level of risk present.[443] The low-risk and smallest firms are normally reviewed off-site through a desk or telephone review.[444]

> In between the formal inspections, ICAEW invites member firms and PC holders to attend masterclasses. ICAEW considers these as a means to maintain contacts with firms in between the formal visits.[445] During these masterclasses, QAD reviewers give practical guidance to member firms and PC holders on key aspects of the PAS and are available to give answers to questions about individual practices. Guidance is also given through the website, e-mails and the organisation of AML roadshows and training events. Member firms and PC holders can obtain advice from a member helpline.[446]

440 ICAEW (2013), *2012/13 AML/CTF Supervision Report: Annual return*, submitted in May 2013 by ICAEW to HM Treasury, par. 46. This report is not publicly available, but has been provided to me during the interview with ICAEW for research purposes. I have been allowed to use and refer to the report for this research: Institute of Chartered Accountants in England and Wales, May 2014.

441 ICAEW (2012) at 7.

442 Ibid., at 6.

443 Ibid., at 3.

444 ICAEW (2013), par. 33.

445 Ibid., par. 10.

446 Ibid., par. 86-92.

The main sources of information for the risk assessment are the annual returns that all member firms and PC holders are required to complete.[447] In these returns they must confirm that they comply with a wide range of professional obligations. Member firms must explicitly confirm that they comply with the Regulations.[448] Other sources of information for the risk assessments concern information regarding the visiting history of the member firm or PC holder, information from the PCD regarding complaints or other cases, information stemming from the media, and in the years 2011-12 information from the benchmarking surveys.[449] Likewise, ICAEW may include intelligence received from other AML supervisors, UKFIU and other law enforcement agencies.

> The AML benchmarking surveys were conducted in 2011 and 2012. Their objective was to provide member firms with a possibility to compare their AML procedures with other firms, to advise firms on good practices and to give recommendations. The surveys also allowed ICAEW to decide on which AML aspects it focusses upon during its reviews. Although this has been a voluntary initiative from ICAEW, possibly explaining its low response rate (in 2011 only 13 of the 150 firms participated), these have enabled ICAEW to formulate recommendations to its member firms. For example, it recommended to review internal AML policies and procedures annually, to train staff regularly, to make more appropriate use of the risk-based approach and to record internal SARs in order to create a documentation trail.[450]

Risk factors that seem to play a role in ICAEW's risk assessment are the size of the member firm, the compliance record, the nature and level of activities undertaken by members, a firm's client pool, and the environment in which the members operate. Specific AML risks observed by ICAEW are firms with clients operating in high-risk jurisdictions or sectors,[451] clients that are politically exposed persons or where a firm has not met the client, engagements with clients where the firm holds high amounts of clients' money and clients introduced by a third party.[452] ICAEW classifies member firms and PC holders as high, medium or low risk. High risk are usually firms that fulfil any of the risk factors above, low-risk firms are usually smaller firms with clients who are locally based, with operations taking place only in the UK and that have long-standing personal clients.[453] All others are classified as medium risk.

447 Ibid. par. 28; ICAEW (2012) at 8.

448 Confirmation 4 in the Annual Return Form, available at: <www.icaew.com/~/media/Files/Members/practice-centre/practice-assurance/current-annual-return.pdf>, last visited on 5 June 2014.

449 ICAEW (2013), par. 28.

450 ICAEW, *About the AML benchmarking survey*, <www.icaew.com/en/technical/legal-and-regulatory/money-laundering/uk-law-and-guidance/about-the-aml-benchmarking-survey>, last visited 22 May 2014.

451 HM Treasury (2013b), *Advisory notice on money Laundering and terrorist financing controls in overseas jurisdictions*, July 2013, <www.gov.uk/government/publications/money-laundering-and-terrorist-financing-controls-in-overseas-jurisdictions-advisory-notice/money-laundering-and-terrorist-financing-controls-in-overseas-jurisdictions-advisory-notice>, last visited on 5 June 2014.

452 ICAEW (2013), par. 34.

453 ICAEW (2012) at 12.

6.8.2.2 Procedure

On the basis of the risk assessment, QAD prepares internal annual supervision plans in which it sets out the number and type of monitoring planned for that period. Low-risk member firms are normally monitored off-site, through desk reviews of the annual returns or telephone conversations.[454] Reviews of medium and high-risk member firms take place via on-site visits.[455] During inspections, QAD reviewers employ a standard checklist for examining AML procedures.[456] Reviewers discuss the AML policies and procedures with the responsible staff and management, such as the appointed money laundering reporting officers who are responsible for (the implementation of) the firms' AML policies and procedures. Reviewers ensure that firms conduct customer due diligence on a risk-sensitive basis, that they recognise the clients and situations for which an enhanced due diligence procedure is required, that internal procedures are in place if a suspicious activity is identified, and that relevant staff have received appropriate training.[457] Reviewers assess information, records and documents to determine whether a firm applies the AML policies consistently and in an appropriate way. QAD reviewers can decide to perform some sample testing of CDD files and transaction files as well. Where information suggests that a member firm or PC holder is non-compliant, reviewers may decide to extend the review and to carry out more research. During inspections, QAD reviewers also aim to provide advice at individual level in order for member firms and PC members to fully understand their legal duties and responsibilities.[458] At the end of each visit, QAD reviewers present the findings to the firm. ICAEW can give four grades to the member firm or PC holder concerned: A – B – C – D. These grades vary from a high level of compliance (A) to serious non-compliance (D). A and B grades indicate that systems are generally sound and that the member firm or PC holder broadly complies with the PAS standards, which makes reference to the Regulations.[459] Monitoring reports graded A or B are usually closed after a dialogue between the QAD reviewers and the member firm or PC holder in which agreements on proposed actions are made, if necessary. Monitoring reports graded C or D are normally forwarded to (the Secretary of) the Practice Assurance Committee. In § 6.8.4, this is further elaborated as part of the disciplinary (sanctioning) procedure.

6.8.2.3 Supervision in numbers

Based on information from the non-public annual AML returns from ICAEW, it appears that ICAEW is highly active in monitoring under the PAS. In 2011, QAD reviewers carried out more than 2,100 visits under the PAS.[460] And in 2012, QAD carried out 1,059

454 The procedure is explained in: ICAEW (2012a), *Practice Assurance desktop review*, available at: <www.icaew.com/~/media/Files/Members/practice-centre/practice-assurance/practice-assurance-desktop-reviews.pdf>, last visited on 22 May 2014.

455 ICAEW (2012b), *Practice Assurance visits*, available at: <www.icaew.com/~/media/Files/Members/practice-centre/practice-assurance/practice-assurance-visit.pdf>, last visited on 22 May 2014.

456 ICAEW (2013), par. 46.

457 Ibid.

458 ICAEW (2012) at 7.

459 Interview Institute of Chartered Accountants in England and Wales, May 2014.

460 ICAEW (2012) at 7.

on-site and 871 off-site visits.[461] These are substantial numbers of visits in light of ICAEW's total supervisory population under the PAS: over 13,000 member firms with 23,000 PC holders, plus approximately 200 firms through a contract.[462] In 2011 ICAEW stated that in less than one per cent of firms visited that year QAD had formally reported serious matters of concern to the PAC, including matters of AML compliance. This, it considered, was comparable to the previous year.[463] For AML-related breaches in 2011, QAD referred 19 member firms to the PAC.[464] The numbers for the year 2012 are somewhat more detailed. Out of the 1,059 on-site and 871 off-site visits, more than half of the member firms and PC holders inspected were considered compliant. Regarding the on-site inspections, 483 member firms were 'generally compliant, with an action plan agreed' and 29 were non-compliant with the MLR 2007. For the off-site inspections, 259 member firms were generally compliant, and 4 were non-compliant with the MLR 2007.[465] In this year, 2% of the cases were formally reported to the PAC. ICAEW only refers cases of serious, high impact or repeated non-compliant behaviour to the PAC: '[i]n firms where we have identified compliance issues, we have generally been impressed with the willingness and effectiveness of the firms' response to our findings and, in accordance with the policy agreed, we do not report these circumstances to our Practice Assurance Committee'.[466] Inspection numbers for the year 2013 were at the time of finalising this chapter not yet available. The Practice Highlights Report, however, indicated that in that year QAD had identified that 7% of the member firms did not have customer due diligence procedures in accordance with the Regulations.[467]

ICAEW has a fairly recent practice of targeted AML supervision, i.e. supervision specifically focused on AML compliance. In 2011 none of the visits performed was instigated due to a higher money laundering risk.[468] In 2012, however, ICAEW reported on the exercise of targeted AML inspections. In that year QAD carried out 28 targeted visits on member firms that held a significant amount of money for their clients.[469] This, as we could observe, is one of the specific money laundering risks that ICAEW observes. In order to avoid that the integration of AML supervision leads to insufficient attention to this matter, the emergence of targeted AML visits is very welcome. ICAEW should think about publishing the results of such visits, as it did with the benchmarking survey and as the FCA does, as a means of guidance for its members. The publication thereof would also enhance transparency and accountability concerning the exercise of its AML supervision.

Likewise, the publication of the annual AML returns would enhance ICAEW's transparency and accountability.[470] This would also be in line with the practice of the other

461 ICAEW (2013), par. 44 and 48.
462 See § 6.4.3.
463 ICAEW (2012) at 9.
464 Ibid., at 14.
465 ICAEW (2013), par. 45 and 49.
466 Ibid., par. 72.
467 ICAEW (2013a), *Practice Assurance Highlights 2013*, at 7.
468 ICAEW (2012) at 7.
469 ICAEW (2013), par. 33.
470 Supra, n. 165 and 439 in which it was stated that the annual reports have been provided for research purposes.

AML supervisors: the FCA has started to publish its detailed AML supervision reports and the OFT has done this in the past as well.

6.8.3 Sanctioning powers

Sanctioning for non-compliance with preventive AML obligations is integrated into ICAEW's disciplinary procedure. Member firms and members, including PC holders, are liable to disciplinary action pursuant to Disciplinary bye-laws 4 and 5.

A wide range of disciplinary sanctions can be imposed on member firms and members.[471] Sanctions can be imposed at two moments in the disciplinary procedure. A consent order can be proposed by the Investigation Committee (hereafter IC) when it is of the opinion that there is a *prima facie* case against a member or member firm. A prima facie case is a case in which the non-compliant behaviour is obvious and the member is willing to admit to the non-compliant behaviour and to accept liability. Through a consent order, the member has the possibility to prevent his case from being forwarded to the Disciplinary Committee (hereafter DC) and coming before a Disciplinary Tribunal, and thereby prevents possible heavier sanctioning. A consent order against a member or member firm can contain a severe reprimand, a reprimand or a fine.[472] Essential for the imposition of a sanction at this stage is that the member (firm) agrees to the order. Alternatively, the IC can offer a caution. This, '(...) is intended to be a more serious step than 'no further action' but less serious than a consent order or referral to the DC [disciplinary committee]. The IC may include in the order a requirement to pay a sum towards costs. This will be a figure for the actual costs incurred up to a maximum of 2,000 [GBP]'.[473] If the offer for an unpublished caution is not accepted, then the matter is still referred to the DC and Tribunal, which do not have this power. The caution is more advantageous for members as it avoids not only further proceedings, but more importantly, potential publicity. It, however, depends on the opinion of the IC whether there is a prima facie case and whether the type and severity of the breach is suitable for an unpublished caution.

Sanctions can also be imposed by the Disciplinary Committee, that is, the Disciplinary Tribunal. This tribunal is the final sanctioning authority. The consent order and the unpublished caution are not available to the Disciplinary Tribunal. It has the following powers: it can decide to exclude accountants from membership, to permanently or temporarily withdraw the practising certificate, to declare the member ineligible for a practising certificate permanently or temporarily, to withdraw or declare the member ineligible for an insolvency licence, to (severely) reprimand the accountant concerned,

471 While this research deals with accountants, sanctions against authorised firms, registered auditors and provisional members are not included here: see bye-laws 22.5 and 22.6 for the applicable sanctions. Also the sanctions that can be imposed as a result of non-compliance with the Insolvency Act are excluded because these cannot be imposed as a result of non-compliance with AML obligations (disciplinary bye-law 22.3(c) and 22.3(d)).

472 Disciplinary bye-law 16.2(a)(i) and (ii). See also: Investigation Committee Regulations 16-18.

473 ICAEW (2013b), *Guidance on Sentencing*, August 2013, at 35. See also: Investigation Committee Regulations 19-21.

or to impose a fine.[474] Member firms can be sanctioned through a temporary prohibition on using the description 'Chartered Accountants', they can be (severely) reprimanded or be ordered to pay a fine.[475] In addition, as a principle, a record of the disciplinary decision is published.[476] The decision should include the name of the defendant and describe the findings and other order(s) made against him.[477] If the Tribunal dismisses a formal complaint against a member firm or member, the decision may be published but only if the defendant so requests.[478] ICAEW publishes the details of a decision in its own member magazine and on its website. Decisions remain on the website for a period of twelve months.[479] Only in exceptional cases is the name of the member in question not published.[480] Consent orders by the Investigation Committee are published as well, but its cautions are not.[481] The publication can be considered an additional sanction as it is a form of naming & shaming.

> The difference between a reprimand and a severe reprimand is that the former is often seen as a warning, while a severe reprimand is a final warning. ICAEW's *Guidance to Sentencing* provides a list of nine relevant considerations for deciding whether to give a warning, such as evidence that the behaviour would (not) have caused direct or indirect harm, no repetition of the behaviour since the incident, or a previous good record. The absence of relevant considerations may influence the decision to impose a severe reprimand or another, more severe, sanction.[482] With respect to the fines, the Disciplinary Tribunal can decide on their amount. No maximum applies, although the Tribunal is required to take into account a set of considerations in deciding the amount of the fine.[483]

The sanctions do not exclude one another and may be imposed simultaneously. In addition, the sanctions may be accompanied by terms and conditions, or in the case of an order for exclusion from membership made against a member, a recommendation that no application for his readmission be considered before the end of a specified period. ICAEW sees these conditions and restrictions as more pragmatic sanctions.[484] A condition can be that a firm must organise training for key staff or allows an external expert to review its (AML) policies and that it has to implement the recommendations of that expert.[485] A possible term or restriction is the limitation on taking on new clients in a particular discipline.[486]

474 Disciplinary bye-law 22.3.
475 Disciplinary bye-law 22.4.
476 Disciplinary bye-law 35.1.
477 Disciplinary bye-law 35.3.
478 Disciplinary bye-law 35.2.
479 ICAEW (2013b) at 32; ICAEW, *FAQs on ICAEW's disciplinary process*, available at: <www.icaew.com/en/about-icaew/what-we-do/act-in-the-public-interest/complaints-process/faqs-on-the-disciplinary-process-for-members>, last visited on 4 June 2014.
480 ICAEW (2013b) at 32 explains that since 2000 this has happened ten times.
481 Ibid., at 36.
482 Ibid., at 29.
483 Ibid., at 29.
484 ICAEW (2012), at 8.
485 Note that this is actually an AML obligation for the regulated sector in Spain: § 4.6.3.3.
486 ICAEW (2012) at 8; Section 6 ICAEW Formal Scheme of Delegations, Appendix 12.7.

6.8.4 Sanctioning policy and practice

6.8.4.1 Disciplinary procedure

Sections 6.4.3.2 and 6.8.3 have already given some insight into ICAEW's sanctioning procedure and the committees that play a role therein. Once the supervision procedure is completed and QAD has given the member or member firm a C or D grade in its monitoring report, the case is forwarded to the (Secretary of) the PAC.[487] The PAC reviews the monitoring reports to consider whether to refer a complaint for investigation in accordance with the disciplinary bye-laws or to accept the member firm's implementation of agreed actions.[488] The PAC may also decide to request a follow-up QAD visit and request the PAC Secretary to notify other authorities with a regulatory interest in the member firm.[489] If it decides to refer the matter to the investigation and disciplinary procedure, it forwards the case to the Professional Conduct Department (hereafter PCD).[490] PCD case managers, consisting of ICAEW staff, will investigate the reported issue and invite the non-complying member or member firm to provide any comments or further evidence. If the case manager deems there is a disciplinary case, the monitoring report and additional information is forwarded to (the Secretary of) the Investigation Committee.[491] Unlike as its name suggests, this Committee does not investigate the case any further. When a matter is referred to it, it shall review a summary of the material facts and matters to which any relevant documentation may be appended.[492] On that basis it considers the case and decides whether or not any of the facts and matters could make the member or member firm concerned liable to disciplinary action.[493] The committee can decide to dismiss a case, to impose a consent order or offer a caution as was indicated in the previous section, or to directly forward the case to the DC. When the case is forwarded to the DC, either directly or when a consent order is denied, the DC meets in a Disciplinary Tribunal. A Tribunal, as explained in § 6.4.3.2, consists of two ICAEW members and one non-accountant member from the DC. The Tribunal arranges a hearing of the formal complaint, in which both ICAEW and the member can be represented.[494] In principle, all hearings are public.[495] If the Disciplinary Tribunal finds that the complaint has been proven in whole or in part, it shall make a finding to that effect and issue a sentencing order. Otherwise it dismisses the case.[496]

487 See about the grades: § 6.8.2.2.
488 Interview Institute of Chartered Accountants in England and Wales, May 2014.
489 ICAEW (2013), par. 46.
490 Disciplinary bye-law 12A.
491 Interview Institute of Chartered Accountants in England and Wales, May 2014.
492 See Investigation Committee Regulation 8.
493 Investigation Committee Regulation 9.
494 Disciplinary bye-law 20. According to Disciplinary Committee Regulation 3, the member firm or member concerned shall be informed within 42 days of the date, time and place of the hearing and of the terms of the formal complaint against him through the issuance of a written notice.
495 Disciplinary Committee Regulation 6. In exceptional cases the hearing may be in private: Disciplinary Committee Regulation 7.
496 Disciplinary bye-law 22.1.

6.8.4.2 Sanctioning policy

ICAEW has adopted a general sentencing policy through the publicly available *Guidance on Sentencing*, which the IC and DC works in tribunals must consider in their decisions on disciplinary action. This policy sets out the key principles, which relate to maintaining the reputation of the profession, correcting and deterring misconduct, upholding proper standards of conduct in the profession and the protection of the public.[497] The main goal is to come to decisions that are 'consistent, proportionate and fair'.[498] Therefore, the sentencing policy provides a step-by-step guide for the committees and Tribunals when they consider whether or not to impose a sanction, and which one is the most appropriate in the light of the circumstances of the case. Where an ICAEW member himself is involved in money laundering, ICAEW's starting point for a sanction is exclusion from membership.[499] Non-compliance with the Regulations is considered a breach of bye-laws and/or regulations. For any failure under the Regulations, ICAEW's Guidance provides that the Tribunal should, as a starting point, impose a severe reprimand and a fine of 5,750 GBP, approximately 7,000 Euros.[500] This is a relatively high starting point compared to the other breaches of bye-laws and/or regulations indicated in the policy.[501] The Disciplinary Tribunal should also weigh any aggravating and mitigating factors in determining the type of sanction. Examples of aggravating factors are repetitive behaviour, the long duration of the offence, the continuation of the offence after the member became aware of it, and intent. Mitigating factors are a short period of time, steps immediately taken after the member became aware of the breach, and minimal work carried out.[502]

> The Guidance provides guidance to Tribunals when they have decided to impose a particular sanction as well. When a Tribunal has, for example, decided to impose a fine for non-compliance with preventive AML obligations, the seriousness of the misconduct and the existence of any aggravating or mitigating factors must be considered. In addition, Tribunals must take into account the circumstances of the defendant and the means available to the member or member firm to pay the fine. Further circumstances which influence the amount of the fine concern, among other things, the question to which extent the member has had an economic gain from the non-compliant conduct, the liquidity of the member firm, and the question whether the fine is to be paid at once or through instalments.[503] Such guidance is also available for the decision to impose a reprimand or severe reprimand, the withdrawal of practising certificates, exclusion from membership and publicity.[504]

497 ICAEW (2013b) at 3-4.
498 Ibid., at 4.
499 Ibid., at 11.
500 Ibid., at 16.
501 Fines indicated for breaches of bye-laws and/or regulations vary from 1,150 to 5,750 GBP. See: ICAEW (2013b) at 16.
502 Ibid., at 16.
503 Ibid., at 29.
504 ICAEW (2013b) at 30-32.

6.8.4.3 Sanctioning in practice

Based on the non-public AML supervision data provided by ICAEW to the Treasury for the years 2011 and 2012, the following observations can be made about ICAEW's practice. In § 6.8.2, we saw that in recent years QAD reported between 1-2% of cases, including AML compliance issues, to the PAC. No data is available on what happened in the different stages of the disciplinary procedure, i.e. how many of the cases ended at PAC, the Investigation Committee or Disciplinary Committee/Tribunal, although ICAEW has stated that 'in rare circumstances the PAC has referred serious cases to the Professional Conduct Department for investigation'.[505] This indicates that after the QAD, which closes many cases after agreement on an action plan, the PAC also acts as a large filter for the following disciplinary procedure. For the year 2011, the number and type of disciplinary actions taken for non-compliance with the Regulations are not included in any report and cannot thus be provided. In 2012, the Disciplinary Tribunals imposed the following sanctions on members:

Table 7 – ICAEW disciplinary sanctions for non-compliance with AML obligations in 2012[506]

Expulsion or removal	4
Fines	3
Reprimands	2

In addition, the Tribunals imposed 15 conditions on member firms and PC holders, such as a mandatory follow-up review or the organisation of AML training for staff, and on eight occasions the Tribunals required member firms to have an independent review of compliance with the laws, regulations and standards applicable to its activities.[507] The sanctions are included as separate individual sanctions, but usually member firms and PC holders are subjected to a combination of sanctions, as indicated in the *Guidance on Sentencing*.

> An example of a case where sanctions are combined is provided by a disciplinary decision dating from the 4th of April 2012. A chartered accountant, who was a former member of ICAEW, had failed to ensure that his firm, between February 2007 and May 2011, complied with the requirements of the Regulations. In particular the firm had failed to complete customer due diligence identification by reference to original documents, there were no procedures in place to carry out CDD on all clients, the firm had not conducted regular compliance reviews and there had been no training for staff and himself on this matter.[508] The Disciplinary Tribunal sanctioned the former member with a severe reprimand, and ordered him to pay a fine of 10,000 GBP and costs of 2,200 GBP. Factors that the Tribunal included in its sentencing order were the fact that the former member already had a disciplinary record, he was uncooperative with ICAEW, and he had wilfully opted out of compliance with the regulatory requirements for the profession that could affect the public's confidence in the profession. These aggravating factors led the Tribunal

505 ICAEW (2013), par. 72.
506 Own table based on information from: ICAEW (2013), par. 68.
507 ICAEW (2013), par. 68.
508 Tribunal of the Disciplinary Committee order against Mr J.M. Johnstone, 7 December 2011. Published on ICAEW's website on the 4th of April 2012 and removed from the website in April 2013.

to decide to expel him from the profession. However, since he was already no longer a member, the most severe sanction that the tribunal could impose was a severe reprimand and a fine.

The table above does not include the number and type of consent orders or cautions by the Investigation Committee. In the period March to December 2012, however, one consent order in relation to non-compliance with the MLR 2007 was published.[509] This order included a severe reprimand, a fine of 5,000 GBP and costs of 1,015 GBP imposed on a chartered account. Two of the four parts of the complaint against the accountant concerned non-compliance with AML obligations. Over a period of nearly seven years, the accountant and his firm had failed to perform adequate customer due diligence procedures. He had failed to ensure that he had sufficient client identification evidence, nor did he always use original documentation.

Although inspection numbers are unknown for the year 2013, the fact that disciplinary decisions are published on ICAEW's website does allow for an overview of the disciplinary actions taken in that year.[510] The Disciplinary Tribunal imposed a sanction for non-compliance with the Regulations twice in 2013. On both occasions this was part of a broader complaint. In the first case, the member concerned had failed to comply with assurances he had given ICAEW that he would perform customer due diligence on all of his clients. The Tribunal issued a reprimand and imposed a fine of 2,000 GBP plus an order to pay costs.[511] In the second case, the accountant in question had no internal policies and procedures in place as required under the MLR 2007. The Tribunal imposed the most severe sanction possible, although this was mostly based on other complaints against the member. The Tribunal decided to withdraw his practising certificate and declared the accountant permanently ineligible for a new practising certificate. In addition, the accountant was reprimanded and a fine of 1,500 GBP was imposed.[512] In 2013, the Investigation Committee issued two consent orders in which non-compliance with MLR 2007 played a role. Sanctions that were part of these consent orders included a severe reprimand and a fine in the one case, and a reprimand and a fine in the other case. In both cases the members were ordered to pay costs as well.[513]

509 Investigation Committee Consent order, no. 006281, 22 June 2012. Published on ICAEW's website on the 1st of August 2012 and removed from the website in August 2013.

510 Search in the database Disciplinary orders and regulatory decisions, available at : <www.icaew.com/en/about-icaew/what-we-do/act-in-the-public-interest/public-hearings>. Reference period: 1st of January 2013 - 31st of December 2013. All disciplinary cases were read to verify whether the cases concerned AML compliance.

511 Tribunal of the Disciplinary Committee order against Mr L. Simans, 22 May 2013. Date of publication on ICAEW's website: 7 August 2013. Due to be removed from the website in August 2014.

512 Tribunal of the Disciplinary Committee order against Mr P.G. Jeffery, 18 June 2013. Date of publication on ICAEW's website: 4 September 2013. Due to be removed from website in September 2014.

513 Investigation Committee Consent order, no. 008566, 23 September 2013. Date of publication on ICAEW's website: 2 October 2013. Due to be removed from the website in October 2014; Investigation Committee Consent order, no. 011732, 16 October 2013. Date of publication on ICAEW's website: 6 November 2013. Due to be removed from the website in November 2014.

6.8.5 Concluding remarks

ICAEW has adequate supervisory powers. Reviewers have the power to compel the production of information, as well as to carry out on-site inspections. Being the professional association, it also has the power to issue further regulations. AML supervision within ICAEW is part of monitoring under the Practice Assurance Scheme. ICAEW applies a four to eight-year cycle for monitoring depending on the size and risk of the firm. The main sources of information for the risk assessment are the annual returns that all member firms and PC holders have to complete and in which they have to declare that they comply with the Regulations. Other sources of information for the risk assessments concern information regard the visiting history, complaints or other cases against the member firm or PC holder, information from the media, the AML benchmarking surveys, information from other AML supervisors, the UKFIU and other law enforcement agencies. AML risk factors are firms with clients operating in high-risk jurisdictions or sectors, clients that are politically exposed persons or where a firm has not met the client, engagements with clients where the firm holds high amounts of clients' money and clients introduced by a third party. ICAEW classifies member firms and PC holders as high, medium or low risk. Off-site monitoring takes place through desk reviews of the annual returns or a telephone conversation. This is only done for the category of low-risk members. Medium and high-risk member firms receive on-site visits. During inspections, QAD reviewers employ a standard checklist for examining AML procedures. They interview responsible staff and look into documents and files. At the end of each visit, QAD reviewers present the findings to the firm. ICAEW can give four grades to the member firm or PC holder concerned, varying from a high level of compliance (A) to serious non-compliance (D). In practice, inspection numbers are substantial in relation to the total number of member firms and PC holders falling under the PAS. Between 1-2% of cases isare forwarded to the PAC. Targeted AML inspections are fairly recent at ICAEW, which is a good development as it ensures that sufficient attention is given to AML compliance. For accountability reasons, as well as the provision of guidance to its members, ICAEW should think about publishing the results of the visits. Besides the monitoring, ICAEW reaches out to its members by giving advice and support to raise their awareness. ICAEW should also consider publishing its AML returns, which it submits to HM Treasury annually.

ICAEW has a wide range of disciplinary sanctions available in case of non-compliance with AML obligations. The Investigation Committee has the power to offer a consent order that includes a (severe) reprimand or fine, or can offer a caution. The Disciplinary Tribunal does not have these powers, but has a wide range of powers varying from a reprimand to exclusion from membership for individual members, and from a reprimand to a fine for member firms. This allows the Tribunal to scale up enforcement action, if necessary. ICAEW has adopted a general sentencing policy through the publicly available *Guidance on Sentencing*, which the IC and DC works in tribunals must consider in their decisions on disciplinary action. From an effective supervision perspective, this is a good thing. In practice it seems that the majority of cases of non-compliance end with an agreed action plan at the QAD or at the PAC. Nevertheless, the statistical and anecdotal information available indicate that the Investigation Committee and Disciplinary Tribunal, when confronted with cases that include non-compliance with the Regulations, are willing to adopt proportionate and dissuasive sanctions. Non-compliance with the MLR 2007 has been sanctioned with relatively mild fines, but has led to removal from office in recent years as well. The Tribunal considers whether mitigating or aggravating factors are present and thereby closely follows the Guidance on Sentencing. Sanctions are published in ICAEW's member magazine and on the website, where the sentences remain online for a year.

6.9 Association of Accounting Technicians

6.9.1 Supervisory powers

Like ICAEW, AAT has regulatory powers and derives its supervisory powers from internal professional norms, most prominently the member in practice regulations (hereafter 'MIP Regulations'). AAT has the power to require the production of information and documents.[514] It can request members information and documents at any time, provided that it needs the documents in the exercise of its functions under the MIP Regulations and Disciplinary Regulations. AAT can require a member to appear before it in order to provide information or documents. Furthermore, members must permit any representative appointed by the AAT to visit their place of business to inspect documents, including, but not limited to, client files, employee files and agents' files, as well as company or partnership files. AAT thus has the power to perform off-site and on-site reviews. This takes place through telephone interviews or desk reviews. Reviews include the monitoring of pre-requested documents and files (off-site), but also sample testing in the case of on-site visits.[515]

AAT has the power to decide at any moment to review a member's compliance with the MIP Regulations, the code of professional ethics and other AAT policies, as well as the Money Laundering Regulations.[516] Members must comply with any reasonable direction by the AAT representative in relation to a review, either before, during and after the review. Members cannot invoke the principle of confidentiality against AAT.[517] If non-compliance with any of the Regulations is identified, AAT may determine that a member must undergo a follow-up review.

6.9.2 Anti-money laundering supervision in practice

AML supervision by AAT is part of the general monitoring procedure under the MIP scheme and is thus always part of a wider supervisory programme. Supervision is exercised by the Conduct & Compliance team (CCT) that consists of AAT staff.[518] As explained, this team operates under the Regulation and Compliance Board. Unlike ICAEW, with a

514 MIP Regulation 16.

515 AAT, *MIP Guidance*, at 32, available at: <www.aat.org.uk/mip-guidance>, last visited on 18 June 2014.

516 MIP Regulation 17.

517 AAT recognises a principle of confidentiality in Section 140 of the Code of Ethics: Section 140.7(iii)(b) states that this cannot be invoked against an inquiry or investigation by AAT or a relevant regulatory body.

518 See § 6.4.4.2.

recent practice of targeted AML supervision, AAT does not carry out such focused AML supervision.

6.9.2.1 Risk-based approach

AAT applies a risk assessment on its members on the basis of which it selects the members that are supervised in a particular year. As AML supervision is integrated in a wider programme, this assessment goes beyond AML risk alone and concerns a wider compliance risk assessment.[519] AAT uses a number of indicators in its risk assessment, varying from the possible existence of complaints against the member, the lack of engagement with AAT, the size and maturity of the firm as well as the fee income and the number of employees, the geographical spread, and the nature and type of services that the accountant and/or firm provides.[520] The risk assessments are based on information that members have to send to AAT annually, the so-called annual returns, as well as information from other AAT departments, the media, intelligence received from other professional bodies and AML supervisors, as well as information received from UKFIU and law enforcement agencies.[521] AAT also considers the diagnostic AML tests which registered members have to pass in order to become a licensed member in its risk-based approach 'as it controls the risk that new members could claim to be unaware of their obligations'.[522] AAT's monitoring activity is targeted at the members or firms that it perceives to have the highest risk. At the same time, AAT randomly selects some members in practice as well, in order to test its risk parameters and hypotheses. This group of randomly selected MIPs provides a reflection of all sorts of AAT members.[523]

6.9.2.2 Procedure

Annual supervision plans are prepared by the CCT. Since 2013 the actual monitoring is carried out by ICAEW under a contract. This means that ICAEW's QAD staff take care of the desk reviews and visits on behalf of the AAT and the administrative tasks surrounding it. The reason for this is that ICAEW already has a well-developed monitoring system and that AAT can spend its resources more effectively by focussing on high-risk firms and giving proactive support to members in practice based on trend information identified through the monitoring activity.[524] Before 2013 AAT had its own reviewers. As a rule of thumb, off-site monitoring is done for MIPs working at firms with a gross fee income of less than 25,000 GBP. MIPs working at firms that have a gross fee income of 25,000 GPB or more are supervised through a review of documentation followed by an on-site visit.

519 Interview Association of Accounting Technicians, May 2014.

520 AAT (2013a), *2012/13 AML/CTF Supervision Report: Annual return*, submitted in May 2013 by AAT to HM Treasury, par. 28. This report is not publicly available, but has been provided to me after the interview with AAT for research purposes. I have been allowed to use and refer to the report for this research: Association of Accounting Technicians, May 2014.

521 Interview Association of Accounting Technicians, August 2012.

522 HM Treasury (2012) at 10.

523 Interview Association of Accounting Technicians, May 2014.

524 Interview Association of Accounting Technicians, May 2014; AAT (2013a), par. 102.

If there is evidence to suggest a (more) serious case, it is likely that an on-site visit follows after a desk review. Verification of AML compliance is always part of the monitoring.

AAT's Guidance for members in practice explains how the monitoring procedure works in practice. The guidance focusses on telephone reviews and on-site visits. Members are normally given four weeks' notice of a review. The notice contains information on the name of the representative who will conduct the review, the format of the review and, if applicable, how long the visit is expected to last.[525] In general, visits take up to one day and assessing AML/CTF compliance is said to take around 50% of the time during a compliance visit.[526] Before a review, the member may be asked to provide documents and records in advance. During an on-site visit, reviewers verify various documents, such as 'practice administration documents and records, (…) anti-money laundering procedures documents and records, and client files'.[527] Once finished, QAD reviewers report back to CCT about the outcomes. The report includes information on which documents and files have been reviewed, which matters have been discussed with the member and the observations and recommendations.[528] The reviewers also give a score to the level of compliance of the member in practice. There are four possibilities varying from a high level of compliance to serious non-compliance (A – B – C – D).[529] When the CCT receives a C report, it will verify whether, and if so which, informal measures should be taken against the member in practice in the first place.[530] When CCT receives a D report, it immediately commences a disciplinary investigation. The procedure that follows hereafter is dealt with in § 6.9.4.

6.9.2.3 Supervision in numbers

Based on the non-public annual AML returns, it appears that AAT's monitoring activity remained stable in the years 2010-2012. In 2010 it undertook a total of 56 reviews under the MIP scheme: 28 on-site visits and 28 telephone interviews.[531] For the year 2011 only the total number is known: 122 inspections.[532] This number, however, consists of reviews carried out under the MIP Scheme as well as investigations carried out on individuals who were within AAT's membership, but not licensed and, therefore, supervised under the MIP scheme and the Regulations. Presumably, the number remained more or less the same as in 2010. In 2012, AAT exercised 27 on-site visits and 25 desk-based reviews, which is similar to the number in 2010.[533] Statistics for the year 2013 are not available at

525 AAT, *MIP Guidance*, at 45, available at: <www.aat.org.uk/mip-guidance>, last visited on 18 June 2014.

526 AAT (2013a), par. 46.

527 AAT, *MIP Guidance*, at 46, available at: <www.aat.org.uk/mip-guidance>, last visited on 18 June 2014.

528 Ibid.

529 This is actually the same as the ICAEW system: see § 6.8.2.2.

530 In accordance with AAT 2012 Disciplinary Regulations 15-17 (informal procedure).

531 AAT (2011a) at 8. This report is not publicly available but has been provided to me after the interview with AAT for research purposes. I have been allowed to use and refer to the report for this research: Association of Accounting Technicians, May 2014.

532 AAT (2012), *HM Treasury AML Supervision Report 2011/2012*, at 18. This report is not publicly available but has been provided to me after the interview with AAT for research purposes. I have been allowed to use and refer to the report for this research: Association of Accounting Technicians, May 2014.

533 AAT (2013a), par. 44 and 48.

the time of finalising this chapter, although representatives indicated that the number had increased to around 100 inspections.[534] Based on a rough calculation for the years 2010-2012, approximately 1.5% of AAT's members were supervised for their compliance with the AML obligations annually.[535] Acknowledging that this number may not be fully accurate, it does give an indication of the likelihood that a member is supervised by AAT. This is a fairly reasonable level of supervision.[536] Nevertheless, in order to build a more robust and effective AML supervisory framework, AAT should also start carrying out inspections which focus specifically on compliance with one or more AML obligations. This form of targeted AML supervision ensures that AAT has a more detailed understanding of the level of compliance with specific obligations, which it may use in its wider monitoring programme. Moreover, this helps to avoid the situation that the integration of AML supervision into the monitoring of its MIP scheme leads to insufficient attention to this matter. AAT should also think about publishing the results of such targeted visits – as the FCA does – as a means of guidance for its members. The publication thereof would also enhance transparency and accountability concerning the exercise of its AML supervision. Although I have just presented information suggesting that around half of the time of on-site visits is spent to assessing AML compliance, this cannot be seen in the figures through which AAT accounts for its supervision. AAT's transparency and accountability would also benefit from the publication of the non-public annual AML returns to HM Treasury.

Finally, it should be pointed out that AAT itself indicates that it expends quite an effort in the provision of guidance and support to its members. According to its annual AML reports, members are provided with a so-called AML toolkit that should help them in developing a risk-based approach to their client bases. In addition, AAT organises and attends events, it has provided specific AML guidance and provides information through its website via blogs, news items and podcasts, as well as via its trade magazine.[537] Members have access to support through telephone and e-mail as well.[538]

6.9.3 Sanctioning powers

AAT's 2012 Disciplinary Regulations demonstrate that non-compliance with the preventive AML obligations is a form of misconduct.[539] Members are therefore liable to disciplinary sanctions. As is the case with ICAEW, sanctions can be imposed at two moments during the disciplinary procedure: they can be proposed by the Investigations Committee (hereafter IC) to which a member may consent, or by a Disciplinary Tribunal.[540] Unlike

534 Interview Association of Accounting Technicians, May 2014.

535 This calculation is based on the average number of inspections in 2010 (56) and 2012 (52), divided by the average number of AAT members subject to AML supervision by AAT in these years (3,633 and 3,386). The numbers for 2011 are not included, for the reason mentioned in the text.

536 Though difficult to compare and without drawing final conclusions from this indication: see § 4.6.2.2 where on average 0.1% of all institutions were supervised annually by SEPBLAC, and § 6.7.2 where the OFT supervised 0.3% of the estate agents in the year 2012.

537 AAT (2012) at 7; AAT (2008), *Guidance on anti-money laundering legislation*, October 2008.

538 AAT (2011a) at 6.

539 AAT 2012 Disciplinary Regulation 13(c).

540 AAT 2012 Disciplinary Regulations 39 and 101.

ICAEW, however, the IC and the Disciplinary Tribunal have exactly the same sanctioning powers.[541] The following range of disciplinary sanctions apply in the case of misconduct:[542]

- expulsion
- suspension of membership
- withdrawal of the practising licence or registration as a student
- declaration of ineligibility for a practising licence
- have the fellow member status removed (if applicable)
- severe reprimand
- reprimand
- disciplinary fine (the sum may not exceed the maximum amount set by the Council)
- obligation to give a written undertaking to ensure that steps are taken to avoid future misconduct
- be debarred from sitting the AAT assessments for a period of time
- have a relevant assessment result declared null and void; or
- be declared unfit to become a full member.

The sanctions do not exclude one another and can be imposed simultaneously.[543] An order in which a sanction is recommended shall, in principle, be published as soon as is practicable.[544] This can be considered an additional sanction as it is a form of naming & shaming. The publication should include the name of the member, the nature of the misconduct and the order made. At present, however, AAT only publishes the sanctioning decisions in its trade magazine. Members receive a copy of this magazine. The decisions are not published on the website or made publicly known elsewhere.[545] This is rather surprising given that the Indicative Sanctioning Guidance states that '[i]t will be normal practice for AAT to publicise the outcome of any disciplinary hearing on its website, membership publications, and to issue a general media "press release" as soon as is practicable'.[546] Although AAT has a wide range of sanctions available, it does not publish sanctioning decisions directly or in an aggregated form so as to be generally available to the public. Only the public annual reports include the total number of sanctions imposed.[547] In line with its policy, but also for reasons of transparency and accountability, the disciplinary decisions should also be made available to the wider public, considering that the Disciplinary Regulations and the Indicative Sanctioning Guidance prove that these sanctions ought to be normal practice within AAT.

541 AAT 2012 Disciplinary Regulation 40.

542 Not all sanctions can be imposed on all members, as some are reserved for full and fellow members – such as sanctions in relation to the practising licence – whereas other sanctions only apply to affiliate and student members – such as the sanctions in relation to assessments. This means that not all sanctions are equally relevant for sanctioning non-compliance with AML obligations, as only full or fellow members may apply to the MIP scheme and only MIPs may perform accountancy services for the public.

543 Inferred from AAT 2012 Disciplinary Regulation 40, which states that 'any one or more' sanctions can be imposed.

544 AAT 2012 Disciplinary Regulation 50.

545 Interview Association of Accounting Technicians, May 2014.

546 AAT (2012a), *Indicative Sanctions Guidance*, July 2012, at 9.

547 E.g. in 2013 AAT imposed 102 sanctions, but which types and for which behaviour is not included: AAT (2013) at 15.

Besides the wide range of formal disciplinary sanctions that AAT bodies may impose, it can also resort to the use of more informal measures, as was indicated in the previous subsection. Such measures can be an (informal) action plan, where a member is given the time to repair identified shortcomings and report to AAT about the steps taken, or an informal warning letter. In the next subsection we will see how AAT makes use of these informal measures.

6.9.4 Sanctioning policy and practice

6.9.4.1 Disciplinary procedure and sanctioning policy

In § 6.9.2 we could read that when the CCT receives a C report, it will verify whether, and if so which, informal measures should be taken against the MIP. During this stage, CCT may decide to give a member an informal warning or to allow the member to agree to an action plan. We could also see that when CCT receives a D report, it immediately commences a disciplinary investigation. It is the task of the Investigations Committee to oversee the investigation conducted against a member by CCT. One Council member from the Investigations Committee and a staff member from CCT jointly form 'the Investigations Team'.[548] The Council member can be actively involved in the investigation, direct the CCT staff to carry out further investigations by making the necessary inquiries, and monitor the progress of any further investigations, if such are needed. The Investigations Team can decide whether or not grounds for disciplinary action are present, make a recommendation on which disciplinary action to take, and whether the action should be accompanied by certain terms and conditions.[549] If the CCT member and Council member do not agree, the latter has a casting vote.[550] If disciplinary action ought to be taken against the member according to the Investigations Team, this may be presented to the member concerned in the form of a consent order.[551] The member can decide to accept or decline the consent order.

If a consent order is declined, the case is handed over to the Disciplinary Committee.[552] As explained, this Committee consists of 12 people who are either AAT members (but not Council members) or independent lay persons who are not professional accountants. Three people from the Committee, one AAT member and two independent lay persons, form a Disciplinary Tribunal.[553] The Tribunal can determine, via a (public) hearing, whether there is a case of misconduct and whether disciplinary action should be taken against the member in practice.[554] If the member in practice does not agree with the decision, the accountant can appeal against the decision to the Appeals Committee. The Appeals Committee appoints an Appeals Tribunal that can decide to uphold or dismiss

548 AAT 2012 Disciplinary Regulations 22 and 23. In certain circumstances this power may be delegated to CCT: AAT 2012 Disciplinary Regulation 25.
549 AAT 2012 Disciplinary Regulation 27.
550 AAT 2012 Disciplinary Regulation 28.
551 AAT 2012 Disciplinary Regulation 39.
552 AAT 2012 Disciplinary Regulations 45-49.
553 AAT 2012 Disciplinary Regulation 70.
554 AAT 2012 Disciplinary Regulations 90-101.

an appeal in whole or in part, foresee in the case itself (as it considers appropriate in the interests of fairness) or refer the case back to the Disciplinary Tribunal.[555]

In determining whether there is a case of misconduct and which sanction to impose, the Disciplinary Tribunal should take into account the following circumstances: the nature and seriousness of the misconduct, the member's character and past behaviour, as well as any other relevant circumstance.[556] 'Other relevant circumstance' could, for example, be the question whether the member has made a large profit from his own non-compliant behaviour. More specifically, the Indicative Sanctions Guidance shows the specific considerations that the Tribunal should take into account for each specific sanction. It states, for example, that for an expulsion the Tribunal must consider whether the behaviour concerns a serious departure from professional standards, whether it is an abuse of one's position and/or trust, whether it is an act of dishonesty or fraud, or whether there is a clear pattern of breaches of professional standards as laid down in AAT's policies, regulations and the Code of Professional Ethics.[557] AAT representatives observe that AAT used to take a more educational stance with regard to identified non-compliance – which could be observed in a number of documents – and applied a rather cooperative style in the first years that the MLR 2007 were in place, but that its ethos has changed.[558] Tribunals are now said to be willing to impose tough sanctions.

6.9.4.2 Sanctioning in practice

The following sanctions were imposed for non-compliance with the Regulations between 2010 and 2012. This information is based on the non-public annual returns from AAT to HM Treasury, which have been provided for research purposes. In 2010 no formal disciplinary sanctions were imposed, but informal action plans were agreed for 16 members reviewed that year, and these were all complied with.[559] In 2011, six members were disciplined by means of formal sanctions imposed by the Investigations Team or the Disciplinary Tribunal, ranging from expulsions to a combination of severe reprimands and fines.[560] In addition, 39 members subject to a review in 2011 were asked to comply with an action plan. Nearly all members complied in full with the requirements of the action plan, while two members decided to surrender their licence.[561] In 2012, AAT subjected 21 members to an action plan and 5 members received an (informal) warning letter.[562] AAT also took disciplinary action for not complying with preventive AML obligations against 29 members in practice in that year. Thereby, the Investigations Team and the Disciplinary Tribunal imposed the following disciplinary sanctions:

555 See about the appeals procedure: AAT 2012 Disciplinary Regulations 107-117.

556 AAT 2012 Disciplinary Regulation 40.

557 AAT (2012), *Indicative Sanctions Guidance*, July 2012, at 6.

558 E.g. AAT (2008) at 45; AAT, *MIP Guidance*, at 49, available at: <www.aat.org.uk/mip-guidance>, last visited on 18 June 2014; Interview Association of Accounting Technicians, May 2014.

559 AAT (2011a) at 9.

560 AAT (2012) at 10.

561 Ibid., at 9.

562 AAT (2013a), par. 74.

Table 8 – AAT disciplinary sanctions for non-compliance with AML obligations in 2012[563]

Expulsions or removal	15
Fines	2
Reprimands	10
Written undertakings	2

Based on the fact that the monitoring activity remained more or less on the same level in the years 2010-2012 and the information above, it can be concluded that AAT is increasingly taking action against members in relation to non-compliance with the MLR 2007. Whereas AAT still applied a highly cooperative enforcement style in 2010 by only imposing informal measures, the numbers for 2011 and, especially, 2012 demonstrate that AAT takes strict disciplinary action if it considers this to be necessary. Particularly expulsions or removal are highly dissuasive sanctions. Nevertheless, if possible, AAT will use informal measures as well in order to keep its enforcement activity proportionate.

6.9.5 Concluding remarks

AAT has adequate supervisory powers. Staff have the power to compel the production of information and to carry out on-site inspections. It also has the power to issue regulations. AML supervision by AAT is part of its general monitoring procedure under the MIP scheme. It is thus always part of a wider supervisory programme. Supervision is exercised by the Conduct & Compliance Team (CCT) that consists of AAT staff. AAT also expends quite an effort in the provision of guidance and support to its members. The basis of AAT's monitoring is the risk assessment. It includes a number of risk indicators, which go beyond the existence of an AML risk alone. Aspects like the existence of complaints against the member, the size and maturity of the firm and the type of services provided by the firm are important for AAT's risk assessments. The assessments are based on the annual returns from members, intelligence from other AAT departments, the media, and other professional or public bodies. Annual supervision plans are prepared by the CCT, but the actual monitoring is outsourced to ICAEW. The QAD performs the reviews and carries out the administrative tasks surrounding these reviews. In the case of visits, around half of the time is said to be spent on assessing AML compliance. Once a review is finished, CCT receives the results from ICAEW. In practice, AAT has had a fairly reasonable level of monitoring, which includes assessing AML compliance, in recent years. Nevertheless, for various reasons AAT should start carrying out targeted AML supervision as well. AAT should also consider publishing its AML returns, which it submits to HM Treasury annually.

The Investigations Team (through a consent order) and the Disciplinary Tribunal have the same wide range of sanctions available. They range from reprimands, to disciplinary fines, or even to expulsion or removal. AAT has a publicly available sanctioning policy, laid down in the Disciplinary Regulations and the Indicative Sanctions Guidance. The Guidance contains the specific considerations that the Tribunal should take into account

563 Own table based on AAT (2013a), par. 68.

for each specific sanction. In practice AAT makes use of this wide variety of sanctions. It has taken more and more disciplinary action against its members for non-compliance with the Regulations. Especially from the last year included in this research, it can be observed that AAT takes strict disciplinary action if it considers this to be necessary. At the same time the numbers demonstrate that, where possible, AAT will use informal measures to overcome non-compliance by its members. This shows that AAT in practice applies dissuasive and proportionate sanctions. AAT, however, should address the aspect of the publication of disciplinary decisions. For reasons of transparency and accountability, and part of the theoretical framework of effective supervision, the disciplinary decisions should be published, especially now that the Disciplinary Regulations and the Indicative Sanctioning Guidance show that the publication of sanctions ought to be normal practice within AAT.

6.10 Supervisory cooperation for the prevention of money laundering

6.10.1 Institutionalised forums for AML cooperation on a policy level

The Anti-Money Laundering Supervisors' Forum (AMLSF) is the most important forum for cooperation between all AML supervisors in the UK. Since its establishment in 2007, it has become an institutionalised setting run by the supervisors themselves. All AML supervisors are expected to participate in the forum and they meet four times yearly.[564] Representatives of the Treasury, the Home Office and the National Crime Agency (UKFIU) attend the plenary meetings as well. Meetings are used, among other things, to discuss and solve supervisory problems, to consider policy developments, to present good supervisory practices and to review the effectiveness of supervision and the sanctions imposed.[565] Individual cases are in principle not discussed here. Three affinity groups operate under the AMLSF. Meetings of these groups take place more regularly than plenary forum meetings.[566] The three affinity groups are Government supervisors (Public), supervisors overseeing the legal profession (Legal) and supervisors overseeing the accountancy, taxation, bookkeeping and insolvency professions (Accountancy).[567] The affinity groups, particularly the Accountancy sector group due to the high number of AML supervisors in this sector, aim to ensure consistency in supervisory practice. Since 2010, ICAEW and AAT have led an initiative for the sharing of information with the aim of having more consistent and effective supervisory and sanctioning practices.[568]

> With the 2012 amendments an explicit legal basis for the exchange of information between AML supervisors was created. More about this follows in the next subsection.

Another institutionalised forum for cooperation on a policy level is the Money Laundering Advisory Committee (MLAC). It is not a forum in which information is exchanged

564 HM Treasury (2013) par. 4.2.
565 Ibid., par. 5.6.
566 Ibid., par. 4.2.
567 Ibid., par. 4.2.
568 HM Treasury (2012) at 16.

between AML supervisors, but rather an advisory committee co-chaired by the Treasury and the Home Office. AML supervisors participate in this committee, but other members also include representatives from law enforcement agencies, as well as Government and industry representatives.[569] MLAC advises the Government on its approach to preventing money laundering in the UK and plays an important role in the acceptance of AML guidance by the Treasury.[570]

A third institutionalised forum in which AML supervisors sit is the SARs Regime Committee, an advisory body to UKFIU on the functioning of the SARs regime. The SARs regime is the UK's reporting regime for suspicions of money laundering and terrorist financing. The Committee was established in 2006 as the result of a review of the regime and meets four times yearly.[571] It is comprised of representatives from the Government and industry. The Committee reviews the SARs regime and its reviews are published in the SARs Annual Reports. Two of the four AML supervisors in this research are members of the SARs Regime Committee: the FCA and ICAEW.[572] Due to its focus and activities, this forum is of less relevance for the exercise of AML supervision and cooperation between the AML supervisors as such.

6.10.2 Cooperation efforts by AML supervisors on an operational level

Besides the possibilities for (general) information sharing through forums, AML supervisors can share information on a case-by-case basis where this is necessary.[573] Since the 2012 amendments, the Regulations have an explicit basis for the exchange of information. This addressed the problem that there was no explicit legal basis for the sharing of information under the preventive regime. For some supervisors, in particular HMRC, the absence of a legal basis was problematic and created uncertainty as to whether and under which circumstances it could provide information to other AML supervisors.[574] The exchange of information is now regulated by Regulation 24A MLR 2007. It allows AML supervisors to liaise with each other by sharing information to the extent that the information is relevant to the functions under the Regulations and, secondly, provided that it is shared for the purposes connected with the effective exercise of the functions of the supervisors under the Regulations. The information may not be further disclosed to other authorities by the receiving supervisory authority unless this is done for purposes connected with the effective exercise of the functions under the Regulations, with a view to the start of any criminal or other enforcement proceedings, or as otherwise required by law. Moreover, the FCA is explicitly allowed to forward information to the PRA where

569 Booth, R., Farrel QC, S., and Bastable, G. (2011), *Money Laundering Law and Regulation: A Practical Guide*, OUP: Oxford, pp. 24-26; FATF (2007a) at 245.

570 HM Treasury (2013a), *Preventing Money Laundering*, policy paper, 5 June 2013, par. 3, available at <www.gov.uk/government/publications/preventing-money-laundering/preventing-money-laundering>, last visited on 18 June 2014.

571 Lander, S. (2006), *Review of the Suspicious Activity Reports Regime*, March 2006; National Crime Agency (2013), *SARs Annual Report 2013*, at 5.

572 National Crime Agency (2013) at 32.

573 HM Treasury (2013), par. 5.6.

574 HM Revenue and Customs (2011), *Anti-Money Laundering Annual Report to Her Majesty's Treasury 2010-2011*, at 11.

the information concerns a PRA-authorised person or a person who has a qualifying relationship with a PRA-authorised person. The Regulation seemingly does not impose any restrictions as to the kind of information that may be exchanged, which suggests that also relevant supervisory information about individual institutions or professionals, or persons related thereto, may be disclosed.

This Regulation does not allow information to be provided by AML Supervisors to UKFIU. The only type of cooperation between supervisors and UKFIU takes place within the AMLSF, where UKFIU attends the plenary meetings. Moreover, Regulation 24(2) obliges AML supervisors to promptly inform the National Crime Agency (UKFIU) when, in the course of carrying out any of the functions under the Regulations, they know or suspect that a person is or has engaged in money laundering or terrorist financing. This provision can serve as a legal basis for the provision of relevant supervisory information about individuals from the AML supervisors to UKFIU; but not the other way around.[575] This is lamentable as this kind of information may be used by AML supervisors as an additional source of information for the verification of compliance with the preventive obligations by their supervisees.[576] UKFIU does reach out to the AML supervisors, although this seems to take place on a more abstract level: 'over the year, the focus has been on engagement with the reporting sectors, especially in relation to achieving the goal of providing effective feedback. This has included working with the Anti-Money Laundering Supervisors' Forum (AMLSF) Affinity Groups regarding implementation, with overall feedback being positive. The UKFIU further liaised with regulators, supervisors and trade associations, who assisted in delivering key messages to their members through their pre-existing secure delivery mechanisms'.[577]

> A more specific provision, Regulation 49A, deals specifically with the disclosure of information from HMRC to the FCA, where the disclosure of relevant information is made for the purpose of enabling or assisting the latter in any of its functions pursuant to the Payment Services Regulations 2009 or the Electronic Money Regulations 2011. The FCA is, in turn, empowered to disclose information to HMRC on the basis of the Payment Services Regulations 2009. In order to cooperate more effectively, the FCA and HMRC have concluded a Memorandum of Understanding (hereafter MOU).[578] This document describes the high-level principles for the exchange of information between the two authorities and explains that for each type of exchange there should be a 'process level MoU'.
>
> As an aside, it can be pointed out that outside the preventive AML policy, AML supervisors engage with each other as well. Particularly the FCA is active in concluding memoranda

575 The confidentiality of information received through SARs is regulated by Home Office Circular 53/2005 on money laundering and it lays down the confidentiality and sensitivity of suspicious activity reports (SARs) and the identity of those who make them. UKFIU acts under this strict regime. The Circular does not seem to allow information on individual SARs to be passed on from UKFIU to relevant AML supervisors.

576 Cf. § 5.9.1.1.

577 National Crime Agency (2013) at 10; FATF (2007a) at 246.

578 Memorandum of Understanding ("MoU") between Her Majesty's Revenue and Customs ("HMRC") and the Financial Conduct Authority ("FCA") in respect of the exchange of information, 22 March 2013, available at: <www.fca.org.uk/static/fca/documents/mou/mou-hmrc.pdf>, last visited on 24 June 2014.

> of understanding with other authorities. It has concluded an MOU with the ICAEW based on FSMA 2000 and the Financial Services and Markets Act 2000 (Disclosure of Confidential Information) Regulations 2001 (as amended).[579] And with the OFT, with whom it shares powers in relation to competition and consumer protection, it concluded an MOU on the basis of various pieces of legislation including FSMA 2000, the Enterprise Act 2002 and the Competition Act 1998. The exchange of information is an integral part of the MOU.[580]

HM Treasury does not keep statistics on the situations and the number of times that information is exchanged based on Regulation 24A MLR 2007. This does not allow one to say something about the question whether – outside the forums for cooperation on a policy level – AML supervisors cooperate in practice on a more operational level. The Treasury does state that the most important instance of the exchange of information concerns the provision of information from the accountancy bodies (that act as an AML supervisor) and the OFT to HMRC: '[t]he sharing of information is particularly important in instances where a firm ceases to be supervised by a professional body and needs to be contacted and supervised by HMRC, the default regulator for accountancy service providers and trust and company service providers. Supervisors should use information gateways available to communicate details of membership and conduct records with default regulators'.[581]

6.10.3 Concluding remarks

In the UK there are three forums for policy cooperation that are of direct importance for the preventive AML policy and the supervisors. The most important forum is the AMLSF, in which all supervisors under the Regulations come together. Representatives from the Treasury, the Home Office and the National Crime Agency (UKFIU) attend the plenary meetings as well, which take place four times yearly. Within the AMLSF and its affinity groups (public, legal and accountancy), AML supervisors share supervisory practices, discuss policy developments and good supervisory practices and review the effectiveness of supervision and the sanctions imposed. Two other forums are the MLAC and the SARs Regime Committee. Some AML supervisors participate in these meetings as well. The 2012 amendments to the MLR 2007 created an explicit legal basis for the exchange of information between AML supervisors. This exchange is subject to a number of limitations, but not as to the type of information that AML supervisors can exchange with each other. This suggests that relevant supervisory information about individual institutions or professionals, or persons related thereto, may be disclosed. The Regulations only regulate cooperation between the AML supervisors, hence the disclosure of information from AML supervisors to the FIU and vice versa is not possible on the basis of this provision. Nevertheless, UKFIU attends meetings of the AMLSF and supervisors are

579 Memorandum of Understanding between the Financial Conduct Authority and the Institute of Chartered Accountants in England and Wales concerning 1. exempt professional firms and 2. authorised professional firms, 12 March 2013, available at: <www.fca.org.uk/static/fca/documents/mou/mou-icaew.pdf>, last visited on 20 May 2014.

580 Memorandum of Understanding between the Office of Fair Trading and the Financial Conduct Authority, 2 April 2013, available at: <www.fca.org.uk/static/fca/documents/mou/mou-oft.pdf>, last visited on 20 May 2014.

581 HM Treasury (2013), par. 5.6.

obliged to inform the National Crime Agency (UKFIU) when, in the course of carrying out supervisory functions under the Regulations, they know or suspect that a person is or has engaged in money laundering or terrorist financing. In turn, UKFIU reaches out to AML supervisors, albeit only on a more abstract level, due to the confidentiality regime under which it operates. Unfortunately, the Treasury does not keep statistics that would allow one to say whether, how often, and which AML supervisors exchange information based on Regulation 24A MLR 2007.

7 Anti-money laundering supervision of banks, real estate agents and accountants in Sweden

7.1 Introduction

Sweden's supervisory architecture in the preventive anti-money laundering policy is of a hybrid nature.[1] Sweden is an interesting country for this research, due to the attention the Swedish Government paid to the matter of supervision during the implementation of the Third Directive.[2] This chapter provides an in-depth analysis of the supervisory system and practice in Sweden with respect to banks, accountants and real estate agents. The legislative, institutional and practical aspects that were identified as part of the theoretical framework of effective supervision are assessed in this chapter.

Section 7.2 describes Sweden's vulnerability for money laundering and the three groups of businesses specifically. This is followed by an outline of the legal framework for the prevention of money laundering (§ 7.3). Both sections aim to purvey the context in which the fight against money laundering takes place in Sweden. Section 7.4 deals with the institutional aspects of the AML supervisors. These are the Swedish Financial Supervisory Authority (*Finansinspektionen*) for banks, the Swedish Estate Agents Inspectorate (*Fastighetsmäklarinspektionen*), the county administrative boards (*Länsstyrelserna*) of Stockholm, Västra Götaland and Skåne regarding accountants, and the Supervisory Board of Public Auditors (*Revisorsnämnden*) for public auditors and audit firms specifically. They must be sufficiently independent in the exercise of their supervisory tasks, and be accountable and transparent about their activities. A discussion on the extent to which banks, real estate agents and accountants are authorised, regulated or required to register with their supervisors or other competent authorities follows in section 7.5. This section aims to answer the question whether the supervisory authorities have, or can have, an adequate knowledge of the institutions or professionals for which they have supervisory responsibility. It also deals with the coverage of the institutions and professionals under the Swedish AML legislation, where this diverges with sectorial legislation. Sections 7.6 to 7.9 analyse the supervisory procedures and practice at the Swedish Financial Supervisory Authority, the Swedish Estate Agents Inspectorate, the three county administrative boards, and the Supervisory Board of Public Auditors.[3] It is verified whether they have adequate supervisory and sanctioning powers, whether they apply them in a proportionate and

1 § 3.4.4.
2 See § 3.4.4 and 7.3.
3 I also refer to these authorities by using their Swedish abbreviations: FI, FMI, LST and RN.

careful manner, and whether they scale up their actions where necessary. Finally, section 7.10 deals with another aspect of effective supervision: the cooperation between supervisors under the AML policy, and to a certain extent with the FIU. There must be no legal barriers to the exchange of information between these supervisors, and with the FIU.

7.2 Vulnerability of Sweden for money laundering

In order to understand the context in which anti-money laundering supervision is exercised, it is relevant to have some ideas about the question whether money laundering is actually a problem in Sweden. This section presents a number of studies that discuss the vulnerability for money laundering, or the scope of the problem, as well as the main predicate offences or sectors that are (considered to be) most at risk in Sweden. Special attention is paid to the banking, real estate and accountancy sectors.

It appears that information about the scope or amounts of money laundered in Sweden is scarce, although there are some studies dealing with this matter. For the year 2009 the ECOLEF study calculated the amount of money laundered in Sweden at 26 billion Euros, which is 5.8% of its GDP.[4] Compared to other EU Member States, this was relatively low.[5] In December 2012 the Swedish Government assigned to a number of authorities the task of performing a national risk assessment on money laundering in Sweden (hereafter the national risk assessment or NRA).[6] The authorities were unable to present exact numbers on the scope of money laundering in Sweden, but provided estimations. In an attempt to translate earlier IMF and UNODC risk assessments to the Swedish conditions, the authorities came to an estimate of 14.5 billion Euros for the year 2012 in Sweden, which is 3.6% of its GDP.[7] The report thereby stressed the uncertainty related to these types of calculations. One can observe a considerable difference between the calculations of the ECOLEF study and the NRA. This can be explained most prominently by the use of different methods, but also by the different periods studied and the sources of information used.[8]

4 Unger and Ferwerda (2014) at 15-16.

5 In the calculations on threat as % of GDP, Sweden ended as 24th out of 27 Member States: Unger and Ferwerda (2014) at 16.

6 Finansinspektionen et al. (2013), *Penningtvätt: En nationell riskbedömning*, Dnr 12-13024. This national risk assessment was undertaken for the first time in 2013: *Regeringsbeslut: Uppdrag till Finansinspektionen m.fl. myndigheter att i samverkan ta fram en nationell riskbedömning avseende penningtvätt och finansiering av terrorism i Sverige*, 29 November 2012, Fi2012/4457 (in English: *Assignment to Finansinspektionen and other agencies to cooperatively develop a national risk assessment of money laundering and terrorist financing in Sweden*). In 2014 the national risk assessment on terrorist financing was published: Finansinspektionen et al. (2014), *Finansiering av terrorism: En nationell riskbedömning*, Dnr 12-13024. No further attention is paid to this risk assessment.

7 Finansinspektionen et al. (2013), at 9 speaks of 128 billion Swedish Crowns (SEK). The NRA stated that the Swedish GDP in 2012 was 3,555 billion SEK. As regards the conversion to Euros: On 5 February 2014 the EUR-SEK exchange rate was 1 EUR = 8.8288 SEK. This means that the exact amount in Euros is 14,475,569,929.

8 We could see in Chapter 4 that the ECOLEF study understood the threat of money laundering as 'the amount of money that could, or might, be laundered in a country if there were no barriers to laundering and there was no 'more attractive place' for the launderer to launder the money', whereas the National Risk Assessment deals with actual estimates of money laundering.

Regarding the main predicate offences and the vulnerability of specific sectors for money laundering, the intelligence report for the year 2012 by the Swedish Economic Crimes Bureau (*Ekobrottsmyndigheten*, hereafter 'SECB') pointed to the fact that cash management brings about a particular money laundering risk in Sweden. It reported on indications that criminals in Sweden have influence over certain companies that are engaged in cash management, currency exchange and money remittance activities.[9] The SECB also indicated that tax fraud is a big problem, because of the profitability of withholding excise duties on the import and sale of cigarettes, alcohol, and mineral oil, and the existing loopholes in legislation and regulations.[10] According to the Swedish FIU (*Finanspolisen*) money laundering through cash, in particular via the gaming industry, and fraud with excise duties are the main typologies of money laundering in Sweden.[11] The FIU explained in its annual report that fraud generates high proceeds and that punishments are relatively low in Sweden. This makes it attractive, especially for organised crime, to engage in this type of criminal activity. Next to the two main typologies, the FIU mentioned drug offences, internet fraud and fraud with respect to transactions to South America as commonly identified money laundering methods in Sweden. Furthermore, it warned against the risk of money laundering via new methods of payments, such as prepaid cards, e-wallets, internet-based payment services, payment services via mobile phones, and virtual currencies such as Bitcoins.[12] The Swedish Financial Supervisory Authority has identified a number of significant deficiencies in compliance with money laundering obligations at firms offering payment services, also suggesting a vulnerability for money laundering in this sector.[13] The national risk assessment confirmed all of the aforementioned typologies and vulnerabilities. In addition it presented some evidence suggesting that Sweden might be an attractive country for laundering via the real estate sector, although it concluded that further studies are needed here.[14] The national risk assessment also stated that a laundering threat stems from sectors such as the construction and restaurant industries as well as – inter alia – hairdressers, brokerage firms and the transport sector.[15] In these sectors, activities can either aim to finance undeclared work or to launder cash. Again it appears that cash brings about a particular money laundering risk in Sweden. Corruption is not considered a big problem in Sweden. The EU Anti-Corruption Report 2014 stated that Sweden is among the least corrupt countries in the European Union.[16]

Based on this information it seems that banks, accountants and, to a lesser extent, real estate agents are not the most vulnerable type of institutions and professions in Sweden. This finding is strengthened by the absence of case law on convictions for money

9 Ekobrottsmyndigheten (2012), *Underrättelsebild 2012*, EBM K-2012/0114, at 8. Cf. NRA (2013) at 22.
10 Ekobrottsmyndigheten (2012) at 8.
11 Finanspolisen (2012), Årsrapport 2012, at 22-23 (in English: *Annual report 2012*). Cf. Interview Finanspolisen, April 2011.
12 Ibid., at 20-21.
13 Finansinspektionen (2013), *Supervision Report 2013*, May 2013, at 18.
14 Finansinspektionen et al. (2013) at 24.
15 Ibid., at 25.
16 European Commission (2014d), *Annex: Sweden to EU Anti-Corruption Report 2014*, COM(2014) 38 final, at 10.

laundering for either of these three types of institutions. Large money laundering scandals that involve banks in Sweden do not exist and the Swedish FIU reported in 2010 that the involvement of bank officials and real estate agents in criminal activities is unusual.[17] Still, the Swedish banking sector is considered to always bear a certain vulnerability for money laundering due to the enormous volumes of money handled by banks.[18] In terms of reporting, it can be observed that of all suspicions of money laundering and terrorist financing reported to the Swedish FIU in 2012 more than 50% of the reports came from banks.[19] This is high, especially compared to the reporting numbers for estate agents and accountants in Sweden. Estate agents' reporting numbers have been low in absolute and relative terms. In 2011 estate agents reported eight times, while in 2012 they disclosed five suspicion reports to the Swedish FIU.[20] This is 0.05% of the total number of reports received by the Swedish FIU in that year. Accountants, not being auditors, reported three times both in the years 2011 and 2012. In those years, auditors (and audit firms) reported four and five times respectively.[21] Information that proves that accountants have been convicted of money laundering or have otherwise been involved in money laundering scandals is absent as well. When the media report on money laundering convictions, this usually concerns lawyers.[22]

The absence of case law might, however, also be explained by the fact that banks, estate agents or accountants have been tried and convicted of underlying predicate offences instead of the money laundering crime itself.[23] Although money laundering is a self-standing offence in the Swedish Criminal Code, in practice it is necessary to prove that an underlying predicate offence has been committed. This makes the prosecution of a separate money laundering offence very difficult and is in practice hardly, if ever, done.[24] It means that launderers are usually convicted of the predicate offence, although they may receive a higher penalty due to the money laundering activity. Legislative amendments are underway, which will be explained hereafter.

7.3 Legal framework for the prevention of money laundering

The core piece of legislation in the Swedish preventive AML policy is the *Penningtvättslag* (hereafter PL or 'AML Act').[25] The Act is the result of the implementation of the Third Directive. It entered into force nearly 18 months later than the implementation deadline

17 Finanspolisen (2010), *Penningtvätt inom den grova organiserade brottsligheten*, RKP Rapport 2010:2 at 15.
18 Finansinspektionen et al. (2013) at 41; Interview Finansinspektionen, October 2013.
19 Finanspolisen (2012) at 27.
20 Ibid.
21 Ibid.
22 Finanspolisen (2010) at 15. Cf: Dagens Juridik, *Ex-advokat fälls för bokföringsbrott och osant intygande – tidigare dömd för penningtvätt*, 4 April 2013, available at: <www.dagensjuridik.se/2013/04/ex-advokat-falls-bokforingsbrott-och-osant-intygande-tidigare-domd-penningtvatt>, last visited on 28 March 2014; Expressen, *Gangsterkungen frias – men advokat döms för penningtvätt*, 30 September 2003.
23 An in-depth study on this point goes beyond the scope of this research and the purpose of this section, which is to purvey the background of supervision in the Swedish preventive AML policy.
24 FATF (2006a) *Third Mutual Evaluation Report on Sweden*, 16 February 2006, at 58-59.
25 *Lag om åtgärder mot penningtvätt och finansiering av terrorism*, SFS 2009:62.

and for this reason Sweden was condemned by the European Court of Justice.[26] Since its entry into force, the AML Act has been amended several times.[27] The main reason for the original delay in the implementation was reported to be caused by discussions on how to design the supervisory system under the AML Act.[28] The Government had ordered the Swedish Agency for Public Management (*Statskontoret*) to investigate the question whether it would be possible and feasible to have a single supervisory authority for all designated institutions and professionals under the preventive policy.[29] The Agency for Public Management advised the Government to retain the supervisory authorities that already exercised anti-money laundering supervision under the previous legislation, and that for the new institutions and professionals, supervision should be carried out by the county administrative boards of Stockholm, Västra Götaland and Skåne.[30]

The AML Act is accompanied by a lower-level Regulation which lays down specific rules for the application of the Act.[31] It regulates in more detail how registration at the Swedish Companies Registration Office (*Bolagsverket,* hereafter BV or 'the Office') should be done, provides rules for the coordination body that oversees measures against money laundering and terrorist financing, and deals with the supervisory competences of the county administrative boards.[32] The AML Regulation also gives the supervisors the power to draft regulations with respect to some obligations. These regulations are specifications concerning the obligations from the AML Act and AML Regulation. They are legally binding on the obliged institutions and professionals.[33] The regulations and general guidelines governing measures against money laundering and terrorist financing from the Financial Supervisory Authority lead the way in this respect.[34] Its regulations are legally binding and directly enforceable, whereas the general guidelines are indirectly enforceable. This means that financial institutions have to comply with the guidelines or explain why they do not do so.[35] FI's regulations and guidelines are to a large extent copied by the other AML supervisors, but at the same time are designed to fit the specific circumstances of each sector.[36]

26 Case C-546/08, *Commission v Kingdom of Sweden* [2009] ECR I-00105.

27 Amendments were made by the following Acts: SFS 2009:716; SFS 2010: 764; SFS 2010:1868; SFS 2011:667; SFS 2011:773; SFS 2011:1051; SFS 2012:376, SFS 2013:580. See § 1.8 for amendments after March 2014.

28 Interview Ministry of Finance and Ministry of Justice, April 2011.

29 Statskontoret gives support to the Government in its efforts to strengthen the capacity of Sweden's public administration to carry out its functions efficiently. More information available at <www.statskontoret.se>.

30 See § 3.4.4.

31 *Förordning om åtgärder mot penningtvätt och finansiering av terrorism*, SFS: 2009:92. Last amended by SFS 2012:24. Hereafter 'AML Regulation'. Translations of Förordning also refer to the term Ordinance. In this research the term ordinance has the same meaning as regulation.

32 See § 7.5.3, 7.8 and 7.10.

33 Section 18 AML Regulation; FATF (2010b), *Fourth Follow Up Report on Sweden*, 22 October 2010, at 5-6; Interview Ministry of Finance and Ministry of Justice, April 2011.

34 FFFS 2009:1 as amended by regulations amending Finansinspektionen's regulations and general guidelines (FFFS 2009:1) governing measures against money laundering and the financing of terrorism, FFFS 2010:5, FFFS 2013:19 and 2013:25. See § 1.8 for amendments after March 2014.

35 Interview Finansinspektionen, April 2011.

36 FATF (2010b) at 22.

There are various other pieces of legislation and regulations which are important in the fight against money laundering. These are, inter alia, the Criminal Code, the Code of Judicial Procedure, and the legislation from which the AML supervisors derive their powers. The Banking and Financing Business Act (hereafter BFBA), the Auditors Act, the Estate Agents Act, and the Public Access to Information and Secrecy Act will be mentioned regularly throughout this Chapter.[37]

Although it is not of direct relevance for this research, it is interesting to point out that Swedish criminal legislation on money laundering is currently undergoing changes.[38] One of the reasons for this is the fact that Sweden is one of the few EU Member States that has not criminalised self-laundering to this day.[39] In 2010 the Swedish Government appointed a Commission to investigate the criminal regulations on money laundering and to consider how these could be made more effective and accessible. In 2012 the official report was presented. It made a number of proposals including the criminalisation of self-laundering, the enactment of a separate act criminalising money laundering, the introduction of an all-crimes approach, the expansion of possibilities to confiscate property related to money laundering, the relieving of the burden of proof regarding the underlying predicate offence, and accession to the Council of Europe Convention on Laundering, Search, Seizure and Confiscation of the Proceeds from Crime and the Financing of Terrorism (Warsaw Convention 2005).[40] In January 2014 the Swedish Council of Legislation responded to the draft text of the Bill in which the majority of the proposals, sometimes amended, are followed.[41] The Bill was laid before Parliament on 20 February 2014 and it should enter into force on 1 July 2014.[42] At the same time the Swedish Police Force is undergoing a reorganisation, which is likely to affect the position of the Swedish FIU.[43]

7.4 The AML supervisors: institutional aspects

The AML Act does not state which authorities have supervisory responsibility under the Act, with the exception of the county administrative boards of Stockholm, Västra Götaland and Skåne.[44] They are the 'default' supervisors and supervise unauthorised or unapproved tax advisors and accountants, independent legal professionals, trust and company service providers, auctioneers and dealers in high-value goods when they receive cash payments

37 *Lag om bank- och finansieringsrörelse*, SFS 2004:297; *Lag om revisorer*, SFS 2001:883; *Fastighetsmäklarlag*, SFS 2011:666; *Offentlighets- och sekreteslag*, SFS 2009:400.

38 See for a brief outline of the Swedish criminal legislation in relation to money laundering: Bergström, M. (2011), 'EU som lagstiftare inom straffrätten och reglerna mot penningtvätt', *Svensk Juristtidning*, issue 4, pp. 357-374, at 370-371.

39 Self-laundering is the process whereby the offender of a predicate offence tries to conceal the illicit origins of the proceeds himself: Magnusson, D. (2009), 'The costs of implementing the anti-money laundering regulations in Sweden', *Journal of Money Laundering Control*, vol. 12, issue 2, pp. 101-112 at 102; FATF (2006a) at 28-29.

40 Swedish Government (2012), *Penningtvätt – kriminalisering, förverkande och dispositionsförbud*, SOU 2012:12.

41 Swedish Council of Legislation (2014), *En effektivare kriminalisering av penningtvätt*, 10 January 2014, available at: <www.regeringen.se/content/1/c6/23/16/84/71b1ac0f.pdf>, last visited on 28 March 2014.

42 *Regeringens proposition* 2013/14:121.

43 Swedish Government (2012a), *En sammanhållen svensk polis*, SOU 2012:13. The reorganisation is foreseen for 1 January 2015.

44 Chapter 6 PL in conjunction with Section 16 AML Regulation.

of 15,000 Euros or more.[45] For the remaining supervisors, Chapter 6, Section 1 PL states that provisions on supervision are contained in the acts governing the institutions subject to the scope of the Act. For banks, Chapter 1, Section 2, first paragraph PL stipulates that it applies to natural and legal persons that run banking or financial businesses under the Banking and Financing Business Act. The BFBA provides supervisory responsibility to the Financial Supervisory Authority, which also makes it the responsible AML supervisor for banks. In addition, the AML Act gives it the statutory responsibility for the AML coordination body (*samordningsorgan för tillsyn över åtgärder mot penningtvätt och finansiering av terrorism*).[46] Due to its supervisory authority under the Estate Agents Act, the Estate Agents Inspectorate can perform the AML supervision of real estate agents.[47] Finally, the Auditors Act provides supervisory responsibility to the Supervisory Board of Public Auditors, which makes it the competent AML supervisor for auditors.[48]

This section provides an analysis of the institutional aspects of the supervisors, most notably their independence and accountability regimes. Regarding the independence and accountability structures, the focus rests with the (relative) political and market independence and corresponding accountability structures, in particular regarding the AML policy.[49] Considering that the independence of administrative authorities is a fundamental principle in the Swedish legal system and that all AML supervisors are administrative authorities, I will first turn to a general outline in § 7.4.1. This section subsequently aims to give an insight into how AML supervision plays a role within the organisations of the Financial Supervisory Authority (§ 7.4.2), the Estate Agents Inspectorate (§ 7.4.3), the Supervisory Board of Public Auditors (§ 7.4.4) and, finally, the three county administrative boards (§ 7.4.5). This section ends with some concluding remarks in § 7.4.6.

7.4.1 The independence of administrative authorities in Sweden and their accountability

Sweden has a long tradition of relatively small ministries and a high number of independent authorities.[50] This has been called a manifestation of dualism in Sweden's political-administrative system.[51] It means that ministries have shifted away from operational matters and generally focus on providing guidance on policy, as well as on performance and

45 Chapter 6, Section 1, first paragraph, PL.

46 Section 13 AML Regulation in conjunction with Section 1 *Förordning med instruktion för Finansinspektionen*, SFS 2009:93 (in English: *Regulation with instructions for Finansinspektionen*). Hereafter 'FI Regulation'. More about the AML coordination body can be found in § 7.10.

47 Section 28 Estate Agents Act.

48 Chapter 1, Section 2, under 10 PL.

49 See § 2.4.2.1 and 2.4.2.2.

50 De Meij, J.M. (2014), *The Kingdom of Sweden*, in: Besselink, L., Bovend'Eert, P., Broeksteeg, H., De Lange, R. and Voermans, W. (eds.), *Constitutional Law of the EU Member States*, Kluwer: Deventer, pp. 1589-1648 at 1614-16; Nergelius (2011) at 87 et seq.; Molander, P., Nilsson J.E., and Schick, A. (2002), *Does anyone govern? The relationship between the Government Office and the agencies in Sweden*, Report from the SNS Constitutional Project, at 6.

51 Niklasson, B. (2012), 'Sweden', in: Verhoest, K., Van Thiel, S., Bouckaert, G. and Lægreid, P. (eds.), *Government Agencies: Practices in Lessons from 30 Countries*, pp. 245-258 at 246 and 248.

results, and holding authorities accountable for meeting the predetermined objectives.[52] The administrative authorities, in the literature also called agencies, have a large degree of discretion in managing their own resources and taking their own decisions. The political independence of administrative authorities is a fundamental principle in Swedish law. Already in 1953 Herlitz pointed out that in Sweden '[g]enerally speaking, State authorities have a more independent position than in other countries'.[53] The independence of the administrative authorities is laid down in the Instrument of Government (IG), which is one of the four fundamental laws of Sweden.[54]

> Together with the Act of Succession, the Freedom of the Press Act and the Fundamental Law on Freedom of Expression, the Instrument of Government forms the 'Swedish Constitutional heritage'. The Instrument of Government deals with the way in which Sweden is to be governed. It is divided into thirteen chapters and contains rules on the realisation of democracy in Sweden and on the division of power between the Riksdag, the Government, municipalities and county councils and courts. It also sets out the fundamental rights and freedoms enjoyed by the people of Sweden.[55]

Chapter 12, Section 2 IG states that no public authority, including Parliament, or decision-making body of any local authority, may determine how an administrative authority shall decide in a particular case relating to the exercise of public authority vis-à-vis an individual or a local authority, or relating to the application of the law.[56] Administrative authorities, in settling individual cases, are bound to observe Chapter 1, Section 9 IG, which determines that courts of law, administrative authorities and others performing public administration functions shall have regard in their work to the equality of all before the law and shall observe objectivity and impartiality.

> According to Nergelius the foregoing means that '(...), ministers do normally not have the power to interfere in the work of public authorities or give detailed instructions to civil servants, though general political guidelines are of course allowed'.[57] He also states that '[o]nly if the minister has known for some time about problems in specific bodies without reacting or doing anything about them (something that was actually discussed in relation to those events) may the minister be held legally or politically accountable'.[58]

Next to the Instrument of Government, the institutional framework of administrative authorities is complemented by the General Authorities Regulation 2007:515, by instruction regulations that apply to each individual administrative authority, as

52 Cf. De Meij (2014) at 1614.
53 Herlitz, N. (1953), 'Swedish Administrative Law', *International and Comparative Law Quarterly*, vol. 2, pp. 224-237 at 225. Cf. Molander et al. (2002) at 11-12.
54 *Regeringsformen*, SFS 1974:152.
55 See for more information about the Instrument of Government: Nergelius (2011) at 13, 24-25.
56 Cf. De Meij (2014) at 1616; Niklasson (2012) at 248.
57 Nergelius (2011) at 85. Cf. Chapter 12, Section 1 IG which states that independent authorities are subordinate to the Government.
58 Ibid., at 85. It should in this context be pointed out that normally ministerial responsibility for the functioning of independent administrative authorities to Parliament is a collective responsibility of the Government. This feature of the Swedish constitutional system precludes individual ministerial responsibility, because ministers do not have individual decision-making powers under the Instrument of Government: Chapter 7, Section 3 IG. Cf. De Meij (2014) at 1615.

well as annual appropriation letters from the Government (*Regleringsbrev*).[59] Annual appropriation letters contain assignments from the Government concerning the goals that an administrative authority should attain in a particular year, how it should report on this, and they specify the budget.[60] Instruction regulations are regulations that specify the main task of an authority and its form of management.[61] They 'fix objectives, and are the centrepiece of the agency's relationship with its parent ministry. They undergo, just like other draft proposals for laws and ordinances, a joint drafting procedure, *i.e.* consultation with other ministries, and the agency itself is also consulted. They are usually quite short, and will include some specifics, such as reporting requirements (which are also often found in appropriation directions)'.[62] Together with these instruments, 'the main instrument available to Government when it comes to steering its public administration is thus the formulation of laws regarding the policy area and instructions'.[63] The Instrument of Government, the General Authorities Regulation, instruction regulations and annual appropriation letters frame the accountability relationships between administrative authorities, their parent ministry and the competent Minister. The exact modality differs per authority.

7.4.2 Financial Supervisory Authority (*Finansinspektionen*)

7.4.2.1 Institutional embedding

The Financial Supervisory Authority (hereafter also FI or 'the Authority') is the Swedish single and integrated regulator for the financial markets. It is a central administrative authority set at a distance from the Ministry of Finance.[64] Its role is to promote stability and efficiency in the financial system as well as to ensure effective consumer protection.[65] It is responsible for the authorisation of financial and credit institutions and it supervises all institutions operating on the Swedish financial markets. It also registers and supervises financial and credit institutions that are not required to be authorised under Swedish legislation, such as currency exchange offices and money remitters. Regarding the promotion of a stable financial system, it shares responsibility with the Swedish Central Bank.[66]

59 *Myndighetsförordningen*, SFS 2007:515.

60 Niklasson (2012) at 252.

61 Ibid., at 245.

62 OECD (2010), *Better Regulation in Europe: Sweden*, at 78, available at: <www.oecd.org/gov/regulatory-policy/45419072.pdf>, last visited on 27 March 2014.

63 Niklasson (2012) at 248.

64 Oliver Wyman (2013), *Organisational effectiveness of financial sector regulators – Benchmarking results: Swedish Financial Supervisory Authority*, at 8, available at: <www.fi.se/upload/10_Om%20FI/10_Verksamhet/undersokningar/effektivitet-tillsynsmyndigheter-internationellt-2013.pdf>, last visited on 28 March 2014.

65 Section 2 FI Regulation.

66 Memorandum of Understanding between Finansinspektionen and the Riksbank concerning a council for cooperation on macro-prudential policy, 17 January 2012, available at: <www.riksbank.se/Documents/Beslutsunderlag/2012/bes_overenskommelse_om_samverkansrad_for_makrotillsyn_120117_eng_revised_120306.pdf>, last visited on 28 March 2014.

Within the Authority supervision is carried out by three operating divisions: Banks, Insurance & Investment funds, and Markets.[67] These divisions take into account aspects of AML obligations during regular supervisory procedures. The extent to which they integrate AML obligations in their regular supervision varies. Under the Markets (*Marknader*) division a special anti-money laundering unit (*Enheten Penningtvätt*) operates.[68] This unit is the expertise body within the Financial Supervisory Authority concerning matters related to money laundering. The unit provides advice to the regular supervisory teams if they have specific questions, it performs (thematic) AML supervision itself, it takes care of international cooperation on this matter, and it is responsible for heading the AML coordination body.[69] The AML supervision of banks is thus carried out by inspectors from the banks operating division within regular supervisory procedures, and by inspectors from the AML unit. With respect to human resources the national risk assessment 2013 spoke of an estimated three to four FTEs for money laundering supervision at the Authority.[70] FI's company register indicates a total of 155 authorised banks for which it has supervisory responsibility.[71] The budget for AML supervision is unknown, as this is entirely integrated into FI's overall budget.[72]

7.4.2.2 *Political independence and accountability*

The Financial Supervisory Authority is a central administrative authority (*styrelsemyndighet*), operating within the limits set by the Government.[73] It is accountable to the Government via the Ministry of Finance, and ultimately to Parliament.[74] Its legal framework consists most prominently of the BFBA, the Obligation to Notify Certain Financial Operations Act,[75] the Deposit Taking Operations Act,[76] and the instruction regulation to the Financial Supervisory Authority and annual appropriation letters. FI is required to act pursuant to a Government assignment (*Regeringsuppdrag*) as well.[77]

67 Finansinspektionen, *Organisation*, available at <www.fi.se/Om-FI/Organisation/>, last visited on 28 March 2014.

68 More specifically under the subdivision 'Uppförande- och infrastrukturtillsyn': Interview Finansinspektionen, October 2013.

69 Section 15 AML Regulation.

70 Finansinspektionen et al. (2013) at 16. Cf. Interview Finansinspektionen, October 2013.

71 FI's Company Register, available at <www.fi.se/Folder-EN/Startpage/Register/Company-register/Company-register-Company-per-category/?typ='BANK++","MBANK+","SPAR++","FILB++'>, last visited on 28 March 2014; Cf. Interview Finansinspektionen, October 2013 and FATF (2006a) at 15.

72 All that is known is that in 2013 the Government provided 4.5 million SEK (app. 510,000 Euros, exchange rate 05/02/2014) to Finansinspektionen for the AML coordination body; this money cannot be spent by FI on its supervisory activities: *Regleringsbrev 2013 Myndighet Finansinspektionen*, 20 December 2012, Fi2012/852, Fi2012/2204, Fi2012/2345 (in English: *Appropriation for the year 2013 concerning Finansinspektionen*). In 2014, the Government increased the budget to 5 million SEK (app. 566,000 Euros, exchange rate 05/02/2014): *Regleringsbrev 2014 Myndighet Finansinspektionen*, 19 December 2013, Fi2013/2853, Fi2013/3226, Fi2013/3404.

73 Section 8 FI Regulation.

74 Section 3 FI Regulation lists a number of reports through which FI must give account to the Government. FI's website indicates that it is accountable to the Ministry of Finance, available at: <www.fi.se/Folder-EN/Startpage/About-FI/>, last visited on 28 March 2014.

75 *Lag om anmälningsplikt avseende viss finansiell verksamhet*, SFS 1996:1006.

76 *Lag om inlåningsverksamhet*, SFS 2004:299.

77 One example of a *Regeringsuppdrag* to Finansinspektionen is the national risk assessment. Supra, n. 6.

The Authority's (political) independence was evaluated by the IMF in 2011, which concluded that its operational independence was not adequately safeguarded.[78] Firstly, the IMF found that the Government could influence FI's supervisory agenda via the annual appropriation letters. As explained above, these letters – together with the instruction regulation – outline the general objectives of the operations and assignments to the Financial Supervisory Authority. At the same time it is a way for the Government to regulate the budget. The budget stemming from the Government is very important, as reflected in FI's annual plan for 2013: the Government's contribution is over 80% of the total budget.[79] According to the IMF, FI 'needs operational independence in being able to set its priorities, make day to day decisions, allocate resources, and to establish a supervisory strategy with a long term horizon. The annual appropriations letter can be amended with updated requests during the year and contains tasks and priorities for FI, thus introducing a degree of uncertainty or even directly impeding FI's ability to plan and execute a supervisory program'.[80] Secondly, the IMF assessed the duality in the powers for the Authority and the Government with respect to the issuance or revocation of (banking) licences. The IMF stated that this created a possibility for the Government to be involved in individual supervisory decisions and recommended that this duality should be removed. The Swedish legislator followed up on this point of criticism.[81] Thirdly, the IMF was concerned by the lack of adequate resources on the side of the Financial Supervisory Authority.[82] It found it troublesome that despite an increase in the levels of funding in recent years, FI would still be too resource-constrained to deliver minimum levels of supervision.[83] In the autumn of 2011 the Government consequently announced that the Authority would receive an increase in resources of around 11.3 million Euros spread over three years.[84]

The IMF's criticism of letters of appropriation is not shared by the OECD. In 2010 the OECD reported that the Swedish Government 'can only influence policy implementation through general prescriptions to the agencies. Each agency has a high degree of freedom in choosing how to use their resources to achieve the results demanded by the government. But they are accountable to the parent ministry on the delivery of results compared with objectives, which is considered a powerful incentive for agency heads to perform well'.[85] On the annual appropriation letters, it stated briefly that '[o]ver 200 of the 447 government agencies regulated by ordinances have annual appropriation directions. These set out

78 IMF (2011b), *Sweden: Financial Sector Assessment Program Update – Detailed Assessment of Observance on Basel Core Principles for Effective Banking Supervision*, IMF Country Report No. 11/281.

79 Finansinspektionen (2013a), *Overall operations plan and internal budget 2013*, Ref.13-48, at 14: out of 432 million SEK, 350 million SEK stems from income via letters of appropriation. At the time of finalising this chapter, the plan for 2014 had not yet been published.

80 IMF (2011b) at 11.

81 *Regeringens Proposition* 2012/13:95 (*Government Bill*). In July 2013 amendments to the Banking and Financing Business Act entered into force. The amendments removed the Government's decision-making powers in the banking and insurance fields and completely transferred this power to Finansinspektionen: *Lag om ändring i lagen (2004:297) om bank- och finansieringsrörelse*, SFS 2013:455; Amendments to Chapter 3, Section 8a BFBA.

82 Cf. Andersson et al. (2013) at 34.

83 IMF (2011b) at 11.

84 Finansinspektionen (2013a) at 14. (11,326,568 Euros, exchange rate 05/02/2014).

85 OECD (2010) at 78.

the goals of each agency, activities, the economic resources at its disposal, and how the funds are to be divided between different operational areas, as well as references to Better Regulation'.[86] Moreover, Niklasson observes that 'the agencies are (…) normally highly involved in the drafting of these letters'.[87] She also states that '[w]ithin the framework set by the instruction and the letter of allocation, Swedish agencies enjoy a high degree of strategic- and operational-managerial autonomy'.[88]

The letter of appropriation 2013 provides a highly transparent and clear framework on its goals and tasks, and the detailed corresponding reporting requirements in order to give accountability on the activities performed. The letter of appropriation 2013 was first issued in December 2012,[89] and amended in March 2013[90] and June 2013.[91] Changes to appropriation letters are not made every year: in the year 2012, for example, no changes were made.[92] The fact that the Government issues publicly disclosed letters of appropriation annually in which it stipulates the main objectives and allocates tasks and reporting requirements to the Financial Supervisory Authority cannot, in light of the theoretical framework of effective supervision, be regarded as too intrusive for the political independence of the supervisory authority. Looking at the content of the letters of appropriation, the instructions are of a general nature and do not involve case-by-case decision making, although – admittedly – it is not excluded that continuous changes to the letters of appropriation might ultimately have this effect.[93] It should also be borne in mind, as Niklasson mentions, that the Financial Supervisory Authority is consulted in the course of the preparation of the appropriation letter and that it can influence the Government's decisions. This, together with the fact that the Swedish Government followed up on the IMF's points of concern regarding duality in power and resources, as well as the fact that independence is guaranteed by the Instrument of Government, leads to the conclusion that FI has an adequate degree of (operational) political independence. The Government, ministers or Parliament cannot influence or modify individual decisions by the Authority. It thus operates at a distance from the political arena. The fact that the Government is empowered by law to give general instructions via an instruction regulation and annual appropriation letters does not detract from this finding.

Legislation on the accountability of the Financial Supervisory Authority to the Government in general does not exist. Nevertheless, clear accountability mechanisms

86 Ibid., at 78.

87 Niklasson (2012) at 252.

88 Ibid.

89 *Regleringsbrev för budgetåret 2013 avseende Finansinspektionen*, Fi2012/852, Fi2012/2204 Fi2012/2345, 20 December 2012.

90 One task added: *Regleringsbrev för budgetåret 2013 avseende Finansinspektionen*, Fi2013/945, 7 March 2013.

91 Specification of a reporting obligation as well as the postponement of the date of submission of the reporting obligation concerning a task: *Regleringsbrev för budgetåret 2013 avseende Finansinspektionen*, Fi2013/2264, 19 June 2013.

92 *Regleringsbrev för budgetåret 2012 avseende Finansinspektionen*, 22 December 2011, Fi2011/1391 Fi2011/4700; Fi2011/5283.

93 This would, however, require a detailed analysis of FI's independence which goes beyond the scope of this research.

are in place. As mentioned, the appropriation letters contain specific instructions with dates on which specific reports must be submitted to the Government and the aspects which must at least be included in these reports. Also the instruction regulation provides a number of obligations concerning FI's accountability vis-à-vis the Government. Section 3 FI regulation stipulates that FI must report to the Government each year by the 15th of April on the costs of the fees for the financing of its operations.[94] It also stipulates that by the 15th of April and the 1st of October each year FI must present proposals for changes with respect to the fees, in respect of past or future regulatory changes at the Authority. The third reporting obligation concerns the obligation for the Financial Supervisory Authority to report by the 1st of June each year in order to account for the authority's experience in the financial supervision of financial stability and consumer protection in the past year and indicate the need for the development of rules in FI's field of activities.[95] Finally, the instruction regulation obliges FI to annually provide the Government with a comprehensive assessment of risks in the financial area where risks to financial stability and consumer protection are shown separately.[96] FI publishes its annual plans and annual reports.[97] In the reports it describes and evaluates the activities during that year, including the cost-effectiveness.[98] The wide variety of reporting obligations stemming from the appropriation letters and the instruction regulation provide the accountability framework from FI to the Government, and the accompanying levels of transparency demonstrate that an adequate accountability structure is in place for FI in order to balance its political independence.

Regarding the preventive AML policy specifically, the instruction regulation does not contain a specific reporting obligation. The annual appropriation letters can instruct the Financial Supervisory Authority to report on the preventive AML policy. The appropriation letter for the year 2012 required FI to describe the actions and results of the work of the AML coordination body. In the annual reports 2012 and 2013 the Authority reported on the number of meetings held in that year, about the organisation of two two-day conferences and on an information campaign.[99] The appropriation for the year 2012 also required a report on the reporting of suspicious transactions to the FIU by obliged institutions and professionals under the AML Act. This instruction could also be found in the appropriation letter for the year 2011 and a follow-up was also required in the appropriation letter for the year 2013.[100] These special reports do not only deal with FI's activities, but also include the activities of all other anti-money laundering supervisors.

94 *Förordning om avgifter för prövning av ärenden hos Finansinspektionen*, SFS 2001:911; and *Förordning om årliga avgifter för finansiering av Finansinspektionens verksamhet*, SFS 2007:1135.

95 Finansinspektionen (2013).

96 Finansinspektionen (2012), *Risks in the financial system 2012*, Dnr 12-12020.

97 Finansinspektionen (2013a).

98 Finansinspektionen (2012a), *Årsredovisning 2012*, Dnr 13-1321; Finansinspektionen (2013b), *Årsredovisning 2013*, Dnr 14-1728.

99 Finansinspektionen (2012a) at 35; Finansinspektionen (213b) at 46.

100 Finansinspektionen (2012b), *Redovisning av uppdrag: Redovisning av Finansinspektionens insatser för att öka rapporteringen till Rikspolisstyrelsen, Fi2010/4920, Fi2010/5063, Fi2010/5322 och Fi2010/5790 (delvis)*, Dnr 12-2798. The annual appropriation letter for 2013 indicated that the Finansinspektionen had to report about the follow-up to this report: Finansinspektionen (2013c), *Redovisning av uppdrag: Uppföljning av rapporten Finansinspektionens insatser för att öka rapporteringen till Rikspolisstyrelsen*, Dnr 13-2864.

This means that this reporting obligation stemming from the annual appropriations to the Financial Supervisory Authority also serves as an indirect reporting obligation for the other AML supervisors.[101] The annual appropriation letters for 2011-13 do not require FI to report about its supervisory activities and any sanctions imposed under the AML Act. The annual appropriation letter for 2014 also does not include a reference to its supervisory responsibility under the preventive AML policy. Although this can in my opinion be regarded as a weak aspect of the accountability structure, this does not mean that the Financial Supervisory Authority never reports about its AML supervision. As instructed in the annual appropriation letter for 2009, the Financial Supervisory Authority reported specifically on the exercise and prioritisation of its AML supervision, and it accounted for the time spent on supervision and the costs involved.[102] The Authority also reports about its AML supervisory efforts on a more voluntary basis. For example, FI's Supervision Report 2013 mentions a few supervisory efforts in the field of the prevention of money laundering.[103] Some specific reports detail its supervisory experience in relation to the preventive AML regime.[104]

If the reports from FI are found to be unsatisfactory, the Government has some limited powers to take action against the Financial Supervisory Authority. Being a board authority *(styrelsemyndighet)* the Authority is headed by a Board of Directors, which consists of ten members, and the Director-General who is the head of the authority.[105] Pursuant to the Authorities Regulation 2007:515, which applies to all central administrative authorities, the Government has the power to appoint the members of the Board of Directors and the Director General of the central administrative authorities.[106] The Government may also appoint the Chairman of the Board of Directors, as well as the vice-chairman.[107] Niklasson states that 'the government's exclusive right to appoint directors general is one way of ensuring that there is a common understanding between political and the administrative top levels'.[108] In the case of the Financial Supervisory Authority, the members of the Board of Directors are selected by the Ministry of Finance.[109] The Director-General is appointed for a period of six years, whereas the Board members are appointed for a minimum of three years.[110] The Government may decide to remove the Director-General from office before the end of the six-year term, but only if he commits a form of misconduct or has a disability impairing the performance of the authority, as defined by law.[111] Where the head of an administrative authority is removed from office, the reasons must be publicly

101 See § 7.7 to 7.9.

102 Finansinspektionen (2010), *Redovisning av Finansinspektionens penningtvättstillsyn*, FI Dnr 10-1002. (in English: *Report on Finansinspektionen's anti-money laundering supervision*).

103 Finansinspektionen (2013) at 18-19.

104 Finansinspektionen (2013d), *Penningtvätt och finansiering av terrorism: En bättre riskhantering*, Dnr 13-4387; Finansinspektionen (2006), *Money Laundering and Terrorist Financing – preventive measures in the finance sector*, Report 2007:17 (summary).

105 Sections 8, 9 and 13 FI Regulation and Section 2 Authorities Regulation.

106 Sections 10, 22 and 23 Authorities Regulation.

107 Section 22 Authorities Regulation; Section 12 FI Regulation.

108 Niklasson (2012) at 255.

109 Oliver Wyman (2013) at 8.

110 IMF (2011b) at 28.

111 Ibid., 27.

disclosed. This intervention mechanism for the Government could be applied where FI severely neglects its duties under the AML Act, but should be applied with great constraint.

7.4.2.3 Market independence and accountability

Overall, Sweden has a strong tradition of transparency and documents from administrative authorities are in principle public in nature.[112] The Freedom of the Press Act applies to every document that is in the possession of administrative authorities and fosters public control over the administration.[113] The right of access to official documents may, however, be restricted if it is necessary for the inspection, control or other supervisory activities of an administrative authority.[114]

The relationship between the Financial Supervisory Authority and the institutions subject to its supervision only concerns financial aspects. They are required to pay fees to the Authority, although this relationship is not as strong as in other Member States.[115] Only roughly 20% of the budget stems from fees levied on institutions subject to its supervision. In its annual reports FI accounts for the spending of its budget. The annual reports are public documents, hence the financial and credit institutions subject to FI's supervision and regulation can access this document. Neither legislation or regulations, nor information stemming from reports or the website of the Authority indicate the existence of panels in which representatives of financial and credit institutions participate. The foregoing leads to the finding that the Authority is adequately independent from the market.

7.4.3 Estate Agents Inspectorate (*Fastighetsmäklarinspektionen*)

7.4.3.1 Institutional embedding

The Swedish Estate Agents Inspectorate (hereafter also FMI or 'the Inspectorate') is the central administrative authority responsible for the registration and supervision of real estate agents in order to ensure compliance with their obligations under the Estate Agents Act.[116] FMI keeps registers of the agents who are registered with it and of those who have faced disciplinary action. It deals with matters of disciplinary action against real estate agents as well. Because FMI is a consumer authority it has responsibility for informing

112 Herlitz (1953) at 227-228.

113 Ibid., at 228.

114 Chapter 2, Section 2, paragraph 3 Freedom of the Press Act. The Swedish Public Access to Information and Secrecy Act details the provisions contained in the Freedom of the Press Act on the right to obtain official documents.

115 *Förordning om avgifter för prövning av ärenden hos Finansinspektionen*, SFS 2001:911; and *Förordning om årliga avgifter för finansiering av Finansinspektionens verksamhet*, SFS 2007:1135. Compare, for example, with the UK Financial Conduct Authority which is fully subsidised by fees paid by financial and credit institutions.

116 Section 28 Estate Agents Act 2011 and Section 1 *Förordning med instruktion för Fastighetsmäklarinspektionen*, SFS 2009:606 (in English: *Regulation concerning instructions for the Estate Agents Inspectorate*). Hereafter 'FMI Regulation'. The FMI Regulation was amended in order to change the name of the Authority: *Förordning om ändring i förordningen (2009:606) med instruktion för Fastighetsmäklarnämnden*, SFS 2012:25.

consumers and estate agents about the content of estate agents' services and to promote sound estate agency practice.[117] Consumers can complain to the Inspectorate when they consider that an estate agent has acted incorrectly.

> *Fastighetsmäklarinspektionen* received its current name in August 2012. Before that, it was called the Board of Supervision of Estate Agents (*Fastighetsmäklarnämnden*). The change was at the instigation of the Inspectorate, which found that the new name would do more justice to its regulatory and enforcement tasks.[118] In 2010 the Government had tasked the Swedish Agency for Public Management to investigate the functioning of the Board of Supervision of Estate Agents.[119] The analysis uncovered a number of internal and external factors that affected its functioning. One factor that hampered an effective exercise of supervision was the limited formulation of the Estate Agents Act in terms of powers for the Board. The report was one of the reasons why the Government drafted a new Estate Agents Act, which repealed the Estate Agents Act 1995. On the 1st of July 2011 the new Act entered into force.[120] It did not change the basic principles of its predecessor, but included a codification of the practice since 1995 and introduced some new requirements in order to strengthen consumer protection. The Act, for example, introduced new transparency and information requirements for estate agents to better inform buyers and sellers as well as requirements regarding the education and training of estate agents.

AML supervision is part of the general supervisory activities carried out by FMI and is based on two tracks. It is a small organisation and there is no single division that works on AML supervision specifically. At the end of 2013, 18 people worked at FMI.[121] In 2011 the size of the authority was the same and representatives indicated at that time that two people worked part time on AML supervision and related matters.[122] The Inspectorate's budget for 2013 was approximately 1.95 million Euros and the annual report indicates that FMI spent a little over 900,000 Euros on supervision during that year.[123] In 2013, there were 6,591 fully registered estate agents.[124]

7.4.3.2 Independence and accountability

The Inspectorate is a central administrative authority (*enrådighetsmyndighet*), headed by an agency head (*myndighetschef*).[125] Its parent ministry is the Ministry of Justice. However, the responsible Minister is the Minister for EU Affairs, who is attached to the Prime

117 Section 2 FMI Regulation.

118 Fastighetsmäklarinspektionen, *Fastighetsmäklarinspektionen blir tydligare*, pressmeddelande 120801, 31 July 2012, available at <www.fmi.se/default.aspx?id=8346>, last visited on 28 March 2014.

119 Statskontoret (2010), *Myndighetsanalys av Fastighetsmäklarnämnden*, Report 2010:18 (in English: *Public-agency analysis of the Swedish Board of Supervision of Estate Agents*).

120 Fastighetsmäklarlag, SFS 2011:666. The Act is accompanied by a Regulation: *Fastighetsmäklarförordning*, SFS 2011:668. Hereafter 'Estate Agents Regulation'.

121 Fastighetsmäklarinspektionen (2013), Årsredovisning 2013, at 12 (in English: *Annual report 2013*).

122 Interview Fastighetsmäklarnämnden, April 2011; Cf. Finansinspektionen et al. (2013) at 17.

123 The budget was 17.2 million SEK as indicated in *Regleringsbrev för budgetåret 2013 avseende Fastighetsmäklarinspektionen*, Ju2012/7931/KO and Ju2012/7905/KO, 13 December 2012. The exact amount is 1,948,169 Euros (exchange rate, 05/02/2014). The annual report 2013 indicates that 7,965,000 SEK (902,161 Euros, exchange rate 05/02/2014) was spent on supervision; Fastighetsmäklarinspektionen (2013) at 29.

124 Fastighetsmäklarinspektionen (2013) at 21.

125 Section 5 FMI Regulation.

Minister's Office.[126] The reason for this construction is that the Minister for EU Affairs is responsible for consumer affairs. Because the Prime Minister's Office is not a ministry, FMI is placed under the Ministry of Justice.[127]

Section 7.4.1 indicated that the independence of administrative authorities is a fundamental principle in Swedish law and in general terms is regulated in the Instrument of Government. This means that FMI's independence is, in principle, safeguarded. In terms of operational independence, the same discussion exists as for the Financial Supervisory Authority. Via FMI's instruction regulation and the annual letters of appropriation the Government provides the general framework under which the Inspectorate operates. The instruction regulation does not provide any reporting obligations that constitute an accountability framework vis-à-vis the Government. The Estate Agents Act and the Estate Agents Regulation remain silent on this matter too. The appropriation letters contain the goals and tasks of FMI, as well as detailed corresponding reporting requirements in order to account for the activities performed. The annual appropriation letters can be amended throughout the year, although in the years 2010-2013 this happened only once. The appropriation for 2013 contains the following goals and assignments and corresponding reporting requirements: FMI is required to make forecasts for the years 2013-17, it must develop a strategy for its supervisory and sanctioning activities as well as the monitoring and evaluation of that strategy, and it must develop a strategy for its communication efforts.[128] In the appropriation letters for the years 2010-2014, not a single reference is made to the activities under the AML Act. The appropriation for 2014 is shorter and only refers to the forecasts.[129] Seemingly on its own motion, FMI publishes annual reports. In these reports it describes how it has conducted its work in relation to the instructions received from the Government, provides statistics, and accounts for the budget and expenditures of the authority.[130] The annual reports are public documents and FMI always pays attention to its activities under the AML Act.[131] Besides, FMI publishes sanctioning yearbooks, so-called årsbocken. These yearbooks publish all decisions by the FMI's Disciplinary Board, including cases concerning non-compliance with AML obligations. Indirectly via the annual appropriation letters 2011-13 to the Financial Supervisory Authority, FMI accounts for the exercise of AML supervision to the Government as well.[132]

The foregoing indicates that the political independence of FMI is adequately safeguarded. The letters of appropriation by the Government contain very broad tasks and reporting obligations for FMI and do not seem to impair the individual decision-making procedures

126 Government Offices of Sweden, *Consumer Affairs*, available at: <www.government.se/sb/d/2112/a/66269>, last visited on 19 February 2014.

127 Interview Fastighetsmäklarinspektionen, August 2013.

128 *Regleringsblev för budgetåret 2013 avseende Fastighetsmäklarinspektionen*, Ju2012/7931/KO and Ju2012/7905/KO, 13 December 2012.

129 *Regleringsblev för budgetåret 2014 avseende Fastighetsmäklarinspektionen*, Ju2013/8523/KO and Ju2013/8661/KO(part), 19 December 2013.

130 Fastighetsmäklarinspektionen, *Årsredovisningen*, available at: <www.fmi.se/default.aspx?id=1912>, last visited on 24 March 2014.

131 FMI's annual reports of 2010, 2011, 2012 and 2013 all contain a considerable amount of information on the activities of FMI in the field of supervision and sanctioning under the PL.

132 See § 7.4.2.2.

and day-to-day activities of the Inspectorate. It is not excluded that regular changes in the letters may ultimately have such an effect, but since 2010 this has only happened once. There are some reporting requirements in place that regulate an accountability framework from FMI to the Government, although these specific obligations only stem from the appropriation letters and not from the law or the instruction regulation. Accountability with respect to FMI's supervisory responsibility under the preventive AML policy is not required by annual appropriation letters, although in practice it publishes annual reports.

A way by which the Government can interfere with FMI when it is not satisfied about the Inspectorate's work concerns the appointment and removal of the agency head and members of the Disciplinary Board. FMI is headed by an Agency head, who is appointed by the Government.[133] Furthermore, the organisation of FMI includes a Disciplinary Board. The Board consists of a chairman, a deputy chairman and not more than six other members and four substitutes.[134] The Chairman of the Disciplinary Board is the Head of FMI. The other members (and deputies) of the Disciplinary Committee are appointed by the Government as well.[135] This power can in theory be used when the Government is dissatisfied with FMI's work under the AML Act, but is to be used with great restraint as explained in relation to the Financial Supervisory Authority above.

In terms of market independence, the only direct relationship between FMI and the estate agents that can be identified is a financial relationship. Estate agents are required to pay fees upon registration as well as annual fees. The amount of the fees is regulated in the Estate Agents Regulation.[136] FMI accounts for its expenditures through the publication of the annual reports. In interviews, the Inspectorate indicated that it cooperates with the branch associations for estate agents in Sweden: the Inspectorate meets twice a year with these organisations to discuss the most outstanding matters in the regulation of estate agents in Sweden.[137] Neither legislation nor any other information indicates the existence of panels of representatives or like bodies at FMI.

7.4.4 Supervisory Board of Public Auditors (*Revisorsnämnden*)

7.4.4.1 Auditing and the accountancy profession

In section 7.5.3 we will see that in Sweden auditing is the only regulated activity and that this is not the case for the wider accountancy profession. This is not uncommon, as the same holds for Spain and the United Kingdom.[138] What makes this situation special is that it makes a difference for AML supervision. Under the previous legal regime accountants did not fall under the scope of the AML legislation, while auditors did.[139] In order to follow up the recommendations from the FATF and to implement the Third Directive

133 Section 23 Authorities Regulation.
134 Section 6(2) FMI Regulation; Fastighetsmäklarinspektionen (2013).
135 Section 8 FMI Regulation.
136 Sections 7 and 8 Estate Agents Regulation.
137 Interview Fastighetsmäklarnämnden, April 2011.
138 § 4.5.3 and 6.5.4.
139 FATF (2006a) at 119.

in full, accountants and accountancy firms that are not approved or authorised public auditors were also brought under the scope of the AML Act. The Supervisory Board of Public Auditors, responsible for the AML supervision of auditors, did not become the supervisor of the wider accountancy profession. Rather, as recommended by the Swedish Agency for Public Management, the county administrative boards became responsible for the AML supervision of accountants not being auditors.[140] They have supervisory responsibility for those accountants or accountancy firms that have registered with the Swedish Companies Registration Office in accordance with the AML Act. If they have not done so, no supervisory jurisdiction for the county administrative boards exists either.[141]

This section is about the Supervisory Board of Public Auditors, being the supervisor of approved or authorised public auditors and audit firms, while section 7.4.5 is about three county administrative boards in their role as AML supervisors for other accountants and accountancy firms.

7.4.4.2 Institutional embedding

The Supervisory Board for Public Auditors (hereafter also RN or 'the Board') is a central administrative authority (*nämndmyndighet*). It is responsible for matters relating to the authorisation, approval or registration of auditors and audit firms, supervision, disciplinary actions, and for the development of ethics and generally accepted auditing standards.[142] The Board is headed by a director who is appointed by the Government for a six-year term and who is accountable to the Government for the Board's activities.[143] The Regulatory Board (*Tillsynsnämnden*) is the decision-making body of RN. It is composed of nine members appointed by the Government for a period of three years.[144] It decides on the regulations, matters of disciplinary action and other matters of principal importance to the Board. Due to its competence under the Auditors Act, it is the competent supervisor under the AML Act.[145]

AML supervision is fully integrated into the Board's quality auditing system. According to the national risk assessment, 'the periodic quality checks include examining the obliged institutions at the enterprise level, their systems and internal procedures to deal with money laundering matters' (*own translation, MB*).[146] The Board has supervisory responsibility for approximately 4,000 auditors and audit firms. In March 2014 the number of authorised and approved auditors was 3,865, plus 148 audit firms.[147] RN has

140 Statskontoret (2008), *Tredje penningtvättsdirektivet – tillsyn och organisation*, 2008:2.

141 See § 7.5.3.1 and 7.9.3 for difficulties related to this finding.

142 Section 3 Auditors Act.

143 Sections 2 and 7 Förordning *med instruktion för Revisorsnämnden*, SFS 2007:1077 (in English: *Regulation with instructions to the Supervisory Board of Public Auditors*). Hereafter 'RN Instruction'. See also Section 8 RN Instruction.

144 Section 8 RN Instruction. Information also available at <www.revisorsnamnden.se>.

145 Chapter 1, § 2, under 10 PL.

146 Finansinspektionen et al. (2013) at 17.

147 Revisorsnämnden (2014), *Auktoriserade och godkända revisorer samt registrerade revisionsbolag 2014-03-03*, available at: <www.revisorsnamnden.se/rn/showdocument/documents/statistik/lopande/statistik_140303.pdf>, last visited on 28 March 2014.

six legal officers and six authorized or approved auditors to carry out audits and including anti-money laundering supervision.[148] It appears, however, that a large number of quality audits are carried out by the professional association of auditors and accountants, called the FAR *(Branschorganisation för redovisningskonsulter, revisorer & rådgivare)*.[149] Pursuant to an arrangement, FAR performs inspections on auditors and audit firms that do not audit listed companies and are members of FAR. The Board oversees this supervision on a systematic basis. FAR has the duty to report material breaches of auditing standards or professional ethics to the Board.[150]

7.4.4.3 Independence and accountability

The Supervisory Board of Public Auditors operates under the Ministry of Justice. As with the other central administrative authorities, its political independence is constitutionally embedded in the Instrument of Government.[151] The Government gives general instructions to the Board via the instruction regulation and annual appropriation letters. The instruction regulation does not lay down any reporting obligations. The annual appropriation letters for 2010-2014 instruct the Supervisory Board of Public Auditors to provide information on:

- the number of applications received;
- the number of decisions on the approval, authorization and registration;
- the number of decisions made in total;
- the number of disciplinary cases brought during the year – how many of those are started on its own initiative and how many can be attributed to the periodic quality control and systematic outreach inspections;
- the number of opened and closed cases decided within the framework of different projects in the systematic outreach inspections;
- the number of open enforcement cases at the end of the year – divided into disciplinary matters and other enforcement cases, and more.[152]

None of the appropriation letters refer to the supervisory responsibility under the AML Act. Understanding that AML supervision is integrated in the general quality audits, it is likely that this, too, is integrated in the figures presented by RN to the Government under its annual appropriations. The annual appropriation letters do not indicate any

148 Ibid., at 17.

149 According to its website: 'FAR is the professional institute for authorized public accountants (*auktoriserade revisorer*), approved public accountants (*godkände revisorer*), and other highly qualified professionals in the accountancy sector in Sweden, available at: <www.far.se/In-English/>, last visited on 28 March 2014.

150 Revisorsnämnden, *The supervisory system in Sweden*, available at: <www.revisorsnamnden.se/rn/english/supervision.html>, last visited on 28 March 2014.

151 De Meij (2014) at 1616. See § 7.4.1.

152 *Regleringsbrev för budgetåret 2010 avseende Revisorsnämnden*, 21 December 2009, Ju2009/10262/DOM; *Regleringsbrev för budgetåret 2011 avseende Revisorsnämnden*, 22 December 2010, Ju2010/9447/DOM, Ju2010/2513/DOM; *Regleringsbrev för budgetåret 2012 avseende Revisorsnämnden*, 22 December 2011, Ju2011/8657/DOM; *Regleringsbrev för budgetåret 2013 avseende Revisorsnämnden*, 20 December 2012, Ju2012/8385/DOM; *Regleringsbrev för budgetåret 2014 avseende Revisorsnämnden*, 12 December 2013, Ju2013/8571/DOM, Ju2013/8610/KRIM (delvis).

specific dates on which the reports must be submitted. It seems that in practice the annual reports are used to give account as these often refer to the annual appropriations.[153] Activities in relation to AML supervision are hardly mentioned in the annual reports. The annual report 2012 only reports that the Board actively participated in the work of the AML coordination body by attending all meetings and that it made contributions in the form of letters and reports.[154] This makes it difficult to analyse what RN actually does in the field of the prevention of money laundering. Indirectly, RN accounts for its AML supervision via the annual appropriation letters of the Financial Supervisory Authority.[155] FI's report contains information about money laundering supervision on a more detailed level than RN's own annual reports.[156] Still, not much information is given as the 2013 report states that RN 'intends to place greater focus on money laundering issues' (*own translation, MB*).[157] Apart from the organisation of some seminars and information on – for example – the Board's AML supervisory policy, the actual exercise of supervision in terms of numbers, the breaches identified and the measures taken in case of identified non-compliance is absent. As no mention is made of the outsourcing of supervision to FAR and how this affects the Board's AML supervision; this is open for discussion. Here the Government also has the power not to prolong the appointment of the director, members or alternates from the Regulatory Board, if it is dissatisfied with the functioning of RN.[158] The power is to be used with restraint.

Only a financial relationship exists with the auditors and audit firms that the Board authorises and regulates. The Supervisory Board of Public Auditors is fully financed by fees and receives no Government funding.[159] The Government, however, determines the amounts of the different annual fees, with the exception of the fees levied for the professional examinations arranged by RN.[160] In the annual reports RN accounts for the expenditures. Neither legislation nor any other information indicates the existence of panels of representatives or like bodies at the Board.

7.4.5 County administrative boards of Stockholm, Västra Götaland and Skåne (*Länsstyrelserna*)

7.4.5.1 Institutional embedding

Sweden is divided into 21 counties (*Län*) that are governed by county councils and county administrative boards.[161] County councils and county administrative boards are situated

153 Cf. Revisorsnämnden (2012), *Revisorsnämndens årsredovisning för räkenskapsåret 2012*, Dnr 2012-1667 (*Annual report for the fiscal year 2012*).
154 *Ibid.*, at 20.
155 See § 7.4.2.2.
156 Cf. Finansinspektionen (2012b); Finansinspektionen (2013c).
157 Finansinspektionen (2013c) at 21.
158 Section 8 RN Instruction.
159 Revisorsnämnden, *Funding*, available at: <www.revisorsnamnden.se/rn/english/approval_authorization_and_registration.html>, last visited on: 28 March 2014.
160 *Förordning om ändring i förordningen (2007:1077) med instruktion för Revisorsnämnden*, SFS 2012:1077.
161 De Meij (2014) at 1634.

between the local level of municipalities and the central Government.[162] County councils form part of the constitutionally embedded framework of local self-government and their members are elected by county citizens.[163] County councils are democratically elected political organs, whereas county administrative boards are Government authorities in the counties.[164] County administrative boards (*Länsstyrelserna*, hereafter also LST or 'the boards') date back to the 17th century and were originally established as tax collecting authorities.[165] They are led by county governors who are appointed by the Government for a six-year period.[166] The other board members are elected by the county councils.[167]

> County administrative boards undertake a wide range of tasks of which the main objective is the coordination of the development of the county in line with the goals set in central government policies and, thus, to represent the Government in the counties. The tasks range from the provision of advice and information, supervision, regulatory tasks (including licensing and the hearing of appeals against municipal decisions), the coordination of the county's resources, to the provision of financial support for various activities such as investment or environmental conservation measures. The policies that they deal with range from 'employment, housing, environment, culture, agriculture, forestry, fishery, food and husbandry, care of sick and elderly, traffic and communications, public relief work, permits and supervision, and competition'.[168]

During the implementation of the Third Directive in Sweden, the question arose how supervision under the AML Act could be designed most effectively.[169] As explained, the Swedish Agency for Public Management considered the possibility and feasibility of a single AML supervisor for all obliged institutions and professionals, but found that this was not the best option.[170] It advised to provide supervisory responsibility for new institutions and professionals under the AML Act to the county administrative boards, because these authorities already had supervisory experience in policies related to

162 Government Offices of Sweden, *The Swedish model of government administration – three levels*, available at <www.government.se/sb/d/2858>, last visited on 28 March 2014.

163 County councils are constitutionally embedded via Chapter 14, Section 1 IG and are part of the framework of democratic local self-government: Chapter 3 of the *Kommunallag*, SFS 1991:900 (in English: *Local Government Act*). Their tasks centre mainly on public health and medical services, but they also have duties regarding public transport and culture.

164 § 1 *Förordning med länsstyrelseinstruktion*, SFS 2007:825 (in English: *Regulation with instructions for the county administrative boards*). Hereafter 'LST Regulation'.

165 Hägerhäll Aniansson, B. and Lohm, U. (2002), 'An Introduction to Östergötland, the Case Region', in: Svedin, U. and Hägerhall Aniansson, B. (eds.), *Sustainability, Local Development and The Future: The Swedish Model*, Kluwer: Dordrecht, pp. 83-98 at 84.

166 Section 41 LST Regulation; LS Stockholm, *County Governor and County Leadership*, available at: <www.lansstyrelsen.se/stockholm/En/om-lansstyrelsen/landshovding-och-lansledning/Pages/default.aspx>, last visited on 28 March 2014.

167 Cf. De Meij (2014) at 1636, who states that 'the nature of this organ is hybrid, since on the one hand it is the county branch of the national government, while on the other hand its 14 members are elected by the county council'.

168 Hägerhäll Aniansson and Lohm (2002) at 84.

169 See § 7.3.

170 Reasons given a great deal of weight by Statskontoret were the sectorial knowledge of existing AML supervisors in Sweden and the costs and efforts associated with the creation of a single authority: Statskontoret (2008) at 43-46 and 48.

money laundering.[171] The boards participate in initiatives for inter-agency cooperation against financial crime as well.[172] The Agency for Public Management advised to provide responsibility to the county administrative boards of Stockholm, Västra Götaland and Skåne specifically, because these counties have the largest industries and are metropolitan areas.[173] The presumption was that most businesses would be concentrated in these areas.[174] Furthermore, in these three counties the regional intelligence centres (RUC) are located. In the regional intelligence centres various authorities such as the tax administration, the Customs Authority (*Tullverket*) and the Swedish Economic Crimes Bureau work together by exchanging intelligence in order to track and prevent financial crime.[175] The legislator followed the recommendations of the Agency for Public Management and gave the county administrative boards of Stockholm, Västra Götaland and Skåne the task to perform AML supervision of unauthorised or unapproved tax advisors and accountants, independent legal professionals, trust and company service providers, auctioneers and dealers in high-value goods when they receive cash payments of 15,000 Euros or more.[176] The AML Regulation stipulates the territorial jurisdictions of each of the three boards.[177] Each county administrative board supervises accountants who are registered in a number of county administrative boards. In addition, the county administrative board of Stockholm supervises branches of foreign institutions and professionals in Sweden.

At Stockholm's county administrative board, AML supervision is carried out by the Supervision Unit. This unit operates under the Department of Legal Affairs and is responsible for the regulatory activities and oversight of foundations, guardians, security video surveillance, pawnbrokers and money laundering.[178] In 2013, it devoted three FTE to AML supervision, while it had supervisory responsibility for a total of 2,807 institutions and professionals, of which an estimated 87% were accountants and accountancy firms.[179] In Länsstyrelsen Västra Götaland the Legal Unit is responsible for AML supervision.[180] In 2013, it had three FTE available for a total of 1,605 institutions and professionals, of which 1,480 were accountants and accountancy firms.[181] In Skåne, AML supervision is carried out by a special AML Unit (3.75 FTE) operating under the Department of Legal

171 Statskontoret refuted the idea that Finansinspektionen could exercise this supervision: Statskontoret (2008) at 52.

172 *Förordning om myndighetssamverkan mot ekonomisk brottslighet*, SFS 1997:899 (in English: *Regulation on inter-agency cooperation against financial crime*).

173 Stockholm County is the region surrounding the capital on the east coast of Sweden. Skåne is the most southern part of Sweden where Sweden is connected to Denmark. Large(r) cities in this county are Helsingborg, Lund and Malmö. Västra Götaland is the region on Sweden's west coast and is the leading region for industry and transportation. The largest city of this region is Göteborg, Sweden's second largest city with the largest harbour in the country.

174 Statskontoret (2008) at 53.

175 Ibid., at 53.

176 *Regeringens Proposition* 2008/09:70 (*Government Bill*).

177 Section 16 AML Regulation.

178 Länsstyrelsen Stockholm, *Organisational chart*, available at: <www.lansstyrelsen.se/stockholm/En/om-lansstyrelsen/organisation/Pages/default.aspx?keyword=Organisational+chart>, last visited on 28 March 2014.

179 Interview Länsstyrelsen Stockholm, September 2013.

180 Länsstyrelsen Västra Götaland, *Organisationplan*, available at: <www.lansstyrelsen.se/vastragotaland/Sv/om-lansstyrelsen/organisation/Pages/Organisationsplan.aspx>, last visited on 28 March 2014.

181 Interview Länsstyrelsen Västra Götaland, September 2013. The data are from 28 August 2013.

Affairs.[182] It supervises a total of 1,372 institutions, of which an estimated 1,164 are accountants and accountancy firms.[183] The foregoing means that the three boards had roughly 9.75 FTE available for the supervision of a total number of 5,809 institutions and professionals in 2013.[184] Around 210,000 Euros per year is available for the performance of AML supervision.[185] The budget is the same for all three boards, even though Stockholm supervises a larger number of institutions and professionals.[186]

7.4.5.2 Independence and accountability

County administrative boards are administrative authorities (*enrådighetsmyndigheter*) headed by a Governor.[187] The Governor is accountable to the Government for the activities of the county administrative board. The boards operate under the Ministry of Social Affairs.[188] Different from FMI, which is the same type of administrative authority, county administrative boards have advisory councils (*insynsråd*).[189] These councils consist of no more than eight members appointed by the Government following a proposal from the Governor. According to Niklasson, advisory councils are used '[w]hen a higher degree of transparency is required (...)'.[190] The advisory councils meet the requirements of democratic accountability and citizen participation. They give advice and provide support to the Governor. They have no decision-making powers.[191] Next to the publication of annual reports and special reports pursuant to appropriations, this is a way for county administrative boards to be accountable and transparent towards the market and the wider public.

County administrative boards' independence is guaranteed by the Instrument of Government.[192] No public authority may interfere with the individual and day-to-day decisions of the county administrative boards.[193] The Government may provide the general framework for the functioning of county administrative boards via the instruction regulation. This regulation does not contain any general reporting obligations through which county administrative boards are accountable to the Government, except for Section 2 which states that the county administrative boards '(...) shall inform the Government on situations that are of particular importance to the Government or on events that occurred

182 Länsstyrelsen Skåne, *Organisational Chart*, available at: <www.lansstyrelsen.se/skane/SiteCollection Documents/Sv/om-lansstyrelsen/organisation/organisationsschema_lst_skane_januari_2013.pdf>, last visited on 28 March 2014.

183 Interview Länsstyrelsen Skåne, September 2013. The data are from 1 August 2013.

184 Cf. Finansinspektionen et al. (2013) at 16-17 that speaks of 8 FTE for 5,500 registered institutions and professionals.

185 Interview Länsstyrelsen Skåne, September 2013.

186 Interview Länsstyrelsen Västra Götaland, September 2013; Interview Länsstyrelsen Stockholm, September 2013.

187 De Meij (2014) at 1635.

188 Finansinspektionen et al. (2013) at 16.

189 Section 13 LST Regulation in conjunction with Section 9 Authorities Regulation.

190 Niklasson (2012) at 251.

191 Ibid.

192 De Meij (2009) at 1616.

193 See § 7.4.1.

in the county' (*own translation, MB*).[194] This seems to be the legal basis for the publication of annual reports. With reference to Section 6, paragraph 8 LST Regulation, which states that the county administrative boards have supervisory responsibility under the AML Act, the three county administrative boards include a section on the exercise of AML supervision in their annual reports.[195] The annual appropriation letters could provide more specific obligations to account for AML supervision. However, the appropriation letters for 2010-2014 do not mention any assignments in relation to AML supervision.[196] Indirectly, the boards also report on their AML supervision via the Financial Supervisory Authority.[197] The accountability of the county administrative boards thus runs via the general obligation in the instruction regulation and indirectly via the annual appropriation to the Financial Supervisory Authority. As pointed out, the Government has the power to dismiss a Governor of a county administrative board before the expiration of the six-year term. This power, however, must be used with great restraint and can only be used if the Governor commits a form of misconduct or has a disability impairing the performance of the authority, as defined by law. Where the head of a government agency is removed from office, the reasons must be publicly disclosed.

There is no (financial) relationship between the county administrative boards and the private sector. Representatives of the private sector may be appointed as members of the advisory council, but this is not necessarily the case.

7.4.6 Concluding remarks

Because the (political) independence of administrative authorities is a fundamental principle in Swedish law, this is adequately safeguarded for all the AML supervisory authorities included in this research. Although there have been comments about the impact of annual appropriation letters on the operational independence of supervisory authorities, this does not unduly hamper the independence of these authorities. The letters are of a general nature and do not involve case-by-case decision making. Moreover, the authorities themselves are consulted in the course of the preparation of the appropriation letters. As a last resort the Government can intervene by using its dismissal powers vis-à-vis the directors, the boards of the authorities or the Governor, but this power should be used with great restraint. As regards market independence, the supervisory authorities

194 Section 2(4) LST Regulation.

195 Länsstyrelsen Stockholm (2012), Årsredovisning 2012, at 126-127; Länsstyrelsen Västra Götaland (2013), *Årsredovisning 2013*, at 20-21; Länsstyrelsen Västra Götaland (2012), Årsredovisning 2012, at 155-156; Länsstyrelsen Skåne (2012), Årsredovisning 2012, at 118-119. At the time of finalising this chapter, the annual reports for the year 2013 of Länsstyrelsen Stockholm and Länsstyrelsen Skåne had not been published.

196 *Regleringsbrev för budgetåret 2014 avseende länsstyrelserna*, 19 December 2013, S2012/2774/SFÖ, S2013/1408/SFÖ, S2013/8584/SAM; *Regleringsbrev för budgetåret 2013 avseende länsstyrelserna*, 28 November 2013, S2013/7202/SFÖ (last amended); *Regleringsbrev för budgetåret 2012 avseende länsstyrelserna*, 15 November 2012, S2012/8011/SFÖ (last amended); *Regleringsbrev för budgetåret 2011 avseende länsstyrelserna*, 15 December 2011, S2011/11086/SFÖ (last amended); *Regleringsbrev för budgetåret 2010 avseende länsstyrelserna*, 2 December 2012, Fi2010/5408, Fi2009/4938(delvis) (last amended).

197 This was already demonstrated for FMI and RN in § 7.4.2 and 7.4.3.

only have (to a certain extent) a financial relationship with their supervisees, if any at all. Account is given through the publication of annual reports. In the county administrative boards, market parties may be represented in the advisory council: a body which can advise the Governor but does not have decision-making powers. All authorities thus have an adequate level of market independence.

Likewise, the annual appropriation letters and instruction regulations establish for the Government an accountability framework with the respective authorities. Specifically with regard to accountability for AML supervision, the requirements vary from authority to authority. Despite the fact that the annual appropriation letters and the instruction regulation have not required the Financial Supervisory Authority to report on its supervisory activities under the AML Act, it has reported regularly about this in the years 2011-13. This varied from reports containing the general results of thematic supervision, its overall AML supervisory experience and the work of the AML coordination body, to reports on an effective reporting regime under a special assignment from the Government. The Estate Agents Inspectorate and the county administrative boards have not been explicitly required to report on their AML supervision via their instruction regulations and annual appropriation letters in the years 2010-2014. Notwithstanding this, they have regularly reported on supervisory activities in their annual reports, in the sanctioning yearbooks (FMI) as well as indirectly via reports from the Financial Supervisory Authority. The same holds true for the Supervisory Board of Public Auditors, but the information provided in the annual reports with respect to AML supervision is close to zero. Activities in relation to AML supervision are hardly mentioned in the annual reports and there are no other reports that give an insight into the Board's AML supervision. The indirect form of accountability via the Financial Supervisory Authority provides some, but still very little information about the exercise of AML supervision by the Supervisory Board of Public Auditors. It should become more transparent in order to be held accountable, for example by specifically paying attention to AML supervision in the annual reports or the issuance of special AML reports.

7.5 The regulation of banks, real estate agents and accountants

This section verifies the extent to which banks, accountants and real estate agents are regulated sectors or professions in Sweden. It gives an insight into the question whether the supervisory authorities have, or can have, an adequate knowledge of their supervisees. This section pays attention to the definition of banks, real estate agents and accountants under the AML Act where this differs from other legislation.

7.5.1 Banks

The authorisation of banks is regulated in the Banking and Financing Business Act.[198] Pursuant to Chapter 1, Section 3, banking is a business which includes the processing of payments through general payment systems, and the acceptance of deposits from the public

198 *Lag om bank- och finansieringsrörelse*, SFS 2004:297.

which are available to the depositor within at most thirty days. Chapter 2, Section 1 BFBA states that the banking or financing business may only be conducted after authorisation, unless stated otherwise. The Financial Supervisory Authority is the designated authority thereto.[199] Upon authorisation banks are included in its public register.[200] Foreign banks established in the EEA may operate directly or through a branch in Sweden when the home state regulator notifies the Authority.[201]

> Chapter 3 BFBA lists the requirements for authorisation, which are further detailed by the Banking and Financing Business Regulation.[202] Upon application banks should indicate the full name, address and social security number, or failing this, the dates of birth of all founders and directors of the bank.[203] The application must be signed by all founders or board members and include a declaration that they are not bankrupt, subject to a trading prohibition, and that they are not subject to guardianship.[204] Applicants must also submit a business plan and a draft of the statutes, regulations or by-laws or amendments thereof.[205] FI's general guidelines regarding the application for authorisation to conduct banking or financing business stipulate in more detail what information the business plan must contain, how the statutes, regulations or by-laws must be drafted, etc.[206] The business plan, for example, should at least contain an organisational diagram, an outsourcing agreement, a group or ownership chart, documentation for ownership and management assessment, annual reports, interim reports, forecasts and lending instructions, guidelines and instructions – including those for acting in accordance with the AML Act.[207] An important aspect for deciding whether a licence should be provided is the assessment as to whether the owners and management are fit and proper for this position.[208] Chapter 3, Section 2 BFBA explicitly states that it should be considered whether there is reason to believe that the holding relates to or increases the risk of money laundering.

7.5.2 Real estate agents

The estate agency profession is a regulated profession in Sweden. The main piece of regulation is the Estate Agents Act and the Estate Agents Regulation.[209] Estate agents are natural persons who on a professional basis perform mediation activities with respect to (parts of) properties, tenant-owned flats, buildings on other persons' land, site leases, and shared owners with regard to flats, leases or rental tenancies.[210] They must always be

199 Chapter 3, Section 8 Banking and Financing Business Act; Cf. § 7.4.2.2 where the (previous) duality in powers between FI and Government was briefly mentioned.

200 FI's Company Register, available at <www.fi.se/Folder-EN/Startpage/Register/Company-register/Company-register-Company-per-category/?typ='BANK++';'MBANK+';'SPAR++';'FILB++'>, last visited on 28 March 2014.

201 Chapter 4 of the Banking and Financing Business Act; See § 1.8 and 4.5.1.

202 *Förordning om bank- och finansieringsrörelse*, SFS 2004:329.

203 Chapter 2, Section 1 Banking and Financing Business Regulation.

204 Under Chapter 11, Section 7 of the Parental Code (*Föräldrabalken*, SFS 1949:381).

205 Chapter 2, Section 2 Banking and Financing Business Regulation.

206 *Allmänna råd om att söka tillstånd att driva bank- och finansieringsrörelse*, FFFS 2011:50.

207 Chapter 2 FFFS 2011:50.

208 See: *Föreskrifter om ägar- och ledningsprövning*, FFFS 2009:3.

209 *Fastighetsmäklarlag*, SFS 2011:666; *Fastighetsmäklarförordning*, SFS 2011:668.

210 Section 1 Estate Agents Act.

registered with the Estate Agents Inspectorate before they can act as an estate agent.[211] There are two types of estate agents in Sweden: estate agents with a full registration under the Estate Agents Act and letting agents.[212] The AML Act only applies to real estate agents with a full registration.[213]

> The profession of estate agent is somewhat different than in the Netherlands, the United Kingdom and Spain where real estate agents normally represent either the selling or buying party. In Sweden estate agents ought to function as a neutral and impartial link between the buyer and seller of a property.[214] Section 15 Estate Agents Act contains a prohibition on acting as a representative of either the buying or selling party. The estate agent's remuneration should be paid by the party that first hired him, although in practice this is usually the seller.[215] During the mediation process the estate agent has the obligation to inform both the seller and the buyer of his own duties, as well as the duties of the seller and buyer towards each other. When the seller and buyer reach an agreement a written contract is drafted by the real estate agent. This also differs from the Dutch, Spanish and UK situation where civil-law notaries or solicitors are involved in the conclusion of property transactions.

Any professional who wishes to be registered as an estate agent must make a written application to FMI containing the applicant's name, civic registration number, address, e-mail address, telephone number and, where relevant, the trading name under which the applicant intends to conduct his or her operations. The application must state whether full registration is being sought or only for letting activities. If the applicant works as an employee, the employer's name, address and telephone number must be provided. If the employer is a legal person, its registration number must be stated as well.[216] Applicants must not be under the age of majority, declared bankrupt or be subject to a trading prohibition, and they must not be subject to guardianship.[217] Further, they must have liability insurance, have obtained adequate training, intend to work professionally as an estate agent, and be sound and otherwise suitable to be an estate agent. Evidence must be submitted that proves that the estate agent complies with all of these requirements. FMI has detailed these requirements in its lower-level regulations.[218]

---

211 Sections 5 and 6 Estate Agents Act. Section 5 contains some minor exceptions for lawyers and estate agents.

212 The difference concerns the level of education: Fastighetsmäklarinspektionen, *Registration of estate agents in Sweden*, available at <www.fmi.se/Sve/Filer/fmi_registration_of_estate_agents_in_Sweden.pdf>, last visited on 28 March 2014.

213 Chapter 1, Section 2, paragraph 8, PL. This will most likely change in the near future, as the proposal for the Fourth Directive, as adopted in its first reading by the European Parliament, includes letting agents under the scope of the AML legislation: *European Parliament legislative resolution of 11 March 2014 on the proposal for a directive of the European Parliament and of the Council on the prevention of the use of the financial system for the purpose of money laundering and terrorist financing,* COM(2013)0045, 2013/0025(COD).

214 Section 8 Estate Agents Act.

215 Section 23 Estate Agents Act therefore speaks of a 'principal' instead of a buyer or seller.

216 Section 1 Estate Agents Regulation.

217 Section 6 Estate Agents Act and Section 2 of the Estate Agents Regulation.

218 *Fastighetsmäklarnämndens föreskrifter om krav för registrering som fastighetsmäklare,* FMN 2012:1.

7.5.3 Accountants

In Sweden, the title accountant does not have statutory protection.[219] Any person can perform activities such as bookkeeping, preparing annual accounts and the provision of (fiscal) advice, provided that they comply with the general requirements laid down in the Annual Accounts Act and the Bookkeeping Act.[220] These Acts provide the general framework for accounting. The Bookkeeping Act regulates, among other things, what accounting records are and how these should be documented. The Annual Accounts Act establishes the format of and the publication of annual accounts and other rules for financial statements and applies to the businesses referred to in Chapter 6, Section 1 Bookkeeping Act. These include, inter alia, limited liability companies, economic associations and companies that have had more than fifty employees in the last two years. Contrary to most accountancy activities, auditing is a regulated activity in Sweden.[221] Auditing can only be exercised by approved public auditors (*godkänd revisorer*) or authorised public auditors (*auktoriserad revisorer*). Both titles receive protection via the Auditors Act.[222] The authorisation for approved and authorised public auditors is done by the Supervisory Board of Public Auditors.

> The Swedish situation is somewhat diffuse because of the use of the term *revisorer*. Translated into English this word means both an auditor and an accountant.[223] Translations from Swedish to English often refer to authorised or approved accountants, where it seems that the word auditor is more appropriate. Professionals providing accounting services other than the regulated activity of auditing could also be referred to as *redovisningskonsulter* (accounting consultant) or *rådgivare* (advisors). For comparative purposes in this research, however, I make a distinction between auditors (*revisorer*) on the one hand, and accountants on the other. This is a reason for referring to the Supervisory Board of Public Auditors instead of Public Accountants.[224]

The Auditors Act governs the authorisation system for individuals and firms that conduct statutory audits.[225] It regulates the requirements for qualification, the professional obligations of public auditors and audit firms, and disciplinary procedures. The request for approval or authorisation should be made in writing to the Board.[226] When the Board

219 Cf. FATF (2006a) at 17.

220 *Årsredovisningslag*, SFS 1995:1554 (in English: *Annual Accounts Act*); *Bokföringslag*, SFS 1999:1078 (in English: *Bookkeeping Act*).

221 See for a sketch of the development of the auditing regulation: Öhman, P. and Wallerstedt, E. (2012), 'Audit regulation and the development of the auditing profession: The case of Sweden', *Accounting History*, vol. 17, issue 2, pp. 241-257.

222 *Revisorslag*, SFS 2001: 883.

223 Cf. FATF (2006a) at 119.

224 The FATF also refers to the Supervisory Board of Public Auditors: FATF (2006a).

225 Under the Companies Act, all Swedish limited liability companies are required to have at least one approved or authorised auditor to examine the company's annual report and accounts as well as the management by the board of directors and the managing director: Chapter 9 *Aktiebolagslag*, SFS 2005:551.

226 Section 7 *Förordning om revisorer*, SFS 1995:665 (Hereafter 'Auditors Regulation').

provides the approval or authorisation, then the name of the auditor or audit firm is included in its register.[227]

> An approved public auditor must carry out audit business professionally; be a resident of Sweden or another EEA Member State or Switzerland; not be declared bankrupt, subject to a trading prohibition, under guardianship, subject to a consultancy prohibition, or be under similar restrictions in another State. He must have the education and experience required for audit business; have passed the examination of professional competence; and be a fit and proper person to carry on audit business.[228] The same requirements apply to authorised public auditors, although the demands in relation to education and examinations are higher than for approved public auditors.[229]

Although the wider accountancy profession does not need to be authorised, we will see in the next subsection that accountants are not entirely unregulated. The AML Act introduced a registration obligation for these professionals allowing the county administrative boards to supervise this group.

7.5.3.1 Accountants under the AML Act

The split between the regulated activity of auditing and the wider accountancy profession had led to the situation that under the previous AML legislation only auditors fell under its scope. As explained, this was criticised by the FATF.[230] The AML Act introduced the obligation for all non-regulated professions to register with the Swedish Companies Registration Office.[231] This obligation applies to accountants or accountancy firms, with the exception of public auditors and audit firms approved or authorised by the Supervisory Board of Public Auditors.[232] Accountants who are not authorised as an auditor but work at a registered audit firm that is authorised by the Board are exempted from registration.[233] The county administrative boards of Stockholm, Västra Götaland and Skåne were designated

227 Section 15 Auditors Regulation details all the information that must be included in the register. For natural persons: name, registration number, personal identification number or date of birth, the private and business address, and business information (name, address and website). For legal persons: business name, corporate structure, contact details, website, addresses of all company offices in Sweden, the name and registration numbers of all authorised or approved auditors working for the company, the name and business address of each director and owner, and registration number of the owners who are auditors (or where this information is available), and the names and addresses of audit businesses in the same network as the registered firm (or where this information is available).

228 Section 4 Auditors Act.

229 Section 5 Auditors Act in conjunction with *Föreskrifter om ändring i Revisorsnämndens föreskrifter om utbildning och prov RNFS 1996:1*, RNFS 2013:1 (in English: *RN's regulations on training and examinations)*. The education and experience required for authorised public auditors is furthermore explained on RN's website, *Utbildning*, available at: <www.revisorsnamnden.se/rn/bli_revisor/utbildning.html>, last visited on 28 March 2014.

230 FATF (2006a) at 119.

231 Hereafter 'Bolagsverket' or BV. Chapter 6, Section 3 PL. This obligation applies to all unauthorised or unapproved tax advisors and accountants, independent legal professionals, trust and company service providers, auctioneers and dealers in high-value goods when they receive cash payments of 15,000 Euros or more.

232 Chapter 1, section 2, under 11 PL.

233 FAR, *Penningtvättsnyhet för skatterådgivar och redovisningskonsulter*, available at: < www.far.se/Du-i-din-yrkesroll/Radgivare-och-specialist/Nyheter/Penningtvattsnyhet-for-skatteradgivare-och-redovisnings konsulter/>, last visited on 28 March 2014.

as the supervisors of this group insofar as this group is registered.[234] If professionals are not registered, the AML Act states that they are not allowed to act.[235]

> The AML Regulation states that registration must be done in writing.[236] If the accountant is a natural person, he should submit his name, social security or coordination number, registered address, and he should indicate the activities for which the notification is made. Accountancy firms must provide their business name, business registration and indicate the activities for which the notification is made.[237] The registration costs of 96 Euros must be paid by the applicant.[238] The Swedish Companies Registration Office is responsible for a public register under the AML Act and should ensure a proper handling of personal data in accordance with the Personal Data Act.[239] The register contains the data mentioned above and the name of the competent county administrative board.[240] Regarding personal data, the register must have the objective of providing data for supervision by the respective county administrative boards exercised under the AML Act and providing public information on operators who have been registered.[241] If an accountant or accountancy firm recorded in the register gives notice that it has ceased activity, the Companies Registration Office should remove it from the register. Upon registration, modifications or removal, the Office must inform the competent county administrative board.[242]

The registration obligation for unregulated accountancy professionals allows the county administrative boards to gather basic information about (the size of) the group. They have the names and addresses of accountants and accountancy firms for which they have supervisory responsibility under the AML Act. A problematic point with this system, however, is the fact that registration cannot be enforced by the boards. As explained before, they only have supervisory responsibility for those professionals that have registered with the Companies Registration Office. This means that they do not have supervisory responsibility for professionals that have not registered. The boards may order accountants or accountancy firms that have not registered to provide information on the activities performed in order to assess whether an obligation to notify exists. If the information is not provided, then they have the power to order the accountant to cease his activities.[243] But when the information requested is provided, the county administrative boards have no powers to take action if they conclude that an accountant or accountancy firm should be registered. In the absence of a legal power that allows the boards to ultimately force the accountant or accountancy firm to register or to cease business, all they can do is to request, inform or advise the accountant or accountancy firm to register with BV.

234 See § 3.4.4.
235 Chapter 6, Section 4 PL.
236 Section 2 AML Regulation. The application form can be found on the BV website: <www.bolagsverket.se/polopoly_fs/1.219!/Menu/general/column-content/pdfFile/705.pdf>, last visited on 28 March 2014.
237 Section 3 AML Regulation.
238 Section 12a AML Regulation. The amount due is 850 SEK (96.28 Euros, exchange rate 05/02/2014).
239 Section 5 AML Regulation.
240 Section 6 AML Regulation.
241 Section 7 AML Regulation
242 Section 12 AML Regulation.
243 Chapter 6, section 4 PL. This may be accompanied with a public law fine (*vite*): Chapter 6, Section 9 of the Act. See more about the sanctioning powers of the county administrative boards: § 7.8.3.

The seriousness of this legal gap is demonstrated by the annual reports of the county administrative boards. Their reports indicate that those professionals who should register with the Companies Registration Office often have not done so. In its annual report 2012 the county administrative board of Skåne states that it believes that many of the operators included in the boards' supervision are not registered, while the annual report for Västra Götaland states that it has recognised that a large number of operators who are required to register have not done so.[244] The annual report 2012 of LST Skåne indicates that of all institutions and professionals registered, approximately 1,300, are based in the counties for which Skåne has supervisory responsibility under the AML Act. Yet at the same time data from the Swedish FIU suggest that this could involve up to 30,000 institutions and professionals.[245]

Specifically with respect to the accountancy sector, the LSTs have received information from the Swedish Tax Authority suggesting that there are at least 20,000 institutions and professionals that provide accountancy services throughout Sweden, although in August 2013 only 5,000 were registered with BV (25%).[246] In 2012, other sources referred to about 15,700 institutions and professionals providing accountancy services in Sweden.[247] In that case, still only 32% would be registered. Already in 2010 the county administrative boards pointed out this legal gap to the Government, and a special report on AML supervision issued by FI in 2012 and the national risk assessment mentioned this problem as well.[248] Notwithstanding this, no legislative action has so far been taken. In the absence of a power to force obliged institutions to register, the county administrative boards send letters and try to inform the non-registered companies about their obligations under the AML Act. The 2012 annual report of LST Västra Götaland stipulates that it made 'approximately 1,150 targeted mailings to operators in the industries covered by the AML Act. Information campaigns have been organised partly in-house, as well as with other agencies such as other county boards, the Companies Registration Office and the Tax Authority and together with professional organisations at their annual meetings' (*own translation, MB*).[249] Likewise, the county administrative board of Skåne 'sent around 2,500 letters to cash traders and accountants who are not connected to either the SRF or the trade organisation for the accountancy profession (FAR) with information on money laundering, the current legislation, and so on' *(own translation, MB)*, thereby pointing at the registration obligation and urging professionals to register at BV.[250] Similar letters were sent to a large number of other obliged institutions as well.

244 Länsstyrelsen Skåne (2012) at 119; Länsstyrelsen Västra Götaland (2012) at 156.
245 Länsstyrelsen Skåne (2012) at 119. It had already noted this in 2011: Länsstyrelsen Skåne (2011), *Årsredovisning 2011*, at 88-89.
246 Interview Länsstyrelsen Västra Götaland, September 2013. The number of registered accountants (5,097) is based on a sum of the number of accountants registered, which stems from information obtained via interviews with the three county administrative boards.
247 Finansinspektionen (2012b) at 27.
248 Länsstyrelsen Stockholm (2011), *Årsredovisning 2011*, at 105; Länsstyrelsen Västra Götaland (2011), *Årsredovisning 2011*, at 116; Finansinspektionen (2012b) at 27; Finansinspektionen et al. (2013) at 32.
249 Länsstyrelsen Västra Götaland (2012) at 156.
250 Länsstyrelsen Skåne (2012) at 119.

The provision of information seems to yield positive results. The annual report of LST Västra Götaland for the year 2013 indicates that after a mailing, another 1,267 institutions and professionals registered during the last four months of that year. The county administrative board believes this is attributable to the mailing.[251]

7.5.4 Concluding remarks

The Financial Supervisory Authority is the competent authority for banking authorisations. It has a good overview of the banks it supervises under the Banking and Financing Business Act, to which Chapter 1, Section 2 PL refers. It knows exactly which banks operate in Sweden and it keeps a public register thereof. Due to the authorisation procedure it has a considerable amount of information on banks, their directors and management, internal policies and procedures. The Estate Agents Inspectorate is the authority that is responsible for the registration of real estate agents. It has available a substantial amount of information on the group of professionals.

A split between the regulated activity of auditing and other accountancy activities exists. This section explained that approved and authorised auditors and audit firms must fulfil a number of criteria in order to be eligible for approval or authorisation by the Supervisory Board of Public Auditors. The Board has a substantial amount of information on the approved and authorised auditors and audit firms. In principle the wider accountancy profession is unregulated, but the AML Act has introduced a registration requirement for all non-regulated professions. Therefore, the county administrative boards of Stockholm, Västra Götaland and Skåne have, in theory, an oversight of accountants and accountancy firms. They should register themselves at the Swedish Companies Registration Office, which is obliged to inform the competent county administrative board of registrations, modifications or withdrawals. Information that must be provided for the registration is basic, but is a starting point for the boards carrying out the AML supervision of the unregulated accountancy profession. It appears, however, that there are serious problems with the registration in practice due to a lack of authority for the boards to enforce registration. This seriously hampers the effectiveness of their AML supervision, since they only have supervisory responsibility for those professionals that are registered at the Companies Registration Office.

7.6 Financial Supervisory Authority (*Finansinspektionen*)

7.6.1 Supervisory powers

Chapter 6, Section 1 PL states that provisions on supervision, exercised by authorities other than the county administrative boards, are contained in the acts governing these parties engaged in those activities. The Authority thus derives its powers from the BFBA in relation to banks. Chapter 13, Section 3 BFBA states that credit institutions and foreign institutions that have branch offices in Sweden must provide FI with all the information

251 Länsstyrelsen Västra Götaland (2013) at 20.

about their activity and related circumstances as required by it.[252] This means that it has the power to compel the production of information and documents. At the same time it entails a duty for the institutions to cooperate. In addition to the power to compel the production of information, the Authority may carry out an investigation at a credit institution where it deems this to be necessary.[253] The Act does not mention the nature of the investigation, but it is generally understood that this means both off-site and on-site inspections.[254] Chapter 16, Section 1, fifth paragraph, BFBA provides that the Government may issue regulations regarding the information that credit institutions must provide to FI for the exercise of its supervisory powers. The Government has delegated this power to the Authority. Specifically with respect to the prevention of money laundering and terrorist financing, Section 18 AML Regulation empowers supervisors to issue regulations on a wide array of obligations, including risk assessments, customer due diligence, auditing and reporting, the training of staff and more.[255] The Financial Supervisory Authority thus has regulatory powers, and it first issued its regulations and guidelines (*föreskrifter och allmänna råd*) in 2009.[256] The regulations are legally binding for the institutions and must be complied with, while the guidelines lack such legal force. Nevertheless, the guidelines do have a certain force, as these concern a comply-or-explain rule.[257] This is, for example, the case in relation to the time period for the keeping of records in relation to reported transactions.

7.6.2 Anti-money laundering supervision in practice

7.6.2.1 The 'two-track' approach to anti-money laundering supervision

Anti-money laundering supervision is carried out via two tracks.[258] Verification of compliance with the obligations stemming from the AML Act can be included in regular supervisory procedures by FI's operating divisions. Moreover, inspectors from the AML Unit perform thematic AML supervision, i.e. focussing on (an aspect of) specific AML obligations. FI does not have a specific AML supervision policy.[259] FI's overall direction of AML supervision is said to focus on the prioritisation of sectors and actors that represent a high(er) risk of money laundering and that are of great importance to the financial system.[260] During interviews, representatives clarified that under the current supervisory strategy, the Authority's policy is that the vast majority of AML supervision is carried out by the AML Unit via thematic supervision, due to the high level of expertise required

252 A branch of a foreign credit institution as referred to in Chapter 4, section 4, of the Act shall be inspected to ensure that the institution complies with the laws and regulations that apply to the institution's activities in this country.

253 Chapter 13, Section 4 BFBA.

254 FATF (2006a) at 100.

255 Chapter 8, Section 1 PL provides this power to the Government, and states that it may delegate this power.

256 *Finansinspektionens föreskrifter och allmänna råd om åtgärder mot penningtvätt och finansiering av terrorism*, FFFS 2009:1. These were last amended on 12 November 2013, FFFS 2013:25. See § 1.8 for developments after March 2014.

257 See: Chapter 5 FFFS 2009:1; Interview Finansinspektionen, April 2011; FATF (2006a) at 101.

258 See § 7.4.1.

259 Interview Finansinspektionen, October 2013.

260 Finansinspektionen (2013c) at 9.

for this type of supervision. It is lamentable that the supervision strategy is not publicly available: effective supervision requires that a public supervision policy is available, as this is an instrument that fosters transparency and accountability by the supervisors, and shows that they apply their powers in a proportionate and risk-based way.[261] One unit within the Banks division focuses on payment services and pays attention to AML compliance more specifically as well.[262]

7.6.2.2 Inclusion of anti-money laundering supervision in regular supervisory procedures

Banking supervision is carried out by the Banks division. Inspectors who perform regular banking supervision can include AML aspects in their supervision, but they are not obliged to do so.[263] After the FATF evaluation in 2006, the Authority established a policy that stated that at least 25% of all regular supervisory procedures must pay attention to AML compliance. According to representatives, in 2007 it amounted to nearly 70% of all regular supervisory procedures. The Swedish Financial Supervisory Authority, however, departed from this ambition in the years thereafter due to resource constraints.[264] Where compliance with the AML Act is nowadays included in regular supervisory procedures the intensity varies on a case-by-case basis. In general terms representatives have indicated that the focus rests on the existence of internal policies and procedures – and less with the execution thereof.[265] Inspectors of regular banking supervision may request the AML Unit for assistance in verifying compliance with the AML obligations, but it seems that this is not always done.[266]

The Financial Supervisory Authority does not keep statistics on the number of times it has included AML supervision in regular inspections of banks. The extent to which the verification of compliance with preventive AML obligations is taken into account during regular supervisory procedures differs as well. This makes it impossible to say at this point whether banks have been supervised for their compliance with the preventive AML policy during regular supervision in recent years, which is lamentable.

7.6.2.3 Thematic anti-money laundering supervision

The AML Unit (*Enheten Penningtvätt*) focuses in its supervision exclusively on compliance with one or more obligations stemming from the AML Act. Within FI it is the leading and expertise unit for AML supervision. Thematic inspections by the AML Unit are usually planned beforehand in annual supervision plans.[267] Annual supervision plans are internal documents that reflect the supervisory choices made for a coming year.[268] These choices are

261 See § 2.4.3.3.
262 Interview Finansinspektionen, October 2013.
263 Interview Finansinspektionen, April 2011; Interview Finansinspektionen, October 2013.
264 Ibid.
265 Ibid.
266 Interview Finansinspektionen, April 2011.
267 Interview Finansinspektionen, October 2013.
268 Interview Finansinspektionen, October 2013.

based on FI's risk analysis, and may be of a structural nature or incident-driven.[269] Publicly available information on how the risk-based approach is actually implemented is absent. The special report 2012 on AML supervision in relation to the reporting levels of supervisees, however, refers to the risk of money laundering and the risk of non-compliance.[270] Sources said to be used for the risk-based approach are publicly available sources, information stemming from regular supervision, other supervisors, and the Swedish FIU.[271] Results of thematic supervision projects are used as input for the risk-based approach as well.[272]

Thematic supervision may take the form of off-site supervision via the use of questionnaires or self-assessments spread among a number of financial and credit institutions, possibly followed by on-site inspections. Examples of thematic projects can, for example, be found in the annual report of 2011, where mention is made of 'an extensive questionnaire focusing on compliance with AML regulations. The study, involving almost 400 businesses, provides valuable input to risk assessments and further enforcement action' (*own translation, MB*).[273] Alternatively, thematic supervision is directly done through the on-site inspections of a limited number of financial and credit institutions.[274] In 2011, this occurred, for example, regarding six securities companies that were the subject of a thematic study.[275] According to representatives the current focus is on on-site inspections.[276]

Comprehensive statistics on the AML supervision of banks by the Financial Supervisory Authority are, unfortunately, not publicly available. Representatives have provided the following data.[277]

Table 9 – Thematic inspections performed by the AML Unit (closed cases)

	On-site inspections total no. of inspections / (of banks)	**Off-site inspections total no. of inspections / (of banks)**
2011	9 / (5)	373 / (42)*
2012	5 / (1)	
2013	5 / (2)	
2014 (until April 2014)	2 / (1)	

This table is based on non-public data provided by the Swedish Financial Supervisory Authority. The table presents the total number of thematic inspections performed by the AML Unit. The number in between brackets indicates the inspections of banks specifically. Representatives have stated that the number of inspections reflect the number of closed supervisory cases. Ongoing on-site and off-site inspections are not included in this table.

* This off-site inspection concerned one self-assessment project, which was just mentioned. In this project institutions were asked to fill in a survey. The project started in 2011 and included 373 businesses in total. The project took three years and was finalised in 2013.

269 Finansinspektionen (2012b) at 15.
270 Finansinspektionen (2012b) at 15.
271 Cf. Interview Finansinspektionen, October 2013.
272 Cf. Finansinspektionen (2012b) at 17; Finansinspektionen (2013c).
273 Finansinspektionen (2011), Årsredovisning 2011, at 24 (in English: *Annual report 2011*); Cf. Finansinspektionen (2012b) at 16.
274 Interview Finansinspektionen, October 2013.
275 Finansinspektionen (2011) at 24; Cf. Finansinspektionen (2012b) at 16.
276 Interview Finansinspektionen, October 2013.
277 The data is used with the permission of the representatives of Finansinspektionen.

Next to the statistics, which demonstrate that banks have been subject to thematic AML supervision since 2011, there is some anecdotal information suggesting that within the thematic supervision projects banks are being supervised for their compliance with the preventive AML obligations. Banks specifically were reported to be the subject of thematic supervision in 2010, when the Authority verified by means of a survey whether banks adhered to the enhanced monitoring of transactions to and from Iran.[278] Likewise, banks were subject to a project in 2012 with respect to compliance with the reporting obligation, together with a wide range of other financial and credit institutions.[279] And the annual report 2013 indicated that four banks were subject to AML supervision in that year.[280] Specific areas that were said to be examined were the management of correspondent banking relationships, politically exposed persons, private banking and legal entities domiciled outside the Nordic countries for tax purposes, including the management of beneficial owners and high-risk transactions.[281] It thus seems that banks' compliance with the AML Act is being supervised within the thematic supervision projects, although it seems that the numbers are somewhat decreasing.

7.6.3 Sanctioning powers

Non-compliance with the obligations stemming from the AML Act can be sanctioned through the powers under the Banking and Financing Business Act.[282] This Act provides FI with sanctioning powers against banks and other financial and credit institutions. The sanctions can only be imposed on the institutions themselves, because FI does not have the power to impose sanctions on the board members or managing directors of those institutions.[283] The Authority can impose the following sanctions:

- Issuance of an order to take measures within a certain time period
- Prohibition on executing a certain decision
- Remark (*anmärkning*)
- Warning (*varning*)[284]
- Reappointment of board member or managing director[285]
- Administrative fee (*straffavgift*)[286]
- Public law fine (*vite*)[287]

278 Finansinspektionen (2009), *Skärpta kontrollåtgärder krävs avseende affärsförbindelser och transaktioner med Iran*, FI Dnr 09-4770; Finansinspektionen (2012b) at 16.
279 Finansinspektionen (2013c) at 8.
280 Representatives have pointed out that the four banks to which the annual report 2013 refers were all thematic AML inspections. For three banks the supervisory activity closed in 2013, while one case is still pending and is not included in the table.
281 Finansinspektionen (2013b) at 27.
282 Chapter 6, Section 1 PL. But not foreign banks supervised by their home state regulator: Chapter 15, sections 15-17 BFBA.
283 Cf. FATF (2006a) at 101.
284 The first four sanctions are laid down in Chapter 15, Section 1 BFBA.
285 Chapter 15, Section 2 BFBA.
286 Chapter 15, Sections 7-9 BFBA.
287 Chapter 15, Section 20 BFBA.

- Revocation of licence[288]
- Late fee (*förseningsavgift*)[289]

One can observe that a wide range of sanctions exist, varying from rather mild sanctions such as a warning or a remark to the revocation of a licence. Not all sanctions can be applied in all circumstances. The late fee can only be imposed when an institution does not comply in time with an order for information, and the public law fine cannot be imposed on a self-standing basis but should accompany an order or prohibition. A subtle difference between the sanctions can be found as well. The difference between a remark and a warning is that for a warning the criteria for the revocation of a licence are met, but that it is considered sufficient to warn an institution. The remark is similar to a warning but can be imposed in those cases where the criteria for the revocation of a licence have not been met. In other words, a remark can be imposed in less serious cases. Warnings and remarks are published on the website of FI when they are imposed.

> The Financial Supervisory Authority is competent to impose various types of fines. The administrative fee (*straffavgifft*) is a punitive sanction that can directly be imposed for a breach with legal obligations.[290] The maximum amount of the fine is 5.7 million Euros.[291] FI must take into account that the administrative fee may not exceed ten per cent of the credit institution's sales immediately preceding the financial year and where the infringement took place during the institution's first year of operation or turnover data is missing or incomplete, it may be estimated. Likewise, the fee may not be so high that the bank on which the sanction is imposed can subsequently no longer meet the requirements of solvency and liquidity. Besides, FI must consider the gravity of the breach and the duration of the infringement.[292] The administrative fee, in combination with a warning or a remark, is said to be the most commonly imposed sanction.[293] It can be compared to regulatory and administrative law fines, and is a well-known sanction in the other three Member States included in this research as well. Different from the administrative fee is the public law fine (*vite*). The main difference is that the vite is not related to the non-compliant behaviour in the first place, but to an order made by a public authority. This means that the public law fine is only payable where an institution fails to comply, within a given timeframe, with an order from a public authority.[294] This sanction may, for example, be relevant in relation to an order to take measures within a certain time, the prohibition on executing a certain decision and the reappointment of a director or manager. This sanction can be compared to an incremental penalty payment in Dutch administrative law as is explained in § 5.6.3.1.

The revocation of a licence is the most deterrent sanction available and must be reserved for the most serious cases of non-compliance. However, there is still discretion in deciding

288 Chapter 15, Sections 1-3 BFBA.
289 Chapter 15, Section 10 BFBA. The maximum amount is 100,000 SEK (approx. 11,325 Euros, exchange rate 05/02/2014).
290 Blanc-Gonnet Jonason, P. (2013), 'Sweden', in: Jansen, O.J.D.M.L. (ed.), *Administrative Sanctions in the European Union*, Intersentia: Antwerp, pp. 553-583 at 557-558.
291 Chapter 15, Section 8 BFBA states that the fine should be between 5000 SEK and 50 million SEK (566 and 5.66 million Euros, exchange rate 05/02/2014).
292 Chapter 15, Section 9 BFBA.
293 Interview Finansinspektionen, October 2013.
294 Blanc-Gonnet Jonason (2013) at 557-558.

whether or not to withdraw a licence. The BFBA states that the Authority may refrain from sanctioning if a violation is minor or excusable, the institution rectifies the breaches or if another authority has already taken action against the institution and these measures are deemed sufficient.[295]

In principle all formal sanctioning decisions that the Financial Supervisory Authority takes are public and are published on its website.[296] The decisions are detailed as they describe the facts and findings of the case, the breaches, and include the name of the offender. The decisions are usually published the day after the sanction is imposed. At that moment the institution concerned can still appeal to the decision. The publication of sanctioning decisions could be regarded as an additional sanctioning instrument, also known as naming & shaming.[297] It seems that the Authority publishes these decisions in order to inform consumers and to promote confidence in the financial markets. Yet at the same time it considers that publication has a strong preventive effect on potential offenders and sees such detailed publications as 'a low cost measure to further increase the effectiveness and the dissuasiveness of the sanctioning regime'.[298]

7.6.4 Sanctioning policy and practice

Non-compliance with preventive AML obligations can be sanctioned, as just observed, with a wide array of sanctions. The question is whether and how FI applies these sanctions where it encounters AML breaches committed by banks. It is important that supervisors issue policies in which they make intelligible their supervisory and sanctioning choices and explain how they will apply their discretion in using these powers.[299] The Authority does not have a specific AML sanctioning policy.[300] A more general sanctioning policy is not publicly available either. This makes it difficult to disentangle the sanctioning principles, goals and style. A representative of the Financial Supervisory Authority explained that the factors which are relevant for determining the type and the amount of the sanctions are the severity of the breach, the number of breaches, and the existence of a follow-up action plan taken by the business in question.[301] Still, each case should be assessed in light of the specific circumstances of the case. It was stated that the Authority punishes harshly where necessary.[302]

295 Chapter 15, section 1, third paragraph, Banking and Financing Business Act.
296 Interview Finansinspektionen, October 2013. The sanctioning decisions can be found at: <www.fi.se/Tillsyn/Sanktioner/Finansiella-foretag/>, last visited on 28 March 2014.
297 See the discussion in the Netherlands about naming and shaming: § 5.6.3.2.
298 Joint Response by the Riksbank and Finansinspektionen to Commission Communication on Supervisory Sanctions, COM (2010) 716 final, 17 February 2011, Dnr 11-195.
299 See § 2.4.3.3.
300 Interview Finansinspektionen, October 2013.
301 Interview Finansinspektionen, April 2011.
302 Ibid.

> From the entry into force of the AML Act in March 2009 until the end of March 2014, FI imposed seven (formal) sanctions directly for non-compliance with AML obligations or as an important aspect of wider non-compliant behaviour.[303] In four cases the sanctions imposed were a warning or a remark, combined with an administrative fee. The amount of the fines varied between 45,000 and 3.4 million Euros.[304] In two cases FI decided to revoke a licence because of the seriousness of the breaches that could result in that the institutions being used for money laundering or terrorist financing.

The Financial Supervisory Authority imposed one sanction on a bank for not complying with the obligations stemming from the AML Act since its entry into force. In April 2013, the Authority imposed a fine on and issued a remark for Nordea Bank AB. Inspections had shown that the bank had insufficient internal procedures for the prevention of money laundering, that it failed to comply with the EU Sanctions Regulation as well as with the enhanced customer due diligence obligations stemming from the AML Act.[305] The sanctioning decision stated that the sanction was the result of a follow-up inspection, but it did not explain whether this was performed in the context of regular or thematic supervision. The Nordea decision gives some insight into the considerations of the Authority on the amount of the administrative fee. It demonstrates that the general factors as mentioned above are indeed included in the assessment. The Financial Supervisory Authority considered that Nordea had breached multiple provisions. These had also existed for a long time, despite the fact that the bank had been informed by the Authority after a previous investigation. Moreover, the fact that Nordea had done nothing to implement corrections to overcome the breaches played an important role. It was considered that '[t]his opens the possibility for the assumption that Nordea did not care that the Bank was in violation of the rules or that the Bank thinks it is too costly to comply with them'.[306] Finally, great weight was attached to the fact that the deficient reporting in relation to the EU sanctions lists meant that the EU Commission had received incorrect information. Altogether, FI set the administrative fee at 30 million SEK (approximately 3.3 million Euros), which was lower than the maximum amount of 50 million SEK (approx. 5.7 million Euros). This sanctioning decision indicates why FI opted to combine the fine with a remark: '[g]iven the fact that the deficiencies have only been identified in the limited area that was investigated, however, there are no grounds to consider the withdrawal of Nordea's authorisation. Likewise, this means that there are no grounds for issuing the Bank with a warning'.[307]

303 This finding is based on a search through FI's sanctioning register on: <www.fi.se/Tillsyn/Sanktioner/Finansiella-foretag/>. Reference period: the 1st of January 2009, until the 28th of March 2014. All sanctioning decisions were read. Results: Sanctioning Decision *Västernorrlandsfonden AB*, 4 October 2010, FI Dnr 10-9365; Sanctioning Decision *Maxima Finans & Försäkringsmäklare AB*, 9 November 2011, FI Dnr 10-6683; Sanctioning Decision *Svensk Kapitalservice & Rådgivning*, 6 December 2011, FI Dnr 11-1104; *Folksam LO Fond AB*, 15 May 2012, FI Dnr 10-7704; Sanctioning Decision *Legio Exchange AB*, 1 October 2012, FI Dnr 11-10359; Sanctioning Decision *Nordea Bank AB*, 15 April 2013, FI Ref. 12-7237; Sanctioning Decision *Exchange Finans Europe AB*, 13 January 2014, FI Ref. 13-399.

304 In SEK between 400,000 and 30 million SEK, exchange rate 05/02/2014.

305 Sanctioning Decision *Nordea Bank AB*, 15 April 2013, FI Ref. 12-7237, at 5.

306 Ibid., at 19.

307 Sanctioning Decision *Nordea Bank AB*, 15 April 2013, FI Ref. 12-7237, at 19.

7.6.5 Concluding remarks

The Financial Supervisory Authority has adequate supervisory powers provided by law. It carries out anti-money laundering supervision via two tracks. The verification of compliance with the obligations stemming from the AML Act can be included in regular supervisory procedures. Unfortunately, comprehensive statistics demonstrating that banks have been supervised for compliance with preventive AML obligations during regular supervisory procedures are not available. Therefore, it is impossible to say whether and to what extent banks are being supervised for their compliance with the AML Act. In the second track inspectors from the AML Unit carry out thematic supervision. The AML Unit is the leading and expertise unit for AML supervision. Thematic projects are planned in annual supervision plans on the basis of a risk-based approach. Thematic supervision may take the form of off-site or on-site inspections, or a combination thereof. Regarding this type of supervision there is information which demonstrates that banks are being supervised for compliance with preventive AML obligations, although it seems that the numbers are somewhat decreasing.

The Banking and Financing Business Act provides a wide range of sanctions, which can be used to sanction non-compliance with preventive AML obligations as well. This ranges from a remark to fines and ultimately to the revocation of licences. FI publishes all sanctions on its website. However, the Authority does not have the power to impose sanctions on board members or the managing directors of those institutions. It does not have a general sanctioning policy, or a specific AML sanctioning policy, which can be considered a weak aspect. For the exercise of effective supervision it is important that supervisors issue policies in which they make intelligible their supervisory and sanctioning choices and explain how they will apply their discretion in using these powers. From the entry into force of the AML Act until the end of March 2014 FI sanctioned one bank, consisting of an administrative fee and a remark, for not-complying with the AML Act.

7.7 Estate Agents Inspectorate (*Fastighetsmäklarinspektionen*)

7.7.1 Supervisory powers

As explained, the AML Act states that provisions on supervision, exercised by authorities other than the county administrative boards, are contained in the acts governing these parties engaged in those activities. This means that the Swedish Estate Agents Inspectorate derives its supervisory powers from the Estate Agents Act. Section 28 states that a registered estate agent is obliged to permit the Inspectorate to inspect files, accounting records and other documents pertaining to the business and to provide the information requested for supervisory purposes. Although formulated as an obligation for estate agents, it shows that FMI has the power to compel the production of documents that are relevant to monitoring compliance, and that it has the power to carry out checks. The Estate Agents Act and Regulation do not provide the Inspectorate with regulatory powers outside the field of training for estate agents.[308] Section 18 AML Regulation,

308 Section 15 Estate Agents Regulation.

however, provides regulatory powers to FMI with respect to certain specific obligations, such as risk assessments, customer due diligence, politically exposed persons, and record keeping.[309] On this basis the Inspectorate issued AML regulations in 2009, which it updated in 2013.[310] The Inspectorate's Disciplinary Board often refers to these regulations in disciplinary cases.[311]

Although it seems that the Inspectorate has adequate supervisory powers, a problem in relation to exercising the power to carry out checks exists. Problematic is the reference to real estate agents in the Estate Agents Act.[312] As we could see in § 7.5.2, real estate agents are defined as *natural* persons who on a professional basis perform mediation activities with respect to (parts of) properties, tenant-owned flats, buildings on other persons' land, site leases, shared owners with regard to flats, leases or rental tenancies. As a result of this formulation, FMI cannot supervise real estate *businesses*.[313] This is problematic in more than one way. Because the Inspectorate can only apply its powers against natural persons, it has no power to perform on-site inspections without contacting a real estate business in advance to request approval for carrying out an on-site visit in order to supervise the individual estate agents that work for the business.[314] Where a real estate business claims that it cannot accommodate FMI inspectors, this must be respected.[315] Moreover, where a business consents to an on-site visit and inspectors identify breaches, the Inspectorate cannot take action against the business. In this sense, on-site inspections have an advisory or awareness-creating function in which FMI can advise businesses about good practices, instead of a true inspection function. This is why FMI's supervisory practice only consists of off-site inspections.[316]

A variety of dangers of the sole use of off-site inspections can be noted. First and foremost, a real estate agent can cheat. He can delete documents relating to a certain transaction or a certain client, he can change the date of transactions or simply decide not to send relevant information to the Inspectorate. Although real estate agents are legally obliged to forward all relevant information as they could lose their registration in case of non-compliance, in the absence of a self-standing power for FMI to conduct on-site inspections, an actual check (or at least the threat thereof) on whether the estate agent has indeed forwarded all the required information cannot be done. A second danger is that FMI is unable to check whether the internal policies that may exist on paper are adhered to in practice. In the absence of a self-standing power to perform on-site inspections, the Inspectorate cannot carry out checks (sample testing) on estate agents' administration to verify whether an estate agent complies with the AML Act in practice. Another problem arises in relation to the obligation to have an internal policy as formulated in Chapter 5, Section 1 PL. Due

309 Via Chapter 8, Section 1 PL.

310 *Fastighetsmäklarinspektionens föreskrifter om åtgärder mot penningtvätt och finansiering av terrorism,* KAMFS 2013:5.

311 For example FMI Cases 2012-01-25:7 and 2012-11-21:17. See about the Disciplinary Board: § 7.7.4.

312 Cf. Finansinspektionen et al. (2013) at 31.

313 See § 5.5.2.1 for a similar discussion.

314 See differently: FATF (2006a) at 130. With respect to unannounced visits: Statskontoret (2010) at 37.

315 Statskontoret (2010) at 41; Interview Fastighetsmäklarinspektionen, August 2013.

316 Interview Fastighetsmäklarnämnden, April 2011; Interview Fastighetsmäklarinspektionen, August 2013.

to the reference to individual estate agents in the Estate Agents Act, in principle each real estate agent has an obligation to individually formulate an AML policy. The provision does state, however, that where institutions subject to the scope of the AML Act are natural persons and run their business as an employee of a legal person, the obligation to maintain procedures applies to the legal person instead. Yet, as explained, this could result in a situation where the Inspectorate supervises an individual estate agent and concludes that the internal policy of the business for which the estate agent works is not adequate. In that case, FMI cannot take action against the business, but only against the individual estate agent. That is, when the Inspectorate is actually allowed to enter the business premises in the first place. Representatives have stated that the focus of FMI's off-site supervision rests with compliance with the obligations to perform the customer due diligence and the keeping of records.[317] The reporting obligation and the obligation to have an internal policy are, in principle, not checked. This can also be inferred from the disciplinary cases. In the years 2010-12, there was only one case in which non-reporting by the real estate agent was a point of discussion.[318]

The problems purveyed here were already present under the previous Estate Agents Act from 1995. The new Act entered into force in 2011. Since the problems related to the exercise of supervision had already been informally brought to the attention of the Ministry of Finance, the Government had the opportunity to overcome these legal problems upon drafting the new legislation.[319] The Government proposal for the new Estate Agents Act, however, does not mention the problems of the scope of the definition of estate agent and the lack of an on-site inspection power for the Inspectorate.[320]

7.7.2 Anti-money laundering supervision in practice

Anti-money laundering supervision is entirely integrated into the work of the Inspectorate under the Estate Agents Act. FMI does not have risk assessments, annual supervision plans, or a specific policy for AML supervision.[321] This suggests that the Inspectorate at present does not carry out its supervision on the basis of a risk-based approach and annual supervision plans.[322] The annual report for 2013 does mention that an enforcement strategy had been submitted to the Government at the end of that year and should serve as the starting point for FMI's supervision.[323] The guiding document for FMI inspectors

317 Interview Fastighetsmäklarnämnden, April 2011.
318 FMI Case 2011-04-27:1.
319 Interview Fastighetsmäklarnämnden, April 2011.
320 *Regeringens Proposition* 2010/11:15 *(Ny fastighetsmäklarlag)* (in English: *Government proposal for the new Estate Agents Act*).
321 Interview Fastighetsmäklarinspektionen, August 2013.
322 Although it does not have its own risk assessments, FMI participated in the national risk assessment on money laundering: Finansinspektionen et al. (2013). See § 2.4.3.3 about the importance of public supervision plans for effective supervision.
323 Fastighetsmäklarinspektionen (2013) at 26.

is the internal manual (*handbok*) which instructs inspectors and explains the procedures that must be followed.[324] Supervision is based on two tracks: complaints and own motion.

7.7.2.1 Supervision on the basis of complaints

Being a consumer authority, the large majority of FMI's supervision and enforcement actions stem from complaints from consumers or third parties, such as banks, or administrative authorities like the Tax Authority.[325] The annual report 2013 states that this method is the starting point of FMI's supervision.[326] Supervision on the basis of complaints is a reactive means of supervision. In 2010 the Swedish Agency for Public Management found that nearly 80% of FMI's supervisory activities stemmed from complaints. It criticised this reliance on complaints and found that supervision had to become more proactive, risk-based and on FMI's own initiative.[327] The passive approach had also been a point of criticism in a report from the Swedish National Audit Office (*Riksrevisionen*).[328] Despite these critical reports, the Inspectorate's supervision actions still originate mostly from complaints (80%).[329] An analysis of all the disciplinary cases concerning non-compliance with the AML Act for the years 2010-2012 provides a similar picture. In all three years roughly 80% of these cases were based on a complaint from a consumer or third party.[330]

In almost all cases stemming from consumer or third party complaints, FMI pays attention to compliance with the customer due diligence and record keeping obligations under the AML Act. The rule of thumb laid down in the internal manual is that complaints should be subject to an extended examination (*utvidgad granskning*) in which FMI investigates AML compliance on its own motion.[331] An analysis of the disciplinary cases from 2010-2011 that deal with non-compliance with preventive obligations demonstrates that in nearly all

324 Fastighetsmäklarinspektionen (2013a), *Handbok om tillsynen over fastighetsmäklare,* 30 April 2013, Dnr. 1.1-1169-13 (not publicly available). The internal manual has been provided for the purpose of this research. FMI representatives have confirmed that the internal manual may be used and referred to.

325 The obligation for administrative authorities to report is laid down in Section 10 of the Estate Agents Regulation. There exists no legal obligation for FMI to conduct supervision on the basis of a complaint, although in practice a complaint is always checked. The internal manual provides for situations where a complaint does not have to be assessed, for example when a complainant is anonymous: Fastighetsmäklarinspektionen (2013a) at 11-12.

326 Fastighetsmäklarinspektionen (2013) at 26.

327 Statskontoret (2010) at 35.

328 Riksrevisionen (2007), *Den största affären i livet, Tillsyn över fastighetsmäklare och konsumenternas möjligheter till tvistelösning,* RiR 2007:7, at 41-43 and 66-68. See in particular Figure 2 of the report.

329 Fastighetsmäklarinspektionen (2013) at 30; Fastighetsmäklarinspektionen, *Hur vi granskar fastighetsmäklare,* available at <www.fmi.se/default.aspx?id=3481>, last visited on: 28 March 2014; Interview Fastighetsmäklarinspektionen, August 2013.

330 Finding based on a search in FMI's sanctioning yearbooks: Fastighetsmäklarinspektionen, *Årsböcker,* available at: <www.fmi.se/1914>, last visited on 28 March 2014. All disciplinary sanctions in the yearbooks 2010-2012 have been read. Results: The Årsbok 2010 shows that 8 out the 10 cases on non-compliance with preventive AML obligations stemmed from a complaint, the Årsbok 2011 shows this for 11 out of the 14 cases. From Årsbok 2012 it can be read that 26 out of 35 AML cases started with a complaint from a consumer or other third party.

331 Fastighetsmäklarinspektionen (2013a) at 16. Fastighetsmäklarinspektionen (2013) at 32 indicates that most complaints concern responses towards the client, a lack of service, or late feedback.

cases the complaints were not about breaches of the AML Act, but concerned buyers who complained that the price of the property was too high or complaints from the seller and/or buyer that the estate agent had not fully informed the parties.[332] In 2012 it occurred on eight occasions that a real estate agent was sanctioned for non-compliance with preventive AML obligations, but not for the original complaint that focussed on other behaviour.[333]

> One illustration is a case where the buyer of a villa complained that the villa had no cellar although the estate agent had mentioned this in the property description. The details of the case show that upon handling this complaint, FMI focused not only on the complaint but on the execution of customer due diligence measures under the AML Act as well. Ultimately, the estate agent received a warning *only* for not complying with the customer due diligence obligations. For the complaint itself, no disciplinary action was taken.[334] In another example the buyers of a house complained that the estate agent had not provided information relating to the fact that the neighbour's carport was to be built in such a manner that it would ruin their view over the lake next to which the house was situated.[335] In reviewing the complaint FMI again included the execution of the customer due diligence measures, and the Disciplinary Board ultimately imposed a warning *only* for not complying with the customer due diligence obligation. The Board stated that there was insufficient evidence to sanction the estate agent for the facts to which the complaint related.

In the aforementioned cases FMI's focus rested on the questions whether the identity checks of sellers and buyers were done before the transaction and whether a copy was made of the identity document. Since 2013, FMI is reported to focus on the wider aspects of customer due diligence, such as grounds for enhanced due diligence.[336] In principle, in supervisory efforts stemming from complaints no attention is paid to the reporting obligation under the AML Act. Only if FMI accidentally comes across this aspect during the review of documentation will it include this in its investigation. As explained, only one case is known for the years 2010-2012.[337]

7.7.2.2 Supervision initiated by FMI

The majority of the supervisory efforts stem from complaints. Roughly 20% of cases originate at the Inspectorate's own initiative. There are essentially four sources on the basis of which FMI can start such inspections: the monitoring of public sources, the periodic review, a follow-up on previous disciplinary decisions or refusals of registration and thematic supervision projects.

332 It should be mentioned that after the filing of the complaint, a consumer or third party plays no further role in the supervisory or disciplinary procedures: Cf. Riksrevisionen (2007) at 44.

333 FMI Cases 2012-01-25:7; 2012-01-25:8; 2012-02-22:4; 2012-02-22:6; 2012-03-28:2; 2012-06-20:7; 2012-06-20:11; 2012-12-12:12.

334 FMI Case 2010-11-24:3.

335 FMI Case 2011-03-31:16.

336 Interview Fastighetsmäklarinspektionen, August 2013.

337 Supra, n. 318.

On the basis of the ongoing monitoring of public sources, FMI can decide to start an inspection.[338] Media messages, the internet, case law from the courts and contacts with other (consumer) authorities can be sources.[339] In the years 2010 and 2011, there was one disciplinary case on non-compliance with the customer due diligence obligation which had come to the knowledge of FMI via a webpage on which the estate agent offered an object.[340] In 2012, the Inspectorate finalised three disciplinary cases in which AML compliance was assessed on the basis of a criminal conviction that had come to its attention, and two on the basis of information received from other public authorities.[341] A second source for supervision on FMI's own motion is the periodic review system.[342] Every five years the Inspectorate checks whether registered estate agents are fit and proper persons. Inspectors look at the existence of criminal records, financial records (debts, the register of bailiffs) and check whether the estate agents have paid their registration fees on time.[343] If there are reasons to suggest that a real estate agent is not fit and proper, FMI performs an extended review by requesting the estate agent to provide various kinds of documents. This always includes a check as to whether the customer due diligence and record keeping obligations under the AML Act are adhered to.[344] In the third place, the Inspectorate follows up on previous disciplinary decisions or refusals of registrations. It carries out checks on estate agents who have previously been warned by the Disciplinary Board, or whose registration has previously been refused, to verify if they have acted in compliance with all legal obligations and sound estate agency practice since that moment. In 2010-2012 there were five such cases in relation to compliance with preventive AML obligations.[345] One example is a case in which FMI decided to perform an extended examination in order to check whether an estate agent had implemented improvements to his practice as a result of a warning issued on him in 2007.[346] In the fourth place, FMI can exercise thematic supervision on its own motion.[347] This is a relatively new method of supervision for the Inspectorate. The head of the Inspectorate may approve thematic projects in which inspectors focus on compliance with particular obligations. This may be a way for FMI to carry out AML supervision on a more self-standing basis and to ensure that it gives sufficient attention to the matter. AML compliance has not yet been subject to a thematic supervision project.[348] Representatives stated that the Inspectorate is considering carrying out a thematic project focusing on the reporting obligation under the AML Act somewhere in 2013-14.[349]

338 Riksrevisionen (2007) at 42; Fastighetsmäklarinspektionen (2013) at 27.
339 Fastighetsmäklarinspektionen (2013a) at 14-15.
340 FMI Case 2011-09-28:8.
341 FMI Cases 2012-02-22:7; 2012-05-23:6; 2012-09-26:17; 2012-11-21:8 and 2012-12-12:26.
342 Fastighetsmäklarinspektionen (2013a) at 29-30; Riksrevisionen (2007) at 42.
343 FATF (2006a) at 130; Fastighetsmäklarinspektionen (2013) at 27.
344 Interview Fastighetsmäklarinspektionen, August 2013. Examples are FMI Cases 2012-03-28:3 and 2012-10-24:5.
345 FMI Cases 2010-06-23:5; 2010-12-15:3; 2011-08-24:1; 2011-12-14:14; and 2012-09-26:5.
346 FMI Case 2010-12-15:3.
347 Fastighetsmäklarinspektionen (2013a) at 24-26. See also the annual report 2013 in which FMI widely reports about the development of the thematic supervision projects: Fastighetsmäklarinspektionen (2013) at 33-34.
348 Fastighetsmäklarinspektionen (2013) at 33-34 explains that in 2013 thematic supervision was aimed at reviewing examination clauses (*besiktningklausuler*) applied by estate agents.
349 Interview Fastighetsmäklarinspektionen, August 2013.

7.7.2.3 Supervision in numbers

The Estate Agents Inspectorate provides general statistics on its website, but these do not include the numbers of (off-site) inspections.[350] The statistics that are useful in relation to AML supervision are the number and outcomes of disciplinary cases dealt with by FMI's Disciplinary Board. These are discussed in § 7.7.4. I will now first turn to the sanctioning powers to analyse whether the Estate Agents Act provides the Inspectorate with adequate powers.

7.7.3 Sanctioning powers

According to Section 29 Estate Agents Act, an estate agent shall be deregistered when he acts in contravention of his or her obligations under this Act. The deregistration may or may not have immediate effect.[351] Alternatively, FMI has the power to issue a disciplinary warning (*varning*) or a reminder (*erinran*). The disciplinary reminder as a sanction came into existence with the new Estate Agents Act in 2011.[352] The reminder is considered a more lenient sanction than a warning.[353] Upon its introduction the Government stated that '[t]he idea is that a reminder shall be given in cases where a warning appears to be an overly harsh penalty, but where the offence is not of such a minor type that one can abstain from imposing a penalty. A reminder can be given when a requirement is not complied with, but the offence is not deemed to be of a serious nature' (*own translation, MB*).[354] A disciplinary reminder could, for example, be used is when an estate agent accidentally enters incorrect data in the description of the property. Estate agents who have knowingly not registered with FMI can be prosecuted and be subjected to a criminal fine or imprisonment for a maximum period of six months upon conviction.[355] Acting as an estate agent without registration is thus enforced via criminal law.

> There could be a discussion on the question whether Section 29 can actually serve as a legal basis for sanctioning non-compliance with the obligations stemming from the AML Act, since it refers to obligations 'under this Act'. Section 28 Estate Agents Act refers to the supervisory responsibility under the Estate Agents Act, too, and adds that within its field of operations FMI shall exercise supervision under the AML Act. This may suggest that the consideration 'under this Act' in Section 29 includes supervision pursuant to the AML Act. The notion of sound estate agency practice reinforces this idea. The Estate Agents Inspectorate has always interpreted the preventive AML obligations as part of sound estate agency practice.[356] In disciplinary cases concerning breaches of AML obligations, the Disciplinary Board often refers to sound estate agency practice. In

7

350 Interview Fastighetsmäklarinspektionen, August 2013; Fastighetsmäklarinspektionen, *Fastighetsmäklarinspektionens statistik per den 31 januari 2014*, available at: <www.fmi.se/Sve/Filer/fmi_statistik_2014-01-31.pdf>, last visited on 28 March 2014.

351 Under the previous regime, the revocation was always imposed with immediate effect. The current practice is that where formal qualifications are breached or where the breach is of a very serious nature, the deregistration has immediate effect. In other cases the revocation does not have immediate effect: Interview Fastighetsmäklarinspektionen, August 2013. Cf. Fastighetsmäklarinspektionen (2013) at 28.

352 *Regeringens Proposition* 2010/11:15 at 2.

353 See also: Fastighetsmäklarinspektionen (2013) at 28.

354 Ibid., at 65-66.

355 Section 31 Estate Agents Act.

356 FATF (2006a) at 130. This general duty of care is now laid down in Section 8 Estate Agents Act.

one case the Board argued that by failing to review a transaction more closely, the estate agent had breached its obligations under the AML act and thereby sound estate agency practice.[357] In another case, where an estate agent had not performed any verification of the representative of the legal entity before signing a contract, this was considered to be a breach of the AML Act as well as being contrary to sound estate agency practice.[358] For these two reasons, breaches of the preventive AML obligations can in my opinion indeed be sanctioned with the powers stemming from the Estate Agents Act. As explained, the sanctions available to FMI are deregistration, the disciplinary warning or a reminder. Criminal enforcement cannot be used for non-compliant behaviour.

Deregistration is a very powerful and dissuasive sanction, whereas the disciplinary warning and reminder are rather mild. The dividing line between a warning and a reminder is very thin and unclear. It is difficult, if not impossible, to point to the differences between the two, or to see how this should make a difference in practice. All disciplinary decisions against estate agents are published in sanctioning yearbooks (*årsböcker)*. All are published in an anonymised manner. This means that, in principle, FMI has no power to name & shame, or at least it does not apply this in practice.[359] There are essentially only three sanctions available to FMI. Moreover, because the difference between a warning and a disciplinary reminder is unclear, it seems that no wide range of sanctions is available. FMI's Disciplinary Board can either turn to deregistration, or issue a warning or reminder. The difference between deregistration, on the one hand, and the warning and reminder, on the other, is extensive. There are no other sanctions that in terms of severity can be placed in between these sanctions, and with the present situation an escalation of sanctions is not possible. Whereas deregistration may be too harsh a sanction for non-compliance with preventive AML obligations, a mere warning or reminder could in certain circumstances be considered too soft. Neither the Government proposal concerning the Estate Agents Act 2011, nor the explanatory memorandum to its predecessor mention the existence of other sanctions.[360] I have been unable to identify why there are no other sanctions available that could provide for a more proportionate sanctioning response in cases where deregistration is disproportionate, but where a warning is too soft. Examples of sanctions that would find themselves in between deregistration and a warning could, for example, be a temporary ban on the exercise of activities or a fine (an administrative fee). As regards a possible escalation of sanctions, it is likewise interesting to look at the formulation of Section 29 Estate Agents Act. It shows that in principle deregistration is the designated sanction, and that FMI may deviate from this standard by issuing a warning or reminder. The Government proposal concerning the Estate Agents Act 1995 explained why deregistration was designed as the primary sanction: 'the possibility of a strong reaction by the supervisor is intended to increase respect for the authority and its orders and should thereby contribute to a speedier resolution of regulatory affairs' *(own translation, MB)*.[361] This conflicts, at least in theory, with the idea that a supervisor escalates in his sanctions by starting with mild, informal sanctions all the way up to the most dissuasive sanctions.

357 FMI Case 2011-03-31:14.

358 FMI Case 2011-03-31:16.

359 Cf. § 7.6.3.

360 *Regeringens Proposition* 2010/11:15; *Regeringens Proposition* 1994/95:14 (*Ny fastighetsmäklarlag*), 8 September 1994.

361 Ibid., at 70.

In practice this formulation may be less relevant: an analysis of the disciplinary cases that deal with non-compliance with AML obligations demonstrates that FMI's Disciplinary Board issues a warning in nearly all cases.[362]

As a result of the narrow formulation of real estate agents in the Estate Agents Act, as discussed in § 7.7.1, FMI has no power to impose sanctions on real estate businesses.

7.7.4 Sanctioning policy and practice

The sanctioning body of the Estate Agents Inspectorate is the Disciplinary Board. Where inspectors find that a breach merits disciplinary action the file is handed over to the agency head, who passes it on to the Disciplinary Board. The Board consists of a chairman, a deputy chairman and no more than six other members and four substitutes.[363] The agency head chairs the Disciplinary Board. It convenes almost every month to adjudicate disciplinary cases; in 2013 it convened nine times.[364] The Estate Agents Inspectorate does not have a sanctioning policy.[365] Besides Section 29 Estate Agents Act that designates deregistration as the standard sanction, only the explanatory memorandum to the former Estate Agents Act gives some indications of the sanctioning principles.[366] Where an estate agent does not comply with the formal requirements to act as an estate agent, or where an estate agent refuses to cooperate with FMI during an inspection, the estate agent shall, in principle, be deregistered.[367] This can be the case where an estate agent has failed to pay the annual fees for registration or does not meet the training requirements. In cases where an estate agent has acted in breach of laws, regulations or sound estate agency practice, the circumstances of the case must be reviewed. Deregistration is suitable when a real estate agent has committed severe breaches or crimes, or where the estate agent engages in repetitive non-compliance. In any case, the Disciplinary Board should always take into account factors that concern the estate agent's suitability. This includes questions on how long the estate agent has been registered and how he has carried out his tasks during that period.

Representatives characterise the Inspectorate as an authority that is willing to impose tough sanctions where the situation at hand so requires.[368] In 2009, when the AML Act

362 Finding based on a search in FMI's sanctioning yearbooks: Fastighetsmäklarinspektionen, *Årsböcker*, available at: <www.fmi.se/1914>, last visited on 28 March 2014. All disciplinary sanctions in the yearbooks 2010-2012 have been read. An analysis of the disciplinary cases from 2010 and 2011 with respect to the AML obligations demonstrates that out of the 19 cases concerning the preventive AML policy in which a sanction was imposed, 17 cases ended with a warning. The warning was either imposed for the breach of customer due diligence obligations itself, or for a combination of offences under the AML Act and the Estate Agents Act (1995). It should be pointed out that in 2010 and the first half of 2011 the Disciplinary Board had no possibility to issue a disciplinary reminder. The disciplinary cases in 2012 in which a sanction was imposed for non-compliance with AML obligations all ended with a warning, despite the possibility of imposing a disciplinary reminder.

363 Section 6(2) FMI Regulation.

364 Fastighetsmäklarinspektionen (2013a), at 37. Fastighetsmäklarinspektionen (2013) at 35.

365 Interview Fastighetsmäklarinspektionen, August 2013. Cf. § 2.4.3.3.

366 *Regeringens Proposition* 1994/95:14.

367 Cf. FMI Case 2012-08-29:5.

368 Interview Fastighetsmäklarnämnden, April 2011.

had just entered into force, FMI gave estate agents some time to adjust their internal policies to the Act. This is no longer the case. As explained, in practice the Board issues warnings to estate agents who do not comply with the preventive AML obligations.[369] The annual reports for 2012 and 2013 show that this non-compliance is one of the deficiencies for which most disciplinary action is taken. In 2010, six estate agents were sanctioned for non-compliance with the customer due diligence obligation. In 2011 this number had increased to 12 and in 2012 even to 33.[370] The annual report for 2013 demonstrates that 15 estate agents were sanctioned for non-compliance with (aspects of) the customer due diligence obligation.[371]

Table 10 – Number of real estate agents sanctioned for breaches of AML obligations[372]

Year	Sanctions imposed on real estate agents
2010	6
2011	12
2012	33
2013	15

It was already mentioned that the analysis of the disciplinary cases for the years 2010-12 demonstrates that most of the cases do not arise from self-initiated supervision but from consumer complaints: 80% versus 20%.[373] It was also explained that the Disciplinary Board generally issued a warning in cases of non-compliance with the AML Act.[374] Only in two cases in which non-compliance with the customer due diligence obligations played a role did the Disciplinary Board decide to revoke the registration of an estate agent. On both occasions, however, this was the result of a combination of offences.[375] In one of these two cases, non-compliance with CDD as such was sanctioned with a warning.[376] The Board has never decided to deregister an estate agent for mere non-compliance with preventive AML obligations, not even the one time where an estate agent had failed to perform customer

369 See § 7.7.3.

370 Fastighetsmäklarinspektionen (2012) at 34. The Årsbok 2012, however, shows a total of 35 cases in which non-compliance with preventive AML obligations was assessed. Because the cases are published in an anonymised fashion, it may be that an estate agent was involved in more than one disciplinary case.

371 Fastighetsmäklarinspektionen (2013) at 38. The Årsbok 2013 was at the time of finalising this chapter not (yet) available.

372 Own table based on FMI's annual reports for the years 2010-2013. Most sanctions are imposed for non-compliance with customer due diligence and/or record keeping obligations.

373 See § 7.7.2.

374 Finding based on a search in FMI's sanctioning yearbooks: Fastighetsmäklarinspektionen, *Årsböcker*, available at: <www.fmi.se/1914>, last visited on 28 March 2014. All disciplinary sanctions in the yearbooks 2010-2012 have been read. An analysis of the disciplinary cases from 2010 and 2011 on AML obligations demonstrates that out of the 19 cases concerning the preventive policy in which a sanction was imposed, 17 cases ended with a warning. The warning was either issued for a breach of customer due diligence obligations itself, or for a combination of offences under the AML Act and the Estate Agents Act (1995). It should be pointed out that in 2010 and the first half of 2011 the Board had no possibility to issue a disciplinary reminder. The disciplinary cases in the year 2012 in which a sanction was imposed for non-compliance with AML obligations all ended with a warning, despite the possibility of a disciplinary reminder. The annual report 2013 indicates that out of the 15 sanctions imposed for non-compliance under the AML Act, 13 were a warning: Fastighetsmäklarinspektionen (2013) at 39.

375 FMI Cases 2010-12-15:11 and 2011-12-14:14.

376 FMI Case 2011-12-14:14.

due diligence and to disclose a suspicion report to the Swedish FIU.[377] Despite the fact that since mid-2011 the Disciplinary Board has the possibility to issue a disciplinary reminder, it had not made use of this until the end of 2012 in AML-related cases. In 2013, it issued a disciplinary reminder twice for deficiencies in the documentation of the customer identification performed.[378]

As an aside, the annual report for 2013 states that of all these decisions in the years 2011-2013, real estate agents have appealed against the sanctioning decision 11 times at the District Court. In nine of these cases the Court ruled in favour of Fastighetsmäklarinspektionen and upheld the sanction imposed.[379]

7.7.5 Concluding remarks

The Estate Agents Inspectorate lacks the power to effectively supervise estate agents. The narrow formulation of estate agents under the Estate Agents Act in combination with the absence of a self-standing power to perform on-site inspections, results in off-site inspections focusing almost exclusively on the performance of the CDD and record keeping obligations only. Resolving these two legal issues by drafting clearer and more precise legislation could allow the Inspectorate to supervise more estate agents with fewer supervisory efforts than it currently does. FMI embeds the verification of compliance with the AML obligations in its wider supervisory activities. Supervision is off-site and mostly reactive. Roughly 80% of the supervisory activities stem from complaints from consumers or third parties. Usually these complaints are not about non-compliance with the AML Act, but the Inspectorate includes the verification thereof in its supervisory activities. The fact that most efforts originate from complaints is worrisome, because not all obligations are adequately checked: the reporting obligation and the obligation to have an internal policy are hardly included, if included at all. The verification of compliance with these obligations requires proactive supervision with on-site inspections and the use of sample testing. Only in this way can FMI truly verify whether the obligations are applied in practice by estate agents. The thematic supervision projects could be a way in which compliance with the reporting obligation under the AML Act can be supervised on a more regular and focused basis in the future. Again, however, the power to perform on-site inspections is very much needed. A second danger of this strong reliance on complaints is that the risks of or associated with money laundering or ongoing non-compliance do not receive adequate attention. The Inspectorate does not perform risk assessments which indicate where money laundering risks in the estate agency sector and activities are greatest. The national risk assessment indicated that more research is needed here.[380]

FMI's Disciplinary Board can impose the dissuasive sanction of deregistration, or the comparatively mild sanctions of a warning or reminder. The dividing line between a warning and reminder is unclear. Because the Inspectorate can either decide to deregister an estate agent or to warn/remind him, there is hardly no possibility for FMI to scale up

377 FMI Case 2011-04-27:1.
378 Fastighetsmäklarinspektionen (2013) at 39.
379 Ibid., at 39-40.
380 Finansinspektionen et al. (2013) at 24.

sanctioning action in a proportionate way in the absence of adequate and proportionate sanctions that are positioned somewhere in between deregistration or a warning. This makes the sanctioning powers inadequate. Moreover, the Inspectorate cannot sanction real estate businesses. FMI does not have a sanctioning policy, but deregistration is, at least in theory, the standard sanction. Sanctioning decisions are always published in an anonymised manner in the sanctioning yearbooks. These prove that in the years 2010-13 real estate agents were regularly sanctioned for not complying with CDD or record keeping obligations. In nearly all cases, the Board sanctioned estate agents with a warning.

7.8 County administrative boards of Västra Götaland, Stockholm and Skåne (*Länsstyrelserna*)

This chapter previously observed the split between auditors and other accounting professionals. Because the group of accountants is larger than auditors, this section first deals with supervision by the county administrative boards of Västra Götaland, Stockholm and Skåne.[381] Although these are three separate authorities, each with a different geographical jurisdiction, this research presents them as one. The reason for this is that they have the same powers, they supervise the same kind of accountants and accountancy firms, and the way in which they operate is very similar. Where variations between the county administrative boards are present, this will be mentioned.

7.8.1 Supervisory powers

Unlike the other Swedish supervisors, the county administrative boards derive their powers directly from the AML Act. Chapter 6, Section 4 PL states that the boards may order professionals who perform any of the activities related to bookkeeping or accounting, tax or legal advice, trust and company service providers and professional dealers of goods to provide information about their activities in order to assess whether an obligation to register with the Swedish Companies Registration Office exists.[382] Chapter 6, Section 7 PL states that the county administrative boards may order the institutions and professionals subject to their supervision to provide information and to grant access to the documents required for AML supervision. The boards may conduct an investigation of institutions and professionals subject to their supervision, that it when they are registered with the Companies Registration Office. This power is formulated broadly and is not further specified. In the explanatory memorandum to the Act, the Government considered that the boards should be able to order their supervisees to submit information and provide access to the documents necessary for supervision, as well as to conduct an inspection on the premises of a supervisee when they consider this to be necessary.[383] From a legality perspective, it would be advisable to clarify this in the AML Act. Besides the power to compel the production of information necessary for supervision and the (implicit) on-site inspection power, the AML Regulation empowers the county administrative boards to

381 See § 7.4.4 and 7.4.5. Based on this data, there are more than 5,000 accountants and accountancy professionals; and around 4,000 auditors and audit firms.

382 This was also mentioned in § 7.5.3.

383 *Regeringens Proposition* 2008/09:70, at 204.

provide regulations on a number of preventive obligations.[384] All three boards have issued AML regulations.[385] These lower-level regulations are legally binding, meaning that those subject to the supervision of the boards must comply with the regulations.[386]

7.8.2 Anti-money laundering supervision in practice

AML supervision by the county administrative boards is not embedded in wider supervisory programmes for which they bear responsibility.[387] When they carry out this supervision, they focus exclusively on compliance with the obligations stemming from the AML Act. All three county administrative boards have (annual) supervision plans, which contain the planned activities for the year.[388] These plans are not public documents, but have been made available for the purpose of this research.[389] None of the supervision plans for the year 2013 provides evidence of a risk-based approach to AML supervision, although there seems to be some movement towards that direction. The supervision plan 2013 of Västra Götaland mentions that a risk analysis should be implemented and that the information sources for it should be intelligence shared within the regional intelligence centre in which the board participates, the media and crime reports, and its own knowledge of existing or potential institutions and professionals subject to its supervision. The county administrative board of Stockholm makes a prioritisation in its wide range of supervisory activities, and designated AML supervision as a whole as a high priority for the year 2013.[390] Whereas the AML Act provides inspection powers to the boards, Section 17 AML Regulation obliges the county administrative boards to do so-called fit and proper tests (*vandalsprövning*) where they have been notified by the Swedish Companies Registration Office that an institution or professional has registered. They *must* perform such verification when an institution or professional makes changes to its registration, and they *may* carry out such tests at other times if needed. Altogether AML supervision by the county administrative boards is given shape as follows: off-site inspections, on-site inspections, mandatory fit and proper tests and the creation of awareness.

384 Chapter 8, Section 1 PL in conjunction with Section 18 AML Regulation.

385 *Länsstyrelsens i Västra Götalands län allmänna föreskrifter om åtgärder mot penningtvätt och finansiering av terrorism,* 14 FS 2009:534; *Länsstyrelsens i Stockholms läns allmänna föreskrifter om åtgärder mot penningtvätt och finansiering av terrorism,* 01 FS 2010:1; *Länsstyrelsens almänna föreskrifter om åtgärdar mot penningtvätt och finansiering av terrorism,* 12 FS 2010:174.

386 Interview Länsstyrelsen Stockholm, September 2013. However, in § 7.8.3 it can be seen that the county administrative boards lack sanctioning powers and cannot enforce compliance.

387 Interview Länsstyrelsen Stockholm, September 2013; Interview Länsstyrelsen Västra Götaland, September 2013; Interview Länsstyrelsen Skåne, September 2013.

388 Länsstyrelsen Stockholm, *Tillsynsplan för Tillsysnsenheten 2013*; Länsstyrelsen Stockholm, *Arbetsplanering 2013 Penningtvätt och kamera*; Länsstyrelsen Västra Götaland, *Tillsynsplan för åtgärder mot penningtvätt under verksamhetsåret 2013*; Länsstyrelsen Skåne, *Länsstyrelsens tillsynsplan avseende penningtvätt 2013*; Länsstyrelsen Skåne, *Verksamhetsplan avseende penningtvätt 2013*.

389 I have been allowed to use and to refer to these reports for the purposes of this research: Interview Länsstyrelsen Stockholm, September 2013; Interview Länsstyrelsen Västra Götaland, September 2013; Interview Länsstyrelsen Skåne, September 2013.

390 Länsstyrelsen Stockholm, *Tillsynsplan för Tillsysnsenheten 2013,* at 1-2.

Off-site inspections are desk reviews of the internal policies that are requested from the institutions and professionals subject to the boards' AML supervision.[391] This allows the county administrative boards to verify, on paper, whether the supervisees have adequate AML policies and procedures in place. The annual supervision plans of the boards sometimes indicate the number of off-site inspections: the supervision plans 2013 of Västra Götaland and Skåne refer to 'supervision on the operators' procedures' and 'control of routines'.[392] On-site inspections allow the county administrative boards to review the implementation of the internal policies in practice. All three annual supervision plans for 2013 indicate the number of planned on-site inspections. The plans, however, do not provide information on how these are divided among the different types of institutions and professionals subject to their supervision. The mandatory fit and proper tests are a different type of off-site inspections. They serve to ensure that the institutions and professionals comply with the fit and properness criteria of Chapter 6, Section 5 PL. Since mid-2013 a computerised system (Visma) allows the boards to check criminal records, debt records or other financial statements, and information on other inappropriate behaviour of the institutions and professionals subject to their supervision. Well-developed practice is not yet present and what 'other inappropriate behaviour' means is still something to be clarified. One clear example, however, concerns the non-payment of taxes for which the Swedish Tax Authority has fined the company or person. This administrative law sanction will not be registered in the criminal records, and therefore falls under the category 'other inappropriate behaviour'.[393]

Finally, the boards pay a great deal of attention to the provision of advice and the raising of awareness, in particular with the purpose of ensuring that the institutions and professionals are adequately registered with the Swedish Companies Registration Office. When the county administrative boards were designated as AML supervisors in 2009, they had to devote their scarce resources to the implementation of a supervisory system and at the same give information and raise awareness among the institutions and professionals that had become subject to the AML Act.[394] In 2010, the FATF stated that, 'it is understandable that at the time of the drafting of this follow-up report the authorities were also still focusing on educating DNFBPs with the requirements of the relatively new AML Act'.[395] The 2011 and 2012 annual reports of the county administrative boards and the special reports from the Financial Supervisory Authority demonstrate that all efforts were put into the provision of information and advice and the raising of awareness.[396] Although the boards still consider the raising of awareness as their main task under the AML Act, the numbers demonstrate that they are focusing more and more on the first three tracks.

391 Länsstyrelsen Västra Götaland, *Tillsynsplan för åtgärdar mot penningtvätt under verksamhetsåret 2013*, shows that it concerns a desk review by stating that it is done via written requests to the institution or professional concerned.

392 In Swedish: *tillsyn av verksamhetsutövares rutiner* and *kontroll av rutiner*.

393 Interview Länsstyrelsen Stockholm, September 2013.

394 Interview Länsstyrelsen Västra Götaland, September 2013.

395 FATF (2010b) at 30.

396 Länsstyrelsen Skåne (2011) at 88-89; Länsstyrelsen Skåne (2012) at 118-119; Länsstyrelsen Västra Götaland (2011) at 116; Länsstyrelsen Västra Götaland (2012) at 155-156; Länsstyrelsen Stockholm (2011) at 122; Länsstyrelsen Stockholm (2012) at 126-127; Finansinspektionen (2012b) at 27-28; Finansinspektionen (2013c) at 13-20.

Supervision in numbers

Concerning the exercise of AML supervision, it appears that the annual reports focus almost exclusively on the activities undertaken with respect to the creation of awareness and the provision of information and advice, although here and there some inspection numbers are mentioned.[397] The special reports for 2012 and 2013 from the Financial Supervisory Authority only report on the efforts put into raising awareness and the provision of information and advice by the boards.[398] Based on data obtained during interviews combined with some information from the annual reports, it can be observed that the supervisory intensity of all three county administrative boards is increasing. For all three county administrative boards off-site inspections are the most important type of inspections. In the period 2011-12 the county administrative board of Stockholm carried out 150 off-site inspections, of which 111 were on accountants and accountancy professionals.[399] Västra Götaland's county administrative board carried out 58 off-site inspections in 2011, 54 in 2012 and 127 in 2013.[400] Unfortunately, representatives could not specify how many of those inspections were aimed at accountants. The county administrative board of Skåne carried out 14 off-site inspections in the year 2011, 35 in 2012, and until August 2013 it had carried out 27 off-site inspections in 2013.[401] These numbers are not specified for accountants, but representatives stated that the inclusion of accountants and accounting professionals increased from an estimated 50% in 2011 to 90% in 2013. This was partially because accountants where a priority group for supervision in 2013 and thus received extra attention.[402]

The fit and proper checks are done regularly. Although the AML Regulation obliges the boards to do such tests upon (changes to) the registration of institutions and professionals and allows them to perform tests at other moments, it seems that all three boards strive to test the institutions and professionals subject to their supervision more often. The annual supervision plan for 2013 of county administrative board Stockholm showed the ambition to do a fit and proper test on all institutions and professionals subject to its supervision, and the intention of the county administrative board of Västra Götaland was to do such tests every two years. The annual report for 2013 of Västra Götaland indicates that the fit and proper check had been conducted on 1,620 registered institutions and professionals; no further distinction was made.[403] Until September 2013, Skåne had undertaken the fit and proper test at 920 institutions and professionals; how many of those were accountants is also not known.[404]

397 E.g. Länsstyrelsen Västra Götaland (2012) at 155, which speaks about 54 off-site inspections.
398 Finansinspektionen (2012b) at 27-28; Finansinspektionen (2013c) at 13-20.
399 Interview Länsstyrelsen Stockholm, September 2013. Cf. Länsstyrelsen Stockholm (2011) and Länsstyrelsen Stockholm (2012) speak in total about 155 supervisory actions, of which 110 were aimed at accountants.
400 Interview Länsstyrelsen Västra Götaland, September 2013; Länsstryrelsen Västra Götaland (2011) at 116; Länsstyrelsen Västra Götaland (2012) at 155; Länsstyrelsen Västra Götaland (2013) at 20.
401 Interview Länsstyrelsen Skåne, September 2013.
402 Ibid.
403 Länsstyrelsen Västra Götaland (2013) at 20.
404 Interview Länsstyrelsen Skåne, September 2013.

The number of on-site visits is low for all three county administrative boards. On-site inspections are said to be of a recent nature and the boards do not have a lot of experience here. The main reasons seem to be the fact that on-site inspections are resource intensive and that the boards were required in the first years to invest a considerable amount of time and effort into raising awareness within the group of obliged institutions and professionals in order to ensure registration. Above we could see that the county administrative boards have only between 3 and 4 FTE available each, while they have supervisory responsibility for a large number of professionals and institutions.[405] In 2011 and 2012, the county administrative board of Västra Götaland carried 0 and 2 on-site inspections, respectively.[406] In 2013, it did 6 on-site visits, of which representatives indicated earlier in that year that at least four of these visits were at accountants or accountancy firms.[407] Länsstyrelsen Stockholm indicated that on-site inspections were carried out for the first time in 2012, but until September none of these had been on accountants.[408] The county administrative board of Skåne seems to have more experience with on-site inspections. It carried out 13 on-site inspections in 2012 and until August 2013 it had performed 24 on-site inspections in that year.[409] How many of those involved accountants could not be said.

In sum, it seems that accountants have been subject to off-site inspections, fit and proper tests and on-site inspections by the county administrative boards. It can be observed that the numbers of on-site inspections are low in comparison to the total number of accountants subject to the county administrative boards' supervision. Resource issues in combination with the fact that a lot of effort had to be expended on ensuring that institutions and professionals are registered are seen as the main reasons for this low level of on-site supervision.

7.8.3 Sanctioning powers

The three county administrative boards are entirely dependent on the AML Act for their sanctioning powers. Chapter 6, Section 9 PL states that orders may be subject to a public law fine (*vite*). There are no minimum or maximum amounts attached to the public law fine. They can decide whether they attach a public law fine to an order, but it is the county administrative court which ultimately establishes that a fine is due.[410]

> As explained in § 7.6.3, a public law fine is 'a sum of money whose amount is fixed beforehand by a court or public authority and which is payable by someone who fails to fulfil, within a certain time limit, a legal obligation as established by the court or public authority and which is payable by someone who fails to fulfil, within a prescribed time limit, a legal obligation as established by the court or public authority concerned'.[411]

405 Interview Länsstyrelsen Stockholm, September 2013; Interview Länsstyrelsen Västra Götaland, September 2013; Interview Länsstyrelsen Skåne, September 2013.
406 Länsstyrelsen Västra Götaland (2011) at 166; Länsstyrelsen Västra Götaland (2012) at 155-156.
407 Länsstyrelsen Västra Götaland (2013) at 20; Interview Länsstyrelsen Västra Götaland, September 2013.
408 Interview Länsstyrelsen Stockholm, September 2013.
409 Interview Länsstyrelsen Skåne, September 2013.
410 Blanc-Gonnet Jonason (2013) at 561.
411 Ibid., at 560.

The AML Act does not provide any other sanctioning powers to the county administrative boards. The fact that the public law fine is the only sanction available makes the sanctioning toolkit highly inadequate. Most problematic is the nature of the sanction in combination with the way in which it is formulated in the AML Act. The result of the current formulation is that boards can only sanction non-compliance with an order that they have issued, and not directly for any non-compliance with the AML Act. This means that in the case of the identification of (serious) breaches of the preventive AML obligations, the county administrative boards cannot sanction immediately – even if the nature of the breach so requires. Offenders that have been caught during an inspection can 'escape' from a sanction if they consequently comply with the order for rectification. Only if an order is not followed are the county administrative boards legally empowered to impose a public law fine. As explained, this fine then still has to be declared due by the county administrative court.

Likewise, the formulation of this sanctioning power in relation to the obligation to register is unfortunate. As explained in § 7.5.3, the boards cannot enforce registration. They lack the legal power to sanction those who refuse to register. They are empowered to require an institution or professional to cease its activities, possibly accompanied with a public law fine, but only when the request to provide information for the purpose of assessing whether registration is required or not is not complied with. Above we saw that this is a major problem in practice, especially because the boards only have supervisory responsibility for those accountants that are registered at the Companies Registration Office, while only an estimated 25% to 32% are registered in practice.

7.8.4 Sanctioning policy and practice

It is impossible to analyse a sanctioning policy when non-compliance cannot be sanctioned in the first place. Although it cannot be established with absolute certainty, the absence of sanctions is most likely the direct result of the lack of sanctioning powers. The boards have no sanctioning policy or practice to rely on. The legal gap in sanctioning powers must first be remedied before the boards can actually develop a specific policy. It is not surprising that the county administrative boards of Stockholm and Skåne have never imposed a sanction in all the years that they have been the AML supervisor. Representatives of the county administrative board of Skåne indicated that orders for information subject to a public law fine have been made, but were all complied with.[412] The county administrative board of Västra Götaland imposed five public law fines. Four were declared due by the county administrative court, of which two were against accountants. The fines were imposed for non-compliance with the order to implement a rectification after the mandatory fit and proper check.[413]

The absence of sanctions is certainly not because accountants are always compliant with the obligations under the AML Act. I already pointed out that only an estimated 25% to 32% of all accountants are registered and, thus, are supervised by the county administrative boards. In addition, the county administrative board of Stockholm indicated that from its

412 Interview Länsstyrelsen Skåne, September 2013.
413 Interview Länsstyrelsen Västra Götaland, September 2013.

inspection activities it appeared that a large variation between the businesses' knowledge of the AML obligations exists, and that in particular accountants appeared to have difficulties in establishing adequate internal procedures on paper.[414] The county administrative board of Skåne indicated a great ignorance regarding the legal obligations with respect to internal policies, as well as how these are to be established and applied.[415] The reporting levels of accountants appear to be very low as well. In 2010 accountants disclosed two reports to the Swedish FIU, and in both 2011 and 2012 three suspicion reports.[416] An argument provided for this reporting behaviour is that accountants do not feel comfortable, or even fear, disclosing money laundering suspicions to the Swedish FIU because they believe that a suspicion report is tantamount to a police report.[417] A second argument is ignorance of the law, despite all information efforts from the county administrative boards.[418]

7.8.5 Concluding remarks

The county administrative boards can compel the production of information for supervisory purposes, perform off-site and on-site inspections, and have regulatory powers via the AML Regulation. They have adequate supervisory powers, although from a legality perspective it would be better to stipulate explicitly in the AML Act that the boards are allowed to perform on-site inspections. In practice the boards build their AML supervision on four tracks: off-site inspections, on-site inspections, mandatory fit and proper tests, and the provision of advice and the raising of awareness. Statistics demonstrate that AML supervision is carried out in practice on accountants, although mostly via the mandatory fit and proper tests or off-site inspections. On-site inspections are of a recent nature, but may constitute resource issues in light of the low number of FTEs compared to the number of institutions and professionals for which the boards have supervisory responsibility. In this respect, it is observed that the boards have not (yet) implemented a risk-based approach to AML supervision. Implementing a risk-based approach with more on-site inspections could improve the AML supervision of accountants. However, the lack of adequate sanctioning powers should first be remedied. The county administrative boards have never imposed a sanction for non-compliance with the preventive AML obligations. Only one sanctioning power – the public law fine – is available to the boards and this power is very limited in terms of its possible application. Identified non-compliant behaviour cannot be sanctioned directly, but is made subject to compliance with an order. In relation to the registration obligation, as was demonstrated in § 7.5.3, the lack of adequate sanctioning powers also results in the situation that they cannot do what they are supposed to be doing. County administrative boards have to invest a great deal of time and resources in persuading institutions and professionals to register with the county administrative boards, before they can start their supervision. This seriously undermines the effectiveness of their supervision.

414 Interview Länsstyrelsen Stockholm, September 2013.
415 Interview Länsstyrelsen Skåne, September 2013.
416 Finanspolisen (2012) at 27. Cf. § 7.2.
417 Finansinspektionen (2013c) at 14, 16 and 19.
418 Ibid., at 16.

7.9 Supervisory Board of Public Auditors (*Revisorsnämnden*)[419]

7.9.1 Supervisory powers

The Auditors Act provides the Board with its supervisory powers. Section 28 states that auditors, registered audit firms and auditors from third countries are obliged to allow the Board, when exercising its supervisory functions, to inspect files, accounts and other documents pertaining to their activities and to provide the information necessary for the supervision. This obligation exists when RN carries out supervision at the request of a competent authority of another State as well. Hence, professional secrecy cannot be invoked against the Board. It can furthermore order a business with particularly strong ties to an audit firm to provide information on the services provided by the audit firm or an auditor from that firm.[420] A public law fine can be attached to such an order. The Board thus has the power to compel the production of information necessary for the exercise of supervision, as well as inspection powers. The Auditors Act does not say anything about the nature of the inspections, but the FATF has observed that 'on-site visits are possible; however, it does not seem that it is often made use of them'.[421] Nevertheless, as considered for the county administrative boards, from a legality perspective it would be more robust to make explicit in the law that the inspections may take place on-site.

Unlike the other Swedish supervisors, the AML Regulation does not empower the Supervisory Board of Public Auditors to draft regulations with respect to certain specific obligations, such as risk assessments, customer due diligence, politically exposed persons, and record keeping. The Government Bill on the AML Act considered that it already follows from the auditors' ethics that auditors should file a complaint when they suspect that a client is laundering money and that, therefore, the Board has regulatory functions to ensure that auditors have procedures in place to report the occurrence of money laundering by clients. The Government stated in the Bill that RN can issue regulations on how auditors should relate their ethics to the preventive AML obligations.[422] The Board's regulatory powers are thus laid down in the Auditors Act. Pursuant to Section 41, the Auditors Regulation provides it with a broad power to issue regulations concerning the authorisation or approval of auditors and the registration of audit firms, the quality control and other conditions for auditors and audit firms.[423] In its regulations on conditions for auditors and registered audit firms the Board refers to the obligation for auditors to comply with the preventive AML obligations and that auditors and audit firms are generally obliged, to the extent of their professional ethics, to take measures to prevent their own operations or principal activities from being used for the purpose of money laundering or terrorist financing.[424] In terms of content the regulations deviate from the regulations of the other

7

419 Please note that no interview took place with the Supervisory Board of Public Auditors and that the information presented in this section stems solely from public information. See: § 1.5.

420 Section 29 Auditors Act.

421 FATF (2006a) at 132.

422 *Regeringens Proposition* 2008/09:70, at 166-167.

423 Section 29 Auditors Regulation.

424 *Revisorsnämndens föreskrifter om villkor för revisorers och registrerade revisionsbolags verksamhet (RNFS 2001:2), uppdaterad t.o.m. RNFS 2013:2.*

Swedish supervisors. These all state in detail how the institutions and professionals subject to their supervision should apply a risk-based approach, perform customer due diligence, etc., whereas the Board decided to leave that to the professional association FAR.[425] This association has developed these regulations as part of its professional ethics.[426] Many authorised and approved auditors, as well as audit firms, are members of FAR.

It can be observed that the Auditors Act provides adequate supervisory powers to the Supervisory Board of Public Auditors, although it would be advisable to make explicit that inspections can be of an on-site nature. We will now see how the Board makes use of the supervisory powers in practice.

7.9.2 Anti-money laundering supervision in practice

AML supervision is an integrated part of the wider quality control system. The Board does not carry out separate AML supervision or targeted AML inspections. It carries out supervision via its systematic and outreach supervision (*systematisk och uppsökande tillsyn, SUT*) and its periodic quality control programme.[427] If inspectors during the exercise of supervision reveal serious shortcomings in auditors' activities, the situation is discussed with the audit firm and the auditor concerned. The Supervisory Board of Public Auditors can then decide to forward the information to its Regulatory Board (*Tillsynsnämnden*) which considers whether disciplinary action is needed.[428]

7.9.2.1 Systematic and outreach supervision

Within the systematic and outreach supervision programme, RN has a number of projects.[429] One project specifically focuses on large audit firms and auditors for listed companies. Other projects are aimed at auditors who refuse to submit to FAR's quality control; auditors who have a large number of audit assignments; auditors about whom doubts emerged when they applied for a renewal of the approval or authorisation; the follow-up monitoring of auditors who have previously been sanctioned for having serious shortcomings in their auditing activities; and other projects. Other projects can be

425 Finansinspektionen (2012b) at 22. Cf. Revisorsnämnden (2010), *Frågor med anledning av framtagande av penningtvättsföreskrifter (Fi dnr 09-8129)*, available at: <www.revisorsnamnden.se/rn/showdocument/documents/yttranden_skrivelser_m_m/2009_1143.pdf>, last visited on 28 March 2014. Loosely translated, RN stated here that the FAR was working on a statement concerning the application of regulations on money laundering to which RN provided comments in terms of comments and design. RN hoped that the statement corresponded to what otherwise should have been subject to regulation by Revisorsnämnden and that it would not need to issue further regulations.

426 *FARS Uttalanden i etikfrågor, EtikU 11: Medlemmarnas tillämpning av lagen om åtgärder mot penningtvätt och finansiering av terrorism*, December 2012, available at: <www.far.se/PageFiles/7025/ETIKU11_dec2012.pdf>, last visited on 28 March 2014 (in English: *FARS Statement in ethics issues, EtikU 11, Members' application of the law on measures against money laundering and financing Terrorism*).

427 The periodic quality controls are based on Section 27a Auditors Act.

428 See §§ 7.4.4.2 and 7.9.3 about this Regulatory Board.

429 Revisorsnämnden, *Mer om SUT och kvalitetskontroll*, available at: <www.revisorsnamnden.se/rn/tillsyn/las_mer_om_systematisk_och_uppsokande_tillsyn_och_kvalitetskontroll.html>, last visited on 28 March 2014.

investigations which have been opened based on information from the media, or for any other apparent reason.

Unfortunately, public information on how these supervisory projects within the SUT programme are planned and exercised remains absent.[430] It is not clear whether supervision within the SUT projects is mostly made up of desk reviews, whether RN carries out on-site inspections, or a combination thereof. It is also not clear for all supervisory projects how these are planned. Are there focal themes in a particular year, or is equal weight given to the aforementioned projects? Likewise, one may wonder whether the Supervisory Board of Public Auditors applies a risk-based approach to its (anti-money laundering) supervision within the SUT. It is not clear whether the systematic and outreach supervision is based on (annual) supervision plans, and how many inspections are carried out annually. Perhaps most importantly with respect to this research, however, is that it is impossible to say to what extent the verification of compliance with preventive AML obligations is included in the projects. The annual reports for 2012 and 2013 do not provide evidence of the prevention of money laundering being a project or focal point within RN's systematic and outreach supervision programme.[431]

7.9.2.2 Periodic quality controls

Periodic quality controls are carried out by the Supervisory Board of Public Auditors and the professional organisation FAR. The Board carries out periodic quality controls on audit firms and auditors of listed companies. In accordance with Section 27a Auditors Act it carries out these controls on the seven largest audit firms in Sweden every three years.[432] It does so by system-oriented quality controls, which are assessments of the audit firms' internal policies. Periodic quality control reports from the Board show that this includes the procedures and internal systems in place for the prevention of money laundering and terrorist financing.[433] The Supervisory Board of Public Auditors also checks a number of specific assignments to see how auditors within the firm apply the policies in practice, which it calls mission-oriented quality control.[434] The FAR performs quality controls on the audit firms and auditors that do not audit listed companies. Such controls must take place at least once every six years.[435] The Board and FAR have signed a supervisory arrangement agreeing that FAR carries out the periodic quality controls on its members. The Board oversees this via sample testing of quality controls performed by FAR in a

430 One exception concerns the project on large audit firms and auditors for listed companies, where in Revisorsnämnden (2012) at 11 states how it carries out its supervision within this project.

431 Revisorsnämnden (2012) at 10; Revisorsnämnden (2013), *Revisorsnämndens årsredovisning för räkenskapsåret 2013*, Dnr 2013-1607 at 11.

432 Revisorsnämnden (2013) at 6.

433 For example: RN Case, *Deloitte AB*, 29 October 2013, Dnr. 2012-56. Other reports are available at: <www.revisorsnamnden.se/rn/tillsyn/kvalitetskontrollrapporter.html>, last visited on 28 March 2014.

434 Revisorsnämnden (2013) at 12; Revisorsnämnden, *Kvalitetskontroll av revisorer som utför lagstadgad revision i börsnoterade företag*, available at: <www.revisorsnamnden.se/rn/tillsyn/kvalitetsgranskning/mer_om_kvalitetskontroll_av_revisorer_som_utfor_lagstadgad_revision_i_borsnoterade_foretag.html>, last visited on 28 March 2014.

435 Section 27a Auditors Act.

particular year.[436] When FAR inspectors identify serious breaches made by an auditor, they should inform the Supervisory Board of Public Auditors. The Board can decide to open a disciplinary case, to carry out a further investigation and to consider taking disciplinary action. Likewise, FAR should report to the Board when FAR members refuse to subject themselves to quality controls by the FAR. The Board carries out the quality controls on that group, as well as on those auditors and audit firms that are not FAR members.

More information about the periodic quality controls is, unfortunately, not available. The Auditors Act establishes the inspection cycle for period quality controls, i.e. three and six years respectively, but how the Supervisory Board of Auditors and FAR plan their controls within these inspection cycles, and how compliance with the AML Act is included, is not clear. There is no information about the existence of a public supervision policy. Although the public quality controls by the Board give the impression that compliance with the obligations to have an internal AML policy is checked, no such information is available about the period quality controls from the FAR. The information on the Board of Supervision of Public Auditors does not prove if, and if so how, compliance with, for example, the reporting obligation under the AML Act is supervised. It is unfortunate that the supervisory arrangement between the Board and the FAR is not publicly available. Therefore, it cannot be verified whether it is concluded on a legal basis, which agreements are made, the binding nature of the arrangement, the nature and procedure of the quality control checks exercised by FAR, the extent to which and the way within which the AML obligations are included in the quality control checks exercised by FAR, and so on. This situation is comparable to the situation in Spain, where the supervisory arrangements between SEPBLAC and the financial regulators with regard to AML supervision are of a confidential nature.[437] Above we saw that in the Netherlands the supervisory arrangement between the Financial Supervision Office and a professional association was not publicly available either.[438]

7.9.2.3 Supervision in numbers

The annual reports for 2012 and 2013 demonstrate that a total of 11 and 21 cases respectively were opened within SUT projects.[439] Whether a case is the same as an inspection with one auditor or audit firm is, however, not explained in the reports. The reports also demonstrate within which projects supervisory action was taken and how many cases were closed and forwarded for disciplinary action. As regards the periodic quality controls on audit firms and auditors for listed companies, the annual report for the years 2012 and 2013 indicate the number of firms and auditors inspected.[440] In 2013, for example, the Board carried out 3 system-oriented quality controls with audit firms and opened 14 mission-oriented quality controls on specific assignments of auditors within the firms. The annual reports for 2012 and 2013 also indicate the total number of audit firms and auditors supervised

436 Ibid.

437 See § 4.6.3.2.

438 But we could also see in Chapter 5 that the text of the supervisory arrangement was provided for the purpose of this research.

439 Revisorsnämnden (2012) at 10; Revisorsnämnden (2013) at 11.

440 Revisorsnämnden (2012) at 11; Revisorsnämnden (2013) at 13.

by FAR and the Supervisory Board of Public Auditors within the periodic quality control programme.[441] In the years 2011-13, the Board and FAR opened the following number of quality controls on authorised and approved auditors (audit firms are excluded):

Table 11 – Periodic quality controls by RN and FAR on auditors[442]

	RN	FAR
2011	16	938
2012	27	477
2013	14	1,238

The annual reports from Revisorsnämnden thus demonstrate that the Supervisory Board of Public Auditors and FAR carry out supervision. They prove that within the periodic quality control programme the number of controls by FAR strongly outweighs those by the Supervisory Board. This makes it even more lamentable that there is so little information about the agreements made between the Board and FAR. The extent to which AML supervision is included in the SUT and period quality control numbers cannot be inferred from the statistics. In the absence of more information, it is not known whether the verification of compliance with the AML obligations is included in all controls on auditors, and which preventive obligations are assessed. Likewise, the statistics do not give an indication of the nature of the supervisory activities, in other words: whether the controls have been merely desk reviews or whether they include on-site inspections as well.

7.9.3 Sanctioning powers

The sanctioning powers are laid down in the Auditors Act. The following sanctions are available to the Board: the revocation of authorisation, a warning or a reminder.[443] Section 32 states that if an auditor is intentionally non-compliant or otherwise acting dishonestly or if an auditor does not pay his fees according to the Auditors Act, the Board shall in principle revoke his authorisation. If there are mitigating circumstances RN may decide to give a warning instead. If an auditor otherwise neglects his duties as an auditor, the Board shall issue a warning. If it is necessary, RN can decide to issue a reminder. If there are aggravating circumstances, however, the Supervisory Board of Public Auditors should revoke the authorisation (or registration). The authorisation of an authorised or approved auditor will also be revoked where the auditor no longer meets the professional requirements.[444] Where an audit firm does not meet the requirements under the Auditors

441 Revisorsnämnden (2012) at 10-11; Revisorsnämnden (2013) at 12.

442 Own table based on Tables 15 and 16 of Revisorsnämnden (2013) at 12. These numbers exclude the audit firms/businesses (*byråer*) that FAR has visited. For the Board the number relates to quality controls on non-FAR members. Periodic controls on FAR members that have refused to submit themselves to periodic quality controls by FAR are included in the RN's SUT programme. This table also excludes the number of quality controls on audit firms and auditors for listed companies mentioned above.

443 Instead of the revocation of authorisation, audit firms can be deregistered: Section 32 in conjunction with Section 34(1) Auditors Act.

444 Section 33 Auditors Act. For audit firms and auditors from third countries RN may decide to suspend their registration.

Act, its registration shall be suspended.[445] Section 35 Auditors Act states that it may decide to order a rectification by an authorised or approved auditor, or an audit firm or auditor from a third country, instead of revoking authorisation or cancelling registration. If the order is not followed, it may still decide to revoke the authorisation or deregister an audit firm in accordance with Sections 32-34 Auditors Act. Revocations of the authorisations of authorised or approved auditors, or the deregistration of audit firms may have immediate effect.[446] Where the Board considers revoking an authorisation or issuing a warning or reminder, it must give the auditor the opportunity in writing to comment on the facts and circumstances of the case.[447] A warning or reminder cannot be issued where the non-compliant or dishonest behaviour of the auditor took place longer than five years before the auditor received a notification of the case.

The sanctioning powers of the Supervisory Board of Public Auditors correspond to the sanctioning powers of the Estate Agents Inspectorate.[448] For that authority it was considered that deregistration is a very powerful and dissuasive sanction, whereas the disciplinary warning and reminder are rather mild and that the dividing line between a warning and a reminder is unclear. For the Estate Agents Inspectorate it was concluded that there is hardly any or no possibility to scale up sanctioning action in a proportionate way in the absence of adequate and proportionate sanctions, that are positioned somewhere in between deregistration or a warning (and a reminder). This should also be concluded for the Supervisory Board of Public Auditors, as it can either revoke an auditor's authorisation, approval or registration (audit firms), which is a highly dissuasive and powerful sanction, or settle the case with a warning or reminder.

> It seems that the Supervisory Board of Public Auditors itself would not agree with the characterisation of a warning and a reminder as rather mild sanctions. The Board itself finds that these sanctions also have a considerable impact, even though the formal legal consequences of the sanctions are limited. In its annual report 2013 it states that 'it is also well known that a warning and reminder are in the auditors' world not generally considered as insignificant measures. The sanctions may be experienced even more harshly by auditors who work in the countryside, where a decision on disciplinary action attracts a relatively high profile in the local press' (*own translation, MB*).[449]

7.9.4 Sanctioning policy and practice

Disciplinary cases originate either from the systematic and outreach supervision, the periodic quality control system, from a complaint by a consumer, company, third party or the FAR, or from other sources such as media reports. Sanctioning decisions are ultimately taken by RN's Regulatory Board, which publishes the anonymised disciplinary decisions on its website. As explained in § 7.4.3.2, this Board is composed of nine members and decides on its regulations, matters of disciplinary action and other matters of principal

445 Section 34(2) Auditors Act. This same applies to auditors from third countries if the requirements for registration are not met: Section 34(3) Auditors Act.
446 Section 35(2) Auditors Act.
447 Section 32(3) Auditors Act.
448 See § 7.7.3.
449 Revisorsnämnden (2013) at 19.

importance to the authority. Disciplinary cases are dealt with in writing. Notwithstanding the origin of the disciplinary case, upon opening such a disciplinary case the Board sends a notification to the auditor in accordance with Section 32, third paragraph, Auditors Act. The auditor is given the opportunity to comment on the facts and circumstances of the case. He can provide the Board with (other) relevant information where the auditor believes that this is necessary or at the request of the Board. Once the auditor has responded to the notification, RN can decide whether a further investigation is needed or whether a disciplinary decision can be delivered. Neither the annual reports, nor the website and the special reports from the Financial Supervisory Authority provide evidence of the existence of a sanctioning policy. This is not in line with the literature and the theoretical framework, which advocate the usefulness of public supervision (sanctioning) plans in relation to effective supervision.[450]

Overall, the Regulatory Board decided 106 disciplinary cases and 139 disciplinary cases in 2013.[451] Of those disciplinary cases in 2012, a little more than 25% originated from the SUT and periodic quality controls by the Supervisory Board of Public Auditors, while the majority of disciplinary cases resulted from complaints or notifications.[452] In 2013, a little more than 20% of the disciplinary cases originated from its own supervisory activities.[453] Of all disciplinary cases that originated in 2013, around two-thirds were written off without a disciplinary sanction.[454] In 2012, this occurred in 52% of the cases.[455]

With respect to sanctions for non-compliance with the obligations stemming from the AML Act specifically, it can be observed that since the entry into force of the AML Act until the end of March 2014, the database of disciplinary decisions provides only one case in which compliance with the obligations from the AML Act was a direct point of discussion.[456] In October 2013, the Regulatory Board for the first time sanctioned an auditor with a warning for not having complied with the basic customer due diligence obligations stemming from the AML Act.[457] Based on a complaint, the Board investigated the authorised auditor concerned. It found that the auditor had not performed an identity check at the time of the conclusion of the audit assignment and had also failed to perform such a check at a later point in time. The auditor was also criticised for other behaviour and altogether the Board decided to issue a warning against the auditor. There are no other cases that concern non-compliance with the AML Act, although RN has decided

450 See § 2.4.3.3.
451 Revisorsnämnden (2012) at 16; Revisorsnämnden (2013) at 17.
452 Revisorsnämnden (2012) at 20.
453 Revisorsnämnden (2013) at 21.
454 Ibid.
455 Revisorsnämnden (2012) at 20.
456 Anonymised disciplinary decisions can be found in Swedish on: <www.revisorsnamnden.se/rn/search/praxis.html>, last visited on 28 March 2014. Reference period: 15th of March 2009 until 28th of March 2014. Search term used: 'penningtvätt'. The database delivered six hits, which all have been translated by myself and subsequently analysed. One case explicitly discussed AML compliance and referred to AML legislation: RN Case D 13, 31 October 2013, Dnr 2012-1522. In two cases, money laundering was mentioned in relation to sound auditing practice, but no reference was made to the AML legislation in place: RN Case D 43/10, 10 December 2010, Dnr 2010-697, and RN Case D 15/11, 5 May 2011, Dnr 2011-409.
457 RN Case D 13, Dnr 2012-1522, 31 October 2013.

on two cases closely related thereto. Both cases followed from the quality control system and in both cases the auditor had not acted in accordance with good auditing practice and professional ethics by failing to consider or investigate whether transactions were used for the purpose of money laundering.[458]

> It is remarkable that while the Board makes no mention – except for a minor reference to the AML coordination body – of its activities in the field of the prevention of money laundering in the annual report for 2012, it discusses this case extensively in its 2013 annual report.[459] In that report the Board stated that for a long time it had a special focus on how auditors take into account their AML obligations as part of their auditing activities within the quality controls and investigations in disciplinary cases. The Board itself concluded that this decision demonstrated that auditors must not only comply with good auditing standards, but also with the obligations stemming from the AML Act.

Recognising that there has been only one sanctioning decision by the Board which concerns compliance with the preventive AML obligations in five years can have various explanations, it still gives the impression that AML supervision and sanctioning is very minimal. Especially when one takes into account that in both 2012 and 2013 the Board decided more than 100 cases and imposed sanctions in between one-third and half of these cases. In any case, it gives the impression that AML supervision by the Supervisory Board of Public Auditors is rather invisible.

7.9.5 Concluding remarks

The Auditors Act provides adequate supervisory powers to the Supervisory Board of Public Auditors. It has the power to compel the production of information relevant to monitoring compliance. The Board can perform on-site and off-site inspections both in respect of auditors and audit firms, although from a legality perspective it is advisable to make the on-site nature of these inspections explicit in the law. The Board also has regulatory powers, which it has partly outsourced to the professional organisation FAR, which has drafted detailed regulations in relation to the risk-based approach, customer due diligence and other obligations, as part of the professional ethics. AML supervision by the Supervisory Board of Public Auditors is integrated into its regular supervision. Within the systematic and outreach supervision programme (SUT), the Board has a number of projects. These projects do not give evidence of the prevention of money laundering being a focal point within the SUT. AML supervision is integrated into the periodic quality controls as well. These controls are exercised by the Board and the professional organisation FAR, for which they have concluded a supervisory arrangement. The Auditors Act establishes the inspection cycle for periodic quality controls, i.e. three and six years respectively. How AML supervision is carried out in practice, however, remains a point of conjecture and an analysis appears impossible. There is, inter alia, no information regarding a risk-based approach to AML supervision by the Board and FAR, the existence of public supervision policies, the on-site or off-site nature of the SUT and periodic quality controls and the extent to which AML aspects are included in

458 RN Case, D 15/11, Dnr 2011-409, 5 May 2011; RN Case, D 43/10, 10 December 2010, Dnr 2010-697.
459 Revisorsnämnden (2012) at 20; Revsirsonämnden (2013) at 18.

the Board's regular supervisory activities. Information on the supervisory arrangement between the Supervisory Board of Public Auditors and the professional organisation FAR on the exercise of periodic quality controls by the latter organisation on its members is unavailable as well. Finally, the limited numbers of general statistics demonstrate that the numbers of periodic quality controls by FAR strongly outweigh those of the Supervisory Board, but the extent to which AML compliance played a role in these controls remains unknown. Despite the fact that the Supervisory Board of Public Auditors itself states that it has had an increased focus on compliance with the preventive anti-money laundering obligations in recent years, the lack of transparency does not point in that direction.[460] The Board is not transparent about the way in which it carries out AML supervision or how it is integrated into its regular supervisory procedures.

The Regulatory Board can impose the dissuasive sanction of the revocation of authorisation or approval, or in the case of audit firms: deregistration, or the comparatively mild sanctions of a warning or reminder. The dividing line between a warning and a reminder is unclear. Because it can either decide to revoke an auditor's authorisation or approval or warn/remind him, there is hardly any or no possibility to scale up sanctioning action in a proportionate way in the absence of adequate and proportionate sanctions that are positioned somewhere in between the revocation or a warning. This makes the sanctioning powers inadequate. Disciplinary cases originate either from the systematic and outreach supervision, the periodic quality control system, or from complaints by consumers, companies or other parties, or from other sources such as media reports. Information on a (publicly available) sanctioning policy at the Board is lacking. Despite the fact that the Regulatory Board takes many sanctioning decisions – in the years 2012 and 2013 more than 100 annually – it has imposed only one sanction for non-compliance with the AML Act in five years' time. The sanction was imposed after the Board had received a complaint and investigated the matter. It gives the impression that AML supervision by the Supervisory Board of Public Auditors is very minimal or at least rather invisible.

7.10 Supervisory cooperation for the prevention of money laundering

7.10.1 Institutionalised forums for AML cooperation on a policy level

In Sweden an important institutional forum for cooperation on a policy level to which all anti-money laundering supervisors participate is the AML coordination body. There are other institutionalised forums for cooperation which are closely related to the AML policy and in which some of the supervisors participate. These institutionalised cooperation efforts, however, are more focused on the criminal investigation side and not primarily on preventing money laundering. For example, the Financial Supervisory Authority participates in the National Economic Crime Council (*Ekorådet*), whereas the county administrative boards participate in the so-called Regional Intelligence Centres

460 Finansinspektionen (2012b) at 23; Finansinspektionen (2013c) at 21; Revisorsnämnden (2013), *Revisorsnämndens årsredovisning för räkenskapsåret 2013*, at 18.

(*Regionala Underrättelsecenter, RUC*).[461] These are intelligence platforms against serious organised crime and work within the national framework for combating serious organised crime.[462] In 2007, the Supervisory Board of Public Auditors was reported to meet regularly with representatives from the Swedish Economic Crimes Bureau and the Swedish Tax Agency (*Skatteverket*) in matters relating to auditors and audit firms and the prevention of financial crime, as well as with the Financial Supervisory Authority.[463]

The AML Act and the AML Regulation established a coordination body.[464] All AML supervisors, except for the Swedish Bar Association, are obliged to participate in this body.[465] In practice, the Bar Association has participated from the beginning as well.[466] Likewise, the Swedish FIU and Swedish Companies Registration Office are also involved by attending meetings of the coordination body.[467] The Financial Supervisory Authority is responsible for the coordination body. Meetings between the representatives of the authorities take place approximately once every two months. In 2012 and 2013, the coordination body convened five times each year.[468]

> The establishment of the coordination body followed from a recommendation from the Swedish Agency for Public Management. In its review of the implementation of the Third Directive and the new supervisory structure, the Agency also considered the question of cooperation between the supervisors. This had appeared to be a concern for the FATF during its evaluation of Sweden as it found that cooperation on a policy level was too reactive. It recommended a more proactive approach.[469] As an alternative to supervisory concentration with one AML supervisor, the Swedish Agency for Public Management advised the setting up of a special advisory board or committee with FI as the responsible authority for the administration thereof. One of the reasons for recommending to provide this responsibility to the Financial Supervisory Authority was because it has the most experience with AML supervision and because it is the authority which implements the most comprehensive regulatory efforts coupled with the AML legislation.[470] The Agency stated that the coordination body should serve as an information hub (*informationsnav*) and bring together the supervisory information from all different sectors. A good knowledge of money laundering, supervision and methodology was not present at all the authorities, it considered.[471] The body would allow for more coherent supervision across the different sectors, which was pointed out by the Agency as a precondition for combating money laundering effectively.[472] The Government Bill shows that the

461 FATF (2006a) at 145; Swedish Government (2007), *Genomförande av tredje Penningtvättsdirektivet*, SOU 2007:23, at 88.

462 Regional intelligence centres form part of a larger national effort in combating serious organised crime. See for more information: Swedish Government (2011), Informationsutbyte *vid samarbete mot grov organiserad brottslighet*, SOU 2011:80 (in English: *Exchange of information on cooperation against serious organised crime*). This is a study commissioned to review and improve the exchange of information between authorities that cooperate in the fight against serious organised crime.

463 Swedish Government (2007), *Genomförande av tredje Penningtvättsdirektivet*, SOU 2007:23, at 86.

464 Sections 13-15 AML Regulation.

465 Section 15 AML Regulation.

466 Finansinspektionen et al. (2013) at 19.

467 Finansinspektionen (2012b) at 3; Finanspolisen (2012) at 9.

468 Finansinspektionen (2012a) at 35; Finansinspektionen (2013b) at 46.

469 FATF (2006a) at 144-145.

470 Statskontoret (2008) at 56.

471 Ibid., at 56.

472 Ibid., at 57.

> Government closely followed this line of reasoning and proposed the establishment of a coordination body in which all AML supervisors should participate.[473]

Section 14 AML Regulation contains the mission and tasks of the coordination body.[474] It has overall responsibility for coordinating the supervisory activities in terms of methods and regulations, as well as for the evaluation and monitoring of the supervision performed. It must provide assistance to the supervisors in terms of education and is responsible for effective cooperation between the supervisors and the FIU concerning the reporting obligation for institutions as well as the registration obligation. The coordination body is tasked to cooperate with and provide support to the Government Office. Finally, it should initiate proposals for changes in legislation, procedures and priorities in order to create more effective supervision. An important function of the coordination body is thus to ensure a coherent, continuous and consistent approach among the AML supervisors.[475] From interviews, it became clear that the coordination body provides a platform for general discussions between supervisors about the interpretation or application of certain provisions of the AML Act, the development of regulations by the supervisors, and practical difficulties that supervisors encounter in the exercise of their supervision.[476] Besides, this coordination body is the place where supervisors meet to discuss (the drafting of) reports pursuant to appropriations and *Regeringsuppdrag*. Examples are the special reports for the years 2011-13 concerning the adequate and effective reporting by the obliged institutions to the FIU and the national risk assessment on money laundering to which all anti-money laundering supervisors contributed.[477]

The coordination body is not used by the supervisors for exchanging relevant supervisory information.[478] This more operational cooperation is no less important for effective AML supervision than cooperation on a policy level, as we have seen in the previous chapters. Inadequate legal powers for supervisors to exchange relevant supervisory information on an operational level with each other seriously undermines the effectiveness of the AML coordination body as well. After all, supervisors may come across information that is relevant for other AML supervisors. If they are not allowed to share this information with other supervisors, then what can really be done within the coordination body? In that case the body would resemble not much more than a discussion forum. We will now take a closer look at the legal powers of AML supervisors to exchange relevant supervisory information with each other, and possibly with the FIU.

473 *Regeringens Proposition* 2008:/09:70 at 165-166.

474 They reflect, to a certain extent, potential tasks that Statskontoret assessed in its report: Statskontoret (2008) at 57-60.

475 Interview Finansinspektionen, April 2011.

476 Interview Finansinspektionen, April 2011; Interview Fastighetsmäklarnämnden, April 2011.

477 Finansinspektionen (2012b) and Finansinspektionen (2013c).

478 Interview Finansinspektionen, April 2011. Interview Länsstyrelsen Stockholm, September 2013; Interview Länsstyrelsen Skåne, September 2013. See § 2.4.3.4 where it is explained what is understood by 'supervisory information'.

7.10.2 Cooperation efforts by AML Supervisors on an operational level

The foregoing demonstrated that AML supervisors have one institutionalised forum for cooperation on a policy level. AML supervisors convene on a two-monthly basis to discuss general supervisory matters. It is interesting to observe that while in the Netherlands and the United Kingdom legislators have recently taken initiatives to strengthen the powers of AML supervisors to exchange relevant supervisory information, the Swedish legislator has exclusively focused on the creation of the AML coordination body. Neither the AML Act nor its Regulation contain provisions on the exchange of supervisory information between the supervisors.[479] The Swedish Agency for Public Management and the Government Bill on the AML Act pointed at the necessity of structural cooperation between the AML supervisors, but neither referred to a legal basis for such cooperation.[480] The absence of a legal provision in the AML Act demonstrates that the supervisors cannot cooperate on an operational level with each other – at least not under this piece of legislation.

For the provision of information from the supervisors to the Swedish FIU this is different. Chapter 3, Section 6 AML Act states that when supervisors discover in the exercise of the supervision of a natural or legal person, or otherwise, a circumstance which is likely to be associated with or constitutes money laundering or terrorist financing, they should inform the FIU of this without delay.[481] For the FIU the regime of the Police Data Act applies, as the Swedish FIU is 'one of the intelligence units of the National Criminal Police within the National Police Board'.[482] Information provided to the FIU by the obliged institutions and professionals is incorporated in its money laundering register.[483] The FIU is not allowed to share the contents of the reported suspicions of money laundering (or terrorist financing) with the AML supervisors. If the analysis of reported suspicions ultimately results in a suspicion of an underlying crime, the FIU can share this information only with the relevant police departments, like the Security Service (*Säkerhetspolisen*), or any of the following law enforcement authorities: the Swedish Economic Crimes Bureau, the Customs Authority (*Tullverket*), the Coast Guard (*Kustbevakningen*) or the Tax Fraud Division (*Skattebrottsenheten*), which is a law enforcement unit of the Swedish Tax Agency.[484] The Police Data Regulation also allows the Swedish FIU to exchange this information with its foreign counterparts.[485] As indicated in the two previous chapters, however, such information may sometimes be beneficial for AML supervisors. They could use this information as an additional source of information for the verification of compliance with the preventive obligations by their supervisees.

479 Compare with § 5.9 and 6.10.

480 Statskontoret (2008); Regeringens Proposition 2008/09:70.

481 Cf. Chapter 10, Section 28 *Offentlighets- och sekreteslag*, which states that confidentiality does not prevent information from being provided to another public authority when an information obligation exists by law or regulation.

482 FATF (2006a) at 51; *Polisdatalag*, SFS 2010:361.

483 Chapter 4, Section 19 Police Data Act. The FIU is in that case allowed to process the personal data contained in the report.

484 Finanspolisen (2012) at 18. Cf. FATF (2006a) at 144 where the FATF speaks about operative co-operation.

485 Section 13 *Polisdataförordning*, SFS 2010:155.

In light of the absence of a legal basis in the AML Act and Regulation for the exchange of information between AML supervisors, the single remark made in the annual report of the county administrative board of Västra Götaland for 2013 is interesting. It stated that: '[c]ooperation is also carried out continuously with the counties of Stockholm and Skåne in monthly collaboration meetings' (*own translation, MB*).[486] What these meetings entail and whether supervisory information obtained during the exercise of AML supervision is exchanged is not explained. This means that other legislation should be consulted in order to find out whether the AML supervisors can exchange relevant supervisory information. When, for example, the Supervisory Board of Public Auditors during a disciplinary investigation of an auditor comes across information concerning the possible involvement of a specific bank in a potential money laundering transaction, can it directly provide information such as the name of the bank, its customer and/or the situation at hand to the Financial Supervisory Authority? The general legal framework for exchanging information between public authorities consists of the Administrative Procedures Act (*Förvaltningslag, FL*) and the Swedish Public Access to Information and Secrecy Act (*Offentlighets- och sekreteslag, OSL*).[487] While Section 6 FL obliges public authorities, to the extent possible, to cooperate and assist each other within the framework of their own activity, the Public Access to Information and Secrecy Act determines that public authorities must provide information in their possession at the request of another public authority, unless the information is confidential.[488] The Act determines which information held by public authorities is confidential and cannot be disclosed.

It seems that the following provisions from the OSL are relevant for AML supervisors. In general terms, Chapter 17, Section 1 OSL states that confidentiality applies to information about the planning or other preparations for supervision, if it can be assumed that the purpose of supervision is counteracted if the information is disclosed. Chapter 30 OSL contains a number of specific provisions on confidentiality for the protection of data about an individual's personal or financial circumstances in the exercise of supervision by public authorities on trade and industry. Section 4 in conjunction with Section 7 regulates the confidentiality regime for the Financial Supervisory Authority. According to the IMF, 'a large proportion of information held by FI is confidential under provisions of this Act and may as such not be disclosed'.[489] Chapter 30, Section 17 OSL specifically regulates confidentiality in relation to auditors and, hence, the Supervisory Board. Confidentiality applies in the case of the approval or authorisation of an auditor or the registration of a firm and in disciplinary actions against an auditor or audit firm, on data on the auditor's or audit firm's financial status or another's personal or financial circumstances, if it can be assumed that the person involved suffers injury or harm if the information is disclosed.

Chapter 30, Section 23 contains a more general confidentiality regime insofar as other provisions have not regulated the matter. It states that confidentiality applies, to the extent that the Government issues regulations, to a public authority's activity consisting

486 Länsstyrelsen Västra Götaland (2013) at 21.
487 *Förvaltningslag*, SFS 1986:23; *Offentlighets- och sekreteslag* SFS 2009:400.
488 Chapter 6, Section 5 OSL.
489 IMF (2011b) at 35.

of supervision or support activities in relation to trade and industry. In the annex to the Regulation issued pursuant to the OSL, one can observe that confidentiality applies to the authorisation and supervision activities of the Supervisory Board of Public Auditors and the Estate Agents Inspectorate, with the exception of their (disciplinary) decisions.[490] The county administrative boards' information in relation to – inter alia – agriculture, fisheries, and questions in relation to trade and industry is confidential, with the exception of formal decisions. It is noticeable that none of the provisions for the county administrative boards in the annex refers to the confidentiality of supervisory information that they obtain under the AML Act. It could be that this is brought under the activity 'in relation to trade and industry', but if the law is not or cannot be interpreted in that way it means that this information from the county administrative boards is not confidential at all. From the theoretical perspective of this research this could be considered to be a positive step in relation to the provision of information to other AML supervisors. However, since the OSL applies to public access to information as well, it would also mean that this information can be requested by citizens and other public authorities. This, I believe, would be an undesirable consequence.[491]

Based on the OSL, I believe that only very little room exists for AML supervisors to exchange supervisory information, as most of the information in relation to the exercise of their supervision remains confidential. Moreover, due to the way in which the OSL is formulated the supervisory authorities cannot exchange information on their own motion, but only provide non-confidential information upon request. This finding is strengthened by the fact that sectoral legislation from which the Financial Supervisory Authority, the Estate Agents Inspectorate and the Supervisory Board of Public Auditors derive their powers for supervision under the AML Act provide no possibilities for the exchange of supervisory information either. And apparently there are no agreements between the AML supervisors on which their cooperation on an operational level could be based.[492]

> Chapter 13, Sections 6a-8 BFBA regulate the powers to exchange supervisory non-confidential information for the Financial Supervisory Authority with other national financial regulators in the EEA and the European Banking Authority. The Act makes no mention of any exchange of information at the national level. More or less the same holds true for the Supervisory Board of Public Auditors, since Section 27b and 27c of the Auditors Act contain some powers for the provision of information to counterparts in the EEA or Switzerland. The Estate Agents Act and the corresponding Regulation do not regulate powers for the exchange of information by FMI. Section 10 Estate Agents Regulation, however, states that where other public authorities consider that there are reasons to issue a disciplinary reminder or a warning to an estate agent, or to revoke registration, they must report this to the Swedish Estate Agents Inspectorate.[493] This could result in some exchange of information from the other AML supervisors or the FIU to the Estate Agents Inspectorate, but not the other way around.

490 Section 9 *Offentlighets- och sekretessförordning*, SFS 2009:641 in conjunction with Annex nos. 24, 31, 88, 103, and 104.

491 Chapter 6, Sections 4 and 5 OSL.

492 For Finansinspektionen this was confirmed: Interview Finansinspektionen, October 2013.

493 Compare with Chapter 10, Section 28 OSL, which states that confidentiality does not prevent information being provided to another authority for information obligations established by law or regulation. Supra, n. 481.

In sum, I have not been able to identify adequate legal possibilities for exchanging relevant supervisory information in individual cases concerning AML compliance between supervisors. A legal basis in the AML Act for such cooperation is lacking. Moreover, pursuant to the Public Access to Information and Secrecy Act a substantial amount of supervisory information is deemed to be confidential. Only the Swedish FIU and the Estate Agents Inspectorate could, in theory, receive relevant supervisory information pursuant to the AML Act and the Estate Agents Regulation.

7.10.3 Concluding remarks

The AML supervisors effectively cooperate on a policy level through the AML coordination body. The AML coordination body allows the supervisors to discuss general supervisory matters on a structural basis. The AML Act, unfortunately, does not provide a legal basis for the exchange of specific supervisory information between AML supervisors. Moreover, pursuant to the Public Access to Information and Secrecy Act a great deal of information held by supervisory authorities is deemed confidential. Only the Swedish FIU and the Estate Agents Inspectorate might receive relevant supervisory information on the basis of the AML Act and the Estate Agents Regulation respectively. AML supervisors are obliged to forward information to the FIU when they discover facts or circumstances likely to be associated with, or which constitute money laundering (or terrorist financing). The Swedish FIU cannot share information that it has received from obliged institutions and professionals with the respective AML supervisors, which is lamentable. It does reach out to them on a more abstract level through its involvement in the AML coordination body.

PART III

8 Synthesis

8.1 Introduction

This synthesis provides a comparison of the supervisory architectures of Spain, the Netherlands, the United Kingdom and Sweden in the preventive AML policy, which were discussed individually in *Part II* of this research. It closely follows the elements of the theoretical framework of effective supervision and should be regarded as a stepping-stone to the answer to the research question in the conclusion.

In the individual country chapters, this research attempted to provide some insight into the background of AML supervision in the respective countries by looking at their money laundering vulnerability, as well as the vulnerability for the specific sectors included in this research. This appeared to be a very difficult exercise, most prominently caused by an absence of information on the one hand, and by the use of studies with different research methods, leading to different outcomes, on the other. Therefore, the vulnerability for money laundering plays a minor role in this synthesis: it is only mentioned where it is of direct relevance.

This chapter starts in Section 8.2 with a discussion on the legal framework for the prevention of money laundering and pays the most attention to the question whether the AML legislation in the countries is of good quality. Section 8.3 addresses the levels of independence of the AML supervisors, the accountability mechanisms that ought to counterbalance this independence and the levels of transparency practised by these authorities. In Section 8.4 AML supervisors' knowledge of the institutions and professionals for which they have supervisory responsibility occupies centre stage. Subsequently, Sections 8.5 to 8.7 discuss the AML supervision of banks, real estate agents and accountants specifically. As an exception to the structure of the theoretical framework of effective supervision, the aspect of the adequacy of resources is dealt with here, because this research has demonstrated that the aspect of resources can best be observed in relation to supervision in practice. Section 8.8 concerns national cooperation between the AML supervisors, and to a certain extent with the FIU. This chapter ends with some concluding remarks (§ 8.9).

Please note that the information used in this comparison is up to date until the 31st of March 2014 and that the findings are valid up until that date. As explained in the introduction to this research, certain developments have taken place after this period and (may) affect the findings of this comparison.[1]

8.2 Legal framework for the prevention of money laundering

Is the legal framework for the prevention of money laundering in Spain, the Netherlands, the United Kingdom and Sweden of good quality? Are the laws sufficiently clear, predictable and, thus, enforceable for AML supervisors?[2] This section deals with these questions by paying attention to the scope of the AML legislation, the substantive norms stemming from the preventive AML policy, as well as other possible conflicts identified. This section does *not* address the legal problems identified in relation to registration systems under the anti-money laundering legislation nor the adequacy of the legal powers provided to the supervisors and possible problems surrounding the application of these powers, as these aspects are dealt with separately in sections 8.4 to 8.8.

Effective supervision requires that (substantive) legislation is clear, precise, foreseeable, predictable and enforceable.

8.2.1 Gaps and conflicts in substantive AML legislation

- *Spain, the Netherlands and, to a lesser extent, Sweden, face gaps or conflicts in their substantive AML legislation. No issues were identified in the United Kingdom.*

Most problematic appears to be the situation in Spain, because of the absence of a Royal Decree implementing provisions from the Spanish AML Act and completing the AML framework. The Decree was already announced in 2010 with the entry into force of the Spanish AML Act, and should complement and clarify a number of substantive norms from the Act. It should have entered into force in April 2011, but up until April 2014 this had not happened.[3] The situation causes a gap in the substantive AML legislation in Spain, but also means that not all international and European norms are fully implemented into national legislation. The absence of the Decree is undesirable from a legality and legal certainty perspective as well: norms that are drafted under the former AML regime and that are incompatible with the norms stemming from the new AML Act have to be set aside. However, guidance as what qualifies as incompatible is not available. The situation negatively affects the enforceability of the norms stemming from the anti-money laundering legislation as well.[4]

1 See § 1.8.
2 See § 2.4.1.
3 Please note, as outlined in § 1.8, that the Spanish legislator ultimately adopted the Royal Decree in May 2014.
4 § 4.2.

A variety of issues could be identified for the Netherlands. A first serious matter concerns the conflict between the anti-money laundering legislation and the Third Directive with regard to legal professional privilege. While the Directive only refers to an exemption from reporting obligations, the consideration 'shall not apply' in the Dutch AML Act results in the complete non-applicability of all AML obligations when legal privilege is invoked. This means that the Dutch exemption is more lenient than the exemption from the Third Directive, which is not allowed.[5] A second conflict concerns the different reporting obligations for accountants working at audit firms. The Dutch AML Act requires accountants to disclose unusual transactions to FIU-NL upon identifying these transactions, without any limitations on the type of activities that may give rise to the unusual nature of these transactions, and prohibits other parties to be informed of this disclosure. The Audit Firms Supervision Act requires audit firms to report suspicions of material fraud to the police and possibly to the Netherlands Authority for the Financial Markets (AFM). Accountants working at audit firms are first required to enter into a dialogue with the client and to give the client the possibility to repair the consequences of the fraud identified during a statutory audit, before they must disclose a report to the authorities and decline the assignment. This means that accountants working at audit firms have to inform their clients about the identified fraud, which may be at odds with the tipping-off prohibition under the AML Act. The conflicting obligations lower the legal certainty of the Acts for audit firms that have to comply with both Acts, as well as the enforceability of the norms for the respective supervisors. The Dutch legislator should clarify how the two obligations should be balanced and how accountants should act when faced with such a conflict.[6]

This research furthermore pointed at the absence of an explicit norm in the Dutch AML Act that requires the obliged institutions and professionals to develop internal AML policies and procedures.[7] Although required by the Third Directive (and the FATF Recommendations), the Dutch AML Act only contains an obligation to train staff. The AML Act does not oblige institutions and professionals to have an internal policy for the prevention of money laundering and terrorist financing, although the AML Guidance issued by the Ministry of Finance considers that an important component of AML supervision is to verify whether institutions have adequate internal organisations and controls. The Guidance, however, is not legally binding. The obligation to have an internal policy can also be created by the instruction power of the AML supervisors, because instructions may require the implementation of internal controls and procedures to prevent money laundering. Nevertheless, this power may only be used upon the identification of non-compliant behaviour in the first place. The absence of this obligation in Dutch legislation appears particularly problematic for the Dutch Tax and Customs Administration/Bureau Supervision Wwft (*Belastingdienst/Bureau Toezicht Wwft*, hereafter Bureau Supervision Wwft or 'the Bureau') and the Financial Supervision Office (*Bureau Financieel Toezicht*, hereafter also 'BFT') as they fully derive their supervisory competence and powers from the AML Act. For them it will be impossible, or at least very difficult, to enforce this in the

5 See § 5.8.1.2.
6 § 5.5.3.1.
7 § 5.6.2.4 and § 5.7.2.4.

absence of a norm establishing such as an obligation for institutions and professionals in the first place.

Another gap discovered in this research concerns the coverage of real estate businesses under the AML legislation in the Netherlands and Sweden. In Sweden the Estate Agents Act clearly defines real estate agents as natural persons. As a consequence, real estate businesses are excluded from the supervisory responsibility of the Swedish Estate Agents Inspectorate under this Act and, hence, under the AML Act as well.[8] The Dutch Commercial Code also defines intermediaries as natural persons.[9] In the absence of a reference in the AML Act to real estate agents being both legal and natural persons, like the Dutch legislator has done for lawyers, accountants and civil-law notaries, the coverage of real estate businesses is doubtful. For real estate agents who also act as valuers of real estate, the situation causes even more uncertainty, because in relation to the valuation of real estate the AML Act does refer to both natural and legal persons. Also from an enforceability perspective this situation is undesirable, as the Bureau Supervision Wwft could face difficulties in determining on whom to impose a sanction.

8.2.2 Clarity and enforceability of substantive AML legislation and related norms

- *Problems regarding the clarity and enforceability of substantive AML legislation and related norms exist in the Netherlands, Spain and the United Kingdom. No issues were identified in Sweden.*

In the Netherlands two norms from the AML Act are unclear. Firstly, the use of the term external accountants is confusing. The AML Act, on the one hand, and the Financial Supervision Act and Audit Firms Supervision Act, on the other, attach different meanings to this term. From a legal certainty perspective, it should be avoided as much as possible that different pieces of legislation use the same term differently. This is especially important when pieces of legislation apply within the same or related areas of the law. Secondly, the partial inclusion of valuers of real estate within the scope of the AML Act causes uncertainty. Although it can be considered a step forward in light of the vulnerability of the real estate sector for money laundering in the Netherlands, the law is not sufficiently clear.[10] The partial inclusion results in uncertainty for real estate agents that provide both mediation and valuation services. In Chapter 5 it was, for example, considered that they might have to develop and to apply two different standards for complying with AML obligations for the two different tasks and that, in practice, they could opt to always comply with the highest standard. This, however, would do away with two of the Government's arguments for a partial inclusion: avoiding higher costs and (sometimes lengthy) procedures. Another argument, namely that for the valuers of real estate the unusual circumstances do not in most cases arise from the client but from the assignment, was not found to be a valid

8 See § 7.7.1.
9 See § 5.5.2.1: it refers to sole traders, partners of firms or directors of bodies corporate, and employees.
10 See § 5.2.

argument.[11] The lack of clarity makes supervision by the Bureau Supervision Wwft more complicated and may result in a lower enforceability of the norms.[12]

For Spain, this research found that legal flaws in relation to the external review system should be overcome in order to strengthen this system. The external review system is potentially a useful instrument for strengthening the AML supervision exercised by SEPBLAC (*Servicio Ejecutivo de la Comisión de Prevención del Blanqueo de Capitales e Infracciones Monetarias).*[13] Nevertheless, the requirements for external experts in terms of the person, education and experience required, should be better regulated. The legislator should also oblige external experts to disclose their reports to SEPBLAC, preferably within a given time frame that is determined by the legislator or SEPBLAC, without the necessity for the latter to request these reports in individual cases.[14] This requires less efforts on the side of SEPBLAC to obtain the information which is relevant for its supervision.

In the United Kingdom, the Money Laundering Regulations 2007 do not require that obliged institutions and professionals lay down their internal policies in writing. Especially the Office of Fair Trading appeared to have difficulties in verifying compliance with this obligation. This research concluded that it would increase the enforceability of the norm if the Regulations would require that the internal policy should be laid down in writing, because this makes compliance with this obligation easier to verify. Furthermore, the creation of a legal basis for the exchange of information or the conclusion of arrangements between HMRC and the National Trading Standards Estate Agency Team (NTSEAT) is recommended. Until April 2014, OFT engaged with the Local Authority Trading Standards for the exercise of the AML supervision of real estate agents. The OFT has now been abolished and its powers under the Regulations have been transferred to HMRC, while its enforcement powers under the Estate Agents Act have been transferred to NTSEAT. Because NTSEAT will have prosecutorial powers in relation to estate agents, also under the Regulations, this research advised to legally allow for engagement between the two authorities.[15] Currently the Regulations lack such a legal basis.

8.3 Independence and accountability of AML supervisors

In their day-to-day activities AML supervisors should be independent from politics (Minister, Government, Parliament) and the market. This is always a *relative* independence, because some form of relationship with politics and the market always exists. For the supervisors of financial and credit institutions there must be a high level of independence from politics and the market. For other AML supervisors the level of independence depends on their nature (external or internal), although a certain degree of independence must always be maintained. At the same time, AML supervisors must be accountable for the exercise of their activities under the preventive AML policy.

8

11 § 5.5.2.1.
12 Cf. § 5.7.2.1 and 5.7.2.4.
13 See § 8.5.1
14 § 4.6.3.3.
15 See § 6.7.5.

Supervisors should thereby take into account the limits that confidentiality regimes may impose on them. The most important way through which supervisors account for the exercise of their AML supervision is by means of annual (supervision) plans and annual reports. Chapter 2 explained that this research pays attention to the legal embedding of mechanisms regulating political and social accountability, as well as the way in which AML supervisors are accountable for their AML supervision in practice.[16] Independence together with accountability together force AML supervisors to act in an objective, neutral and professional way in effectively performing their supervisory tasks.

Effective supervision requires an adequate level of political and market independence. The powers of politics or the market may not go as far as influencing the individual decision-making procedures and the day-to-day practice within the supervisory authority. Effective supervision also requires that supervisors account for the exercise of their AML supervision. They must at least be transparent about the reasons for performing supervision, the supervisory goals, they must make their choices in supervision visible, and provide information about the procedures and results.

8.3.1 Political independence and accountability

- *The political independence and accountability mechanisms in Spain and, to lesser extent, the Netherlands are not well regulated for (all) AML supervisors. The lack of political independence is particularly worrisome in Spain, because SEPBLAC is the only AML supervisor and its lack of independence thus affects the entire supervisory architecture. This research found that in Sweden and the United Kingdom no issues of political independence and minor issues of accountability, if any at all, exist.*

8.3.1.1 Spain and the Netherlands

In Spain, where SEPBLAC is the formal AML supervisor for the entire range of institutions and professionals under the preventive AML policy, an adequate level of political independence is not sufficiently guaranteed. As we could see in Chapter 4, SEPBLAC is a dependent support body of the Commission for the Prevention of Money Laundering and Monetary Offences (*Comisión de Prevención del Blanqueo de Capitales e Infracciones Monetarias*). This Commission is a dependent collegiate body falling under the authority of the Secretariat of State for the Economy and Business Support. The Secretariat of State, in turn, belongs to the Spanish Ministry of Economy and Competitiveness.[17] A wide variety of public authorities are represented within the Commission, which is chaired by the Secretary of State for Economy and Business Support. The Commission, possibly through its Standing Committee, has a wide range of powers with respect to the functioning of SEPBLAC. Among these powers are the power to appoint SEPBLAC's director, to decide on its budget, to guide its actions, to conclude supervisory arrangements with financial regulators, and to approve SEPBLAC's organisational structure, operational guidelines and annual supervision plans. Particularly the formal approval of annual supervision plans is

16 § 2.4.2.1.

17 § 4.4.1.1 and 4.4.1.2. See Figure 2 for an illustration of the institutional embedding in Spain.

a far-reaching power.[18] The inadequate level of political independence is accompanied by the finding that norms on accountability for SEPBLAC are largely absent and its accountability practice can be called poor as well. The AML Act contains one general obligation for SEPBLAC to submit to the Commission any reports that it requests, but it is doubtful whether this can be used for an *ongoing* accountability relationship. This finding, combined with a lack of transparency in practice, demonstrates that two important institutional requirements for effective supervision are absent in Spain.

The Dutch Tax and Customs Administration/Bureau Supervision Wwft has an inadequate level of political independence as well. This is caused by the fact the Dutch Tax and Customs Administration is an executive organ of the Ministry of Finance and is thus ultimately headed by the Minister of Finance. The system of access to databases provides the Bureau with some operational independence, because it has access to the databases of other DTCA divisions whereas its own database is protected, but this is insufficient to alter the finding. The conclusion that an adequate level of political independence is lacking is accompanied by the absence of a legal obligation in the AML Act or lower-level regulations for the Bureau Supervision Wwft to account for the exercise of its AML supervision. Like SEPBLAC, the Bureau Supervision Wwft has a poor accountability practice. The annual reports from the Ministry of Finance and the Dutch Tax and Customs Administration do not mention the Bureau's work at all, whereas the annual (supervision) plans and reports from the Bureau Supervision Wwft itself are internal documents. This means that in practice no account is given to the general public about the exercise of AML supervision by the Bureau and that it acts in a highly non-transparent manner.

The conclusion of an inadequate level of political independence is especially worrisome for Spain. This directly results from the fact that Spain applies the FIU model in its AML supervisory architecture, thus providing full supervisory responsibility to a single authority. SEPBLAC's lack of independence thus affects the entire supervisory architecture. In the Netherlands, the external AML supervisors share final responsibility for AML supervision. The lack of an inadequate level of political independence for the Bureau Supervision Wwft is compensated by adequate levels of political independence for the Dutch Central Bank (*De Nederlandsche Bank, DNB*) and the Financial Supervision Office.[19] Dutch legislation has established both authorities as so-called 'independent administrative authorities'. They are positioned at arm's length from their responsible Ministers, yet the latter do have powers to oversee the general functioning of these authorities. The responsible Ministers cannot in principle interfere with the individual decisions of the two authorities, although the Minister of Justice and Security does have some far-reaching powers in relation to the Financial Supervision Office. The most far-reaching power is the annulment of individual decisions made by the BFT. Nevertheless, legislation provides enough safeguards to ensure that the Minister only uses these far-reaching powers as a last resort and with great restraint. The DNB is positioned at a greater distance than the BFT, which is reflected in the more limited powers of the Minister of Finance against the DNB. Both the DNB

18 § 4.4.2.

19 § 5.4.1.2 and 5.4.3.2. Please note that the fourth AML supervisor, the Netherlands Authority for the Financial Markets (*Autoriteit Financiële Markten, AFM*), has not been included in this research. See § 1.3.

and BFT are legally obliged to draft annual reports and to send them to the responsible Minister(s), as well as Parliament and the Senate. In practice, their annual reports include information about the exercise of AML supervision and are published on their respective websites. Other accountability mechanisms are parliamentary investigations and inquiries, which have been used for the DNB although not in the context of AML supervision, and investigations by the Court of Audit. The Court of Audit has twice investigated the effectiveness of the fight against money laundering and terrorist financing in the Netherlands, in which all AML supervisors' activities were assessed at a more abstract level.[20]

8.3.1.2 Sweden and the United Kingdom

The political independence of the Swedish administrative authorities is laid down in the Instrument of Government, which is one of the four fundamental laws of Sweden.[21] Although there have been comments about the impact of annual appropriation letters on the (operational) independence of supervisors, this research concluded that they do not unduly hamper the level of political independence required. The annual appropriation letters are of a general nature and do not involve individual decision making. Moreover, the supervisors themselves are consulted in the course of the preparation of the appropriation letters. Together with the instruction regulations the letters provide the Government with a way to establish an accountability framework with the authorities. With respect to accountability for AML supervision, the requirements vary from authority to authority. The annual appropriation letters and the instruction regulation have not required the Swedish Financial Supervisory Authority (*Finansinspektionen, FI*) to report about its activities under the AML Act in recent years, but it has nevertheless accounted for its work. This has varied from reports with results of thematic AML supervision and the work of the AML coordination body, to special reports on an effective reporting regime under a special assignment from the Government. The Estate Agents Inspectorate (*Fastighetsmäklarinspektionen, FMI*) and the county administrative boards (*Länsstyrelserna*, hereafter also 'the boards') have not been explicitly required to report about their AML supervision either, but in practice they have accounted for their AML supervision through their annual reports, sanctioning yearbooks (FMI) and indirectly via FI's special reports. The Supervisory Board of Public Auditors' annual reports, however, contain hardly any to no information on the Board's AML supervision. Activities in relation to AML supervision are hardly mentioned in the annual reports and there are no other reports that can give an insight into its AML supervision.[22] This research, therefore, found that the Supervisory Board of Public Auditors (*Revisorsnämnden*, hereafter also RN or 'the Board') should become more transparent about its AML activities.

The AML supervisors from the United Kingdom included in this research all have an adequate level of political independence. AML supervision is partly exercised by public bodies. This research includes two public bodies, namely the Financial Conduct Authority

20 § 5.4.1.2, 5.4.2.2 and 5.4.3.2.
21 § 7.4.1.
22 § 7.4.4.3.

(FCA) and the Office of Fair Trading (OFT). The FCA is a non-departmental public body, positioned at a great distance from the Government and Parliament and a very high level of independence. The OFT is a non-ministerial government department. Most political independence, and at the same time most legal accountability obligations to counterbalance this independence, exist for the FCA. The wide range of accountability obligations for the FCA are only to some extent used for the exercise of AML supervision. The OFT is obliged to publish annual plans, which are subject to consultation, and annual reports. Here too, it appeared that the OFT hardly uses these plans and reports to account for its AML supervision. AML supervision is also exercised by a large number of professional associations. These do not form part of the UK's system of public bodies, but even between the two professional associations included in this research the level of political independence and formal accountability obligations differ. The Association of Accounting Technicians (AAT) seems to be positioned at the greatest distance from the Government in terms of independence and accountability. In contrast to the FCA, where the high level of independence is counterbalanced by a wide variety of accountability mechanisms embedded in the law, no formal accountability obligation on the exercise of the public task of AML supervision vis-à-vis the Government exists for the AAT. The Institute of Chartered Accountants in England and Wales (ICAEW) has more connections with the Government than the AAT, because of the existence of a legal obligation to account for the regulation of statutory auditors. Moreover, ICAEW has agreed with the Financial Reporting Council to consider recommendations in relation to (the supervision of) non-statutory accountancy activities as well. Important for all AML supervisors in the UK is the voluntary accountability system to HM Treasury as developed under the Regulations.[23] Chapter 6 explained that this is not a formal obligation, although all supervisors are expected to send annual returns on the exercise of their AML supervision to the Treasury. In practice the four AML supervisors included in this research have reported annually about their AML supervision, although only the FCA and the OFT have published (some of) these reports online. Each year HM Treasury publishes an aggregated AML supervision report as well.

Compared to the other three countries, it can be observed that with this *voluntary* mechanism AML supervisors in the UK are in practice most transparent about and accountable for the exercise of their AML supervision. However, from the perspective of effective supervision, ICAEW and AAT should publish their annual returns to the Treasury. This research also recommended that a legal embedding of this voluntary accountability mechanism in the Regulations should be considered, thereby giving the Treasury some minimum powers to ensure that all AML supervisors are equally transparent and accountable in practice, and to allow it to publish more intelligible and meaningful aggregate reports.

23 § 6.4.1.2.

8.3.2 Market independence and accountability

- *The strongest relationship between AML supervisors and the market can be found in the United Kingdom. This is the result of the fact that the preventive AML policy is required to be self-funding and because of the strong involvement of professional associations as AML supervisors. This research identified an inadequate level of market independence for one professional association acting as an AML supervisor in the UK. No problems were identified in the other three countries.*

The finding that the strongest relationship between AML supervisors and the market can be found in the United Kingdom is not surprising, given that the AML supervisors of the other three countries included in this research are all external supervisors and can thus be found at a more distanced position from the institutions and professionals for which they have supervisory responsibility. In the UK, all institutions and professionals subject to the AML legislation pay fees to their AML supervisors, whether public bodies or professional associations, in order to be registered and supervised. Some of the AML supervisors in the Netherlands and Sweden are (partially) funded by the private sector as well.[24] In order to manage this financial relationship, the supervisors normally publish annual reports in which they account for the expenditures and supervisory choices made. In addition, some AML supervisors have given more powers to the sector, particularly through the presence of panels. These were identified in the Netherlands for the DNB, for the FCA in the UK, and to a lesser extent for the county administrative boards in Sweden.[25] In all cases, the panels can provide insights from the sector and advice to the AML supervisors, but they do not have binding or decision-making powers.

This research discovered one issue of an inadequate level of market independence in the United Kingdom. This issue did not arise from the financial relationship between the supervisor and the private sector, but concerns the participation of members in the governance structure of professional associations. Upon presenting the supervisory models in Chapter 3, the nature of AML supervisors was addressed. Arguments in favour of and against self-regulation were discussed, as well as the pros and cons of the involvement of professional associations as supervisors in the preventive AML policy. Although it may be advantageous that professional associations have close relationships with their members in terms of knowledge of the sector, it was considered that a downside is that they run the risk that they are not adequately independent from their members. Critics may refer to 'chaps regulating chaps' and a conflict of interest may arise between furthering the quality of the profession as a whole and fighting money laundering for the public interest.[26] This research identified that within the Institute of Chartered Accountings in England and Wales (ICAEW), members have a large majority presence in those committees that are responsible for investigations and disciplinary procedures. Moreover, the disciplinary tribunal that ultimately decides on the disciplinary action consists of a two-thirds majority

24 These are the Dutch Central Bank (the Netherlands), the Swedish Financial Supervisory Authority, the Swedish Estate Agents Inspectorate and the Supervisory Board of Public Auditors (Sweden).

25 § 5.4.1.2; § 6.4.1.3 and § 7.4.5.2.

26 § 2.4.2.1.

of members as well.[27] Because the committees and tribunal decide on the disciplinary action, also in the case of AML supervision, this provides members with too much influence in the AML supervisory procedure of ICAEW. In order to avoid (the appearance of) any lack of independence on the side of ICEAW, this research recommended that a better balance should be found between members and independent lay persons, or alternatively, to make ICAEW's disciplinary committee and tribunal entirely independent from its governance structure. In this respect, it could draw inspiration from the other professional association included in this research. AAT members also play a role throughout investigations and disciplinary procedures, but unlike the case for ICAEW, they never represent a majority. The AAT particularly differs from ICAEW in the independence of the disciplinary committee from AAT's governance structure and the fact that the disciplinary tribunal consists of a majority of independent lay persons.[28]

The foregoing demonstrated a higher vulnerability of market independence issues for countries that apply the internal model in their AML supervisory architectures. It does not stem from the financial relationship between AML supervisors and the private sector, but rather from the participation of members within governance structures of the professional associations. Countries that apply the FIU, external and, to lesser extent, the hybrid models do not face this problem at all. Nevertheless, this research also proved that when professional associations act as AML supervisors this does not *automatically* result in an inadequate level of market independence. It all depends on how the membership and governance of professional associations is regulated by each individual association. This is a highly casuistic matter and does not allow for a general conclusion on the effectiveness of the internal model. This finding should be read with great vigilance as well, because this research only included two professional associations that are both active in the United Kingdom, a country which is known for its long history of and experience with self-regulation.[29]

8.4 Knowledge of AML supervisors of their supervisory population

An adequate knowledge of the group of institutions for which an authority has supervisory responsibility is of fundamental importance for the effectiveness of that supervision. Especially the level of regulation of a profession is considered a preventive enforcement tool, because it may keep out the so-called bad apples. This research, therefore, looked at the level of regulation of banks, real estate agents and accountants in the four Member States.[30] Regulation increases the likelihood that AML supervisors know the institutions and professionals for which they have supervisory responsibility. If a sector or profession is unregulated, this research verified the existence of other mechanisms that may limit the practical disadvantages of non-regulation for the AML supervisor.

27 § 6.4.3.2.
28 § 6.4.4.2.
29 Bartle and Vass (2005) at 7-8.
30 See § 1.3 as to why this research has selected these three sectors.

Effective supervision requires that AML supervisors know the size of the group of institutions and professionals for which they have supervisory responsibility, and that they have some basic information on them as a starting point for their supervision.

8.4.1 The regulation of banks, real estate agents and accountants

- *Banking is a highly regulated activity in the four countries and the AML supervisors all have a good knowledge of the banks for which they have supervisory responsibility.*

The high level of regulation is the result of the strong influence of the European Union in this field. Applicants for a banking licence must provide a wealth of information to the authorising authorities varying from business information, the existence of internal policies, liquidity and solvability to information regarding whether directors and (senior) management are fit and proper persons. In the Netherlands, Sweden and the United Kingdom the AML supervisors of banks are also the responsible authorities for the authorisation of banks, or share this responsibility with another authority. In Spain this is not the case, but legislation determines that SEPBLAC must be consulted by the Bank of Spain (*Banco de España*) in the authorisation procedure for banks.[31] Banks are always incorporated in a public register.

- *Only in Sweden is the real estate profession a regulated profession.*

The AML supervisor for real estate agents in Sweden is also the authority responsible for their authorisation.[32] The Swedish Estate Agents Inspectorate receives a lot of information from real estate agents upon registration. It lists all the estate agents that it has registered in a public register. This means that the Inspectorate complies with the adequate knowledge requirement. The real estate profession in Spain, the Netherlands and the United Kingdom is fully liberalised. The title of real estate agent is not protected in these countries and membership of professional associations only exists on a voluntary basis. For all three countries, it appeared that not all real estate agents are members of these professional associations. The lack of regulation concerning the real estate profession may also affect the AML supervisors' knowledge of the real estate agents for which they have supervisory responsibility. More about this follows in § 8.4.2.

31 See § 4.5.1.

32 As explained in Chapter 7, the real estate profession in Sweden differs from the Netherlands, the UK and Spain where real estate agents normally represent either the selling *or* the buying party. In Sweden estate agents ought to function as a neutral and impartial link between buyers and sellers of property. Another difference is that real estate agents in Sweden conclude written contracts on property, whereas in the other three countries civil-law notaries or solicitors are normally involved in the conclusion of property transactions. This might explain why the profession is regulated in Sweden, and not in the other countries.

- *The regulation of the accountancy profession shows a diverse picture. In the Netherlands, the accountancy profession is a fully regulated profession. This is not the case for Spain, Sweden and the United Kingdom, where only aspects of the accountancy profession are regulated.*

The Dutch Accountancy Profession Act requires accountants to be incorporated in the accountants register of the Dutch Institute of Chartered Accountants (*Nederlandse Beroepsorganisatie van Accountants, NBA*) in order to use the title of registered accountant or accounting consultant. Upon registration, applicants must provide a wide range of information to demonstrate, among other things, that they comply with the minimum standards of education required. The legal framework for accountants is complemented by the Audit Firms Supervision Act that applies to (accountants working at) audit firms, and the Accountants Disciplinary Law Act. The Dutch AML supervisor for accountants, the Financial Supervision Office, does not have a role under the accountancy legislation. It does have access to the public register of accountants held by the NBA. This means that it has an overview of the group of accountants for which it has supervisory responsibility under the AML Act.

In Spain and Sweden, the only regulated area for accountants is auditing. The title of auditor has statutory protection in these countries. For Sweden the split between the wider accountancy profession and the audit profession is very interesting, because it has resulted in a situation where different authorities have AML supervisory responsibility: the county administrative boards supervise non-regulated accountancy professionals, while the Supervisory Board of Public Auditors supervises auditors and audit firms.[33] The latter authority is also the authority responsible for the authorisation of auditors and audit firms and has, therefore, substantial knowledge of this group. The Spanish AML supervisor (SEPBLAC) has no role in the authorisation procedure for auditors and audit firms, but it can access the official public register of auditors. This means that it has an adequate knowledge of this particular group of accountants. In the United Kingdom the wider accountancy profession is unregulated and professional associations play an important role here. There are, nevertheless, three reserved areas for which minimum qualifications and training are required by law: audit, insolvency and investment business. The Government has established the regulatory framework through legislation for these areas. The professional associations have an adequate knowledge of their supervisory population, since they supervise their own members or carry out AML supervision on a contractual basis.

The foregoing obviously raises the question of whether the fact that the real estate and accountancy professions are not or not fully regulated in the four countries, means that the responsible AML supervisors do not have an adequate knowledge of their supervisory population.

33 § 7.5.3.1.

8.4.2 Initiatives from national legislators to overcome (potential) problems of non-regulation

- *This research demonstrated that in the absence of the regulation of particular sectors or professions, the legislators in Spain, Sweden and the United Kingdom have created different kinds of requirements enabling the AML supervisor(s) to gather basic knowledge on the group of institutions and professionals for which they have supervisory responsibility. This finding is particularly interesting, because neither the Third Directive, nor the FATF Recommendations, provide for such obligations.*

In Spain, all institutions and professionals subject to the preventive AML legislation are obliged to designate a representative to SEPBLAC as a part of their internal control measures for ensuring an effective reporting regime.[34] SEPBLAC keeps the names of the institutions and their representatives in a special register. Although SEPBLAC gathers this information via its function as the national FIU, SEPBLAC inspectors can use this information for supervisory purposes as well. All staff fall under the same confidentiality regime and this research found no evidence to suggest that this practice is forbidden. Provided that all obliged institutions and professionals comply with the law, SEPBLAC thus has a complete oversight of banks, accountants and estate agents through its function as an FIU. Non-compliance with the obligation to appoint a representative to SEPBLAC is considered a serious breach and can be sanctioned accordingly.

The Swedish AML Act contains a registration obligation for institutions and professionals that fall under the Act and that are not subject to any kind of regulation. Upon registration, the county administrative boards become the responsible AML supervisors for the group of non-regulated institutions and professionals.[35] As the wider accountancy profession is unregulated in Sweden, this obligation therefore also applies to those accountants and firms that do not perform auditing. Registration takes place at the Swedish Companies Registration Office and not at the county administrative boards. In principle, however, the boards can obtain names, addresses and some basic information on the accountants and accountancy firms from the Office. This system thus allows the county administrative boards to gather basic knowledge on the size and composition of the group of accountancy professionals for which they have supervisory responsibility. As pointed out in Chapter 7, a problematic aspect of this system is that the county administrative boards have no power to enforce registration by non-regulated institutions and professionals that fall under the scope of the AML Act. The legislation allows them to order accountants or firms (or other professionals) that have not registered to provide information on the activities performed for the purpose of assessing whether an obligation to register exists. If this is not provided, then the county administrative boards have the power to order them to cease their activity. But when the information requested *is* provided, the boards have no powers to take action when they conclude that an accountant or firm (or other professional) should be registered. The county administrative boards only have AML supervisory responsibility for those institutions and professionals that are registered, but in the absence of a legal power that

34 § 4.5.4.
35 § 7.5.3.1.

allows them to ultimately enforce registration, all that can be done is to request, inform or advise accountants and accountancy firms to register with the Companies Registration Office. This research found that this is a considerable problem in practice and means that the boards have to invest a considerable amount of time and resources in persuading everyone to register, before they can even start to engage in supervision. This obviously diminishes the effectiveness of their AML supervision.

The Money Laundering Regulations 2007 in the UK contain registration obligations for institutions and professionals that belong to unregulated sectors or professions. The registration system applies to some institutions and professionals that fall under the scope of the Regulations and that have the Financial Conduct Authority, the Office of Fair Trading (until the 1st of April 2014) or Her Majesty's Revenue and Customs (HMRC) as their AML supervisors.[36] Institutions that already undergo a more extensive authorisation procedure, like banks, are not subject to this registration obligation. Institutions and professionals that are obliged to register under the Regulations are not allowed to carry out their business or profession if they are not properly included in the supervisor's register. The registration system applies to estate agents, which are obliged to register with their AML supervisor, the Office of Fair Trading (OFT).[37] Upon registration they are included in the OFT's public register. The registration obligation also applies to accountants who do not perform any of the three reserved activities and who are not a member of a professional association, like ICAEW or AAT.[38] They are required to register with HMRC.

The registration system solves the aforementioned problem that institutions and professionals are subject to the Regulations but not supervised for that purpose, and ensures that the supervisors have an adequate knowledge of the institutions and professionals for which they have responsibility. There is an area for improvement for the English system as well. The OFT would benefit from a more in-depth registration obligation for real estate agents. At present, estate agents are only requested to provide a minimum level of business information.[39] However, because it concerns an unregulated profession, no integrity or quality checks are performed on this sector. Combined with the indication that estate agents in the UK bear a certain level of AML vulnerability, this shows the necessity of the introduction of a requirement to demonstrate the fit and proper nature of estate agents working at a firm or as sole practitioners. This obligation ensures that the OFT receives more relevant information than at present and allows the registration system and its supervision to become more effective. It would particularly benefit OFT's information position and risk assessments. This finding also applies to HMRC, which took over the AML supervision of estate agents on the 1st of April 2014.

36 § 6.5.1.

37 On the 1st of April 2014, HMRC became the AML supervisor for estate agents. From that date estate agents have to register with their new supervisor.

38 § 6.5.4.

39 § 6.5.3.

- *The Netherlands is the only one of the countries included in this research where anti-money laundering legislation does not provide some kind of registration system for non-regulated sectors and professions, like the real estate profession.*

The Bureau Supervision Wwft is the competent AML supervisor for the real estate profession, as well as a number of other unregulated sectors and professions, like dealers in goods. In the absence of the regulation of the real estate profession, it runs the risk of not having an accurate knowledge of this sector. Whether the absence of a registration obligation in the AML Act is problematic for the Bureau is subject to discussion, however. As explained in Chapter 5, the Bureau is part of the Dutch Tax and Customs Administration and derives its internal information for the exercise of AML supervision from the tax database. This could suggest that the Bureau has an adequate knowledge of the real estate sector. Nevertheless, this research demonstrated that the use of the tax database for the purpose of AML supervision brings about some difficulties.[40] One problem is that businesses are registered only for their *principal* business activity. Theoretically, this means that if a real estate agent has another principal activity, such as project development, he acts under another sectoral code. And valuers of real estate, which partially fall under the scope of the AML Act, do not have their own sectoral code at all. This research also concluded already that it is questionable whether real estate businesses actually fall under the scope of the AML Act in the first place.[41] This leads to the finding that, although the tax database is a useful starting point, the Bureau runs the risk of not having an adequate knowledge of the entire group of real estate agents. The reliance on the tax database also requires quite an effort from the Bureau to obtain a full picture of the supervisory population, since it has to carry out searches for all the institutions and professionals for which it has this responsibility.

The differences between Spain, Sweden and the United Kingdom, on the one hand, and the Netherlands, on the other, cannot be related to the choice of supervisory models under the preventive AML policy. It rather seems to be a lack of recognition on the side of the Dutch legislator that unregulated sectors and professionals are not easy to identify, as well as the fact that this takes (sometimes considerable) efforts on the side of the responsible supervisor. The comparative viewpoint presented in this research clearly proves that some form of registration in the Dutch AML Act may be an useful instrument for the Bureau Supervision Wwft to obtain, on a self-standing basis, relevant information on the real estate sector (as well as on the other unregulated businesses and professionals for which it has supervisory responsibility, such as dealers in goods). The information available in the tax database can be used next to or compared with information that the Bureau has obtained through the registration, which makes the information position of the Bureau stronger and may make its supervision more effective as well.

Ideally, norms in relation to registration systems would in the future be considered by the EU and FATF when revising their norms or expanding the scope of the preventive AML

40 § 5.7.2.1.
41 See § 8.2.1.

policy to other unregulated sectors and professions. They can draw inspiration from the different systems applicable in Spain, Sweden, the United Kingdom, and perhaps other EU Member States that are not included in this research.

8.5 Anti-money laundering supervision of banks

Is the anti-money laundering supervision of banks in Spain, the Netherlands, the United Kingdom and Sweden effective? This section compares the competences of the AML supervisors on banks and the way in which they apply these powers. The AML supervision of banks is exercised by the financial regulators in the Netherlands, the United Kingdom and Sweden: the Dutch Central Bank, the Financial Conduct Authority and the Swedish Financial Supervisory Authority. Only in Spain is the financial regulator, the Bank of Spain, not formally responsible for the AML supervision of banks as SEPBLAC is given this responsibility for the entire range of obliged institutions and professionals. The Bank of Spain is however involved in the exercise of AML supervision through the conclusion of an arrangement with the Commission for the Prevention of Money Laundering and Monetary Offences.

Effective supervision requires that AML supervisors have adequate supervisory and sanctioning powers provided by law.[42] AML supervisors should apply these powers in practice and do so in a proportionate and careful manner. With respect to sanctioning, AML supervisors must speak softly where possible and hard where necessary. Ultimately the sanctions must be capable of providing a deterrent effect. The existence of public supervision (sanctioning) policies is a precondition for effective supervision. Such policies should include an explanation of the legal framework, the supervisory goals, the desired level of compliance, the principles followed by the supervisor for its activities, as well as a general description of the procedures applied.

8.5.1 Supervision

8.5.1.1 Supervisory powers

- *The AML supervisors of banks in the Netherlands, the UK and Sweden have adequate supervisory powers. The Spanish AML supervisor lacks regulatory powers.*

The Dutch Central Bank, the Financial Conduct Authority and the Swedish Financial Supervisory Authority all have the power to compel (the production of) information relevant to the monitoring of compliance, the power to perform on-site inspections and they have regulatory powers as well. The supervisory powers are either provided by AML legislation, by sectoral legislation, or by a combination of these pieces of legislation. The Swedish Financial Supervisory Authority derives its supervisory powers in full from sectoral legislation.[43] Although both the DNB and the FCA obtain most of their supervisory powers from the AML legislation, they are provided with regulatory powers

42 See Table 1 for the concrete interpretation of adequate supervisory and sanctioning powers.
43 § 7.6.1.

by sectoral legislation. In Spain, SEBLAC obtains its supervisory powers directly from the AML Act. It has adequate inspection powers, but lacks the power to issue rules or regulations. This power is provided to the Commission for the Prevention of Money Laundering and Monetary Offences, or its Standing Committee, under whose authority SEPBLAC acts. Problems in relation to the application of the supervisory powers have not been identified for any of the AML supervisors of banks.

8.5.1.2 AML supervision of banks in practice

- *The financial regulators (DNB, FCA and FI) that exercise the AML supervision of banks all follow a two-track approach. This is different for the Spanish AML supervisor of banks.*

A two-track approach means that on the one hand the financial regulators integrate the verification of AML compliance into the regular supervisory procedures, and on the other hand that they exercise thematic AML supervision.[44] In the United Kingdom thematic AML supervision is integrated into the FCA's broader financial crime supervision programme, whereas in the Netherlands it is an integral part of the thematic supervision programme focussing on integrity. The Swedish Financial Supervisory Authority has the most focused type of AML supervision. It has a specific AML Unit (*Enheten Penningtvätt)* that exercises thematic AML supervision by focusing on aspects of specific AML obligations, and assists the regular supervision team when they identify possible AML issues. SEPBLAC only has supervisory tasks in relation to the prevention of money laundering and terrorist financing, hence its activities are completely focused on compliance with the preventive AML obligations.

This difference can be explained by the supervisory models applicable in these countries: in Spain the FIU is the authority that is ultimately responsible for the AML supervision of banks. The Bank of Spain has only been given a secondary role in the AML supervision of banks. In the Netherlands, the United Kingdom and Sweden, the supervisory models allow for the possibility to appoint the financial regulators as the authorities with final responsibility for the AML supervision of banks.

- *When anti-money laundering supervision is integrated into wider supervisory programmes, the financial regulators are not transparent about this. On the contrary, they do provide information and account for the exercise of their thematic supervision. The DNB, FCA and the Swedish Financial Supervisory Authority have regularly supervised banks for their compliance with AML obligations in recent years.*

Regarding integration into wider supervisory programmes, it appears that the supervisors cannot or simply do not give an insight into the extent to which verification with preventive AML obligations is included in the supervisory procedures. The most commonly identified reason is the fact that it is generally up to the individual inspectors' discretion whether and to what extent they integrate the verification of compliance with preventive AML

44 § 5.6.2; § 6.6.2; § 7.6.2.

obligations into their regular supervisory procedures. From the perspective of effective supervision, this lack of information is lamentable. The absence of information and statistics have as a consequence that outsiders do not really know what is being done here and that the supervisors cannot be held accountable for the exercise of AML supervision in this track. Information on the exercise of thematic AML supervision is primarily seen as a means to account for the exercise of AML supervision, and serves as a tool for the provision of guidance at the same time.[45]

In its public annual thematic supervision plans the DNB indicates which thematic projects it plans to undertake. Thematic AML supervision of banks had been planned in the years 2012-14, and in one of the announced AML reviews the DNB would include 75 banks. From this research it appeared that the DNB strongly focuses on the existence of adequate internal policies and procedures for the prevention of money laundering. Unfortunately, the outcomes of the DNB's thematic AML projects are not provided in the annual reports, special thematic reports or published on its website. In this respect, it can learn from the Financial Conduct Authority that reports annually about the exercise of its AML supervision. In recent years the FCA's specialist financial crime supervision team has carried out a high number of on-site inspections and investigations of banks annually, in particular through the ongoing Systematic Anti-Money Laundering Programme (SAMLP) and thematic reviews.[46] Until 2014 the FCA also published four reports with the results of thematic AML supervision. In the two most relevant reports, a total of 44 banks were inspected. In addition, the specialist team has carried out event-driven AML supervision on a risk-based approach. Like the FCA, the DNB could publish the results of thematic AML inspections of banks in an aggregated version or publish special reports with good and bad practices. The Swedish Financial Supervisory Authority is not very transparent about the exercise of thematic AML supervision of banks either. Annual plans are not public and information on the outcomes of the thematic AML reviews performed and the inclusion of banks therein is fragmented. Sometimes it includes this information in the annual reports, while at other times it publishes special reports. Although it may learn from the DNB in relation to the publication of annual (thematic) supervision plans and the way in which the FCA accounts for the exercise of its thematic AML supervision of banks, there is nevertheless enough evidence to support the finding that banks operating in Sweden have been subject to AML inspections through thematic supervision. However, because the numbers seem to be decreasing, it should keep ensuring that enough attention is paid to AML compliance by banks.

45 Cf. § 7.6.2.3.

46 The SAMLP is an ongoing supervision programme on 14 major retail and investment banks operating in the UK and until July 2013 the team had carried out in-depth on-site inspections on five banks, see: § 7.6.2.3.

- *SEPBLAC exercises its anti-money laundering supervision in a highly non-transparent manner. It may have supervised banks, but this cannot be concluded with certainty. Overall, this research discovered that AML supervision by SEPBLAC is practically non-existent, even if a risk-based approach is followed. Resource issues may be an explanation for this.*

Information on the way in which SEPBLAC exercises its supervision is not available. Annual supervision plans are privileged, evidence of the existence of a supervision policy is absent, and in its public annual reports SEPBLAC does not even account for the exercise of its AML supervision.[47] Supposedly SEPBLAC applies a risk-based approach, but there is no information that explains how it has implemented this approach in its supervision. Based on the limited statistical data available, which even diverges between different sources, it seems that SEPBLAC carried out a number of on-site inspections on credit institutions in the years 2010 to 2012. How many of those institutions were banks cannot be said. They may have been subject to AML inspections, but this is not necessarily the case. This research discovered that on average 0.1% of the total number of obliged institutions and professionals were supervised on-site annually by SEPBLAC in the years 2010 to 2012. The low number of inspections is most likely caused by serious resource issues. Chapter 4 demonstrated that roughly around 11 FTE are available at SEPBLAC for the AML supervision of 22,000 institutions.[48] This imbalance prevents SEPBLAC from carrying out AML supervision effectively.

The Spanish AML legislation does contain a number of tools that have the potential to strengthen SEPBLAC's AML supervision. These are SEPBLAC's FIU-related functions, the possibility for the Commission for the Prevention of Money Laundering and Monetary Offences to enter into supervisory arrangements with the Bank of Spain and two other financial regulators, and the obligation for institutions and professionals to have their internal policies for the prevention of money laundering and terrorist financing assessed by external experts on a regular basis.[49] The FIU-related functions allow SEPBLAC inspectors to have access to a wide range of databases and information on the reporting behaviour of obliged institutions and professionals, thus creating a strong information position. The external review system also allows SEPBLAC to gather additional information on the supervisory population and to use these reports in various ways in its supervision. Yet as mentioned in § 8.2.2, the system of external review reports would benefit from amendments to the legislation in force. Finally, the conclusion of supervisory arrangements by the Commission may remove part of the supervisory work from SEPBLAC and avoids the 'double supervision' of financial and credit institutions. A lack of transparency, however, prevents any insight into the content and functioning of these arrangements, the relationship and mutual responsibilities of SEPBLAC and the arrangement partners, as well as legal safeguards that accompany these agreements. From the perspective of effective supervision it is lamentable that the supervisory arrangements are privileged. This research showed that in practice the Bank of Spain has not, or to a

47 § 4.2.
48 § 4.4.1 and 4.6.2.2.
49 § 4.6.3.

very limited extent, carried out AML inspections on banks. It does not refer at all to the carrying out of AML supervision in its annual banking supervision reports for the years 2011 and 2012, while information from the Commission for the Prevention of Money Laundering and Monetary Offences states that the Bank of Spain carried out 12 on-site inspections in the period 2010-2012.

This research demonstrated that compared to the AML supervision of banks in the three other countries included in this research, banks operating in Spain have not or have hardly been supervised for the purpose of AML compliance, either by SEPBLAC or the Bank of Spain. This finding may be related to the choice for the FIU model in Spain. This research demonstrated that providing a single authority with final responsibility for AML supervision may bring about a high(er) risk of resource issues that can (seriously) affect supervision in practice. Whereas the DNB, the FCA and the Swedish Financial Supervisory Authority can focus their AML supervisory efforts on banks (and a limited number of other financial and credit institutions) specifically, SEPBLAC's supervisory population is so large and diverse that it can only select a number of institutions or professionals to be supervised in a single year. Without adequate resources, this may result in a complete absence of AML supervision for certain types of institutions and professionals. As mentioned above, it has been impossible for SEPBLAC to ensure an adequate level of supervision in practice. In relation to banks, however, this finding could have been different if the Bank of Spain had actually carried out a high(er) number of AML inspections of banks in the period studied.

8.5.2 Sanctioning

8.5.2.1 Sanctioning powers

- *Overall the AML supervisors of banks have adequate sanctioning powers. Only in the Netherlands and Sweden do some particular problems exist. The Spanish AML Act provides adequate sanctioning powers as well, although not to SEPBLAC but to other (political) organs. This is due to the Spanish doctrine of punitive administrative law.*

The AML supervisors of banks obtain their sanctioning powers either from the AML Act or from sectoral legislation. Before they resort to the imposition of formal sanctions, however, all AML supervisors of banks can turn to a variety of informal measures varying from signalling meetings, informal warnings to action plans, in order to persuade banks to comply with the legislation without the use of formal sanctions.

The Dutch AML Act provides the DNB with the power to impose incremental penalty payments, administrative fines and instructions. The administrative fine has a statutory cap of 4 million Euros per breach or twice the amount of money the breach has yielded, if the gain of not complying is more than 2 million Euros.[50] Based on lower-level regulations, however, it appears that breaches of the AML Act can be sanctioned with a maximum administrative fine of 1 million Euros per breach, depending on the category in which

50 Please note, as outlined in § 1.8, that the Dutch AML Act was amended in August 2014. It now provides for tougher sanctioning powers for the DNB for the most serious cases of non-compliance by banks.

the offence is included.[51] In the most serious cases, the DNB can decide to file a criminal complaint for breaches under the AML Act. The incremental penalty payment and administrative fine can be imposed on legal persons as well as on natural persons, provided that the latter have either ordered the offence or had actually controlled the forbidden act. Dutch administrative law makes a distinction between reparatory and punitive sanctions, which may result in the imposition of a combination of sanctions.[52] The powers stemming from the AML Act provide a considerable range of sanctions and possibilities to scale up enforcement action. The DNB can, however, also rely on its sanctioning powers from the Financial Supervision Act (*Wet op het financieel toezicht, Wft*). In particular the power to publish sanctioning decisions and public warnings and the power to amend, revoke in full or partly, or restrict licences or registrations are dissuasive sanctions. In relation to natural persons, the DNB can also instruct an institution that a manager, director, or other person involved in policy-making may no longer exercise his function within the institution due to a lack of trustworthiness. Although the Acts are highly interrelated, this research found it debatable whether the DNB can (always) sanction offences under the AML Act via the Financial Supervision Act. There are various arguments that favour this approach, but at the same time it is difficult to understand why the Dutch legislator has provided the DNB with a separate set of sanctioning powers under the AML Act without making any explicit reference to the Wft. This research therefore found that the AML Act is unclear and unforeseeable on this point, which has a negative effect on legal certainty. The legislator should either make a connection between the Wft and the AML Act, opt for a combination of the two Acts, or explicitly state that this practice is not allowed.

The Swedish Financial Supervisory Authority fully derives its sanctioning powers for breaches of the preventive AML obligations from sectoral legislation.[53] It may issue an order to take measures within a certain time, which is comparable to the DNB's power to issue instructions. Furthermore, it may prohibit the execution of a certain decision, issue a remark or warning, order the reappointment of a board member or managing director, impose an administrative fee (fine), a public law fine or a late fee. The administrative fee has a statutory minimum of approximately 577 Euros and a cap of 50 million SEK, around 5.7 million Euros.[54] A public law fine is comparable to the incremental penalty payment in the Netherlands. In the most serious cases, it may also decide to revoke licences. Although this is a wide range of powers, it may only impose these sanctions on legal persons. The Financial Supervisory Authority does not have the power to impose these sanctions on the board members or directors of those institutions. This is not in line with the Third Directive which requires Member States to ensure that also natural persons can be held liable.[55] The Swedish legislator should ensure that this provision is implemented into national legislation.

51 § 5.6.3.1.

52 A combination between a punitive administrative sanction and a reparatory administrative sanction, or between a criminal sanction and a reparatory administrative sanction, is possible. This means, for example, that the incremental penalty payment can be combined with an administrative fine. See § 5.6.3.1.

53 See § 7.6.3.

54 Please note, as outlined in § 1.8, that this statutory cap was removed in August 2014.

55 Article 39(3) Third Directive.

Under the Money Laundering Regulations 2007, the FCA only has the power to impose a civil penalty (fine) in case of non-compliance. There is no statutory cap on this fine, although the FCA must ensure that it is appropriate. The fine can be imposed on both legal and natural persons. The FCA has a wide range of sanctioning powers stemming from sectoral legislation as well. Unlike for the DNB, there is no discussion as to whether or not this is allowed: the prevention of money laundering belongs to the efforts to tackle financial crime, which fall under the FCA's operational goal of protecting the integrity of the UK's financial sector. The Financial Markets and Services Act 2000 provides for public censures (formal warnings), financial penalties (fines), the suspension of or restrictions on the authorisation, the withdrawal of an authorisation or the imposition of requirements thereto, as well as enforcement action through the civil and criminal courts. The FCA even has prosecutorial powers: Section 402 FSMA 2000 explicitly states that it may institute proceedings for an offence under the prescribed regulations relating to money laundering. In addition, the FCA can prohibit a natural person from operating in financial services, declare that he is not fit and proper, and decide to prohibit him from undertaking specific regulated activities.

Finally, as explained the Spanish AML Act does not provide sanctioning powers to SEPBLAC. This is due to the doctrine of punitive administrative law, which is a very important doctrine in the Spanish legal system.[56] It is strongly reflected in the preventive AML policy as well, as the supervision and sanctioning phases are strictly separated. Supervision is carried out by SEPBLAC, whereas the sanctioning powers rest with the Council of Ministers, the Minister of Economy and Competitiveness and the Director-General for the Treasury and Financial Policy of the Ministry of Economy and Competitiveness, depending on the seriousness of the breaches. The Spanish AML Act distinguishes in great detail between the types of offences (very serious, serious or minor), the corresponding sanctions and the limitation periods. The Act provides a wide range of sanctions varying from private warnings to fines and public warnings, as well as the revocation of licences. For the most serious offences, the fine has a minimum amount of 150,000 Euros and a statutory cap of the highest of these figures: either 5% of the net worth of the institution or professional covered by the AML Act, twice the economic substance of the transaction, or 1.5 million Euros. The amount applies to each individual breach, which means that in the case of several breaches the amounts may be multiplied. What makes the sanctioning powers under the AML Act (even more) dissuasive is that legislation determines that for very serious offences a fine *must* be accompanied by either a public warning or the revocation of the licence. Such an obligation to combine sanctions does not exist in the other countries. Sanctions can be imposed on the non-complying institutions and professionals, as well as their managers or directors who are responsible for the breaches. For the category of very serious offences, they can be fined or be forbidden from holding an administrative or management position in the same institution or any institution covered by the AML Act for a maximum period of ten years. The maximum amount of the fine is 60,000 Euros per individual breach.

56 § 4.7.1.

8.5.2.2 Public supervision (sanctioning) policies

- *None of the AML supervisors of banks has a specific AML supervision (sanctioning) policy. The FCA and DNB do have general public supervision (sanctioning) policies, while the Spanish authorities and the Swedish Financial Supervisory Authority do not.*

From an effective supervision perspective, policies should be public and contain an explanation of the legal framework, the goals of supervision and/or sanctioning, the desired level of compliance, the general principles of the supervisor for its activities and a description of the procedures. This research demonstrated that none of the AML supervisors of banks has a specific AML supervision or sanctioning policy. The DNB and FCA do have general public supervision (sanctioning) policies that are applied in AML-related cases as well. The Spanish authorities and the Swedish Financial Supervisory Authority do not have public supervision policies at all. The DNB has a joint sanctioning policy with the Netherlands Authority for the Financial Markets. This public policy contains the goals and underlying principles for sanctioning, and explains which factors the DNB takes into account in the application of its sanctioning powers under various pieces of legislation, including the Financial Supervision Act and the AML Act. In the UK, the FCA has a very detailed public supervision policy (Enforcement Guide), in which it explains how it makes use of its supervisory and sanctioning powers. For the application of specific sanctions this is further detailed in the public Decision Procedure and Penalties Manual. The Swedish Financial Supervisory Authority does not have a public policy at all. This makes it impossible for outsiders to disentangle FI's sanctioning principles, goals and style. There is also no public sanctioning policy available for the competent sanctioning authorities under the Spanish AML Act. This is caused, to a certain extent, by the fact that the punitive administrative law doctrine and the AML Act already provide information on the sanctioning procedure and the underlying principles.

8.5.2.3 Sanctioning in practice

- *The Spanish authorities and the DNB are not transparent about their AML sanctioning activity.*

From the perspective of effective supervision it is lamentable that information concerning the numbers, types and the severity of the sanctions imposed for breaches of the preventive AML obligations is not provided in an intelligible way. The DNB, for example, only publishes information on the number of sanctions imposed on banks in general statistics and does not make a distinction as to the breaches for which the sanctions have been imposed. Likewise, in Spain the authorities keep very general statistics on the number of sanctions imposed under the AML Act, without making clear on which specific type of institutions the sanctions were imposed. In both cases this makes it difficult to hold the AML supervisors accountable for the exercise of their anti-money laundering supervision.

- *All four supervisors have taken informal and/or formal action for breaches of the preventive anti-money laundering obligations against banks. Compared to the other supervisors included in this research, the DNB is soft in sanctioning banks for non-compliance with the AML Act.*

Possible explanations for this finding may be sought in the DNB's sanctioning style and the *de facto* cap of 1 million Euros for administrative fines. The DNB's sanctioning policy and practice demonstrates that DNB prevents the use of formal sanctions as much as possible and that it strongly relies on informal measures like signalling meetings and informal warnings. Sometimes the mere intention of imposing a formal measure has been enough to overcome breaches, according to the DNB itself.[57] The cap on administrative fines for AML breaches is the lowest in all four countries included in this research. Spain has a statutory cap for administrative fines: for very serious breaches a maximum amount is set at 1.5 million Euros per breach and Sweden has a statutory cap of around 5.7 million EUR.[58] In the UK, the amounts are left to the discretion of the FCA. Legislation establishes that the fines must be appropriate, meaning 'dissuasive, proportionate and effective', but within this framework the FCA can determine the amount of the fines. Acknowledging that the DNB's soft approach may have other reasons which have not all been purveyed (in full) in this research, the finding is nevertheless remarkable in light of the fact that the Dutch financial sector is considered to be highly vulnerable to money laundering due to the attractive financial climate and size of the financial sector.[59]

Within the period studied the DNB used its power to issue instructions on a number of occasions in relation to non-complying banks. Based on media messages it also appeared that it imposed one administrative fine of 27,225 Euros on a bank for breaching the customer due diligence obligations stemming from the AML Act. Compared to the formal sanctions taken by the other AML supervisors against banks, this illustrates the soft approach that the DNB follows. Especially the FCA has been active in imposing formal sanctions on banks for breaches of preventive AML obligations, besides an increasing use of informal measures like early interventions. The fines on banks for breaches of the Money Laundering Regulations 2007 varied from between approximately 355,000 to more than 10 million Euros.[60] The use of informal measures besides the average of 4.5 million Euros per fine – which already exceeds the statutory cap on fines under the legislation in the Netherlands – and the fact that the FCA normally publishes its penalty decisions with full reference to the name of the institution sanctioned, demonstrate both the proportionality and the dissuasiveness of the FCA's regime at the same time. Regarding the publication of sanctions, it should be pointed out that the FCA is in principle obliged to publish its decisions. Interestingly, the DNB also has an obligation (or a restrained power) to publish the decisions of administrative fines or incremental penalty payments under the Financial Supervision Act. But while in recent years the FCA has published these decisions, even at the time when it was the single financial regulator in the UK, the DNB has mostly

57 § 5.6.4.2.
58 Please note, as outlined in § 1.8, that this statutory cap was removed in August 2014.
59 § 5.2.
60 § 6.6.4.2 (the amounts were 294,000 GBP and 8.75 million GBP).

relied on the exception ground. The one fine that the DNB (supposedly) imposed for non-compliance with the AML Act was not made public. It is thus unknown whether the DNB used the power to impose an administrative fine under the Wft or the AML Act. The AML Act does not provide for an obligation or power to publish sanctioning decisions.[61] Like the DNB, the Swedish Financial Supervisory Authority has not taken much formal action against banks either. Nevertheless, the one fine that was imposed on a bank was a great deal harsher than the fine imposed by the DNB, around 3.3 million Euros, accompanied by a remark (warning) and a full publication on the website as well. In Spain, banks have faced strong formal action for acting in breach of the preventive AML obligations. This is remarkable given the low level of AML inspections on banks in recent years. Sanctioning decisions under the AML Act are in principle not published in any form in Spain, with the exception of public warnings that can be imposed for the category of very serious offences. Although it has been difficult to find out exactly which formal actions have been taken against banks, since the entry into force of the AML Act in 2010, at least three banks were publicly warned and fined for acting in breach of (the predecessor) of the AML Act. The fines varied from 1.11 to 2.1 million Euros. In all three decisions, two or more fines were imposed and the amounts determined for each individual fine were added up, explaining why the fines exceeded the statutory cap. The FCA and the Spanish authorities also took formal action against natural persons working at financial institutions, like managers and money laundering reporting officers. There is no such information available for the DNB and the Swedish Financial Supervisory Authority.

The soft approach taken by the DNB compared to the other AML supervisors of banks included in this research may send out a wrong signal to banks with bad intentions. Especially where the financial sector is considered to be highly vulnerable to money laundering, one would expect that firm action would be taken in case of non-compliance. The DNB has an adequate range of sanctioning powers, but this comparative research proved that it could, and from an effective supervision perspective should, apply these powers in a more dissuasive way.

8.6 Anti-money laundering supervision of real estate agents

Is the anti-money laundering supervision of real estate agents in Spain, the Netherlands, the United Kingdom and Sweden effective? This section compares the competences of the AML supervisors of real estate agents and the way in which they apply these powers. Supervision is without exception exercised by the Government or public (administrative) bodies. This is not surprising, given that the Third Directive does not allow the real estate sector to be supervised by professional associations.[62]

61 More about this in § 8.6.2.1, as the lack of such a power affects the two other Dutch AML supervisors more.

62 This will (most likely) change with the adoption of the Fourth Directive, as discussed in § 2.3.3 and § 6.4.2.4.

Effective supervision requires that AML supervisors have adequate supervisory and sanctioning powers provided by law.[63] AML supervisors should apply these powers in practice, and do so in a proportionate and careful manner. With respect to sanctioning, AML supervisors must speak softly where possible and hard where necessary. Ultimately, the sanctions must be capable of providing a deterrent effect. The existence of public supervision (sanctioning) policies is a precondition for effective supervision. Such policies should include an explanation of the legal framework, the supervisory goals, the desired level of compliance, the principles followed by the supervisor for its activities, as well as a general description of the procedures applied.

8.6.1 Supervision

8.6.1.1 Supervisory powers

- *This research found that none of the AML supervisors of real estate agents has adequate supervisory powers. The most serious lack of adequate powers can be found in Sweden.*

The supervisors of real estate agents in the UK, the Netherlands and Spain obtain their supervisory powers directly from the AML legislation. Although the UK's Office of Fair Trading has powers under other pieces of legislation as well, the AML regime is dealt with as a separate supervisory regime.[64] The Dutch Tax and Customs Administration/ Bureau Supervision Wwft and SEPBLAC only have supervisory responsibility under the preventive anti-money laundering policy and thus derive their powers in full from this legislation. The OFT, the Bureau Supervision Wwft and SEPBLAC all have the power to compel (the production of) information which is relevant to the monitoring of compliance and the power to perform on-site inspections. However, national AML legislation does not provide them with regulatory powers. In Spain, this power is provided for the Commission for the Prevention of Money Laundering and Monetary Offences under whose authority SEPBLAC acts.

The Swedish Estate Agents Inspectorate (FMI) does have regulatory powers. It is given this power via the Swedish AML Regulation. The FMI obtains its other supervisory powers from the Estate Agents Act. However, due to the narrow formulation of real estate agents under this Act, as pointed out in § 8.2.1, and the absence of a self-standing power to perform on-site inspections, the Inspectorate has no power to carry out on-site AML inspections. As a result, AML supervision currently consists of off-site inspections focusing almost exclusively on the performance of customer due diligence and the record keeping obligations.[65] In Chapter 7 it was considered that if these two problems are solved by drafting clearer and more precise legislation, this would allow the FMI to carry out AML supervision on more real estate agents than it currently can and does.

63 See Table 1 for the concrete interpretation of adequate supervisory and sanctioning powers.

64 On the 1st of April 2014, the Office of Fair Trading was abolished. From that date, supervisory responsibility for estate agents rests with HM Revenue and Customs. See § 6.4.2.4.

65 § 7.7.2.

8.6.1.2 AML supervision of real estate agents in practice

- *For all AML supervisors of real estate agents, public information on the exercise of their AML supervision is scarce or is not intelligible. All authorities should become more transparent about the procedures and outcomes of AML supervision in order to be held accountable. Based on the limited information available, the weakest AML supervision of real estate agents is in Spain. The Dutch AML supervisor has been the most active supervisor in terms of (on-site) AML inspections.*

SEPBLAC, the Bureau Supervision Wwft, and the OFT all carry out AML supervision on a self-standing basis. Only the Swedish Estate Agents Inspectorate integrates anti-money laundering supervision into a wider supervisory programme.

In relation to the AML supervision of banks we could already observe that SEPBLAC is highly non-transparent about the exercise of its AML supervision.[66] Moreover, this research demonstrated that AML supervision by SEPBLAC is practically non-existent, even if it follows a risk-based approach.[67] More importantly, however, between 2010 and 2012 SEPBLAC did not carry out a single inspection of any of the 4,720 real estate agents that were registered with it in the year 2012.[68] In the absence of any supervision activity on real estate agents, SEPBLAC clearly does not comply with the requirement that AML supervisors must apply their supervisory powers in practice, and do so in a proportionate and careful manner. The Commission for the Prevention of Money Laundering and Monetary Offences has no power to enter into supervisory arrangements with authorities that are involved in the regulation and supervision of the real estate profession. Due to a lack of transparency there is no information about the (possible) use of the external review system by SEPBLAC either. The fact that real estate agents have not been supervised for their compliance with the preventive obligations is even more remarkable in light of the high vulnerability of the sector for money laundering.[69]

Anti-money laundering supervision by the Swedish Estate Agents Inspectorate is entirely off-site and mostly reactive in nature. The FMI does not follow a risk-based approach. Exact numbers are not available, but roughly 80% of all supervisory activities stem from complaints from consumers or third parties, which in most cases are not even about non-compliance with AML obligations in the first place.[70] When it receives complaints, the Inspectorate includes the verification of AML compliance on its own motion in the supervisory activities. The fact that most efforts originate from complaints is worrisome, because not all obligations are adequately checked: the reporting obligation and the obligation to have an internal policy are hardly included, if they are included at all. Moreover, the risks of or associated with money laundering or ongoing non-compliance by real estate agents do not receive adequate attention. The verification of compliance with

66 § 4.4.2 and § 8.5.1.2.

67 See § 8.5.1.2 where it was considered that overall SEPBLAC had supervised 0.1% of the entire population for which it has supervisory responsibility in the years between 2010 and 2012.

68 § 4.6.2.2.

69 § 4.2.

70 § 7.7.2.

the reporting obligation and the obligation to have an internal policy require proactive, risk-based supervision with on-site inspections and the use of sample testing. Only in this way can FMI verify whether the obligations are actually applied in practice. Of course, the current lack of adequate supervisory powers has prevented the Inspectorate from exercising its supervision in this way. Thematic supervision projects, which the FMI has started to carry out, is a way in which compliance with the reporting obligation under the AML Act can be supervised on a more regular and focused basis in the future. Again, for this the Inspectorate first needs a legal power to perform on-site inspections.

The Office of Fair Trading carries out risk-based AML supervision of real estate agents in the UK. Based on risk assessments in which it uses a wide range of internal and external information, the OFT prepares internal annual supervision plans.[71] The Code of Practice details how it exercises on-site inspections. Information on the number of AML inspections of real estate agents is scarce. Based on the limited information available, it seems that the activity is rather low in light of the total number of real estate agents in the UK. In the year 2012, approximately 0.3% of the total number of real estate agents were supervised by the OFT. AML legislation permits the OFT to enter into arrangements with Local Authority Trading Standards Services, allowing LATSS officers to exercise AML supervision as well.[72] The Money Laundering Regulations 2007, however, do not stipulate what the arrangements should comprise of and how the arrangements should be concluded and maintained. The only matter that is clear is that the OFT is ultimately responsible for AML inspections exercised by LATSS officers. From the viewpoint of transparency and accountability, as well as legality and legal certainty, this research found that formal arrangements between the OFT and LATSS should be concluded in writing. These should also regulate in more detail the relationship between the authorities under the AML regime. AML supervision by LATSS seems to be in its infancy: LATSS carried out some on-site visits as part of a pilot project and the OFT concluded one informal agreement with a LATSS. More information on AML supervision by the LATSS in practice is not available. The OFT should be more transparent about its own AML supervision in practice, as well as about activities carried out by LATSS in relation to the AML policy.

The Dutch AML supervisor of real estate agents, the Bureau Supervision Wwft, applies a risk-based approach in its AML supervision, although its implementation was found to be a difficult task. The main problems in relation to real estate agents appears to be the unregulated nature of the profession and the fact that real estate agents who perform valuation activities only partially fall within the scope of the AML Act. Despite the difficulties, the non-public annual reports demonstrate that real estate agents have been given supervisory priority in recent years resulting in a high inspection intensity both in project-based an individual supervision.[73] Between 2011 and 2013 it carried out more than 1,000 on-site AML inspections involving approximately 900 real estate agents and businesses. This is a lot more than the other AML supervisors of real estate agents involved in this research. The Bureau should, not surprisingly, become transparent about

71 § 6.7.2.1.
72 § 6.7.2.2.
73 § 5.7.2.2 and 5.7.2.3.

its supervisory activities. Despite the high inspection intensity, this research discovered that the Dutch AML Act complicates the exercise of AML supervision by the Bureau Supervision Wwft in two ways. The Bureau makes a distinction between smaller and larger institutions in its supervisory approach. For smaller institutions it focuses on dossiers on a transaction and client level. For larger institutions, it verifies whether the institutions have adequate internal policies and procedures. However, in the absence of such an obligation in the AML Act, the Bureau cannot enforce this obligation against the larger institutions. In order to make the Bureau's supervision more meaningful, decisive and effective, the Dutch legislator should introduce an explicit obligation in the AML Act concerning internal controls and policies. Moreover, the partial inclusion of valuers of real estate also makes the supervision of real estate agents performing valuation activities unnecessarily complicated.[74]

The finding that Spain is the weakest in the AML supervision of real estate agents in practice can be explained, as was the case for its supervision of banks, by the choice for the FIU model. SEPBLAC does not have the resources to carry out AML supervision of the entire range of obliged institutions and professionals in Spain, even if it would apply a risk-based approach. Unlike the case of the AML supervision of banks, the Commission for the Prevention of Money Laundering and Monetary Offences is not allowed to enter into supervisory arrangements with regulators or professional associations active in the real estate sector. This means that there is no other authority that can (partly) take over the AML supervision of real estate agents or exercise it on SEPBLAC's behalf. The finding that the Dutch AML supervisor has been the most active AML supervisor of real estate agents does not, on the other hand, seem to be related to the choice for the external model. After all, in all four countries AML supervision is exercised by external supervisors. Rather, it could be explained by the extra focus that the Bureau Supervision Wwft has placed on real estate agents after the mutual evaluation of the FATF on the Netherlands in 2010.[75] Also the fact that the Swedish Estate Agents Inspectorate does not have adequate supervisory powers could be an explanation for the different levels of supervision in practice between the Dutch and Swedish AML supervisors.

8.6.2 Sanctioning

8.6.2.1 Sanctioning powers

- *This research found that most problems in relation to the adequacy of sanctioning powers exist for the Swedish Estate Agents Inspectorate.*

The Inspectorate does have three different types of sanctions available, but these do not always allow the Inspectorate to act in a proportionate way. The deregistration of real estate agents is a far-reaching and highly dissuasive sanction, whereas the warning or reminder are very soft sanctions and the dividing line between these two sanctions is

74 See § 8.2.2.
75 See § 5.7.2.2.

unclear.[76] Legislation establishes deregistration as the standard sanction. This makes the sanctioning powers inadequate in light of effective supervision, which requires that AML supervisors must sanction in a proportionate and careful manner and escalate their sanctions where necessary. The narrow formulation of real estate agents also prevents the FMI from sanctioning real estate businesses.[77] This is not in line with the requirement that AML supervisors must be able to apply sanctions against both legal and natural persons.

The OFT has two sanctions available: the imposition of a civil penalty (fine) and prosecution. This is not a wide range of sanctions, but nevertheless allows the Office to scale up its activities, if needed. The amount of the fine is entirely left to the discretion of the OFT, as long as it can be considered appropriate. Both sanctioning powers can be used against legal and natural persons. As already explained in § 8.5.2, SEPBLAC does not have sanctioning powers. These powers rest with the Council of Ministers, the Minister of Economy and Competitiveness and the Director-General for the Treasury and Financial Policy, depending on the seriousness of the breaches. A wide range of sanctions are available, which can be applied against legal and natural persons. The Dutch AML Act provides the Bureau Supervision Wwft with the power to impose incremental penalty payments, administrative fines with a (*de facto*) maximum of 1 million Euros per breach, and instructions. This is a considerable range of powers and allows the Bureau to resort to more dissuasive sanctions, if necessary. At present, however, it is questionable whether these sanctions can be imposed on real estate businesses, since these are not explicitly included in the scope of the AML Act.[78] The Dutch legislator should act on this point. In order to make the range of powers wider and more dissuasive the AML Act should also consider providing a discretionary power for supervisors to publish sanctioning decisions. These are two important elements in the theoretical framework of effective supervision. AML supervisors can reserve this power for the most serious cases of non-compliance.

8.6.2.2 Public supervision (sanctioning) policies

- *The only AML supervisor of real estate agents with a public supervision (sanctioning) policy is the Office of Fair Trading.*

Besides its Code of Practice, the public documents on AML enforcement principles and the approach to penalties under the Money Laundering Regulations 2007 deal with the OFT's AML policy in general. The OFT's interim penalty policy details which steps it takes in determining whether to impose a penalty and to determine the amount thereof.[79] Unlike the other AML supervisors of real estate agents, the OFT is highly transparent. In line with the theoretical framework, the policy contains an explanation of the legal framework, the supervision goals and principles and sets out the procedures to be followed. The policy should, however, be improved by including an explanation of the OFT's use of prosecutorial powers, as this is missing in the policy. Likewise, the policy should contain

76 § 7.7.3.
77 See § 8.2.1.
78 See § 8.2.1.
79 § 6.7.4.1.

information on the use of prosecutorial powers by the LATTS and the relationship with sanctions imposed by the OFT under the AML policy. The three other AML supervisors of real estate agents should become more transparent about their own AML supervision (sanctioning) policies. They could learn from the Office of Fair Trading in this respect. This is also an aspect that HMRC should take into account when taking over the AML supervision of real estate agents.[80]

8.6.2.3 Sanctioning in practice

- *This research identified a wide variety in the sanctioning practices against non-complying real estate agents. Especially the Spanish and Dutch AML supervisors do not seem to perform well compared to their counterparts in the United Kingdom and Sweden.*

Based on the limited information available and considering that between 2010 and 2012 real estate agents were not supervised by SEPBLAC at all, it is highly unlikely that real estate agents or real estate businesses have been sanctioned in Spain since 2010. Information on the use of informal measures is completely absent as well. Judgments of the Spanish Supreme Court do demonstrate that some real estate businesses have been sanctioned for non-compliance with preventive AML obligations in the past, but the facts of these cases date from far before the entry into force of the current legislation.[81]

Based on the information stemming from the non-public annual reports of the Bureau Supervision Wwft, this research found that the Bureau's practice does not comply with the requirement that sanctions must ultimately be capable of providing a deterrent effect. Despite the fact that it has encountered a considerable number of breaches during inspections of real estate agents in recent years, the Bureau has only once resorted to the imposition of a formal sanction. Another real estate agent was prosecuted by the Dutch Public Prosecution Service for acting in breach of the reporting obligation. The non-public annual reports did demonstrate that the Bureau has made use of informal measures like signalling meetings and issuing informal warnings.[82] The Bureau's cooperative style may be adequate upon the identification of minor offences. Nevertheless, even for very serious offences like the failure to report to the FIU, the Bureau still gives real estate agents the opportunity to overcome the breach without any consequences or being directly backed by a formal measure. Under circumstances this may be understandable, but such should not be the standard. This research concluded that the Bureau Supervision Wwft should start applying these powers in the case of (serious) infringements in order to demonstrate to the sector that it takes the matter seriously and to deter future non-compliance.

The Office of Fair Trading's sanctioning activity shows that it has imposed a considerable number of civil penalties on real estate agents until early 2014. Information on the informal measures taken is not available, however. The OFT's formal sanctions have become more dissuasive over the years (especially between 2012 and 2014) in terms of the amount of fines

80 § 6.7.5.
81 § 4.7.4.
82 § 5.7.4.

and the publication of the sanctioning decisions.[83] The Office of Fair Trading has moved from imposing sanctions merely for acting in breach of the registration obligation, to the imposition of sanctions for breaches of the wider range of preventive AML obligations. In the absence of information indicating otherwise, it seems that the OFT and the LATSS have never prosecuted an estate agent for acting in breach of the Regulations.

The sanctioning practice of the Swedish Estate Agents Inspectorate is remarkable in light of the way in which it exercises its AML supervision, which was criticised in the previous section. Despite the lack of proactive and risk-based supervision, a lack of adequate sanctioning powers and the impossibility to sanction real estate businesses, the FMI's sanctioning yearbooks, that include all disciplinary decisions in an anonymised fashion per year, demonstrate that the Inspectorate's Disciplinary Board sanctioned a high number of real estate agents in the years between 2010 and 2013 for acting in breach of the customer due diligence or record keeping obligations. In nearly all cases, however, a warning was issued. This confirms the absence of adequate sanctioning powers that allow the FMI to sanction in a proportionate and careful manner and to escalate its sanctions where necessary.

8.7 Anti-money laundering supervision of accountants

Is the anti-money laundering supervision of accountants in Spain, the Netherlands, the United Kingdom and Sweden effective? This section compares the competences of the AML supervisors of accountants and the way in which they apply these powers. The supervision of accountants in the four countries is from an institutional perspective more diverse than the AML supervision of banks and real estate agents. In the UK, 11 professional associations have AML supervisory responsibility for the accountancy sector, whereas Swedish AML legislation provides supervisory responsibility for accountants to the Supervisory Board of Public Auditors and three county administrative boards. In practice, the Supervisory Board of Public Auditors (hereafter also 'the Board' or 'RN') also engages with the professional association for authorised and approved public auditors and other highly qualified professionals in the accountancy sector in Sweden (*Branschorganisation för redovisningskonsulter, revisorer & rådgivare, FAR*). Although in the Netherlands the Financial Supervision Office is formally designated as the AML supervisor for accountants, professional associations are indirectly involved in carrying out AML supervision as well. Only in Spain is it clear that one authority, SEPBLAC, carries out the AML supervision of accountants.

Effective supervision requires that AML supervisors have adequate supervisory and sanctioning powers provided by law.[84] AML supervisors should apply these powers in practice, and do so in a proportionate and careful manner. With respect to sanctioning, AML supervisors must speak softly where possible and hard where necessary. Ultimately, the sanctions must be capable of providing a deterrent effect. The existence of public supervision (sanctioning) policies is a precondition for effective supervision. Such policies

83 § 6.7.4.2.
84 See Table 1 for the concrete interpretation of adequate supervisory and sanctioning powers.

should include an explanation of the legal framework, the supervisory goals, the desired level of compliance, the principles followed by the supervisor for its activities, as well as a general description of the procedures.

8.7.1 Supervision

8.7.1.1 Supervisory powers

- *The anti-money laundering supervisors of accountants in the United Kingdom have adequate supervisory powers. The other AML supervisors all have, to a different extent, issues in relation to the adequacy of their powers, or the application thereof in practice.*

The Dutch AML supervisor, the BFT, lacks regulatory powers and may encounter some difficulties in the application of its powers due to legal professional privilege. Accountants are allowed to directly invoke, under certain circumstances, the legal privilege exemption laid down in the AML Act, or indirectly when they act under the assignment of a lawyer. The law is insufficiently clear on how, particularly, the derived professional privilege and the duty of secrecy work through the AML supervision exercised by BFT. It has itself developed a way through which it aims to marginally check whether an accountant justifiably invokes the (derived) privilege. When it finds an abuse, the BFT must make a reasonable case that there is actually an abuse.[85] It is desirable that Dutch legislation clarifies in which circumstances accountants may invoke their legal professional privilege under or in relation to the AML policy and which requirements they must fulfil. The Dutch legislator can draw inspiration from the other three countries included in this research as legal professional privilege – if in place for accountants and/or auditors at all – does not hamper the AML supervision.

As mentioned, the Spanish AML Act provides SEPBLAC with adequate inspection powers, but SEPBLAC lacks the power to regulate. The Swedish Supervisory Board of Public Auditors has adequate supervisory powers, although from a legality perspective it would be advisable to explicitly lay down in the Auditors Act that the Board is allowed to perform on-site inspections. The three county administrative boards carry out the AML supervision of accountants and accountancy firms, with the exception of public auditors and audit firms approved or authorised by the Board. They have adequate supervisory powers provided by the AML Act, including the power to compel (the production of) information which is relevant for supervision, the power to carry out inspections and regulatory powers. Nevertheless, also here it would be advisable to state explicitly that the boards are allowed to perform on-site inspections, because now this can only be inferred from the explanatory memorandum to the AML Act, which merely expresses the Government's opinion.

ICAEW and AAT derive their supervisory powers from their own professional norms. In both cases the powers of the professional associations are formulated as obligations for their

85 § 5.8.1.

members. Staff have the power to compel (the production of) relevant information and to carry out on-site inspections. Both ICAEW and AAT, being professional associations, have regulatory powers as well. No problems could be identified in relation to the application of these powers, meaning that both associations fully comply with the requirement that AML supervisors must have adequate supervisory powers. It is interesting to observe that only the professional associations have no issues at all with the (application of) supervisory powers in practice. One possible explanation for this is that by applying the internal model to the AML supervisory architecture, all professional associations in the UK appointed as AML supervisors derive the supervisory powers from their own internal professional norms. These norms may be less prone to flaws or errors than is the case with legislation, and may be more flexible than legislation as well.

8.7.1.2 AML supervision of accountants in practice

- *Compared to the AML supervision of accountants in the Netherlands, the United Kingdom and by the Swedish county administrative boards, the weakest AML supervision is in Spain. Due to a lack of transparency the Supervisory Board of Public Auditors' supervisory practice could not be included in this analysis.*

Supervision is exercised differently by the AML supervisors of accountants included in this research. SEPBLAC (Spain), the Financial Supervision Office (the Netherlands) and the three county administrative boards (Sweden) carry out AML supervision on a self-standing basis. This is because they do not have other supervisory responsibilities, as is the case for SEPBLAC, or they do have wider supervisory responsibility, but not in relation to accountants. To the contrary, the Swedish Supervisory Board of Public Auditors and the two professional associations in the UK acting as AML supervisors for their members (ICAEW and AAT) integrate AML supervision into their regular supervisory procedures. The Board carries out supervision via its systematic and outreach supervision and the periodic quality control programme, whereas ICAEW and AAT integrate AML supervision in their ongoing quality assurance procedures. In order to ensure that despite this integration adequate attention is given to AML compliance, ICAEW has recently started to perform targeted AML inspections.[86] The Supervisory Board of Public Auditors and AAT do not have such a practice.

As observed above, SEPBLAC is highly non-transparent concerning the exercise of its supervision.[87] Moreover, anti-money laundering supervision by SEPBLAC is practically non-existent, even if a risk-based approach is followed. In relation to accountants, SEPBLAC did not carry out a single inspection of accountants between the years 2010 and 2012. In the absence of any supervision activity vis-à-vis accountants, SEPBLAC does not comply with the requirement that AML supervisors must apply their supervisory powers in practice, and do so in a proportionate and careful manner The Spanish AML Act does not allow the Commission for the Prevention of Money Laundering and Monetary Offences to enter into supervisory arrangements with other authorities or professional

86 § 6.8.2.
87 § 4.4.2.

associations that have a regulatory or supervisory role in the accountancy sector, like the Accounting and Auditing Institute (*Instituto de Contabilidad de Auditoría de Cuentas, ICAC*).[88] Because of a lack of transparency, information on the possible use of the external review system by SEPBLAC is completely absent as well.

The Swedish Supervisory Board of Public Auditors is equally non-transparent. It does not provide any information on the way in which it carries out AML supervision and how the verification of AML compliance is integrated into its regular supervisory procedures. An analysis of its supervisory practice is therefore impossible.[89] Within the systematic and outreach supervision programme, the Board exercises a number of projects. There is no evidence that (the prevention of) money laundering has been a focal point within the SUT in the years 2012 and 2013. AML supervision is also integrated into the periodic quality controls. These controls are exercised by the Board itself and by a professional organisation (FAR) for which they have entered into a supervisory arrangement. In this instrument parties have agreed that FAR performs quality controls on the audit firms and auditors that do not audit listed companies and which are members of this association. The Swedish Auditors Act establishes the inspection cycles for periodic quality controls of three and six years respectively, but how the Supervisory Board of Auditors and FAR plan their controls within these inspection cycles, what the nature of their controls is and how compliance with the AML Act is included, is not clear. Although the public quality controls by the Board give the impression that compliance with the obligation to have an internal AML policy is checked, no such information is available for the FAR. Numbers of periodic quality controls by FAR strongly outweigh those of the Supervisory Board, but the extent to which AML compliance played a role in these controls remains unknown.[90] Despite the fact that the Supervisory Board of Public Auditors itself stated that it has had an increased focus on compliance with the preventive AML obligations in the last few years, the lack of transparency does not support this statement. The Board should publish more information about its anti-money laundering supervision and the outcomes thereof, and make the supervisory arrangement with the FAR publicly available.

This research observed that the county administrative boards in Sweden exercise AML supervision through off-site inspections, on-site inspections, mandatory fit and proper tests and the raising of awareness. In the last few years they have not used a risk-based approach, although this research found some movement in that direction. Since 2011, the supervisory intensity of all three county administrative boards has increased, which is a positive sign.[91] Off-site inspections are the most important type of inspections and particularly the mandatory fit and proper tests have been undertaken regularly. Based on the limited data available, this research found that accountants have been subject to off-site inspections, fit and proper tests and on-site inspections by the county administrative boards. The number of on-site inspections is low in comparison to the total number of accountants subject to their supervisory responsibility under the AML Act. The main

88 § 4.6.3.2.
89 § 7.9.2.
90 § 7.9.2.3.
91 § 7.8.2.

reason is that the few resources that the county administrative boards had available had to be spent on persuading institutions and professionals to register. This means that the requirement that AML supervisors must have adequate resources is not being complied with. Implementing a risk-based approach with more on-site inspections will improve the (effectiveness of) anti-money laundering supervision by the county administrative boards.

The Dutch Financial Supervision Office applies a three-track approach in its AML supervision: the raising of awareness, the conclusion of supervisory arrangements with professional associations and the exercise of regular and risk-based supervision. Regarding the third track, this research concluded that the risk-based supervision of accountants is highly dependent on external signals provided by the police, the Dutch Tax and Customs Administration, the Public Prosecution Service, other AML supervisors and professional associations. The BFT's overall supervision data demonstrated that the regular visits outweighed the risk-based visits in the years between 2010 and 2012.[92] This gives the impression that the BFT's risk-based approach in its AML supervision has been rather reactive and has played a limited role. Accountants were included in both regular and risk-based visits, but the inspection intensity appeared low in light of the high number of accountants that fall under the BFT's supervisory responsibility. Resource issues could be an explanation for this, as the BFT has a small number of staff in relation to the total supervisory population and the fact that it puts a considerable effort into the anti-money laundering supervision of civil-law notaries for which it has broader supervisory responsibilities. From the perspective of effective supervision it seems that the requirement that AML supervisors must have adequate resources is not being (fully) complied with. The second track, supervisory arrangements, could overcome these findings and could be an instrument to strengthen the BFT's AML supervision in practice. Like the Swedish Supervisory Board of Public Auditors, the BFT has entered into such an arrangement with a professional association in the accountancy sector called *Samenwerkende Registeraccountants en Accountants-administratieconsulenten* (SRA). This supervisory arrangement is not publicly available, although, from the perspective of effective supervision, it should be published. The arrangement covers around 20% of the total number of accountancy firms. It lays down the tasks and responsibilities of both SRA and BFT, but requires one amendment. This concerns the obligation for SRA to forward, upon request, privileged information that it obtained during its reviews to the BFT. This undermines the professional privilege of accountants and creates an unequal level playing field with other accountants, which, as we could see, are allowed to invoke legal professional privilege against the BFT in certain circumstances.[93] At the time of finalising this research no data was (yet) available on the practical implementation of this arrangement. The BFT has no such arrangement with the Dutch Institute of Chartered Accountants (NBA), which is regrettable. Its quality audits could help to diminish the resource tensions that the BFT seems to face and at the same time provide input for its risk-based supervision of accountants. It is important that the Dutch legislator starts to act

92 § 5.8.2.1.
93 § 5.8.2.2.

by creating a legal basis for the NBA to forward supervisory information to the BFT and that both authorities are convinced of the need for cooperation on this point.

In the United Kingdom, both ICAEW and AAT have a well-developed practice of AML supervision. ICAEW's AML supervision is embedded within its Practice Assurance Scheme (PAS). It applies a four to eight-year cycle for monitoring, depending on the size and risk of the firm. ICAEW has access to a wide range of information for its risk assessments; the main source of information is the annual returns that all member firms and PC holders are required to complete. ICAEW classifies member firms and PC holders as high, medium or low risk. Off-site monitoring takes place through desk reviews of the annual returns or a telephone conversation. This, however, is only done for the category of low-risk members. Medium and high-risk member firms always receive on-site visits from reviewers of the Quality Assurance Department (QAD). In practice, the inspection numbers are substantial in relation to the total number of member firms and PC holders falling under the PAS.[94] Between 1-2% of the cases are forwarded to the Practice Assurance Committee for further consideration. As just mentioned, targeted AML inspections are fairly recent at ICAEW, which is an instrument to ensure that sufficient attention is given to AML compliance. For accountability reasons as well as the provision of guidance to its members, ICAEW should think about publishing the results of its targeted visits. ICAEW should also consider publishing its AML returns, which it submits to HM Treasury annually (see § 8.3.1.2). At AAT, AML supervision is the responsibility of the Conduct and Compliance Team (CCT). Also here, the basis of monitoring is a risk assessment, which includes aspects like the existence of complaints against the member, the size and maturity of the firm and the type of services provided by the firm. The assessments are based on the annual returns from members, intelligence from other AAT departments, the media, and other professional or public bodies. The carrying out of monitoring visits is outsourced to ICAEW.[95] Information demonstrates that AAT has had a fairly reasonable level of monitoring, which includes assessing AML compliance, in recent years. Nevertheless, for reasons considered in § 6.9.2.3, AAT should start carrying out targeted AML supervision like ICAEW, and publish the outcomes thereof. Finally, AAT should consider the publication of its AML returns, which it submits to HM Treasury annually.

The finding that the AML supervision of accountants is the weakest in Spain, may be the result of the choice for the FIU model. As explained, SEPBLAC does not have the resources to carry out AML supervision on the entire range of obliged institutions and professionals, even if it would apply a risk-based approach. As was the case for real estate agents, the Commission for the Prevention of Money Laundering and Monetary Offences is not allowed to enter into supervisory arrangements with regulators or professional associations active in the accountancy sector, meaning that no other authority can (partly) take over the supervision of accountants or exercise it on SEPBLAC's behalf.

94 § 6.8.2.3.
95 § 6.9.2.2.

8.7.2 Sanctioning

8.7.2.1 Sanctioning powers

- *This research found that most problems exist in Sweden regarding the adequacy of sanctioning powers.*

The Supervisory Board of Public Auditors has inadequate sanctioning powers. It essentially faces the same problem as was pointed out for the Swedish Estate Agents Inspectorate in § 8.6.2. In case of non-compliance with the preventive AML obligations, it can either impose the highly dissuasive sanction of the revocation of authorisation (or deregistration), or the comparatively mild sanctions of issuing a warning or reminder. In the absence of sanctioning powers that find themselves in between these sanctions, there is hardly any to no possibility for the Board to scale up its actions and sanctions proportionately. The disciplinary decisions are published in an anonymised fashion on the Board's website. More problematic, however, are the sanctioning powers of the county administrative boards that are responsible for the AML supervision of the wider accountancy profession. They only have one sanction available, the public law fine, which is also very limited in terms of its (possible) application. They cannot directly sanction non-compliant behaviour, as this is made subject to compliance with an order made by the boards. The lack of any power to enforce registration was already considered in § 8.4.2. The foregoing obviously does not comply with the requirement of effective supervision that AML supervisors must have adequate sanctioning powers.

The AML supervisors in Spain, the UK and the Netherlands have adequate sanctioning powers. As explained, SEPBLAC has no sanctioning powers itself. The AML Act provides other (political) organs with a wide range of adequate sanctioning powers.[96] The two professional associations in the UK involved in this research can both resort to a wide range of disciplinary powers in case of non-compliance with preventive AML obligations. At ICAEW, the Investigation Committee can offer a consent order that includes a (severe) reprimand or fine, or it can offer a caution. The Disciplinary Tribunal does not have these powers, but its powers vary from a reprimand to exclusion from membership for individual members, and from a reprimand to a fine for member firms. At AAT the Investigations Team (through a consent order) and the Disciplinary Tribunal have the same wide range of sanctions available, varying from reprimands to disciplinary fines or even to expulsion or removal. This research found that the wide range of sanctions vary from relatively mild sanctions to highly dissuasive sanctions of exclusion from membership allowing the Investigation Committee (ICAEW), the Investigations Team (AAT) or the disciplinary tribunals of the two professional associations to speak softly where possible and hard where necessary. The Dutch AML Act provides the BFT with adequate sanctioning powers vis-à-vis accountancy firms.[97] As mentioned, however, the AML Act should also provide for a discretionary power for AML supervisors to publish sanctioning decisions imposed under

96 Cf. § 8.5.2 and 8.6.2

97 See § 8.6.2 as these are the same powers that the Bureau Supervision Wwft has been given by the Dutch AML Act.

the AML Act. For sanctions against individual accountants, the BFT should resort to the use of disciplinary law (until the law is amended[98]). Disciplinary law sanctioning is the task of the Accountants' Chamber, which in principle has a wide range of sanctions available.[99] This research found that there may be some reservations concerning the dissuasiveness of the disciplinary law sanctions. This is especially due to the low maximum amount of a disciplinary fine compared to fines that can be imposed under the AML Act, and the fact that judgments, if published in the first place, are published in an anonymised fashion.[100]

8.7.2.2 Public supervision (sanctioning) policies

- *None of the AML supervisors of accountants has a specific AML supervision (sanctioning) policy. Only the two professional associations from the United Kingdom included in this research, ICAEW and AAT, have a public general sanctioning policy that applies to AML supervision as well.*

ICAEW has adopted a general Guidance on Sentencing, which the Investigation Committee and disciplinary tribunals ought to consider in determining sanctions. The AAT's public sanctioning policy is laid down in the Disciplinary Regulations and the Indicative Sanctions Guidance. The latter document demonstrates the specific considerations that the disciplinary tribunal should take into account for each specific sanction. The AML supervisors of accountants in Spain, the Netherlands and Sweden do not have a public supervision (sanctioning) policy at all. The Financial Supervision Office has no public supervision policy, which is particularly lamentable in relation to the way in which it deals with identified non-compliant behaviour under the supervisory arrangement. As explained in § 8.5.2.2, there is no public supervision (sanctioning) policy available in Spain. The Swedish county administrative boards do not have a public policy either. This is not surprising, as we have just considered that they cannot sanction non-compliance in the first place. This legal gap must first be remedied before the boards can actually develop a policy that can be followed in practice. Finally, the Supervisory Board of Public Auditors does not have a public supervision (sanctioning) policy either. The Dutch, Spanish and Swedish AML supervisors should become more transparent about their supervision policies. They can draw inspiration from the way in which their counterparts in the United Kingdom have done so.

8.7.2.3 Sanctioning in practice

- *In terms of the sanctioning practice, it appears that the Spanish and Swedish supervisors perform less well than the professional associations from the United Kingdom. Information concerning sanctions imposed by the BFT are insufficiently intelligible to be included in this synthesis.*

98 See § 3.4.2.
99 See about the Accountants' Chamber: § 5.8.3.2.
100 § 5.8.3.2.

This finding is not surprising. Based on the limited information available, it seems highly unlikely that accountants in Spain have been sanctioned for acting in breach of the AML legislation since its entry into force in 2010. As we could just read, accountants have not been subjected to AML inspections since that year and there is no information in the Official State Gazette or case law from the Supreme Court that demonstrates that sanctions have been imposed on accountants either. The Swedish county administrative boards have never sanctioned accountants for non-compliance with the preventive AML obligations. This is (most likely) the direct result of the lack of sanctioning powers for these authorities. A total of two public law fines imposed by a county administrative board on accountants were declared due by a court, but these were imposed for non-compliance with orders to implement rectifications after fit and proper checks and not directly for non-compliance.[101] The Supervisory Board of Public Auditors has, despite the high number of sanctions annually, only imposed one sanction for non-compliance with the Swedish AML legislation in five years' time. Moreover, this case did not result from the Board's own supervision, but from a complaint.

ICAEW and AAT have taken disciplinary action against accountants for not complying with AML obligations. For ICAEW, it seems that the majority of cases ended with informal measures, such as an agreed action plan. The limited information available, however, also showed that the Investigation Committee and the Disciplinary Tribunal are willing to take proportionate and dissuasive sanctions. Non-compliance has been sanctioned with relatively mild fines, but has also led to the withdrawal of membership. The sanctioning decisions have also been published with the names of the accountants concerned in ICAEW's member magazine and on its website, giving the sanctions an extra level of dissuasiveness.[102] The AAT's sanctioning bodies have taken more and more disciplinary action against its members for acting in breach of the AML legislation. At the same time AAT uses informal measures in order to keep its sanctioning activity proportionate as well. AAT sanctioning in practice complies with the requirement that AML supervisors must sanction in a proportionate and careful manner, and escalate their sanctions. The AAT, however, should address the publication of disciplinary decisions, especially because its own policy indicates that publication ought to be normal practice.[103]

Within this research it appeared impossible to give an outline of the sanctions imposed against accountancy firms by the Financial Supervision Office. For various reasons mentioned in § 5.8.4, however, it is presumed that the sanctioning activity against accountants was not high in the years 2010-12.[104] Regarding disciplinary law sanctions, this research demonstrated that the Dutch Institute of Chartered Accountants (NBA) has been far more active than the BFT in starting proceedings against accountants for not complying with preventive AML obligations. The NBA started seven disciplinary cases, whereas BFT initiated one case. The BFT should become more transparent about its

101 § 7.8.4.
102 § 6.8.4.3.
103 § 6.9.1.
104 § 5.8.4.

sanctioning practice and provide more intelligible information, which would allow it to be held accountable.

The finding that the two professional associations in the UK have done better in terms of sanctioning in practice than their counterparts in the Netherlands, Sweden and Spain seems to be the result of various factors. One of these is that in Spain accountants have not been supervised at all in recent years, which leads to no sanctioning activity against these professionals. In Sweden, a lack of sanctioning powers has prevented the county administrative boards from directly sanctioning non-compliance by accountants. And for the Netherlands, it was presumed that the sanctioning activity was not high, but a lack of transparency prevented an analysis on this point.

8.8 Supervisory cooperation for the prevention of money laundering

Do the AML supervisors cooperate with each other and allow AML supervision to become (more) effective? This research focusses on the existence of legal bases for the exchange of supervisory information between AML supervisors and, to an extent, with the FIU, in the AML legislation or other relevant legislation. Supervisory information is specific individual information about an institution that possibly acts in contravention of its AML obligations or is otherwise involved in a money laundering transaction. The exchange of supervisory information is a delicate issue since it may include different types of business information or personal data for which different confidentiality regimes exist. It is equally important that AML supervisors cooperate in practice. This research has paid attention to cooperation efforts on a policy level and on an operational level.[105] This section compares the findings with regard to forums and possibilities for cooperation.

Effective supervision requires that AML supervisors have adequate cooperation powers provided by law, and that they use these powers in practice.

8.8.1 Institutionalised forums for AML cooperation on a policy level

- *In all countries, except for Spain, one or more forums for cooperation between AML supervisors exist. The most institutionalised forum for cooperation between AML supervisors can be found in Sweden where AML legislation establishes and regulates this forum.*

The absence of forums for cooperation on a policy level in Spain can be explained by the supervisory model: SEPBLAC is the only AML supervisor and FIU at the same time. All staff fall under the same secrecy provisions in the AML Act, which means that FIU data can be used for supervision purposes as well.[106]

Cooperation on a policy level between the Swedish AML supervisors takes place within the AML coordination body. All AML supervisors, except for the Swedish Bar Association, are

105 § 2.4.3.4.
106 § 4.5.4.

obliged to participate in this body.[107] The Financial Supervisory Authority is responsible for the coordination body and meetings between representatives of the authorities take place regularly. The AML Regulation tasks the coordination body with the overall responsibility for the coordination of the supervisors in terms of methods and regulations, as well as for the evaluation and monitoring of the supervision performed. The AML coordination body should provide assistance to the supervisors in terms of education and is responsible for effective cooperation between the supervisors and the FIU concerning the reporting obligation for institutions as well as the registration obligation. The coordination body is furthermore tasked to cooperate with and provide support to the Government Office. Finally, it should initiate proposals for changes in legislation, procedures and priorities in order to create a more effective supervision. The coordination body is not used by the AML supervisors to exchange relevant supervisory information with each other. Other forums for cooperation, in which some of the AML supervisors participate, also exist in Sweden. Yet these focus more on the criminal investigation side and are not primarily in place to prevent money laundering.[108]

In the Netherlands, there are four cooperative efforts that are (in)directly related to the preventive AML policy: the AML coordination meeting, the Financial Expertise Centre, the National Task Force on Tackling the Misuse of Real Estate and the Committee on the duty to disclose unusual transactions. This research found that some (legal) improvements should be made in relation to these forums. The most important and direct forum is the AML coordination meeting, in which all four AML supervisors and the FIU participate. The forum is not established by law, and is thus of a voluntary nature. Meetings take place regularly. Within this forum, the AML supervisors and the FIU share information of general interest. They discuss legislative developments, trends and typologies. The FIU cannot share information with the AML supervisors concerning the content of individual disclosures or the subjects mentioned in these disclosures. Especially information on unusual transaction reports that have been declared suspicious by the Dutch FIU cannot be shared with the AML supervisors. Such information, however, would increase the effectiveness of AML supervision. Especially the Bureau Supervision Wwft would benefit from this information, since its information position is relatively weak and its supervision with respect to smaller businesses focusses on a transaction or client-file level. The AML supervisors are obliged to inform the FIU when they, in the course of their supervisory activities, discover facts that may be an indication of money laundering or terrorist financing. The second forum is the Financial Expertise Centre (FEC). This is a network comprising of various public authorities in which information on the integrity of the financial sector is exchanged. The forum is based on an agreement and the statutory confidentiality regimes of the individual FEC partners apply. It is not a forum which directly acts under the preventive AML policy, but (the prevention of) money laundering is an important matter for the FEC. The DNB participates in this network, but the Bureau Supervision Wwft and the BFT do not. The lack of a legal basis for the sharing of supervisory information under the AML Act used to be the main reason for this. Since January 2013, however, AML supervisors are allowed to share supervisory information

107 In practice, the Swedish Bar Association has always participated.
108 § 7.10.1.

with each other and with their foreign counterparts.[109] This legal basis is an improvement compared to the old situation, but it insufficiently acknowledges the role of professional associations in the BFT's anti-money laundering supervision. And although this provision provides a limited basis for cooperation for the Bureau Supervision Wwft and the BFT, participation in the FEC will be of little added value since they cannot share information with FEC partners other than the AML supervisors, with whom they already cooperate in the AML coordination meeting and with whom they can liaise on an individual basis. Depending on the legal framework of the other FEC partners, the Bureau Supervision Wwft and the BFT might be allowed to receive some information. Regarding the third forum for cooperation, the National Task Force on Tackling the Misuse of Real Estate, this research advised that the Bureau Supervision Wwft should join this task force alongside its parent organisation DTCA, although it should still respect the limitations attached to Section 22 Wwft. All Dutch AML supervisors participate in the Committee on the duty to disclose unusual transactions, but due to its focus and activities, this forum is less relevant for cooperation between AML supervisors as such.

Similar to the AML coordination meeting in the Netherlands, the United Kingdom has a forum for cooperation on a policy level in which all AML supervisors participate: the Anti-Money Laundering Supervisors' Forum (AMLSF). This forum has been set up by the supervisors themselves. Within the AMLSF the supervisors share their supervisory practices, discuss policy developments and review the effectiveness of supervision and the sanctions imposed. The AML supervisors meet more regularly within the three affinity groups: legal, public sector and accountancy.[110] An exchange of supervisory information does not take place within the AMLSF or the affinity groups. Representatives from the Treasury, the Home Office and the National Crime Agency (UKFIU) attend the plenary meetings as well. Two other forums for cooperation are the Money Laundering Advisory Committee (MLAC) and the SARs Review Committee. The latter is similar to the Dutch Committee on the duty to disclose unusual transactions. Some, but not all, AML supervisors participate in these forums.

8.8.2 Cooperation efforts by AML supervisors on an operational level

- *In the Netherlands and the United Kingdom the anti-money laundering legislation contains a legal basis for the exchange of supervisory information between supervisors. This is not the case in Spain and Sweden. Especially in Sweden the lack of a legal basis may affect cooperation between the AML supervisors on an operational level. Information on the exchange of information between anti-money laundering supervisors in practice is absent in all countries.*

As just explained, the Dutch AML Act provides, since January 2013, a legal basis for the exchange of supervisory information between the AML supervisors, as well as with foreign counterparts. This legal basis, it was considered, should be improved in order to adequately acknowledge the role of professional associations in the BFT's

109 Section 22 Wwft.
110 § 6.10.1.

AML supervision. Unfortunately, data concerning the application of the exchange of information between the AML supervisors is not available. It is thus impossible to verify whether and to what extent the AML supervisors cooperate with each other on an operational level in practice. Nevertheless, there are some operational liaisons for the AML supervisors involved in this research. Especially the project 'Non-reporters' (*'Niet-melders'*), within which the Bureau Supervision Wwft and the BFT participate, gives some indications about supervisory cooperation in practice. Cooperation with the FIU was already discussed in the previous section. In the United Kingdom, the 2012 amendments to the Money Laundering Regulations 2007 created an explicit legal basis for the exchange of supervisory information between the AML supervisors. The exchange is subject to a number of limitations, but not as to the type of information that can be exchanged. Unfortunately, data concerning the application of the exchange of information between the AML supervisors is not available either. Cooperation with the FIU is not covered by this legal basis. The cooperation between the UKFIU and the AML supervisors on an operational level is more or less similar to that in the Netherlands. The AML supervisors are obliged to inform the National Crime Agency (UKFIU) when, in the course of carrying out supervisory functions under the AML legislation, they know or suspect that a person is or has engaged in money laundering or terrorist financing.[111] We just saw that on a policy level the FIU attends the plenary meetings of the AMLSF. Information from the FIU to the supervisors is abstract, due to the confidentiality regime under which it operates. This does not allow UKFIU to disclose information on individual SARs to the relevant AML supervisors.

The Swedish AML Act does not provide a legal basis for the exchange of supervisory information between the AML supervisors. Sectoral legislation from which the Financial Supervisory Authority, the Estate Agents Inspectorate and the Supervisory Board of Public Auditors derive their powers for their anti-money laundering supervision do not contain powers for the exchange of supervisory information with other AML supervisors either. Based on the general legal framework for the exchange of information by public authorities, this research concluded that only little room exists for AML supervisors to exchange supervisory information, as most of the information in relation to the exercise of their supervision is deemed confidential. Moreover, it seems that they cannot exchange information on their own motion, but only provide non-confidential information upon request. There are no agreements on which the AML supervisors could base their operational cooperation either.[112] As in the Netherlands and the UK, the AML supervisors are obliged to inform, without delay, the Swedish FIU when they discover, during the exercise of supervising a natural or legal person, or otherwise, a circumstance which is likely to be associated with or constitutes money laundering or terrorist financing. The Swedish FIU, in turn, can only reach out to the AML supervisors on a more abstract level through its involvement in the AML coordination body.

The Spanish AML Act or the Royal Decree at the level below the Act do not contain provisions on the exchange of supervisory information. This is obviously less pressing

111 Regulation 24A MLR 2007.
112 § 7.10.2.

than is the case in Sweden, because of the application of the FIU model. The Commission for the Prevention of Money Laundering and Monetary Offences is empowered to enter into supervisory arrangements with three financial regulators, in which the aspect of cooperation could be regulated. Given that these arrangements are privileged, it is impossible to verify to what extent the exchange of supervisory information between SEPBLAC and the financial regulators, in particular the Bank of Spain, is allowed and takes place in practice.

8.9 Concluding remarks

This synthesis has presented the comparative findings of AML supervision in Spain, the Netherlands, the United Kingdom and Sweden. All aspects of the theoretical framework of effective supervision were included and discussed on a systematic basis. These findings will now be considered in the concluding chapter of this research in which an answer to the research question is given.

9 Conclusion

9.1 Introduction

This chapter is the concluding piece of this research. It summarises and brings together the most important findings. By doing so, it gives an answer to the central question of this research that was formulated in the first chapter:

In which of the Member States of the European Union is supervision within the preventive anti-money laundering policy the most effective, and what can other Member States do to reach the same level of effectiveness?

In order to come to an answer to this question, attention will first be paid to the question of when supervision is considered effective (§ 9.2). This is followed by an outline of how EU Member States are different in designing their supervisory regimes under the preventive anti-money laundering policy (§ 9.3). Subsequently, section 9.4 contains a summary overview of the AML supervision of banks, real estate agents and accountants in Spain, the Netherlands, the United Kingdom and Sweden. Section 9.5 contains an answer to the research question and formulates a number of recommendations that follow from this answer. The conclusion and findings are put into perspective in section 9.6. What does this research teach us about the theoretical framework of effective supervision, and the underlying principle of effectiveness? And what does the conclusion mean for the supervisory models identified within the preventive anti-money laundering policy in the European Union? Does it allow one to say something about the effectiveness of the models as such, are the models useful and should we keep these differences within the European Union or strive for more harmonisation? Finally, this chapter ends with an epilogue that provides a short reflection on this research (§ 9.7).

9.2 Effective supervision

In order to analyse the effectiveness of anti-money laundering supervision, it is of fundamental importance to have clear in our minds what makes supervision effective. The first supportive question of this research – when is supervision effective, principally viewed from a legal perspective? – has served as a means for the development of the theoretical framework of this research. Based on the principle of effectiveness as a good governance and EU principle, the minimum requirements stemming from the Third Directive, as well as a common core of requirements identified in relevant literature, Chapter 2 discussed what effective supervision requires. The requirements can be divided into three categories: legislative requirements, institutional requirements and requirements concerning the competences of anti-money laundering supervisors and their application in practice. These requirements were extensively discussed in the synthesis (Chapter 8) as well, and will hereafter be presented in a summary fashion.

The first category requires that legislation is clear, precise, foreseeable, predictable and, hence, enforceable. The absence of a clear legal basis or a lack of clarity in substantive legislation affects the enforceability of the norms. The enforceability is important, because if norms are not enforceable, supervision can never be effective in the first place. The second category (institutional requirements) places conditions on the anti-money laundering supervisors in terms of independence from politics and the market, accountability and transparency, the availability of adequate resources and the knowledge of the institutions and professionals for which the supervisors have supervisory responsibility. The institutional position of AML supervisors can affect their information position, and thus, the effectiveness of their supervision. The third category of requirements includes that anti-money laundering supervisors have adequate supervisory, sanctioning and cooperation powers. Effective supervision requires that AML supervisors must apply these powers in practice, and do so in a proportionate and careful manner. Regarding the activity of sanctioning, AML supervisors must speak softly where possible and hard where necessary. Ultimately, however, the sanctions must be capable of providing a deterrent effect. Finally, AML supervisors must have in place public supervision (sanctioning) policies that include an explanation of the legal framework, the supervisory goals, the desired level of compliance, the principles followed by the supervisor for its activities, as well as a general description of the procedures. Public policies foster transparency and accountability. By displaying how they apply their powers in practice, AML supervisors can improve their credibility, and even their legitimacy.

9.3 Institutional differences in AML supervision in the European Union

The second supportive question concerned the design of anti-money laundering supervision in the European Union. Understanding that the Third Directive left this design mostly to the Member States, their choices have been influenced by factors such as national politics, culture, the legal system, the economy and finances. As a result of these influences, a patchwork of AML supervisory architectures exists within the European Union. Based on two criteria, four models of AML supervision could be identified within the EU. The first criterion concerned the number of authorities involved in anti-money laundering supervision combined with final responsibility for this supervision, and the second criterion concerns the nature of these authorities (internal vs external).[1] Chapter 3 provided the following figure of the application of these four models within the EU. It gives a comprehensive overview of the institutional differences in AML supervision.

1 § 3.2.2.

Figure 5 – AML Supervisory Architectures in the European Union

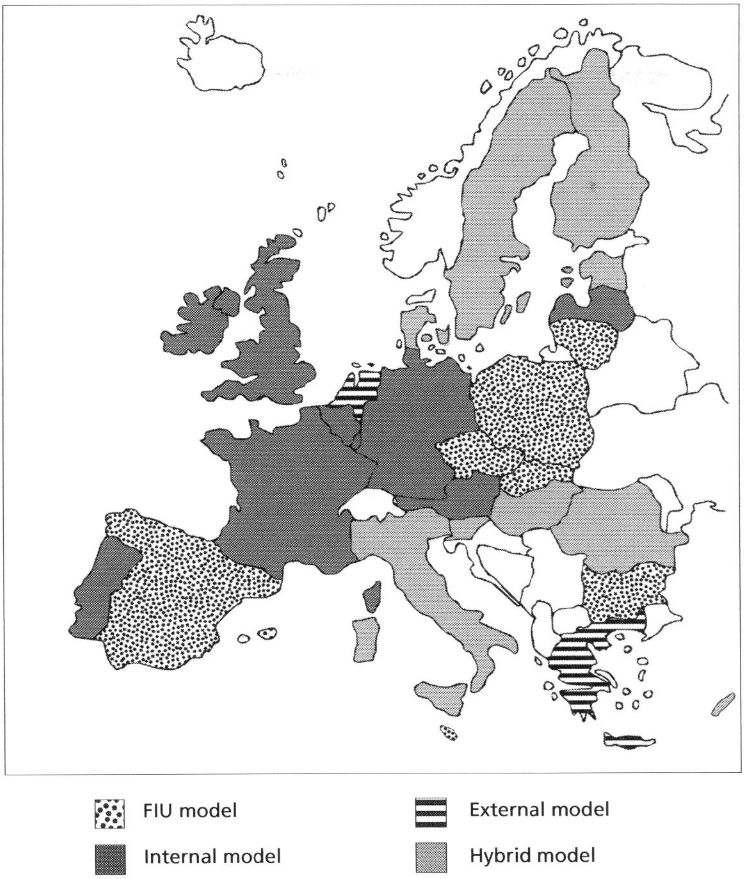

The first model identified is the FIU model. This model's main characteristic is that the financial intelligence unit (FIU) is the national authority with final responsibility for AML supervision. FIUs are (part of) the national authorities that are primarily responsible for receiving, analysing and disseminating financial intelligence submitted through suspicion reports by obliged institutions or professionals. Spain is considered to be one of the purest examples of the model and has therefore been included in this research. Under the second model, the external model, AML supervision is formally exercised by public administrative or Government authorities that have no direct or professional relationship with the supervisees. Final responsibility for this supervision is shared between these authorities. In practice, an informal role can be played by professional associations in the supervision and sanctioning of legal and fiscal service providers. As the figure above shows, the external model only applies in Greece and the Netherlands. For reasons of practicality, linguistics and a knowledge of the legal system, the Dutch system has been further studied in this research.

The internal model is the most widespread model in the European Union. Here, anti-money laundering supervision is mainly carried out by professional associations, with the exception of the supervision of financial and credit institutions and casinos. The guiding principle of this model is that where AML supervision can be performed by internal supervisors, these will be assigned this task. All supervisors involved share final responsibility. The United Kingdom, having 22 professional (and trade) associations carrying out AML supervision out of a total of 28 supervisors, demonstrates how the internal model can be implemented at the national level and is included in this research. The last model identified is the hybrid model. This model combines, in different gradations, elements of the other three models. So far, mixtures between internal and external supervisors, and between internal and external supervisors and the FIU have been identified. Here, too, final responsibility is shared between all the AML supervisors involved. In Sweden, with a mixture of one internal and external supervisors, a great deal of attention was paid to the matter of supervision during the implementation of the Third Directive and was, therefore, considered as the most interesting country for this research.

9.4 Anti-money laundering supervision in the Member States

What does supervision look like at the national level? This was the last supportive question formulated in the first chapter. *Part II* of this research discussed the implementation of the models at the national level and described with a great level of detail how the AML supervision of banks, accountants and real estate agents is legally embedded and exercised in practice in Spain, the Netherlands, the United Kingdom and Sweden. It was demonstrated that the Member States are very different from each other in terms of the types and numbers of formal supervisors and professional associations involved in the AML supervision. It appeared, moreover, that they face different legal and practical difficulties. The synthesis compared the national systems based on the requirements stemming from the theoretical framework of effective supervision. That is why this section only briefly addresses the institutional settings of AML supervision in the four Member States.

Chapter 4 explained that anti-money laundering supervision in Spain is carried out by SEPBLAC (*Servicio Ejecutivo de la Comisión de Prevención del Blanqueo de Capitales e Infracciones Monetarias*). SEPBLAC is Spain's financial intelligence unit and has supervisory responsibility for the entire range of institutions and professionals that fall under the Spanish legislation. It acts under the authority of the Commission for the Prevention of Money Laundering and Monetary Offences (*Comisión de Prevención del Blanqueo de Capitales e Infracciones Monetarias*). This Commission is competent to enter into arrangements with the three Spanish financial regulators with the aim of coordinating and harmonising their AML inspections and supervisory activities with those carried out by SEPBLAC. The general idea is that the regulators integrate AML supervision into their general supervision programmes and send their supervision reports to the Commission Secretariat, which is another support body of the Commission. If breaches of the preventive obligations are identified, the Commission Secretariat can decide to start a sanctioning procedure. SEPBLAC, however, remains ultimately responsible for the exercise of anti-money laundering supervision. The supervisory arrangement between the Commission and the Bank of Spain (*Banco de España*) is particularly relevant for the AML supervision of banks.

Overall, anti-money laundering supervision in the Netherlands, as discussed in Chapter 5, is exercised by four authorities: the Dutch Central Bank (*De Nederlandsche Bank, DNB*), the Netherlands Authority for the Financial Markets (*Autoriteit Financiële Markten, AFM*), the Financial Supervision Office (*Bureau Financieel Toezicht, BFT*) and the Dutch Tax and Customs Administration/Bureau Supervision Wwft (*Belastingdienst/Bureau Toezicht Wwft, 'the Bureau'*). Banks and real estate agents are supervised by the DNB and the Dutch Tax and Customs Administration/Bureau Supervision Wwft respectively. The Financial Supervision Office has supervisory responsibility for a wide range of legal and fiscal service providers, including accountants. Through the conclusion of supervisory arrangements, professional associations are indirectly involved in the exercise of anti-money laundering supervision of professionals for which BFT has formal supervisory responsibility.

Chapter 6 dealt with anti-money laundering supervision in the United Kingdom. The UK has by far the highest number of supervisors in the EU. As explained, no less than 22 professional (and trade) associations have supervisory competence, besides the six public bodies designed as AML supervisors. These are the Financial Conduct Authority (FCA), the Office of Fair Trading (OFT), the Gambling Commission, Her Majesty's Revenue and Customs (HMRC), the Department of Enterprise, Trade and Investment in Northern Ireland and the Secretary of State – in practice the Insolvency Service. The FCA has AML supervisory responsibility for banks and a range of other financial institutions. Estate agents were until the 1st of April 2014 supervised by the OFT. On that date the OFT was abolished and AML supervisory responsibility for estate agents was transferred to HMRC. Within this research it was impossible to include this transfer, but where relevant reference is made to it. Accountants are supervised by their professional associations. Two of the eleven professional associations in the accountancy sector are studied in this research: the Institute of Chartered Accountants in England and Wales (ICAEW) and the Association of Accounting Technicians (AAT).

Finally, Chapter 7 discussed the AML supervisory architecture of Sweden. Overall, supervision is exercised by the Swedish Financial Supervisory Authority (*Finansinspektionen, FI*), the Gaming Board, the Swedish Bar Association, the Supervisory Board of Public Auditors (*Revisorsnämnden, RN*), the Estate Agents Inspectorate (*Fastighetsmäklarinspektionen, FMI*) and the country administrative boards of Stockholm, Västra Götaland, and Skåne. The anti-money laundering supervision of banks is exercised by the Financial Supervisory Authority, while real estate agents are supervised by the Estate Agents Inspectorate. The Supervisory Board of Public Auditors has supervisory responsibility for auditors and audit firms, and the county administrative boards for accountants, not being auditors or audit firms.

9.5 The most effective anti-money laundering supervision

9.5.1 Answer to the research question

From the synthesis it has become clear that, viewed from the perspective of effective supervision, no AML supervisory architecture is perfect. The four EU Member States included in this research each have their own strengths and weaknesses. At times these could be related to the choice for a particular supervisory model, while at other times these strengths or weaknesses reflected national realities. Notwithstanding this, it can be concluded that the most effective AML supervision can be found in the United Kingdom. No serious issues in relation to the institutional requirements could be identified for this country. Except for one professional association, the AML supervisors appeared to have adequate levels of political and market independence. The legislator, however, should continue to be aware of the fact that in the UK the strongest relationship between AML supervisors and the market exists. This research also did not identify resource issues for any of the anti-money laundering supervisors included in this research, and the AML supervisors' knowledge of their supervisees outside the regulated sectors and professions is covered by an extensive registration obligation laid down in the Money Laundering Regulations 2007. The synthesis also demonstrated that the AML supervisors from the UK are in practice most transparent about and accountable for the exercise of their supervision. In the synthesis it could also be observed that, unlike for the other three Member States, no gaps and conflicts in the substantive AML legislation were identified in the United Kingdom. The legislation could benefit from some clarifications, as argued in § 8.2.2, but compared to the other Member States, the legal framework appeared to be rather clear and complete.

Zooming in more deeply on the specifics of the anti-money laundering supervision of banks, real estate agents and accountants, the synthesis demonstrated the effectiveness of the UK system. It proved that the AML supervision of banks is most effectively carried out by the Financial Conduct Authority. The FCA has adequate supervisory and sanctioning powers provided by law and, comparatively, it is the most active AML supervisor of banks in practice as well. It has the highest inspection activity and its sanctioning activity, which is laid down in a general public sanctioning policy, can be regarded as both dissuasive and proportionate. Its sanctioning activity demonstrated an increasing use of informal measures, like early interventions, but at the same time it contained fines of up to more than 10 million Euros on banks for breaching the Money Laundering Regulations 2007.[2] The anti-money laundering supervision of estate agents in the UK was found to be effective as well. The Office of Fair Trading is especially doing well in relation to the requirements of the public supervision policy and sanctioning in practice. Concerns were nevertheless raised here on the comparatively low inspection activity in light of the total number of estate agents in the UK. Finally, the synthesis demonstrated that the AML supervision of accountants is most effective in the United Kingdom. The two professional associations included in this research, ICAEW and AAT, are the only AML supervisors of accountants included in this research that were found to have adequate supervisory powers and a

2 See § 8.5.2.3.

well-established practice of anti-money laundering supervision. The two professional associations are, moreover, the only AML supervisors of accountants included in this research with a public supervision (sanctioning) policy, although these general policies go beyond sanctioning for breaches of the preventive anti-money laundering obligations alone. Finally, they were also considered the most active AML supervisors of accountants in terms of sanctioning. Their practices showed that both authorities have regularly resorted to the use of informal measures, but have been willing to take proportionate and dissuasive sanctions when necessary.

Not only can it be concluded that anti-money laundering supervision is most effective in the United Kingdom, it also appears that it is least effective in Spain. This is caused by a combination of factors, but is most prominently the result of the choice for appointing the financial intelligence unit as the only formal AML supervisor, and the way in which SEPBLAC's institutional position is regulated. The synthesis found that SEPBLAC has an inadequate level of political independence. Because it is the only AML supervisor in Spain, the lack of an adequate level of independence affects the entire supervisory architecture.[3] SEPBLAC also suffers from serious resource issues, which have led to *de facto* no supervision. In the years 2010-2012 only 0.1% of the entire supervisory population were supervised. Banks have presumably been inspected, but real estate agents and accountants were not supervised at all. Here, too, the fact that it is the only authority responsible for AML supervision means that the lack of adequate resources affects the entire supervisory architecture in Spain. This conclusion could have been different for banks, because the Commission for the Prevention of Money Laundering and Monetary Offences has entered into a supervisory arrangement with the Bank of Spain. However, this research found that the Bank of Spain has not, or to a very limited extent, as public information on this matter diverges, carried out AML inspections of banks.

The foregoing naturally leads to the formulation of a number of recommendations that aim to strengthen anti-money laundering supervision. This essentially answers the second part of the research question, which is what other Member States can do to reach the same level of effectiveness.

9.5.2 Recommendations

This section contains the most important general recommendations that follow from the answer to the research question. These recommendations are not only directed to the national legislators, but also to the European legislator, and are presented on a step-by-step basis. After each set of recommendations, the recommendations are further expounded to place them in the right context. Recommendations that are specific for the banking sector or real estate or accountancy professions, as well as recommendations for the individual AML supervisors, can be found in the concluding remarks of the respective country chapters and in the synthesis and are not further discussed here.

3 See § 8.3.1.1

EU legislator

1. Consider the incorporation of an obligation for Member States in future directives that concerns the creation of a registration obligation for institutions and professionals that are not regulated or supervised under other pieces of national legislation;
2. Require Member States to ensure that all AML supervisors, whether external or internal in nature, have an adequate level of political and market independence and set some minimum requirements in this respect;
3. Require Member States to regulate the accountability of AML supervisors towards the Government, Parliament and the general public, whereby supervisors should practise a certain level of transparency;
4. Require Member States to provide all AML supervisors with the power to perform on-site inspections;
5. Consider the incorporation in future directives of an obligation for Member States to regulate national cooperation between AML supervisors, in particular the power to exchange supervisory information.

The *first recommendation* is prompted by the discovery that it can be difficult for AML supervisors with responsibility for non-regulated professions, like the accountancy or real estate professions, to identify the professionals for whom they have this responsibility. Three of the four Member States already have mechanisms in their AML legislation, enabling these AML supervisors to find out who they should supervise, and allowing them to obtain some basic information that can be used as a starting point for their supervision. Considering the presence of these mechanisms at the national level, it is advisable that the European legislator includes an obligation for all Member States to make sure that so-called default AML supervisors have an adequate knowledge of their supervisees. This can be considered a form of 'bottom-up' harmonisation. This research also demonstrated that considerable institutional problems exist, which prevent an effective exercise of anti-money laundering supervision. Therefore, the *second and third recommendation* aim at providing a minimum level of requirements in relation to the political and market independence of AML supervisors, as well as accountability mechanisms to counterbalance this independence. The EU legislator can think about drafting norms that determine that national Ministers may not have powers in relation to individual decisions from AML supervisors. It can also consider regulating the influence of members in the governance structures of professional associations when they exercise anti-money laundering supervision, for example by fixing a maximum threshold for the involvement of members in committees that are responsible for investigation and disciplinary matters. In relation to accountability, the EU legislator could think about requiring Member States to ensure that AML supervisors draft and publish annual reports, and that they publish their supervision (sanctioning) policies. Understanding that such interference from the EU legislator limits the national procedural autonomy of Member States, it will nevertheless prevent, to a certain extent, that supervision is not or less effective because of institutional problems at the national level. The *fourth recommendation* concerns the power for AML supervisors to perform on-site inspections. Requiring on-site inspections for all AML supervisors does more justice to the wide scope of the preventive AML policy. The current formulation in the directive suggests that on-site inspections are only important for supervisors for the financial markets and casinos. Yet without on-site inspection powers, supervision becomes superficial, notwithstanding the sector to be supervised. Finally, this research demonstrated that not all Member States have legal gateways in place that allow for the exchange of supervisory information between AML supervision. Effective supervision requires good co-operation between AML supervisors on an operational level as well. It is therefore important that the European Union legislates in this area (*recommendation five*).

Considering that the proposal for the Fourth Directive already contains provisions on administrative sanctions with the aim of ensuring a minimum level of harmonisation, no recommendations are here made in relation to sanctions.

Spain

1. Remove SEPBLAC as an AML supervisor, or allow it to be the default supervisor, and appoint one or more independent authorities as AML supervisors. Alternatively, provide SEPBLAC with more political independence and increase the number of staff available for the exercise of supervision;
2. Create a legal obligation in the AML Act for SEPBLAC (and possibly for other AML supervisors) to draft annual reports, to forward these to the Commission for the Prevention of Money Laundering and Monetary Offences, the Government and Parliament, and to publish these reports;
3. Provide SEPBLAC, instead of the Commission for the Prevention of Money Laundering and Monetary Offences, with the power to enter into arrangements on the exercise of AML supervision and allow arrangements with regulators and professional associations that are active outside the financial sector as well. Ensure that all supervisory arrangements are made public and can be consulted;
4. Enact, as soon as possible, the Royal Decree and ensure that all substantive and procedural aspects are fully regulated by the Spanish AM Act and Royal Decree[4];
5. Improve the system of external expert reviews by regulating which requirements external experts should meet, and that they should always disclose their reports within a given timeframe to SEPBLAC without the necessity for the latter to request these reports.

Because of the serious issues that the implementation of the FIU model has caused at the national level, it is advisable that the Spanish legislator reconsiders its supervisory architecture. It can decide to entirely remove SEPBLAC as an AML supervisor and appoint one or more sectoral supervisors as AML supervisors, or designate SEPBLAC as the default supervisor for unregulated sectors and professions. If the Spanish legislator wants to retain SEPBLAC as the only formal AML supervisor, then it should allocate more political independence to SEPBLAC and increase its resources for an effective exercise of anti-money laundering supervision. More political independence can especially be achieved

4 Please note that this recommendation has already been complied with: see § 1.8.

by removing the powers of the Commission for the Prevention of Money Laundering and Monetary Offences ('the Commission') to formally approve SEPBLAC's operational guidelines and annual supervision plans (*first recommendation)*. In order to exercise an adequate level of transparency and to account for the exercise of anti-money laundering supervision, *recommendation two* advises to legally oblige SEPBLAC, and other AML supervisors should the supervisory architecture be revised, to draft and publish annual reports. The *third recommendation* advises that the power to enter into arrangements concerning the exercise of AML supervision should be directly provided to SEPBLAC, as more self-standing powers also enhance SEPBLAC's independence from the Commission. Moreover, SEPBLAC should not only be allowed to enter into arrangements with financial regulators, but also with other sectoral supervisors or professional associations. This is a possible way of reducing the resource tensions that SEPBLAC has encountered in recent years. For the accountancy sector a supervisory arrangement could possibly be concluded with the Accounting and Auditing Institute (*Instituto de Contabilidad de Auditoría de Cuentas, ICAC*) as this Institute already has regulatory and supervisory powers in relation to auditors. In order to ensure an adequate level of transparency and to increase the predictability and foreseeability of the exercise of AML supervision for the supervisory population and the general public, the legislator should ensure that those kinds of arrangements are made public. This research demonstrated that the absence of the Royal Decree caused gaps in the substantive AML legislation as well as serious issues of legal certainty, and for this reason it is recommended to enact, as soon as possible, the Royal Decree under the AML Act (*recommendation four*). Finally, we could observe that anti-money laundering supervision by SEPBLAC can become more effective if the external review system is strengthened. To that effect, *recommendation five* advises the Spanish legislator to set requirements for the person and education of external experts, as well as to oblige external experts to forward their external review reports to SEPBLAC within a timeframe determined by the legislator or SEPBLAC.

The Netherlands

1. Remove the Bureau Supervision Wwft from its parent organisation or assign another authority with more political independence as the AML supervisor. Alternatively, create a more independent position for the Bureau within the Dutch Tax and Customs Administration in a law or regulation. If the Bureau remains as the supervisor, it should be legally obliged to draft annual reports, to forward these to the Government and Parliament, and to publish these reports;
2. Consider the introduction of a registration obligation for those sectors and professions that are not regulated or supervised under other pieces of legislation in order to strengthen the Bureau Supervision Wwft's information position;
3. Create a legal basis for the AML supervisors (or the Financial Supervision Office specifically) to enter into arrangements with professional associations on the exercise of AML supervision complementary to or on behalf of the AML supervisors (or the Financial Supervision Office specifically) and ensure proper cooperation between professional associations and AML supervisors by amending Section 22 AML Act and by providing a legal basis for the provision of supervisory information in relation to the prevention of money laundering from the Dutch Institute of Chartered Accountants to the Financial Supervision Office;
4. Introduce a self-standing obligation in the AML Act for institutions and obligations to develop and maintain internal policies and procedures and to keep these in writing;
5. Consider the creation of a legal basis for the provision of information on (the content of) individual disclosures from FIU-NL to the AML supervisors.

The *first recommendation* concerns the choice of the Dutch legislator for the Dutch Tax and Customs Administration/Bureau Supervision Wwft as an AML supervisor. This research demonstrated that the Bureau has an inadequate level of political independence. Therefore, it is advised to remove the Bureau Supervision Wwft from the organisation of the Dutch Tax and Customs Administration, or to assign another authority with more political independence as the AML supervisor. Alternatively, if the legislator wants to retain the Dutch Tax and Customs Administration/Bureau Supervision Wwft as the AML supervisor, then it should create a more independent position for the Bureau within the organisation of the Tax and Customs Administration and a legal obligation in the AML Act for the Bureau to account for the exercise of its AML supervision. Unlike for the DNB and BFT, no such legal obligation currently exists for the Bureau or the Dutch Tax and Customs Administration. The legislator can draw inspiration from Section 18 Autonomous Administrative Authorities Framework Act. This research furthermore demonstrated that the Netherlands is the only country included in this research without some kind of registration system that allows the AML supervisor for the unregulated sectors and professions to gather basic knowledge on this group. Therefore, *recommendation two* advises the Dutch legislator to consider the introduction of a registration obligation for those sectors and professions that are not regulated or supervised under other pieces of legislation in order to strengthen the Bureau Supervision Wwft's information position.

It could look at the registration systems in the United Kingdom and Sweden. Regarding the involvement of professional associations in AML supervision, this research indicated that the BFT enters into supervisory arrangements with professional associations. For the accountancy sector, the arrangement with the SRA was found to be of importance. From the perspective of effective supervision, it is advisable to embed this possibility in the AML Act. In order to ensure good cooperation between professional associations and the AML supervisors or BFT specifically, the Dutch legislator should amend Section 22 of the AML Act that regulates the exchange of supervisory information between AML supervisors. This research concluded that this provision insufficiently recognises the role of professional associations in the AML supervision of accountants. Because an important, indirect role in the AML supervision of accountants is played by the Dutch Institute of Chartered Accountants (NBA), the Institute should be allowed to forward supervisory information to the BFT. A legal basis could be created in the Accountancy Profession Act or the AML Act. This research considered that it is important that both the NBA and BFT are convinced of the need for cooperation on this point. Another aspect that requires action from the Dutch legislator is the absence of an explicit norm in the AML Act on the obligation to develop internal AML policies and procedures. This research concluded that this negatively affects enforceability and, hence, supervision by the Bureau Supervision Wwft and the BFT since they fully derive their supervisory competence and powers from the AML Act. Therefore, *recommendation four* advises the introduction of this self-standing obligation in the Act. The *fifth recommendation* is prompted by the impossibility for FIU-NL to provide information on suspicions of money laundering disclosed by obliged institutions and professionals to the AML supervisors. For supervisors, however, such information may be useful. It, for example, allows them to compare records and files obtained from the obliged institutions themselves with the disclosures as received from the FIU.

The United Kingdom

1. Ensure that when professional associations act as AML supervisors, they have an adequate level of market independence. Members should not have a majority role in the governance structures of professional associations, especially not in the committees involved in the investigation and disciplinary procedures;
2. Consider a legal embedding of the voluntary accountability mechanism in the Money Laundering Regulations;
3. Stipulate in the Money Laundering Regulations that arrangements made between the Office of Fair Trading and the Local Authority Trading Standards Services should be made in writing and be publicly available. (After the 1st of April 2014 this applies to arrangements made between HM Revenue and Customs and the National Trading Standards Estate Agents Team.);
4. Create a legal basis in the Money Laundering Regulations for the exchange of supervisory information between HM Revenue and Customs and the National Trading Standards Estate Agents Team;
5. Consider the creation of a legal basis for the provision of information on (the content of) individual disclosures from UKFIU to the AML supervisors.

The *first recommendation* is prompted by the discovery of an inadequate level of market independence for the Institute of Chartered Accountants in England and Wales. In order to avoid (the appearance of) a lack of independence from the market, all professional associations acting as AML supervisors should restrict the influence of their members within their organisation, especially at the investigation and disciplinary stages. Inspiration can be drawn from the AAT, which proved that professional associations can have an adequate level of market independence. The UK legislator should ensure that this is the case for all internal AML supervisors. A second aspect concerned the voluntary accountability mechanism. Although it was identified as the most important accountability mechanism for AML supervision, it appeared that at present not all supervisors account for the exercise of their supervision to the general public, nor are they equally transparent. Therefore, the *second recommendation* concerns the embedding of this mechanism in the Regulations. This makes it possible that minimum powers are given to HM Treasury to ensure that all AML supervisors are in practice accountable and transparent about their supervision. At the same time a legal embedding allows the Treasury to publish aggregated annual AML supervision reports that contain more intelligible information than is presently the case, and that are meaningful for the general public as well.

The *third recommendation* aims at increasing transparency on the arrangements concluded under the Regulations. While the OFT entered into arrangements with the LATSS, this power has now been transferred to HMRC. The publication of the arrangements increases the predictability and foreseeability of the exercise of AML supervision for the supervisory population and the general public, as they (better) know what can be expected from these arrangements. It also creates more awareness and understanding of the role of LATSS (and NTSEAT) in the anti-money laundering supervision of estate agents. *The fourth recommendation* follows from the previous recommendation. At present the Regulations only provide for a legal basis for the exchange of supervisory information between AML supervisors. The powers in relation to the Estate Agents Act 1979 and the Money Laundering Regulations used to be concentrated at the Office of Fair Trading, but this is no longer the case. In order to allow for effective cooperation between HMRC and NTSEAT in light of their respective tasks under the Estate Agents Act 1979 and the Money Laundering Regulations 2007, they need to be allowed to exchange information with each other. *Recommendation five* concerns the provision of information from UKFIU to the AML supervisors. As explained, information on disclosed suspicions of money laundering from obliged institutions and professionals may be useful for AML supervisors.

Sweden

1. Require in annual appropriation letters or instruction regulations that the supervisors report more structurally about the exercise of their anti-money laundering supervision;
2. Do not allow the supervisory responsibility of the county administrative boards to depend on the question whether the institutions or professionals have registered at the Swedish Companies Registration Office and, more importantly, provide the county administrative boards with adequate powers to enforce the registration obligation for institutions and professionals that ought to register;
3. Provide adequate powers to the AML supervisors: provide the Estate Agents Inspectorate with the power to perform on-site inspections; make it explicit that the Supervisory Board of Public Auditors and the county administrative boards have on-site inspection powers; and provide adequate sanctioning powers to the Estate Agents Inspectorate, the county administrative boards, the Supervisory Board of Public Auditors and the Swedish Financial Supervisory Authority;
4. Create a legal basis in the AML Act that allows supervisors to exchange supervisory information with each other;
5. Consider the creation of a legal basis for the provision of information on (the content of) individual disclosures from the Swedish FIU to the AML supervisors.

This research did not identify any issues with the levels of political and market independence of the AML supervisors in Sweden. However, there are no structural accountability mechanisms that require AML supervisors to account for the exercise of their supervision. Therefore, the *first recommendation* advises the Swedish Government to require AML supervisors in annual appropriation letters or instruction regulations to report structurally about the exercise of this supervision. The *second recommendation* concerns the registration obligation under the Swedish legislation. What caused concern is the fact that the county administrative boards' AML supervisory responsibility depends on whether institutions and professionals have actually registered with the Swedish Companies Registration Office, combined with a lack of adequate powers to enforce registration. This research demonstrated that this is a serious problem, also in relation to accountants, and for this reason it is advised not to allow the responsibility of the county administrative boards to depend on registration, and to provide adequate powers to enforce registration. This can be realised, for example, by providing the county administrative boards with the power to impose an administrative fine (*straffavgift*) directly on the institution or professional that has not registered. It furthermore appeared that Swedish legislation does not always provide adequate supervisory or sanctioning powers to the AML supervisors. Therefore, *recommendation three* advises the Swedish legislator to strengthen the powers of AML supervisors, sometimes by creating new powers and at other times by making powers more explicit. Whereas the supervisors cooperate with each other in the AML coordination body on a policy level, the AML Act does not provide them with powers to exchange supervisory information. This is why *recommendation four* advises the creation of such a legal basis. The legislator could draw inspiration from the legal gateways that were created in the United Kingdom and the Netherlands. Finally, the *fifth recommendation* concerns the provision of information from the Swedish FIU to the AML supervisors. Information on disclosed suspicions of money laundering from obliged institutions and professionals may be useful for AML supervisors.

9.6 Conclusions in perspective

9.6.1 Effective supervision and the principle of effectiveness

The principle of effectiveness has been used as a stepping-stone for the development of the theoretical framework of effective supervision. What does the development of this theoretical framework mean for the principle of effectiveness? And what does it mean for legal research dealing with effectiveness?

We have seen in Chapter 2 that no single meaning can be attached to the principle of effectiveness. Within the notion of good governance the principle of effectiveness requires that goals are set and that those goals are accomplished as effectively as possible. There should be no legal hindrances, or factual hindrances that may bear legal consequences, that make the application of the law and regulations by the public administration more burdensome, as a result of which legislative or regulatory goals cannot be achieved. The principle of effectiveness as a good governance principle is influenced by the meaning attached to the principle of effectiveness within EU law, where that principle is most elaborated. In the European Union the principle of effectiveness concerns the implementation, application and enforcement of EU law at the national level. National norms must not render virtually impossible or excessively difficult the exercise of rights conferred by the European legal order. More specifically in relation to enforcement, the EU principle of effectiveness is linked to proportionality and dissuasiveness. Despite the different meanings and scope that these two concepts attach to the principle of effectiveness, in both cases the principle of effectiveness has a strong instrumental character. It is therefore not surprising that the theoretical framework of effective supervision has such a character as well. It contains the presupposition that when the requirements of the theoretical framework are complied with, supervision will be effective. Compliance with the requirements of effective supervision does not, however, *automatically* mean that supervision is effective in the sense that the actual goal(s) of supervision is (are) attained. Rather, the requirements give an indication of the potential of reaching that goal. In relation to AML supervision this means the following. As expounded in Chapter 3, the main goal of AML supervision is to ensure compliance by the private sector with the obligations set by legislation in order to prevent them from being used or involved in money laundering and terrorist financing transactions.[5] Whether the goal is attained is a factual question and requires a different type of research that uses effectiveness as a standard for measuring whether the goal is reached (outcome). By researching the effectiveness of supervision from a legal perspective instead, the focus rests on the process of supervision and not on its outcome.[6] That is why legal research on the effectiveness of a policy, a norm or a mechanism is

5 See § 3.2.2.
6 Compare § 2.1.

valuable alongside the existence of effectiveness studies as known in other disciplines. This research has demonstrated that legal research provides insights other than effectiveness studies, which purely focus on the question whether goals have been attained or which effects are created by the application of a policy, norm or mechanism, would be able to give.

The development of the theoretical framework of effective supervision furthermore demonstrated that the principle of effectiveness does not operate in isolation. Rather, in order to analyse effectiveness from a legal perspective, other (legal) principles and related notions give effectiveness its substance. For supervision, effectiveness includes aspects like independence, accountability, transparency, the quality of legislation (legality, legal certainty, and enforceability), the adequacy of resources, and knowledge. These aspects are very diverse in nature, but have in common that the literature considers these to be of fundamental importance for exercising supervision. In Chapter 2 this was purveyed on a more abstract level to a certain extent. Herein, it was stated that within the notion of good governance the principles of effectiveness, accountability and transparency reinforce one another in the field of supervision. And the EU principle of effectiveness in an enforcement context relates to the notions of proportionality and dissuasiveness. We can observe that when effectiveness is used as an evaluative concept in legal research, the principle of effectiveness essentially functions as an umbrella term.

9.6.2 Supervisory models in the preventive AML policy

This research clearly gives room for thought on the application of the supervisory models in the preventive anti-money laundering policy. What do the findings and conclusion of this research mean for the supervisory models in the preventive AML policy as identified in the European Union? Should the EU Member States that apply the FIU model in their supervisory architectures, like Spain, do away with this model and all adopt the internal model, or not? Which role is there for the EU?

An important delineation of this research is that only one country per model is studied. In the introduction and Chapter 3 this choice was explained. There, I expressed the idea that it would be possible to generalise the outcomes of this research from the country level to the level of the models. That, unfortunately, appears to be very difficult. The main argument for that is, as just explained in answering the research question, that the synthesis demonstrated that not all issues identified in the selected Member States can be (directly) related to the choice for a particular supervisory model. Sometimes issues originated from poor national legislation or a lack of recognition from the national legislator that a matter should be regulated. Likewise, the use of powers by the AML supervisors in practice could lead to the finding that a country did not (fully) comply with a requirement stemming from the theoretical framework of effective supervision. This thus means that the conclusion that the United Kingdom has the most effective AML supervision of banks, accountants and real estate agents compared to the Netherlands, Spain and Sweden, does not *mutatis mutandis* mean that the internal model is also the most effective model. A second important delineation of this research is that the findings and answer to the research question are restricted to a specified time frame. Understanding that the AML policy is a rapidly developing policy, numerous changes affecting the (effectiveness of) anti-money laundering supervision in the Member States have occurred after the 31st of March 2014.[7]

Taking these delineations into account it is nevertheless possible to purvey some of the (im)possibilities of the models or to ponder on their future. The implementation of the FIU model in Spain demonstrated that this model is highly prone to resource issues. We could also see that this particularly affects the exercise of supervision in practice, possibly even leading to *de facto* no supervision at all. Spain is the second largest country in Western Europe and the European Union. It is large in terms of its territory, as well as the size of its population, and consequently in the number of institutions and professionals subjected to the preventive AML policy. In those circumstances the centralisation of AML supervision at a single authority appears not to be optimal. It may, however, be the case that the FIU model is suitable for small(er) countries in terms of geography, population and/or size of the financial sector. The FIU model should thus not be disregarded immediately because of the fact that it is not optimal for Spain. Rather, it would be worthwhile to conduct research on the implementation of the FIU model at the national level in countries that are considerably smaller than Spain, in order to discover whether the same problems exist or whether the FIU model may be effective in those countries.

Essentially the same holds true for the internal model. This research included the United Kingdom because it is an outstanding example of the internal model. The UK has the most internal supervisors in its AML supervisory architecture within the European Union. The conclusion that AML supervision in the UK is the most effective makes one think whether other Member States should opt for the internal model as well. During this research, I considered on various occasions that the UK has a rich history and a great deal of experience with self-regulation. This research demonstrated that the two professional associations included in this research are really convinced of the necessity of fighting money laundering. Nevertheless, the foregoing does not necessarily mean that the internal model functions equally optimally in other EU Member States. How optimal is the internal model in Member States that do not have such a high level of experience with self-regulation? Or how optimal is this model for Member States where professional associations prefer to act as 'defenders of the profession' and distrust the Government? What happens when the internal model is applied in countries where the professional associations are not so convinced of the need for preventing money laundering by members of their profession? Also the legal system may play a role: while the United Kingdom is known for its common law tradition, one may wonder how the internal model would function in countries with a civil law tradition. Although it has not been the aim of this research to compare the legal systems as such, indirectly they may have played a role. All of the foregoing questions show once more that the implementation of the models at the national level is a very casuistic matter, depending on a country's characteristics in terms of culture, national politics, legal system, finances and so on. It may thus be the case that the implementation of the internal model in other Member States leads to very different results.

7 See § 1.8.

A common problem for external supervisors in this research appeared to be a lack of regulation of the real estate or accountancy sector. The unrelated nature of the sectors in combination with the distanced position of external supervisors makes it a challenge for the supervisors to effectively carry out anti-money laundering supervision. This research demonstrated that in order to make the external model, and to lesser extent the FIU and hybrid models, work at the national level it is important that Member States that choose this model actually provide mechanisms that enable the responsible AML supervisors to supervise the unregulated sectors. This research at various times mentioned and explained the existence of different kinds of registration obligations.

This research also demonstrated that the separation of the models, as presented in Chapter 3, becomes somewhat blurred with the implementation of these at the national level. We could, for example, see that in Spain the Commission for the Prevention of Money Laundering and Monetary Offences is allowed to enter into supervisory arrangements with the three financial regulators in Spain. Under this arrangement, the financial regulators can also carry out anti-money laundering supervision. Then the only difference with the external model is that the final responsibility for this supervision still remains SEPBLAC, instead of a shared final responsibility for all authorities exercising anti-money laundering supervision. For the external model, in turn, the informal involvement of internal supervisors in the Netherlands actually seems to be a first step towards a departure from this model. Having internal supervisors as AML supervisors may be beneficial at times, as this research demonstrated, so it is not unimaginable that Member States which apply the FIU and external models will slowly abandon these models in the future and move to a more hybrid variant where external supervisors and professional associations formally share AML supervisory responsibility for certain sectors. This would even mean the creation of a new hybrid variant.

Does the foregoing mean that more harmonisation should be brought into the supervisory architectures of the Member States in the preventive AML policy by the European legislator? This research has proved that this is indeed necessary. Of course, it is hoped that this research already leads to more voluntary convergence. Likewise, the future Fourth Directive already contains steps towards more harmonisation, particularly with the introduction of a minimum set of administrative sanctions for supervisors. Nevertheless, more harmonisation could – and as the recommendations for the European legislator showed should – also be pursued in relation to the institutional aspects of AML supervisors. Although this touches upon the national procedural autonomy of the Member States, which, admittedly, is a sensitive issue, this research clearly demonstrated that an important part of the problems identified in relation to effective supervision, like independence and accountability, originate from the national level. The above recommendations therefore advise the EU legislator to include some minimum institutional requirements in future directives. If this is a step too far, the European Union could first address the most pressing issues via guidance documents in order to help Member States in making the right choices in relation to the supervisory architecture that meets the specific needs and questions, as well as traditions, in those countries.

9.7 Epilogue

I hope that it has become clear that the supervisory models in the preventive anti-money laundering policy as presented in this research are not a given, fixed concept. They should rather be considered as concepts based on which on a systematic basis insight can be given in the matter of supervision in this policy. The models themselves could be susceptible to changes: they could branch out over time, be replaced by other models or simply vanish entirely. Moreover, this research has repeatedly demonstrated that most important is the actual implementation of the models at the national level. This depends for a large part on the priority that Member States give to combating money laundering. Personally, I think it can even be claimed that if a Member State does not give priority to the fight against money laundering in the first place, anti-money laundering supervision will by definition be ineffective, or indeed less effective. So, eventually, that is what it all comes down to: the true conviction of national Governments that money laundering should be prevented.

Summary

Introduction

The process of concealing illegally obtained proceeds, better known as money laundering, is criminalised virtually all around the world and has been a law enforcement priority since the early 1990s. The international nature of money laundering, combined with estimations on the scope and the distorting effects it may bring about, make it a grave danger to national and international financial markets. At the same time money laundering is considered a danger to society due to its strong interaction with organised drugs and white-collar crime. Therefore, there is a general consensus that money laundering should be combated. Over the years a 'twin-track approach' has been developed.[1] On the one hand, this approach consists of a preventive policy, which aims at the prevention of money laundering through the setting of identification and reporting obligations for financial institutions, designated non-financial institutions and legal professionals like lawyers and civil-law notaries. On the other hand, the twin-track approach consists of a repressive policy whose objective is to punish the money launderers. Efforts against money laundering can be found at the international, the regional (such as the European Union), and the national level.

Definition of the problem and the research question

Money laundering has attracted a great deal of attention from the academic world. In the broad field of the study of money laundering by far the most attention has been devoted to measurements of the amounts of money laundered and to the effects of money laundering. Supervision within the preventive anti-money laundering (hereafter also 'AML') policy is, however, an aspect that has remained underexposed in research. This means that an insight into the contours and contents, the similarities and differences between countries, let alone into the effectiveness thereof, is largely absent. The aim of this research is therefore to obtain an insight into the differences in the supervision within this policy, to analyse these on a systematic basis and to compare the supervisory architectures of countries to identify which one is the most effective, as well as to create a learning effect for other countries in order to strengthen their systems. This research focuses on the anti-money laundering supervision in the European Union (hereafter also 'EU'). The main research question is in which of the Member States of the European Union is supervision within

1 Stessens, G. (2000), *Money Laundering: A New International Law Enforcement Model*, Cambridge University Press: Cambridge, at 82 and 108-112.

the preventive anti-money laundering policy the most effective, and what other Member States can do to reach the same level of effectiveness. More specifically, this research is about the anti-money laundering supervision of banks, accountants and real estate agents. These institutions are selected as representatives of the different categories of institutions under the preventive AML policy: the financial and credit institutions, the legal and fiscal service providers and the category of non-financial businesses and non-legal professionals.

Effective supervision

Based on the principle of effectiveness as a good governance principle and EU principle, the minimum requirements stemming from the EU Directive on the prevention of the use of the financial system for the purpose of money laundering and terrorist financing (hereafter the 'Third Directive'[2]) as well as a literature study, a common core of requirements for effective supervision can be identified. These can be distinguished into three categories: the legislative requirements, the institutional requirements and the category of requirements regarding the competences of anti-money laundering supervisors and the application thereof in practice.

The **first category** requires that the legislation is clear, precise, foreseeable, predictable and, hence, enforceable. The absence of a clear legal basis or a lack of clarity in the substantive legislation affects the enforceability of the norms. The enforceability is important, because if norms are not enforceable, supervision can never be effective in the first place. The **category of the institutional requirements** places conditions on the AML supervisors in terms of their independence from politics and the market, their accountability and transparency, the availability of adequate resources and their knowledge of the institutions and professionals for which they have supervisory responsibility. The institutional position of supervisors can affect their information position, and thus, the effectiveness of their supervision. The **third category**, concerning the competences of anti-money laundering supervisors and the application thereof in practice, essentially requires that AML supervisors have adequate supervisory, sanctioning and cooperation powers. Effective supervision requires that supervisors must apply these powers in practice, and do so proportionately and with care. In their sanctioning activity, the AML supervisors must speak softly where possible and be hard where necessary. Ultimately, however, the sanctions must be capable of providing a deterrent effect. Finally, AML supervisors should have public supervision (sanctioning) policies in place that include an explanation of the legal framework, the supervisory goals, the desired level of compliance, the principles followed by the supervisors, as well as a general description of the procedures. Public policies foster transparency and accountability. By displaying how they apply their powers in practice, the supervisors can improve their credibility, and even their legitimacy.

2 Directive 2005/60/EC of the European Parliament and of the Council of 26 October 2005 on the prevention of the use of the financial system for the purpose of money laundering and terrorist financing, [2005] OJ L 309/15.

Anti-money laundering supervision in the European Union

Understanding that the Third Directive has left the design of supervision mostly to the EU Member States, their choices have been influenced by factors such as national politics, culture, the legal system, the economy and finances. As a result of these influences, a patchwork of anti-money laundering supervisory architectures exists in the EU. Based on two criteria, four models of AML supervision can be identified within the EU. The first criterion concerns the number of authorities involved in anti-money laundering supervision combined with the final responsibility for this supervision. The second criterion refers to the nature of these authorities. Supervisors can either be internal or external, viewed from the perspective of the supervised institutions and professionals. Professional associations are internal supervisors, whereas external supervisors are public (administrative) or Government authorities.

The first model identified is the **FIU model**. This model's main characteristic is that the financial intelligence unit (FIU) is the national authority with the final responsibility for AML supervision. FIUs are (a part of) national authorities that are primarily responsible for receiving, analysing and disseminating financial intelligence submitted through suspicion reports by the obliged institutions or professionals. In the second model, the **external model**, AML supervision is formally exercised by public administrative or Government authorities that have no direct or professional relationship with the supervisees. The final responsibility for this supervision is shared between these external supervisors. In practice an informal role can be played by professional associations in the supervision and sanctioning of legal and fiscal service providers. The third model, the **internal model**, is the most widespread model in the EU. Here, anti-money laundering supervision is mainly carried out by professional associations, with the exception of the supervision of financial and credit institutions and casinos. The guiding principle of this model is that where AML supervision can be carried out by internal supervisors, these will be assigned with this task. All the supervisors involved share the final responsibility. The last model identified is the **hybrid model**. This model combines, in different gradations, different elements of the aforementioned models. So far, mixtures between internal and external supervisors, and between the internal and external supervisors and the FIU have been identified. Here, too, the final responsibility is shared between all the supervisors involved.

Evaluation of the models in the light of effective supervision

The EU Member States that have been selected for further analysis in this research are Spain, the Netherlands, the United Kingdom (hereafter also the 'UK') and Sweden. They each represent one of the four models. Their supervisory architectures have been analysed based on the theoretical framework of effective supervision. Hereafter follows a concise account of these supervisory architectures and the most important findings from the perspective of effective supervision.

Spain

The Spanish financial intelligence unit (*Servicio Ejecutivo de la Comisión de Prevención del Blanqueo de Capitales e Infracciones Monetarias, SEPBLAC*) has supervisory responsibility for the entire range of institutions and professionals that fall under the AML legislation. SEPBLAC acts under the authority of the Commission for the Prevention of Money Laundering and Monetary Offences (*Comisión de Prevención del Blanqueo de Capitales e Infracciones Monetarias*). This Commission has a wide range of powers vis-à-vis SEPBLAC and is competent to enter into arrangements with the three Spanish financial regulators with the aim of coordinating and harmonising their anti-money laundering inspections and supervisory activities with those carried out by SEPBLAC. The general idea is that the regulators integrate AML supervision into their general supervision programmes and send their supervision reports to the Commission Secretariat, which is another support body of the Commission. SEPBLAC, however, remains ultimately responsible for the exercise of AML supervision. The supervisory arrangement between the Commission and the Bank of Spain (*Banco de España*) is particularly relevant for the supervision of banks. This research identified a number of problems affecting the effectiveness of SEPBLAC's supervision. The two main problems are the inadequate level of political independence of SEPBLAC and the fact that the financial intelligence unit has been appointed as the only formal AML supervisor. Serious resource issues on SEPBLAC's side led to *de facto* no anti-money laundering supervision in Spain in the period 2010-2012. Despite the supervisory arrangement, this research observed that the Bank of Spain's publicly available supervision statistics do not show any AML(-related) inspection of banks in 2011 and 2012 either.

The Netherlands

Anti-money laundering supervision of banks, accountants and real estate agents in the Netherlands is exercised by the Dutch Central Bank (*De Nederlandsche Bank, DNB*), the Financial Supervision Office (*Bureau Financieel Toezicht, BFT*) and the Dutch Tax and Customs Administration/Bureau Supervision Wwft (*Belastingdienst/Bureau Toezicht Wwft, 'the Bureau'*) respectively.

For anti-money laundering supervision of **banks**, the most remarkable finding is that DNB is soft in sanctioning banks for non-compliance with the AML obligations in comparison to its counterparts in Spain, the United Kingdom and Sweden. As far as anti-money laundering supervision of **real estate agents** is concerned, this supervision faces a number of problems. Important problems originate from the coverage of real estate agents under the Dutch AML legislation, the absence of an explicit obligation to have an internal policy for the prevention of money laundering and terrorist financing in the AML legislation, the inadequate level of political independence for the Bureau Supervision Wwft and its relatively weak information position vis-à-vis the sector. A strong aspect, however, is the intensity with which the Bureau has supervised real estate agents in recent years. With regard to anti-money laundering supervision of **accountants**, it appears that the Financial Supervision Office faces some resource issues. This could be solved by entering into arrangements with professional associations through which the latter become indirectly involved in the exercise of anti-money laundering supervision of accountants. Regarding its supervisory arrangement with the professional association SRA, however, this research finds that BFT is insufficiently transparent about this (important) aspect of its AML supervision. This research identifies a number of other problems as well, including difficulties in the application of supervisory powers due to legal professional privilege, the absence of a public supervision policy, and the lack of a legal basis for the Dutch Institute of Chartered Accountants (*Nederlandse Beroepsorganisatie van Accountants, NBA*) to forward relevant supervisory information to the Financial Supervision Office.

Cooperation between AML supervisors takes place through institutional forums and on a more operational level. In the Netherlands, four cooperative efforts are (in)directly related to the preventive AML policy: the AML coordination meeting, the Financial Expertise Centre, the National Task Force on Tackling the Misuse of Real Estate and the Committee on the duty to disclose unusual transactions. Regarding the exchange of supervisory information, this research concludes that the legal basis for the exchange between the AML supervisors should be amended in order to adequately acknowledge the role of professional associations in BFT's anti-money laundering supervision.

United Kingdom

With 22 professional (and trade) associations and six public bodies acting as AML supervisors, the UK has by far the highest number of supervisors in the EU. Anti-money laundering supervision of banks is carried out by the Financial Conduct Authority (FCA). Until the 1st of April 2014, estate agents were supervised by the Office of Fair Trading (OFT). On this date, this Office was abolished and AML supervisory responsibility for real estate agents was transferred to Her Majesty's Revenue and Customs (HMRC). Within this research it was impossible to fully include this transfer but, where relevant, reference is made to it. Accountants are in principle supervised by their professional associations. Two out of the eleven professional associations in the accountancy sector have been included in this research: the Institute of Chartered Accountants in England and Wales (ICAEW) and the Association of Accounting Technicians (AAT).

Anti-money laundering supervision of **banks** by the FCA is integrated into the regular supervisory procedures on the one hand, and a specialist financial crime supervision team on the other. While this research finds that more information should be provided about the integration of AML supervision in the FCA's regular supervisory procedures, it also concludes that the specialist team carries out a high number of on-site inspections and investigations of banks annually, in particular through the ongoing Systematic Anti-Money Laundering Programme (SAMLP) and thematic studies on banks' compliance with AML obligations. The FCA has a wide range of sanctioning powers, it has a detailed public supervision policy and the sanctions are laid down in final or decision notices which are, in principle, always published by the FCA. Recent years have shown that the FCA has been active in terms of imposing sanctions on banks that do not comply with AML obligations, while it has made use of early interventions and informal measures against banks as well. For anti-money laundering supervision of **estate agents**, an interesting aspect is that despite the fact that the real estate profession in the UK is a non-regulated profession, the Office of Fair Trading has a good oversight of this group of professionals. The Money Laundering Regulations require all non-regulated professionals to register with their competent AML supervisor. This obligation, which is not required by the Third Directive, effectively ensures that all supervisors have adequate knowledge of their supervisees. The OFT has nevertheless faced some problems. One of the concerns in this research was the intensity of the Office's AML supervision in recent years, as this was rather low in light of the total number of estate agents. Under the Regulations the OFT has the possibility to enter into arrangements with Local Authority Trading Standards Services (LATSS), but this research argues that these arrangements should be made in writing and be publicly available. A strong aspect is the OFT's high level of transparency: the Office is the only AML supervisor of real estate agents included in this research with a specific public supervision (sanctioning) policy. This research recommends HMRC to apply the same level of transparency as the Office of Fair Trading. Regarding the activity of sanctioning, it appears that the OFT's sanctions have become more dissuasive over the years in terms of the amount of the fines and the publications of the sanctions, and that it has moved from imposing sanctions for acting in breach of the registration obligation to imposing sanctions for non-compliance with the wider range of preventive obligations.

For anti-money laundering supervision of **accountants**, this research concludes that ICAEW and AAT generally have a well-developed practice of supervising their members. Yet, some changes are still required. Important examples are the lack of an adequate market independence for ICAEW and the carrying out of targeted AML supervision. Whereas this research recommends that ICAEW should publish the outcomes of its targeted inspections, it recommends AAT to start carrying out these targeted inspections to ensure and to demonstrate that an adequate level of attention is given to AML compliance. In terms of sanctioning, this research concludes that both professional associations do well in comparison with the AML supervisors of accountants in Spain, the Netherlands and Sweden.

The United Kingdom has a forum for cooperation on a policy level in which all AML supervisors participate: the Anti-Money Laundering Supervisors' Forum (AMLSF). Within the AMLSF the supervisors share their supervisory practices, discuss policy developments and review the effectiveness of supervision and the sanctions imposed. Two other forums for cooperation are the Money Laundering Advisory Committee (MLAC) and the SARs Review Committee. Some, but not all, AML supervisors participate in these forums. The 2012 amendments to the Money Laundering Regulations 2007 created an explicit legal basis for the exchange of supervisory information between the AML supervisors.

Sweden

The Swedish AML supervisors of banks and real estate agents are the Financial Supervisory Authority (*Finansinspektionen, FI*) and the Estate Agents Inspectorate (*Fastighetsmäklarinspektionen, FMI*). Anti-money laundering supervision of accountants is carried out by different supervisors: the Supervisory Board of Public Auditors (*Revisorsnämnden, RN*) has supervisory responsibility for auditors and audit firms, whereas the county administrative boards of Stockholm, Västra Götaland, and Skåne supervise accountants, not being auditors or audit firms.

As far as anti-money laundering supervision of **banks** is concerned, this research concluded that the Swedish Financial Supervisory Authority has carried out thematic AML supervision of banks in recent years, but that it should become more transparent about the exercise of this supervision. Annual plans are not public and information on the outcomes of thematic reviews and the inclusion of banks therein is fragmented. The Financial Supervisory Authority also lacks a public supervision (sanctioning) policy. Regarding the anti-money laundering supervision of **real estate agents** in Sweden, a lot can be improved. The Estate Agents Inspectorate lacks adequate supervisory powers due to the narrow formulation of real estate agents under the Estate Agents Act Act and the absence of a self-standing power to carry out on-site inspections. AML supervision is therefore entirely off-site and mostly reactive in nature. Most of the Inspectorate's supervisory activities stem from complaints from consumers or third parties, which are in most cases not even about non-compliance with preventive anti-money laundering obligations in the first place. The fact that most efforts originate from complaints is worrisome, because not all obligations are adequately checked: the reporting obligation and the obligation to have an internal policy are hardly included, if included at all. It is surprising that despite the lack of proactive and risk-based supervision, and a lack of adequate supervisory and sanctioning powers, the Inspectorate's Disciplinary Board sanctioned a high number of real estate agents between 2010-2013 for acting in breach of the customer due diligence or record keeping obligations.

For anti-money laundering supervision of **accountants**, this research concludes that the lack of transparency by the Swedish Supervisory Board of Public Auditors is most problematic. The Supervisory Board does not provide information about the way in which it carries out AML supervision of auditors and audit firms, and how the verification of AML compliance is integrated into its regular supervisory procedures. An analysis of its supervisory practice therefore appeared impossible within the context of this research. The county administrative boards' supervisory responsibility for accountants that are not auditors depends on the actual registration of these professionals at the Swedish Companies Registration Office. Worrisome, however, is the lack of powers for the county administrative boards to enforce registration. Their number of on-site inspections are low as well. Most likely this has to do with the fact that the few resources that the county administrative boards had available, had to be spent on persuading institutions and professionals to register. This research concluded that implementing a risk-based approach with more on-site inspections will improve the (effectiveness of) AML supervision by the county administrative boards. It is thereby of the utmost importance that the Swedish legislator provides the boards with adequate sanctioning powers, because at present they cannot enforce registration and directly sanction non-compliance with the preventive obligations.

The most institutionalised forum for cooperation between AML supervisors can be found in Sweden where AML legislation establishes and regulates this forum. The Swedish AML

Act does, however, not provide a legal basis for the exchange of supervisory information between the AML supervisors. Based on the general legal framework for the exchange of information by public authorities, this research concluded that only little room exists for AML supervisors to exchange supervisory information.

Conclusion

After the comparison of the anti-money laundering supervision of banks, accountants and real estate agents in Spain, the Netherlands, the United Kingdom and Sweden in the synthesis, this research finally concludes that the most effective anti-money laundering supervision can be found in the United Kingdom. No serious issues in relation to the institutional requirements can be identified for this country. Except for one professional association, the AML supervisors included in this research all appear to have adequate levels of political and market independence. There are no resource issues for any of the supervisors either and the knowledge of their supervisees outside the regulated sectors and professions is covered by an extensive registration obligation. The supervisors from the UK are in practice most transparent about and accountable for the exercise of their AML supervision in comparison to their counterparts in the other three countries. And, finally, the legal framework in the UK appears to be rather clear and complete. At the same time, this research concludes that the least effective anti-money laundering supervision can be found in Spain. This is the result of a combination of factors, but most prominently results from the choice for appointing the financial intelligence unit as the only formal AML supervisor in combination with resource issues and the way in which SEPBLAC's institutional position is regulated. Based on this conclusion, this research comes with a number of recommendations for the EU legislator and the national legislators of Spain, the Netherlands, the United Kingdom and Sweden to strengthen the anti-money laundering supervision and to make it more effective.

With the formulation of the research question it was anticipated that the findings on the effectiveness of the anti-money laundering supervision in the four EU Member States would allow definitive conclusions to be drawn on the effectiveness of the models as such. This research, however, has demonstrated that although some effectiveness issues at the national level originated from the choice for a particular supervisory model, a number of issues arose from purely domestic matters as well, such as poor legislation or the actual use of the powers by the AML supervisors. So, in the end, the effectiveness of the supervision largely boils down to the actual implementation of the anti-money laundering supervisory models in the national legal systems.

Samenvatting

Introductie

Het verhullen van illegaal verkregen vermogen, beter bekend als witwassen, is in vrijwel de hele wereld strafbaar gesteld en is sinds het begin van de jaren negentig een handhavingsprioriteit. Het internationale karakter van witwassen, in combinatie met schattingen over de omvang en de verstorende effecten die ermee gepaard gaan, maakt witwassen een grote bedreiging voor nationale en internationale financiële markten. Witwassen wordt bovendien als een gevaar voor de samenleving beschouwd omdat het sterk samenhangt met georganiseerde drugs- en witteboordencriminaliteit. Daarom bestaat er algemene consensus dat witwassen moet worden tegengegaan. De afgelopen jaren is er een zogenoemd tweesporenbeleid ontwikkeld.[1] Dit bestaat enerzijds uit een preventief beleid, dat zich richt op de preventie van witwassen door middel van identificatie- en meldplichten voor financiële instellingen, voor juridische en fiscale dienstverleners zoals advocaten en notarissen, en voor aangewezen niet-financiële instellingen.[2] Anderzijds bestaat dit uit een repressief beleid, met het doel om witwassers te pakken en te bestraffen. Initiatieven voor de bestrijding van witwassen zijn terug te vinden op internationaal, regionaal (zoals de Europese Unie) en nationaal niveau.

Probleemstelling en onderzoeksvraag

Witwassen heeft veel aandacht gekregen vanuit de academische wereld. In onderzoek naar witwassen is de meeste aandacht uitgegaan naar metingen van de omvang van witwassen en van de effecten ervan. Toezicht binnen het preventieve anti-witwasbeleid is echter een aspect dat tot dusverre onderbelicht is gebleven. Dit betekent dat er weinig tot geen inzicht is in de structuren en inhoud van het toezicht, de overeenkomsten en verschillen tussen landen, laat staan de effectiviteit van het toezicht. Het doel van dit onderzoek is daarom om inzicht te verkrijgen in de verschillen in toezicht binnen dit beleid, om deze verschillen op systematische wijze te analyseren en om de verschillende toezichtsystemen van landen met elkaar te vergelijken om vast te stellen welke toezichtstructuur het meest effectief is. Het doel is tevens om een leereffect voor andere landen te creëren, waardoor zij hun

1 De Engelse term 'twin-track approach' komt onder meer naar voren in het werk van Stessens, G. (2000), *Money Laundering: A New International Law Enforcement Model*, Cambridge University Press: Cambridge, p. 82 en 108-112.

2 Bijvoorbeeld handelaren in goederen van grote waarde (auto's, juwelen, kunst) en makelaars.

toezichtsystemen kunnen versterken. Dit onderzoek richt zich op het anti-witwastoezicht binnen de Europese Unie (hierna ook 'EU'). De onderzoeksvraag is in welke lidstaat van de Europese Unie het toezicht binnen het preventieve anti-witwasbeleid het meest effectief is, en wat andere EU-lidstaten kunnen doen om hetzelfde niveau te bereiken. Meer in het bijzonder richt dit onderzoek zich op het anti-witwastoezicht op banken, accountants en makelaars. Deze instellingen vertegenwoordigen de categorieën instellingen die onder de anti-witwasregelgeving vallen: de financiële en kredietinstellingen, de juridische en fiscale dienstverleners, en de categorie van niet-financiële en niet-juridische en fiscale professionals.

Effectief toezicht

Op basis van het effectiviteitsbeginsel als beginsel van *good governance* en EU-beginsel, de minimum vereisten die voortvloeien uit de EU Richtlijn tot voorkoming van het gebruik van het financiële stelsel voor het witwassen van geld en de financiering van terrorisme (hierna 'Derde richtlijn'[3]), en een literatuurstudie, kan een aantal kernvereisten voor effectief toezicht worden geformuleerd. Deze vereisten kunnen worden onderscheiden in drie categorieën: juridische vereisten, institutionele vereisten en vereisten met betrekking tot bevoegdheden van toezichthouders en de feitelijke toepassing daarvan.

De **eerste categorie** vereist dat de wetgeving duidelijk, precies, voorzienbaar, voorspelbaar en daarmee handhaafbaar is. De afwezigheid van een duidelijke juridische basis of een gebrek aan duidelijkheid in de materiële wetgeving heeft invloed op de handhaafbaarheid van de normen. De handhaafbaarheid is belangrijk, want als normen niet handhaafbaar zijn, dan zal het toezicht nooit effectief kunnen zijn. De **categorie met institutionele vereisten** stelt voorwaarden aan de anti-witwastoezichthouders op het punt van onafhankelijkheid van de politiek en de markt, hun verantwoording en transparantie, de beschikbaarheid van adequate middelen en de kennis van instellingen en professionals voor wie de toezichthouders verantwoordelijkheid dragen. De institutionele positie van toezichthouders kan invloed hebben op hun informatiepositie en daarmee ook op de effectiviteit van het door hen uitgevoerde toezicht. De **derde categorie**, met betrekking tot bevoegdheden van toezichthouders en de feitelijke toepassing daarvan, vereist in essentie dat de anti-witwastoezichthouders adequate toezicht-, sanctionerings- en samenwerkingsbevoegdheden hebben. Effectief toezicht vereist dat toezichthouders deze bevoegdheden daadwerkelijk toepassen op een proportionele en zorgvuldige wijze. Bij het opleggen van sancties moeten anti-witwastoezichthouders rekening houden met het adagium 'zacht waar het kan, hard waar het moet'. Sancties dienen echter uiteindelijk vooral een afschrikwekkend effect te hebben. Tot slot moeten anti-witwastoezichthouders een openbaar handhavingsbeleid te hebben, waarin ten minste aandacht dient te worden besteed aan een uitleg van het juridische kader, de doelstellingen die in dit toezicht worden nagestreefd, het gewenste nalevingsniveau, de beginselen die door de toezichthouders worden gevolgd, en een algemene beschrijving van de te volgen

3 Richtlijn 2005/60/EG van het Europees Parlement en de Raad van 26 oktober 2005 tot voorkoming van het gebruik van het financiële stelsel voor het witwassen van geld en de financiering van terrorisme, [2005] Pub. L 309/15.

toezicht- en sanctioneringsprocedures. Openbaar beleid bevordert de transparantie en verantwoording. Door inzicht te geven in de manier waarop de bevoegdheden in de praktijk worden toegepast, kunnen toezichthouders hun geloofwaardigheid en zelfs hun legitimiteit vergroten.

Anti-witwastoezicht in de Europese Unie

Omdat de Derde richtlijn wat betreft de vormgeving van het toezicht veel aan de lidstaten heeft overgelaten, zijn hun keuzes beïnvloed door factoren als nationale politiek, cultuur, het rechtssysteem, de economie en financiën. Door deze verschillende invloeden bestaat er nu een lappendeken (*patchwork*) van anti-witwastoezichtsystemen in de EU. Op basis van twee criteria kunnen vier modellen van anti-witwastoezicht worden geïdentificeerd. Het eerste criterium betreft het aantal autoriteiten betrokken bij het anti-witwastoezicht in combinatie met de eindverantwoordelijkheid voor dit toezicht. Het tweede criterium betreft de aard van de toezichthouders. Toezichthouders kunnen ofwel intern ofwel extern zijn, gezien vanuit het perspectief van de ondertoezichtstaande instellingen en professionals. Beroepsorganisaties zijn interne toezichthouders, en externe toezichthouders zijn bestuursorganen of andere overheidsorganen.

Het eerste model is het **FIU-model**. Het hoofdkenmerk van dit model is dat de financiële inlichtingeneenheid de nationale autoriteit is met eindverantwoordelijkheid voor het anti-witwastoezicht. Financiële inlichtingeneenheden, in het Engels *financial intelligence units* genoemd, zijn (onderdeel van) nationale autoriteiten die primair belast zijn met het ontvangen, opvragen, analyseren en het verspreiden onder bevoegde autoriteiten van meldingen van verdachte transacties die zijn gedaan door instellingen en professionals die vallen onder de werking van de anti-witwasregelgeving. In het tweede model, het **externe model**, wordt het anti-witwastoezicht formeel uitgevoerd door bestuursorganen of overheidsorganen die, zoals gezegd, geen directe relatie of beroepsrelatie hebben met ondertoezichtstaande instellingen of professionals. De eindverantwoordelijkheid voor het anti-witwastoezicht wordt gedeeld door deze externe toezichthouders. In de praktijk kan door beroepsorganisaties een informele rol worden gespeeld bij het uitvoeren van toezicht of het opleggen van sancties op juridische en fiscale dienstverleners. Het derde model, het **interne model**, is het meest toegepaste model binnen de EU. Anti-witwastoezicht wordt hier voornamelijk uitgevoerd door beroepsorganisaties, met uitzondering van het toezicht op financiële en kredietinstellingen en casino's. Het leidende beginsel is dat waar anti-witwastoezicht kán worden uitgevoerd door interne toezichthouders, zij deze taak ook zullen krijgen. Alle toezichthouders delen de eindverantwoordelijkheid voor het anti-witwastoezicht in dit model. Het laatste model is het **hybride model**. Dit model combineert in verschillende gradaties de verschillende elementen van de drie eerdergenoemde modellen. Tot nu toe zijn er combinaties van interne en externe toezichthouders gevonden, en van interne en externe toezichthouders en de FIU. Ook hier wordt de eindverantwoordelijkheid voor het anti-witwastoezicht gedeeld door alle toezichthouders.

Evaluatie van de modellen in het licht van effectief toezicht

De EU-lidstaten die zijn geselecteerd voor verder onderzoek zijn Spanje, Nederland, het Verenigd Koninkrijk (hierna ook 'VK') en Zweden. Elk land vertegenwoordigt een van de vier bovengenoemde modellen. De toezichtstructuren van deze lidstaten zijn geanalyseerd op basis van het theoretisch kader voor effectief toezicht. Hierna volgt een beknopte weergave van deze toezichtstructuren en de meest belangrijke bevindingen vanuit het perspectief van effectief toezicht.

Spanje

De Spaanse financiële inlichtingeneenheid (*Servicio Ejecutivo de la Comisión de Prevención del Blanqueo de Capitales e Infracciones Monetarias, SEPBLAC*) is verantwoordelijk voor het anti-witwastoezicht op alle instellingen en professionals die onder het preventieve anti-witwasbeleid vallen. SEPBLAC opereert onder de verantwoordelijkheid van de Commissie voor de Preventie van het Witwassen van Geld en Monetaire Delicten (*Comisión de Prevención del Blanqueo de Capitales e Infracciones Monetarias*). Deze Commissie heeft een breed scala aan bevoegdheden ten opzichte van SEPBLAC en is bevoegd om over dit toezicht afspraken te maken met de drie Spaanse toezichthouders op de financiële markten met als doel hun anti-witwasinspecties en toezichtactiviteiten te coördineren en deze te harmoniseren met die van SEPBLAC. Het idee is dat de financiële toezichthouders het anti-witwastoezicht integreren in hun algemene toezichtprogramma's en dat zij hun bevindingen toesturen aan het Secretariaat van de Commissie (*Secretaría de la Comisión*), een ander orgaan dat onder de verantwoordelijkheid van de Commissie opereert. SEPBLAC blijft echter de eindverantwoordelijke voor de uitvoering van het anti-witwastoezicht. Het convenant tussen de Commissie en de Spaanse centrale bank (*Banco de España*) is in het bijzonder relevant voor het toezicht op banken. Dit onderzoek heeft een aantal problemen geconstateerd dat invloed heeft op de effectiviteit van het toezicht door SEPBLAC. De twee grootste problemen zijn de onvoldoende mate van politieke onafhankelijkheid van SEPBLAC en het feit dat de financiële inlichtingeneenheid als enige anti-witwastoezichthouder in Spanje is aangewezen. Een ernstig gebrek aan adequate middelen voor SEPBLAC heeft ertoe geleid dat er in de periode tussen 2010 en 2012 *de facto* geen anti-witwastoezicht plaatsvond. Ondanks de afspraken met de Spaanse centrale bank over het uitvoeren van toezicht constateert dit onderzoek dat de openbaar toegankelijke statistieken wat betreft het toezicht van de Spaanse centrale bank ook geen blijk geven van anti-witwasinspecties bij banken in de jaren 2011 en 2012.

Nederland

Het anti-witwastoezicht op banken, accountants en makelaars wordt in Nederland uitgevoerd door De Nederlandsche Bank (DNB), het Bureau Financieel Toezicht (BFT) en de Belastingdienst/Bureau Toezicht Wwft.

Voor het anti-witwastoezicht op **banken** is de meest in het oog springende bevinding dat DNB in vergelijking met diens tegenhangers in Spanje, het Verenigd Koninkrijk en Zweden zacht optreedt bij het sanctioneren van banken die zich niet houden aan de verplichtingen uit het anti-witwasbeleid. Het anti-witwastoezicht op **makelaars** in Nederland ondervindt een aantal problemen. Belangrijke problemen komen voort uit de bepalingen aangaande makelaars in de Wwft, de afwezigheid van een expliciete verplichting in de Wwft dat instellingen en professionals een intern beleid ter voorkoming van witwassen en financiering van terrorisme dienen te hebben, de onvoldoende mate van politieke onafhankelijkheid voor Bureau Toezicht Wwft en diens relatief zwakke informatiepositie ten opzichte van de sector. Een sterk punt, daarentegen, is de toezichtintensiteit van Bureau Toezicht Wwft op makelaars in de afgelopen jaren. Met betrekking tot het anti-witwastoezicht op **accountants** lijkt het Bureau Financieel Toezicht te maken te hebben met een gebrek aan middelen. Dit kan worden opgelost door het sluiten van toezichtarrangementen met beroepsorganisaties, waardoor deze organisaties indirect betrokken kunnen worden bij het anti-witwastoezicht op accountants. Ten aanzien van het bestaande toezichtarrangement met de organisatie Samenwerkende Registeraccountants en Accountants-administratieconsulenten (SRA), concludeert dit onderzoek dat het BFT onvoldoende transparant is over dit (belangrijke) aspect van diens anti-witwastoezicht. Dit onderzoek constateert daarnaast een aantal andere problemen, waaronder problemen met de toepassing van toezichtbevoegdheden door het beroepsgeheim en (afgeleide) verschoningsrecht, de afwezigheid van een openbaar handhavingsbeleid, en het ontbreken van een wettelijke basis voor de Nederlandse Beroepsorganisatie van Accountants om relevante toezichtinformatie te verstrekken aan het BFT.

De samenwerking tussen de toezichthouders vindt plaats op institutioneel niveau (fora) en op een meer operationeel niveau. Er bestaan vier samenwerkingsverbanden die (in)direct betrekking hebben op het preventieve anti-witwasbeleid: het Wwft Toezichthoudersoverleg, het Financieel Expertise Centrum, de Nationale Regiegroep Aanpak Misbruik Vastgoed, en de Commissie inzake de meldingsplicht ongebruikelijke transacties. Met betrekking tot de onderlinge uitwisseling van informatie concludeert dit onderzoek dat de wettelijke basis moet worden aangepast zodat de rol van beroepsorganisaties in het anti-witwastoezicht van het Bureau Financieel Toezicht voldoende wordt erkend.

Verenigd Koninkrijk

Met 22 beroepsorganisaties en zes overheidsorganen heeft het Verenigd Koninkrijk binnen de EU veruit het grootste aantal anti-witwastoezichthouders. De *Financial Conduct Authority* (FCA) is verantwoordelijk voor het anti-witwastoezicht op banken. Tot 1 april 2014 hield de *Office of Fair Trading* (OFT) toezicht op makelaars. Deze organisatie is sindsdien opgeheven en de verantwoordelijkheid voor het anti-witwastoezicht op makelaars is overgedragen aan *Her Majesty's Revenue and Customs* (HMRC). Binnen dit onderzoek was het onmogelijk om deze verandering mee te nemen, maar waar relevant wordt hier naar verwezen. In beginsel houden beroepsorganisaties toezicht op accountants. Twee van de in totaal elf beroepsorganisaties zijn in dit onderzoek betrokken: het *Institute of Chartered Accountants in England and Wales* (ICAEW) en de *Association of Accounting Technicians* (AAT).

Anti-witwastoezicht op **banken** wordt enerzijds door de FCA uitgevoerd als onderdeel van reguliere toezichtprocedures en anderzijds door een gespecialiseerd team dat financiële criminaliteit bestrijdt (*specialist financial crime supervision team*). Hoewel uit dit onderzoek blijkt dat er meer informatie moet worden verstrekt over de integratie van het anti-witwastoezicht in de reguliere toezichtprocedures van de FCA, wordt er ook geconcludeerd dat het gespecialiseerde team jaarlijks een groot aantal inspecties en onderzoeken ter plaatse doet bij banken. Dit gebeurt in het bijzonder binnen het doorlopende *Systematic Anti-Money Laundering Programme* (SAMLP) en middels thematisch toezicht op de mate van naleving van de verplichtingen uit het preventieve anti-witwasbeleid door banken. De FCA heeft een breed scala aan sanctiebevoegdheden. De FCA heeft ook een openbaar handhavingsbeleid en de opgelegde sancties worden, in beginsel, altijd gepubliceerd. De laatste jaren is de FCA actief geweest in het sanctioneren van banken die de verplichtingen uit het anti-witwasbeleid niet hadden nageleefd, terwijl het tegelijkertijd ook gebruik heeft gemaakt van vroege interventies en informele maatregelen. Met betrekking tot het anti-witwastoezicht op **makelaars** is het interessant om te zien dat, ondanks het feit dat het makelaarsberoep in het Verenigd Koninkrijk geen gereguleerd beroep is, de OFT een goed overzicht en kennis heeft van deze groep professionals. De Britse anti-witwasregelgeving verplicht alle professionals van niet-gereguleerde beroepen om zich te registreren bij hun toezichthouder. Deze verplichting, die niet terug te vinden is in de Derde richtlijn, zorgt ervoor dat alle toezichthouders een adequaat overzicht en kennis hebben van de (omvang van) de groep ondertoezichtstaanden. Desondanks heeft de OFT wel problemen gehad. Een van de zorgen die in dit onderzoek worden geuit betreft de lage toezichtintensiteit op makelaars in de afgelopen jaren ten opzichte van het totaal aantal makelaars. Onder de anti-witwasregelgeving heeft de OFT de mogelijkheid om afspraken te maken met de lokale overheidsdiensten voor handelsvoorschriften (*Local Authority Trading Standards*). Dit onderzoek betoogt dat deze afspraken schriftelijk moeten worden vastgelegd en openbaar moeten worden gemaakt. Een sterk aspect van het anti-witwastoezicht van de OFT is diens transparantie: de OFT is in dit onderzoek de enige anti-witwastoezichthouder op makelaars met een openbaar handhavingsbeleid dat speciaal voor het anti-witwasbeleid is ontworpen. Dit onderzoek beveelt de HMRC aan om dezelfde mate van transparantie te betrachten. Met betrekking tot de sanctionering valt het op dat de door de OFT opgelegde sancties bij makelaars steeds afschrikwekkender zijn geworden qua hoogte van de boetebedragen en de publicatie van opgelegde sancties. Ook is de OFT steeds vaker gaan sanctioneren voor niet-naleving van andere anti-witwasverplichtingen dan de registratieplicht.

Voor het anti-witwastoezicht op **accountants** concludeert dit onderzoek dat de ICAEW en de AAT in het algemeen een goed ontwikkelde toezichtpraktijk hebben. Er zijn echter wel enkele wijzigingen noodzakelijk. Belangrijke aandachtspunten zijn het gebrek aan voldoende marktonafhankelijkheid van de ICAEW en het uitvoeren van gerichte anti-witwasinspecties. Voor de ICAEW adviseert dit onderzoek om de uitkomsten van diens gerichte anti-witwastoezicht te publiceren. Voor de AAT wordt aanbevolen om dergelijke gerichte inspecties uit te voeren om te waarborgen dat er voldoende aandacht wordt geschonken aan de naleving van anti-witwasverplichtingen door de leden, en om dit aan de buitenwereld te laten zien. Op het gebied van sanctionering doen beide beroepsorganisaties het goed in vergelijking met de anti-witwastoezichthouders op accountants in Nederland, Spanje en Zweden.

Ook in het Verenigd Koninkrijk vindt de samenwerking tussen de anti-witwastoezichthouders plaats op institutioneel en operationeel niveau. Belangrijk is het *Anti-Money Laundering Supervisors' Forum (AMLSF)* waarin de toezichthouders hun ervaringen uit de praktijk delen, beleidsontwikkelingen bespreken en waarin zij de effectiviteit van hun toezicht en opgelegde sancties evalueren. Daarnaast bestaan er twee andere fora, waar enkele toezichthouders aan deelnemen: het *Money Laundering Advisory Committee* en *SARs Review Committee*. In 2012 werd in de Britse anti-witwasregelgeving een wettelijke basis gecreëerd waarmee de uitwisseling van informatie tussen de toezichthouders mogelijk werd gemaakt.

Zweden

De Zweedse anti-witwastoezichthouder op banken is de financieel toezichthouder *Finansinspektionen* (*FI*) en voor makelaars is dat de *Fastighetsmäklarinspektionen* (*FMI*). Het anti-witwastoezicht op accountants wordt door verschillende toezichthouders uitgeoefend. De *Revisorsnämnden* (RN) is verantwoordelijk voor het toezicht op accountants en accountantsorganisaties die bevoegd zijn om wettelijke controles uit te oefenen, terwijl de provinciebesturen (*Länsstyrelserna*) van Stockholm, Västra Götaland, en Skåne verantwoordelijk zijn voor het anti-witwastoezicht op de groep overige accountants.

Wat betreft het anti-witwastoezicht op **banken** concludeert dit onderzoek dat de Zweedse financieel toezichthouder de afgelopen jaren thematisch anti-witwastoezicht heeft uitgevoerd, maar dat deze transparanter moet worden over de inrichting en uitvoering van dit toezicht. Jaarplannen zijn niet openbaar, en de resultaten van de thematische onderzoeken naar de naleving van de anti-witwasregelgeving alsmede de mate waarin dit toezicht bij banken heeft plaatsgevonden zijn gefragmenteerd. De *Finansinspektionen* heeft bovendien geen openbaar handhavingsbeleid. Wat betreft het anti-witwastoezicht op **makelaars** in Zweden valt er veel te verbeteren. De *Fastighetsmäklarinspektionen* ontbreekt het aan adequate toezichtbevoegdheden, door de beperkte definitie van makelaars onder de Zweedse makelaarswetgeving en het ontbreken van een onafhankelijke bevoegdheid tot het uitvoeren van inspecties ter plaatse. Het anti-witwastoezicht is daardoor geheel *off-site* en voornamelijk van reactieve aard. De meeste toezichtactiviteiten van de *Fastighetsmäklarinspektionen* vloeien voort uit klachten van consumenten of derden-partijen, die in de meeste gevallen niet eens (primair) op de niet-naleving van de preventieve anti-witwasregelgeving zien. Het feit dat de meeste inspanningen voortkomen uit klachten is zorgelijk, omdat niet alle anti-witwasverplichtingen op een adequate manier (kunnen) worden nagegaan: de meldplicht en de verplichting tot het voeren van een intern beleid ter voorkoming van witwassen en financiering van terrorisme worden nauwelijks gecontroleerd, als deze überhaupt al worden meegenomen in het toezicht. Het is verrassend dat, ondanks het gebrek aan een proactief en risicogeoriënteerd toezicht en een gebrek aan adequate toezicht- en sanctioneringsbevoegdheden, het tuchtorgaan van de *Fastighetsmäklarinspektionen* tussen 2010 en 2013 een groot aantal makelaars heeft gesanctioneerd voor het niet naleven van de identificatieverplichting of de bewaarplicht.

Ten aanzien van het anti-witwastoezicht op **accountants** concludeert dit onderzoek dat het gebrek aan transparantie aan de zijde van *Revisorsnämnden* het meest problematisch is. De toezichthouder verstrekt geen informatie over de manier waarop deze het anti-witwastoezicht uitoefent en hoe het nagaan van naleving met de anti-witwasregelgeving geïntegreerd is in de reguliere toezichtprocedures. Een analyse van diens toezichtpraktijk bleek daardoor onhaalbaar binnen dit onderzoek. Voor de groep accountants die geen wettelijke controles uitvoeren hangt de toezichtverantwoordelijkheid van de drie provinciebesturen af van de vraag of deze professionals zich bij de Zweedse autoriteit voor de registratie van bedrijven (*Bolagsverket*) hebben geregistreerd. Het is echter zorgelijk dat de provinciebesturen geen bevoegdheden hebben om registratie af te dwingen. Het aantal inspecties ter plaatse is ook laag; dit heeft waarschijnlijk te maken met het feit dat de beperkte middelen door de provinciebesturen zijn aangewend om instellingen en professionals geregistreerd te krijgen. Dit onderzoek concludeert dat de invoering van risicogeoriënteerd toezicht in combinatie met meer toezicht ter plaatse (de effectiviteit van) het toezicht door de provinciebesturen zal verbeteren. Het is hierbij van groot belang dat de Zweedse wetgever voorziet in adequate sanctioneringsbevoegheden voor de provinciebesturen, omdat zij momenteel geen registratie kunnen afdwingen en ook niet direct kunnen sanctioneren bij het constateren van overtredingen van de anti-witwasregelgeving.

Op beleidsniveau kent Zweden het meest geïnstitutionaliseerde samenwerkingsverband tussen toezichthouders in het preventieve anti-witwasbeleid. De Zweedse anti-witwasregelgeving kent echter geen juridische basis voor de uitwisseling van toezichtinformatie tussen de toezichthouders. Op basis van de algemene wet- en regelgeving op het gebied van de uitwisseling van informatie door bestuursorganen lijkt de uitwisseling van toezichtinformatie tussen de anti-witwastoezichthouders slechts beperkt mogelijk.

Conclusie

Na een vergelijking van het anti-witwastoezicht op banken, accountants en makelaars in Spanje, Nederland, het Verenigd Koninkrijk en Zweden, kan worden geconcludeerd dat het meest effectieve anti-witwastoezicht te vinden is in het Verenigd Koninkrijk. Daar bestaan geen serieuze problemen in relatie tot de institutionele vereisten. Met uitzondering van één beroepsorganisatie hebben alle Britse anti-witwastoezichthouders in dit onderzoek een adequaat niveau van onafhankelijkheid van de politiek en van de markt. Geen van de toezichthouders heeft te maken met een gebrek aan middelen en het nodige overzicht en kennis van de (omvang van) de groep ondertoezichtstaanden wordt geregeld door een uitgebreide registratieplicht voor instellingen en professionals. De Britse toezichthouders zijn in de praktijk ook het meest transparant en leggen de meeste verantwoording af over het door hen uitgevoerde anti-witwastoezicht in vergelijking met de toezichthouders uit de andere drie landen. Tot slot is het juridische kader in het Verenigd Koninkrijk ook behoorlijk duidelijk en compleet. Dit onderzoek concludeert tegelijkertijd dat het minst effectieve anti-witwastoezicht kan worden gevonden in Spanje. Dit is het resultaat van een combinatie van factoren, maar volgt voornamelijk uit de keuze voor de financiële inlichtingeneenheid als enige anti-witwastoezichthouder in combinatie met een gebrek aan adequate middelen en de institutionele positie van SEPBLAC. Op basis van deze conclusie formuleert dit onderzoek een aantal aanbevelingen aan de Europese wetgever en de nationale wetgevers van Spanje, Nederland, het Verenigd Koninkrijk en Zweden om tot een sterker en effectiever anti-witwastoezicht te komen.

Bij de formulering van de onderzoeksvraag werd verondersteld dat de bevindingen over de effectiviteit van het anti-witwastoezicht in de vier EU-lidstaten het ook mogelijk zouden maken om conclusies te trekken over de effectiviteit van de modellen als zodanig. Dit onderzoek heeft echter aangetoond dat, hoewel kwesties omtrent de effectiviteit op nationaal niveau soms waren ontstaan door de keuze voor een bepaald toezichtmodel, sommige kwesties het gevolg waren van puur nationale aspecten, zoals slechte wetgeving of de toepassing van bevoegdheden door toezichthouders in de praktijk. Uiteindelijk hangt de effectiviteit van het toezicht dus voor een groot deel af van de implementatie van de modellen van anti-witwastoezicht in de nationale rechtsorde.

Bibliography

Literature

Accetto and Zleptnig (2005)

Accetto, M. and Zleptnig, S. (2005), 'The Principle of Effectiveness: Rethinking Its Role in Community Law', *European Public Law*, vol. 11, issue 3, pp. 375-403

Adamski (2014)

Adamski, D. (2014), 'Access to Documents, Accountability and the Rule of Law – Do Private Watchdogs Matter?', *European Law Journal*, vol. 20, issue 4, pp. 520-524

Addink (2005)

Addink, G.H. (2005), 'Principles of Good Governance: Lessons from Administrative Law', in: Curtin, D.M. and Wessels, R.A. Good *Governance and the European Union: Reflections on concepts, institutions and substance*, Intersentia: Antwerp 2005, pp. 21-48

Addink (2008)

Addink, G.H. (2008), 'Goed Bestuur: een norm voor het bestuur of het recht van een burger?', in: Addink, G.H., Jurgens, G., Langbroek Ph. M. and Widdershoven, R.J.G.M., *Grensverleggend Bestuursrecht*, Kluwer: Deventer, pp. 3-25

Addink (2009)

Addink, G.H. (2009), *Local and Regional level participation in Europe: A comparative exploratory study on the application of the participation principle at local and regional level within the framework of the Council of Europe*, Utrecht University

Addink (2010)

Addink, G.H. (2010), *Goed Bestuur*, Kluwer: Deventer

Addink et al. (2010)

Addink, G.A., Anthony, G., Buyse, A. and Flinterman, C. (2010), *Source Book on Human Rights and Good Governance*, SIM Special no. 34

Addink (2011)

Addink, G.H. (2011), 'De doorbraak van het beginselenrecht in het bestuursrecht: enkele opmerkingen over een conceptueel beginselenrecht', in: De Gier, T. et al. (eds.) (2011), *Goed verdedigbaar: vernieuwing van bestuursrecht en omgevingsrecht* (liber amoricum prof. mr. P.J.J. van Buuren), Kluwer: Deventer, pp. 3-16

Addink (2012)

Addink, G.H. (2012), 'Het concept 'goed bestuur' in het bestuursrecht en de praktische consequenties daarvan', *Ars Aequi*, April 2012, pp. 266-275

Addink (2014)
Addink, G.H. (2014), 'Europees bestuursrecht in ontwikkeling: op weg naar een Europese Awb', *Nederlands Tijdschrift voor Bestuursrecht* 2014-24
Addink (2015)
Addink. G.H. (2015), *Good Governance: Concept and Context*, OUP: Oxford (forthcoming)
Adriaanse et al. (2008)
Adriaanse, P.C. et al. (2008), *Implementatie van EU-handhavingsvoorschriften*, WODC: The Hague
Adriaanse et al. (2008a)
Adriaanse, P.C. et al. (2008a), 'Implementation of EU Enforcement Provisions: Between European Control and National Practice', *Review of European Administrative Law*, vol. 1, issue 2, pp. 83-97
Aelen (2014)
Aelen, M. (2014), *Beginselen van goed markttoezicht: Gedefinieerd, verklaard en uitgewerkt voor het toezicht op de financiële markten*, Boom Juridische uitgevers: The Hague (doctoral thesis Utrecht University)
Aelen and Van den Broek (2014)
Aelen, M. and van den Broek, M. (2014), 'De dubbele rol van het recht bij de effectiviteit van het financieel toezicht', *Tijdschrift voor Financieel Recht*, issue 1/2, pp. 12-22
Alldridge (2003)
Alldridge, P. (2003) *Money laundering law: forfeiture, confiscation, civil recovery, criminal laundering and taxation of the proceeds of crime*, Oxford: Hart Publishing
Alldridge (2008)
Alldridge, P. (2008), 'Money Laundering and Globalization', *Journal of Law and Society*, vol. 35, issue 4, pp. 437-463
Amrani (2012)
Amrani, H. (2012*), The Development of Anti-Money Laundering Regime: Challenging issues to sovereignty, jurisdiction, law enforcement, and their implications on the effectiveness in countering money laundering*, doctoral thesis Erasmus University Rotterdam, available at: <http://hdl.handle.net/1765/37747>
Andersson et al. (2013)
Andersson, M. Cerps, U. and Noréus, M. (2013), 'The Case for Analytical Supervision: The Swedish Perspective', in: Kellerman, A.J., De Haan, J. and De Vries, F. (eds.), *Financial Supervision in the 21st Century*, Springer Publishing, pp. 33-46
Argentiero et al. (2008)
Argentiero, A., Bagella, M. and Busato, F. (2008), 'Money Laundering in a Two-Sector Model: Using Theory for Measurement', *European Journal of Law and Economics*, vol. 26, issue 3, pp. 341-359
Arnull (2011)
Arnull, A. (2011), 'The Principle of Effective Judicial Protection in EU Law: an Unruly Horse?', *European Law Review*, vol. 36, pp. 51-70

Ayres and Braithwaite (1992)
Ayres, I. and Braithwaite, J. (1992), *Responsive Regulation: Transcending the Deregulation Debate*, Oxford University Press: New York

Bachmaier and del Moral García (2010)
Bachmaier, L. and del Moral García, M. (2010), *Criminal Law in Spain*, Kluwer Law International: Alphen aan den Rijn

Bagella et al. (2013)
Bagella, M., Busato, F. and Argentiero, A. (2013), 'Using dynamic macroeconomics for estimating money laundering: a simulation for the EU, Italy and the United States', in: Unger, B. and Van der Linde, D. (eds.), *Research Handbook on Money Laundering*, Edward Elgar Publishing Ltd: Cheltenham, pp. 207-223

Baldwin and Black (2008)
Baldwin, R. and Black, J. (2008), 'Really Responsive Regulation', *Modern Law Review*, vol. 71, issue 1, pp. 59-94

Bannier et al. (2008)
Bannier, F.A.W. et al. (2008), *Heeft de lokale deken een geheimhoudingsplicht en een verschoningsrecht?,* advies in opdracht van de Algemene Raad van de Nederlandse Orde van Advocaten

Bannier et al. (2008a)
Bannier, F.A.W., Duijst-Heesters, W. and Fanoy, N.A.M.E.C. (eds.) (2008), *Beroepsgeheim en verschoningsrecht: handboek voor de advocaat, medisch hulpverlener, notaris en geestelijke*, Sdu Uitgevers

Bannier and Fanoy (2010)
Bannier, F.A.W. and Fanoy, N.A.M.E.C. (2010), *Visie leerstoel advocatuur op toezicht door BFT,* advies in opdracht van de NOvA

Bar Cendón (2000)
Bar Cendon, A. (2000), 'Accountability and Public Administration: Concepts, Dimensions, Developments', in: Kelly, M. (ed.), *Openness and Transparency in Governance: Challenges and Opportunities*, Maastricht: EIPA, pp. 22-61

Bartle and Vass (2005)
Bartle, I. and Vass, P. (2005), 'Self-regulation and the regulatory State: A survey of policy and practice', *CRI Research report* 17

Becker (1968)
Becker, G.S. (1968), 'Crime and Punishment: An Economic Approach', *Journal of Political Economy*, vol. 76, pp. 169-217

Beck Jørgensen and Bozeman (2007)
Beck Jørgensen, T. and Bozeman, B. (2007), 'Public values: an inventory', *Administration & Society*, vol. 39, issue 3, pp. 354-381

Benito Sánchez (2006)
Benito Sánchez, C.D. (2006), 'Blanqueo de capitales y fraude inmobiliario', in: Sanz Mulas, N. (ed.), *El Desafío de la Criminalidad Organizada*, Comares Editorial: Granada, pp. 95-129

Bergström (2011)
Bergström, M. (2011), 'EU som lagstiftare inom straffrätten och reglerna mot penningtvätt', *Svensk Juristtidning*, issue 4, pp. 357-374

Betancor Rodríguez (1994)
Betancor Rodríguez, A. (1994), *Las administraciones independientes*, Tecnos: Madrid
Bingham (2007)
Bingham, T. (2007), 'The Rule of Law', *Cambridge Law Journal*, vol. 66, issue 1, pp. 67-85
Birkinshaw et al. (1990)
Birkinshaw, P., Harden, I., Lewis, N. (1990), *Government by moonlight: the hybrid parts of the state*, Unwin Hyman: London
Black (1996)
Black, J. (1996), 'Constitutionalising self-regulation', *Modern Law Review*, vol. 59, pp. 24-55
Blanc-Gonnet Jonason (2013)
Blanc-Gonnet Jonason, P. (2013), 'Sweden', in: Jansen, O.J.D.M.L. (ed.), *Administrative Sanctions in the European Union*, Intersentia: Antwerp, pp. 553-583
Blanco Cordero (2009)
Blanco Cordero, I. (2009), 'Eficacia del sistema de prevención del blanqueo de capitales: estudio del cumplimiento normativo (compliance) desde una perspectiva criminológica', *Eguzkilore*, issue 23, pp. 117-138
Blomberg and Michiels (1997)
Blomberg, A. and Michiels, F.C.M.A. (1997), *Handhaven met effect*, VUGA: Den Haag
Blomberg (2000)
Blomberg, A.B. (2000), *Integrale handhaving van milieurecht*, Boom Juridische uitgevers: The Hague (doctoral thesis Utrecht University)
Blomberg (2008)
Blomberg, A. (2008), 'European Influence on National Environmental Law Enforcement: Towards an Integrated Approach', *Review of European Administrative Law*, vol. 1, issue 2, pp. 39-81
Blomberg (2013)
Blomberg, A. (2013), 'Handhaving en toezicht', in: Michiels, F.C.M.A. and Muller, E.R. (2013), *Handhaving*, Kluwer: Deventer, 2nd edition, pp. 33-62
Booth et al. (2011)
Booth, R., Farrel QC, S., and Bastable, G. (2011*), Money Laundering Law and Regulation: A Practical Guide*, OUP: Oxford
Botchway (2001)
Botchway, F.N. (2001), 'Good Governance: The Old, The New, The Principle and The Elements', *Florida Journal of International Law*, vol. 13, pp. 159-210
Bovens (2007)
Bovens, M. (2007), 'Analysing and Assessing Accountability: A Conceptual Framework', *European Law Journal*, vol. 13, issue 4, pp. 447-468
Bovens (2010)
Bovens, M. (2010), 'Two Concepts of Accountability: Accountability as a Virtue and Accountability as a Mechanism', *West European Politics*, vol. 33, issue 5, pp. 946-967.

Bovens et al. (2012)
Bovens, M.A.P., 't Hart, P. and Van Twist, M.W.J. (2012), *Openbaar bestuur: beleid, organisatie en politiek*, Deventer: Kluwer
Braithwaite (2002)
Braithwaite, J. (2002), *Restorative Justice and Responsive Regulation*, Oxford University Press: New York
Bröring (2005)
Bröring, H.E. (2005), *De bestuurlijke boete*, Kluwer: Deventer
Brouwer (2013)
Brouwer, D. (2013), 'De forensische accountant als Paard van Troje?', *Accountancynieuws*, issue 3, 15 February 2013
Buijze (2009)
Buijze, A. (2009), 'Effectiviteit in het bestuursrecht', *Nederlands Tijdschrift voor Bestuursrecht* 2009-31
Buijze (2013)
Buijze, A. (2013), *The Principle of Transparency in EU law*, Boxpress: 's-Hertogenbosch (doctoral thesis Utrecht University)
Buisman (2011)
Buisman, S. (2011), 'The Influence of the European Legislator on the National Criminal Law of Member States: It Is All in the Combination Chosen', *Utrecht Law Review*, vol. 7, issue 3, pp. 137-155
Burkens et al. (2012)
Burkens, M.C, Kummeling, H.R.B.M., Vermeulen, B.P. and Widdershoven, R.J.G.M (2012), *Beginselen van de democratische rechtsstaat*, Kluwer: Deventer
Burrell et al. (2007)
Burrell, P. and Meakin, K. (2007), 'United Kingdom', in: W.H. Muller, C.H. Kälin and J.G. Goldworth, *Anti-Money Laundering: International Law and Practice*, John Wiley & Sons Ltd., pp. 369-380
Busuioc (2010)
Busuioc, M. (2010), *The Accountability of European Agencies: Legal Provisions and Ongoing Practices*, Eburon: Delft (doctoral thesis Utrecht University)
Busuioc and Groenleer (2014)
Busuioc, M. and Groenleer, M. (2014), 'The Theory and Practice of EU Agency Autonomy and Accountability: Early Day Expectations, Today's Realities and Future Perspectives, in: Everson, M., Monda, C. and Vos, E. (eds.), *European Agencies in Between Institutions and Member States*, Kluwer: Alphen aan de Rijn, pp. 175-200
Cañibano and Ucieda (2005)
Cañibano, L. and Ucieda, J.L. (2005), 'Accounting and financial reporting in Spain', *Research Paper UAM*, at 7, available at: <www.uam.es/personal_pdi/economicas/jlucieda/sci/canibano_ucieda_2005.pdf>
Caro (2010)
Caro, M.A. (2010), 'La ley crea un registro de expertos externos en blanqueo', Expansión, *suplemento 'Asesores de Empresas'*, pp. 33-36, available at: <www.ciss.es/expansion/>

Chowdhury and Skarstedt (2005)
Chowdhury, N. and Skarstedt, C.E. (2005), 'The Principle of Good Governance', *CISDL Draft Legal Working Paper*, Oxford
Cole (2005)
Cole, M. (2005), 'Quangos: The Debate of the 1970s in Britain', *Contemporary British History*, vol. 19, issue 3, pp. 321-352
Costa (2008)
Costa, S. (2008), 'Implementing the new anti-money laundering directive in Europe: Legal and enforcement issues – The Italian Case', *Global Business and Economics Review*, vol.10, issue 3, pp. 284-308
Costas-Pérez et al. (2012)
Costas-Pérez, E., Solé-Ollé, A., and Sorribas-Navarro, P. (2012), 'Corruption scandals, voter information and accountability', *European Journal of Political Economy*, vol. 28, issue 4, pp. 469-484
Craig (2008)
Craig, P.P. (2008), *Administrative law*, Sweet & Maxwell: London
Craig (2012)
Craig, P.P. (2012), *Administrative Law*, Sweet & Maxwell: London, 7th edition
Craig (2013)
Craig, P. (2013), 'A General Law on Administrative Procedure, Legislative Competence and Judicial Competence', *European Public Law*, vol. 19, issue 3, pp. 503-524
Craig and De Búrca (2008)
Craig, P. and De Búrca, G. (2008), *EU law: Text, Cases and Materials*, Oxford University Press: Oxford, 4th edition
Curtin and Dekker (2005)
Curtin, D.M. and Dekker, I. (2005), 'Good Governance: The concept and its application by the European Union', in: Curtin, D.M. and Wessels, R.A., Good *Governance and the European Union: Reflections on concepts, institutions and substance*, Intersentia: Antwerp, pp. 3-20
Curtin (2009)
Curtin, D. (2009), *Executive Power of the European Union: Law, Practices, and the Living Constitution*, Oxford University Press
Dal Bó (2006)
Dal Bó, E. (2006), 'Regulatory Capture: A Review', *Oxford Review of Economic Policy*, vol. 22, issue 2, pp. 203-225
Debelle and Fischer (1994)
Debelle, G. and Fischer, S. (1994), 'How independent should Central Banks be?', *Conference paper Federal Reserve Bank of Boston*
De Graaf et al. (2013)
De Graaf, G., Huberts, L. and Smulders, R. (2013), *Publieke waarden: De beginselen van goed bestuur in de dagelijkse praktijk van ziekenhuis en gemeente*, onderzoek in opdracht van het Ministerie van Binnenlandse Zaken en Koninkrijksrelaties

De Lange (2014)
De Lange, R. (2014), 'The United Kingdom of Great Britain and Northern Ireland', in: Besselink, L., Bovend'Eert, P., Broeksteeg, H., De Lange, R. and Voermans, W. (eds.), *Constitutional Law of the EU Member States*, Kluwer: Deventer, pp. 1651-1693
Deleanu (2014)
Deleanu, I. (2014), 'FIUs in the European Union – facts and figures, functions and facilities', in: Unger et al., *The Economic and Legal Effectiveness of the European Union's Anti-Money Laundering Policy*, Edward Elgar Publishing Ltd: Cheltenham, pp. 97-124
Deleanu and Van den Broek (2014)
Deleanu, I. and Van den Broek, M. (2014), 'International cooperation', in: Unger et al., *The Economic and Legal Effectiveness of the European Union's Anti-Money Laundering Policy*, Edward Elgar Publishing Ltd: Cheltenham, pp. 147-161
De Leeuw (2013)
De Leeuw, J. (2013), *Onderzoek naar de herpositionering van ZBO's*, research commissioned by the Ministry of Interior Affairs and Kingdom Relations, May 2013
Delicostopoulos (2003)
Delicostopoulos, J.S. (2003), 'Towards European Procedural Primacy in National Legal Systems', *European Law Journal*, vol. 9, issue 5, pp. 599-613
De Meij (2014)
De Meij, J.M. (2014), 'The Kingdom of Sweden', in: Besselink, L., Bovend'Eert, P., Broeksteeg, H., De Lange, R. and Voermans, W. (eds.), *Constitutional Law of the EU Member States*, Kluwer: Deventer, pp. 1589-1648
Demmke (2001)
Demmke, C. (2001), 'Towards Effective Environmental Regulation: Innovative Approaches in Implementing and Enforcing European Environmental Law and Policy', *Jean Monnet Working Paper* 5/01
De Moor-van Vugt (2001)
De Moor-Van Vugt (2001), *Toezicht achter matglas: Over de betekenis van transparantie voor toezicht op de naleving van regelgeving*, Boom Juridische uitgevers: The Hague
De Moor-van Vugt (2003)
De Moor-Van Vugt, A.J.C. (2003), 'Europese criteria voor milieutoezicht', in: Biezeveld, G.A. (ed.), *Handhaving van milieurecht vanuit Europees perspectief*, Boom Juridische uitgevers: The Hague, pp. 85-103
De Moor-van Vugt (2011)
De Moor-Van Vugt, A.J.C. (2011), 'Netwerken en de europeanisering van het toezicht', *SEW: Tijdschrift voor Europees en Economisch Recht*, issue 3, pp. 94-102
De Moor-van Vugt et al. (2009)
De Moor-Van Vugt, A.J.C., Du Perron, C.E. and Krop, P.J. (2009), *De bevoegdheden van De Nederlandsche Bank inzake Icesave*, research commissioned by the Dutch Ministry of Finance
De Moor-van Vugt et al. (2012)
De Moor-Van Vugt, A.J.C. et al. (2012), *Gegevensuitwisseling door Toezichthouders*, WODC: The Hague, research commissioned by the Ministry of Security & Justice

Dickson (2013)
Dickson, J. (2013), 'Supervision: Looking Ahead to the Next Decade', in: Kellerman, A.J., De Haan, J. and De Vries, F. (eds.), *Financial Supervision in the 21st Century*, Springer Publishing, pp. 221-232

Diekman (2010)
Diekman, P. (2010), 'Meldplichten voor accountants: Complex Spoorboekje', *De Accountant*, March 2010

Docters van Leeuwen and Korte (2006)
Docters van Leeuwen, A.W.H. and Korte, H.W.O.L.M. (2006), 'Toezichtautoriteiten, in het bijzonder de AFM', in: Michiels, F.C.M.A. and Muller, E.R. (eds.), *Handhaving*, Kluwer: Deventer, pp. 335-355

Docters van Leeuwen (2010)
Docters van Leeuwen, A. (2010), *Het bestaande is geen alternatief: een verkenning naar verbeteringen in het toezicht op de advocatuur*, NSOB.

Doorenbos (2007)
Doorenbos, D.R. (2007), *Naming & Shaming*, Serie Onderneming en Recht, no. 38

Dougan (2011)
Dougan, M. (2011), 'The Vicissitudes of Life at the Coalface: Remedies and Procedures for Enforcing Union Law before the National Courts', in: Craig, P. and de Búrca, G., *Evolution of EU Law*, 2nd edition, Oxford: Oxford University Press, pp. 693-746

Doyle (1997)
Doyle, C. (1997), 'Self-Regulation and Statutory Regulation', *Business Strategy Review*, vol. 8, issue 3, pp. 35-42

Duijkersloot (2007)
Duijkersloot, A.P.W. (2007), *Staats- en Bestuursrecht: Toezicht op gereguleerde markten*, Ars Aequi Libri

Duijkersloot (2013)
Duijkersloot, A.P.W. (2013), 'Handhaving door marktautoriteiten', in: Michiels, F.C.M.A. and Muller, E.R. (eds.), *Handhaving*, Kluwer: Deventer, 2nd edition, pp. 341-360

Duijkersloot and Kummeling (2012)
Duijkersloot, T. and Kummeling, H. (2012), 'Onnodig en onwenselijk: de geheimzinnigheid van DNB', *Nederlands Juristenblad*, 2012/5.

Duijkersloot and Kummeling (2012a)
Duijkersloot, T. and Kummeling, H. (2012a), 'Parlement en geheime toezichtinformatie', in: Kummeling, H.R.B.M., de Morree, P.E., Nehmelman, R., Ortlep, R. and Widdershoven, R.J.G.M. (eds.), *De samengestelde Besselink: Bruggen bouwen tussen nationaal, Europees en internationaal recht*, Wolf Legal Publishers, pp. 75-82

Dyrberg (2002)
Dyrberg, P. (2002), 'Accountability and Legitimacy: What is the Contribution of Transparency?', in: Arnull, A. and Wincott, D. (eds.), *Accountability and Legitimacy in the European Union*, Oxford University Press, pp. 81-96

Eckart (2008)
Eckart, S.E. (2008), 'The US regulatory approach to terrorist financing', in: Biersteker, T.J. and Eckart, S.E. (eds.), *Countering the financing of terrorism*, Routledge, pp. 218-219

Eijlander (1993)
Eijlander, Ph. (1993), *De wet stellen: Beschouwingen over onderwerpen van wetgeving*, Tjeenk Willink: Zwolle

Esty (2006)
Esty, D.C. (2006), 'Good Governance at the Supranational Scale: Globalizing Administrative Law', *The Yale Law Journal*, vol. 115, issue 7, pp. 1490-1562

Faraldo Cabana (2007)
Faraldo Cabana, P. (2007), 'Legal professionals and money laundering in Spain', *Journal of Money Laundering Control*, vol. 10, issue 3, pp. 318-336

Faure et al. (2009)
Faure, M., Nelen, H. and Philipsen, N. (2009), *Evaluatie tuchtrechtelijke handhaving: Wet ter voorkoming van witwassen en financiering van terrorisme en haar voorlopers*, Boom Juridische uitgevers: The Hague

Faure (2010)
Faure, M.G. (2010), 'Effective, Proportional and Dissuasive Penalties in the Implementation of the Environmental Crime and Ship source Pollution Directives: Questions and Challenges', *European Energy and Environmental Law Review*, vol. 19, issue 6, pp. 256-278

Fernández Rojas (2005)
Fernández Rojas, G. (2005), 'Las Administraciones Independientes de Regulación y Supervisión en España', *Vniversitas*, issue 109, pp. 419-460

Ferran and Babis (2013)
Ferran, E. And Babis, V. (2013), 'The European Single Supervisory Mechanism', *University of Cambridge Faculty of Law Legal Study Research Papers* 10/2013

Ferro Veiga (2012)
Ferro Veiga, J.M. (2012), *Propriedad inmobiliairia: Blanqueo de capital y crimen organizado*, ECU: Alicante

Ferwerda et al. (2007)
Ferwerda, H. et al. (2007), *Malafide activiteiten in de vastgoedsector: Een exploratief onderzoek naar aard, actoren en aanpak*, research commissioned by the Dutch Ministry of Justice

Ferwerda (2012)
Ferwerda, J. (2012), *The Multidisciplinary Economics of Money Laundering*, Tjalling C. Koopmans Dissertation Series, USE 007 (doctoral thesis Utrecht University), at 5 and 29-38

Ferwerda (2013)
Ferwerda, J. (2013), 'The Effects Of Money Laundering', in: Unger, B. and Van der Linde, D. (eds.), *Research Handbook on Money Laundering*, Edward Elgar Publishing Ltd: Cheltenham, pp. 35-46

Ferwerda (2014)
Ferwerda, J. (2014), 'Definitions of money laundering practice', in: Unger et al., *The Economic and Legal Effectiveness of the European Union's Anti-Money Laundering Policy*, Edward Elgar Publishing Ltd: Cheltenham, pp. 87-96

Ferwerda (2014a)
Ferwerda, J. (2014a), 'Collection of statistics', in: Unger et al., *The Economic and Legal Effectiveness of the European Union's Anti-Money Laundering Policy*, Edward Elgar Publishing Ltd: Cheltenham, pp. 162-186

Ferwerda (2014b)
Ferwerda, J. (2014b), 'Cost-benefit analysis', in: Unger et al., *The Economic and Legal Effectiveness of the European Union's Anti-Money Laundering Policy*, Edward Elgar Publishing Ltd: Cheltenham, pp. 205-219

Feteris (2009)
Feteris, M.W.C. (2009), *Formeel belastingrecht*, Kluwer: Deventer

Flinders (1999)
Flinders, M.V. (1999), 'Setting the Scene: Quangos in Context', in: Flinders, M.V. and Smith, M.J. (eds.) (1999), *Quangos, Accountability and Reform*, MacMillan Press Ltd, pp. 3-16

Frankel (1989)
Frankel, M.S. (1989), 'Professional Codes: Why, How and with What Impact?', *Journal of Business Ethics*, vol. 8, pp. 109-115

Friedman and Philips (2004)
Friedman, A. and Phillips, M. (2004), 'Balancing strategy and Accountability: A Model for the Governance of Professional Associations', *Nonprofit management and Leadership*, vol. 15, issue 2, pp. 187-204

Gallardo Castillo (2008)
Gallardo Castillo, M.J. (2008), *Los Principios de la Potestad Sancionadora: Teoría y práctica*, Iustel: Madrid

García Sanz and San Pedro (2007)
García Sanz, J. and G. San Pedro (2007), 'Spain', in: Muller, W.H., C.H. Kälin and J.G. Goldsworth (eds.), *Anti-Money Laundering: International Law and Practice*, John Wiley & Sons Ltd., pp. 513-526

García Ureta (2006)
García Ureta, A. (2006), *La potestad inspectora de las Administraciones públicas*, Marcial Pons

Gay (1996)
Gay, O. (1996), 'The Quango Debate', *Research Paper* 96/72, House of Commons Library

Gerbrandy (2009)
Gerbrandy, A. (2009), *Convergentie in het mededingingsrecht*, Boom Juridische uitgevers: The Hague (doctoral thesis Utrecht University)

Gilardi (2005)
Gilardi, F. (2005), 'The Formal Independence of Regulators: A Comparison of 17 Countries and 7 Sectors, *Swiss Political Science Review*, vol. 11, issue 3, pp. 139-167

Gilmore (2011)
Gilmore, W.C. (2011), *Dirty Money: the evolution of international measures to counter money laundering and the financing of terrorism*, Council of Europe Publishing, 4th edition
Goodhart and Schoenmaker (1998)
Goodhart, C. and Schoenmaker, D. (1998), 'Institutional Separation Between Supervisory and Monetary Agencies', in: Goodhart, C.A.E. (ed.), *The Emerging Framework of Financial Regulation*, Central Banking Publications: London, pp. 133-212
Goodhart et al. (1998)
Goodhart, C.A.E., Hartmann, Ph., Llewellyn, D., Rojas-Suaréz, Weisbrod (1998), *Financial Regulation: Why, how and where now?*, London: Routledge
Greve et al.(1999)
Greve, C., Flinders, M. and Van Thiel, S. (1999), 'Quango's: What's In A Name?: Defining Quango's from a Comparative Perspective', *Governance: An International Journal of Policy and Administration*, vol. 12, issue 2, pp. 129-146
Grilli et al. (1991)
Grilli, V. Masciandaro, D. and Tabellini, G. (1991), 'Political and monetary institutions and public financial policies in the industrial countries', *Economic Policy*, vol. 6, issue 13, pp. 342-392
Grønbech-Jensen (1998)
Grønbech-Jensen, C. (1998) 'The Scandinavian Tradition of Open Government and the European Union: Problems of Compatibility?', *Journal of European Public Policy*, vol. 5, issue 1, pp. 185-199
Grundmann-van de Krol (2012)
Grundmann-van de Krol, C.M. (2012), *Koersen door de Wet financieel toezicht*, Boom Juridische uitgevers: The Hague
Hägerhäll Aniansson and Lohm (2002)
Hägerhäll Aniansson, B. and Lohm, U. (2002), 'An Introduction to Östergötland, the Case Region', in: Svedin, U. and Hägerhall Aniansson, B. (eds.), *Sustainability, Local Development and The Future: The Swedish Model*, Kluwer: Dordrecht, pp. 83-98
Harding (1997)
Harding, C. (1997), 'Member State Enforcement of European community Measures: The Chimera of 'Effective Enforcement', *Maastricht Journal for European and Comparative Law*, vol. 4, issue 5, pp. 5-24
Harvey (2005)
Harvey, J. (2005), 'An evaluation of money laundering policies', *Journal of Money Laundering Control*, vol. 8, issue 4, pp. 339-345
Hatje (2001)
Hatje, A. (2001), *Loyalität als Rechtsprinzip in der Europäischen Union*, Nomos: Baden-Baden
Hawkins and Thomas (1984)
Hawkins, K. and Thomas, J.M. (1984), 'The Regulatory Process: Issues and Concepts', in: Hawkins and Thomas, *Enforcing Regulation*, Kluwer: Boston, pp. 3-23

Helikoski and Leino (2006)
Heliskoski, J. and Leino, P. (2006), 'Darkness at the break of noon: The case law on Regulation 1049/2001 on access to documents', *Common Market Law Review*, vol. 43, issue 3, pp. 735-781

Helsloot and Haverkate (2013)
Helsloot, I. and I.L. Haverkate (2013), 'Handhaving van brandveiligheid; een pars pro toto?', in: Michiels, F.C.M.A. and Muller, E.R. (eds.), *Handhaving*, Kluwer: Deventer, 2nd edition, pp. 461-482

Henretty et al. (2012)
Henretty, C., Larouche, P., Reindl, A. (2012), *Independence, accountability and perceived quality of regulators: a CERRE Study*, Brussels, available at: <www.cerre.eu/sites/default/files/report_container.pdf>

Héritier (2003)
Héritier, A. (2003), 'Composite democracy in Europe: the role of transparency and access to information', *Journal of European Public Policy*, vol. 10, issue 5, pp. 814-833

Herlitz (1953)
Herlitz, N. (1953), 'Swedish Administrative Law', *International and Comparative Law Quarterly*, vol. 2, pp. 224-237

Hofmann and Mihaescu (2013)
Hofmann, H.C.H. and Mihaescu, C. (2013), 'The Relation between the Charter's Fundamental Rights and the Unwritten General Principles of EU Law: Good Administration as the Test Case', *European Constitutional Law Review*, vol. 9, issue 1, pp. 73-101

Houben (2013)
Houben, A. (2013), 'Aligning Macro- and Microprudential Supervision', in: Kellerman, A.J., De Haan, J. and De Vries, F. (eds.), *Financial Supervision in the 21st Century*, Springer Publishing, pp. 201-220

Huberts and Van Hout (2011)
Huberts, L.W.J.C. and Van Hout, E.J.Th. (2011), 'Goed bestuur: kiezen of delen?', *Bestuurskunde,* vol. 20, issue 2, pp. 53-62

Hunter (1984)
Hunter, J. (1984), 'Development of the Rule against Double Jeopardy', *Journal of Legal History*, vol. 5, issue 1, pp. 1-19

Hüpkes et al. (2005)
Hüpkes, E.H.G., Quintyn, M. and Taylor, M.W. (2005), 'The Accountability of Financial Sector Supervisor: Principles and Practice', *IMF Working Paper*, WP/05/51

Jacobstein and Mersky (1990)
Jacobstein, J.M. and Mersky, R.M. (1990), *Fundamentals of legal research*, Foundation Press: New York

Jans et al. (2007)
Jans, J.H., De Lange, R., Prechal, S. and Widdershoven, R.J.G.M. (2007), *Europeanisation of public law*, Europa Law Publishing: Groningen

Jansen (2013)

Jansen, O.J.D.M.L. (2013), 'The Netherlands', in: Jansen, O.J.D.M.L. (ed), *Administrative Sanctions in the European Union*, Intersentia, pp. 317-465

Jerez Darías et al. (2012)

Jerez Darías, L.M., Martín Martín, V.O. and Pérez González, R. (2012), 'Aproximación a una geografía de la corrupción urbanística en España', *Ería*, issue 87, pp. 5-18

Joerges et al. (2001)

Joerges, C., Meny, Y.and Weiler, J.H.H. (eds.), 'Mountain or Molehill? A critical appraisal of the Commission's White paper on Governance', *Jean Monnet Working Paper*, No. 6/01.

Kagan and Scholz (1984)

Kagan, R.A. and Scholz, J.T. (1984), 'The "Criminology of the Corporation" and Regulatory Enforcement Strategies', in: Hawkins and Thomas (eds.), *Enforcing Regulation*, Kluwer: Boston, pp. 68-95

Kapteyn (2008)

Kapteyn, P.J.G., VerLoren van Themaat, P. (2008*), The law of the European Union and the European Communities*, Kluwer: Deventer

Katz (2007)

Katz, E. (2007), 'Implementation of the Third Money Laundering Directive – an overview', *Law and Financial Markets Review*, vol. 1, issue 3, pp. 207-211

Kernaghan (2003)

Kernaghan, K. (2003), 'Integrating Values into Public Service: The Values Statement as Centerpiece', *Public Administration Review*, vol. 63, issue 6, pp. 711-719

Kolkman and Reckweg (2012)

Kolkman, D.S. and Reckweg, C.A. (2012), 'WWFT wijzigingen 2013', in: Bureau Financieel Toezicht, *Nieuwsbrief Toezicht*, vol. 8, issue 2, winter edition, pp. 8-11

Kómarek (2008)

Komárek, J. (2008), 'Legal Professional Privilege and the EU's fight against Money Laundering', *Civil Justice Quarterly*, vol. 27, issue 1, pp. 13-22

Kremers and Schoenmaker (2010)

Kremers, J. and Schoenmaker, D. (2010), 'Twin Peaks: Experiences in the Netherlands', *LSE Financial Markets Group Paper Series*, Special Paper 196, December 2010

Kruisbergen et al. (2012)

Kruisbergen, E.W., Van de Bunt, H.G. and Kleemans, E.R. (2012), *Georganiseerde criminaliteit in Nederland: vierde rapportage op basis van de Monitor Georganiseerde Criminaliteit*, research commissioned by the Dutch Ministry of Security & Justice

Lander (2006)

Lander, S. (2006), *Review of the Suspicious Activity Reports Regime*, March 2006

Langbroek et al. (2012)

Langbroek, Ph., Buijze, A. and Remac, M. (2012), *Designing Administrative Pre-Trial Proceedings*, Eleven International Publishing

Lavrijssen (2006)
Lavrijssen, S.A.C.M. (2006), *Onafhankelijke mededingstoezichthouders, regulerende bevoegdheden en de waarborgen voor good governance*, Boom Juridische uitgevers: The Hague (doctoral thesis Utrecht University)
Leeuw (2011)
Leeuw, F.L. (2011), 'Can legal research benefit from evaluation studies?', *Utrecht Law Review*, vol. 7, issue 1, pp. 52-65
Leftwich (1993)
Leftwich, A. (1993), 'Governance democracy and development in the Third World', *Third World quarterly*, vol. 14, issue 3, pp. 605-624
Lehmann Nielsen (2006)
Lehmann Nielsen, V. (2006), 'Are Regulators Responsive?', *Law & Policy*, vol. 28, issue 3, pp. 395-416
Leliveld (2007)
Leliveld, J.T.C. (2007), 'De toezichtbepalingen van de Wft', *Tijdschrift voor Financieel Recht*, issue 7-8, pp. 216-220
Llewellyn (2006)
Llewellyn, D.T. (2006), *Institutional structure of financial regulation and supervision: the basic issues*, Paper presented at the World Bank seminar 'Aligning Supervisory Structures with country needs', Washington DC, 6-7 June 2006
López Menudo (1992)
Lopéz Menudo, F. (1992), 'Los principios generales del procedimiento administrativo', *Revista de Administración Pública*, issue 129, Sept-Dec 1992, pp. 19-76
López Torralba (2005)
López Torralba, V. (2005), 'Breve estudio en torno al Procedimiento Administrativo Sancionador y sus garantías', *Revista Jurídica de la Comunidad de Madrid*, issue 22, September 2005, pp. 181-244
Luchtman et al. (2002)
Luchtman, M.J.J.P. Vervaele J.A.E. and Jansen, O.J.D.M.L (2002), *Informatie-uitwisseling in het kader van het Financieel Expertise Centrum*, research commissioned by the Ministry of Finance
Luchtman and Van der Hoeven (2009)
Luchtman, M.J.J.P and Hoeven, R. van der (2009), 'Case C-305/05, Ordre des barreaux francophone et germanaphones et al. v Conseil des Ministre, judgment of 26 June 2007, Grand Chamber ; [2007] ECR I-5305', *Common Market Law Review*, vol. 46, issue 1, pp. 301-318.
Lumpkin (2002)
Lumpkin, S. (2002), 'Supervision of Financial services in the OECD Area', *OECD Working paper*
Magide Herrero (2000)
Magide Herrero, M. (2000), *Límites constitucionales de las administraciones independientes*, INAP: Madrid

Magnusson (2009)
Magnusson, D. (2009), 'The costs of implementing the anti-money laundering regulations in Sweden', *Journal of Money Laundering Control*, vol. 12, issue 2, pp. 101-112

Masciandaro (2013)
Masciandaro, D. (2013), 'Money Laundering And Its Effects on Crime: A Macroeconomic Approach', in: Unger, B. and Van der Linde, D. (eds.), *Research Handbook on Money Laundering*, Edward Elgar Publishing Ltd: Cheltenham, pp. 47-56

Mascini and Van Wijk (2009)
Mascini, P. and Van Wijk, E. (2009), *Responsive regulation door de Voedsel en Waren Autoriteit: Een empirisch onderzoek naar de theoretische veronderstellingen*, Boom Juridische uitgevers: The Hague

Matusitz (2013)
Matusitz, J. (2013*), Terrorism and Communication: A Critical Introduction*, Sage Publications Inc.

May (2004)
May, P. J. (2004), 'Compliance Motivations: Affirmative and Negative Bases', in: *Law and Society Review*, vol. 38, issue 1, pp. 41-68

May and Wood (2003)
May, P.J. and Wood, R.S. (2003), 'At the Regulatory Front Lines: Inspectors' Enforcement Styles and Regulatory Compliance', *Journal of Public Administration Research and Theory*, vol. 13, issue 2, pp. 117-139

McEldowney (2013)
McEldowney, J. (2013), 'United Kingdom', in: Jansen, O.J.D.M.L. (ed.), *Administrative Sanctions in the European Union*, Intersentia: Antwerp, pp. 585-604

Mendes (2009)
Mendes, J. (2009), 'Good Administration in EU Law and the European Code of Good Administrative Behaviour', *EUI Working Papers Law* no. 2009/09.

Michiels (2006)
Michiels, F.C.M.A. (2006), *Houdbaar Handhavingsrecht*, Kluwer: Deventer

Michiels (2007)
Michiels, F.C.M.A. (2007), '"Naming and Shaming" in het markttoezicht', *Nederlands Tijdschrift voor Bestuursrecht* 2007-3, pp. 85-95

Michiels (2013)
Michiels. F.C.M.A. (2013), 'Handhavingsrecht en handhavingsbeleid', in: Michiels, F.C.M.A. and Muller, E.R. (eds.), *Handhaving*, Kluwer: Deventer, pp. 21-31

Mitchell et al. (1998)
Mitchell, A., Sikka, P., Willmot, H. (1998), *The Accountants' Laundromat*, Monograph, Southgate Publishers

Mitchell et al. (1998a)
Mitchell, A., Sikka, P., Willmot, H. (1998), 'Sweeping it under the carpet: The role of accountancy firms in money laundering', *Accounting, Organizations and Society*, vol. 23, issue 5/6, pp. 589-607

Mitsilegas (2003)

Mitsilegas, V. (2003) *Counter-measures in the European Union: A New Paradigm of Security Governance versus Fundamental Legal Principles*, Kluwer Law International: The Hague-Boston-London

Mitsilegas (2009)

Mitsilegas, V. (2009) 'The third wave of third pillar law: which direction for EU criminal justice?', *Queen Mary University of London, School of Law Legal Studies Research Paper* No. 33/2009

Mitsilegas and Gilmore (2007)

Mitsilegas, V. and Gilmore, W.C. (2007), 'The EU legislative framework against money laundering and terrorist finance: A critical analysis in the light of evolving global standards', *International and Comparative Law Quarterly*, vol. 56, issue 1, pp. 119-140

Molander et al. (2002)

Molander, P., Nilsson J.E., and Schick, A. (2002), *Does anyone govern? The relationship between the Government Office and the agencies in Sweden*, Report from the SNS Constitutional Project

Møller (2005)

Møller, L.H.E. (2005), 'Hoe ver reikt het zogenoemde 'informele verschoningsrecht?', *Weekblad Fiscaal Recht*, 6606, pp. 3-8

Mowbray (2007)

Mowbray, A. (2007), *Cases and Materials on the European Convention on Human Rights*, Oxford University Press: Oxford

Mulig and Smith (2004)

Mulig, E.V. and Smith, M. (2004), 'Understanding and Preventing Money Laundering', *Internal Auditing*, vol. 19, issue 5, p. 22-25.

Nergelius (2011)

Nergelius, J. (2011), *Constitutional law in Sweden*, Kluwer Law International

Nieto (2002)

Nieto, A. (2002), *Derecho administrative sancionador,* 3rd edition, Tecnos: Madrid

Niklasson (2012)

Niklasson, B. (2012), 'Sweden', in: Verhoest, K., Van Thiel, S., Bouckaert, G. and Lægreid (eds.), *Government Agencies: Practices in Lessons from 30 Countries*, pp. 245-258

Öhman and Wallerstedt (2012)

Öhman, P. and Wallerstedt, E. (2012), 'Audit regulation and the development of the auditing profession: The case of Sweden', *Accounting History*, vol. 17, issue 2, pp. 241-257

Oldenziel (1998)

Oldenziel, H.A. (1998), *Wetgeving en rechtszekerheid:*
een onderzoek naar de *bijdrage* van het *legaliteitsvereiste aan* de *rechtszekerheid* van de burger, Kluwer: Deventer (doctoral thesis University of Groningen)

Ottow (2006)
Ottow, A.T. (2006), *Telecommunicatietoezicht. De invloed van het Europese en Nederlandse bestuurs(proces)recht*, Boom Juridische uitgevers: The Hague (doctoral thesis University of Amsterdam)
Ottow (2011)
Ottow, A. (2011), 'Europeanisering van het markttoezicht', *SEW: Tijdschrift voor Europees en Economisch Recht*, issue 1, pp. 3-17
Ottow (2011a)
Ottow, A. (2011a), 'Het Europese toezicht op de financiële markten', *Regelmaat* 2011/4, pp. 202-212
Ottow (2013)
Ottow, A.T. (2013), 'The different levels of protection national supervisors' independence in the European landscape', in: Comtois, S. and De Graaf, K.J. (eds.), *On Judicial and Quasi-Judicial Independence*, Boom Juridische uitgevers: The Hague, pp. 139-155
Ottow (2014)
Ottow, A. (2014), 'The New European Supervisory Architecture of the Financial Markets', in: Everson, M., Monda, C. and Vos, E. (eds.), *European Agencies in Between Institutions and Member States*, Kluwer: Alphen aan de Rijn, pp. 123-143
Ottow and Lavrijssen (2011)
Ottow, A.T. and Lavrijssen, S.A.C.M. (2011), 'Het Europese recht als hoeder van de onafhankelijkheid van nationale toezichthouders', *Tijdschrift voor Toezicht*, vol. 2, issue 3, pp. 34-50
Ottow and Lavrijssen (2012)
Ottow, A. and Lavrijssen, S. (2012), 'Independent Supervisory Authorities: A Fragile Concept', *Legal Issues of Economic Integration*, vol. 39, issue 4, pp. 419-445
Ottow and De Cock Buning (2013)
Ottow, A.T. and De Cock Buning, M. (2013), 'Juridisch ruggengraat toezicht mag niet ontbreken', *Tijdschrift voor Toezicht*, vol. 4, issue 4, pp. 33-38
Paláez Martos (2009)
Paláez Martos, J.M. (2009), *Fraude Fiscal, Blanqueo de capitales y corrupción en el Sector Inmobiliario*, Kluwer España
Paterson et al. (2003)
Paterson, I., Fink, M. and Ogus, A. (2003), *Economic impact of regulation in the field of liberal professions in different Member States: Regulation of Professional Services*, Study for the European Commission DG Competition
Perelló Domenech (1994)
Perelló Domenech, I. (1994), 'Derecho administrativo sancionador y jurisprudencia constitucional', *Jueces para la democracia*, issue 22, pp. 76-81
Pernice (2013)
Pernice, I. (2013), 'The Right to Effective Judicial Protection and Remedies in the EU', in: Court of Justice of the European Union, *The Court of Justice and Construction of Europe: Analyses and Perspectives on Sixty-Years of Case Law*, Asser Press: The Hague, pp. 381-397

Pheijffer (2000)
Pheijffer, M. (2000), *De forensisch accountant: het recht meester*, Koninklijke Vermande: The Hague (doctoral thesis Leiden University)
Ping (2004)
Ping, H. (2004), *The fight against money laundering: a comparative perspective*, doctoral thesis Erasmus University Rotterdam
Polinsky and Shavell (2000)
Polinsky, A.M. and Shavell, S. (2000), 'The Economic Theory of Public Enforcement of Law', *Journal of Economic Literature*, vol. 38, pp. 45-76
Ponce (2005)
Ponce, J., (2005), 'Good Administration and Administrative Procedures', *Indiana Journal of Global Legal Studies*, vol. 12, issue 2, pp. 551-588
Prechal and Widdershoven (2011)
Prechal, S. and Widdershoven, R. (2011), 'Effectiveness or Effective Judicial Protection: A Poorly Articulated Relationship, in: Baumé, T., Oude Elferink, E., Phoa, P. and Thiaville, D. (eds.), *Today's Multilayered Legal Order: Current Issues and Perspectives,* Paris Legal Publishers: Zutphen, pp. 283-296
Quintyn and Taylor (2003)
Quintyn, M. and Taylor, M.W. (2003), 'Regulatory and supervisory independence and financial stability', *CESifo Economic Studies*, vol. 49, issue 2, pp. 259-294
Quintyn et al. (2007)
Quintyn, M., Ramirez, S., and Taylor, M.W. (2007), 'The Fear of Freedom: Politicians and the Independence and Accountability of Financial Sector Supervisors', *IMF Working Paper*, WP/07/25
Quintyn (2009)
Quintyn, M. (2009), 'Independent agencies: More than a Cheap Copy of Independent Central Banks?', *Constitutional Political Economy*, vol. 20, issue 3, pp. 267–295
Quirk (1996)
Quirk, P.J. (1996), 'Macroeconomic implications of money laundering', *IMF Working Paper*, no. 96/66
Rebollo Puig et al. (2013)
Rebollo Puig, M., Izquierdo Carrasco, M., Alarcón Sotomayor, L. and Bueno Armijo, A. (2013), 'Spain', in: Jansen, O.J.D.M.L (ed.), *Administrative sanctions in the European Union*, Intersentia: Antwerp, pp. 515-551
Reuter (2013)
Reuter, P. (2013), 'Are Estimates of The Volume of Money Laundering Either Feasible Or Useful?', in: Unger, B. and Van der Linde, D. (eds.), *Research Handbook on Money Laundering*, Edward Elgar Publishing Ltd: Cheltenham, pp. 224-231
Rietbroek (2013)
Rietbroek, S. (2013), 'De Zeven AML Zonden van HSBC', *Tijdschrift voor Compliance*, issue 1, pp. 56-59
Rietbroek (2013a)
Rietbroek, S. (2013a), 'De Zeven Anti-Money Laundering Zonden van HSBC', *Tijdschrift voor Compliance*, issue 2, pp. 168-170

Rietrae (2007)
Rietrae, J. (2007), 'The 3rd EU anti-money laundering directive: main issues and intriguing details', in: Van Duyne, P.C., Maljevic, A., Van Dijck, M., Von Lampe, K. and Harvey, J. (eds.), *Crime Business and Crime Money in Europe. The Dirty Linen of Illegal Enterprise*, Wolf Legal Publishers, pp. 15-42

Rivero Ortega (1999)
Rivero Ortega, R. (1999), *El estado vigilante*, Editorial Tecnos

Roberge (2011)
Roberge, I. (2011), 'Financial Action Task Force', in: Hale, T. and Held, D. (eds.), *The Handbook of Transnational Governance: Institutions and Innovation*, Polity Press: Cambridge, pp. 45-50

Rogier (1992)
Rogier, L.J.J. (1992), *Strafsancties, administratieve sancties en het una-via beginsel*, Gouda Quint (doctoral thesis Erasmus University Rotterdam)

Ross and Hannan (2007)
Ross, S. and Hannan, M. (2007), 'Money laundering regulation and risk-based decision making', *Journal of Money Laundering Control*, vol. 10, issue 1, pp. 106-115

Roth (2008)
Roth, G.P. (2008), 'De stille curator in de Wet op het financieel toezicht: Een kritische verkenning van een buitenissige rechtsfiguur', *Tijdschrift voor financieel recht*, issue 9, pp. 289-298

Santamaría Pastor (2000)
Santamaría Pastor, J.A. (2000), *Principios de Derecho Administrativo*, Volumen II, Editorial Centro de Estudios Ramón Areces, S.A.

Sauvé (2010)
Sauvé, A.M.P.J.H. (2010), *Naming and Shaming: Een onderzoek naar de juridische mogelijkheden en beperkingen voor de Arbeidsinspectie om op het terrein van de Arbeidsomstandighedenwet, de Arbeidstijdenwet, de Wet arbeid vreemdelingen en de Wet minimumloon en minimumvakantiebijslag haar inspectiegegevens te openbaren en haar boetebeschikkingen te publiceren*, Uitgeverij Paris

Scheltema (1974)
Scheltema, M. (1974), *Zelfstandige bestuursorganen*, Tjeenk Willink: Groningen

Scheltema and Scheltema (2003)
Scheltema, M.W. and Scheltema, M. (2003), *Gemeenschappelijk recht: Wisselwerking tussen publiek- en privaatrecht*, Kluwer: Deventer

Schlössels and Zijlstra (2010)
Schlössels. R.J.N. and Zijlstra, S.E. (2010), *Bestuursrecht in de sociale rechtsstaat*, Kluwer: Deventer, 6th edition

Schneider (2010)
Schneider, F. (2010), 'Turnover of organized crime and money laundering: some preliminary empirical findings', *Public Choice*, vol. 144, issue 3-4, pp. 473-486

Scholten (2011)
Scholten, M. (2011), 'Independent, hence unaccountable?', *Review of European Administrative Law*, vol. 4, issue 1, pp. 5-44

Scholtes (2012)
Scholtes, E. (2012), *Transparantie, icoon van een dolende overheid*, Boom Lemma (doctoral thesis Tilburg University)
Schrama (2011)
Schrama, W. (2011), 'How to carry out interdisciplinary legal research: Some experiences with an interdisciplinary research method', *Utrecht Law Review*, vol. 7, issue 1, pp. 147-162
Seelig and Novoa (2009)
Seelig, S. and Novoa, A. (2009), 'Governance Practices at Financial Regulatory and Supervisory Agencies', *IMF Working Paper*, WP/09/135
Seerden and Wenders (2011)
Seerden, R. and Wenders, D. (2011), 'Administrative law in the Netherlands', in: Seerden, R. (ed.), *Administrative law of the European Union, its Member States and the United States: A comparative analysis*, Intersentia, pp. 101-176
Shears (2008)
Shears, P. (2008), 'Hang your shingle and carry on: estate agents – the unlicensed UK profession', *Property Management*, vol. 27, issue 3, pp. 191-211
Sijbrand and Rijsbergen (2013)
Sijbrand, J. and Rijsbergen, D. (2013), 'Managing the Quality of Financial Supervision', in: Kellerman, A.J., De Haan, J. and De Vries, F. (eds.), *Financial Supervision in the 21st Century*, Springer Publishing, pp. 17-32
Smits et al. (2009)
Smits, J., Struiksma, N. and Van den Heuvel, M. (2009*), Systeem in zaken: een evaluatie van de effectiviteit en doelmatigheid van het Bureau Financieel Toezicht*, research commissioned by the Ministry of Justice
Snijders-Kuiper and Tilleman (2013)
Snijders-Kuiper, B. and Tilleman, A.T.A. (2013), 'Nieuwe witwaswetgeving! Overzicht van de belangrijkste wijzigingen voor de notariële praktijk', *Weekblad voor Privaatrecht, Notariaat en Registratie*, issue 6972
Snyder (1993)
Snyder, F. (1993), 'The Effectiveness of European Community Law: Institutions, Processes, Tools and Techniques', *Modern Law Review*, vol. 56, issue 1, pp. 19-54
Stessens (2000)
Stessens, G. (2000), *Money Laundering: A New International Law Enforcement Model*, Cambridge University Press: Cambridge
Stigler (1970)
Stigler, G. (1970), 'The Optimum Enforcement of Laws', *Journal of Political Economy*, vol. 78, issue 3, pp. 526-536
Stigler (1971)
Stigler, G. (1971), 'The theory of economic regulation', *Bell Journal of Economics and Management Science*, vol. 2, issue 1, pp. 3-21.
Stouten (2011)
Stouten, M. (2011), 'Een ongebruikelijke uitleg van de witwasmeldplicht: Tijd voor een wetswijziging', *Nederlands Juristenblad*, issue 31, pp. 2020-2025

Stouten (2012)

Stouten, M. (2012), *De witwasmeldplicht: Omvang van handhaving van de Wwft meldplicht voor juridische en fiscale dienstverleners*, Boom Juridisch uitgevers: The Hague (doctoral thesis Utrecht University)

Stouten and Tilleman (2013)

Stouten, M. and Tilleman, A. (2013), 'Reporting Duty for Lawyers versus Legal Privilege: Unresolved Tension', in: Unger, B. and Van der Linde, D. (eds.), *Research Handbook on Money Laundering*, Edward Elgar Publishing Ltd: Cheltenham, pp. 426-434

Streeck and Schmitter (1985)

Streeck, W. and Schmitter, P.C. (1985), 'Community, Market, State – and Associations? The Prospective Contribution of Interest Governance to Social Order', in: Streeck, W. and Schmitter, P.C. (eds.), *Private Interest Government: Beyond Market and State*, Sage: London, pp. 1-29

Suurmond and Van Velthoven (2004)

Suurmond, G. en Van Velthoven, B.C.J. (2004): *Handhaven: eerst kiezen dan doen. Economische mogelijkheden en beperkingen (Interim Report IV)*, Expertisecentrum Rechtshandhaving, Ministerie van Justitie

Taekema and Van Klink (2009)

Taekema S. and Van Klink, B. (2009), 'Dwarsverbanden: Interdisciplinair onderzoek in de rechtswetenschap', *Nederlands Juristenblad*, issue 36, pp. 2559-2566

Thony (1996)

Thony, J.F. (1996), 'Processing Financial Information in Money Laundering Matters: The Financial Intelligence Units', *European Journal of Crime, Criminal Law and Criminal Justice*, issue 4, pp. 257-282

Tillema and Doets (2007)

Tillema, A.J.P. and Doets, C.A. (2007), 'Bestuursrechtelijke handhaving', in: Busch, D. et al., *Onderneming en financieel toezicht*, Serie Onderneming en Recht, no. 40, Kluwer: Deventer, pp. 493- 545

Tilleman (2007)

Tilleman, A. (2007), 'Money laundering and the professional sector. Supervision of lawyers and civil-law notaries in the Netherlands – what about professional secrecy?', in: Van Duyne, P.C., Maljevic, A., Van Dijck, M., Von Lampe, K and Harvey, J. (eds.), *Crime Business and Crime Money in Europe. The Dirty Linen of Illegal Enterprise*, Wolf Legal Publishers, pp. 43-68

Tilleman (2009)

Tilleman, A.T.A (2009), 'Notariaat en Toezicht', *Ponder*, issue 27, p. 17

Tridimas (2006)

Tridimas, T. (2006), *The General Principles of EU Law*, Oxford EC Law Library, 2nd edition

Unger et al. (2006)

Unger, B. et al. (2006), *The amounts and effects of money laundering*, Report for the Dutch Ministry of Finance

Unger (2006a)
Unger, B. (2006a), 'De omvang en effecten van witwassen', *Justitiële Verkenningen*, vol. 32, issue 2, pp. 21-33
Unger (2007)
Unger, B. (2007), *The Scale and Impacts of Money Laundering*, Edward Elgar Publishing Ltd: Cheltenham
Unger and Ferwerda (2014)
Unger, B. and Ferwerda, J. (2014), 'Threat of money laundering', in: Unger et al., *The Economic and Legal Effectiveness of the European Union's Anti-Money Laundering Policy*, Edward Elgar Publishing Ltd: Cheltenham, pp. 9-19
Unger and Van den Broek (2014)
Unger, B. and Van den Broek, M. (2014), 'Implementing international conventions and the Third EU Directive', in: Unger et al., *The Economic and Legal Effectiveness of the European Union's Anti-Money Laundering Policy*, Edward Elgar Publishing Ltd: Cheltenham, pp. 46-61
Unger et al. (2014)
Unger, B., Ferwerda, J, Van den Broek, M. and Deleanu, I. (2014), *The Economic and Legal Effectiveness of the European Union's Anti-Money Laundering Policy*, Edward Elgar Publishing Ltd: Cheltenham
Van Buuren and Borman (2009)
Van Buuren, P.J.J. and Borman, T.C. (eds.) (2009), *Tekst en Commentaar Algemene Wet Bestuursrecht*, Kluwer: Deventer, 6th edition
Van Buuren et al. (2011)
Van Buuren, P.J.J., Jurgens, G.T.J.M. and Michiels, F.C.M.A. (2011), *Bestuursdwang en dwangsom*, Kluwer: Deventer
Van de Bunt et al. (2007)
Van de Bunt, H., Van Erp, J. and Van Wingerde, K. (2007), 'Hoe stevig is de piramide van Braithwaite', *Tijdschrift voor Criminologie*, vol. 49, issue 4, pp. 386-399 at 386-387
Van de Bunt et al. (2011)
Van de Bunt, H. et al. (2011), *Bestuurlijke rapportage vastgoedfraudezaak 'Klimop'*, Final Report, June 2011
Van den Berg (2012)
Van den Berg, A. (2012), *Integriteitsbeoordelingen in advocatuur, notariaat en accountancy: een juridisch onderzoek naar informatiegebruik bij de bestrijding van integriteitsschendingen in de vastgoedsector*, Boxpress: 's-Hertogenbosch (doctoral thesis VU University Amsterdam)
Van den Broek (2010)
Van den Broek, M. (2010), *New Governance: The exchange of information within the Dutch Financial Expertise Centre from a Good Governance Perspective*, Research Master thesis, Utrecht University: August 2010 (not published, available on request)
Van den Broek (2011)
Van den Broek, M. (2011), 'Gelijkwaardigheid in het antiwitwasbeleid: de FATF en de EU', *SEW: Tijdschrift voor Europees en Economisch Recht*, vol. 59, issue 10, pp. 422-428

Van den Broek (2011a)
Van den Broek, M. (2011a), 'The EU's preventive AML/CFT policy: asymmetrical harmonisation', *Journal of Money Laundering Control*, vol. 14, issue 2, pp. 170-182

Van den Broek (2011b)
Van den Broek (2011b), 'Effectiviteit, publieke verantwoording en transparantie van het Financieel Expertise Centrum', *Tijdschrift voor Compliance*, issue 4/5, pp. 230-238

Van den Broek (2014)
Van den Broek, M. (2014), 'Supervisory architectures in the preventive AML policy', in: Unger et al., *The Economic and Legal Effectiveness of the European Union's Anti-Money Laundering Policy*, Edward Elgar Publishing Ltd: Cheltenham, pp. 62-86

Van den Broek (2014a)
Van den Broek, M. (2014a), 'Harmonization of substantive norms in preventive AML policy', in: Unger et al., *The Economic and Legal Effectiveness of the European Union's Anti-Money Laundering Policy*, Edward Elgar Publishing Ltd: Cheltenham, pp. 20-45

Van den Broek and Popping (2012)
Van den Broek, M. and Popping, D. (2012), 'De governance van het Financieel Expertise Centrum', in: Nederlands Compliance Instituut, *Jaarboek Compliance 2013*, NCI, pp. 143-165

Van den Broek and Addink (2013)
Van den Broek, M. and Addink, G.H. (2013), 'Prevention of money laundering and terrorist financing from a good governance perspective', in: Unger, B. and Van der Linde, D. (eds.), *Research Handbook on Money Laundering*, Edward Elgar Publishing Ltd: Cheltenham, pp. 368-378

Van den Broeke and Hoff (2008)
Van den Broeke, P.J. and Hoff, R.J. (2008), *Memo Wet ter voorkoming van witwassen en financieren van terrorisme*, Kluwer: Deventer

Van der Jagt (2006)
Van der Jagt, J.A.E. (2006), *Milieuconvenanten gehandhaafd: Een juridisch onderzoek naar handhaafbaarheid en handhaving van Nederlandse milieuconvenanten en in het bijzonder van klimaatconvenanten in het licht van de democratische rechtsstaat*, Boom Juridische uitgevers: The Hague (doctoral thesis Utrecht University)

Van der Wal (2008)
Van der Wal, Z. (2008), *Value solidity: Differences, similarities and conflicts between the organizational values of government and business*, Enschede: Print partners Ipskamp (doctoral thesis VU University)

Van Duyne (1994)
Van Duyne, P.C. (1994), 'Money Laundering: Estimates in Fog', *Journal of Financial Crime*, vol. 2, issue 1, pp. 58-74

Van Duyne et al. (2005)
Van Duyne, P. C., Groenhuijsen, M.C. and Schudelaro, A.A.P. (2005), 'Balancing Financial threats and legal interests in money-laundering policy', *Crime, Law and Social Change*, vol. 43, issue 1-2, pp. 117-147

Van Erp (2009)
Van Erp, J. (2009), *Naming en shaming in het markttoezicht*, Boom Juridische uitgevers: The Hague
Van Gerwen (2000)
Van Gerven, W. (2000), 'Of rights, remedies and procedures', *Common Market Law Review*, vol. 37, issue 3, pp. 501-536
Van Montfort (2008)
Van Montfort, C. (2008), *Besturen van het onbekende: Goed bestuur bij publiek-private arrangementen*, Uitgeverij Lemma: The Hague
Van Ommeren (2010)
Ommeren, F.J. van (2010), 'Het legaliteitsbeginsel als hoeksteen van het staats- en bestuursrecht', *Ars Aequi*, September 2010, pp. 6-8
Van Onzenoort (2013)
Van Onzenoort, D. (2013), 'Meldplicht ongebruikelijke transacties', *Accountancynieuws*, no. 14, August 2013, pp. 22-24
Van Thiel (2010)
Van Thiel, S. (2010), *Bestuurskundig Onderzoek: Een methodologische inleiding*, Uitgeverij Coutinho: Bussum
Van Wijk/Konijnenbelt & Van Male (2014)
Van Wijk/Konijnenbelt & Van Male (2014), *Hoofdstukken van het bestuursrecht*, Kluwer: Deventer
Vega Serrano (2011)
Vega Serrano, J. M. (2011), *La Regulación Bancaria*, La Ley
Verhey and Verheij (2005)
Verhey, L.F.M. and Verheij, N. (2005), 'De macht van de marktmeesters: Markttoezicht in constitutioneel perspectief', in: Preadvies NJV, *Toezicht*, Kluwer, pp. 139-332
Verhoeven (2011)
Verhoeven, M. (2011), *The Costanzo Obligation: The obligations of national administrative authorities in the case of incompatibility between national law and European law*, Intersentia: Antwerp (doctoral thesis Utrecht University)
Vermeer (2001)
Vermeer, F.R. (2001), 'De beginselplicht tot handhaving en de ruimte om te gedogen', *JBPlus* 2001, pp. 76-85
Versluis (2003)
Versluis, E. (2003), *Enforcement matters: Enforcement and compliance of European Directives in Four Member States*, Eburon: Delft (dissertation Utrecht University)
Vervaele (2013)
Vervaele, J. (2013), 'Economic crimes and money laundering: a new paradigm for the criminal justice system?', in: Unger, B. and Van der Linde, D. (eds.), *Research Handbook on Money Laundering*, Edward Elgar Publishing Ltd: Cheltenham, pp. 379-396
Viñals and Fiechter (2010)
Viñals, J. and Fiechter, J. (2010), *The Making of Good Supervision: Learning to say 'no'*, IMF Staff Position Note, SPN/10/08

Voermans (2005)
Voermans, W. (2005), 'De communautarisering van toezicht en handhaving', in: Barkhuysen, T., den Ouden, W. and Polak, M., *Recht realiseren: Bijdragen rond het thema adequate naleving van rechtsregels*, Kluwer: Deventer, pp. 69-88

Vos (2005)
Vos, E. (2005), 'Independence, Accountability and Transparency of European Regulatory Agencies', in: Geradin, D., Muñoz, R. and Petit, N., *Regulation through Agencies in the EU: A new Paradigm of Governance*, Edward Elgar Publishing Ltd: Cheltenham, pp. 120-140

Wade and Forsyth (2014)
Wade, H.W.R. and Forsyth, C.F., *Administrative Law*, Oxford University Press: Oxford, 11th edition

Wagemakers (2005)
Wagemakers, M. (2005), 'Verscherpt integriteittoezicht in de financiële sector', *Tijdschrift voor Financieel Recht*, issue 7, pp. 185-189

Wakefield (2007)
Wakefield, J. (2007), *The right to good administration*, Kluwer: Deventer

Walker (1999)
Walker, J. (1999) 'How Big is Global Money Laundering', *Journal of Money Laundering Control*, vol. 3, issue 1, pp. 25-37

Walker and Unger (2009)
Walker, J. and Unger, B. (2009), 'Measuring Global Money Laundering: "the Walker Gravity Model"', *Review of Law and Economics*, vol. 5, issue 2, pp. 821-853

Webley and Samuels (2012)
Webley, L. and Samuels, H. (2012), *Complete Public Law: Text, Cases, and Materials*, Oxford University Press: Oxford

Welp (2012)
Welp, P. (2012) 'Effectiviteit van toezicht: tijd voor *responsive evaluation*', *Tijdschrift voor Toezicht*, issue 2, pp. 7-22

Widdershoven (2002)
Widdershoven, R.J.G.M. (2002), 'Encroachment of criminal law in administrative law in the Netherlands', in: *Electronic Journal of Comparative Law*, vol. 6, issue 4, pp. 445-461

Wilks (2007)
Wilks, S. (2007), 'Boardization and Corporate Governance in the UK as a Response to Depoliticization and Failing Accountability', *Public Policy and Administration*, vol. 22, issue 4, pp. 443-460

Winter (2013)
Winter, H. (2013), 'Regulatory enforcement in the Netherlands: Struggling with Independence', in: Comtois, S. and De Graaf, K.J. (eds.), *On Judicial and Quasi-Judicial Independence*, Boom Juridische uitgevers: The Hague, pp. 157-166

Winter and May (2001)
Winter, S. and May, P.J. (2001), 'Motivation for Compliance with Environmental Regulations', *Journal of Policy Analysis and Management*, vol. 20, issue 4, pp. 675-698

Wouters and Ryngaert (2005)
Wouters, J. and Ryngaert, C. (2005) 'Good Governance: Lessons from international organizations', in: Curtin, D.M. and Wessels, R.A., Good *Governance and the European Union: Reflections on concepts, institutions and substance*, Intersentia: Antwerp, pp. 69-104
Wymeersch (2007)
Wymeersch, E. (2007), 'The Structure of Financial Supervision in Europe: About Single Financial Supervisors, Twin Peaks and Multiple Financial Supervisors', *European Business Organization Law Review*, vol. 8, issue 2, pp. 237-306
Yang Lim and Lian Teo (2013)
Yang Lim, A. and Lian Teo, S. (2013), 'Developments in Supervisory Enforcement', in: Kellerman, A.J., De Haan, J. and De Vries, F. (eds.), *Financial Supervision in the 21st Century*, Springer Publishing, pp. 103- 110
Yasin (2004)
Yasin, N.M. (2004), 'Lawyers, legal privilege and money laundering: The UK and Malaysian experience', *Journal of Banking Regulation*, issue 5, pp. 364-386
Zijlstra (2009)
Zijlstra, S.E. (2009), *Bestuurlijk organisatierecht*, Kluwer: Deventer
Zijlstra (2009a)
Zijlstra, S.E. (2009a), 'Toezichthouders', in: Huizink, J.B. and Schoenmaker, D. (eds.), *Leerboek Wft*, Maklu, pp. 87-109

Reports and policy documents

AAT (2008)
AAT (2008), *Guidance on anti-money laundering legislation*, October 2008
AAT (2011)
AAT (2011), *Annual report and financial statements of the group for the year ending 31 December 2011*
AAT (2011a)
AAT (2011a), *HM Treasury AML Supervision Reporting 2010/2011,* (not publicly available)
AAT (2012)
AAT (2012), *HM Treasury AML Supervision Reporting 2011/2012,* (not publicly available)
AAT (2012a)
AAT (2012a), *Indicative Sanctions Guidance*, July 2012
AAT (2013)
Association of Accounting Technicians (2013), *Annual report and financial statements of the group for the year ending 31 December 2013*
AAT (2013a)
AAT (2013a), *2012/13 AML/CTF Supervision Report: Annual return*, submitted in May 2013 by AAT to HM Treasury (not publicly available)

Algemene Rekenkamer (2005)
Algemene Rekenkamer (2005), *Essentials of Good Governance*, The Hague
Algemene Rekenkamer (2008)
Algemene Rekenkamer (2008), *Goed Bestuur in uitvoering: de praktijk van onderwijsinstellingen, woningcorporaties, zorgorganisaties en samenwerkingsverbanden*, The Hague
Algemene Rekenkamer (2008a)
Algemene Rekenkamer (2008a), *Bestrijden witwassen en terrorismefinanciering, Parliamentary papers II*, 2007-08, 31 477, nrs. 1-2
Algemene Rekenkamer (2008a)
Algemene Rekenkamer (2008a), *Bestrijden witwassen en terrorismefinanciering, Parliamentary papers II*, 2007-08, 31 477, nrs. 1-2
Algemene Rekenkamer (2011)
Algemene Rekenkamer (2011), *Toezicht van DNB op de stabiliteit van banken*, November 2011
Algemene Rekenkamer (2012)
Algemene Rekenkamer (2012), *Rapport Kaderwet zbo's: reikwijdte en implementatie*, June 2012
Algemene Rekenkamer (2014)
Algemene Rekenkamer (2014), *Bestrijding witwassen: stand van zaken 2013*, March 2014
Audit Commission (1999)
Audit Commission (1999), *Measure for measure: the best value agenda for Trading Standard Services*, December 1999
Banco de España (2011)
Banco de España (2011), *Report on Banking Supervision in Spain 2011*
Banco de España (2012)
Banco de España (2012), *Report on Banking Supervision in Spain 2012*
Bank of England and FSA (2013)
Bank of England and FSA (2013), *A review of requirements for firms entering into or expanding in the banking sector*, March 2013
Basel Committee on Banking Supervision (2012)
Basel Committee on Banking Supervision (2012), *Core Principles for Effective Banking Supervision*, available at: <www.bis.org/publ/bcbs230.pdf>
Belastingdienst (2011)
Belastingdienst (2011), *Beheerverslag 2011, Parliamentary Papers II*, 2011-12, 33 000-IXB, no. 24
Belastingdienst Holland-Midden/Unit MOT-Ordening (2009)
Belastingdienst Holland-Midden/Unit MOT-Ordening (2009), *Visiedocument "Waarheen... waarvoor...?" Handhaving in de jaren 2009-2012*, 6 January 2009
Belastingdienst/Bureau Toezicht Wwft (2011)
Belastingdienst/Bureau Toezicht Wwft (2011), *Jaarverslag 2011* (not publicly available)

Belastingdienst/Bureau Toezicht Wwft (2012)
Belastingdienst/Bureau Toezicht Wwft (2012), *Jaarverslag 2012* (not publicly available)
Belastingdienst/Bureau Toezicht Wwft (2013)
Belastingdienst/Bureau Toezicht Wwft (2013), *Jaarverslag 2013* (not publicly available)
British Institute of International and Comparative Law (2006)
British Institute of International and Comparative Law (2006), *Comparative Implementation of EU Directives (II): Money Laundering*, City Research Series, no. 10, City of London
Bureau Financieel Toezicht (2008)
Bureau Financieel Toezicht (2008), *Jaarverslag 2008*
Bureau Financieel Toezicht (2010)
Bureau Financieel Toezicht (2010), *Jaarverslag 2010*
Bureau Financieel Toezicht (2011)
Bureau Financieel Toezicht (2011), *Jaarverslag 2011*
Bureau Financieel Toezicht (2012)
Bureau Financieel Toezicht (2012), *Jaarverslag 2012*
Bureau Financieel Toezicht (2013)
Bureau Financieel Toezicht (2013), *Nieuwsbrief Toezicht*, no. 1, winter edition
Cabinet Office (2012)
Cabinet Office (2012), *Public Bodies 2012*
Cabinet Office (2013)
Cabinet Office (2013), *List of Ministerial Responsibilities: Including Executive Agencies and Non-Ministerial Departments*, December 2013
Carsberg review (2008)
Carsberg Review (2008), *Review of residential property*, Final Report, June 2008
Commissie De Wit (2010)
Tijdelijke Commissie Onderzoek Financieel Stelsel (Commissie De Wit) (2010), *Verloren Krediet, Parliamentary Papers II, 2009-10, 31980*, no. 4
Commissie De Wit (2012)
Parlementaire Enquêtecommissie Financieel Stelsel (Commissie De Wit) (2012), *Verloren Krediet II – De balans opgemaakt, Parliamentary Papers II,* 2011-12, 31 980, no. 61
Commissie Horizontaal Toezicht Belastingdienst (2012)
Commissie Horizontaal Toezicht Belastingdienst (2012), *Fiscaal toezicht op maat: Soepel waar het kan, streng waar het moet*, The Hague
Commissie Kaderstelling en Toezicht Woningcorporaties (2012)
Commissie Kaderstelling en Toezicht Woningcorporaties (2012), *Eindrapportage*, 17 December 2012
Commissie Michiels (1998)
Commissie Michiels (1998), *Handhaven op Niveau*, W.E.J. Tjeenk Willink: Deventer

CPBCIM (2013)
Comisión de Prevención del Blanqueo de Capitales e Infracciones Monetarias (2013), *Memoria de Información Estadística 2010-12* (in English: *Statistical report 2010-12*)
De Larosière (2009)
De Larosière (2009), *The High-Level Group on Financial Supervision in the EU*, 25 February 2009, available at: <http://ec.europa.eu/internal_market/finances/docs/de_larosiere_report_en.pdf>
Deloitte (2011)
Deloitte (2011), *Final Study on the Application of the Anti-Money Laundering Directive*, Service Contract ETD/2009/IM/F2/90
Department for Business, Innovation & Skills (2013)
Department for Business, Innovations & Skills (2013), *Enterprise and Regulatory Reform Act 2013: Policy Paper*, June 2013
DNB (2009)
DNB (2009), *The Seven Elements of an Ethical Culture Strategy and approach to behaviour and culture at financial institutions 2010-2014*, November 2009
DNB (2010)
DNB (2010), *Visie op Toezicht 2010-2014*, March 2010
DNB (2011)
DNB (2011), *ZBO-verantwoording 2011* (in English: *Annual report 2011*)
DNB (2012)
DNB (2012), *Thema's DNB toezicht 2012*, January 2012
DNB (2012a)
DNB (2012a), *FOCUS! De vernieuwde toezichtaanpak van DNB*, April 2012
DNB (2012b)
DNB (2012b), *ZBO-verantwoording 2012* (in English: *Annual report 2012*)
DNB (2013)
DNB (2013), *Thema's DNB toezicht 2013*, January 2013
DNB (2013a)
DNB (2013a), *ZBO-verantwoording 2013* (in English: *Annual report 2013*)
DNB (2014)
DNB (2014), *Good practices bestrijden corruptie*, 25 June 2014
DNB (2014a)
DNB (2014a), *Thema's DNB toezicht 2014*, January 2014
Egmont (2004)
Egmont (2004), *Information Paper on Financial Intelligence Units and the Egmont Group*, September 2004
Ekobrottsmyndigheten (2012)
Ekobrottsmyndigheten (2012), *Underrättelsebild 2012*, EBM K-2012/0114
European Commission (2001)
European Commission (2001), *White Paper on European Governance*, COM(2001) 428 final

European Commission (2005)
European Commission (2005), *Press Release: Commission takes action to ensure that 12 Member States implement EU rules*, IP/10/305, 18 March 2005
European Commission (2011)
European Commission (2011), *Commission Staff Working Paper on Anti-money laundering supervision of and reporting by payment institutions in various cross-border situations*, SEC(2011) 1178 Final
European Commission (2012)
European Commission (2012), *Report from the Commission to the European Parliament and the Council on the application of Directive 2005/60/EC on the prevention for the use of the financial system for the purpose of money laundering and terrorist financing*, COM(2012) 168 final
European Commission (2012a)
European Commission (2012), *Feedback Statement: Summary of comments on the report from the Commission to the European Parliament and the Council on the application of Directive 2005/60/EC*, available at <http://ec.europa.eu/internal_market/company/docs/financial-crime/072012_feedback_statement_en.pdf>
European Commission (2014)
European Commission (2014), *EU Anti-Corruption Report 2014*, COM(2014) 38 final
European Commission (2014a)
European Commission (2014a), *Annex: Spain to EU Anti-Corruption Report 2014*, COM(2014) 38 final
European Commission (2014b)
European Commission (2014b), *Annex: Netherlands to EU Anti-Corruption Report 2014*, COM(2014) 38 final
European Commission (2014c)
European Commission (2014c), *Annex United Kingdom to the EU Anti-Corruption Report*, COM(2014) 38 final
European Commission (2014d)
European Commission (2014d), *Annex: Sweden to EU Anti-Corruption Report 2014*, COM(2014) 38 final
Evaluatiecommissie Bureau Financieel Toezicht (2009)
Evaluatiecommissie Bureau Financieel Toezicht (2009), *Toezicht en inzicht: Een helder denkraam*, August 2009
Fastighetsmäklarinspektionen (2012)
Fastighetsmäklarinspektionen (2012), *Årsredovisning 2012*
Fastighetsmäklarinspektionen (2013)
Fastighetsmäklarinspektionen (2013), *Årsredovisning 2013*
Fastighetsmäklarinspektionen (2013a)
Fastighetsmäklarinspektionen (2013a), *Handbok om tillsynen over fastighetsmäklare*, 30 April 2013, Dnr. 1.1-1169-13 (not publicly available)
FATF (2006)
FATF (2006), *Third Mutual Evaluation Report on Spain*, 23 June 2006

FATF (2006a)
FATF (2006a) *Third Mutual Evaluation Report on Sweden*, 17 February 2006
FATF (2007)
FATF (2007), *Money laundering and terrorist financing through the real estate sector*, Paris
FATF (2007a)
FATF (2007a), *Third Mutual Evaluation Report on the United Kingdom of Great Britain and Northern Ireland*, 29 June 2007
FATF (2010)
FATF (2010), *Fourth Follow Up Report on Spain*, 22 October 2010
FATF (2010a)
FATF (2010), *Third Mutual Evaluation Report on Germany*, 19 February 2010
FATF (2010b)
FATF (2010b), *Fourth Follow Up Report on Sweden*, 22 October 2010
FATF (2011)
FATF (2011), *Third Mutual Evaluation Report on the Netherlands*, 25 February 2011
FATF (2012)
FATF (2012), *High-Level Principles and Objectives for FATF and FATF-style regional bodies*, October 2012
FATF (2012a)
FATF (2012a), *International standards on combating money laundering and the financing of terrorism & proliferation: The FATF Recommendations*, February 2012
FATF (2014)
FATF (2014), *Money laundering and terrorist financing through trade in diamonds*, January 2014
FATF (2014a)
FATF (2014a), *Virtual Currencies: Key Definitions and Potential AML/CFT Risks*, June 2014
FATF (2014b)
FATF (2014), *Second Follow Up Report: Mutual Evaluation on the Netherlands*, February 2014
FCA (2013)
FCA (2013), *Anti-money laundering annual report 2012/13*, July 2013
FCA (2013a)
FCA (2013a), *Corporate Governance at the Financial Conduct Authority*, April 2013
FCA (2013b)
FCA (2013b), *How the Financial Conduct Authority will investigate and report on regulatory failure*, April 2013
FCA (2013c)
FCA (2013c), *Transparency*, Discussion Paper DP13/1**, March 2013
FCA (2013d)
FCA (2013d), *Risk Outlook 2013*, March 2013
FCA (2013e)
FCA (2013e), *Business Plan 2013/14*, March 2014

FCA (2013f)
FCA (2013f), *Banks' control of financial crime risks in trade finance*, TR13/03
FCA (2013g)
FCA (2013g), *Anti-Money Laundering and Anti-Bribery and Corruption Systems and Controls: Asset Management and Platform Firms*, TR13/09
FCA (2014)
FCA (2014), *Business Plan 2014/15*, March 2014
Financieel Expertise Centrum (2012)
Financieel Expertise Centrum (2012), *Jaarverslag 2012-2014 voor het jaar 2012*
Finansinspektionen (2006)
Finansinspektionen (2006), *Money Laundering and Terrorist Financing – preventive measures in the finance sector*, Report 2007:17 (summary)
Finansinspektionen (2009)
Finansinspektionen (2009), *Skärpta kontrollåtgärder krävs avseende affärsförbindelser och transaktioner med Iran*, FI Dnr 09-4770
Finansinspektionen (2010)
Finansinspektionen (2010), *Redovisning av Finansinspektionens penningtvättstillsyn*, FI Dnr 10-1002
Finansinspektionen (2011)
Finansinspektionen (2011), *Årsredovisning 2011* (in English: *Annual report 2011*)
Finansinspektionen (2012)
Finansinspektionen (2012), *Risks in the financial system 2012*, Dnr 12-12020
Finansinspektionen (2012a)
Finansinspektionen (2012a), *Årsredovisning 2012*, Dnr 13-1321
Finansinspektionen (2012b)
Finansinspektionen (2012b), *Redovisning av uppdrag: Redovisning av Finansinspektionens insatser för att öka rapporteringen till Rikspolisstyrelsen, Fi2010/4920, Fi2010/5063, Fi2010/5322 och Fi2010/5790 (delvis)*, Dnr 12-2798
Finansinspektionen (2013)
Finansinspektionen (2013), *Supervision Report 2013*, May 2013.
Finansinspektionen (2013a)
Finansinspektionen (2013a), *Overall operations plan and internal budget 2013*, Ref.13-48,
Finansinspektionen (2013b)
Finansinspektionen (2011), *Årsredovisning 2013*, Dnr 14-1728
Finansinspektionen (2013c)
Finansinspektionen (2013b), *Redovisning av uppdrag: Uppföljning av rapporten Finansinspektionens insatser för att öka rapporteringen till Rikspolisstyrelsen*, Dnr 13-2864
Finansinspektionen (2013d)
Finansinspektionen (2013c), *Penningtvätt och finansiering av terrorism: En bättre riskhantering*, Dnr 13-4387
Finansinspektionen et al. (2013)
Finansinspektionen et al. (2013), *Penningtvätt: En nationell riskbedömning*, Dnr 12-13024

Finansinspektionen et al. (2014)
Finansinspektionen et al. (2014), *Finansiering av terrorism: En nationell riskbedömning*, Dnr 12-13024
Finanspolisen (2010)
Finanspolisen (2010), *Penningtvätt inom den grova organiserade brottsligheten*, RKP Rapport 2010:2
Finanspolisen (2012)
Finanspolisen (2012), *Årsrapport 2012* (in English: *Annual report 2012*)
FIU Nederland (2012)
FIU Nederland (2012), *Jaaroverzicht 2012 (*in English: *Annual report 2012)*
FSA (2009)
FSA (2009), *The Turner Review: a regulatory response to the global banking crisis*, March 2009
FSA (2011)
FSA (2011), *Banks' management of high money-laundering risk situations: How banks deal with high-risk customers (including politically exposed persons), correspondent banking relationships and wire transfers*, June 2011
FSA (2012)
FSA (2012), *Banks' defences against investment fraud: detecting perpetrators and protecting victims*, June 2012
FSA (2013)
FSA (2013), *Annual report 2012-13*
FSA (2013a)
FSA (2013a), *Enforcement Annual Performance Account 2012/13*
Gambling Commission (2011)
Gambling Commission (2011), *Money laundering: the prevention of money laundering and combating the financing of terrorism. Guidance for remote and non-remote casinos*, 2nd edition
Group of Thirty (2008)
Group of Thirty (2008), *The structure of financial supervision: Approaches and challenges in a global marketplace*, Washington DC
Hampton Review (2005)
Hampton Review (2005), *Reducing Administrative Burdens: Effective Supervision and Enforcement*, Final Report
HM Revenue and Customs (2010)
HM Revenue and Customs (2010), *Anti-money laundering guidance for high value dealers*, July 2010
HM Revenue and Customs (2011)
HM Revenue and Customs (2011), *Anti-Money Laundering Annual Report to Her Majesty's Treasury 2010-2011*
HM Revenue and Customs (2013)
HM Revenue and Customs (2013), *Annual report and accounts 2012-13*
HM Revenue and Customs (2014)
HM Revenue and Customs (2014), *Guidance: Supervision of Estate Agency Businesses by HMRC*, January 2014

HM Treasury (2001)
HM Treasury (2001), *An Independent And Accountable FSA*, available at: <http://webarchive.nationalarchives.gov.uk/+/www.hm-treasury.gov.uk/newsroom_and_speeches/press/2001/press_144_01.cfm>
HM Treasury (2007)
HM Treasury (2007), *Implementing the Third Money Laundering Directive: Draft Money Laundering Regulations 2007*, January 2007
HM Treasury (2011)
HM Treasury, *Anti-Money Laundering and Counter Terrorist Finance Supervision Report 2010-11*, November 2011
HM Treasury (2011a)
HM Treasury (2011a), *White Paper: A new approach to financial regulation – the blueprint to reform*, Cm8083
HM Treasury (2011b)
HM Treasury (2011b), *Consultation on proposed changes to the money laundering regulations 2007: Summary of Responses*, November 2011
HM Treasury (2012)
HM Treasury (2012), *Anti-Money Laundering and Counter Terrorist Finance Report 2011-12*
HM Treasury (2013)
HM Treasury (2013), *Anti-Money Laundering and Counter Terrorist Finance Supervision Report 2012-13*, available at: <www.gov.uk/government/publications/anti-money-laundering-and-counter-terrorist-finance-supervision-reports/anti-money-laundering-and-counter-terrorist-finance-supervision-report-2012-13>
HM Treasury (2013a)
HM Treasury (2013a), *Preventing Money Laundering*, policy paper, 5 June 2013
HM Treasury (2013b)
HM Treasury (2013b), *Advisory notice on money Laundering and terrorist financing controls in overseas jurisdictions*, July 2013
ICAEW (2012)
ICAEW (2012), *Effective AML/CTF Supervision 2011*, submitted in May 2012 by ICAEW to HM Treasury (not publicly available)
ICAEW (2012a)
ICAEW (2012a), *Practice Assurance desktop review*, available at: <www.icaew.com/~/media/Files/Members/practice-centre/practice-assurance/practice-assurance-desktop-reviews.pdf>
ICAEW (2012b)
ICAEW (2012b), *Practice Assurance visits,* available at: <www.icaew.com/~/media/Files/Members/practice-centre/practice-assurance/practice-assurance-visit.pdf>
ICAEW (2013)
ICAEW (2013), *2012/13 AML/CTF Supervision Report: Annual return*, submitted in May 2013 by ICAEW to HM Treasury (not publicly available)
ICAEW (2013a)
ICAEW (2013a), *Practice Assurance Highlights 2013*

ICAEW (2013b)

ICAEW (2013b), *Guidance on Sentencing*, August 2013

ICAEW et al. (2013)

The Institute of Chartered Accountants in England and Wales, The Institute of Chartered Accountants of Scotland and the Institute of Chartered Accountants in Ireland (2004), *Designated Professional Body Handbook 2004*, updated until 1 April 2013, available at: <www.icaew.com/~/media/Files/Members/Regulations-standards-and-guidance/dpb%20handbook/DPB_handbook.pdf>

IMF (2004)

IMF (2004), *Financial Intelligence Units: An Overview*, Washington DC

IMF (2011)

IMF (2011), *Financial Sector Assessment Program Update: Kingdom of the Netherlands-Netherlands*, June 2011

IMF (2011a)

IMF (2011), *United Kingdom: Basel Core Principles for Effective Banking Supervision Detailed Assessment of Compliance*, IMF Country Report No. 11/233, July 2011

IMF (2011b)

IMF (2011b), *Sweden: Financial Sector Assessment Program Update – Detailed Assessment of Observance on Basel Core Principles for Effective Banking Supervision*, IMF Country Report No. 11/281

Independent Commission on Good Governance in Public Services (2004)

Independent Commission on Good Governance in Public Services (2004), *The Good Governance Standard for Public Services*: OPM: London

KLPD (2008)

KLPD (2008), *Witwassen: Verslag van een onderzoek voor het Nationaal dreigingsbeeld 2008*, October 2008

KLPD (2013)

KLPD (2013), *Criminaliteitsbeeldanalyse 2012: witwassen*

KVoT (2005)

Ministerie van Binnenlandse Zaken en Koninkrijksrelaties (2005), *Kaderstellende Visie op Toezicht: Minder last, meer effect: Zes principes van goed toezicht*, The Hague

Länsstyrelsen Skåne (2011)

Länsstyrelsen Skåne (2011), *Årsredovisning 2011*

Länsstyrelsen Skåne (2012)

Länsstyrelsen Skåne, *Årsredovisning 2012*

Länsstyrelsen Stockholm (2011)

Länsstyrelsen Stockholm (2011), *Årsredovisning 2011*

Länsstyrelsen Stockholm (2012)

Länsstyrelsen Stockholm (2012), *Årsredovisning 2012*

Länsstyrelsen Västra Götaland (2011)

Länsstyrelsen Västra Götaland (2011), *Årsredovisning 2011*

Länsstyrelsen Västra Götaland (2012)

Länsstyrelsen Västra Götaland (2012), *Årsredovisning 2012*

Länsstyrelsen Västra Götaland (2013)

Länsstyrelsen Västra Götaland (2013), *Årsredovisning 2013*

Law Society of England and Wales (2009)
Law Society of England and Wales (2009), *The costs and benefits of anti-money laundering compliance for solicitors: Response by the Law Society of England and Wales to the call for evidence in the Review of the Money Laundering Regulations 2007*, December 2009

Law Society of England and Wales (2011)
Law Society of England and Wales (2011), *Response to the HM Treasury Consultation on the Money Laundering Regulations 2007*, August 2011

Macrory Review (2006)
Macrory Review (2006), *Regulatory Justice: Making Sanctions Effective*, Final Report

Markttoezichthoudersberaad (2011)
Markttoezichthoudersberaad (2011), *Effectief markttoezicht: bijdrage voor de herziening van de Kaderstellende Visie op Toezicht*, available at: <www.cbpweb.nl/downloads_med/med_20111114-effectief-toezicht.pdf>

Markttoezichthoudersberaad (2013)
Markttoezichthoudersberaad (2013), *Criteria voor goed toezicht: visie markttoezichthoudersberaad*, 23 April 2013, available at: <www.afm.nl/~/media/Files/publicatie/2013/criteria-goed-toezicht-mtb.ashx>

Ministerie van Binnenlandse Zaken en Koninkrijksrelaties (2009)
Ministerie van Binnenlandse Zaken en Koninkrijksrelaties (2009), *Nederlandse Code voor Goed Openbaar Bestuur: beginselen van deugdelijk overheidsbestuur*, The Hague

Ministerie van Financiën (2011)
Ministerie van Financiën (2011), *Toezicht op afstand: de relatie tussen de minister van Financiën en de financiële toezichthouders De Nederlandsche Bank (DNB) en de Autoriteit Financiële Markten (AFM) 2011-2016*, February 2011

Ministerie van Financiën (2011a)
Ministerie van Financiën (2011a), *Jaarverslag en slotwet 2011, Parliamentary Papers II*, 2011-12, 33 240 IXB, no. 1

Ministerie van Financiën (2012)
Ministerie van Financiën (2012), *Jaarverslag en slotwet 2012, Parliamentary Papers II*, 2012-13, 33 605 IXB, no. 1

National Audit Office (2008)
National Audit Office (2008), *Effective inspection and enforcement: implementing the Hampton vision in the Office of Fair Trading*, March 2008

National Crime Agency (2013)
National Crime Agency (2013), *Suspicious Activity Reports (SARs) Annual Report 2013*

National Crime Agency (2014)
National Crime Agency (2014), *National Strategic Assessment of Serious and Organised Crime 2014*

Nationale Ombudsman (2005)
Nationale Ombudsman (2005), *De maakbare overheid: jaarverslag 2005*, The Hague

Nederlandse Beroepsorganisatie van Accountants (2012)
Nederlandse Beroepsorganisatie van Accountants (2012), *Jaaroverzicht 2012* (in English: *Annual report 2012*)
OECD (2007)
OECD (2007), *Report on tax fraud and money laundering vulnerabilities involving the real estate sector*, Centre for Tax Policy and Administration.
OECD (2009)
OECD (2009), *Better Regulation in Europe: United Kingdom*, available at: <www.oecd.org/regreform/regulatory-policy/44912232.pdf>
OECD (2010)
OECD (2010), *Better Regulation in Europe: Sweden*, available at: <www.oecd.org/gov/regulatory-policy/45419072.pdf>
OFT (2009)
OFT (2009), *Money Laundering Regulations 2007: Core Guidance*, OFT954
OFT (2010)
OFT (2010), *Home buying and selling: A Market Study*, OFT1140b
OFT (2011)
OFT (2011), *Anti-Money Laundering Annual Report to HM Treasury 2010-11*, June 2011
OFT (2011a)
OFT (2011a), *OFT Anti-Money Laundering Registration Policy*, OFT1104
OFT (2011b)
OFT (2011b), *Money Laundering Regulations 2007: The OFT's approach to penalties*, OFT1326
OFT (2011c)
OFT (2011c), *Visits to businesses under the Money Laundering Regulations 2007: Code of Practice*, OFT1386
OFT (2011d)
OFT (2011d), *The Money Laundering Regulations 2007: OFT Response to HM Treasury's Review*, OFT1362
OFT (2011e)
OFT (2011e), *FAQ on MLR 2007 Supervision by OFT: Version 7*
OFT (2011f)
OFT (2011f), *Money Laundering Regulations 2007: Interim Penalty Policy*, OFT1271
OFT (2011g)
OFT (2011g), *Anti-Money Laundering Enforcement Principles: Money Laundering Regulations 2007*, May 2011, OFT1094
OFT (2012)
OFT (2012), *Annual Report and Accounts 2011-12*, OFT1347
OFT (2013)
OFT (2013), *Annual Report and Accounts 2012-13*, OFT1490
OFT (2013a)
OFT (2013a), *Anti-Money Laundering Enforcement Principles: Money Laundering Regulations 2007*, May 2011 (updated May 2013), OFT1094

Oliver Wyman (2013)
Oliver Wyman (2013), *Organisational effectiveness of financial sector regulators – Benchmarking results: Swedish Financial Supervisory Authority*, available at: <www.fi.se/upload/10_Om%20FI/10_Verksamhet/undersokningar/effektivitet-tillsynsmyndigheter-internationellt-2013.pdf>

Pliatzky (1980)
Pliatzky, L. (1980), *Report on Non-departmental Public Bodies*, CMND 7797: 1980

Raad voor Toezicht NBA (2012)
Raad voor Toezicht NBA (2012), *Verslag van werkzaamheden 2012*

Regioplan Beleidsonderzoek (2012)
Regioplan Beleidsonderzoek (2012), *Naar een beleidsmonitor bestrijding witwassen*, WODC: The Hague, research commissioned by the Dutch Ministry of Security & Justice

Riksrevisionen (2007)
Riksrevisionen (2007), *Den största affären i livet, Tillsyn över fastighetsmäklare och konsumenternas möjligheter till tvistelösning*, RiR 2007:7

Revisorsnämnden (2012)
Revisorsnämnden (2012), *Revisorsnämndens årsredovisning för räkenskapsåret 2012*, Dnr 2012-1667

Revisorsnämnden (2013)
Revisorsnämnden (2013), *Revisorsnämndens årsredovisning för räkenskapsåret 2013*, Dnr 2013-1607

SEPBLAC (2008)
SEPBLAC (2008), *Tipologías de blanqueo de capitales*, January 2008

SEPBLAC (2012)
SEPBLAC (2012), *Memoria Anual 2012* (in English: *Annual report 2012*)

SEPBLAC (2013)
SEPBLAC (2013), *Recomendaciones sobre las medidas de control interno para la prevención del blanqueo de capitales y de la financiación del terrorismo*, 4 April 2013

Serious Organised Crime Agency (2009)
Serious Organised Crime Agency (2009), *Estate Agents – Identifying Risks to your Business and Reporting Suspicious Activity*

Serious Organised Crime Agency (2011)
Serious Organised Crime Agency (2011), *Suspicious Activity Reports Regime: Annual Report 2011*

Serious Organised Crime Agency (2012)
Serious Organised Crime Agency (2012), *Suspicious Activity Reports Regime: Annual Report 2012*

Spanish Government (2013)
Spanish Government (2013), *The National Security Strategy: Sharing A Common Project*, NIPO 002130352

Statskontoret (2005)
Statskontoret (2005), *Principles of Good Administration in the Member States of the European Union*, 2005:4.

Statskontoret (2008)
Statskontoret (2008), *Tredje penningtvättsdirektivet – tillsyn och organisation*, 2008:2
Statskontoret (2010)
Statskontoret (2010), *Myndighetsanalys av Fastighetsmäklarnämnden*, Report 2010:18
Swedish Council of Legislation (2014)
Swedish Council of Legislation (2014), *En effektivare kriminalisering av penningtvätt*, 10 January 2014
Swedish Government (2012)
Swedish Government (2012), *Penningtvätt – kriminalisering, förverkande och dispositionsförbud*, SOU 2012:12
Swedish Government (2012a)
Swedish Government (2012), *En sammanhållen svensk polis*, SOU 2012:13
OHCHR (2007)
OHCHR (2007), *Good Governance Practices for the Protection of Human Rights*, New York-Geneva
Organización profesional de Inspectores de Hacienda del Estado (2007)
Organización profesional de Inspectores de Hacienda del Estado (2007), *Fraude, Corrupción y Blanqueo de Capitales en España*, November 2007
UK House of Commons (1985)
UK House of Commons (1985), *Lifting the Burden: White Paper*, Cmnd 9751
UNODC (2011)
UNODC (2011), *Estimating Illicit Financial Flows Resulting From Drugs Trafficking and Other Transnational Organized Crimes: Research Report*, Vienna, October 2011
US Department of State (2014)
US Department of State (2014), *International Narcotics Control Strategy Report: Volume 2 Money Laundering and Financial Crimes*, March 2014
Van Dijkhuizen et al. (1998)
Van Dijkhuizen, C. et al. (1998), *Rapport van de MDW-werkgroep makelaars*, Ministerie van Economische Zaken: The Hague
World Bank (1989)
World Bank (1989), *Sub-Saharan Africa: From Crisis to Sustainable Growth*, Washington DC
World Bank (1992)
World Bank (1992), *Governance and Development*, Washington DC
World Bank (1994)
World Bank (1994), *Good Governance and Fiscal Transparency*, Washington DC
World Bank (1997)
World Bank (1997), *Corruption and Good Governance*, Washington DC
World Bank (2009)
Chatain, P., et al. (2009), *Preventing Money Laundering and Terrorist Financing: A Practical Guide for Bank Supervisors*, World Bank: Washington DC

Newspapers

Expressen, *Gangsterkungen frias – men advokat döms för penningtvätt*, 30 September 2003

The Guardian, *Regulation of estate agents ruled out after OFT inquiry*, 18 February 2010

Financial Times, *ABN Amro admits sanctions breach*, 10 May 2010

The Telegraph, *Tax-payer owned RBS pays $500m to settle ABN money laundering case*, 11 May 2010

NRC Handelsblad, *Hoofdverdachte vastgoedfraude betaalt miljoenenschikking*, 28 October 2010

De Volkskrant, *Vastgoedhandelaar Joep J. met gezin opgepakt*, 21 juni 2011

Het Financieele Dagblad, *OM houdt treasurer van corporatie Vestia aan*, 16 April 2012

De Telegraaf, *Malafide makelaar gepakt*, 10 May 2012

The Guardian, *HSBC sets aside $700m for money-laundering fines*, 30 July 2012

Het Financieele Dagblad, *Reeks vastgoedbonzen fêteerde Hooijmaijers*, 12 October 2012

El País, *Maite Zalvídar declara que acusó a Julián Muñoz por despecho*, 15 October 2012

The Guardian, *HSBC pays record $1.9bn fine to settle US money-laundering accusations*, 11 December 2012

USA Today, *HSBC will pay $1.9 billion for money laundering*, 11 December 2012

Dagblad De Limburger, *Zaak Van-Rey: Invallen bij Van Pol en makelaar*, 28 January 2013

BBC News, *Lawyer and book keeper convicted of laundering £1.8m*, 29 January 2013

Het Financieele Dagblad, *Maak advocaten leidend bij fraude*, 4 February 2013

Dagens Juridik, *Ex-advokat fälls för bokföringsbrott och osant intygande – tidigare dömd för penningtvätt*, 4 April 2013, available at: <www.dagensjuridik.se/2013/04/ex-advokat-falls-bokforingsbrott-och-osant-intygande-tidigare-domd-penningtvatt>

El País, *El Banco de España refuerza el control de sueldos y blanqueo de capitales*, 4 April 2013

El País, *Isabel Pantoja condenada por blanqueo a 24 meses de prisión*, 18 April 2013

The Guardian, *Rics calls for estate agents tests*, 4 May 2013

Trouw, *Opsporingsdiensten pakken witwassen via makelaar aan*, 07 July 2013

Het Financieele Dagblad, *DNB beboet ABN om Vestia-fout*, 19 August 2013

NRC Handelsblad, *ABN-Amro boete van DNB om Vestia-fout*, 19 August 2013

RtvES, *El 'caso Malaya', la operación más importante en España contra la corrupción urbanística*, 2 October 2013

ABC Andalucía, *El cerebro del caso Malaya, Juan Antonio Roca, condenado a once años de cárcel*, 5 October 2013

Trouw, *OM zet jacht op verzakende poortwachters door*, 8 October 2013

Het Financieele Dagblad, *Priester Vaticaan aangeklaagd wegens witwassen*, 21 January 2014

Marca, *Messi caught up in 1m money laundering mess*, 8 June 2014, available at: <www.marca.com/2014/06/08/en/football/barcelona/1402228989.html>

The Independent, *Spanish Princess Cristina de Bourbon charged with money laundering and fraud in major corruption investigation*, 25 June 2014

El Mundo, *Corrupción en Marbella*, availabe at: <www.elmundo.es/especiales/2006/04/espana/corrupcion_marbella/trama.html>

Case law and sanctioning decisions

Court of Justice of the European Union (ECJ)

Case 33/76 *Rewe* [1976] ECR-1989

Case C-45/76 *Comet BV v Produktschap voor Siergewassen* [1976] ECR 2043

Case 61/79 *Denkavit* [1980] ECR I-1205

Joined Cases 66/79, 127/79 and 128/79 *Salumi* [1980] ECR 1237

Case 199/82 *San Giorgio* [1983] ECR I-3595

Case 14/83 *Von Colson and Kamann* [1984] ECR 1891

Case 222/84 *Johnston* [1986] ECR 1651

Case 222/86 *Heylens* [1987] ECR 4097

Case 309/85 *Barra* [1988] ECR I-355

Case 240/87 *Deville* [1988] ECR I-3513

Case C-68/88 *Commission v Greece* (*Greek Maize*) [1989] ECR 2965

Case C-7/90 *Vandevenne* [1991] ECR I-4371

Case C-271/91/ *Marshal II* [1993] ECR I-4367

Joined Cases C-430-431/93 *Van Schijndel and Van Veen* [1995] ECR I-4705

Case C-312/93 *Peterbroeck* [1995] ECR I-4599.

Case C-265/95 *Commission v France (Spanish Strawberries)* [1997] ECR I-6959

Case C-188/95 *Fantask* [1997] ECR-6783

Case C-29/95 *Pastoors* [1997] ECR I-285

Case C-246/96 *Magorrian* [1997] ECR I-7153

Case C-260/96 *Spac* [1998] ECR I-4997

Case C-228/96 *Aprile* [1998] ECR I-07141

Case C-326/96 *Levez* [1998] ECR I-7835

Case C-354/99 *Commission v Ireland* [2001] ECR-07657

Case C-424/99 *Commission v Austria* [2001] ECR I-9285

Case C-50/00 P *Unión de Pequeños Agricultores v Council* [2002] ECR I-6677

Case C-62/00 *Marks & Spencer* [2002] ECR I-6325

Case C-255/00 *Grundig Italiana* [2002], ECR I-8003

Case C-63/01 *Evans* [2003] ECR I-14447

Case C-129/00 *Commission v Italy* [2003] ECR I-14637

Case C-327/00 *Santex* [2003] ECR I-1877

Case C-147/01 *Weber's Wine World* [2003] ECR I-11365

Joined Cases C-387/02, C-391/02, and C-403/02 *Berlusconi and Others* [2005], Opinion of AG Kokott, delivered on 14 October 2004 [2004] ECR I-3565

Case C-295-298/2004 *Manfredi* [2006] ECR I-6619

Case C-432/05 *Unibet* [2007] ECR I-2271

Case C-305/05 *Ordre des barreaux francophones et germanophones and Others v Conseil des Ministres* [2007] ECR I-05305

Case C-63/08 *Pontin* [2009] ECR I-10467

Case C-2/08 *Olimpiclub* [2009] ECR I-7501

Case C-502/08 *Commission v Spain* [2009] ECR I-00161

Case C-546/08 *Commission v Kingdom of Sweden* [2009] ECR I-00105

Case C-279/09 *DEB* [2010] ECR I-13849

Joined Cases C-317/08 - C-320/08 *Alassini* [2010] ECR I-02213

Case C-212/11 *Jyske Bank Gibraltar Ltd against Spain* [2013] ECR I-00000

Joined Cases C-141/12 and C-372/12 *Y.S. v Minister voor Immigratie*, Opinion AG Sharpton, delivered on 12 December 2013

European Court of Human Rights (ECtHR)

ECtHR, 15 September 2009, *Moskal v Poland*, app. no. 10373/05
ECtHR, 20 October 2011, *Rysovskyy v Ukraine*, app. no. 29979/04
ECtHR, 16 May 2013, *Maksymenko and Gerasymenko v Ukraine*, app. no. 49317/2007, in: *EHRC*, 2013/153 annotated by Henk Addink
ECtHR, 26 November 2013, *Bogdel v Lithuania*, app. no. 41248/06

Spain

Constitutional Court (Tribunal Constitucional)

STC 18/1981 of 8 June 1981
STC 13/1982 of 1 April 1982
STC 77/1983 of 3 October 1983
STC 89/1995 of 6 June 1995
STC 14/1999 of 22 February 1999
STC 54/2003 of 24 March 2003
STC 74/2004 of 22 April 2004

Supreme Court (Tribunal Supremo)

STS 6457/2009 of 4 November 2009
STS 2028/2010 of 23 April 2010
STS 4812/2011 of 18 July 2011
STS 7085/2011 of 8 November 2011
STS 7055/2012 of 6 November 2012
STS 529/2013 of 5 February 2013
STS 1338/2013 of 12 March 2013
STS 2174/2013 of 21 April 2013
STS 1996/2013 of 29 April 2013
STS 4808/2013 of 30 September 2013
STS 5917/2013 of 17 December 2013

District court of Málaga (Audiencia provincial de Málaga)

Audiencia Provincial de Málaga, Sentencia no. 179/13, 16 April 2013
Audiencia Provincial de Málaga, Sentencia no. 535/2013, 4 October 2013

Public warnings (amonestación pública)

Resolution 7232 of 26 April 2010 against Jyske Bank Gibraltar Limited (*Resolución de 26 de abril de 2010, de la Dirección General del Tesoro y Política Financiera, por la que se publica las sanciones impuestas a Jyske Bank Gibraltar Limited por infracciones muy graves de la Ley 19/1993, de 28 de diciembre, sobre determinadas medidas de prevención del blanqueo de capitales*), BOE no. 110, 6 May 2010, 40285-40286

Resolution 6575 of 13 May 2013 against HSBC Bank Plc (*Resolución de 13 de mayo de 2013, de la Secretaría General del Tesoro y Política Financiera, por las que se publican las sanciones impuestas a HSBC Bank Plc, Sucursal en España, por infracciones muy graves de la Ley 19/1993, de 28 de diciembre, sobre determinadas medidas de prevención del blanqueo de capitales*), BOE no. 144, 17 June 2013, 45771-45771

Resolution 7465 of 27 June 2013 against Moneygram Payments Systems Spain SA (*Resolución de 27 de junio de 2013, de la Comisión de Prevención del Blanqueo de Capitales e Infracciones Monetarias, por la que se publica el Acuerdo del Consejo de Ministros de 2 de noviembre de 2012, por el que se sanciona a Moneygram Payments Systems Spain SA, por infracción muy grave de la normativa sobre prevención del blanqueo de capitales*), BOE, no. 162, 18 July 2013, 50828-50828

Sweden

Estate Agents Inspectorate (Fastighetsmäklarinspektionen)

Årsbok 2010
2010-11-24:3
2010-06-23:5
2010-12-15:3
2010-12-15:11

Årsbok 2011
2011-04-27:1
2011-03-31:16
2011-09-28:8
2011-08-24:1
2011-12-14:14
2011-03-31:14

Årsbok 2012
2012-01-25:7
2012-11-21:17
2012-01-25:8
2012-02-22:4
2012-02-22:6
2012-03-28:2
2012-06-20:7
2012-06-20:11
2012-12-12:12
2012-02-22:7
2012-05-23:6
2012-09-26:17
2012-11-21:8
2012-12-12:26
2012-03-28:3
2012-10-24:5
2012-08-29:5

Financial Supervisory Authority (Finansinspektionen)

Västernorrlandsfonden AB, 4 October 2010, FI Dnr 10-9365
Maxima Finans & Försäkringsmäklare AB, 9 November 2011, FI Dnr 10-6683
Svensk Kapitalservice & Rådgivning, 6 December 2011, FI Dnr 11-1104
Folksam LO Fond AB, 15 May 2012, FI Dnr 10-7704
Legio Exchange AB, 1 October 2012, FI Dnr 11-10359
Nordea Bank AB, 15 April 2013, FI Ref. 12-7237
Exchange Finans Europe AB, 13 January 2014, FI Ref. 13-399

Supervisory Board of Public Auditors (Revisorsnämnden)

RN Case, D 43/10, Dnr 2010-697, 10 December 2010
RN Case, D 15/11, Dnr 2011-409, 5 May 2011
RN Case, *Deloitte AB,* Dnr 2012-56, 29 October 2013
RN Case D 13, Dnr 2012-1522, 31 October 2013

The Netherlands

Supreme Court (Hoge Raad)

HR 25 October 1983, ECLI:NL:HR:1983:AG4685, *NJ 1984/132* annotated by A.C. 't Hart
HR 14 June 1985, ECLI:NL:HR:1985:AC9068, *NJ 1986/175* annotated by W.L. Haardt
HR 6 May 1986, ECLI:NL:HR:1986:AB9404, *NJ 1986/813* annotated by W.L. Haardt
HR 29 March 1994, ECLI:NL:HR:1994:ZC9693, *NJ 1994/552* annotated by A.C. 't Hart
HR 12 March 1997, *BNB/1997/146c* annotated by P.J. Wattel
HR 12 February 2002, ECLI:NL:HR:2002:AD4402, *NJ 2002/440* annotated by Y. Buruma

Council of State Administrative Jurisdiction Division (Afdeling Bestuursrechtspraak Raad van de State)

ABRvS 2 February 1998, ECLI:NL:RVS:1998:ZF3176, *AB 1998/181* annotated by F.C.M.A. Michiels

ABRvS 30 June 2004, ECLI:NL:RVS:2004:AP4683, *JB 2004/293* annotated by C.L.F.G.H. Albers

ABRvS 4 June 2014, ECLI:NL:RVS:2014:1982

ABRvS 25 June 2014, ECLI:NL:RVS:2014:2303

Trade and Industry Appeals Tribunal (College van Beroep voor het bedrijfsleven)

CBb 10 November 2005, ECLI:NL:CBB:2005:AU6169, *JOR 2006/47* annotated by R.H. Maatman

CBb 23 November 2009, ECLI:NL:CBB:2009:BK4209, *AB 2010/117* annotated by M. Stouten

CBb 20 June 2010, ECLI:NL:CBB:2010:BN4700, *AB 2010/242* annotated by I. Sewandono

CBb 15 June 2011, ECLI:NL:CBB:2011:BQ8708, *JB 2011/182* annotated by G. Overkleeft-Verburg

District Court Rotterdam (Rechtbank Rotterdam)

Rb. Rotterdam, ROT12/1391, 30 May 2013

Accountants' Chamber (Accountantskamer)

Case 10/1991 Wtra AK, 9 May 2011, ECLI:NL:TACAKN:2011:YH0167

Case 12/1168 en 12/1169, 8 February 2013, ECLI:NL:TACAKN:2013:YH0342

Case 12/1955 Wtra AK, 1 July 2013, ECLI:NL:TACAKN:2013:2

Case 12/2450 Wtra AK, 30 September 2013, ECLI:NL:TACAKN:2013:47

Case 12/2338 Wtra AK, 30 September 2013, ECLI:NL:TACAKN:2013:45

Case 13/852 Wtra AK, 11 November 2013, ECLI:NL:TACAKN:2013:64

Case 13/1145 Wtra AK, 2 December 2013, ECLI:NL:TACAKN:2013:67

Case 13/1476 Wtra AK, 20 December 2013, ECLI:NL:TACAKN:2013:75

Case 12/2337 Wtra AK, 20 December 2013, ECLI:NL:TACAKN:2013:78

Case 13/2415 Wtra AK, 14 March 2014, ECLI:NL:TACAKN:2014:24

Sanctioning decisions AFM

AFM, *Boetebesluit KPMG*, 21 February 2011, available at: <www.afm.nl/~/media/files/boete/2013/kpmg/primair-boetebesluit-kpmg-art8-lid-1-bta.ashx>

AFM, *Boetebesluit KPMG II*, 21 February 2011, available at: <www.afm.nl/~/media/files/boete/2013/kpmg/primair-boetebesluit-kpmg-art8-lid-2-bta.ashx>

AFM, *Boetebesluit Ernst & Young*, 9 November 2011, available at: <www.afm.nl/~/media/files/boete/2012/ernst-young-compliance.ashx>

AFM, *Boetebesluit Deloitte*, 15 February 2012, available at: <www.afm.nl/~/media/files/boete/2012/deloitte.ashx>

Other

Hof van Discipline 11 September 2009, ECLI:NL:TAHVD:2009:YA0027

United Kingdom

Case law

AGIP (Africa) Limited v Jackson & Others [1990] 1 Ch. 265
R v Pattinson [2007] EWCA Crim 1536 [2008] 1 Cr App R (S) 51
R v Waya [2012] UKSC 51
R v Charalambous [2010] Blackfriars CC (2011).
R v Doshi [2011] EWCA Crim 1975

Sanctioning decisions FCA (and predecessor FSA)

FSA Final Notice: Coutts & Company, Ref. no. 122287, 23 March 2012

FSA Final Notice: Mr Syed Itrat Hussain, Ref. no. SIH 01010, 4 May 2012

FSA Final Notice: Habib Bank AG Zurich, Ref. no. 113991, 4 May 2012

FSA Decision Notice: Turkish Bank (UK) Ltd, Ref. no. 204566, 2 August 2012

FSA Final Notice, EFG Private Bank Ltd, Ref. no. 144036, 28 March 2013

FCA Final Notice: Guarantee Trust Bank (UK) Limited, Ref. no. 466611, 8 August 2013

FCA Decision Notice: Standard Bank Plc, Ref. no. 124823, 22 January 2014

Disciplinary decisions ICAEW (Investigation Committee and Disciplinary Tribunal)

Tribunal of the Disciplinary Committee order against Mr J.M. Johnstone, 7 December 2011 (published 4 April 2012, removed April 2013)

Tribunal of the Disciplinary Committee order against Mr L. Simans, 22 May 2013 (published 7 August 2013)

Tribunal of the Disciplinary Committee order against Mr P.G. Jeffery, 18 June 2013 (published 4 September 2013)

Investigation Committee Consent order, no. 006281, 22 June 2012 (published 1 August 2012, removed August 2013)

Investigation Committee Consent order, no. 008566, 23 September 2013 (published 2 October 2013)

Investigation Committee Consent order, no. 011732, 16 October 2013 (published on 6 November 2013)

Table of interviews

Country	Authority	Date	Location	ECOLEF
The Netherlands	Ministerie van Financiën	28 April 2010	Den Haag	x
	Bureau Financieel Toezicht (BFT)	28 April 2010	Utrecht	x
	De Nederlandsche Bank (DNB)	4 May 2010	Amsterdam	x
	Belastingdienst Holland-Midden, Unit MOT	6 July 2010	Hoofddorp	x
	Belastingdienst/Bureau Toezicht Wwft	17 April 2013	Hoofddorp	
	De Nederlandsche Bank (DNB)	13 May 2013	Amsterdam	
	Samenwerkende Registeraccountants en Accountants-administratieconsulenten (SRA)	27 May 2013	Nieuwegein	
	Bureau Financieel Toezicht (BFT)	11 June 2013	Utrecht	
	FIU-Nederland	11 June 2013	Zoetermeer	
	Nederlandse Beroeporganisatie van Accountants (NBA)	20 June 2013	Amsterdam	
Spain	Ministerio de Economía y Hacienda	28 October 2011	Madrid	x
	Servicio Ejecutivo de la Comisión de Prevención del Blanqueo de Capitales e Infracciones Monetarias (SEPBLAC)	31 October 2011	Madrid	x
	Servicio Ejecutivo de la Comisión de Prevención del Blanqueo de Capitales e Infracciones Monetarias (SEPBLAC)	30 November 2011	Vienna	x
	Servicio Ejecutivo de la Comisión de Prevención del Blanqueo de Capitales e Infracciones Monetarias (SEPBLAC)	13 October 2013	Madrid	

Country	Authority	Date	Location	ECOLEF
Sweden	Finanspolisen	18 April 2011	Stockholm	x
	Finansdepartementet & Justisdepartementet	19 April 2011	Stockholm	x
	Finansinspektionen (FI)	20 April 2011	Stockholm	x
	Fastighetsmäklarnämnden	20 April 2011	Stockholm	x
	Fastighetsmäklarinspektionen (FMI)	27 August 2013	Telephone interview	
	Länsstyrelsen Stockholm	17 September 2013	Telephone interview	
	Länsstyrelsen Västra Götaland	20 September 2013	Telephone interview	
	Länsstyrelsen Skåne	24 September 2013	Telephone interview	
	Finansinspektionen (FI)	30 October 2013	Telephone interview	
United Kingdom	Financial Services Authority (FSA)	18 April 2012	London	x
	HM Treasury and Home Office	19 April 2012	London	x
	Institute of Chartered Accountants in England and Wales (ICAEW)	16 May 2012	London	x
	Association of Accounting Technicians (AAT)	3 August 2012	Telephone interview	x
	HM Revenue and Customs (HMRC)	19 May 2014	London	
	HM Treasury	20 May 2014	London	
	Financial Conduct Authority (FCA)	21 May 2014	London	
	Association of Accounting Technicians (AAT)	21 May 2014	London	
	Institute of Chartered Accountants in England and Wales (ICAEW)	22 May 2014	London	

Curriculum Vitae

Melissa van den Broek was born in 1987 in Haarlem, the Netherlands. She graduated from high school (vwo) at Het VeenLanden College in 2005. She studied law at Utrecht University from 2005-2010. As an undergraduate, Melissa visited the University of Granada in Spain on an exchange programme for a period of five months. After receiving her Bachelor's degree (cum laude), she enrolled in Utrecht University's Master's degree in Legal Research. The title of her Master's thesis was 'New Governance: The exchange of information within the Dutch Financial Expertise Centre from a Good Governance Perspective'. After she graduated (cum laude) in 2010, she started to work on her PhD research at Utrecht University's Institute for Jurisprudence, Constitutional and Administrative Law. During this period she was involved as a legal researcher in the EU-funded research project 'ECOLEF: The Economic and Legal Effectiveness of Anti-Money Laundering and Combating Terrorist Financing Policy', carried out by the Schools of Economics and Law at Utrecht University. She authored and co-authored a number of articles that were published in various (inter)national books and academic journals, and taught a bachelor's course on the administrative enforcement of law. Since the 1st of October 2014 Melissa has been working as a policy officer at the Netherlands Authority for the Financial Markets (Autoriteit Financiële Markten, AFM).